CROSBY, STILLS, NASH & YOUNG

CROSBY, STILLS, NASH & YOUNG

THE WILD, DEFINITIVE SAGA *of* ROCK'S GREATEST SUPERGROUP

DAVID BROWNE

DA CAPO PRESS

Da Capo Press
Hachette Book Group
1290 Avenue of the Americas, New York, NY 10104
dacapopress.com
@DaCapoPress, @DaCapoPR

Printed in the United States of America
First Edition: August 2019

Published by Da Capo Press, an imprint of Perseus Books, LLC, a subsidiary of Hachette Book
Group, Inc. The Da Capo Press name and logo is a trademark of the Hachette Book Group.

The Hachette Speakers Bureau provides a wide range of authors for speaking events. To find
out more, go to www.hachettespeakersbureau.com or call (866) 376-6591.

The publisher is not responsible for websites (or their content) that are not owned by the
publisher.

Editorial production by Christine Marra, Marrathon Production Services.
www.marrathoneditorial.org

Book design by Jane Raese
Set in 10-point Century ITC

Library of Congress Cataloging-in-Publication Data has been applied for.
ISBN 978-0-306-90328-1 (hardcover), ISBN 978-0-306-92264-0 (ebook)

LSC-C

10 9 8 7 6 5 4 3 2 1

To my father, Cliff,

my mother, Raymonde, and

my sister Linda Virginia,

who were all with us when I discovered this music

and who bought some of these records for me.

I always think of you when I hear this music,

and you are all deeply missed.

CONTENTS

PART FOUR
ON THE WAY HOME

PREFACE

"What a story," Graham Nash said to me, shaking his head, during an interview for this book. "What a fucked-up foursome." It was late 2017, and at that moment, Crosby, Stills and Nash—and sometimes Young—appeared to be shattered for good, the result of beefs and grievances that had been festering for years and had finally discharged. Even after nearly five decades of upheaval, you could only shake your own head at the disarray of it all.

But way back in more innocent times, it was the voices, not the drama, we noticed. On a family drive sometime in the early '70s, I can still recall turning on the AM radio on the dashboard and the inside of the car unexpectedly being engulfed in massive, densely packed harmonies, the lyrics saying something about returning to some sort of garden. Instantly drawn to the sound, I reached forward from the back seat to pump up the volume dial, probably to my parents' annoyance. Afterward, the DJ informed us we had just heard a group called "Crosby, Stills, Nash and Young."

As one of those kids who often walked around with a transistor radio and its white, one-ear bud, I must have heard some of the records each of them had been a part of before: the Byrds' "Mr. Tambourine Man" or "Turn! Turn! Turn!"; the Hollies' "Bus Stop"; Buffalo Springfield's "For What It's Worth." I'd probably chanced upon Crosby, Stills and Nash's "Marrakesh Express" or the shortened version of "Suite: Judy Blue Eyes" on New York's biggest AM station. All I knew was that, from the singing to the grinding organ to the jabbing guitar solo midway through, I'd never heard anything quite like "Woodstock" before. It made everything outside the window, especially the dreary car dealership on Route 35 in New Jersey where my mother worked, seem somehow more uplifting—an early power-of-song moment.

Not long after, thanks to birthday-gift money and whatever allowance I could scrounge up in my entering-teen days, I joined the millions of people who had already bought copies of the evolving group's first two LPs, *Crosby, Stills & Nash* and *Déjà vu.* The covers reflected their different moods. On the former, three guys, dressed hippie-casual in denim and boots and lounging on a tattered couch, stared directly at the camera; they looked like more charismatic versions of my friends' older brothers. On the latter album, those three were joined by three more people—and a dog—in a duskier, Old West setting, none of them looking happy. Using the songwriting credits as my guide, I was struck by the way David Crosby, Stephen Stills, Graham Nash and Neil Young each sang in a distinctive voice and had a songwriting style his own, yet still managed to create a unified sound together. The lyrics had an unguarded directness I wasn't accustomed to hearing in much rock at the time. Getting into Bob Dylan's head on his records was a challenge, as was discerning his intention; with these people, their feelings of confusion, romantic anguish or anger were entirely out in the open. You never forget how eerily chill and singular a song like "Guinnevere" sounded or how Young's voice on "Helpless" was so fragile, high and spooky.

I read what I could on them at the time, mostly in magazines like *Rolling Stone* and its scrappier music competitors *Creem, Circus* and *Hit Parader.* I learned that the group featured members of Buffalo Springfield, the Byrds and the Hollies. Some writers called them a "supergroup," whatever that was. They were ubiquitous and mythological, and I also learned they were already defunct.

I spent the next few years buying everything else of theirs I could find. It was like entering the world of an extended musical family but with siblings who were all from different clans. How could the person who made a rattled and jittery record like Young's *Time Fades Away* be in the same band with the guy who made Nash's far more crafted and precise *Songs for Beginners*? How could both harmonize with a guy like Stills, whose force-of-nature voice and musicianship almost swallowed up albums like *Stephen Stills*? And how could any of them bond with the indolently blissed-out hippie at the center of Crosby's *If I Could Only Remember My Name*? This was a *band*?

Well, it was and it wasn't, as many of us came to realize. I'd read in 1974 that they were playing together again. To my eternal regret, I didn't go to the concert; my parents frowned on me venturing to nearby Jersey City, warning it was an awful place. Once that tour was over, we all awaited a new album from them—but it never came. Instead they went back to their separate worlds. I first saw them onstage in 1977, when Crosby, Stills and Nash, no Young, reformed for an album and tour. Even in the nosebleed seats where my friend Chris and I sat, it was pretty thrilling to behold them in person and watch Stills run around the parameters of the stage by way of a wireless guitar. (How did he *do* that, we thought?) But a year later they'd shattered again. And so it went: they would reform as a trio or a quartet (Young generally seemed to keep as much distance as possible), resurrect their songs and vocal interplay, make more money than most of us would in a lifetime, then burst into pieces and go about their own business before starting up the cycle again. One of their former employees told me they'd broken up eight times during his tenure with them.

Over the years that followed, this experience was at once fascinating, exasperating and disheartening. The records they made separately or in pairs alternated between tremendous and enervated, and as the decades wore on, they increasingly looked and sounded ravaged by their lifestyles. As anyone who recalls the full quartet's deflating reunion at 1985's Live Aid will attest, the sight wasn't always pretty. Their relationships surely weren't as exquisite as their music, which seemed to sum up something about all of them: How could a group so identified with harmony fall into such regular discord and disarray?

And, just as important, why have so many of us remained riveted by this saga despite the merry-go-round of glories, letdowns and buzzkills? Naturally, the music they made remains the fundamental reason. Fifty years on, their finest moments are permanently interwoven with the fabric of rock history. Stills' chilly voice and Young's two-note guitar on "For What It's Worth." The rush of voices and guitars at the start of "Suite: Judy Blue Eyes." Crosby's warm-blanket harmonies on "Mr. Tambourine Man," and Nash's on the Hollies' "On a Carousel." Later Nash-written hits, like "Wasted on the Way" and "Just a Song Before I Go," now soft-rock

talismans. Entire albums, like *Rust Never Sleeps* or *Déjà vu* (along with
plenty of others that should be considered classics but aren't). Crosby's
fringed jacket. Stills' immortal words at Woodstock ("We're scared shitless!"). Young's guitar, Old Black. Their collective sideburns. The mere
sight of the four of them sitting onstage with their chairs and acoustic
guitars, like some sort of adult campfire summit. For all the imitators
who came in their wake, no one ever sounded quite like them, and on a
good night, the combination of their voices remained peerless. And just
when you were ready to count them out, they somehow managed to un-
leash a song or performance that gave new meaning to the phrase "keep
hope alive" well into the current century.

Nonmusical reasons lured us into their legend, too. Feuding rock
bands are nothing new, and pop history is larded with tales of rancor,
splendor and excess. But few such sagas have stretched out over five
decades and had as many twists and turns as that of Crosby, Stills, Nash
and Young—rock's longest-running soap opera, starring its most eternally
dysfunctional musical family. Long before social media, they were duking
it out in public in interviews and even in song; one could compile an entire album of the barbed tunes they wrote about each other. As Crosby
told me during one of our conversations, "It's always been strange. It
never wasn't strange. Right from the beginning."

Their story is also unique in the way it has mirrored so much of what
was happening around them and us. From the never-cut-my-hair '60s to
the solipsism of the '70s to the way excesses caught up to their generation in the '80s to the lessons learned along the way, their narrative, for
better and sometimes worse, is that of the baby-boom generation. If the
boomers were coddled, few were indulged more in the industry than
these four. Along the way, they encountered and reacted to everything
around them, from Vietnam to the antinuke movement to the Iraq War,
chronicling those events in song.

But why else do we still care? It's a question I posed one day to
a friend, fellow author, and group chronicler, Dave Zimmer. We both
mulled it over before Dave said, aptly, "Because they're such *characters.*"

He was right, of course, and I would take a step further. Another
part of the ongoing Crosby, Stills, Nash and Young allure lies with each
being an archetype we can relate to or even want to be. Crosby was

the shoot-from-the-hip rebel who couldn't help but stick it to the man. Stills, especially during his early years, was the driven careerist—always on the go, go, go—as well as the eternally unrequited romantic. Nash was the sensitive lady killer with the taste for quality possessions, the proto-yuppie. Young was the elusive, changeable outsider who couldn't quite commit to any one thing at any one time.

How those public personae jibed with reality was another matter; they weren't always the people their fans thought they were. But it's easy to suppose that many could, and still do, relate to at least one of those prototypes and their foibles. We've all had the wind at our backs and blown opportunities. We've all had hotheaded moments. We've all had times when we've wanted to be team players and others when we craved alone time. We've all said hurtful things to friends or family members, maybe without intending to. We've all worn clothes that seemed fashionable at the time but that we later regretted. We've all struggled with one compulsion or another (even if not to their extremes). To paraphrase Nash, we've all been fuckups at some point. They are us, we are them, and telling their story allows us to understand why.

PART ONE
THE GARDEN

CHAPTER 1

EARLY YEARS–DECEMBER 1968

The experiment began almost by accident and, befitting the way it would toggle between love and something far from it, on Valentine's Day. February 14, 1968, had been an overcast midwinter day in Los Angeles, but the weather didn't deter the city's pop music royalty from making its way to the Sunset Strip that evening. Commandeering the corner of Sunset Boulevard and Clark Street in West Hollywood, the hulking Whisky a Go Go had been a Bank of America branch until the building was transformed into a dance-crazy pop nightclub in 1964. Since then, the five-hundred-seat nightspot, with its incongruously old-fashioned awning over the front door, had hosted rock-and-roll mavericks as well as more soul and R&B acts than any other club in town; it was the place to catch everyone from the Doors and Frank Zappa's Mothers of Invention to Stevie Wonder, Otis Redding and the Miracles, often with woozy lights and bubbles projected on the wall.

Crammed next to each other at one table tonight were David Crosby, best known for his affiliation with the Byrds, and Cass Elliot, the beloved and gregarious member of the Mamas and the Papas, whose enveloping harmonies had done their best to calm the country down over the past three years. Nearby were Nancy Sinatra, Frank's pop-singer daughter, former Lovin' Spoonful frontman John Sebastian, and at least three of the Monkees, the fabricated but socially connected TV pop band. Stephen Stills of Buffalo Springfield, one of the most beloved if combustible of Los Angeles pop bands, was also in the crowd; one account also placed his bandmate Neil Young there. All were primed for a rare Hollywood performance by peers from across the ocean named the Hollies.

In light of the grim drumbeat of the nightly news, it made sense to want to escape for an evening. The war in Vietnam was thousands of miles away but hitting closer to home by the day. Weeks before, North Vietnam had stunned the world with the Tet Offensive, a barrage of surprise attacks on over a hundred cities in South Vietnam. That February day, just after it was announced that peace talks between North Vietnam, the United States and other nations had collapsed, the beleaguered US President, Lyndon Johnson, signed off on sending another 10,500 troops into war. Asked if nuclear bombs would be used to defend Marine outposts in South Vietnam, the chairman of the Joint Chiefs of Staff "refused to speculate." (Decades later, it would be revealed that Johnson had vetoed a plan that week to install nukes in South Vietnam as a last resort against the North.) Even the local news was unsparing: an eighteen-year-old living near the University of Southern California had been arrested for allegedly shooting his father in the face with a 16-gauge shotgun after a family argument.

Little intruded on the festivities at the Whisky a Go Go. In their native England, the Hollies had played the Cavern Club in Liverpool right after the Beatles; starting in the now far-off 1963, they had become a hit-making machine all their own. In the States, the Hollies were a regular pop radio presence—with kicky, full-voiced charmers like "Bus Stop" and "Carrie Anne"—but had yet to fully graduate to the counterculture world of FM radio. At the Whisky, one reason why they hadn't was clear: they looked sharp in now-unfashionable matching dark jackets, and only one of them, goateed rhythm guitarist and harmony singer Graham Nash, sported facial hair. But the band's even sharper-cut vocalizing, courtesy of Nash, lead singer Allan Clarke and lead guitarist Tony Hicks, was dazzlingly precise; onstage, the Hollies sounded exactly as they did on record, no easy feat in the sound-system-challenged days of the '60s. Slicing through the arrangements, Nash's keening, high-pitched voice, which Paul McCartney had once mistaken for a trumpet, was particularly impressive.

When the show ended, Stills and Crosby, who had been circling each other over the past year, two ambitious musicians in search of a magic combination to vault them to the top, loitered on the sidewalk outside the Whisky, near its yellow awning. Each was at a crossroads. Crosby exuded a sun-baked, up-for-anything gusto—"What's the most fun we can have in 20 minutes?" would be his most devilish and successful pickup line—and his droopy mustache, occasional cape and hair flipping down to his shoulders made him one of the most recognizable figures on the city's music scene, a naughty boy prince of pop. But at twenty-six, the now former Byrd faced an uncertain future after having been fired four months before from one of rock's leading and most innovative bands. With Buffalo Springfield faltering and at least two of its members regularly missing in action, the blonder Stills—whose flashes of good-old-boy grins and phlegmy laughs could easily give way to an intimidating, penetrating stare that signaled his displeasure—could never tell if his band would exist much longer. When a newspaper reporter asked him a few months later about the state of the Springfield, Stills, all of twenty-three, mentioned a planned fall European tour but added: "I don't know, though. You never can tell. You know, we might break up tomorrow." Although Young had joined him at the Whisky, he was generally off somewhere else, which didn't surprise Stills in the least; even then, no one could keep tabs on Young.

For all the uncertainty gripping their careers, Crosby and Stills were now caught up in what they'd just witnessed inside the Whisky. Joined by Elliot, who seemed to know everyone in town and delighted in moving around musical chess pieces, Stills and Crosby talked elatedly about Nash's performance that night. "Maybe we can steal him," Crosby said out loud, according to one of many varying accounts. Crosby had already met Nash; they'd bonded in Los Angeles and London and had gotten stoned together. The only thing they hadn't done together was sing, but in front of the Whisky, Stills and Elliot weren't sure that was an option. In the rules-oriented world of pop in 1968, swiping a member of another group was fairly unthinkable, an affront to the bonds of a rock-and-roll band; legally and morally, there were still rules.

Whether they realized it or not that evening, Crosby, Stills and Nash were each dogged with insecurities; in one form or another, they were in search of acceptance, validation and victory. In due time, those needs, and how they intersected with financial concerns, would also pull in Young. But at the moment, they were men of radically different voices, temperaments and features (Stills and Nash chiseled, Crosby more baby-faced, even at his age) who were hungry for someone to complete them. They wanted what they wanted, and they decided that the established rules would not apply to them.

FOR NASH AND his school friend Harold Clarke, their first taste of a different, less suffocating world beyond working-class Salford, a suburb northwest of Manchester, arrived inside a pub. The two had met in elementary school (Nash had raised his hand when the newly arrived Clarke had shown up in class and needed a seat next to *someone*), and the two had first noticed the comfortable way their voices blended while singing "The Lord Is My Shepherd" at a school concert. It wasn't long before they had hustled up guitars and together started singing skiffle—scruffy folk that had originated in the States but had undergone a revival in the United Kingdom—in the Clarke or Nash homes. When Clarke's older brother overheard them, he thought the two kids, now in their teens, should try singing in public—specifically, at a nearby workingmen's bar, the Devonshire Sporting Club. Clarke's brother introduced them to the owner, who asked them to play him a few songs. Satisfied with what he'd heard, he told them they could play at the bar that same day, immediately after a juggling act. "We came offstage and the guy came up to us and said, 'We like that and here's 10 bob,' a half pound in those days, quite a lot of money," Clarke recalls. "Graham and I looked at each other and said, 'This is okay.'"

For Nash, the moment would be formative, his first taste of rising above his surroundings and feeling less like an outsider. He'd been born amid the rubble of World War II; the Christmas 1940 bombings of Manchester and Salford had forced expectant mothers to relocate to hospitals in nearby Blackpool, where Nash arrived on the second day of February 1942. (Adolf Hitler had spared Blackpool, thinking it would make for an ideal seaside vacation spot once he had conquered Great Britain.) Nash would long be haunted by memories of the thick "blackout curtains" his family used at night so enemy bombers wouldn't be able to determine where the towns and villages lay below.

In his teen years, Nash's face grew lean, and his hair became an overgrown version of a Presley pompadour. But he could never escape the feeling that he was a societal black sheep. His father, William, cast metal in a local foundry. At the Nash family home in Ordsall, the gritty, blue-collar section of Salford, the bathroom was outside and hot water was in short supply. Unlike the more cultured types in London, two hundred miles to the south, Nash didn't have fashionable clothes; his

Manchester-area accent, combined with his frequent salty-sailor exple-
tives, made his working-class roots even more pronounced. One of the
few things that made him less than blue collar was music. "I definitely
wasn't cool," he says. "If the leather wore out on the bottom of my shoes,
I wore a pair of my mother's manly-looking shoes. But when I started
to play guitar and sing Everly Brothers and Buddy Holly songs, people
started to treat me a little differently, strangely enough. And I realized
that. I recognized the power in being popular. And so because I wasn't
'cool' in my normal life, this one little area of playing and singing made
me feel a little cooler than I was. And I *liked* that."

Once their schooldays had ended, Nash and Clarke both followed
their supposed accepted paths in life, working day jobs that, for Nash,
included the post office. But their desire to play music and escape their
lives was unquenchable. By their later teens, they were giving themselves a string of different names—the Two Teens, the Guyatones (named
after the mass-produced Japanese guitar manufacturer), or the Everly
Brothers–inspired Ricky and Dane Young—and playing regularly in whatever club or pub would have them. Clarke, who would soon rename himself Allan, had a strong, nasal tone that demanded he be the lead singer,
and Nash had startlingly high harmonies that softened Clarke's delivery.
Additional musicians were added until, in 1962, the full group, first named
the Deltas, transformed into the Hollies. The name was partly a nod to
their hero Buddy Holly; it was also a reference to the Christmas decora-
tions in a club they were playing. Asked to come up with a name before
they took the stage, Clarke looked around and told the announcer, "We're
the Hollies," and it stuck.

An EMI Records executive saw them at the Cavern Club in December
1962. A month later they had followed the Beatles to EMI and were recording their first single, a peppy, breathless cover of the Coasters' "(Ain't
That) Just Like Me" that hit no. 25 and set the tone for their original
sound. "Our lives changed completely," Clarke marvels. Suddenly, the two
childhood friends who'd grown up feeling less than hip were seeing their
songs—covers of R&B hits like "Searchin'," "Stay" and "Just One Look"—on
the British charts, and singing before throngs of squealing young women.

In early 1966, the Hollies broke through in America with "Look Through
Any Window," which played to their most charming qualities—swelling

vocal harmonies, picturesque lyrics, and drummer Bobby Elliott's kinetic rhythms. Whether written in-house or by outsiders, the singles that followed—the weather-driven love story "Bus Stop," the belly-dancer-inspired "Stop! Stop! Stop!," the Marianne Faithfull nod "Carrie Anne"—were impossibly magnetic radio candy and, deservedly, hits on both sides of the ocean. Nash had a hand in writing many of them, and momentarily, life felt grand: in 1963, he left the Manchester area behind and moved to London, marrying his girlfriend, Rose Eccles, the following year. By then, he and Clarke had even spent an inebriated evening in the studio with the Rolling Stones and Phil Spector, singing warbly backup on throwaways like "Andrew's Blues."

For all those accomplishments, the Hollies could never score an aura of hipness. In 1965, they released "Too Many People," a politely political commentary describing how a million people died in an unnamed war. In fact, the song had its roots in news reports about the Mau Mau, a terrorist organization of the late '50s and '60s that was killing white farmers in Kenya to protest their settlements. It didn't make the Hollies rebels, but it was a start. When the multi-hued late '60s came into view, the band snazzed up its wardrobe with floral-patterned shirts and beads. "We went along with the flower-power stuff because that's what was happening," says Clarke. "We would have gone along with anything if we wanted a hit record." But the band's unhipness, the way it now made him feel as out of sorts as he had in grade school, gnawed at Nash, who longed for the credibility of the London scene. "Graham was going down to London and to the clubs and seeing things there that hadn't come into his life before, like drugs," says Clarke. "If there was anything happening, Graham wanted to be there. I was enjoying the '60s, but Graham wanted to take it further."

In the middle of 1966, the Hollies flew to Los Angeles for the first time to promote one of their records. If the palm trees and beaches he saw from the plane weren't enticing enough for Nash, the immediate bear hug of the Hollywood music scene was. At a party, he met Elliot, known as Mama Cass, the queen bee of the scene, and Nash took her up on an invitation to attend a recording session for the Mamas and the Papas. To complete Nash's trip to LA—and to fulfill her desire to make everyone feel connected—Elliot invited him to visit a friend of hers who lived in a wooden house on Lisbon Lane in Beverly Glen Canyon. There, Nash encountered a mustached man sifting through a box of weed–David Crosby of the Byrds–and Crosby promptly got his new acquaintance higher than he'd ever been. "I had better pot than anybody else," Crosby says. "I got him whacked." Although Nash didn't know it at the time, Crosby stashed some of his drugs behind secret cupboards, along with guns and knives.

The trip was a grand awakening for Nash: people like Crosby and Elliot knew who he was and loved his singing. In a heartbeat, he felt hipper, more like an insider, than ever before (the Hollies dabbled in drugs but mostly stuck to drinking). Simultaneously, Nash began to take greater charge of steering the Hollies' ship. At the same time–and in the same Abbey Road studio where the Beatles were concocting *Sgt. Pepper's Lonely Hearts Club Band* in early 1967–the Hollies began recording *Evolution*, the first of two self-consciously psychedelic albums they would make. Nash played an even larger role in the same year's *Butterfly*, which was stuffed with Indian sitars, a song about a flying horse, and another song titled, with trippy pretensions, "Elevated Observations." They made a valiant effort to sound high, but they still came across as too chipper and perky, and *Butterfly* would be one of their least successful albums.

That summer Nash brought in his most ambitious undertaking, "King Midas in Reverse," a self-lacerating account of his own infidelities and growing personal confusion. With its trilling strings and intentionally swervy, hallucinatory harmonies on the chorus, the record was the most ambitious the Hollies had ever made, although not everyone in the band approved. "The producer told us it wasn't going to be a hit, but Graham was quite adamant," says Clarke. "He was trying to be the Beatles. Everything but the kitchen sink was on that record. But it wasn't the Hollies' approach." Although a sonic accomplishment, the single peaked at no. 18 on the British charts–about a dozen spots lower than "Carrie Anne" or the equally contagious "On a Carousel." Although Clarke denies it, Nash feels the song's lack of impact made the Hollies begin questioning his judgment and decisions.

By then, Nash was already keenly aware of an alternative universe he longed for. Sometime before the "King Midas in Reverse" recording, the

Byrds, with Nash's new acquaintance Crosby in tow, flew into London for promotion. Nash invited his new American friend to stay with him and his wife, then to accompany him to a Hollies interview. To Nash's astonishment, Crosby was curt and rude to the British reporter. "A lot of it was my own natural feistiness," Crosby recalls. "I didn't like show business. It was very appealing to me to be completely different about that." The Hollies would have never been so improper—they played by the rules—but Nash was stunned and intrigued by Crosby's insolence. He saw for himself that Crosby was truly one of pop's savviest players and realized he wanted some of that integrity for himself.

FROM AN EARLY AGE, Crosby was enthralled by the sound, the *idea*, of people working together to create musical beauty, even as another part of him rebelled against collaboration. As a child, his nurturing mother, Aliph, had taken him to a symphony orchestra concert—in the late '40s, rock and roll did not yet exist—and the sight of a large ensemble working in tandem to create an overwhelming sound would stay with him for decades. "I had never heard an orchestra," he says. "I had never been to a rock concert. Nobody had. But this was huge, and the strength of it was all of them together, making this big thing."

But finding partners in musical or even personal harmony would rarely come easily for him. Compared to Nash, Crosby was a child of privilege. His father, Floyd, came from the social circles of New York; he was born in 1899, graduated from the Naval Academy in Maryland, and briefly worked in the cotton business in the South and at a brokerage firm in New York. His life changed when he accompanied an expedition to Haiti to take photographs, a trip so inspiring that it led to a career as a cameraman on documentaries. That phase extended well into the '30s, and in 1931 he won an Oscar for the cinematography on *Tabu*, a silent film shot in Tahiti. He met and married Aliph in New York and moved with their two sons—Floyd Jr., later known as Ethan, born in 1937, and David, born four years later, August 14, 1941—to Los Angeles.

The youngest member of the Crosby family would remember his mother as "a really good parent" who encouraged her son's love of music, but Floyd, who played mandolin on the side, would be a fleeting, sometimes disapproving presence in David's life. Thanks to Floyd's job making films for the Air Transport Command during World War II, he wasn't around for his youngest son's first three years. Even when the war ended, Floyd was gone again, this time to shoot a film on ice patrols in the northern part of the Atlantic. Though Floyd preferred working on exotic-locale documentaries and didn't care much for Hollywood back-patting, he was awarded a Golden Globe for cinematography for his work on *High Noon*, the 1952 Gary Cooper western. Several years later, after being blacklisted for associating with left-wing filmmakers, he began the first of many collaborations with future B-movie king Roger Corman.

By then, the Crosby clan was living in Santa Barbara, an enclave one hundred miles north of Los Angeles that attracted Hollywood types in search of less clogged surroundings. Yet despite the trappings and Floyd's steady work, the distance between father and son rarely im-proved. "I knew my father as a very straight crusty old guy, not much of a father," Crosby says. "Being around and being warm and concerned weren't his thing." Insecure, often chubby, and increasingly an expert at "fighting authority," as his older brother once said, Crosby began making a name for himself in school in the most inharmonious ways. At Crane Country Day School, he realized the power of an audience's love when he took a role in a production of Gilbert and Sullivan's comic opera *H.M.S. Pinafore*. But at his next school, the Cate School, he was kicked out for disconnecting a bell as a prank. The Laguna Blanca School deemed him of "dubious moral character" after it was discovered he was having sex with several girls in his class; he was soon ousted from that institution as well. He eventually managed to graduate from high school and enroll at Santa Barbara City College, though he was suspended after being arrested as part of an ad hoc burglary posse—and only able to re-enroll after ongoing therapy.

They didn't realize it at the time, but he and Nash had a ruptured family in common. When his son was a teenager in the '50s, William Nash was arrested on the grounds of possessing a stolen camera—which he insisted he'd bought second-hand from a friend. Unwilling to di-vulge that person's identity to the authorities, the elder Nash was sen-tenced to a year in jail: first at Strangeways, the daunting brick-wall prison in Manchester with a permanent—but now unused—gallows, then a minimum-security jail in Bela River. Overnight, Graham had to become the premature man of the household, presiding over his mother and two younger sisters, Elaine and Sharon. William Nash was released in 1960, but by then he was, as his son recalled, a broken man. He died six years later—shortly before his son came upon the startling sight of his mother kissing another man.

Crosby's family difficulties erupted when his parents divorced in 1960. Dropping out of college and relocating to LA (into an apartment that his father, now based in Ojai, kept for trips into Los Angeles), Crosby at first seemed intent on an acting career. But he ran afoul of his teacher, Jeff Corey, who, despite being a friend of Floyd's, still kicked Crosby out of the class for acting up. During his high school years in Santa Barbara, Crosby had begun singing folk music in local coffeehouses, discovering immediately the power that a supple voice and a strummed guitar had over young women. In Los Angeles, he frequented the folk clubs, although hardly singing the type of hale-and-hearty ballads common to that post–Kingston Trio era in pop music. As she later recounted, one early girlfriend characterized her boyfriend's downbeat performance style, prophetically, as: "I'm really horrible, everybody hates me, I'm different, isn't it sad, I can get attention this way and self-destruct in the end."

In July 1960, a clean-cut guitarist and banjo player named Jim (later Roger) McGuinn found himself at the Ash Grove, LA's fairly new and already prominent folk club, playing a nearly weeklong stint with the folk-pop group the Limeliters. Originally from Chicago and born in 1942, McGuinn was the son of two writers (his parents, Jim and Dorothy McGuinn, had coauthored the 1947 advice book *Parents Can't Win*); a private-school kid, he'd been pulled into rock and roll as a teen before switching to folk during rock's fallow years in the early '60s. The young McGuinn had landed a job backing the Limeliters as soon as he'd graduated from high school, and Crosby had approached him at their Ash Grove show. Crosby struck McGuinn as an aspiring actor who dabbled in music, so he showed Crosby a few chords and played him a couple songs by Chicago folk legend Bob Gibson. Crosby invited McGuinn up to his family home in Santa Barbara, and the two zipped up the highway in Crosby's convertible, complete with woven fabric seat belts that reminded McGuinn of airplane seat buckles. McGuinn stayed at the Crosby home for a few days, relishing Aliph Crosby's lamb-and-avocado sandwiches, but he already sensed his new friend was trouble. "He was a little bit unruly," McGuinn says. "Substance abuse problems even then. Not illicit drugs, no pot, but mostly beer. I remember him having too much alcohol." A Crosby friend warned McGuinn to stay away from him.

Trouble not only followed Crosby to Los Angeles but made him leave. In 1961, he learned that his girlfriend, Celia Ferguson, was pregnant. Unable to handle the news and not wanting the responsibility, he immediately left for Arizona and then Colorado; from there he ventured to New York, passing the hat at folk clubs, before continuing his travels to New England, Canada and eventually Miami. By late 1962, he was back in California—this time San Francisco, where he befriended fellow stoned folkies Paul Kantner, David Freiberg and Dino Valenti, and all four made their way down to Los Angeles. In 1962, Travis Edmonson of the duo Bud and Travis—who introduced Crosby to weed—recorded Crosby's first song, a languid ballad called "Cross the Plains" that would contain the first hints of his irregular-cadence approach to songwriting. Crosby, along with his older brother, Ethan, was then hired as part of a shanty-voiced folk group, Les Baxter's Balladeers, but like his father, Crosby bristled at conformity; he soon left to resume his scuffling around Los Angeles. Jim Dickson, an army veteran and aspiring producer, heard Crosby on the folk circuit and recorded four songs with him—folk-blues tracks like "Come Back Baby" and "Willie Gene" that showcased Crosby's high, pliable voice yet didn't lead to a record contract.

At the Troubadour, one of the city's leading folk clubs, Crosby met up again with McGuinn, who was now performing with Gene Clark, a transplanted Missouri singer-songwriter. Clark, like Crosby, had tried his hand at mainstream folk (in his case, the New Christy Minstrels). At the front part of the club, Crosby joined them and, uninvited, began singing along. "He wanted to be in the band," McGuinn says. "And I was like, 'I'm not sure I want to do this.'" McGuinn remembers Crosby's reputation for being a "problem child" but was willing to table his concerns for the time being when Crosby told them he knew someone—Dickson—who had a studio they could use. "He bribed me and said, 'We've got a recording

studio we can use for free!'" says McGuinn. "And I said, 'You're in!'" Paul
Potash, a folksinger and fledgling actor, was also present and advocated
for Crosby coming aboard, and the Jet Set—McGuinn, Crosby and Clark—
was hatched.

Like many others, including Stills, McGuinn and Crosby saw the Beatles' *A Hard Day's Night* that year and realized the future was not in
vernacular ballads but in rock and roll; McGuinn, who had already begun playing Beatles songs in folk clubs, to the consternation of some in
the audience, would always recall the sight of Crosby excitedly twirling
around a lamppost after they saw the movie together. With the addition of
Chris Hillman, a bluegrass mandolinist handed a bass, and Michael Dick
(later renamed Clarke) on drums, the Jet Set was now a rock-and-roll
band. With his orchestral memories in mind, Crosby tried to be as much
of a team player as possible. McGuinn recalls his sometime-roommate
bringing donuts and chocolate milk to rehearsals for breakfast. The two
would idle away the time at the Los Angeles airport on a runway, and
eventually, inspired by watching the planes zoom over them, they eventually wrote "The Airport Song."

Throughout 1964, led by McGuinn's twelve-string Rickenbacker guitar,
Gene Clark's often doleful pop songs, and their harmonies, the band
bore down on becoming a Beatles-influenced rock band. Initially called
the Beefeaters once the Jet Set was discarded, they recorded one failed
single for Elektra but were given a second chance by Columbia, which
signed the band in late 1964. Their manager, Eddie Tickner, suggested "the
Birds" as a name, but McGuinn opted for the snazzier alternate spelling.
Two months later, in January 1965, the newly renamed Byrds, abetted
by studio musicians, recorded a celestial cover of Bob Dylan's "Mr. Tambourine Man." (Hillman had beat them to the Dylan punch when his
bluegrass band, the Hillmen, did a version of Dylan's "When the Ship
Comes In," but that version wasn't electrified.) Dickson had received a
demo of "Mr. Tambourine Man" from Dylan's publisher, a recording with
Ramblin' Jack Elliott singing out of tune on the harmony. They added
what McGuinn calls a "Beatle beat"—4/4 time—and deleted several verses;
Crosby worked out the high harmonies, and pop radio devoured it. The
single sold nearly a million copies in the summer of 1965 and the Byrds
were overnight pop stars. Soon they were flying in a chartered DC-3 and,

like the Hollies thousands of miles away, straining to hear themselves over the screams of female fans.

Unlike the early years of the relatively harmonious Hollies, the Byrds' flight was tumultuous almost from launch. By early 1966, months after the success of "Mr. Tambourine Man," Clark was out of the band, a victim of his own neuroses (Crosby had whittled away at Clark's self-confidence by taking the rhythm-guitar role, leaving Clark as the lead singer). Starting with their third album, *Fifth Dimension*, Crosby began to find his voice as a writer. On that album and the following year's *Younger Than Yesterday*, he began contributing songs that stood apart in their beautiful bareness ("Everybody's Been Burned"), confused state-of-mind reflections ("What's Happening?!?!"), and ancient-world splendor ("Renaissance Fair"). If McGuinn was the reserved, analytical, brainy heart of the band, Crosby was its searching, breaking-bad soul, and the unconventional quality of his melodies, rooted more in jazz than rock, embodied pop's new, open-ended future. Crosby was the most musically adventurous of the Byrds, as Mark Naftalin, keyboard player for the Paul Butterfield Blues Band, saw for himself when he visited Crosby at his apartment in 1965: showing him a photo of George Harrison holding a sitar, Crosby told him, "Change is where it's at."

On Byrds albums, Crosby's harmony parts encased each song in a warm glow, but his personality could be discordant. Smuggling pot onto the Byrds' tour buses, often sporting one of his trademark green or brown suede capes, Crosby, perennially outspoken, began living up to Billy James' description of him, in the liner notes of the band's first album, as a "troublemaker." At a press conference in Los Angeles to debut the band's single "Eight Miles High"—a rumbling supersonic jet of a song co-written by Clark, McGuinn and Crosby—Crosby barked out, "Rev it up *loud.*" In March 1966, a review of a Byrds show at Lawrence University in Wisconsin noted the elevated decibel level of Crosby's guitar, which "literally made the chapel doors vibrate and in the process removed all chances of hearing either leader Jim McGuinn or Crosby sing." Those same pushy traits began alienating him from McGuinn and Hillman, and one by one, quality Crosby numbers, like the half-spoken "Psychodrama City" and two sensual, erotic songs—the dreamy, floaty "It Happens Each Day" and the love-triangle revel "Triad"—were recorded but, to Crosby's frustration, omitted from Byrds albums. "I was into Eastern religion and being goody-two-shoes about that song," McGuinn admits of "Triad." "I should have let it go."

For Crosby, the Byrds were no longer offering him the support and ego-stroking he needed on a regular basis. To him, they were square, the worst possible designation, and he began searching for other options. He didn't have to look terribly far. One afternoon in 1967, McGuinn and Crosby visited the home of Stills; Buffalo Springfield had opened for the Byrds on several occasions, so the two bands knew of each other. Stills and McGuinn cradled their guitars and Stills played a blues lick.

"Can you do that?" he said to McGuinn.

"It's not my style, man," McGuinn, an inveterate folkie, said.

Stills turned to Crosby: "*See?*"

THAT SPRING, WITH the Monterey International Pop Festival approaching, Stills had his own pressing need—another guitarist. Buffalo Springfield was once again on shaky ground: their eccentric bass player, Bruce Palmer, had been busted for pot, and their co-lead guitarist, Young, had bolted the band in the spring, right before they were scheduled to hobnob with Johnny Carson on *The Tonight Show*. Months earlier, the Springfield had scored its first—and eventually only—Top 40 hit with Stills' "For What It's Worth," inspired by demonstrations on the Sunset Strip. A slot at Monterey Pop, which would be filmed for a concert documentary, would vault them even further toward the stardom Stills craved. With Young out of the picture, Stills was in search of an additional player who could fill out the sound of the band and lend the support and encouragement he always seemed to require.

Commotion and irregularity were deeply rooted in Stills' life. Although he had been born in Dallas, on January 3, 1945, that city had only been a blip in his roundabout upbringing. As Crosby, Stills and Nash biographer Dave Zimmer would unearth, William Stills, his father, had been raised in the South but had wound up in Illinois, booking concerts by big bands. The elder Stills' skills as an engineer soon led to construction work and overseeing early tract-housing projects in that state. According to his son, speaking with writer David Fricke, William Stills was "an entrepreneurial kind of guy—he'd start something up and be real successful, then get bored and start something else." (For decades afterward, rumors swirled that William Stills was either a "career diplomat" or worked for the CIA, where, as Nash told one interviewer, he "had to change countries every ten minutes." Informed of this comment, Stills was stunned and insisted his father was an engineer.)

After Illinois, the family was on the move again, down to Louisiana and finally to Florida, where William Stills went into the retirement-home business. There, during the 1956–1957 school year, his son Stephen, a sixth-grader, was sent to the Admiral Farragut Academy, which would instill a military-style precision and bossiness into his brain (along with an occasional fantasy). "I loved the drill," he told Fricke. "It was really a relief to have some organization because my house was always in such chaos." The constant relocation also gave the teenage Stills an inordinately wide musical palette: he played drums in school bands, heard local bluesmen playing in informal backyard settings, and joined a band early in high school in Gainesville, Florida. (His fellow guitarist was Don Felder, later of the Eagles.) During his Florida high school years, he discovered blues records by way of his friend Michael Garcia, along with open tunings and country and bluegrass songs like the railroad-disaster chronicle "Wreck of the Old 97." Like Crosby and many other musicians before and after, he also saw the way music easily attracted women: he and his friends would sit in their cars, play guitars and watch local girls gather around and applaud. The sound of the crowd and the support made up for whatever he felt missing in him growing up in a home with a hard-living mother, Talitha, who wished her son was more refined. (He also had two sisters, Hannah and Talitha.)

As Zimmer also documented, Stills was soon on the move again, this time to join his family in Costa Rica's capital, San Jose, after he was falsely accused of stealing two textbooks at a high school in Florida (Stills, just sixteen at the time, contended he had picked them up by accident with a pile of other books). The rest of his family had already moved there because William Stills, who his son would later say had a bad temper and a fondness for alcohol, had become involved in the construction of storage tanks in El Salvador. Amid the mountains, cattle ranches and banana plantations of Costa Rica, where the Stills family would live for nearly a decade, Stills was exposed to jazz, folk and, naturally, Latin music. He would always remember the musician at a hotel in Panama who played a mighty Wurlitzer organ with a salsa beat. After an aborted attempt at college in Florida and a falling-out with his father, he wound up in New Orleans in early 1964. Stills had begun singing in a folk band in Costa Rica, exposing a prematurely grainy voice, but in New Orleans his musical talents expanded. With a local singer, Chris Sarns, he landed a gig in a bar, the Bayou Room, just around the corner from the New Orleans Playboy Club; it wasn't unusual to see off-duty Bunnies stopping in for a drink.

After six months, Stills was on the move again, this time following Sarns up to New York City to become part of the burgeoning folk scene in Greenwich Village. He found an apartment in the area and hit up all the usual open-mic clubs, sometimes with Peter Thorkelson, a similarly sandy-haired musician and singer from Connecticut who had relocated after graduating from Carleton College in Minnesota. Dylan was gone by then, but the Village still had its share of characters, including the gentle, beatific Manhattan-born singer, guitarist and harmonica player John Sebastian and the blues-rooted singer, songwriter and guitarist Fred Neil, who advised Stills to grow out his thumbnail to improve his guitar playing.

At one or another coffeehouse, Stills met Richie Furay, a wide-eyed, newly transplanted Ohio kid. By the summer of 1964, both had been swept up into a short-lived folk music revue called *America Sings* at a theater on MacDougal Street. After the show closed, the troupe was booked into the Village club called Café Au Go-Go. The band rechristened itself as the Au Go-Go Singers and recorded an album titled *They Call Us Au Go-Go Singers*. On the one song that spotlighted his singing, "High Flyin' Bird," Stills, all of nineteen, revealed a husky voice that could soar into a wail (and fly above the hokey folk-chorus choir behind him); a guitar solo on another track also hinted at his potential. "Stephen was head and shoulders above most of the guitarists playing the Village at that time," recalls Sebastian. "He had soul, and that was one of the things you really had to look for, especially in the folk movement. There were soulful people like Ronnie Gilbert of the Weavers. But being a fluid lead guitarist wasn't really a folk job." In an homage to Chuck Berry pianist Johnnie Johnson, Stills was later known as the "take-off man," the type who takes a song to a new level by turning up a guitar "and taking your head off," as Sebastian put it.

The Au Go-Go Singers disbanded in 1965, and Stills, eager to get his career going, was at loose ends. He briefly toured Canada with the Company, an offshoot of the Au Go-Go Singers. There, in a club in Ontario in April, the group shared a bill with the Squires, led by a lanky singer and guitarist, Neil Young. Young introduced himself, and the two promptly went out, got drunk and plotted putting a band together. Like Stills and Crosby, Young had also been inspired by *A Hard Day's Night*; folk was out, and amped-out rock and roll was in. But Young flaked out on Stills, opting for a solo act, and Stills was back in the Village hunting for work. Through it all, Stills retained a sense of drive, a hunger for success, that many others lacked or hid. Meeting him on the club circuit in the Village, before the Butterfield band, Naftalin jammed one day in Stills' apartment and heard him tell a friend that Naftalin was the bass player in his band, even though no such band existed.

Stills soon became part of the great westward migration, which would bring at least two hundred thousand Americans to California each year between 1960 and 1965, though the numbers sharply declined for the rest of the decade. With his parents' marriage over, he then made his way back to New Orleans, where he picked up his mother and one sister and drove with them to San Francisco. Relocating to Los Angeles, Stills was approached about a job on an upcoming TV pilot about a fictional rock band, but he passed when he heard he would have to sell the rights to his songs; Stills' recessed, non-camera-ready front left tooth probably didn't help. (He would later recommend his friend Thorkelson, who, after some initial hesitation, took the job; Thorkelson moved to Los Angeles and became Peter Tork on *The Monkees*.) Calling Furay, who was still in New York, Stills told him to fly out to California to join the band he was forming, but when Furay arrived, he realized, as Naftalin had, that there was no actual group.

But there soon would be. In what would become one of rock and roll's most divine accidents, Stills and Furay were driving on Sunset Boulevard in early April 1966 when they saw a hearse with Canadian plates, and Stills instantly remembered Young drove that type of vehicle. Pulling up behind the hearse, Stills and Furay shouted for the car to stop, and Young and Palmer, who had been kicking around in Los Angeles after a long drive from Canada and were on their way to San Francisco, pulled over. In what felt like no time, they decided to pool their talents, hiring a seasoned drummer, Dewey Martin, along the way. Young soon wrote to his mother in Canada: "We have formed a group in which we'll do all our own material. . . . The group is called Buffalo Springfield, for no particular reason." (A reason actually did exist: they'd seen it on the side of a steamroller on Fountain Avenue.) A mere month after that meeting on the streets of Los Angeles, they were playing at the Whisky a Go Go and had two managers, Charlie Greene and Brian Stone, as well as a contract with Atco Records, a subsidiary of Atlantic.

On paper, the Springfield would seem a jumble of a band: Stills wrote and sang pleading or cautious love songs; Young contributed spooky tunes that Furay, who had a more commercial voice, sang; and Palmer would play with his back to the audience. But those same clashing personalities and styles immediately made them stand apart in the Los Angeles club scene, and they had terrific material to boot. Released late in 1966, *Buffalo Springfield*, their debut, had songs that ranged from Stills' bubbly "Sit Down I Think I Love You" to Young's addled "Out of My Mind." With its muffled sound, the album didn't entirely do them justice, but its green effervescence was impossible to deny.

The Strip would come to their rescue. In the fall of 1966, clubgoers began descending on it, irritating area residents and upscale boutiques, and the Los Angeles Police Department instigated a 10:00 P.M. curfew for anyone under eighteen. On the night of November 12, a local radio station announced a protest at a club called Pandora's Box, complete with a fake funeral procession. A fight broke out for reasons unrelated to the curfew: a car carrying a group of Marines was bumped by another vehicle. Egged on by that brawl, the protesters (some of them carrying placards that read "We're Your Children! Don't Destroy Us") trashed a city bus and threw bottles and rocks at storefronts. Inspired by that night—with the Vietnam War in the back of his mind and a few songs by the band Moby Grape in mind as well—Stills drove home and quickly wrote what came to be known as "For What It's Worth." In a sign of how fast things were happening, the band recorded it a few weeks later. With its emphasis on Stills' rattled voice, Martin's ominous snare drum, and

Young's warning-bell two-note guitar part in the verse, the recording was gaunt and unsettling, capturing the uneasy mood of the moment that extended beyond Los Angeles to the whole country. At the suggestion of Ahmet Ertegun, the erudite head of Atlantic Records, the single was rush-released with an amended title. "For What It's Worth (Stop, Hey What's That Sound)" peaked at no. 7.

Thanks to the creative overdrive of both Stills and Young at that point, the Springfield broke as much artistic ground in as short a period of time as any rock band in history. From their first demo sessions in the summer of 1966 through the following summer, they wrote and recorded a dizzying array of songs that touched on country, rock and nearly everything in between. Onstage, Stills and Young—decked out as a dressy cowboy and a fringe-laden Native American, respectively—egged each other on, and off-stage it was even more intense. Furay was the earnest-voiced front man of the band, but Stills and Young almost seemed in a race to be the first to elongate the group's sonic range. Young was its dark psyche, casting a prematurely jaundiced eye on fame in "Burned" and "Mr. Soul"; without the rest of the band around, he took his music into opulent orchestrated places with "Expecting to Fly." With his musical schooling in South America and Latin America, Stills was leading the band into Latin rhythms and horns ("Uno Mundo"), stomping rock ("Special Care") and hungover cocktail-lounge jazz ("Everydays"); in terms of sheer musical diversity, few of his generation had his range at such a young age. By their second album, 1967's shape-shifting *Buffalo Springfield Again*, the members of the Springfield were already recording songs without the others. Furay sang and played "Sad Memory" alone when no one else showed up in the studio that day, and Stills recruited outside players for his experiments.

Taking a similar route as the Byrds, the Springfield began flying apart shockingly fast. Palmer, who was increasingly indulging in psychedelics, was busted for pot early in 1967; Young, dealing with both epileptic fits and the stress of success at the age of twenty-one, began flaking out. Amid the chaos, Stills tried to herd the band in the direction he wanted for it. "Stephen and Neil both respected each other's work, but they were ambitious and there was always this rivalry," says Nurit Wilde, a friend of the band members at the time. "Stephen was much more open about it. Neil was more passive-aggressive about his ambitions. Their guitar styles were quite different. Their managers thought they could get more out of them creatively, more songs, and would say, 'Well, maybe such-and-such a song would be side A,' and you could see the hackles going up. It wasn't who wrote the better songs but whose song was going to get out there." In a 1969 interview with the *Detroit Free Press*, Young placed the blame on Martin: "We just couldn't hack him anymore. He was on an ego thing and thought he could sing and always wanted to. It just bugged the hell out of us."

One May 1967 evening, Buffalo Springfield was scheduled to fly to New York to tape *The Tonight Show Starring Johnny Carson*, which hadn't yet relocated to Burbank, California. Instead, that evening, Young left the band. Buffalo Springfield was still slotted to play the Monterey Pop festival, with guitarist Doug Hastings filling in for Young. Stills nevertheless felt the need for someone else to have his back.

MONTEREY POP WASN'T the first rock festival of the Summer of Love: the Fantasy Fair and Magic Mountain Music Festival in Marin County, a week earlier, had staked out that turf, complete with an appearance by the Byrds. But Monterey's organization and lineup easily vaulted past the Fantasy Fair. It began when manager and Dunhill Records head Lou Adler found himself talking about jazz and folk festivals—like the respected ones at Newport—with Paul McCartney, Cass Elliot and Mamas and Papas singer, songwriter, guitarist and libertine guru John Phillips. "It was all about the fact that rock and roll wasn't considered an art form in the way jazz was," Adler remembered. Everyone realized that pop music should have a comparable festival of its own, and Adler and Phillips (who took over from the original planners) concocted an ambitious plan: three days of pop, rock, soul and world music at the Monterey County Fairgrounds, with a capacity for seven thousand concertgoers. Over the course of three harmonious days, the weekend of June 16 to 18, 1967, musicians hung out backstage, eating lobster and steak and sharing dope, while the seated crowd took in Otis Redding, the Grateful Dead, Big Brother and the Holding Company (with their frontperson Janis Joplin), Ravi Shankar, and both the Byrds and Buffalo Springfield.

Monterey Pop was intended as a statement of solidarity and harmony in the new pop landscape, but the Byrds and the Springfield came to the festival in various stages of disarray. McGuinn, Hillman and Michael Clarke were growing increasingly irritated with Crosby, and they arrived already testy, having just fired Jim Dickson, their co-manager and mentor. "They were at a point where there was so much separation there and angst between everyone," Adler recalls. In full rock-Cossack look—fur hat, mustache, mischievous "STP" sticker on his guitar—Crosby was center stage and dominant during the Byrds' set that Saturday night; he was also high, and, in McGuinn's memory, "so grumpy at us." At one point, Crosby quoted a line from Paul McCartney that "all statesman and politicians in the world" should be dosed with LSD to prevent future wars. Before the Byrds started up "He Was a Friend of Mine," a traditional folk song updated with John Kennedy–related lyrics, Crosby again addressed the crowd: "I'm sure they'll edit this out. I want to say it anyway even though they will edit it out." As McGuinn and Hillman stood silently on either side of him, Crosby told the audience that Kennedy was "not killed by one man," that there was a conspiracy to keep it hidden. "He was going beyond the scope of what we were about," McGuinn recalls. "We weren't running for office. 'Everyone should take LSD.' I took LSD but I wasn't sure everybody should—it could be *dangerous* to some people."

Crosby also didn't fill McGuinn in on his plans for the following day. Debate still rages over Crosby's initial impressions of Buffalo Springfield when he and Hillman saw them at the Whisky a Go Go in the spring or summer of 1966. Hillman and Stills would maintain that Crosby was dismissive of the band ("Ah, they suck—I don't like them," Crosby supposedly said to Hillman), although Crosby disputes those reports: "I liked the Springfield right away. The quality was obvious—the songwriting and the singing. Way ahead of everybody else." Whatever his initial impression, Crosby was spending more time with Stills by the time thousands began streaming into Monterey Pop. With Crosby providing an introductory part, Stills had already written and was in the midst of arranging a new song, "Rock & Roll Woman," partly about Jefferson Airplane's Grace Slick. "My lick," Crosby says with a laugh. "I showed it to him because I had thought of it and he swiped it."

Few, if any, Monterey concertgoers took note when the Springfield walked onstage without Young but with Crosby, now wearing a black cowboy hat. Unlike during his time onstage with the Byrds, Crosby

stayed comparatively subdued with the Springfield, remaining mum between their six songs and strumming and harmonizing as best he could
under the circumstances. "Stephen asked me," Crosby says. "And I was
there. The Byrds were coming apart at the seams, and I was very taken
with Stills. He was cocky. As a young guitar player, he probably thought
he was better than he was, but he was good. But I didn't have a plan. I
knew their songs and they were fun to sing. I didn't care how Roger and
Chris would react. It was fun filling in."

Other members of both bands were less than happy, though. Hillman
was rattled by the thought of his bandmate allying himself with another,
competitive band ("One just didn't do that then," he told Zimmer), and
Palmer told a Canadian journalist, John Einarson, that Crosby "stunk to
high heaven" and "embarrassed us to the max." Asked about Crosby's
cameo months later by a New Jersey reporter, Stills was nonchalant: "He
sat in with us a couple of times and he played with us at the Monterey
thing, and everyone started thinking all these horrendous and heavy
things. It was just that he could jam with us, whereas some of the other
Byrds couldn't."

No matter what discord they were sowing, Stills and Crosby were
increasingly being pulled into each other's orbits. On June 22, just a
week after Monterey Pop, the Springfield began cutting the shimmery,
sweet-to-tough "Rock & Roll Woman," which they'd played at the festival.
(Crosby has been credited with singing backup harmonies, although he
can't confirm he actually did sing on the record.) Late June 1967 was a
time of rising convulsions in Los Angeles. On June 23, President Johnson
arrived in town for a fundraiser only to find protesters outside the hotel
where the event was taking place. Organizers were so concerned for his
safety that plans were made to airlift him out by helicopter if a riot ensued; fortunately, the protesters simply marched.

On the Strip, a different type of protest, this one cultural, was taking
place the following weekend. Stills and Crosby again found themselves
on the same stage, this time at a hopping club called the Hullabaloo.
The three nights of performances, technically billed as Springfield shows,
amounted to free-for-all sessions that included most of the Springfield
(even, on the first night, a cameo by Young, who met Crosby for the first
time), Byrds drummer Michael Clarke, and African American power-

house drummer Buddy Miles. On the second night, Crosby again stepped onstage with Stills, this time singing the garage rocker "Hey Joe" (a song he'd recorded with the Byrds) and pitching in with Furay on harmonies on Stills' "Bluebird."

"We may be breaking some rules tonight," Crosby told the crowd on the second night. "But it's about time someone started experimenting."

ASKED ABOUT HIS future at a 1966 Byrds press conference, Crosby had casually retorted, "I want to retire in five years and sail off in a big schooner." His wish would be granted sooner than he planned. As his interactions with Stills became increasingly creative, McGuinn began to feel that Stills was trying to pull Crosby away from the Byrds. At the same time, Crosby became more and more vocal about his unhappiness with the band. Over the summer and into the fall, the band was at work on a new and ambitious album, a swirling song-sound collage called *The Notorious Byrd Brothers*. When "Triad" was recorded, but deemed unworthy of inclusion, Crosby pouted, sitting on a studio couch and refusing to sing on its likely replacement, a cover of Carole King and Gerry Goffin's wistful "Goin' Back." The last straw for McGuinn came when Crosby, who'd spent time in London with George Harrison and an orchestra, remarked that the Byrds weren't good enough musicians for him. "We thought, 'Oh, really?'" McGuinn remembers. "Chris got mad."

In late September 1967, Crosby was at his home in Beverly Glen Canyon when McGuinn and Hillman pulled up in matching Porsches. (Crosby says they called first; McGuinn says it was a surprise.) There, the two Byrds bluntly informed Crosby that they were tired of him and he was out of the band. "It wasn't *my* plan," Crosby says. "I said, 'It's short-sighted, but okay.'" In Crosby's memory, McGuinn told him, "We can do better without you"; McGuinn insists he said, "We can continue to make music without you." Either way, Crosby was now unemployed, rejected by yet another institution. One announcement declared that he was "complying with a request to resign."

Later that day, Crosby tooled around in his Porsche with the Monkees' Peter Tork, reiterating the party line: "They asked me to resign today," he told Tork. But in Tork's mind, Crosby seemed more bemused than distraught. "He was still in some kind of shock," Tork told *Rolling*

Stones's Brian Hiatt, "but he always wondered what was going to happen next, and of course, he was set up well enough that he didn't have to worry about eating in the immediate future." Later, McGuinn would express regret about the decision. "It was a bad marriage, and it was painful to hang out with him," he says. "But in retrospect, it wasn't the best career move for the Byrds. It would've been better to keep him in the band and make it work."

But as Tork sensed, Crosby accepted the decision, telling Columbia president Clive Davis he was quitting the business to go sailing. (Davis called McGuinn to confirm the statement.) Crosby was proud of the fact that the label bought his rationale. In fact, few at Columbia minded the change; Crosby was viewed as an agitator who was hindering the band. When *The Notorious Byrd Brothers* was released in January 1968, Crosby was surprised—and more than a little appalled—to see the three surviving members of the band pictured alongside a horse, which he interpreted as representing him.

Crosby would have mixed feelings about his forced exit from the Byrds. "There was regret because I loved that band and enjoyed it," he says. "But there was also a certain freedom, a door opening. Now I'd got a clean slate and could go in any direction I wanted." With a chunk of cash—McGuinn recalls a $50,000 settlement, although Crosby feels he borrowed $25,000 from Peter Tork—Crosby returned to Florida, bought a seventy-four-foot sailboat made of Honduran mahogany, the *Mayan*, and lived the life of an adrift pop star mulling over his options. Flying down to visit, Paul Kantner, Crosby's folkie pal and now cofounder and guitarist of Jefferson Airplane, helped his friend write a new song that caught the anxiety of life in the nuclear age. "Wooden Ships" opened with a line about the common language of smiling—inspired by a saying Crosby had seen on a church sign in Florida—and turned into the dialogue of two survivors recounting the screams they heard and the silver-suited radiation suits they witnessed. Crosby and Kantner were both science-fiction buffs, and Stills, who also saw Crosby in Florida during this period, pitched in with writing it as well. Although Crosby would soon be in need of cash and a new direction, life after the Byrds was already revealing what it could offer artistically—collaborations with anyone he wanted, the no-rules ethic at work.

When Crosby stopped by the Gaslight Cafe in Coconut Grove one night in late September, a different potential partner revealed herself. Billing itself as home to "the finest folk," all for $1.75 admission on many nights, the club was hosting a relative newcomer, Joni Mitchell. Born Roberta Joan Anderson, the twenty-three-year-old had lived several lives by the time she stepped onto the Gaslight stage: a childhood in several towns in Canada, a case of polio when she wasn't yet ten, a club performer and fledgling songwriter by her teens, an unexpected mother at age twenty-one, a wife after she married folksinger Chuck Mitchell (not the father of her child), followed by stints in Detroit and, after leaving Mitchell, in New York. Soon came a career-making performance at the 1967 Newport Folk Festival.

Crosby, who'd never heard Mitchell's name before, had stepped into the Gaslight to see another act on the bill, teenage folksinger and guitarist Estrella Berosini. As Berosini told author Sheila Weller, Crosby caught sight of Mitchell onstage and initially dismissed her as "just another blonde chick singer." But that perception changed when he listened more closely. "You walk into a club in Florida and she's singing 'Michael from Mountains' or 'Both Sides Now' or one of those early songs," Crosby recalls. "I instantly fell in love with her. Some of it was lust, but I certainly had a crush on her and thought she was the best thing I'd heard."

The feelings were initially mutual, and by Christmas, both Crosby and Mitchell had moved to Los Angeles, where Crosby helped arrange Mitchell's first record deal, with Reprise. The two had a brief romance, and Crosby would act as producer for the album; he would also revel in presenting her to his friends, treating her like a prized, talented possession. "I discovered sensimilla early on and I had it before anybody else did," he recalls. "So I would get people wrecked and then say, 'Hey, Joni, sing 'em a song.' It was fun." (Mitchell would later claim she felt uncomfortable in those situations. "It was kind of embarrassing . . . as if I were his discovery," she told biographer David Yaffe.) Mitchell would later complain about the sonics of her first album, *Joni Mitchell*, also known as *Song to a Seagull*, but Crosby adequately captured the spiraling purity of her soprano and a few of her strongest early songs, including "Night in the City" (which featured Crosby's new pal Stills on bass guitar).

Life as a producer, though, wasn't enough to satisfy Crosby or pay his bills. Never one to churn out songs, by early 1968 he nonetheless had enough to record a demo for a possible record contract of his own. The songs he put on tape one night that March, with no accompaniment but his own guitar, continued the meditative, rhythmless, puzzled-by-life journey he had begun in the Byrds. "Games" questioned relationships and his own motivations; the skeptical "Laughing" was triggered by George Harrison's devotion to the Maharishi. "Wooden Ships" didn't yet have all its lyrics, but Crosby nonetheless put down its surging, cresting melody on tape. Like "Wooden Ships" itself, the tape was intriguing but unfinished, waiting for something or someone to complete it.

That same spring, Buffalo Springfield was wobbling on its last legs. Finally the band held a meeting with Ertegun to tell him it was over. In his mid-forties, two decades older than the Springfield members, Ertegun had been the band's biggest cheerleader. With his heavy-lidded, jazz-cat aura, the Turkish-born record head and social aristocrat had launched Atlantic in the late 1940s and had signed pioneers such as Ray Charles and, more recently, the British power trio Cream. He saw a future for the band, especially Stills, whom he regarded with something akin to reverence.

At the meeting, Ertegun was visibly shaken, almost in tears. But Stills, like Crosby, was already thinking ahead. Bill Halverson, a husky, blond, twenty-five-year-old native Californian, had long been enamored of vocal groups; after working his way into audio recording, he had helped record portions of the Monterey Pop Festival. At the time, he was managing Wally Heider's studio in Los Angeles when he heard Stills wanted to book time. Halverson had already met Stills, during the Springfield era, and it hadn't gone well: when Stills had asked him to turn up the volume in his headphones during an overdub session, the headphones had squealed horrific feedback and Stills had chewed out Halverson. The studio reunion in mid-1968 was more productive—and further revealed Stills' talents to Halverson. Playing every instrument himself, Stills meticulously constructed a song called "49 Reasons," then instructed Halverson to turn the tape over so he could record another guitar part backward. "This is *nuts*," Halverson thought to himself, but it worked, adding a slithering, psychedelic-trip aspect to the punchy song about lost love.

Work like that should have augured the start of Stills' own career, in much the way his now former bandmate Young was bearing down on his own first album without the Springfield. But Stills was unsure of his voice, imagining himself a better guitarist than singer. Fortunately for him, another collaborative partner was willing to join him and bolster his confidence. Crosby had similar doubts about his own viability as a solo act and was still drawn to the idea of a band—"like a brotherhood or a marriage," he says. In Stills, he saw a simpatico character. "I liked that he was cocky," Crosby says. "He believed in himself. He believed he was good, so he would step forward and bite a chunk out of life, and I felt the same way." As spring led into summer, the Crosby and Stills friendship began firming up. The two musicians had little to do but spend time in one another's homes, playing guitars, getting high and plotting a way to make themselves stars.

In Crosby, Stills found a collaborator who was everything he could want at the time: supportive in a stoned-cheerleader way but not nearly as threatening or dominating as Young could be. With Crosby, there would be no arguments over guitar solos or, at least at that moment, leadership. Crosby, meanwhile, was open to a partner with a similar lifestyle and an even more open-minded musical sensibility. "The Byrds could swing, sort of," Crosby says. "But we were a bit awkward at it. I wanted to swing like a Motown record, and Stills could. I liked that. I wanted me some of that." Crosby had his first taste of that input as soon as the two began working together that summer. "Long Time Gone" had tumbled out of Crosby immediately after Robert Kennedy's horrific assassination in Los Angeles on June 5. "It wasn't just about Bobby," he says. "He was the penultimate trigger. We lost John Kennedy and Martin Luther King, and then we lost Bobby. It was discouraging, to say the least. The song was very organic. I didn't plan it. It just came out that way." A mere eight days after Kennedy's death, he and Stills put the first version of the song on tape, Stills again handling the majority of the in-struments. It was instantly apparent what Stills could bring to Crosby's music. From Stills' assertive bass to his crisp drumming, the song didn't meander or glisten the way Crosby's songs with the Byrds did; instead, "Long Time Gone" sounded like a switchblade, sharp and dangerous, and even Crosby's voice exhibited an added grit.

By still mysterious means, B. Mitchel (sometimes spelled Mitchell) Reed, the influential forty-two-year-old DJ at KMET, Los Angeles's leading rock radio station, got ahold of a copy of the song and began playing it on air, introducing it as the work of "The Frozen Noses." No matter who came up with the ad hoc band name, its meaning was obvious: Stills and Crosby had both begun sampling cocaine, which has a numbing effect on the nose ("freeze your nose" was an in-vogue phrase for doing the drug). "We could've done without that [name]," Crosby says, but by then, the duo was already associated with the drug. "[Cocaine] started happening right when we started to make the [first] album, before we even started," Crosby later told *Rolling Stone* writer Andy Greene. In 1968, Americans spent only an estimated $5 million on cocaine, a pittance next to the estimated $100 million on marijuana, but the drug was on the rise, especially in the music business.

The recordings Stills and Crosby made, which also included Crosby's "Guinnevere," partly inspired by Mitchell, had potential, but it was left to Cass Elliot, who prided herself on uniting like-minded talents, to determine what was missing. By now, her Hollywood pop social circles also included Stills' old Village folk pal John Sebastian. In the years since he and Stills had encountered each other on the coffeehouse circuit, Sebastian had become more successful than any of his peers; thanks to Sebastian songs like the bubbly "Do You Believe in Magic" and the atypically granular "Summer in the City," his band, the Lovin' Spoonful, had scored bigger hits than anyone outside the Mamas and the Papas. But by 1968, Sebastian had left and relocated from New York to California. At one or another hang-out session at someone's home that summer, Sebastian overheard a conversation between Elliot, Stills and Crosby over the way an even higher voice than Crosby's, someone like a Phil Everly of the Everly Brothers, could enhance Crosby and Stills. "I probably wasn't the only one who said it, but I said, 'You probably can't have him, but you might be able to get Graham Nash, who's even more fluid as a singer,'" says Sebastian. "It was all part of that running conversation."

No one knew it at the time, but when the Hollies rolled onstage at the Whisky that mid-February night in 1968, Nash had one leg out the door. To compensate for the poor chart performance of "King Midas in Reverse," he and Allan Clarke had concocted "Jennifer Eccles," a too-perky, more mechanical pop love song that Nash detested. He went along with recording and promoting it, but for him, it represented a step backward, another sign that the Hollies were behind the times. (The record trade magazine *Cashbox* dubbed it "a cutie with terrific appeal for younger pop listeners," which must have also made Nash's teeth gnash.) He'd already presented the Hollies with a few new songs—including the hippies-gone-Middle-East travelogue "Marrakesh Express," written during a trip he and his wife, Rose, had made to Morocco the previous summer—and the band seemed indifferent, although they recorded a half-hearted instrumental version of it. Instead, plans were in the works for an album of Dylan interpretations. Nash participated in the first recording, a horn-driven, Vegas-friendly remake of "Blowin' in the Wind" that disgusted him even further. "I was pretty down on myself," Nash says. "I was feeling pretty useless. I thought 'Marrakesh Express' was a decent song, but my bandmates didn't like it, so it must not be very good."

At some point during their conversations with Elliot, Crosby or Stills must have flashed back to the Hollies' Whisky a Go Go show the previous Valentine's Day evening. As soon as the show ended, Nash had joined Stills and Crosby outside the club. The three had walked down Sunset Strip, eventually winding up in Stills' Bentley (nicknamed the "Dentley" for all its scratches and nicks). As Stills drove, Nash and Crosby in the back seat, and all sharing a joint, Stills (according to Zimmer) turned to Crosby and asked, mischievously, "Which one of us is gonna steal him?" (Clearly he was referring to Crosby's earlier comment outside the club when Nash wasn't around.) Allan Clarke recalls the three men showing up at the Hollies' hotel room, where they sat around and possibly sang together. Not considering himself a good enough musician to grab a guitar and join in, Clarke went to bed. "I thought everyone was having a good time and getting on and the Hollies will go back and everything will be all right," Clarke says. "I just thought Graham was interested in other musicians. He always was. But all the signs were there. I just didn't see what was coming."

IN THE END, it was Joni Mitchell as much as Cass Elliot who clinched the deal. A month after the Hollies' Los Angeles show, on March 15, 1968, the group found itself in Ottawa, Canada, for a show at a local theater.

By coincidence, Mitchell had just begun a twelve-night run at a local folk club, Le Hibou. Crosby had told her about Nash, and vice versa, and after the Hollies' performance, Mitchell wound up at a party for the band at a local Holiday Inn, where Nash was smitten by her looks and the combination music box and photo album she was carrying. Always up for a chat with an attractive woman, he instantly introduced himself. Clarke remembers hearing a knock at the band's hotel room door, opening it, and seeing Mitchell, who asked for Nash and added, "David sent me." Nash was an engaged and attentive conversationalist: "He is aware and alert, and if he asks a question, he always listens to the answer," observed the *Ottawa Journal* after interviewing him during this time. Not surprisingly, he and Mitchell wound up spending the night together. All evening, Clarke could hear Mitchell singing her songs to Nash in the room next door.

By summer, Mitchell and Nash had committed to each other. Mitchell's relationship with Crosby had run its course, and by then, Crosby was in love with Christine Gail Hinton. A blonde with a winning smile and a father who was in the army, Hinton had been the founder of the Byrds' fan club, which soon became, in the words of a friend, "a David Crosby fan club." Determined to meet Crosby, she even took an apartment across the street from the Whisky a Go Go when the Byrds played there. She and Crosby had hooked up before he'd met Mitchell, but after Mitchell and Crosby were less of an item, Hinton and Crosby were together again. "Joni found out about that and came to a party at Tork's house and was very angry and said, 'I've got a new song,'" Crosby says. "'*Ooh*, Joni's got a new song.' She sat down and sang 'That Song About the Midway.'" With its references to a man's sky-high harmonies and the way she had caught him cheating on her more than once, there was no question about the subject of the song. "It was a very 'goodbye David' song," he says. "She sang it while looking right at me, like 'Did you get it? I'm really mad at you.' And then she sang it again. Just to make sure."

With money she had earned from her first, Crosby-produced album, which was rolled out in early 1968, Mitchell was now a homeowner. Given that houses on Lookout Mountain Avenue were generally priced in the affordable range of $25,000 to $40,000, she was able to buy a cozy place with a fireplace, paneled walls, stained-glass windows, and antique lamps and clocks. Guitarist Robert "Waddy" Wachtel, a New York–born musician newly arrived in town with his own band from Rhode Island, was driving down Sunset Boulevard and spotted two recognizable figures, Nash and Mitchell, and pulled over. Nash, who was carting a large bag of weed, asked for a ride to their home.

As Crosby and Nash remember it, Mitchell's home was the setting for the historic moment that came next. Crosby and Stills visited one evening, and as the two began singing one of Stills' new songs, "You Don't Have to Cry," Nash listened, asked them to sing it one more time (it only had one verse), and, on the third go-round, joined in harmony. Both Crosby and Stills were taken aback by how naturally Nash's high register blended with their lower tones. "I didn't think much of the Hollies because it was a purely pop band," says Crosby. "No substance at all. The harmonies were good. But when he sang with us, it was startling. The third time he put on the harmony [on 'You Don't Have to Cry'], you couldn't forget it. Stills and I looked at each other and we knew we wanted him to sing with us right then. Immediately."

Stills has recalled it differently, with the vocal hookup taking place at Elliot's cozy, white-fenced home on Woodrow Wilson off Mulholland. She had encountered Stills at a club one night and told him Crosby would soon be inviting him to her house, and Stills should go along. ("Do it—that's all I'm going to tell you," she said.) In Stills' memory, the "You Don't Have to Cry" moment occurred there, where Stills felt less inhibited about performing one of his own songs than in front of a young master like Mitchell. (In another version of events, Stills said in a 1982 radio interview that the "Who will steal him?" comment came after they'd first sung together.)

Others claim to have had their own sightings of the trio's initial moment of harmony—almost as if it were a sort of musical Yeti. Sebastian thinks it was at a home with a swimming pool, either his or Elliot's. "They called out 'You Don't Have to Cry,'" Sebastian says, suggesting it was not the first time, "and it was instantly, 'Crap, that sounds like the Four Lads or Four Freshman—it sounds like a unit.'" Wherever it happened—and it's likely there were many impromptu performances that summer and into the early fall—the sound of the three intertwining, very different voices (Stills' on the bottom, Nash's high register on top, and

Crosby's meaty middle) made for unison singing unlike anything anyone had experienced. "We took it 'on the road,'" Nash says. "We went to Peter Tork and [producer] Paul Rothchild and Sebastian and Cass. We knew immediately. We *knew*. It was just ridiculous. That sound didn't exist before that sound."

Emotionally and physically, Nash was ready to bolt the Hollies for a new, more welcoming world, and those ad hoc performances were his ticket out. Crosby had already sent Nash a copy of the solo tape he'd recorded, and Nash was struck by the unusual quality of the songs, how freeform and unstructured they were compared to the airtight pop of the Hollies' work. Now, singing alongside two of Los Angeles's most respected singers, songwriters and musicians, he was being welcomed into a hipper, more exclusive universe, complete with the supportive brothers he never had growing up. Within two weeks, they'd decided where their future lay. Wachtel ran into Crosby, whom he'd already met on the scene. "I'm going to ask you something," Wachtel recalls Crosby saying. "What would you think if I put together a band with Nash and Stills?"

In August, Nash returned to London and, as if nothing had happened, continued to work on new Hollies songs. They recorded two by outside writers, singer-songwriter-guitarist Terry Reid's "Man with No Expression" (also known as "Horses Through a Rainstorm") and songwriter Tony Hazzard's "Listen to Me" (which would sound like an early version of the '90s Brit pop band Oasis). The band, Clarke in particular, knew Nash was unhappy, but felt they were resuming as always; the Hollies were nothing if not productive. The group was planning more concerts as well as a benefit at year's end for the Invalid Children's Aid Association. Clarke was therefore stunned when, crossing the road near home, he encountered a friend who informed him that Nash had left the Hollies and had formed a new group with his friends in California. Clarke had known Nash for a dozen years; when the Hollies toured, Nash's wife would move into the Clarke home for company. But this news (which Nash admits he avoided telling the band in favor of letting their producer know first) was the first Clarke was hearing of his friend's sudden new life.

BACK IN LONDON, Nash, closing in on twenty-seven, began dismantling his life. He left his wife, Rose, although the divorce would not be finalized until January 1971 ("on the grounds of her misconduct with a married man," according to reports at the time). Nash moved into an apartment with Larry Kurzon, a William Morris agent who was also, at one point, interested in managing the potential trio of Crosby, Stills and Nash. The Hollies had confronted Nash about the rumors, and he admitted he was exiting: "He said, 'I want to leave, and I'm going whether you like it or not,'" as Clarke recalls. (Nash says he gave notice.) Stills and Crosby soon joined Nash in London, decamping to an apartment on Moscow Road and woodshedding individual songs that could be adapted to a trio format.

In that geographical context, Crosby and Stills' American brashness could be jolting. Chris O'Dell, an Apple Records employee who spent time with them at their shared apartment, was stunned when a bag of cocaine accidentally spilled onto the floor and Crosby and Stills dropped to the carpet to snort it. "I was thinking, 'Oh my God, is this for real?'" she says. A neighbor complained about Stills playing too loud. At the Hollies' last show, the charity performance at the London Palladium on December 8, Crosby appeared backstage, much to Nash's amusement and the Hollies' displeasure. ("He wasn't in *my* dressing room," says Clarke.) In Crosby's mind, he'd stolen Nash away from the Hollies in much the way he'd snatched that bell from his old high school.

Based on the Frozen Noses demo, Ahmet Ertegun had forked over seed money to the trio, which gave them funds for traveling to the United Kingdom, but he didn't necessarily have the rights to the band. Then again, no one was 100 percent certain there would be a band. Part of the reason for Stills and Crosby's London getaway was to make sure Nash *would* leave the Hollies, but they also planned to audition for Apple, the Beatles' recently launched label. George Harrison and Peter Asher, the former Peter and Gordon member in charge of signing acts to Apple, dropped by the apartment and listened as the trio played acoustically for them. The two said little and left, and the trio later heard Apple was passing. "Crosby, Stills and Nash were already established, in a way, and Apple was looking for nonestablished new talent," says O'Dell. "And each of them had already been in a band that had made it." ("They didn't get it," Crosby counters. "Everyone makes mistakes. They made a mistake. We were good.") O'Dell also wonders if Paul McCartney, who was seen visiting the flat at least once, may have been rattled by the amount of cocaine, a drug that was not yet prevalent in England.

Still, the trio knew what they had, in terms of the combination of talent, and they knew they needed a rapacious team to ensure that the industry met their demands for such a musical merger. Acerbic and enamored of a good joint himself, Elliot Rabinowitz had grown up in the Bronx, but by the time he was working as a young agent at the William Morris Agency he'd renamed himself Elliot Roberts, and one of his first clients was Mitchell. While at William Morris he had met another agent, David Geffen, an even sharper rising mover and shaker who had worked his way up from the agency's mailroom. Geffen, a Brooklyn native, had moved on to the Ashley Famous Agency, where he had worked solely on their music acts. Roberts planned to manage the trio himself by way of his new company, Lookout Management, which had a total of three employees, including himself, but he realized there was a complication: Crosby was a free agent after the Byrds, but the Hollies were signed to Epic (in America), and Stills had signed with Atlantic as part of Buffalo Springfield.

Realizing he didn't have the record company contacts Geffen had, Roberts reached out to him. Legend has it that Crosby, who tended to be initially wary of outsiders and kept them at arm's length until he felt comfortable with them, almost killed the deal when they met with Geffen at an apartment he was subletting on Central Park South in New York. Scanning the LP collection in the home, Crosby, according to Geffen biographer Thomas L. King, saw rows of mainstream pop albums and freaked out. "Is this what you listen to?" Fearing he had blown his chance to manage the trio, Geffen called his friend and client, singer-songwriter Laura Nyro, and begged her to come over and play her songs on the piano in the apartment as a way of bolstering Geffen's credibility. (Crosby doesn't recall the incident and says it may be apocryphal.) According to King, Crosby wasn't initially convinced of Geffen but was talked into it by Stills. But when Geffen and Roberts decided to join forces, at Geffen's insistence, everything began to click. "Elliot we knew and liked a lot, but we thought to ourselves, 'We're in a shark pool and need our own shark,'" says Crosby. "We met Geffen and said, 'There's one. Okay, those two guys. Elliot will be the mensch and David will be the wolf and that'll be fine.' They were both the wolf, it turned out, but that was okay."

For Geffen, securing the new group a record contract presented both a challenge and a showcase for his canny negotiation skills. Their Laurel Canyon friends were stoked at the idea of this musical conglomerate, but Geffen and Roberts were still dealing with fairly unknown quantities when it came to the trio's name recognition. The Byrds and the Hollies had had hit singles, but few outside the business knew Crosby's and Nash's names; Buffalo Springfield had largely been an underground act with only one hit to its credit. Geffen's first choice for a deal was Columbia, and Clive Davis, the avuncular head of the label who always craved the respect of the rock crowd, expressed his interest. Visiting the rambunctious Atlantic A&R man Jerry Wexler to ask that Stills be let out of his deal, Geffen was physically thrown out of Wexler's office, then told Stills that that company was run by "animals." Capitol Records was attracted to the idea of the trio, but, according to Leslie Morris, who worked for the label at the time, "Capitol wouldn't touch it. It was sticky because it was multiple record companies. So they were hands off."

In the end, they wouldn't need Capitol or any of the others. When Atlantic's Ertegun heard about Geffen's meeting with Wexler, he swooped back in and charmed Geffen. Stills was already thinking ahead: he knew his former Springfield bandmate, Richie Furay, had formed a spunky, country-leaning band, first called Pogo and then changed to Poco for legal reasons. Stills sensed that a band rooted in that genre would be more at home on Columbia than on the R&B-leaning Atlantic and called Furay with the idea of switching labels. Furay was amenable, and Geffen made an offer: Nash would leave Epic, the Hollies' label, for Atlantic, and Furay would leave Atlantic for Epic. "Sort of like a baseball deal," Stills said later. According to King, Ertegun suggested that Atlantic and Columbia partner: the former label would release the unnamed trio's first album, Columbia would release the second, and so forth, but Davis was understandably not interested in such a peculiar deal.

Ertegun hedged a bit. "Ah, man, the trouble you cause me," he told Stills when the idea of swapping labels for Nash was brought up. "Why do you make me go through all this trouble with Sir Joseph [Lockwood, chairman of EMI, Capitol's parent company] and Clive Davis just because you want harmony?" He also wondered aloud to Geffen whether Stills' new band would be as big as another harmony-driven group, the Association. Ertegun later admitted that, had negotiations dragged on, he would have let the trio go to another company. But he valued Stills and, in the end, offered them a six-album deal. "Geffen manipulated the outcome," says Ron Stone, who was then working for the newly renamed Geffen-Roberts Company. "It was not so much a legal process as a kind of ballsy move, and David was quite brilliant. He was playing chess, many years ahead of us."

In the last month of 1968, Jerry Pompili, the house manager of the Fillmore East, New York's preeminent rock theater, heard from a box-office clerk that a strange-looking guy was standing beneath the marquee, not moving or talking. It wasn't a completely uncommon sight, but Pompili went to check on the situation and, to his surprise, recognized the loiterer—David Crosby of the Byrds. Introducing himself, Pompili invited Crosby in to hear whatever band was playing that night, but Crosby said no, he just wanted to stand outside. Pompili was confused, but Crosby told him he had just landed an amazing deal and couldn't tell anyone yet. His way of celebrating, he told Pompili, was to travel downtown to the Fillmore and stand in front of it.

Finally, two days before New Year's Eve, 1969, the respected and music-savvy *San Francisco Chronicle* columnist Ralph J. Gleason broke the news: "David Crosby of the Byrds, Graham Nash of the Hollies, and Steve Stills of the Buffalo Springfield will form a special trio to record together." Refugees from three disjointed families had come together to form a new one, with its own unique rules. It was now a matter of making the new family and brotherhood work in ways the old ones hadn't.

CHAPTER 2

JANUARY 1969–DECEMBER 1969

Even though they knew what they were doing, they still began in the dark. Early in 1969, Bill Halverson was again at work, managing Wally Heider's Studio 3, when he took a call from an underling at Atlantic Records. The label wanted to book time for one of its new acts. Halverson wasn't given the name of the band—apparently, they didn't have one yet—but was told it was a self-contained unit that would need three to four weeks at the studio. Halverson, who offered to work on the sessions himself, told the label fine, he'd be prepared.

As mysterious as the project was, Halverson was even more puzzled when a green Volkswagen bus, outfitted with a revved-up Porsche engine, rolled up in front of the studio on Cahuenga Boulevard in Hollywood in early February. Out stepped Stills and Crosby, both of whom he knew, and Nash, whom he didn't. The three were hauling various guitars and basses, but no one else accompanied them. Was this a full band or not? After small talk, they instructed Halverson, seated in the control booth, to set up a microphone but no music stand in the recording room.

Walking into the space with one of his acoustic guitars, Stills told Halverson to kill the lights. Halverson couldn't see Stills at all but could hear him warming up, and Crosby, standing beside Halverson, swung his arm over his head, what Halverson calls the universal signal for "we're recording." As Stills started playing a slippery opening in an open D modal tuning, every string tuned to an A or D, Halverson thought it sounded off, with no bottom end. But Stills kept going, and when he finished, still enshrouded in darkness, Halverson heard Stills putting his guitar down followed by the sound of high-fiving. "That's the sound I've been looking for forever," Stills told Halverson, who soon learned that the multipart, seven-and-a-half-minute guitar performance he'd just put on tape was the foundation for a song called "Suite: Judy Blue Eyes."

Besides being unaware of what they would call themselves, Halverson also hadn't realized how much the trio had prepared in the short, insanely concentrated time since they'd first harmonized together. Two months before, they'd been in another studio, the Record Plant in New York, where they'd congregated with producer Paul Rothchild, best known at that moment for his work with the Doors. What transpired over the course of one day set the tone for their future dealings with other potential overseers. Although untested in many ways—they still hadn't performed in front of people who weren't their friends—the trio was inordinately confident in its abilities and had little interest in outside input. With Stills handling percussion, they put two songs on tape, "You Don't Have to Cry" and another Stills ballad, "Helplessly Hoping," instigated by an alliteration exam he'd taken in high school. Both mid-tempo, both acoustic, both quieter than anything their previous bands had done, the recordings were striking—a new harmonic blend in a new context.

The recordings were satisfactory, but to Nash, Rothchild came across as too controlling and prescriptive. Rothchild's interest in taking a cut of any profits if he were to be their full-time producer was also off-putting, and David Geffen convinced Crosby, Stills and Nash that they could handle the production chores themselves—and keep the extra cash as well. "We worked with Rothchild to see if he was okay," says Crosby. "It was okay, but not good enough. We didn't need him. We'd all three made records. We didn't need a producer. We saw that very quickly. We cut him out." Although those tapes soon helped secure their future, Rothchild would long be resentful about what he felt was a raw deal—his first indication that money was beginning to matter as much as music in his business. "He was very bitter about that," says Dave Rao, who would later work for Stills and met Rothchild. "He said, 'They're *baaaad* people,' which I didn't agree with."

After the Rothchild episode, the trio stayed on the East Coast. Already sensing they were attracting unwelcome hangers-on and could easily fall prey to distractions, John Sebastian had suggested they relocate there from Los Angeles to refine their approach. Sebastian made the case for Sag Harbor, a former whaling port on the far eastern end of Long Island, where he lived with his wife, Loretta (Lori for short), and their four dogs, five cats and organic garden. Crosby, Stills and Nash agreed and rented an A-frame home with a fireplace where they could rehearse and get as stoned as possible without any interruptions.

At the airport on the way to Long Island, they coincidentally met Sebastian's new drummer, a twenty-year-old from San Antonio who'd played in a quasi-psychedelic band, Clear Light, that Sebastian had heard and liked. Already married with two young children, Dallas Taylor arrived with his own baggage—to combat stomach issues when he was a child, his mother had given him medicine laced with paregoric, a form of opium—but he also came with a limber, jazz-influenced style. His dark hair, cut in a bowl shape, gave him a distinctive look. Taylor and Stills had gotten off on the wrong foot earlier when, Taylor said, he worked with Stills and hadn't been paid, forcing him to report Stills to the American Federation of Musicians (AFM). But Taylor heard the trio was looking for a drummer, and he and Stills reconnected as buddies in frenetic, relentless jamming. Nash quickly realized that his initial hope for Crosby, Stills and Nash—an acoustic folk album—wasn't to be. "Stephen was pushing them to do a rock-and-roll record instead of a folk album because he was the electric guy," Taylor recalled later. "He was a rocker. He wanted to play."

Between snorts of cocaine, the trio rounded up a few other musicians, including bass player Harvey Brooks and keyboardist Paul Harris. (Stills and Brooks had worked together earlier in the year on *Super Session*, a jam album with singer and multi-instrumentalist Al Kooper and white-blues guitar hero Michael Bloomfield that was a surprise hit; Stills' wah-wah guitar on his and Kooper's version of Donovan's "Season of the Witch" became a major presence on FM radio that summer of 1968.) Songs were beginning to tumble out. Crosby wrote a hippie statement of purpose, "Almost Cut My Hair," at the Sag Harbor house. "At the time we were very rebellious," Crosby recalls. "We were the counterculture, so the idea was, 'Don't give in, stay with it, don't cop out from the attitude that we're different and want it another way.' Hair was only a symbol. It was a statement of independence. We're not going to shave it and put on a button-down shirt and become like you." Nash would pen "Right Between the Eyes," about sleeping with a friend's partner, that referred circuitously to his feelings for Sebastian's wife. (According to Nash, those feelings weren't consummated until later, and Sebastian was accepting, given the shaky status of his marriage at that time: "Once you realize you're not well paired," Sebastian says, "it's a lot less painful when you find out there's someone else involved.")

During this period, Sebastian's name was floated as a possible addition to the band. During a practice session in Sag Harbor, he slipped behind a drum kit to tap out a gentle rhythm. "I got a little brushes thing going and they said, 'Hey, he could sing below and we'll have another songwriter in the fold,'" Sebastian recalls. "It sounded good that afternoon, but it was just that afternoon. It was a really brief idea that faded quickly. I dodged a bullet." Meanwhile, Stills, an accomplished bass player himself, wasn't hearing the sound or tone he wanted, and Brooks learned of his dismissal when he arrived at an airport to pick up a plane ticket to join them for recording in Los Angeles—and discovered there *was* no ticket.

Now ensconced at Heider's studio on a bustling Hollywood street, Crosby, Stills and Nash had the songs they wanted to record or remake, like "Long Time Gone" from the Frozen Noses moment. (Halverson remembers someone bringing up that name, so it hadn't yet been completely dismissed.) They also knew exactly how they wanted to sound. In a matter of months, they'd worked out most of their vocal arrangements and sounded like they'd been harmonizing together for years. But knowing they had to prove their worth on record, they also realized they had to concentrate, so certain rules were laid down. No friends or groupies were allowed; nor were any representatives from the American Federation of Musicians, which routinely kept tabs on recording dates for financial reasons. "That was normally what happened in the '60s," says Nash. "The union was a big presence in the studio making sure the drummer was being paid right, and so on. We said, 'We don't want anybody here. Leave us the fuck alone.'" (As a result, no official AFM paperwork has turned up for those sessions.) Not for the first or last time, they were accommodated, allowed to get away with something few had before.

As they worked from early afternoon into the early hours of the morning, day after day, the album began taking shape. One early idea—a double album, half acoustic and half electric—was abandoned, but "Guinnevere," which Crosby had first attempted on his own, was reborn as a Crosby and Nash duet. Crosby recorded two guitar parts, Stills played a mellowed bass line, and Crosby and Nash added intertwined harmonies with breathy, brotherly precision. (They also recorded it with drums but, realizing the song felt too conventional that way, erased them; Halverson would still hear a bit of the percussion in the background of the recording.) Such creative interactions fueled the sessions. Crosby and Nash faced each other at a microphone and sang Nash's "Lady of the Island" (which Sebastian also sensed may have been about his wife, the "island" being Long Island). When Crosby struggled with a few of the introductory lines in "Wooden Ships," Stills stepped in, making the first part of the song a duet that enhanced the postapocalyptic dialogue of the lyric. The trio sang a version of Stills' rousing "Change Partners" with round-robin vocals that recalled the Hollies' "On a Carousel," and cut a version of the Beatles' "Blackbird," but opted to leave them both off the record. Nash made fried-chicken runs; as a way to cement their new bond, Crosby bought Stills a Fender Precision bass. "It was a lot better than I thought it would be," says Crosby of the songs emerging. "It was kind of startling. I didn't know how good we would be at creating tracks. A lot of it was Stills. He was terrific."

Now decisively in charge of his music and destiny, Stills worked with a manic drive, playing most of the guitars as well as every note of bass guitar and keyboard, since Paul Harris had ultimately not been enlisted, either. (Even the percussion toward the end of "Suite: Judy Blue Eyes" was Stills thwacking away on the back of his Martin guitar.) He toyed with varied guitar tones on "Suite: Judy Blue Eyes," including lazy-day country licks he eventually discarded. Thanks to Stills, Nash was finally able to hear "Marrakesh Express" the way he wanted it, with Stills' fizzy organ and slithering guitar pushing the song down the tracks. "It was amazing to watch," says Sebastian, who dropped in one evening. "Stephen was, 'Here's a guitar. Now I'll play bass on it. Now it needs a little more guitar in this other part. Now I'll put on some B3 organ.' Stephen really made that whole album."

Unable to make the "Marrakesh Express" session, Taylor was temporarily replaced by session drummer Jim Gordon, a handsome surfer type who was as talented as he was peculiar. Years later, after he had played with Eric Clapton and co-written "Layla" as part of Derek and the Dominos, Gordon half-jokingly told Taylor he had wanted to "cut his [Taylor's] hands off" and do the rest of the Crosby, Stills and Nash album himself—a chilling admission given that, over a decade later, Gordon would be imprisoned for stabbing his mother and bashing in her head with a hammer.

Crosby was confronted with Stills' pushed-to-the-max work ethic when they hit an impasse. After five weeks, "Long Time Gone," so important to Crosby, was proving difficult to nail; the whip-crack feel of the Frozen Noses version was discarded, but nothing was emerging to take its place, and the song was almost left for dead. Finally, on the night of March 11, Stills told Crosby and Nash to go home; he wanted to work on the arrangement. "Graham and David would come and go, but Stephen was obsessed," says Halverson. "The sound would be in his head, and he had so many ideas it was just a matter of 'How quick can I get these down?' As quick as I could rewind to another track, he was onto something else. You just had to keep up."

When Crosby and Nash arrived back at Heider's the next morning, Stills was still there—he'd been up all night, no doubt aided by one stimulant or another—and played them the track. Again, he'd handled everything except the drums, and out of the speakers emerged an organ that throbbed menacingly and jabs of guitar that sounded like snarling dogs. Overjoyed, Crosby grabbed a bottle of wine, tossed down a few gulps and sang the song with a new, deeper tone, almost as if he were underwater and struggling for air. As writer Ellen Sander, who was on the scene and was the only writer invited to watch them at work, observed of that moment, "Stills . . . had his eyes down, and when he raised them, the expression on his face said plainly and silently: *I arranged your song better than you could have in a thousand years. And don't you forget it.*"

As Nash recalls: "Yes, that's absolutely true."

DESPITE THE NO-OUTSIDERS decree, plenty of friends still managed to drop into Heider's over the course of those weeks and heard bits of what Crosby, Stills and Nash were secretively creating. Ertegun arrived in a limo, dragging along an eerily quiet Phil Spector. Joni Mitchell and Cass Elliot stopped in; when Nash couldn't make it, Elliot would substitute for him on early versions of songs, and her voice eventually made its way into a bit of "Pre-Road Downs," a polite rocker that was Nash's attempt at preparing Mitchell for when the band would leave Los Angeles behind and go on tour. Revisiting the backwards-guitar idea he had used with Halverson the year before, Stills threaded his serpentine solo through the song like a needle.

Then there was the woman who inspired, to various degrees, most of the Stills songs on the album. By the summer of 1968, when she left New York for Los Angeles to make her first rock-influenced album, Judy Collins had already been a performer for a decade, first in her native Colorado. On 1966's *In My Life*, she was progressing beyond the folk ballads and shanties of her early work into art song and pop. Rightly lauded by many media outlets as a folk "goddess," Collins exerted a siren-like pull with her pure soprano, enchanting blue eyes and long brown hair. Now, with the help of producer David Anderle, who wanted to loosen her up, she was hoping to inject country and rock and roll into her pristine folk.

When he heard she was recording, Stills "bugged Anderle [to enlist him] until David said okay," Collins recalls. The two would long disagree on where in Los Angeles they first met, but the immediate attraction, musically and physically, was undeniable; Collins thought he was one of the most handsome men she'd ever seen. Stills' impact on her music was equally immediate: for the album that came to be called *Who Knows Where the Time Goes*, he added gentle strums on Collins' version of British singer-songwriter Sandy Denny's title song, chicken-scratch guitar swipes behind her slow, churning version of the traditional murder ballad "Pretty Polly," vibrato twang to "First Boy I Loved," and a loping bass on her take on Ian Tyson's "Someday Soon," which Stills had suggested. Flying back to New York, Collins, who at twenty-eight was five years older than Stills, told her boyfriend they were over and a new man was in her life.

Stills and Collins gave off the air of a music-textbook folk-rock couple. She would visit California, where they would talk of getting a home together; he would join her band onstage for shows, including at Carnegie Hall, to promote her album. Although women visitors were frowned upon during Crosby, Stills and Nash's Sag Harbor practices, Collins recalls bringing along a copy of *Music of Bulgaria*, a collection of vocally astounding harmony singing from the '50s that her record company boss, Elektra's Jac Holzman, had just released on his sister Nonesuch label. (Crosby thinks he turned Nash onto the album; Nash recalls receiving a copy from Paul Simon.) "A huge influence on me," says Crosby of the sound of the massed Eastern European female voices heard on the record. "I don't think Stills or Neil ever listened to it, but the harmonies are brilliant. It was stuff people hadn't even tried, let alone pulled off. It was as important to me as the Beach Boys."

But the Stills and Collins affair would burn itself out quickly. Collins, who lived in New York, was five years into psychotherapy and had no desire to move west; Stills wanted to stay in California. Both were headstrong careerists, and Collins—rightly, it turned out—felt that *Who Knows Where the Time Goes* would take her music to a larger audience, and she didn't want to miss the opportunity to promote it. "Stephen didn't like therapy and New York, and I was in both," she says. "That was kind of a parting flag that went up. And I was determined to make sure that this career that was beginning to actually happen had to be paid attention to." In an effort to change her mind, Stills began crafting songs to her, first and foremost, probably in the summer of 1968, "Suite: Judy Blue Eyes"— three different tunes he merged into one, based on a series of notebook musings about his feelings for Collins. In it, he pleaded for reconciliation, felt sorry for himself, begged her to remember the good times, melodramatically admitted he was suffering, and in general tried to convince her that the two had a connection. "You Don't Have to Cry," which told of how wrecked she'd left him in favor of her work phone calls and music business matters, began as a love letter to Collins.

By the time of the Crosby, Stills and Nash sessions, their relationship was teetering, but Collins stopped by the studio nonetheless around March 12, when she was in Los Angeles for the Grammy Awards. (She walked away with a "Best Folk Performance" award for her chamber-pop version of Mitchell's "Both Sides Now.") Collins and Mitchell visited Heider's together, and Collins, who'd received word that her on-again, off-again beau had started a new band, was suitably floored by what she heard. "It was just thrilling to be there and hear them sing," Collins says. "All these songs were pouring out. That harmony was astonishing; you couldn't help but be drawn into it. It was a way for Stephen to realize a lot of his dreams of songwriting and arranging. You could hear this was Stephen's thing; he'd found a way to realize it with these guys. In the beginning, it was magical."

But Collins didn't stay long. Ten years into an alcohol problem, she didn't want to be pulled into what she sensed was a potentially dangerous situation. "It was a struggle for me making sure I didn't get sucked into the scene out there," she says. "I knew it would do me in—the music scene and everything with Stephen, my producer, the drugs. I knew that if I stayed out there, I would not make it."

Collins returned to California in early May, shortly before the scheduled release of Crosby, Stills and Nash's completed album, to play at the Santa Monica Civic Auditorium. Visiting her Holiday Inn hotel room, Stills, still lovestruck, gifted her with a Martin guitar and sang and played "Suite: Judy Blue Eyes" for her in its entirety. Collins, who hadn't yet heard the song, was stunned and touched, recognizing the subtle reference to the days of her therapy appointments (Thursdays and Saturdays) in the lyrics. "He must have been reading my diaries," she says wryly. She told him it was a wonderful song but that it wouldn't win her back.

By LATE MARCH, the first Crosby, Stills and Nash album was finished, and the time had come to finalize what name or names would appear on the cover. Given the unpleasant experiences each had had with previous bands, the idea of a formal group name felt distasteful and restrictive, not to mention perilous. "If you have a band name, you can be replaced," says Crosby. "We'd each had some experience with that. It needed to be an equivalent situation, not a bullshit situation."

They decided to use their names, like a law firm, as a way to ensure everyone knew who they were individually and to signify that they could splinter and work with others at any time. Calling themselves Crosby, Stills and Nash would also announce their experiment to the world, what an Allentown, Pennsylvania, newspaper writer pegged as "the latest trend in groups—that is, non-groups . . . an ever-changing membership to suit its needs, along with the rights for the members to do whatever they please." The non-group would be the ultimate symbol of '60s values, a world in which one could do anything, with anybody, without facing consequences as long as it suited one's needs.

The *order* of their names proved a stickier matter. On February 22, 1969, as the making of the record was under way, a *Billboard* article on Atlantic's new signings referred to the trio as "Stills-Crosby-Nash"—not surprisingly, Stills' choice for their name. But while he was adamant, Stills couldn't deny that the handle sounded better as Crosby, Stills and Nash. "Try saying it any other way," says Crosby. "It was blatantly obvious to anyone who understood that kind of thing that that's how it would be." Adds Nash, "Stephen was pissed because me and Crosby said no. But Stills-Crosby-Nash just doesn't work." Crosby had another rationale: "At the time I was the one with the biggest name—the Byrds, hits. The Hollies might have had more but not of the same caliber. So at the beginning, to people who were concerned, I was the most important one."

The debate had an unintentionally comical postscript when the three gathered for a cover photo. To amplify the organic, earthy quality they saw in themselves and their music, they wanted a jacket that felt homey, and Nash and Gary Burden, a thirty-six-year-old former Marine and architectural design student who had been encouraged by (naturally) Cass Elliot to fashion album covers instead, found the ideal location: a derelict home at 815 Palm Avenue in West Hollywood. Although the property was just off the hectic Santa Monica Boulevard, the house, complete with a run-down sofa out front, felt worlds removed from Hollywood. To photograph it, the trio recruited photographer and fellow musician Henry Diltz. The son of an Army Air Corps recruit, Diltz, thirty, had lived all over the world, from Tokyo to Bangkok to Hawaii, and had attended West Point for a year. At school in Hawaii, Diltz had begun singing in a coffeehouse, and he had become a founding member (on banjo) of the Modern Folk Quartet (MFQ). He had moved with the group to Los Angeles in the early '60s, where they made the rounds of folk clubs. Diltz met Stills in Greenwich Village around 1964, when the MFQ briefly relocated there. Genial, bespectacled and rarely given to drama, Diltz was able to easily ingratiate himself into the already stormy Crosby, Stills and Nash world. Shooting them at Heider's during the making of the album, he made sure to time the clicking on his camera with the drums so that his picture taking wouldn't interrupt anything.

Diltz photographed the trio on the ratty couch on Palm Avenue, making for a homespun image of approachable rock stars who could have been mistaken for members of their audience. But when everyone looked at the prints in the days that followed, one major error announced itself: they were sitting in the wrong order from left to right—Nash, then Stills, then Crosby. "We were panicked about it: 'How could you have Crosby's name over Graham Nash?'" says Ron Stone of the Geffen-Roberts Company. When Diltz and the trio returned to the same spot the next day to retake the photo, they discovered the house had been torn down, leaving them no choice but to use the original. The group and Burden also convinced Atlantic to bend to their wishes on the texture of the cover itself; they wanted it to feel rough, not smooth. "It was the first album with that feeling," Diltz says. "The record company freaked out and went *nuts*. It wasn't any more expensive. They just hated anything new and different." On the back cover, they stripped in a photo of Dallas Taylor as if he were staring out the window. For decades, many would mistake Taylor for Neil Young.

In the hills of Laurel Canyon, anticipation for the album was building as music industry insiders (and Crosby and Nash themselves) played advanced pressings for friends and fellow musicians. Other musicians may not have wanted to witness the reactions, but Crosby and Nash reveled in sitting back and watching the euphoric responses to their work. Word was also spreading east. When the Who played a few nights at the year-old Fillmore East theater in May, two weeks before the album's scheduled release, promoter and owner Bill Graham emerged from the wings and told the crowd he had something no one else in the world had heard: the first music from Crosby, Stills and Nash, directly from the band itself. "I think you're gonna like it," he told them, and "Suite: Judy Blue Eyes" blasted out over the PA. "Needless to say, all in attendance, myself included, were thoroughly mind-blown," says Binky Philips, a Who devotee at the show that night. When it was over, the song received a standing ovation.

For all the careful deliberation and construction that went into the making of the album, no one could have planned how well timed it would be. The previous year had been relentlessly brutalizing: the assassinations of Robert Kennedy and Martin Luther King Jr.; the chaotic, violent Democratic National Convention in Chicago in which protesters were clubbed; the Tet Offensive in Vietnam; and, most deflatingly, the election of Richard Nixon in November, the first Republican president since Dwight Eisenhower roughly a decade before. Even rock and roll was mystifying: on their White Album, the Beatles seemed to be growing up and splintering before everyone's eyes, and Dylan, in the last month of 1967, had reemerged as a more obliquely political folkie on *John Wesley Harding.*

Triumphs trickled out: for the first time, Mississippi allowed women to be jurors, and Shirley Chisholm became the first African American woman in Congress, winning the race for the 12th Congressional District in her native Brooklyn. But into 1969, such victories seemed few and very far between. In the days and weeks leading up to the release of *Crosby, Stills & Nash,* four hundred American soldiers died overtaking Dong Ap Bia Mountain, or Hill 937, in Vietnam; the battle was so bloody that the mission was nicknamed "Hamburger Hill." At the all-black Dudley High School in Greensboro, North Carolina, a junior who advocated for black power wasn't allowed to be placed on the ballot for student council. Other students protested, leading to tear-gas-wielding police arriving at the school. The clashes soon spread to the nearby North Carolina Agricultural and Technical State University, and gunfire battles erupted between the National Guard and unidentified protesters. Although it was never determined who fired the fatal shot, Willie Grimes, a twenty-year-old sophomore, died from a bullet to the back of his head.

Into this increasingly dire scenario arrived *Crosby, Stills & Nash* on May 29, 1969. At Ertegun's insistence, the album had been remixed at the last minute by engineer and producer Tom Dowd to boost the voices; Ertegun wanted to replicate what he'd heard when he'd visited Crosby, Stills and Nash at work, and he had mostly remembered their singing. The band protested, but, according to Halverson, they had no choice: "Ahmet signs our paycheck," Stills told him. The impact of that demand was easily heard on the finished record: the voices, not Stills' guitars, keyboards, or bass, or Taylor's drums, stood out the most. The decision may not have enhanced the band's rock-and-roll credibility, but it would be a wise move. Whether he realized it or not, Ertegun knew what would make the trio stand apart: their carefully entwined voices.

Anyone reading the fold-out lyric sheet inserted with the album— another uncommon perk—wouldn't have sensed much joy. Even without explicitly mentioning any member of the Kennedy family or King, "Long Time Gone" conveyed the frustration of attempting to speak truth to power in the late '60s. "Wooden Ships," which Jefferson Airplane would also record that year, spoke to that part of the generation that wanted to escape the planet; in their alternating parts in the introduction, Stills and Crosby played battle-weary warriors from opposite sides now sharing food and hopes of survival. "You Don't Have to Cry" and "Suite: Judy Blue Eyes" read like chronicles of adults working out their relationship issues; "49 Bye-Byes" was a farewell to an affair. Even in its hazy depiction of three women in Crosby's life—Christine Hinton, Joni Mitchell and another he would never reveal—"Guinnevere" had an undertone of longing more than sexual connection; all three women seemed apart, in their own worlds, unreachable.

But starting with the skittering riff of "Suite: Judy Blue Eyes," followed by the sound of the multitracked voices in unison, *Crosby, Stills & Nash* immediately radiated something desperately needed in pop at the time: a luminous hint of hope. Harmony singing was nothing new in pop, and in many ways *Crosby, Stills & Nash* picked up where classic vocal harmony pop bands like the Four Seasons, the Beach Boys and even the Hollies had left off, albeit with their own supergroup twist. Instead of the water-tight unison harmonies of those bands, however, Crosby, Stills and Nash sang together and, in a way, separately; in a typical mix, it was still easy to pick out each of their individual voices. Thanks to that singing, *Crosby, Stills & Nash* was akin to a floor-to-ceiling, sun-drenched window. For all the personal anguish and hard labor that went into it, "Suite: Judy Blue Eyes" was seamless—what critic Robert Christgau, reviewing the album for the *New York Times*, called a "structural triumph." As it moved through its three sections—upbeat and feisty to slow and anguished and back to fast again, with Stills' acoustic and electric guitar parts flying in and out—the song was in keeping with rock's newfound ambition: songs that stretched past the accepted two- or three-minute mark. In its closing "doo doo doo" section, it also captured rock's ebullience.

Reflecting the camaraderie with which it was made, *Crosby, Stills & Nash* was also startlingly of a piece. Each man may have had a distinct personality (and look, judging from the cover photo), but the album had a cohesive flow, and that pacing allowed the songs to breathe. The cheery

bounciness of "Marrakesh Express" contrasted with the bestilled exqui-
siteness of the subsequent "Guinnevere," which paved the way for Stills'
folk guitar trot on the following "You Don't Have to Cry." Lyrically, "Wooden
Ships" was bleak, but the moment when Crosby and Nash's harmonies
joined Stills in the chorus was anything but despairing. The same went
for "Long Time Gone." The original version that Stills and Crosby had recorded as a duo had a certain crackle, but the merged, fussed-over voices
on the chorus of the trio version chased away the blues of the times.

Thanks in part to Halverson's careful attention to microphone tech-
niques, the album also came off as strikingly direct; on "Lady of the Island,"
his love-by-the-fireplace serenade, Nash's voice sounded inordinately up
close and personal, and the pirouette of his and Crosby's voice throughout the song was more common to jazz vocalese than anything heard in
rock. "It was that intimacy we wanted," says Nash. "Taking it down to
the essence. We drew our audience closer to us with the lyrics and the
gentleness of how we presented it." The concluding "49 Bye-Byes" found
Stills merging two different songs: the first half, "49 Bye-Byes," was sulky,
almost pouty, with Stills' organ prodding the arrangement only so much,
but the second portion, originally called "Bye Bye Baby," used Crosby
and Nash's multitracked harmonies as the ultimate, I'm-okay-now send-
off to a relationship. The song embodied everything the album offered:
splendor and optimism during a time that needed both.

The reviews were largely enthusiastic. "Success is insured for this
new group," announced *Billboard*, while Christgau called it "as perfect
as has been expected" (while also noting that overall, "the wildness that
should liberate great rock" was noticeably absent). In *The Saturday Review*, Ellen Sander called it "nothing short of a treasure," adding, "It is
packed with songs of the changes that have made searchers of all of
us." Immediately, the group was crowned as the multiheaded voice of
its generation, and *Crosby, Stills & Nash* earned a gold record with sales
of five hundred thousand copies. Now, all they had to do was live up to
those expectations.

ALTHOUGH NASH HAD first crashed in Crosby's house when he moved to
Los Angeles, they were now living separately. Stills hunkered down in a
hovel on Beachwood Drive in the Hollywood Hills, so far from the main

road that friends weren't always inclined to visit. Nash and Joni Mitchell were living together at her home in a blend of domesticity and oncoming pop fame. When a *New York Times* reporter visited them in April, Diltz had just dropped by with the photo of the trio's album cover and Elliot Roberts was making plans for Mitchell. Later, they went to a studio, where Nash watched as Mitchell recorded "That Song About the Midway," her kiss-off to Crosby. "Do you want to pack it in, luv?" Nash asked her after she was having trouble landing the right take on another new song, "Chelsea Morning." With a smile, she replied, "Just sit there and look groovy."

Their domestic life would be immortalized in song that same spring, when, at his insistence, Mitchell bought a vase for herself. Back home, Nash tossed some wood in their fireplace and, with an idea for a song, sat down at her piano; in an hour's time, he'd written "Our House," an homage to their togetherness that blended details of their home with a chord pattern and descending bass line that evoked Baroque pieces like Pachelbel's *Canon in D*. When he began playing the song in concert later that year, he would often introduce it as "about my woman" without naming her; the phrase, later seen as chauvinistic, was barely greeted as such at the time.

In Mitchell's compact driveway, barely wide enough for two cars, Crosby was killing time waiting for Nash and Mitchell to return home one day when Neil Young, who lived not far away, drove by, stopped and asked Crosby what he was doing. Crosby told him not much. As Crosby recalls it, Young asked if he could sing Crosby a few songs. Pulling out a guitar he played "Helpless," a turtle-paced reminiscence of growing up in his native Canada, all moons and birds, and "Country Girl," a suite made up partly of fragments of songs from the Buffalo Springfield days. Crosby knew who Young was and had spent a bit of time with him, but the ad hoc performance was a revelation—and helped the new group resolve a lingering issue.

The rules of the music business dictated that the trio would have to promote the album with live shows despite having only sung together in friends' living rooms. By then, ads for summer Crosby, Stills and Nash concerts, like the one at the Greek Theatre in Los Angeles, had begun appearing in newspapers. (Amusingly, the *Los Angeles Times*, of all places, announced the concert would present "a newly formed combination of singers from England.") But they would need help. Crosby and Nash were adequate guitarists and Taylor would be their drummer, but they required a bass player and, in Stills' mind, another musician to fill out their sound, preferably on keyboards.

The search began. Visiting England, Stills and Taylor ran into George Harrison at Basing Street (also known as Island) Studio and brashly brought up the idea of the Beatle as one of their accompanists; Harrison had no reaction. The two men clomped through rain and mud to visit the country home of Steve Winwood, who was then in the midst of a disorienting experience with Eric Clapton in their supergroup, Blind Faith. As respected as Stills and the *Crosby, Stills & Nash* album were among their peers, Stills' intensity could be intimidating—to the point where, Taylor recalled, "Winwood was scared to death and locked himself in his bedroom." Stills later claimed he asked Mark Naftalin, who had just left his keyboard slot in the Paul Butterfield Blues Band, to join Crosby, Stills and Nash, but Naftalin later had no memory of such a request, though he says he might well have taken the job had it been offered. (Two years earlier, Stills had asked him to join the Springfield to replace the newly busted Bruce Palmer, who had been deported to Canada; Naftalin had started as a bass player. But Naftalin politely turned him down and remained with Butterfield.) Nash says John Sebastian was also on their mind, but he still resisted; by then, Sebastian was about to set sail on his post-Spoonful career.

With a planned summer tour in the works, they were fast running out of options. Someone had to make a decision, and that person would be Ertegun. Although he remained very much in Stills' corner, a part of Ertegun missed Buffalo Springfield, and the thought of Stills and Young reunited had stayed with him. During a dinner with Stills and Geffen at his apartment on Manhattan's Upper East Side (or, as Crosby would recall in his first memoir, he and Roberts), Ertegun slyly played a few Springfield songs on his stereo.

Finally, Ertegun posed the question outright: What about asking Young to join? "There's something about Neil Young that goes with this," he said to Stills, according to an interview Ertegun later gave to author Dave Zimmer. After all, he argued, Stills and Young had "something special" in the Springfield. Ertegun even offered to call Young himself.

(Another possible reason to inject some revamped-lineup news into the situation: while *Crosby, Stills & Nash* was a hit album, neither "Marrakesh Express" nor an edited-down version of "Suite: Judy Blue Eyes" had broken into the Top 10.) For any number of reasons, it was the one idea no one had considered before.

TWO WEEKS BEFORE Crosby, Stills and Nash began putting their artistic union on tape at the Heider studio, Young was in the same facility beginning the next chapter of his career. He had a new group of players behind him—three members of the Rockets, a band that had kicked around in several previous incarnations, including an LA doo-wop group, before morphing into their bustling pop-garage sound. Much to the dismay of lead guitarist George Whitsell, Young had begun rehearsing with the other Rockets—singer and guitarist Danny Whitten, drummer Ralph Molina and bassist Billy Talbot. They had rechristened themselves as Crazy Horse and, with him, had recorded two monolithic epics in January 1969. "Down by the River" and "Cowgirl in the Sand" were both relatively simple in structure and musicianship; both were long and spacious enough to allow Young to roam free on his guitar; and both augured a new, stripped-down, primal sound for Young. They also cut "Everybody Knows This Is Nowhere," which would wind up the title song of the record they were making.

After a break—and once Crosby, Stills and Nash had vacated the premises after finishing their record—Young and Crazy Horse returned in March to tape another song, the fever-dream-fueled "Cinnamon Girl," which was more concise than their previous tracks but had a densely packed power. Few remember Young crossing paths with Crosby, Stills and Nash at the time, although Young and Roberts did visit the trio's sessions as they wrapped up to hear "Suite: Judy Blue Eyes"; in a photo that exists of that moment, Young looks noticeably wide-eyed and impressed at what he's hearing. Standing near him, Stills has the expression of someone who knows what he's achieved.

In some ways, though, it was inevitable that Young would end up connecting with the three of them. Born in Toronto on November 12, 1945, ten months after Stills, he shared traits with each of his future partners. Like Stills, he had a mother—Edna, known to all as Rassy—who was a tough, life-of-the-party type, and a father—Canadian journalist, sportswriter and novelist Scott Young—who was in and out of his life (much like Floyd Crosby, William Nash and William Stills with their sons). As with the Stills clan, the Young family had moved around for several years, living in the small town of Omemee, Ontario, which Young—who was also coping with a diagnosis of polio at the age of five—would later revisit in "Helpless." After Scott Young began straying from his wife, Young was told his parents were divorcing; it was 1960, the same year Crosby's parents broke up. Like Floyd Crosby, Scott Young wasn't known to be especially supportive of his son's musical ambitions.

Moving to Winnipeg with his mother and his brother, Bob, Young garnered a reputation as quick witted but sensitive. Like Crosby, he had his mischievous side; like all three of them, he realized soon enough that playing guitar and singing made him stand out, especially with girls. The young Neil Young was elusive even in his youth. As one of his high school classmates later told writer John Einarson, Young once bolted from school as soon as the bell rang, right out a window instead of the classroom door: "That was kind of his philosophy," she said. Young's first instrument was the ukulele, but by Winnipeg he had moved to an acoustic guitar and then an electrified one. He tried joining local bands, but soon after starting high school in 1961, he formed his earliest group, the Squires, which played concerts as early as 1963, when Young was all of seventeen. Like Nash at the same age, Young was indoctrinated into the world of bars and clubs early on. The songs the Squires played and recorded—quasi-surf instrumentals, smitten-teen ballads ("I'll Love You Forever") and twangy throbbers ("I Wonder," which would later morph into "Don't Cry No Tears")—displayed Young's range and devotion to craft. With the encouragement of his mother but his father's hesitation, he dropped out of high school before graduating to pursue the dream of becoming a professional musician.

The Squires slogged on, moving to Fort William in Ontario (where Young turned nineteen and wrote one of his most important early songs, "Sugar Mountain"), then back to Winnipeg. Young and Stills met during this period. By the fall of 1965, the Squires had collapsed and Young had shifted to solo, Dylan-influenced songs, such as "The Rent Is Always Due." Traveling to New York City with Stills' Greenwich Village address in hand, Young learned that his new friend had left for California, but Stills' roommate and music buddy Richie Furay happened to be in the apartment. He filled Young in on Stills' whereabouts, and several false starts followed. Young recorded some of his new songs for Elektra, which passed, and thanks to a Canadian friend, Bruce Palmer, Young found himself at the Motown building in Detroit. Palmer enlisted Young in the Mynah Birds, a woolly rock band fronted by an African American lead singer—Ricky James Matthews, later known as Rick James. Preliminary recordings were made, but Matthews was AWOL from the US Navy Reserve and eventually turned himself in and spent time behind bars. With the Mynah Birds shut down and his Canadian music prospects looking dimmer by the day, Young, with Palmer and some other friends, piled into his new car—his second used hearse—and headed for California. It was the beginning of spring in 1966. The hearse wasn't the ideal car for a cross-country road trip, but if he hadn't bought it, and if Stills hadn't noticed it and its Canadian plates on Sunset Boulevard, Young's career may well have gone in another, less rewarding direction.

Young's tenure with the Springfield made for an even rougher ride than the hearse. To Stills' consternation, Young seemed to be in and out of the band on a regular basis. Even once he rejoined the group after dropping out before the Monterey Pop Festival, he remained his own, solitary man. During a group interview in Connecticut in the fall of 1967, the band members reveled in a party that was thrown for them, bouncing around and chatting up everyone—all except Young, who was dressed in black and quietly sipped a glass of milk in a different part of the room. After the Springfield's farewell concert in Long Beach, California, in May 1968, Young began assembling his own team, including a crazed but inspired producer, arranger and musician named Jack Nitzsche and an ornery producer named David Briggs. Young also married for the first time, to a Topanga waitress named Susan Acevedo, in late 1968.

During the same period when Crosby, Stills and Nash were first harmonizing in the homes of Laurel Canyon, Young was huddled with Briggs and Nitzsche to make his first album, *Neil Young*, released in early 1969. Unlike anything he'd made before or would make after, *Neil Young* took the layered musical textures of the Springfield to another level. The songs were often melancholic, stacked with pipe organs, multiple guitar parts, gospel backup singers, even rodeo hoedown strings. In "I've Loved Her So Long" and "Here We Are in the Years," the album established the vibe—that of the high-voiced, lonely-guy balladeer—that would follow Young around, often to his dismay, for years.

Neil Young made the smallest of splashes, not even making *Billboard*'s Top 200 album chart, but true to his restless spirit, Young was already looking ahead. The same month it was released, he was already at work with Crazy Horse. *Everybody Knows This Is Nowhere* was more basic, far more cohesive and far more down home than *Neil Young*; billing Crazy Horse on the cover, Young could be both boss and one of the guys in the band. But at least initially, it, too, fell short of expectations. Released the same month as *Crosby, Stills & Nash*, *Everybody Knows This Is Nowhere* peaked at no. 127 on the *Billboard* chart. Although he never wavered in his support of Crazy Horse during those early days, Young also had to consider other options.

When Ertegun broached the idea of his former bandmate augmenting Crosby, Stills and Nash, a huge red flag immediately unfurled in Stills' mind. "I went, 'Why would we *do* that?'" he has said. "'You know him—he has control issues.' As a trio, we worked pretty well." Yet other factors were in play. For all his cockiness, Stills harbored doubts about his abilities as a lead guitarist (which he later told Zimmer were "kind of silly"). Stills also couldn't deny the financial ramifications of a so-called supergroup: "I knew this was going to be a monster and it would make *scads* of money," he told David Fricke three decades later. "And that maybe the thought of being multi-millionaires would soothe, would balm, some of these old wounds." It's possible that the power-play dynamic also appealed to him: Stills would be asking Young to join *his* very successful band and would thereby have the upper hand.

Not everyone was sold on the idea. Geffen and Roberts worried about tinkering with the trio, a formula that was clearly working. In his memoir *Waging Heavy Peace*, Young enthused that Crosby, Stills and Nash "sounded like a new car coming off the assembly line!" Young also worried that Stills would "overplay" and "step on me," much like in the Springfield. Meanwhile, their friends scratched their heads at the thought of Young joining up. "I thought, '*That's* an odd pairing,'" says Sebastian. "Here was this perfect vocal unit. Nothing against Neil, but I didn't see the need to add to it. I just felt that's such a complete unit and now they're going to get it more complicated again."

Far more problematically, Crosby and Nash were at first ambivalent, and rightly so. Nash, who'd been smitten with Young's Springfield mini-epic "Expecting to Fly" and had played the recording endlessly on a portable stereo during a Hollies tour, asked for a meeting with Young. "Neil wasn't a superstar then—he was the guitar player in the Buffalo Springfield," he says. "I said, 'You want someone to join the band I've never fuckin' met? I don't know if I'll like the way he smells or whatever.'" The two sat down for breakfast in Greenwich Village, near where the trio were beginning to rehearse at the Village Vanguard jazz club when it was empty during the day, and Young charmed Nash with his sense of humor. Crosby was also on the fence. But after hearing Young perform in Nash and Mitchell's driveway, he was won over. "I said, 'Oh, shit! We need him in the band,'" Crosby says. "Not just because he was a guitar and keyboard player but because of the songs. They were completely different from ours and I knew what they would do. So I flipped and said, 'I want him in.'"

Young couldn't deny the musical blend that Crosby, Stills and Nash had created, especially when he heard them rehearsing; nor could he discount how much he enjoyed exchanging guitar parts with Stills, whose talent he still respected. Taylor recalled a night he and Stills jammed with Young in a club somewhere on the East Coast. "We said, 'Wow, that was great,' and Neil said, 'Really cool,'" Taylor recalled. "Neil wanted to find out if he and Stephen could share a stage without hitting each other and if I was any good." Driving to Young's boxy redwood home on Skyline Trail in Topanga, where he lived with his wife, Susan, Stills made the offer to Young. For several weeks, the deal hung in the balance when Young insisted he receive equal billing in the name, as opposed to none at all (the group still wanted to be known as Crosby, Stills and Nash). In what would not be the last time, they consented to his demand, and in mid-July, the word was out, thanks to Ralph J. Gleason of the *San Francisco Chronicle* and other writers: Crosby, Stills and Nash were now Crosby, Stills, Nash and Young. "Nothing Neil does is an accident," says Crosby. "We were the hottest thing at that point. He knew, and he knew exactly how to work it. He's a very bright guy."

Ertegun had his wish for a partial Springfield reunion and Young had a project that could elevate him in the public eye in new ways. How it would benefit the other three members of what was now a quartet was open to question. "They had the tiger by the tail on the first album, and it all looked great," says Stone. "I don't think anyone could have comprehended where it was headed by bringing in Neil. I don't think they understood the potential in what was about to happen to them. It was risky to throw that element in. High risk, high reward."

When reviewing *Crosby, Stills & Nash*, a writer from the *Detroit Free Press* said, "If the heavens ever descend upon us with musical gifts, they include Crosby, Stills and Nash." Then he noted the unexpected addition of Young: "One could fear the extra man may upset the beautiful balance already existing."

No SOONER HAD Young merged with Crosby, Stills and Nash than they began rehearsing and even recording new material, and many of those rehearsals took place at a white, gated compound at 3615 Shady Oak Road on the north side of Laurel Canyon. Formerly owned by dweebish actor Wally Cox, and then by Peter Tork of the Monkees, the house became the expanded band's home base. At the top of a curvy driveway for maximum seclusion, it came with all the Hollywood-star amenities of the time: a pool, a sauna, a pool house with an apartment above it, marble floors and staircase, and a multicar driveway. In between the kitchen and living room was a large room that had been converted into a music practice space, its walls covered in rugs to muffle the sound.

Although it was technically Tork's house (he was in and out), the bedrooms were always filled and the vibe remained hippie casual. During breaks while recording their debut album, Crosby, Stills or Nash would stop by the pool for a quick dip; the house was so high in the hills that no other homes overlooked it, so nude swims were a daily, private occurrence. Stills—and sometimes his musical running buddy Dallas Taylor, who would often crash at the house—would seclude themselves in the music room and jam for hours upon hours, with friends slipping candy bars under the door for Stills to help him keep up his energy. One evening, ornate tapestries were spread across the living room floor for a casual banquet for the band and two dozen friends, including Joni

Mitchell, who came bearing paint brushes and an easel, part of her other life as a painter.

One of the Shady Oak bedrooms was occupied by Salli Sachse, a comely twenty-three-year-old actress who had entranced teenagers the world over in beach-party movies like *How to Stuff a Wild Bikini* and *Bikini Beach.* Sachse had lost her first husband in a flying accident in 1966, after which she had dated Dean Martin's agent. The freewheeling, anything-goes Shady Oak scene was a radically different and even more liberal-minded version of the Hollywood she thought she knew. "There was nude swimming and a lot of people running around without any clothes on," she says. "It was a different set of norms, totally against all the values I grew up with in San Diego. Someone would always be pushing the limits of public decency in the kitchen."

Crosby, Stills, Nash and Young still needed a bass player, and former Springfield bassist Bruce Palmer was the first who came to mind for Stills and Young. But the plan quickly hit a speedbump. Crosby and Nash weren't convinced Palmer was up for the task; they may have also been concerned about what was essentially a Springfield reunion in their midst. Palmer had a history of drug busts and deportations, most recently in early 1968. Luckily, a replacement was practically in their backyard. The legends of how a teenaged but already seasoned Motown bass player named Greg Reeves came into the fold vary. Reeves, who was sharing a house with Rick James, remembered Crosby and Nash visiting one day and literally pulling him into their world; James himself would recall running into Stills at a local club, which led to Reeves being invited to a band audition at Shady Oak. No one could agree on his age, either: everyone thought Reeves was nineteen, thanks to what turned out to be a phony ID card, but in fact he was about three years younger. "We always wondered why he was a little immature," said Taylor. "But he was tall. You couldn't tell how old he was." What wasn't debatable was the way Reeves' bass lines added an extra, funky thrust to the rhythm section. After Reeves was invited to sit in with them at Shady Oak, James knew his protégé had landed the job when James was tossed a vial of pure cocaine as a thank-you gesture from the band.

With a full-band lineup now in place, the group began prepping for what promised to be a feverishly hectic summer and fall: concerts, a smattering of TV appearances, photo shoots behind the house on Shady Oak, even a follow-up record to make with Young in tow, which Atlantic was already hoping to release in time for Christmas. In the early summer of 1969, the full band set up in the driveway to play outside with their stacks of amplifiers. Crosby discouraged it, fearing it would bring the police, and he was right: at sundown, squad cars arrived to tell them the band could be heard several canyons over and they needed to stop, immediately.

But between the gold-record award, the fame, the pressure and an audience that was suddenly hanging onto their every utterance about life, music and politics, the scenario was heating up like the pots of rice people always kept on the boil in the kitchen. Bobby Hammer—a former Army Security Agency employee who had moved to California to pursue a completely different career, in photography and film—was one of many at Shady Oak who grappled with the group's curious dynamic. (Hammer, who had arrived first, lived in the apartment above the poolhouse with Sachse, who was then his girlfriend.) In the kitchen one day, Stills and Crosby flew into a heated debate about something Stills had read about turtles and how long they could survive underwater. "It was some silly thing and they got into a really big argument about it," Hammer says. "I wondered, 'What are they *really* trying to say to each other here? What's the real undercurrent?'" Another time, Hammer was filming Crosby as he reclined in the white rope hammock in the driveway; Crosby was pontificating about one topic or another when in stormed Stills, shouting at Crosby. All Hammer could decipher was that Crosby and Stills were already angry with each other: Crosby wasn't happy that Stills was late, and Stills wasn't happy that Crosby had missed a day or two of rehearsal when he was sick. Crosby criticized Stills for not thinking enough about the group as a whole. Stills, continuing his shouting, said, "You walked out two fuckin' days in a row, you fuckin' hypocrite—you piss me off!" Then he stalked off.

Years later, Stills felt the argument had stemmed from Crosby's uneasiness at being booked on TV shows like *This Is Tom Jones*, where the Welsh pop singer had joined them for a riotous "Long Time Gone" that fall. (Geffen pushed for as much mainstream exposure as possible.) But it almost didn't matter what had instigated the clash. "It wasn't shocking," says Sachse, who also witnessed the argument. But she felt uneasy about the "bad vibes." Hammer also observed the other part of their relationship. Whether it was a rehearsal or a concert, the group would always play expertly after one of their blow-outs, as if they were kissing and making up in song.

As MICHAEL LANG learned, few in the group's camp doubted their potential, even before *Crosby, Stills & Nash* arrived in record stores. Only twenty-four, Lang, whose halo of dark curls surrounded an impish mug, was in the early stages of co-producing a summer festival in Woodstock, New York. Having already organized a successful outdoor rock gathering at a racetrack in Miami the previous year, Lang was learning what it took to mount such happenings, from arranging artists' fees to providing bathroom facilities. Working out of the Manhattan office of an agent and friend at the William Morris Agency, Lang was introduced one spring day to Geffen, who eagerly played him a test pressing of the trio's album.

As a fan of the Byrds and Buffalo Springfield, Lang was already primed, but the majesty of the music won him over, and he knew he wanted the band at the Woodstock Music & Art Fair—but he also sensed Geffen was going to play hardball. "Geffen knew what he had, put it that way," Lang recalls. "He was like the cat who had swallowed the canary. You knew this was going to be huge." When Geffen demanded the group receive $10,000, the second-largest fee Lang was offering, Lang agreed on the spot. Although the biggest acts, like Jimi Hendrix, were being paid $15,000, it was a good deal for Crosby, Stills and Nash (Young was added after the initial agreement was made). Their payday put them on the same level as Jefferson Airplane and Creedence Clearwater Revival, bands with many hit singles and gold albums under their belts by 1969. Stills would later tell writer Alan di Perna that they'd had to talk Geffen into including them in the festival; Geffen was worried they wouldn't get paid, but Stills and Crosby were convinced it would be the place to be that summer. Woodstock was to open its gates in the middle of August.

Crosby, Stills, Nash and Young's stage debut had been scheduled for New York's Fillmore East. The downtown theater was only a year old, but it bestowed immediate counterculture credibility on anyone who played there. Yet that show, and a planned set at the Atlantic City Pop Festival, had to be postponed when Nash developed throat polyps.

Instead, their public debut would be in Chicago's 3,800-seat Auditorium Theatre on August 16. There, they received three standing ovations, one after the very first song, "Suite: Judy Blue Eyes." Even the group, which hadn't yet performed together in public, appeared to be taken aback by the response. "Golly, we needed that," Nash told them.

At those shows and others for the remainder of the year, audiences basked in a band that, on multiple levels, was unlike anything they'd seen before. Starting with their clothing, each embodied an archetype of the moment. With his fringed jackets, his head nodding up and down with the music, and his decidedly opinionated between-song patter, Crosby was the counterculture agitator, the free-love spokesman, the benevolent hippie-philosopher. More straitlaced in his garb (sweaters, white-collared shirts) and the most severe in his onstage demeanor, Stills was the down-to-business professional. Nash, the genial stage host with the voice, air and occasional embroidered vest of British gentry, despite his working-class origins, appeared to be the sensitive, worldly soul many audience members probably wanted to be themselves; he was also the band member female fans tended to crush on the hardest. Taking in his surroundings with hooded eyes, Young, the last-minute addition, was both part of the show and apart from it—the one who, like many other members of their generation, didn't quite want to commit to anything at the moment.

The format of their shows wasn't unique. Once Bob Dylan had fully invested in electrifying his sound a few years earlier, he'd begun splitting his shows between unaccompanied acoustic songs and high-voltage sets with the Hawks. Crosby, Stills, Nash and Young used a similar format, albeit with their anti-group twist. They would open the shows with the founding trio, strumming out a song or two, and then be joined by Young, at which point they'd play pop musical chairs, performing separately or in pairs. "It's up to each individual, you know, whatever songs they want to lay down to people, and sometimes it gets a bit difficult," Nash told the audience in Houston. In fact, their set lists were largely established. They would always begin with "Suite: Judy Blue Eyes," often followed by the Beatles' "Blackbird," a showcase for the original trio's harmonies. Crosby and Nash would wrap their voices around "Guinnevere"; Crosby would quiet the crowd with a solo version of "Triad," often dissing the Byrds' rejection of the song in the process. (In Detroit he told the crowd, "A certain member got red-faced, stormed out of the room and said, 'That's a freak-out orgy song and I won't sing it!'") Stills would use an acoustic blues number, "Black Queen," to showcase pins-and-needles guitar runs. By fall, he had also devised a novel move, segueing from a solo-piano version of "49 Bye-Byes" into a crowd-pleasing, stomp-your-feet take on "For What It's Worth" that hammered home the group's socially aware image. (After one of those performances, someone in the crowd yelled, "Stills in '72!" three years before the next presidential election.) Young would often accompany himself on "Country Girl."

After an intermission, Reeves would emerge, Taylor's drum kit would be rolled out, and all six would fire up the electric second half of the show. As intimate and hushed as the acoustic set could be, the second bristled with amplification and tension. The harmonies were nowhere near as precise and full as they were on record—even four voices couldn't duplicate the sound they'd captured in the studio—but the plugged-in sets offered another side of the band. During "Long Time Gone," Young's lead guitar and Stills' throat-shredding cameo in the chorus seemed to vie for attention. Stills reveled in notice-me gestures, like the way he would throw his right arm back after he hit a note on the guitar. The group rendition of "Down by the River" became a forum for tennis-match guitar parts between Stills and Young.

Threaded throughout the show, especially the first half, were gags and in-jokes, ranging from amusing to alarmingly self-satisfied for such a new act. When Young walked on, Stills would coyly introduce each to the other in a drawl ("Mr. Young, meet Mr. Nash," and so forth). Minutes could pass between songs as they joked or tuned up. Any other act would have been booed or criticized for such indulgences, but for these four, each witticism or bit, spontaneous or not, was greeted with cheers and interjections of "Right on!" from the crowd.

The day after their Chicago debut, Nash and Taylor were being helicoptered toward the Woodstock festival when Taylor asked the pilot the name of the lake over which they were flying. The pilot informed him it was no waterway but an audience. By the time all six musicians had assembled at the grounds—Young arrived by car with Jimi Hendrix—several hundred thousand people had settled in with their tickets or crashed the gates, and the enormity of the event overcame them. In a backstage tent, they were met by John Sebastian, who sensed their anxiety. (As they well knew, it was only their second concert.) "They're looking around going, 'Holy shit,'" recalls Sebastian, who shared his weed to calm them down. "And I'm going, 'Don't panic, guys. This is a great situation. You just have to go with it.'"

Upon his arrival, Crosby witnessed a seemingly miraculous sight: a New York State trooper in pressed pants and black, shiny shoes walking nonplussed into a mudbank to rescue a girl who'd cut her bare foot on a shard of glass. When the police cruiser became stuck in the muck, Crosby watched as a dozen of his fellow hippies helped push the car out. "I thought, 'Okay, this is working,'" Crosby says. "'This is what I want. This is different and I like it.'"

But everyone arrived with his own baggage. Taylor and Nash's helicopter nearly crash-landed after it scraped an electrical wire; when all seemed lost for a moment, Taylor considered kicking in what he called Nash's "smug, English face" before it went down. Stills worried that the rainstorms that had soaked the festival grounds that afternoon would ruin their instruments or screw up their tunings. Young had his doubts about such a circus before he arrived, and they stayed with him. *Rolling Stone* magazine had launched two years before, almost immediately becoming the journalistic heart of the counterculture, and as part of its team coverage of the festival, writer Greil Marcus found himself by the side of the stage that evening, where he encountered Young taking in the crowd. "He was quiet and circumspect," recalls Marcus. "It was dark and he kept saying, 'I wish I could see all the way out.'" (Meanwhile, Mitchell, who had been their opening act in Chicago, missed the festival entirely. Early reports portrayed it as a traffic-clogged mudfest, and since Mitchell was scheduled to tape the all-important *Dick Cavett Show* the following day, Geffen argued that she should avoid Woodstock.)

Their sixteen-song set, which began at 3:00 A.M. on the last of Woodstock's three days, wasn't without its glitches. The harmonies and guitars were not always in tune, and an inspired idea—Young and Stills reprising "Mr. Soul" as an acoustic duet—lacked the fire of the Springfield version. Yet Lang and the band's peers who gathered to watch them by the sides of the stage were startled by how serene the now tens of thousands remaining in the crowd were during the set and how intimate it felt despite the surroundings. "That was remarkable," Lang says. "Nobody captured the moment like they did in terms of that connection. It was so quiet. You feel they were really connected."

When the film version of the concert was released, an announcer would be heard introducing them as "Crosby, Stills, Nash . . . ," as if the "and Young" had been edited out. In fact, it had. Only after their set had begun had Young made it clear he didn't want to be captured on camera. "Neil would threaten to deck anybody who did," Nash says. "Or so I heard, *after* the fact." Since the movie used the trio version of "Suite: Judy Blue Eyes," his absence wasn't immediately noticeable, but his decision—"a huge mistake," says Crosby—was the first sign that Young was already having second thoughts two months after hooking up with the others. Stills later said, only half joking, that Young's light blue suit may have been the issue in terms of camera shyness, but Young told his biographer Jimmy McDonough that Woodstock was "a bullshit gig. . . . I think Stephen was way overboard into the huge crowd. Everybody was on this Hollywood trip with the fuckin' cameras." Keeping to his original plan to alternate between his own career and his band membership, Young had recorded a few tracks with Crazy Horse—including the almost desperate "I Believe in You," a cover of country singer Don Gibson's "Oh, Lonesome Me"—shortly before the festival.

Musical and personal matters improved during the group's multi-night stand at their hometown venue, the Greek Theatre in Los Angeles. With its emphasis on mainstream entertainers—they were bookended by pop crooner Johnny Mathis and Hawaiian crossover act Don Ho—the Greek wasn't normally receptive to rock and roll, and the Geffen-Roberts crew slyly ensured that Crosby, Stills, Nash and Young would be the first rock act to play the six-thousand-seat venue by way of a half-truth. "The sales pitch was that, for the most part, the show was acoustic, but that was a lie," says Stone. "They knew there was going to be an electric section, but they didn't know it would be so loud and ferocious. By the time it was resolved, the show was over."

Beyond financial reasons—the band was paid $70,000 for those shows—the risk was worth it: after playing the Greek (in a show that *Los Angeles Times* critic Robert Hilburn called "a triumph of the first order" and "a staggering display of individual and collective talent"), the group was newly legitimized in the eyes of promoters eager to book them into similar non-rock venues. (Among those in the audience at the Greek, at the invitation of Geffen, was up-and-coming promoter Jerry Heller, who would later work on duo outings by Crosby and Nash; much later, he would become the notorious manager of the West Coast rap act N.W.A.) Other signs of mainstream acceptance were cropping up: when Bayou West, a "hip" clothing store in Chula Vista, opened its doors, the local newspaper coverage noted that the inside "features Crosby, Stills and Nash instead of the more conventional Lawrence Welk as background music."

A few weeks later, the annual Big Sur Folk Festival should have been a placid and mellow gig, and in many ways, it was. Crosby took part in a hot-tub session with naked men and women; the quartet shared a stage with Sebastian, Joan Baez and former Traffic guitarist Dave Mason, among others; and the group played in front of a pool, with ocean views behind them. But it wasn't without problems: on the first of their two days at the festival, they had barely finished their first song, "Helplessly Hoping," when a stoned heckler began berating them for their fur coats and rock-star image. Crosby reminded him (and the audience) that the group was playing for free, having canceled a TV appearance to be there: "If you didn't pay, shut up," Crosby told the guy, to cheers from the crowd.

But as Crosby tried to reason with him, Stills' temper flared. He stepped off his stool and approached the heckler, hoping at first to make him chill out. "Peace and love, peace and love—kick his ass," Crosby joked, although in a tone that implied he wasn't kidding. Nash implored Stills: "If you push him in the pool, Stephen, I'll never forgive you!" and the crowd laughed. Young simply muttered, "Positive . . . positive . . . positive" into his microphone.

Before anyone could fully grasp what was happening, the two men were in a tussle. The crowd quieted. "Wasn't that great?" Crosby recalls. "Stills was ready to punch that motherfucker out. It was hysterical. I was perfectly happy with him wanting to punch his lights out." Stills was quickly pulled away, and their set resumed. (Five years later, talking about the documentary that was made about the festival, Stills admitted, "I did give him a knee in the old solar plexus, but they didn't put that in the movie.") Onstage, Stills rambled on about how "we think about that shit that that guy was saying," and how the group could fall into that "same old trap." As one reporter mistily noted, "Stills was ministered to in a loving fashion and scores of spectators cried at the senselessness of the confrontation and the beauty of the music." Befitting the way they could lurch from madness to magic and back again, they then performed a flawless "You Don't Have to Cry" with pitch-perfect harmonies.

IN HER CAR, Salli Sachse was navigating the canyons of Topanga, listening to the radio, when the station's disc jockey, B. Mitchel Reed, broke the inconceivable news that Christine Hinton, Crosby's main love, was dead. Sachse and Bobby Hammer—who together had just moved out of the Tork house, since the free-for-all environment had become too much for them—called Crosby at his new home in Marin County, and whoever answered confirmed the report. The two then drove north to stay in Crosby's house and help him through the most traumatic episode of his life.

Crosby and Hinton had moved to a rented house in Novato a few months before, in the summer of 1969. Crosby had grown weary of Los Angeles for several reasons. On the night of August 8, about half a mile from his LA home, the members of Charles Manson's cult had slaughtered five people: the pregnant actress Sharon Tate; coffee heiress Abigail Folger; Jay Sebring, a hairdresser; a writer, Wojciech Frykowski; and a teenager, Steven Parent, who knew the caretaker for the estate. Tate and her husband, film director Roman Polanski, who was in Europe making a movie, were renting the home where the murders took place; eerily, the house belonged to Terry Melcher, the son of Doris Day and a record producer who had worked on the first two Byrds albums. The next night, Manson himself, along with several of his followers, had killed a supermarket executive, Leno LaBianca, and LaBianca's wife, Rosemary, in their home south of Griffith Park. Manson was known by some in musical circles for his friendship with Dennis Wilson of the Beach Boys, among others; Manson played guitar and had written and recorded several songs. When Young heard the songs, he thought they were "fascinating" and suggested that Mo Ostin, head of Reprise Records (where Young recorded on his own), meet Manson. Manson had already spent time in prison after being convicted on a variety of charges over a period of many years, but few expected him to transform into the darkest, grisliest incarnation of the counterculture. Crosby immediately bought a 12-gauge shotgun to protect himself, and he and Hinton decided it was time to leave Los Angeles.

Crosby and Hinton seemed inseparable, especially when Crosby was off the road. "She rolled the best joints, and she was tolerant of his ways," says Hammer. "She could make him laugh, and intellectually she could keep up with him. When others were around, she knew it was David's show and she pretty much stayed in the background. She always made him feel stronger and better." Given Crosby's liberal attitude toward relationships, it was hardly surprising when Debbie Donovan, a friend of Hinton's barely out of her teens, settled into the house as well.

On the morning of September 30, Crosby seemed to have it all: his career had taken off, and he had found the woman who appeared to be his soul mate. The Grateful Dead's Mickey Hart was preparing to deliver a horse to Hinton, but in the meantime, she and one of her close friends, Barbara Langer, were taking Hinton's cats to the vet. On her way out the door, Hinton passed a few hand-rolled joints to Crosby and Nash, who was visiting that day. (Nash later claimed that, earlier, he had slept with Hinton with Crosby's knowledge.) Hinton and Langer then climbed into Crosby's green VW bus.

In a normally harmless moment that would come to derail the course of Crosby's life and change his demeanor for over a decade, the two women were driving to the veterinarian's office when one of the cats escaped Langer's grip and jumped onto Hinton; distracted, Hinton crashed the vehicle directly into an oncoming school bus. She was killed instantly. Since Crosby lived near members of the Dead—and had been encouraging and coaching them on their harmony singing for what would be their next album, *Workingman's Dead*—a member of the Dead's crew, Ray Slade, drove Crosby to the hospital to identify the body. On the way, Crosby saw his mangled VW bus by the side of the road. In the hospital parking lot, an attendant was washing down a parked ambulance. When Hart heard about the accident, he rushed to the hospital too. (He and Langer had recently ended a relationship.) When he arrived, he found her wrapped in bandages, "like the Mummy," he says. Hinton, whom he didn't see, had already passed away. She was only twenty-one.

Crosby's friends filled his home almost instantaneously, seeking to help and comfort him. "It brought everybody down to earth," says Hart. "Everybody's high and stoned, and we didn't have many fatalities. This was a real wake-up call. We were moving a thousand miles a second. And all of a sudden this just stopped the clock. Certainly for David." Members of the Dead dropped by with drugs; Sachse made chocolate chip cookies and mended jeans for Crosby, Stills, Nash and Young when they returned from gigs. "Things like that kept David busy," she says. "He was doing everything he could to avoid thinking about it. There was so much going on—the speed of all this and having to deal with his grief. Her parents would call and say, 'Is there going to be a funeral?' It was painful." (Crosby would eventually spread Hinton's ashes in San Francisco Bay, early in 1970.)

Although Crosby was shaken—"His entire world had been yanked from under him," says Nash—neither Crosby nor anyone else in the band had time to completely process what had happened. A scheduled concert the night of Hinton's death at Winterland in San Francisco was canceled, but in several weeks' time, the group was due to continue recording its first record as a quartet. Preliminary work had been done in Los Angeles, but they had booked three weeks at the Wally Heider studio in San Francisco's grimy Tenderloin neighborhood with a holiday release still in mind. Stills, Nash and Young took rooms in the nearby Caravan Lodge Motel; for added lunacy, Young brought along two pet bush babies, who scampered around his room. (According to Halverson, Ertegun decreed that the second group album must include Young now that he had appeared with them at Woodstock. The festival transformed from muddy joke to cultural talisman almost overnight when *Rolling Stone* rushed out an in-depth story cementing its importance.) As soon as they finished the album, they would have to begin jetting around the country for concerts, from Pittsburgh to Hawaii. There would be no time to mourn.

As Stephen Barncard would see for himself, the next group album would not echo the fluid creation of *Crosby, Stills & Nash*. Hired as Bill Halverson's assistant for the recording sessions in San Francisco, the twenty-two-year-old Barncard, who'd cut his teeth recording bands in Kansas City before relocating to the Bay Area, was more than eager to work on the first record by Crosby, Stills, Nash and Young, but it wouldn't always be what he expected. One day when Barncard looked through the glass into the recording room, he spied Crosby screaming into Nash's ear from two inches away, although he couldn't hear what he was saying. "It was frightening because the music was so good," he says, "and it was frightening because of the tension between them."

As Barncard also observed, there would be no dearth of material. Before the band arrived, their preliminary Los Angeles work tapes were shipped north. "Usually one or two reels come in on a project," Barncard recalls, "but here, there was a cart stacked with tapes." Nash brought "Our House," his ode to life with Mitchell, and "Teach Your Children." Written the previous year, the latter had been inspired by a Diane Arbus photograph, "Child with a Toy Hand Grenade in Central Park, N.Y.C. 1962," showing a young boy flashing a playful grimace while holding a plastic weapon. The advice-to-parents-and-kids song, which captured Nash's straightforwardly melodic style, had poured out of him while he was under the influence of hash. He taught it to the band one day in the studio while walking around holding his guitar, as if he were a serenading waiter. Among his contributions, Stills had "Bluebird Revisited," a slowed-down, nearly pleading update of the Springfield's "Bluebird," along with "So Begins the Task," a despondent but stoically gentle farewell to Judy Collins that he had actually written before their breakup.

The album seemed to get off on the correct musical foot. On the first day of recording, with Mitchell watching, the full band tackled "Woodstock," her look back at the festival she hadn't been able to attend. Mitchell's version, which would arrive in stores around the same time as the band's, was misty and spectral, an idealized homage to a new-world moment she hadn't experienced firsthand. Woodstock co-producer Michael Lang heard an altogether different arrangement when he was visiting LA; as he walked down Sunset Strip, Stills pulled up alongside him and asked him to accompany him back to the Shady Oak house. There, in the music room, Stills and Taylor, on organ and drums, respectively, blasted out a rocked-out version of the song. "Mind-boggling," Lang recalls. "I had no clue it was even written." (During a trip to New York in September, Stills worked up a version with Jimi Hendrix that captured the wild-cat intensity of Stills' voice.)

The Crosby, Stills, Nash and Young take, cut in October, picked up where that jacked-up version left off; in a promising sign, they recorded the instrumental and vocal tracks in one day. "There was steam coming off the floor," says Barncard, who watched awestruck. Yet other songs were rarely that easy. Over the following two months, many tracks were recorded, including a rash of solid if unexciting Stills numbers, such as "30 Dollar Fine" and "Everyday We Live"; Nash's "You're Wrong, Baby," a comment on his early relationship with Mitchell that recalled Paul Mc-Cartney's twee music-hall moments; and Young's organ-driven "Sea of Madness" and "Everybody's Alone." Crosby, crushed by Hinton's death, couldn't bring himself to write new music and brought three songs he'd written the year before: "Déjà vu" and "Almost Cut My Hair" ended up on the final album, but the band quickly abandoned "Laughing" when they couldn't grapple with its chord changes. "Déjà vu" had its origins in a ride on a friend's sailboat that felt eerily familiar. "It's as if I had done it before," Crosby recalls. "I knew way more about it than I should have. I knew how to sail a boat right away. Not an instinctive thing. It doesn't make sense. I wasn't thinking about that specifically when I wrote the song. It just came, but in hindsight, the song was informed by those experiences. I felt then and now that I have been here before. I don't believe in God but I think the Buddhists got it right—we do recycle."

Crosby's situation was the most tragic, but the others were struggling with personal turmoil of their own. Nash was beginning to realize that his romance with Mitchell, now a year old, was suffering from his work demands; he would also claim she was reluctant to marry him. Mitchell herself would say her heart was more shattered than his when things began going south, and that she told him he had to come to terms with his mother's affair: "Until you forgive your mother, your relationships with women are going to be difficult," she told Nash, according to biographer David Yaffe. Then again, observant friends like Hammer felt that Nash was more besotted of Mitchell than she was of him. "He was madly in love with her and she liked him and thought he was an okay guy, and that was about it," says Hammer. "She did not have the same commitment and devotion."

Meanwhile, Dallas Taylor had left his wife and had briefly moved in with Neil and Susan Young. Stills remained wounded after his breakup with Collins. The same month he played "Suite: Judy Blue Eyes" for her in California, Collins had met the intensely rugged actor Stacy Keach, her costar in a Joseph Papp production of Henrik Ibsen's *Peer Gynt* in New York. She and Keach had quickly begun an affair before the show opened that summer. Stills continued sending her "crazy, love-filled, disjointed letters," Collins says. Returning to her Upper West Side apartment with Keach one night after dinner, she found Stills hovering outside her building. "We had a confrontation in the street," she recalls. "Stephen was quite persistent and I was in the other direction." Again, she brushed him off.

With so many headstrong, creative chefs in the kitchen, most of them in various fragile emotional states, the making of their second album exhibited little of the focus of *Crosby, Stills & Nash*. They drove each other to distraction, attempting songs without always giving them the same degree of rehearsal time that had gone into the first album. Stills' meticulous approach to layering and overdubbing voices and instruments to create the ideal recording grated on Young, who thought Stills shouldn't have changed part of his original, rougher vocal on "Woodstock." Nash would think a song was complete, leave for the night, then return the next day to hear a noticeable difference. He would think he was losing his mind, when, in fact, Stills had tweaked the song after everyone left. Not averse to making demands of his own, Nash wanted a different low note on the piano to end "Our House," forcing Halverson to fly down to Los Angeles to use a different keyboard in a different studio for one sustained *ommmm*.

Stills, who had run a tight musical ship on the first album, saw his control slipping away. When Halverson showed up to work in San Francisco, the sessions had already started without him. Halverson's first instructions were to set things up so the band could play an electric version of Crosby's "Almost Cut My Hair" live in the studio. The finished version, edited down from a nearly nine-minute jam, captured the snappish fire of the Stills and Young interplay. Stills thought Crosby's voice was too raw, but Crosby wanted it that way. "David thought it was perfect," says Barncard. "It was what it was." (As laughable as many considered the lyrics, including, later, Crosby himself, the rasp in his voice also expressed his anguish after Hinton's death.) "I didn't want anyone to be in charge," says Crosby. "I didn't like that. Right from the start I knew I was not going to let Stephen be the leader of the group. Which he wanted to be. I didn't want it myself, but I didn't want anyone else to be either. Which was deeply frustrating for Stephen."

The gloom that hovered over the session led to one noticeable sacrifice. They recorded a cover of Terry Reid's "Horses Through a Rainstorm" that Nash had once attempted with the Hollies. Fueled by Stills' burbling church organ and trio harmonies that extended the ray-of-light high spirits of their first album, "Horses Through a Rainstorm" was almost a spiritual follow-up to "Marrakesh Express." But it was deemed too sunny, too commercial, for the comparatively moodier new album, and the group relegated the recording to Atlantic's vault. Another lost treasure would be many attempts to record "So Begins the Task," one of Stills' most fluid and moving songs. "It's like, 'What was wrong with us? What were we thinking?'" Stills has said. "We were brimming with songs. But we would go into the studio and write there, which turned out to be a dreadful mistake as studio costs and discipline go." (Adds Crosby of the band abandoning that song, "Mistakes—lots of mistakes. That was Stills at his best.")

Meanwhile, Young made his bandmates accommodate his particular creative wishes. "Neil was all business," says Barncard. "He would only show up for the tracking and doing his vocals, and then disappear. I didn't see him around a lot." Young had first tried recording "Helpless" with them over the summer in Los Angeles (also with Crazy Horse, without satisfying results). Now, in the fall, they tried it again, and again, and again. Young felt that Taylor and Reeves—Taylor specifically—were overplaying, rushing the tempo. He knew the song required a slower, sludgier pace. With that in mind, Young kept them going in the studio for hours until, just before dawn, when they were all drained, he had the take he wanted. Later, Stills overdubbed a shimmery, sustained guitar that he made to sound like a sleepy fiddle. On the last day, according to Barncard, Young asked Barncard for his two songs—"Helpless" and "Country Girl"—to be removed from the master reel so he could take them to a studio in Burbank to remix or add other instruments, including a pipe organ on "Country Girl." "It was bedlam, man," Stills has said. "It was everybody doing whatever they wanted. It didn't start that way, but it ended that way."

Before Hinton's death, Crosby had been on top of planning and preparation, the one the management team consulted first. After Hinton's passing, he was suddenly unable to handle those responsibilities, which now fell upon Nash. "Graham was easygoing and sensible and gentlemanly—he had an air of English sophistication," says Sachse. "He had manners and knew right from wrong, and he could say to them, 'Oh, come on, now.' He wasn't a hothead like Stephen and David." In the way it harked back to the days when Nash had to oversee his family after his father's imprisonment, the role was a natural one for him. But it also taxed his patience. "Stephen and Neil were back at each other, and coke was making us all nuts," said Taylor. "I remember Graham crying in the studio: 'Guys, what are you doing? Why are you doing this? You're destroying this.' He couldn't understand why things were self-destructing so quickly. I was kind of dumbfounded. I thought, 'This is not good.'" One day, Nash was seen walking around the studio holding a spoon that cradled an inch-and-a-half-high pile of cocaine. "By the time we got to *Déjà vu* and we'd snorted eighty pounds of cocaine," Nash said later, "things were a little different."

Grudges began piling up. At Heider's one night, they successfully turned "Teach Your Children" into a sparkling country-style song with the help of the Dead's Jerry Garcia, who overdubbed a pedal steel guitar. Young didn't sing on the track (many don't recall him being there), nor did he participate in Nash's "Our House," much to Nash's irritation. "From day one, I don't think the other guys in the band gave Graham the credit he deserved," says Stone. "All the hits were Graham's songs. They were determined to be a rock-and-roll band, but Graham turned out to be the most successful pop songwriter." For his part, Taylor, who was lapsing deeper into drug use, was growing increasingly resentful that Young received billing in the group name, while he did not.

In another indication that his commitment to the group wasn't as solid as the others had hoped, Young didn't appear at all on several other tracks. When Nash told Stills the album needed an ear-grabbing opener along the lines of "Suite: Judy Blue Eyes," Stills overnight wrote "Carry On," a cathartic sign that he was regrouping after his breakup with

Collins. Playing all the instruments himself, other than Taylor on drums and Nash thumping on a conga, Stills was back in his preferred captain's seat. (He also paired it with a revival of his Springfield-era "Questions.") Crosby had written "Déjà vu" the year before, and the trio had tried to cut it for the first album, to no avail. Given that the meter changed dramatically, from 6/8 to 4/4, and Crosby used an unusual tuning (E, B, D, G, A, D, from low to high), it was a tricky song to wrestle with. But they kept at it until the wee hours of the morning, and Stills slowly overdubbed parts on top of it, sometimes when Crosby was asleep.

For all the fragmentary nature of the work, the potential for greatness together nevertheless poked out. Nils Lofgren, an impish, teenaged Maryland-based singer and guitarist who'd met Young at the Cellar Door, a club in Washington, DC, had tracked Young down again in Topanga Canyon. He was working with his own band, Grin, and Young's producer, David Briggs, that fall. One day Young, along with Crosby, Stills and Nash, came bounding into the studio. "The door flies open and CSNY come blowing in, all with matching two-foot-thick polar-bear fur coats," Lofgren recalls. "Obscene furs. They say, 'Briggs, can we play you something?'" Briggs had little time or use for the group—he was in Young's camp, not theirs—but agreed, and the band put on a tape of their completed version of "Woodstock." Starting with Young's wrenching guitar, the song embodied the way he could energize the band, and the harmonies never sounded fuller or more overpowering. "We put it on 10 and were pinned by the volume," Lofgren says. "It was impressive, especially those high harmonies. They were very proud of it." At such moments, maybe the chaos was worth it.

MEANWHILE, THE BUSINESS of the band churned around them, with both rewarding and fraught results. Elliot Roberts wisely set up separate publishing companies for each man, but they soon began squabbling over who would get how many songs on the album and make more money as a result. (Even the musician designated bandleader for each session, a union rule, earned more. In one of the few bits of paperwork that seem to exist, the group cut several songs at Heider's in Los Angeles in July, including a version of "Helpless"; Stills, as the leader, earned $171 for the day, whereas the others were paid $86 each.) Halverson would watch in frustration as Geffen and Roberts arrived packing paperwork and discussing plans for the rollout of what was now one of rock's most eagerly anticipated albums. "When the managers would come in with the contracts, it would only take fifteen minutes," says Halverson. "But somebody wasn't getting their way and the business would get in the way of the creativity. The vibe would change and it would take us two days to get it back."

No sooner had they wrapped up most of the work on the album, before Christmas 1969, when they had to pack their bags for a series of concerts around the country. That task alone was no small enterprise: the group's show in Arizona would be delayed when twelve thousand pounds of equipment needed to be set up. The Winterland shows that had been canceled after Hinton's death were rescheduled for November. Robert Greenfield, a young music journalist covering the show for *Fusion* magazine, recalls that "Crosby's face was so sad you could cry." But they returned triumphantly to Chicago, where the *Chicago Tribune* noted the "homogenous" audience—"almost to a man bell-bottomed, pea-jacketed, fringed, and long haired"—and were again greeted by standing ovations and shouts of "Right on!" At an outdoor stadium outside San Diego, they had to overcome overhead airline noise, even tuning up as the audience watched.

Seeds of discord were already sprouting up. At the Hawaii International Center Arena, Young showed up late, joining them midway into the acoustic set (and apologizing to the crowd for it). The group was invited to participate in the Vietnam Moratorium in San Francisco's Golden Gate Park that November; along with an earlier such protest, it would call for the immediate withdrawal of all American troops from Southeast Asia. Further reinforcing the connection between themselves and their audience, who were enraged by the war in Vietnam, the group performed a short set. Stills told the crowd: "Politics is bullshit! Richard Nixon is bullshit! Spiro Agnew is bullshit! Our music *isn't* bullshit!" Young, however, didn't make the event.

In early December, they were enlisted to join the Dead, Jefferson Airplane, Santana and the Flying Burrito Brothers (the country-rock band that included Crosby's former Byrdmate Chris Hillman) in a free concert headlined by the Rolling Stones at the Altamont Speedway. Originally planned for Golden Gate Park, the event had been moved twice to end up at its current locale, a dust bowl east of San Francisco. Promoters had dubbed the daylong event "Woodstock West," but by the time the band arrived by helicopter on the grounds, the mood was anything but festive. The crowd, which shut down roadways and mushroomed to several hundred thousand, seemed to be everywhere. Leo Makota, a burly, red-headed, lumberjack-like member of the band's road crew, was forced to hot-wire a truck and drive through the audience to the stage while Stills yelled out the band's name to clear a path. ("Leo worked his ass off," says Hammer of Makota's crucial role in helping the band during this period. "They couldn't find their way to a hot-dog stand without Leo.")

The size of the crowd wasn't the worst of it. Whoever's idea it was—the Stones, the Dead, even, by one claim, Jefferson Airplane—the local chapter of the Hells Angels had been hired as security. Some of the Angels were "prospects," not regular Angels, but no matter; the combination of gang members and sun-dazed, wasted fans was a bad one. As Crosby, Stills, Nash and Young played in the afternoon, hours before the Stones, Hells Angels milled around menacingly. Stills was accidentally poked in the leg by a motorcycle spoke—"Streams of blood streaked his legs and soaked through his pants," reported author Joel Selvin—and Crosby told the crowd, "Hey, crazy people, stop hurting each other," to no avail.

They managed to make it through an abbreviated set that culminated in a lengthy "Down by the River" jam. Since they were scheduled to play a show that same night at the University of California at Los Angeles, they had to leave almost immediately, and Makota hot-wired the same truck to drive them to the airport. On the way out, they crossed paths with Hart, who remembers them as "just wide-eyed, scared shitless." The band was out and gone before anyone seemed to know it (and before Meredith Hunter, an eighteen-year-old African American man, charged the stage with a gun and was knifed and killed by an Angel). "It went really fast, and we were glad to get out of there," says Sachse, who accompanied them to and from the show and photographed them onstage. In fact, Crosby, Stills, Nash and Young's set was so fleeting that most of the day-after newspaper coverage failed to mention their performance.

Altamont was unlike any other show or event they experienced that year, yet, in a way, the bedlam of that day was of a piece with the crazy rush of the year they'd just endured. As Young wrote later, "I could feel the music dying." Less than six months after they'd finished their first album and become a quartet, they needed a serious break from each other before the sea of madness fully engulfed them.

CHAPTER 3
JANUARY 1970–JANUARY 1971

L ike many who were orbiting the group's world, Henry Diltz had already grown accustomed to never knowing what to expect. The previous summer, in 1969, he'd taken a call at home from two New Jersey kids who loved his photographs on *Crosby, Stills & Nash.* They were calling themselves the "Henry Diltz Fan Club." In the middle of March 1970, an even more mysterious call came to Diltz's home. Amid crackling static, he could decipher, barely, the voice of art director Gary Burden cutting in and out, saying something about being on Crosby's boat off the coast of Mexico. He knew that Crosby, Stills and Nash had blown off the Grammys—the ceremony was considered square and old-fashioned, and none of the three were in Los Angeles that March night anyway. In another week or two, Diltz was scheduled to photograph Young—but with his *other* band, Crazy Horse. Diltz had no idea what was happening, but then, he was hardly alone in wondering about the state of rock's most exalted non-group.

To Ahmet Ertegun's disappointment, the first album by Crosby, Stills, Nash and Young would not be delivered to record stores in time for Christmas 1969. Thanks to the various obstacles, sessions and final touches, the completion of the album dragged on past New Year's 1970. The graphics themselves wouldn't have been ready in time for the holidays. On an early November 1969 afternoon, the entire band, including Taylor and Reeves, convened at Crosby's Novato home for a photo shoot for the cover. Given that it was the home where Crosby had lived with Christine Hinton, who had died less than two months before, the setting couldn't have been more somber. But after a late coffee-and-eggs breakfast and a few lines of cocaine—and with cheerleading from their friend Grace Slick, who was visiting—the group changed into cowboy costumes they rented at the Western Costume Company in North Hollywood and gathered in the backyard. The photographer, Tom O'Neal, then using his birth name, Gundelfinger, had been tasked by Stills and Burden to make the band appear as if they were in a Mathew Brady–style photo from the Civil War. "Ahmet would whine, 'That's gonna cost a lot!'" Stills has said. "But it was this whole concept I had. If you went to the wrong part of town with long hair, guys would attack your car. We felt like we were in the Civil War because of the times."

As the group congregated in front of a gnarled tree in the backyard, Nash refused to hold a gun. But Crosby had grown up around weapons—he "joined the Junior NRA and went through their whole riflery program" as a youth, he would later recall—and he had no such issues carrying a musket. Nodding to his southern heritage, Stills picked out a Confederate outfit—which wouldn't be the only nod to those times. To fully capture the North-versus-South mood they wanted, O'Neal had rented a well-preserved wooden-box camera that dated back over one hundred years. The exposure time was two and a half minutes, so he also brought along a modern camera as insurance. Sure enough, the photo that would ultimately make the cover would be taken with that new model and then chemically treated to make it appear as if it were a century old. But that was only stage one of the process. The band demanded that the photo be hand-glued onto simulated-leather cardboard covers—part of Stills' demand that the packaging resemble an antique hymnal. Workers at multiple pressing plants around the country were enlisted for the task, postponing the record's release until nearly spring.

Yet no amount of delays could dampen the expectations for the album they'd decided to call *Déjà vu*. Everything in the zeitgeist appeared to be lining up in their favor. Boosted by their first album, sales of fretted instruments, including acoustic guitars, had leapt from $106 million to $160 million between 1969 and 1970. *Crosby, Stills & Nash* had been nominated for Album of the Year and the trio for Best New Artist. In an instance of brilliant timing that made record companies and managers drool, the Grammy ceremony would be held the week of the new album's release. "I hear a group like CSN and understand how free and expressive they are," an unnamed Eastern teenager commented in a Gilbert Youth Poll conducted early in 1970. "This is how we should all be."

Two weeks after *Déjà vu* was scheduled to be displayed in record stores, the movie of the Woodstock festival was set to open. Thanks to David Geffen, who wanted to make sure the group's presence was played up as much as possible, the group would not only be seen in a performance segment, but "Long Time Gone" would accompany the opening footage of crews setting up the Woodstock stage, and the film would end with their version of "Woodstock." "It was perfect for the film," says festival co-organizer Michael Lang. "There wasn't much push-back." To further promote the album, Geffen and Elliot Roberts were in the midst of organizing a national tour, including two nights in Chicago and six in New York City.

Déjà vu was a guaranteed moneymaker. Atlantic had already scored $2 million in preorders, and the label was certain it would be one of its most lucrative releases in years. In the weeks leading up to the release, record stores across the country laced ads in their local newspapers exclusively for *Déjà vu.* Two Guys, a mostly Eastern-based department store chain, made it the only LP featured in its full-page ads alongside everyday products like a Hoover upright vacuum cleaner ($49.97) and Presto hair curlers ($16.99). Even though one band member was British and another Canadian, the phrase "American Beatles" began appearing in the media about them. "That was tragic," Stills has said. "What an absurd, stupid, Hollywood-manager thing to say." But with the Beatles seemingly evaporating before the public's eye, the public was eager to embrace another quartet of distinct personalities crammed together in one band—with the added expectation that they would represent liberty and social justice for all.

As MUCH AS they were looking for a reprieve from the crush of the previous year, now would not be the time. Early in 1970, they shipped their amplifiers and gear across the ocean for a few concerts in Europe. Their performance at the Royal Albert Hall in London was especially nerve-wracking, since Nash felt he would be judged for having left his beloved previous band. "I'd committed the sin of leaving the Hollies, and the English people didn't like that particularly," he says. "So I really wanted to be good. I really wanted to shine and let England know that there was a good reason I left." Stills worried that the time they often spent onstage tuning would also be frowned upon.

At that point, they needn't have worried. The sold-out venue, which included Paul McCartney and Donovan, seemed to adore them as much as American audiences had the year before. As in the States, they opened with "Suite: Judy Blue Eyes," joked repeatedly among themselves (Stills slapped an "L" handbill—the British learner's permit for driving lessons— on Crosby's back on the way to the stage), and ended with a "Down by the River" jam. But after two additional shows in Scandinavia, they more than ever realized they needed time apart from each other. More a drinker than a toker, Stills was growing irritated by his bandmates' devotion to weed, and they were tiring of his bossy tendencies. Greg Reeves was beginning to act abnormal, carrying around what seemed like witch-doctor paraphernalia that inevitably led to drawn-out airport security searches. Even worse, in their book, he began asking if they could perform some of the songs he'd written. Like Taylor, he assumed that the rhythm section was an integral part of the band—they were featured on the cover of *Déjà vu*, too—but both men would soon learn that was not the case.

Once their European obligations were met, they scattered. In a pattern that would repeat itself over decades, Stills and Young each immersed themselves in work while Crosby sought to escape with the help of his close friend Nash. Entranced by England, Stills decided to stay there a bit longer. He rented a room at the Dorchester Hotel and began dropping into nightclubs and pubs, quickly ingratiating himself with the likes of Eric Clapton and Ringo Starr. When Starr was looking for someone to lease Brookfield House, his home in Elstead outside of London, Stills was given a tour of the property by Starr's wife at the time, Maureen, who had taken Ringo's real last name, Starkey. Stills was captivated by what he saw: a 350-year-old estate with chandeliers, a wine cellar, a pond that was home to ducks and geese, and a living room with beams made from the wood of Spanish Armada ships. Thanks to one of its previous owners, actor Peter Sellers, it also had a movie theater for private screenings. From the sight and sound of his bandmates to the upheaval in America, Stills was tired of the States. Brookfield House was the sort of property one would associate with pop royalty, and Stills, who was newly wealthy and valued his privacy, quickly rented it and moved in.

Always driven to prove himself and ward off the feelings of self-dislike that derived from his upbringing, Stills had barely settled in when he got back to work. Even though *Déjà vu* wasn't yet in stores, he decided to initiate an album of his own, becoming the first to take advantage of their anti-band concept following the success of *Crosby, Stills & Nash.* With over a dozen newly written songs in hand, he began spending dusk-to-dawn nights at Island Studios in London, zipping back and forth from Elstead at pushing-the-limit speeds in one of his Ferraris or Mercedes.

His new musical connections helped: Clapton overdubbed a guitar solo on "Go Back Home," a blues piece that allowed Stills to show off his Hendrix-inspired skills on wah-wah guitar. Starr arrived one day, set up before everyone else had arrived, and played on several songs, including "As I Come of Age," in which Stills, all of twenty-five, was already assessing his mistakes. (Starr later invited Stills to join him and George Harrison on one of Starr's first solo singles, "It Don't Come Easy," recorded that spring; Stills played piano.) At a party, Billy Preston, the African American singer and keyboardist who had pitched in on the Beatles' *Let It Be,* was talking with Stills about women and casually said, "If you can't be with the one you love, love the one you're with," inspiring Stills to write—and soon record—a driving, pulsating song with that title in London in March.

Stills and Jimi Hendrix had been endless-jam buddies for several years. "Stephen came to me full of praise for Jimi, saying this guy made him swing the hardest and jam the hardest he'd ever jammed," said Peter Tork. Hendrix and Stills would convene in the music room at the house on Shady Oak in Los Angeles and play for hours. In London, where Hendrix was now based, the two reconnected—hitting the clubs, indulging together, and recording, in one feverish take, "Old Times Good Times," Stills' swampy look back at his youth. His organ and Hendrix's guitar sidled up along each other with a natural ease. Afterward, Hendrix implied to Stills that they'd make an album together.

For his part, Young, having done about six months' time in the Crosby, Stills, Nash and Young world, was eager to regroup with Crazy Horse. As if cleansing his palette, he and the band were on the road just weeks after the last CSNY show in Copenhagen. While playing acoustic sets before being joined by the Horse, Young made it explicitly clear he wasn't bound by his deal with Crosby, Stills and Nash. In Cincinnati in February, he introduced a performance of "Helpless" with a wry chuckle, calling it a song from "a new album on Atlantic Records" and not mentioning the names of the others. (At that and other shows, his between-song comments were generally droll and self-deprecating, another contrast with his partners.) Eager to complete *After the Gold Rush*, the album he'd started the previous summer, Young went in search of what Nils Lofgren called "a clear, direct sound" and recruited Lofgren, Crazy Horse drummer Ralph Molina and Greg Reeves. During the same weeks that Stills was frantically recording and pulling musical all-nighters in London, logging up to 160 hours in the studio, Young was on fire too. Over the course of one week at his home studio in Topanga—a down-home space beneath a porch—he and his musicians recorded more than half an album: a contemplative beauty called "After the Gold Rush"; "Only Love Can Break Your Heart," his song to Nash about his growing troubles with Mitchell; a rare political-zinger diatribe, "Southern Man"; and a few lightweight throwaways, including "Till the Morning Comes." "CSNY was this storm gathering on the horizon, this super-band Neil was part of," Lofgren says. "We were happy for him. But we didn't go with him to those sessions. In our world, he was focused on *Gold Rush*."

Still grappling with the aftermath of Hinton's death, Crosby opted to fulfill a dream he'd long had—sailing his boat an inordinately long distance—and, along the way, he would put Hinton's ashes to rest. Retrieving his sailboat, the *Mayan*, in Florida in late January 1970, he enlisted an initially wary Nash, who'd never been on a boat but wanted to support his friend, to go along. Also joining them was a rotating cast of band crew members (including road manager Leo Makota), bona fide sailors and a few musicians, including singer-songwriter Ronee Blakey (later known for her role in Robert Altman's *Nashville*).

Setting sail from Fort Lauderdale, Crosby and Nash effectively dropped off the music business radar for over a month. They sailed from Florida and the Bahamas to the West Coast by way of Cuba, Jamaica, the Panama Canal and Mexico. On the trip from Jamaica to the Panama Canal, they were joined by Joni Mitchell, who'd been invited by Crosby and didn't know Nash would be aboard. By the time the *Mayan* arrived at the Panama Canal, Nash and Mitchell were barely on speaking terms. ("It was just unpleasant," Nash says. "I wasn't grown up enough. It was tense.") They stopped at a yacht club, went to Mexican banks for cash, witnessed an eclipse, saw whales springing up through the waves, and got endlessly high along the way on pot and a canister of cocaine.

Few knew where they were, including Geffen and Roberts. "Elliot was freaked," Crosby says. "We were wasting time sailing around on that damn boat. We were supposed to be working. It made no sense to him at all." But the trip would prove cathartic to Crosby, "good medicine," as he put it, that would also solidify his bond with Nash. After they made their way up the West Coast, Crosby completed the trip as he had hoped, spreading Hinton's ashes from aboard the *Mayan* not far from the Golden Gate Bridge.

BY THE TIME the completed tapes of *Déjà vu* were submitted to Atlantic in February, the music betrayed little of the second-guessing and the turbulence that had plagued its creation. The album's mix was crisper and more upfront than on *Crosby, Stills & Nash*. Since the band no longer had to take sonic orders from Ertegun, the guitars and percussion were more pronounced, and the individual instruments were clearly delineated. "Woodstock" was a perfect example: after opening with Young's guitar, the other instruments—Stills' organ, Reeves' bass, Crosby's scraping-rake rhythm guitar and Taylor's drums—slid in one by one. The moment when Nash's and Stills' voices each swelled up behind Crosby's in "Déjà vu" had a similar lucidity. As well made as it was, the first album almost sounded muddy next to the sonic clarity of *Déjà vu.* For sheer record-making skill, it was hard to top "Carry On," from its exclamatory verses to the array of guitars and keyboards Stills layered throughout.

What *Déjà vu* lacked, not surprisingly, was the cohesion of the first album. None of the songs on *Crosby, Stills & Nash* featured a single voice with no accompanying harmony, yet several on *Déjà vu* did. Alone with just his guitar, Stills had sat down in an LA studio and played "4 + 20," about an imaginary old man looking back on his tattered life. He sang it in the same solemn timbre from start to finish, lending the song a repressed undercurrent. The take felt so right, so perfect, down to a telling pause between "I" and "embrace," that Crosby and Nash decided to keep it that way and not add their voices to it. "Crosby and I were watching when he was recording, and Stephen really felt it," says Nash. "When he came to that line and took that gulp, he wanted to cut it again—which he did, without the gulp. But Crosby and I loved it. It was so human, and on such a human song. We convinced Stephen to use the first take."

Through the magic of overdubbing, *Déjà vu* could *sound* like a band effort. After taking the basic tapes of the medley back with him to Los Angeles, Young and collaborator David Briggs worked their magic on "Country Girl (Whiskey Boot Hill, Down Down Down, Country Girl [I Think You're Pretty])," adding a pipe organ and other instruments. With Crosby and Nash harmonizing with Young on one verse, and Stills and Young blending together on another, the song was transformed into a hippie-choir ensemble piece, a Laurel Canyon symphony with an accompanying, otherworldly vocal crescendo. By and large, though, *Déjà vu* felt more like a revue and less like a working band. As it should: in the end, Young played on only five of its ten songs and sang on just two, his own. His guitar, however, noticeably upped the energy levels on "Woodstock" and "Almost Cut My Hair."

Yet from the moment it started, with a bustle of Stills acoustic guitars and burst of massed harmonies on "Carry On," the glummer *Déjà vu* tapped into the mood of the moment as much as its predecessor had. Five days before the album's release, a townhouse in New York's Greenwich Village suddenly exploded; in the weeks that followed, it was learned that in its basement, members of the Weather Underground had been building bombs to possibly attack a military base. Meanwhile, Richard Nixon's approval rating, after just a year in office, was approaching 60 percent, despite his announcement that he was sending troops into Cambodia. A sense of powerlessness began taking over the counterculture, and few knew what a new decade augured.

In that context, *Déjà vu* struck many chords at once. "Almost Cut My Hair" now seemed like a defiant statement of purpose. "Helpless" may have been about Canada, but that word rarely implied more in a pop song than it did at that moment. "Woodstock" was one of the band's meatiest moments, living up to Mitchell's celebratory lyrics, but with Altamont now in the rear-view mirror, the fantasy of half a million hippies living in harmony was back to being a dream. Nash's "Our House" and "Teach Your Children" were cheery, but the concluding "Everybody I Love You," masterfully cobbled together by Halverson from two different recordings, was so rushed that it sounded desperate, as if they were trying to convince each other and the country that everything was on track.

Finally released on March 11, 1970—if Ertegun didn't have Christmas, at least he had Easter—*Déjà vu* wasn't immune to criticism. *Rolling Stone* published a sarcastic piece about fans awaiting its release, then took sharp jabs at the album, calling its worked-over harmonies and arrangements "too perfect to be true." (Given the tumult that went into its making, the magazine wasn't far off in that regard.) But the so-called straight press, from the *Los Angeles Times* to the *Tampa Tribune*, called it the best rock album of the year to date, and a New York college radio station played the LP in its entirety most of the day.

As much as they were reveling in their time apart, band duties beckoned. Crosby and Nash were reminded of the work that lay ahead when Roberts and Burden flew to Mexico, on an especially rickety plane, to ensure they signed contracts for concerts that would earn them $25,000 and 65 percent of the gross—an especially sweet deal for the pop-concert business of 1970. At a typical arena that charged an average of $5 a seat, that percentage could amount to as much as an extra $50,000 a night. And as Diltz would soon learn, here was the reason for the mysterious ship-to-shore call to his home. Someone had finally tracked down Crosby and Nash, and the group, such as it was in March 1970, now had to fulfill its obligations to their management and their record company, if not to each other.

"PUBLIC NOTICE" BLARED an advertisement with imposing black letters in the May 18 edition of the *Minneapolis Tribune*. Beneath that warning was the startling news: "The entire national concert tour of Crosby, Stills, Nash & Young has been cancelled due to illness." Over the next few days, similar reports sprouted up in newspapers in Chicago, Detroit and St. Louis for performances in those cities. Each ad similarly mentioned an unnamed illness along with an address for mailing tickets back for a refund. It was a rare—and catastrophic—announcement for a major act whose album was no. 1 in the country that week (and the second biggest-selling record in the eight-track tape and cassette formats).

As soon as everyone had reassembled in Los Angeles in April to rehearse, everything about the group suddenly had felt jinxed. While Mitchell had been on vacation in Greece, she had telegrammed Nash, who was still at her house, to formally end their relationship. Returning from London and driving home from the Los Angeles airport on April 14, Stills saw a police car in his rear-view mirror, was temporarily distracted, and rammed his car into a parked vehicle, fracturing his left hand. In what would amount to the first of many delays of rehearsals, Stills' broken wrist was now in a cast, and he fled to Hawaii to recuperate. (Although he could only move two fingers on his left hand, he still managed to write several songs.) After two weeks, he returned, but now the group had to deal with Reeves. His mysterious ways and his request to have them sing his own material irked Crosby, Stills and Nash, if not Young or some of their friends. "He was a bit eccentric, but from where I could see it didn't affect his relationship with the band," says Bobby Hammer. "He had some bizarre cultish religious beliefs, but he was a really quiet guy and could play all their songs. He was really good."

Still, the decision was made to fire Reeves. "He did something that drove David crazy," Stills has said. "It was, 'This has to change.'" Opposed to the idea yet still supportive of Reeves' musicianship, Young accepted their decision but vowed to keep working with him. (At Young's behest, Reeves and Taylor had also been awarded 1 percentage point of *Déjà vu*'s royalties.) Reeves was indignant but accepted the situation. "Being a medicine man or not (which is when I was more a practitioner of the Native American way of life) has nothing to do with the fact that they needed me to make the 'track' portion of their records complete," he said later. Either way, he was out, and with their first concert less than a week away, a new bass player was needed, and immediately. Stills flashed on Calvin "Fuzzy" Samuel (then Samuels), a black Jamaican bassist he'd met in London. At twenty-two, Samuel, nicknamed for the way he played his bass through a fuzz pedal for a distorted tone, had logged time in R&B and ska bands. A frequent presence at London's Olympic Studio, he had asked Stills' roadie Bruce Berry to set up a bass in the studio where Stills was working, and soon the two were jamming together—and, to Samuel's surprise, the notoriously demanding Stills seemed to like his playing. With his friend, drummer Conrad Isidore, Samuel ended up participating on Stills' own in-progress album.

Told to track down a "bass player named Fuzzy" in London, Ron Stone of Geffen-Roberts somehow managed to find the possible new bass player. Homeless at the time, Samuel often wound up crashing at Olympic, so it may not have been too difficult. Though Samuel didn't have the money for a plane ticket (Stone recalls he did get him a visa), he went to Heathrow Airport anyway. In a scenario that could have only happened at that moment in history, Samuel took advantage of a distraction and sneaked aboard a flight to Los Angeles, then fled the plane when it landed. He was driven to meet the band at a rehearsal space, and the next day, flew with them to their first show, at the Denver Coliseum on May 12. "We didn't rehearse," Samuel says. "We got on the plane and flew straight to Colorado to play. All in one night."

The stage was set for a less than almighty return, which the band more than delivered. "We haven't seen each other for six weeks!" Crosby announced early in the show, words that rang true in light of the group's shambolic performance. Stills hobbled around on crutches (he'd hurt his leg skiing, adding to the delays), and the sound system crackled and fed back; Crosby warned the audience that the crew was "struggling with it." Samuel, who was not intimately familiar with the group's repertoire, had to learn to play their material as thousands of faces bore down on him. At one point, Crosby rolled out his usual adulatory introduction of Stills—who was nowhere to be found and didn't emerge from the wings for five minutes.

But the group was nevertheless greeted with adoration—screams of "Right on!" punctuated the air, references to Woodstock were cheered, and the crowd seemed to happily forgive mistakes, including a fumbled "Teach Your Children." During a particularly time-consuming moment in the electric set, Crosby warned the crowd that they'd have to watch the band get in tune. "And you get to get stoned!" came the approving response of one fan. Their bond with their fans was reinforced by elliptical comments about protests, the war, and the debut of a newly written Nash song, "Chicago," inspired by the group receiving an invitation to play a benefit for the Chicago Eight, the protesters who had been arrested in the aftermath of the demonstrations at the Democratic National Convention the previous year. Jerry Rubin, Abbie Hoffman, Tom Hayden, Lee Weiner, John Froines, Bobby Seale, Renee Davis and David Dellinger had all been charged with conspiracy to "incite, organize, promote, encourage, participate in and carry on a riot." (Seale had been bound and gagged in the courtroom and chained to a chair to keep him from interrupting the proceedings. The first line of the song is a reference to him.) The Chicago Eight had gone to trial in September 1969, and in February 1970 they were found guilty of contempt of court and, except for two of them, intent to riot; most were fined $5,000. Not for the first time, Nash talked to his partners in song; the song was actually addressed to Stills and Young, who opted against appearing at the benefit, particularly in the line pleading with them to come to Chicago to sing.

In Denver, before playing "Helpless," Young told the crowd, "It's good to be back on the boards." Inside he was seething, initially about the PA. "The monitor system really sucks, you know," he grumbled out loud, for all to hear. "It's driving me crazy." He was also displeased with Stills, who had returned to his preferred role of leading—or, as the others interpreted it, dominating—the band. Young, still unhappy over the firing of Reeves, now had to cope with a rhythm section made up entirely of Stills' players and a set list dominated by Stills songs, since Samuel was more familiar with those than with Crosby, Nash or Young material. (Five years later, Stills pooh-poohed those tales of friction to writer Barbara Charone, saying, "Remember all those stories about who was the *lead guitarist* in CSN&Y? Well, that discussion lasted through the first guitar break in the first day of rehearsal the first time we did 'Carry On.' Neil walked over and said, 'You're the lead guitar player.'") Stills also played more solo songs (three) than the others. Before the penultimate song of the night, "Long Time Gone," Young unplugged his guitar and stalked off—to the shock of the others, who remained onstage, made it through the song without a lead guitar part, bid their goodbyes and left without playing another song.

Before they all went to bed, Taylor was called to a meeting in Young's Denver hotel room, where he also found Nash and Crosby. In an extraordinary—and reckless—move that exposed the fragility of their union, they told the drummer that they no longer wanted to work with Stills and were canceling the tour and flying back to Los Angeles. "If the music's not there, why the fuck would we want to do it in front of people?" Nash says. "And it wasn't there. We had a partner who was going off the deep end. It was too much. And it was definitely too much for Neil." Taylor pledged his allegiance to Stills, who, uninformed of what had taken place, flew to their next gig in Chicago by himself and arrived at the auditorium only to find the crew packing up.

Four hours before show time, the two Chicago concerts were officially called off, with "illness" initially cited as the cause. Atlantic then announced that the cancellations were due to "the sore throats of David Crosby and Graham Nash." Stills and Taylor flew back together to Los Angeles; Taylor tried to console his shaken bandmate by arguing that they should form their own group and forget about the others. As dance students at Sonoma College in Santa Rosa, California, performed a routine to "Déjà vu," and a survey of Indiana high school students revealed that their favorite song was the group's recording of "Woodstock," what promised to be one of the most profitable rock concert tours of its time was effectively over after one inadequate performance.

STARTING WITH AN onstage meltdown and the immediate breakup, Crosby, Stills, Nash and Young would sprint through a stunning gamut of experiences in the nine days that followed the Denver show.

For the June 6 issue of *Billboard*, Atlantic rushed out a statement denying the group was disbanding, blaming the cancellations on Stills' "wrist and knee injuries" and Nash's recurring throat issues. The label also began preparing ads like the one that would run in the *Minneapolis Tribune* announcing the cancellation of the entire tour. In reality, nobody, least of all the business types who worked for them, wanted to scratch the shows; breakup rumors could deter fans from buying tickets to future concerts. Three days after Denver, on May 15, the four musicians were summoned to the Geffen-Roberts offices with their dual managers and a flummoxed Ertegun. "We told Elliot that was it and he had to undo the tour and figure out how long it would be before we talked to one another again," Nash recalls. Instead, the four were read the rock-and-roll version of a riot act and told that they risked lawsuits and other financial crises if they didn't resume. This time, the money truly talked. "We had to face the consequences," says Nash. "It was a lot of money. We had to make sure the promoters who were so kind to us on the first tour weren't hurt."

But at least one compromise had to be reached between the band members, and Young made it clear that Taylor had to go. In the worst possible timing, Taylor arrived at the office as the meeting was wrapping up and watched as the somber-faced bandmates emerged. Stills apologized and said they had no choice; Taylor was out, to be replaced by a drummer to be named. "The deal had already happened, and Neil got his way," Taylor claimed. "It was the worst day of my life. I was dumbfounded. It had nothing to do with my playing. Neil was pissed at me for not saying I would tour without Stephen." (Counters Crosby: "Dallas was canned because Neil could get and should have had a better drummer"; Taylor also claimed that Young's wife, Susan, was "flirty" with him, which, Taylor added, annoyed Young.)

The group scattered briefly to lick its collective wounds, with Crosby and Young heading north to San Francisco and then driving south to road manager Makota's house in redwoods-encased Pescadero. On the morning of May 19, four days after the band meeting, someone at the house went for groceries. At the time, the country's most popular photo-driven newsweekly was *Life*, which had a weekly circulation of over eight million copies—one of which was dropped into the bags of food. "Tragedy at Kent" read the cover line, next to a photo of students leaning over the body of a fallen man. As everyone already knew by then, four students at Kent State had been shot and killed on May 4 by National Guardsmen. At that moment, the circumstances and timelines remained murky, but the fatalities were horrifically undeniable, and the photos that took up eleven pages of the magazine offered a visceral chronicle of the event. As Crosby watched, Young picked up a guitar and, in short order, wrote and sang a song he called "Ohio," about soldiers, Nixon, and students being gunned down.

When the group reassembled in Los Angeles two days later, May 21, to begin rehearsals, they had a revived sense of purpose, along with a replacement percussionist. Also staying at Makota's home had been Johny (then Johnny) Barbata, a lanky, Jersey-born drummer who must have heard his beats on the radio a million times when he was a member of the Turtles (and played on their biggest hit, "Happy Together"). The Crosby, Stills, Nash and Young tour was already being rescheduled, and Barbata was witness to discussions over who would replace Taylor. "They were a bit in disarray," Barbata recalls. "We talked about Dewey Martin, but he wasn't good enough. Then at that point, Leo said, 'Why don't you do it, John?'" With little time to spare and rehearsals days away, the choice seemed obvious, and Barbata was offered a sizable amount, $1,500 a week, for the month-long tour.

That first day, the four of them, along with Barbata and Samuel, reconvened at the Warner Brothers studio lot for five or six days of rehearsals. *They Shoot Horses, Don't They?*, a movie about a Prohibition-era contest where couples danced until they dropped, had finished filming on the same soundstage, and a sign from the set—"How Long Will They Last?"—hung ominously over the stage. Adding to the discomfort was the presence of Taylor, who had been asked to drop by and help Barbata learn the drum parts. "Like a dummy, I did it," Taylor said. "'Awkward' is the word. It was horrible. I was in my own nightmare, awake." The tension was broken at least once, when comedian Bill Cosby, who was also working on the lot, appeared with a prop whip and, snapping it, ordered them to get to work; finally, everyone laughed.

At the end of rehearsals, Halverson, working at the Record Plant studio on Stills' album, received a call asking him to prepare for a group recording session instead. Later that night, the six musicians arrived and took their places with their instruments. They were in a smallish space in the studio that was normally home to a string section, and practically on top of each other. In just a few takes, they taped Young's "Ohio," which they'd been practicing all day at the Warners lot.

Over the months they'd spent on *Déjà vu*, they'd labored to create a unified group sound, but starting with Young's funeral-march introduction, soon joined by Crosby's rhythm guitar and Stills' steely lead lines, they achieved cohesion in just a few takes of "Ohio." (Stills would always feel the song needed another verse, though.) Even the vocal parts were recorded live, without their customary layers of overdubs. During the extended chant at its conclusion, Crosby improvised a part—"How many, how many more?" "I went to the end of it and was so into it and I was just screaming that stuff at the end," he recalls. "I'm very proud of that. If that's what CSNY gets remembered for, fine. That's good."

The previous decade had been rife with protest songs, but from its timeliness to the way the intertwined guitars crackled with brittle, amplified menace, few felt as immediate as "Ohio." Ertegun pushed to release it as a single. For the flip side, they gathered around and recorded "Find the Cost of Freedom," a one-verse, hymn-like meditation Stills had written for the previous year's *Easy Rider* that had been rejected. Again they gathered close—"It was like the four of them at a card table, that close," recalls Halverson—and sang in effortless four-part harmony. (As was often the case, Young took the highest part.) The tapes were quickly shipped to New York in order to press and release the songs as soon as was mechanically possible.

With "Ohio" and "Find the Cost of Freedom" quickly in the can, they had not only both sides of a timely single but a renewed sense of commitment. In the course of little over a week, they had played, fought, broken up, disbursed, fired a drummer, hired a new one, reunited and forged a new bond. It had been a whirlwind 216 hours since the Denver concert.

FOR THE COUNTRY, 1968 and 1969 had been soul-shattering years, piled high with race riots, deeper involvement in Vietnam, Manson's death-cult murders, and assassinations of beloved political leaders. What remained of the legacy of the '60s seemed to erode even further as 1970 wearily dragged on. Kent State was a chilling example of the potentially violent consequences of protesting the war, and the Weather Underground's townhouse explosion disgusted many on both the right and the left. After NASA had landed a man on the moon in 1969, the Apollo 13 mission in the spring of 1970 nearly stranded astronauts in space. The Manson trial that summer put the grisly details of the murders on display, even dragging the Beatles into the fray (prosecutor Vincent Bugliosi learned that Manson had read apocalyptic signs into their so-called White Album, which had even been played for the jury while they were deliberating). Already teetering on a breakup, the Beatles themselves appeared to publicly collapse in the spring, when McCartney released a solo album complete with a self-written question-and-answer session in which he seemed to dismiss the thought of working with John Lennon again in the near future.

Just as 1970 tried to hold itself together, so did Crosby, Stills, Nash and Young as they resumed their tour in Boston on May 29, about a week after recording "Ohio." During rehearsals, the set list for the upcoming tour was carved into particularly tough stone, ensuring that each man (and his songs) received equal stage time and exposure. "Suite: Judy Blue Eyes" would still open each show, followed by Young joining them for "On the Way Home" from his Springfield days. Some of the onstage gags were repeated. During their six-night stand at the Fillmore East in New York, workers at the theater were initially charmed to see Stills grab a standup bass and act as if it were a regular guitar; the others, acting surprised, yucked it up. The band then did the same shtick the following nights.

The second, electric set would have nearly the same lineup of songs each night, centered around extended, dozen-minute-plus versions of "Carry On" and Young's new, vitriolic tongue-lashing "Southern Man," which allowed Stills and Young to turn it up and lob guitar solos back and forth. "It was entertaining," Stills has said. "We'd try to imitate what the other guy was playing and that worked out really good. We'd go off and come back to the original theme. The word 'dueling' never came from me. Musicians don't duel. It ain't a competition. It ain't NASCAR. I said, 'Neil, are we doing that or not?' And he said, 'No, we're just trading off.'" Sticking a lit cigarette in the tip of his guitar or mugging during solos, Stills had the tendency to overdo his stage moves, but he also felt the businessmen around them were egging him and Young on: "It was destructive and it probably contributed to our demise: 'He's a better guitar player!' Thanks, guys."

Drama continued to ensnare them. Although he had sung "Our House" on stage at many shows the year before, Nash, still shaken from his breakup with Mitchell, didn't play the song on the entire tour, fearing he wouldn't be able to get through it. At the Fillmore East, when Dylan came in a back door and sat in the sound booth, Stills played more solo songs than the group permitted, leading to a backstage confrontation in which Nash accused him of hogging the spotlight. The others watched silently, Stills crushing a beer can in his hand and glowering. (To coerce them into an encore and out of their locked dressing room, Graham started slipping $100 bills under the door.) Three days after the last of the Fillmore East shows, they played the Spectrum in Philadelphia, where critic Jack Lloyd of the *Inquirer* noted that "needlessly bitter barbs came zinging out between songs periodically." But in the wee hours of the morning after the performance, Stills and Nash reversed course yet again; in search of a pool table, they hired a limousine to drive them to the suburban home of a teenager, Joel Bernstein, and his family.

Bernstein, who had just graduated from high school before the group's Fillmore shows, had met and photographed Mitchell the previous fall, when she had played in Philadelphia; taken with his work, Mitchell had invited him to be her official portrait taker. In no time, the affable, chatty teen was drawn into their world. His photos of Young would grace the front, back and inside of Young's next album, *After the Gold Rush.* Arriving at his family's house after the Spectrum, Stills and Nash first congregated in his bedroom; when Nash sat on Bernstein's bed, a photo of Mitchell on the wall seemed to hover behind him. They relocated to the basement, where Bernstein watched as the two rock stars snorted and played pool for hours. Bernstein's father, Stanley, buzzed down to the basement to ask his son what exactly was going on before finally popping in, in his robe, and introducing himself. At times like those, the group could almost live up to the just-folks image on their first album cover.

As the tour resumed, their talking-to after Denver clearly had its desired, scared-straight effect. Especially during the electric set, where they were grounded by Barbata's sturdy, rigid beats, the band sounded sharper and more focused than they had in Denver. (Unfortunately, some of the highlights of that show, including Crosby's solo version of "Everybody's Been Burned," from his Byrds days, and an attempt at "Everybody I Love You," from *Déjà vu,* were not to be repeated.) Nash's "Chicago" and Stills' medley of "49 Bye-Byes" and "For What It's Worth" (renamed "America's Children" for the over-the-top poem/exhortation he included in it) felt newly plugged into the times in light of the Kent State massacre. Most of *Déjà vu* was left unplayed, but the sets featured a slew of songs the public hadn't yet heard: Young's "Don't Let It Bring You Down" and "Tell Me Why"; Stills' "Love the One You're With" and "As I Come of Age"; Nash's "Right Between the Eyes"; and Crosby's "The

Lee Shore," a sailing soundscape that served as another showcase for the way his and Nash's harmonies circled each other. A nightly highlight was the newly released "Ohio"; for kinetic crackling energy, the concert version easily surpassed the studio rendition.

As enthusiastic as the crowds were—"Youth Await Their Heroes" proclaimed one headline—early signs of a backlash were beginning to surface. In their lifestyle, wardrobe and political views, Crosby, Stills, Nash and Young staked their claim to being interchangeable from their audience, but those fans had the first of several rude awakenings when tour dates and prices were announced in April. The best seats at the Metropolitan Sports Center in Bloomington, Minnesota, were an inordinately high ten dollars (the equivalent of sixty or seventy dollars several decades later), leading Barry Knight, a twenty-one-year-old student at St. Paul's Macalester College, to launch a boycott of the concert. "No one can afford to hear music anymore," Knight told the *Minneapolis Tribune*. In response, five record stores in the city opted out of selling tickets to the show. "Crosby writes about how he almost cut his hair but finally let his 'freak flag fly,'" commented a local writer. "Well, let him cut his prices instead." He added that the situation augured "a feeling of disappointment, as though a trusted friend had betrayed you. . . . Their heads are close to ours. It's our music."

The tactic worked—before the concert was ultimately canceled in May, the venue's promoter reduced the price of some of the cheapest Met Center seats from five dollars to two. But a newfound suspicion toward the group remained.

In late June, the group returned to their Los Angeles home base for two nights at the Forum. As ever, they walked their own particular tightrope. Heading from their dressing rooms to the stage on opening night, Crosby, Stills and Nash decided to warm up then and there, in the hallway. Breaking into the line from "Suite: Judy Blue Eyes" that compared Collins to a sparrow, they hit all the notes, looked at each other and giggled. "Well, that takes care of the sound check," they cracked. A poet and friend, Charles John Quarto, who was strolling around with them, was stunned by how much that small portion sounded precisely like the recorded version of the song.

Before and after the Forum shows, they were afforded a sliver of downtime prior to heading back to the Midwest to play the rescheduled shows. Ever the workaholic, Stills used the days off to complete the solo album he'd started in London, running up costs of over $500,000 due to its across-the-pond sessions. A few of the songs, including "Love the One You're With" and a majestic plea for brotherhood, "We Are Not Helpless," cried out for a choir. (The latter had been triggered by the 1962 novel *Fail-Safe*, about a clash between the United States and the Soviet Union that threatens to go nuclear: "Man has been made into a helpless spectator," warns one character.) Stills invited a slew of his friends—including Crosby, Nash, Cass Elliot and John Sebastian—to join in, along with a relative newcomer to the scene. At twenty-five, Rita Coolidge had a sweet but sultry voice, alluring Native American looks, and plenty of professional experience under her belt, including background vocals for Joe Cocker's *Mad Dogs and Englishmen* tour earlier that year. She and Stills had met when he had been invited to play on the first album she released under her own name. (He played all the guitars on the unplugged "Second Story Window.") In turn, Stills invited her to be part of the choir on his album.

It was at the Stills session where Coolidge first met Nash, who was clearly smitten and immediately asked her to be his date at the band's Forum show the following night. (As Mitchell would later say, it didn't take Nash long to move on to a new partner: "Well, my heart was much more broken than his," she told biographer David Yaffe. "He just jumped right back into dating.") By then, Nash was crashing at Stills' Shady Oak home, so he gave Coolidge the phone number. When she called the next day to finalize the arrangements, she says, Stills answered and told her Nash wasn't at home but that he'd left a message: Nash wouldn't be able to take her to the show, but he, Stills, would be happy to do so. (She didn't know it at the time, but Stills had been so taken with Coolidge the night he met her that he'd written and recorded a song about her, "Cherokee," that very evening; she and Judy Collins also shared the same birthday, May 1.) "I said okay," Coolidge says. "I wasn't in love with anybody. I just wanted to see CSNY." Backstage at the show, Nash, unaware of the machinations, and thinking Coolidge had bailed on him, pointedly ignored her the whole evening.

Before matters grew more tangled on that front, the band was back on the road to play their rescheduled concerts. Minor irritations ensued: The first show, in St. Louis, started an hour late, after the equipment trucks suffered several flat tires on the drive from California to Missouri. The review of the first of their two Chicago shows noted that Stills was "brooding" by the side of the stage and that Crosby seemed distracted. But in a standard example of the make-up-sex aspect of their rapport, both men were excitedly bouncing in sync during the concluding "Carry On" jam.

When they arrived in Minnesota for their final performance, on July 9, the sour aftertaste of the initial boycott of that show lingered. A writer for *Hundred Flowers*, the city's leading underground newspaper, encountered Crosby on the afternoon of the show in Dinkytown, on the edge of the University of Minnesota's Minneapolis campus. After first denying he was who he was, Crosby admitted he was eyeing the female co-eds passing by: "The love of my life for the night may be wandering around these hallowed halls." Students recognized Crosby and began asking him about the high prices of the concert. "My first reaction was fuck 'em," he told them. "My second was 'we won't play,' and my third was 'we'll get sued.'" Crosby's tattooed bodyguard paid for the *Hundred Flowers* writer's dinner and offered him a free ticket.

Although the band sounded more cohesive than they had at the chaotic Denver show, Stills remained dissatisfied with the tour that summer. "We got through it okay," he has said. "We weren't very good, though. We were real sloppy. It was drifting toward Grateful Dead bedlam. I don't care for that. I remember feeling, 'This is almost right but nobody's *finishing* anything.' It never had that craftsmanship quality." Halverson, who recorded shows in Chicago and New York, agrees about the lack of fine-tuning on some of the stage arrangements: "They didn't do a lot of rehearsing or 'let's go play it again because we want to.' It was 'you have enough.'"

After the Minneapolis show, they gathered in a hotel room for a celebratory, end-of-tour dinner, with Young's mother, Rassy, in tow. Joining and photographing them, Diltz caught "various energies between people, feelings good *and* bad." They had just hit the two-year mark as an anti-band, and the time felt right to continue the part of the experiment where each could now go off on his own.

JAMES MAZZEO, A freewheeling artist also known as Sandy Castle, was hanging out at his commune south of San Francisco one fall day in 1970 when Neil Young, of all people, drove up. Young had bought a nearby ranch and, while tooling up State Route 35, had come upon a group of local hippies. "Hi, my name's Neil—I moved into the neighborhood," he told them. The women told him he just had to meet Mazzeo.

Raised in northern California, a former member of the Coast Guard who'd then drifted into the bohemian world, constructing psychedelic light shows, Mazzeo was Young's type of nonconformist. By chance, he'd worked the sound system for a 1967 Buffalo Springfield show at the Ark, a ferry boat that had been converted into a performance space in Sausalito. Mazzeo remembered Young as the enigmatic, black-garbed member of the Springfield who stood in the darkened portion of the stage but still managed to command as much attention as Stills or Furay. Standing in the back of the room at the sound board, Mazzeo heard audience members asking each other, "Who's the guy in back?"

Mazzeo's commune, the Star Hill Academy for Anything, was home to several dozen wayward adults and kids. As Young and Mazzeo became reacquainted, Mazzeo got a sense of what had drawn Young to the northern part of the state, four hundred miles away from Los Angeles. "He told me he really didn't like doing CSNY because it was too big," Mazzeo says. "At those concert places, they weren't getting good sound, and he felt like he was ripping off 30,000 people. With Crazy Horse, Neil felt he could jump into the shadows. With CSNY he felt under the microscope."

Despite Young's concerns about the overwhelming popularity of the band, Crosby, Stills, Nash and Young remained very much an ongoing business and cultural presence as 1970 began winding down. *Woodstock*, an instant box-office draw when it was released in the spring, continued to play in movie houses across the country, eventually becoming the fifth highest-grossing film of the year and cementing the band's connection to the festival and all it represented. A few of their songs were included on the soundtrack of *The Strawberry Statement*, a heavy-handed riots-on-campus drama that was released that summer. "Ohio" had initially struggled to get radio play—stations in Detroit and Chicago declined to air it—but it hit enough of a nerve to reach no. 14 on the charts. As if they were a normal band that operated on a traditional schedule, Atlantic announced that a two-record set recorded in concert would be in stores by the end of 1970. Ertegun insisted to the press that the group had not disbanded, and that they were working on a new album and planning to hit the road again in the spring of 1971.

Yet by the fall, they were more scattered than they'd ever been, aided by the financial windfall of the previous year. Between tour revenue and record sales—*Crosby, Stills & Nash* and *Déjà vu* had sold a combined 3,050,000 copies that year alone—each man had made as much as $7 million after taxes. In the spring of 1967, as a member of Buffalo Springfield, Young had received a six-month royalty statement of exactly zero cents. Thanks to Crosby, Stills and Nash, he could now afford to fork over $340,000 in cash for a 140-acre spread near the Santa Cruz Mountains. At least for the time being, he would be living there without his wife; he and Susan, who struggled to deal with her husband's fame and popularity, broke up as he was moving north, and their divorce was finalized that fall. When Nash visited the Youngs at their Topanga home before the breakup, he noticed a photo he'd taken of Neil pinned to the corkboard in the kitchen with push pins through the eyes. "When I saw that, I went, 'This marriage is over,'" Nash says.

Starting with Young's Broken Arrow Ranch, their respective new homes became mirror images of their divergent personalities. Preparing to make his move up north, Young enlisted roadie Bruce Berry and one of Berry's high school friends, Guillermo (later Felix) Giachetti, to help him. Arriving at the Chateau Marmont in Los Angeles to start the trip, Giachetti met Young for the first time. "He looked like a wreck and a drug addict, but he wasn't," he says. Driving north in two cars, the men arrived in the early morning hours at Young's new home, a low-rent place with a fireplace and not much else. Young and Giachetti began the process of renovating the house by hand, starting with ripping out the carpeting by hand, as well as the ceiling, which looked like old cottage cheese, taking the house down to its studs. "Crazy thing to do when you're a guitar player," recalls Giachetti, who sensed a reclusive side to his new boss.

True to his own image as a free-living hippie bard, Crosby had moved out of the Novato home where he had lived with Hinton and Debbie Donovan and onto his sailboat, the *Mayan*, now docked in a Sausalito harbor. Women, including two look-alike teenagers, came and went on the boat, which contained bunks for half a dozen; Crosby always kept a stash of cash, about $2,000, for drugs or to lend to anyone who might need it. Among those who crashed on the *Mayan* was Jackson Browne, a rising singer-songwriter whom Crosby had championed in the pages of *Rolling Stone.* "I was stoned and happy and getting laid a lot," Crosby recalls. "I didn't have a plan."

As if taking up where the domestic coziness of "Our House" had left off, Nash had bought a four-story Victorian townhouse in San Francisco's Haight Ashbury district. When his relationship with Mitchell soured, he decided to move into the house by himself. Hiring road-crew members like Makota as carpenters, Nash had the home remade from the inside; by the time he was finished, it had velvet curtains, a studio in the basement and, on the fourth floor, a bathtub made of black walnut. The upstairs bathroom featured a stream, complete with live goldfish, between the tub and the sink. "The floor was all water and you had to step on stones so you wouldn't get your feet wet," says producer Ron Albert, who visited. "It wasn't the type of bathroom you'd want to get to in the middle of the night." As disillusionment with so-called revolution was setting in after Kent State and other traumas, Nash had plugged into another reemerging part of the zeitgeist: as historian Bruce J. Schulman put it, "sixties radicals found it easier to build new homes for themselves than to rebuild American political culture."

Nash, Crosby and Young were all "in the same general area, but living so completely apart," says Ron Stone. "Three completely different worlds." The most famous Los Angeles–based pop band of the moment was now far from that city, and Stills' world was even farther removed. After a brief stay at a rented home in the Colorado Rockies—where, to his shock, he received a call saying his friend Jimi Hendrix had been found dead in a hotel room in London, after which he stayed up all night playing piano—Stills returned to his house outside London, which he'd bought from Ringo Starr for a quarter of a million dollars (about $1.6 million in 2018 value). (At the last minute, the business manager of the Beatles, Allen Klein, had tried unsuccessfully to up the price.) Stills continued to be attracted to the British countryside and lifestyle, but he had an additional motivation for retreating across the pond in September 1970: the incestuous California rock world had made a direct hit on him.

Soon after the Crosby, Stills, Nash and Young tour wound down, Stills and Rita Coolidge continued seeing each other, although Coolidge was less than enchanted by Stills' seemingly out-of-control lifestyle, which involved everything from recreational drugs to manic horse racing. From Nash, she finally learned the truth of what had happened the night of the "Love the One You're With" recording—and, at the same time, realized that she and Nash were drawn to each other. Wanting to be upfront with Stills, Nash suggested he and Coolidge tell Stills to his face that they were in love. "Stephen was adorable, but he had all these different things going on," she says. "Being with Graham was as easy as breathing." Driving to the Shady Oak place and finding Stills poolside, they told him what had transpired, and Stills, angered and shocked, spit at Nash. No longer welcome at that house, Nash immediately moved out, taking a room at the Chateau Marmont in West Hollywood.

Nash, dubbed "Mr. Sex of the Hollies" in a story on Crosby, Stills and Nash the year before, had a reputation for easily wooing women, which Stills now understood all too well. "It's a terrible thing when a best friend snakes your lady," Stills told Diltz. Already shaky, the group now ceased to exist over the Coolidge incident. "It didn't help," says Crosby. "Girls fell quite naturally in love or in lust with Graham. He had that lovely British accent and he was a good lover and a gentleman. Stephen had tried everything he knew to get Rita's attention. So he wasn't happy with Graham walking off with the prize without any effort at all, which is probably how he saw it." (Or, as Stills put it later, "She didn't break us up. *He* broke us up.") With a flair for drama, Stills went off the deep end. On August 14, the front desk clerk at a La Jolla motel saw a man "crawling along the floor" in a hallway and called an ambulance. When police arrived, Stills was found babbling incoherently on the bed; two grams of cocaine and some barbiturates were found in the room, along with a twenty-two-year-old woman friend. (According to Coolidge, Stills had also written "I love you Rita" on the bathroom mirror, which she interpreted as his way of getting her attention.) Stills and the woman he was with were both arrested, and Stills spent the night in jail. Eventually he was freed on $2,500 bond, and the following spring, the charges were reduced to a $1,000 fine and a year's probation.

No sooner had Stills finalized and submitted his first album to Atlantic than he was at work on its follow-up, a planned double album that would integrate all his musical passions and then some. He would do so in England, moving there for good (or at least for the foreseeable future), wishing to be as far from Crosby, Nash and Young—and Coolidge—as possible. "When Stephen was in the studio back then, it was guitars, not girls," says Halverson. "With Crosby, sometimes it was with girls. But with Stephen, he got to the studio and said, 'What am I going to sing or play next?'" Staying up for days at a time, welcoming guests—including Bill Wyman of the Rolling Stones—Stills and his loyal engineer, Halverson, recorded acoustic blues, flew the esteemed Memphis Horns to London for his stab at the big-band rock newly being popularized by acts like Chicago, and finally succeeded at reworking Buffalo Springfield's "Bluebird" into an overwrought but passionate breakup song, "Bluebird Revisited." "He was more and more obsessed with doing everything," says Halverson. "There were days when I would get there on a Tuesday and leave on a Thursday and do some more amphetamines. I was starting to lose perspective." When the sessions moved to Criteria studios in Florida a few months later, Nils Lofgren, who had been invited to play keyboards, saw the differences between working with Stills and with Young: for one thing, the Stills jam sessions extended from midnight to dawn. Moreover, "Neil was very focused," he says, whereas "Stephen was just feeling songs out." But with Stills, there was "hellacious jamming" and plenty of rock-life perks: "People came in and cooked and cleaned," Lofgren added. "It was heaven."

One frenetic day in November, Stills drove his Mercedes onto a ferry to go to Paris; there, fellow drag-race aficionado Steve McQueen was filming the racecar movie *Le Mans*, for which Stills was hoping to score the soundtrack. Realizing he'd just missed McQueen, Stills instead partied with Ertegun at his Paris home. (The following summer, he and Ertegun would be among the guests at Mick and Bianca Jagger's wedding in St. Tropez, France.) Soon after visiting Ertegun, Stills drove for five hours to get to an airport and hopped on a KLM flight to Amsterdam, where he literally walked right onto the stage to sit in with the Stones before carousing until dawn with Jagger and Keith Richards. Arriving back in London, Stills then spent thirty-three straight hours recording. Piles of empty wine bottles accumulated in the yard of the Brookfield House. "It was so much fun," Stills has said. "It was wicked dangerous because there were nasty things crawling about. And I managed to walk that razor's edge. Probably not without making an utter fool of myself."

Crosby and Nash saw the hazardous side of Stills' lifestyle for themselves when they flew to England in October. Forgiving Nash at least for the moment, Stills recruited him to sing harmonies on a few of his new recordings. To his shock, Nash witnessed Stills almost overdosing. But little was slowing Stills down at that moment. Visiting a horse farm, he bought a steeplechase horse he called Major Chance, but a little Appaloosa pony also kept following him around. "You've got to buy that little horse too," said Diltz, who accompanied him on the trip. Eventually, Stills did, naming the animal, of all things, Crazy Horse. "It was wild times," Stills has said. "That's when it started to be a four-way street, four horses pulling in different directions. Which is the method they used to use for executions."

By CHRISTMAS 1970, all four were back in the States. Stills had returned to the States temporarily earlier in the month, but that didn't necessarily mean a reunion was imminent. Young had begun experiencing back pain, and a few days before Christmas, he was admitted to a Los Angeles hospital for a slipped disc. Among his visitors were Crosby and Carrie Snodgress, an Illinois-born actress whose deft performance in *Diary of a Mad Housewife*, from the summer of 1970, was about to lead to an Oscar nomination. Giachetti had seen the film and told Young about it, and the two had gone to see it together. "We were like a couple of groupies," Giachetti says. He and roadie Bruce Berry sent her a note about Young, and she and Young (whose marriage was about over by then) soon hooked up.

Up to that point, Young had been riding the headwinds of his association with Crosby, Stills and Nash. In the aftermath of *Déjà vu*, he would be the first of the four to embark on his own series of concerts. In the fall of 1970, he hit the road for a series of solo performances that included a headlining stand at New York's Carnegie Hall. Although its versions

of "Down by the River" and "Cowgirl in the Sand" were by then staples
on FM radio, *Everybody Knows This Is Nowhere* had barely registered
in sales terms when it first came out. Now that Young's name was more
widely known, thanks to *Déjà vu*, the album reentered the pop charts in
the summer of 1970, finally busting into the Top 40. Young's investment in
working with Crosby, Stills and Nash began paying off. "As good as Neil
was—and make no bones, he was good—he's never really been in the
group in his mind," Crosby says. "It wasn't that thing you hoped for, that
feeling of brotherhood, committed to this thing we're building together.
He was a comrade-in-arms. But it was part of his plan. The plan was to
use us as stepping-stones to become an enormous star. And it worked.
It's not like he was sneaky about it. It was pretty easy to see how he
wanted it to go. It's ironic since he was solo and he wanted to come with
us on tour, but it would have been unrealistic for me to look at it any
other way."

After the Gold Rush, the Young album that arrived in the fall of 1970,
included songs he'd either played onstage with the trio or had tried recording with them. Stills had even sung backup on a few tracks, although
some of those parts were either wiped out or lowered in the final mix.
What the album made profusely clear was that Young didn't need any
of them. Although *After the Gold Rush* had been cobbled together from
different months and sessions, the album was so seamless, so airtight,
that only the most careful listener would have known. As self-indulgent
as Crosby, Stills, Nash and Young could be onstage, *After the Gold Rush*
didn't contain even one wasted note. As it made its way from the opening "Tell Me Why" through a crackling version of "Southern Man" and
back to the delicate rumination of songs like "Birds," framed by piano
and harmonies, the record made it clear that Young could have it both
ways—pensive, soul-searching singer-songwriter one minute, scream-
ing-guitar rocker the next. With Jack Nitzsche seemingly striking random
piano notes and chords, "When You Dance, I Can Really Love" captured
the brawny thunder of Crazy Horse and an unabashedly sexual side
of Young's writing. On the other side, "After the Gold Rush" evoked the
dazed-and-confused feel of a generation that had just hesitatingly left one
vital era in American history and was entering a new, less defined, more
unknowable one. Young could have it all. Nor was his sense of humor

missing in action: "Cripple Creek Ferry" was a stoner's sea shanty. But with the help of Bernstein's photography—especially the shot of Young in his Philadelphia dressing room, which took up the entire inside spread of the LP, showcasing his patched jeans and deep-in-thought scowl—the album buttressed Young's image as one of pop's leading lonely guys, a bard of brooding. That fall, it became his first individual album to break into the Top 10.

With his back issues, the work slowed down, but only temporarily. Even while restricted to a hospital bed, Young was busy planning a fifteen-song live album from both his solo and Crazy Horse tours and mapping out plans for his first movie, which he planned to write and begin filming late in 1971. As for Crazy Horse, they were recording without him. ("Neil likes to play in groups, but basically he's a solo artist," Horse singer-guitarist Danny Whitten said at the time. "I don't think he'll ever stay with any group for very long. Deep down, he knows he has to do the gig by himself.") When a visiting reporter started asking about the state of Crosby, Stills, Nash and Young, a nurse conveniently appeared to take Young away for more physical therapy. Early in 1971, Young was released from the hospital in time to start a one-man tour of the States and Canada. After arriving at an airport in Toronto in his lumberjack jacket and work boots, Young was searched by customs agents, who even rifled through his harmonica boxes looking for drugs. But the shows, which included homecoming concerts in Winnipeg and Toronto, featured exquisite versions of new and older material and backstage reunions with family members. When asked in interviews about the "bigger band" he was part of, Young offered little comment about its status or future.

Their managers weren't sure about that situation, either. By those early months of 1971, the offices of the Geffen-Roberts Company, now on Sunset Boulevard, were the bustling, weed-friendly center of West Coast rock—which, at the time, seemed to be most of rock. With Geffen working the phones and Roberts chilling and schmoozing with their acts, new and established clients flitted in and out—Joni Mitchell, Jackson Browne, singer-songwriter Ned Doheny, members of a newly formed and inordinately success-hungry band called the Eagles. Geffen-Roberts continued to cater to their clients. Roberts' newly hired assistant, Leslie

Morris, would attend to coffee and flowers; now and then, she would cup headphones over her ears and listen intently to Mitchell's latest album so she could transcribe every word for an album package.

But few of their acts loomed larger than Crosby, Stills, Nash and Young. A year and over a million copies later, *Déjà vu* had been nominated for a Grammy for Album of the Year (it would wind up losing to Simon and Garfunkel's *Bridge over Troubled Water*). England's *Melody Maker* had crowned CSNY the best rock group of 1970. But Morris only saw the group members occasionally and always separately. "They'd had their big moment and they were not getting along too well and were going their separate ways," she recalls. "Neil certainly could easily do it on his own and wanted to. If it wasn't fun, he wouldn't do it. That's the message I kept getting."

At that moment, the situation was doubly challenging for Bill Halverson, who'd been tasked with compiling the live album of the group's summer tour. Since each man was living in a different city, Halverson, in those pre-Internet and pre-MP3 days, had to fly from one home to another to get each of the four to sign off on the songs and versions to be included. To ensure that Stills' and Young's guitar solos were of equal length, Halverson, with Nash pitching in, worked diligently to edit the longer jams; Nash recalls "Southern Man" as particularly tricky to whittle down. Unhappy with the record, especially the occasionally off-key harmonies, Stills lobbied for overdubbing but was overruled, especially by Crosby. "We made the mistake of recording and I listened to it and said, 'Some of this is horribly out of tune—we should just redo the vocals,'" Stills has said. "And Crosby says, 'No, *maaan*, keep it real!' I found that album really embarrassing." Halverson was under the distinct impression that he was the only person in contact with all four of them.

The harmonic blends heard throughout *4 Way Street* rarely approached the precisely layered harmonies on the studio versions. A vocally ragged version of "Carry On" was an occasionally wince-inducing case in point. But the album, which replicated the half-unplugged, half-electric format of their shows, captured both the living-room-hang ambience and the high-voltage authority of the group at its peak. The original trio and Young rarely blended onstage as naturally as they did on Young's "On the Way Home," complete with Stills' call-and-response harmony and fluid acoustic solo. The exchanges between Stills and Young on "Carry On" and "Southern Man"—the way they would alternate solos like jazz musicians, with Crosby comping chords, before all three guitars and the rhythm section built to frenzied climaxes after roughly a dozen minutes—benefited from Halverson's crisp recording.

4 Way Street preserved the band's no-rules mandate, its collective civil-disobedience voice and its ever-impending sense of implosion. Many of the double LP's highlights were solo or duo configurations that spotlighted the individuals over the collective: Crosby and Nash's exquisite duet of "The Lee Shore," which bobbed and weaved like a boat on the ocean; Crosby's commanding take on "Triad"; Young's solo "Cowgirl in the Sand," shorn of Crazy Horse's electrified backing but spookier than ever; and Stills' merciless, pastor-voiced medley of "49 Bye-Byes" and "America's Children," which immortalized both his all-consuming intensity and his tendency to go way over the top. With Crosby harmonizing, Nash finally unveiled "Right Between the Eyes," his somewhat guilt-ridden rumination on his feelings for John Sebastian's wife.

As its title implied, *4 Way Street* was the sound of men preparing to go their separate ways, as if they'd finished what they'd set out to do together and were ready to get on with the rest of their lives. It would also be the last album of newly recorded material that Crosby, Stills, Nash and Young would release for seventeen years.

PART TWO
MANY-COLORED BEASTS

CHAPTER 4

FEBRUARY 1971–MARCH 1973

The first week of February 1971, all Ben Keith knew was that an out-of-town musician needed a pedal steel guitar player for his record. At thirty-three, the tall, ruggedly handsome Keith had already staked out his turf as one of country music's leading session men, starting with Patsy Cline's "I Fall to Pieces" and extending to Ringo Starr's country album in 1970. He was familiar with Crosby, Stills, Nash and Young—everyone seemed to be—but didn't make the connection when he received the call for some studio work that week. Tim Drummond, one of the musicians at the session, mentioned that he knew a steel player, Keith, who lived only a few blocks away.

When Keith arrived for work, he still didn't realize who the singer-songwriter was who was leading the session. Recording had already begun, so he slipped in, took a seat at a pedal steel rack and played along for at least two songs before he even met Young. Keith added a poignant ascending note to the verse of "Old Man," a plaintive song inspired by the caretaker on Young's ranch; on "Heart of Gold," Keith's alluring steel guitar lines curled and slid around the chunky guitar chords. Young, it turned out, had been invited to appear on Johnny Cash's network variety show; while he was in Nashville for the taping, he recruited local musicians, including Louisiana-born bass player Drummond and now Keith, to nail down the first few songs for what would be his next album. After the session, Keith was finally able to meet and speak with Young, who was friendly, if somewhat aloof, especially about his past. "I'd heard of CSNY, but I didn't know this was him," Keith said. "He didn't mention them at all."

As Ahmet Ertegun had announced, Crosby, Stills, Nash and Young were writing and recording throughout the fall of 1970 and into the following year. What Ertegun hadn't expected was that each man would be working on his own. Hurt feelings, psychodrama and poor communication kept them apart, but each was nonetheless on a creative roll, and the albums— all on Atlantic except Young's—began pouring out. And much in the way their separate residences captured facets of their personalities, so did the music. Starting with Crosby's *If I Could Only Remember My Name* in February 1971, each individual project—in line with the dawn of the "solo album" in pop, another affront to the idea of a united band—would echo and amplify the psyches of the men who created them.

Of the four, few sought more refuge in record making at that point than Crosby. Other than aboard the *Mayan*, he still felt most comfortable in a studio. Now wealthy enough to rent one out for days at a time, whether he was working there or not, Crosby retained San Francisco's Wally Heider compound as his own personal sonic playground. Friends from the Grateful Dead, Santana and Jefferson Airplane lived in the area and popped in, happy to help Crosby cope with Hinton's passing by focusing on music. With the Dead in an adjoining Studio C making *American Beauty*, the cross-pollination was, as Crosby had sung, free and easy. "Whoever showed up every night was on the record," he says. "It was the only place I could safely be. Every night I'd go in there and do whatever came. It was no rules, no-holds-barred. I did whatever made me happy." The casual jams were given a name, the Planet Earth Rock & Roll Orchestra, PERRO for short.

The music that emerged extended the rules-challenged lifestyle he'd fashioned for himself, starting during his later days in the Byrds and continuing through his merger with Nash, Stills and Young. The night before Halloween in 1970 was typical of Crosby's creative process on his first solo album. He began picking notes on his guitar and was soon joined by Jerry Garcia, who played lithe, circular lines around Crosby. As the tape rolled, others—Young, Dead bassist Phil Lesh—wandered in, took a hit off a joint and began joining in. The music rolled along, stammering guitar notes striking off in different directions; like a snowball rolling down a hill and slowly massing, the sound became more potent and focused. Later, during a plane flight, Crosby wrote down musings on the people controlling the country, titled "What Are Their Names?," and realized they fit as lyrics for the music he'd put on tape.

Crosby had a few leftover songs from the band days, including "Laughing," which he finally fleshed out with the magnanimous help of Garcia, his new cohort in song. A ubiquitous presence at Crosby's sessions, Garcia further nudged his friend's exploratory, improvisatory side. The two men, and whoever else was around, would play guitars for hours on end, winding up with interstellar, and proudly out-there, pieces of music. With Garcia's sweetly lush steel guitar riding over Crosby's full-bodied twelve-string chords, "Laughing" transformed into a waterfall-high wall of sound, complete with an overdubbed Joni Mitchell vocal trill that enhanced its splendor. (Garcia also encouraged Crosby's bad-boy side: Dead roadie Steve Parish recalled Crosby "snorting up a long line of cocaine that he had used to spell out Jerry's name on a coffee table.") During one jam, someone placed a stash of pharmaceutical cocaine in Dead drummer Mickey Hart's cylindrical tom-tom. When Hart slammed his stick onto the drum, the flakes sailed up in the air, everyone sniffing them on the way down.

Starting with its title and its story about outlaws betrayed by a "sweet little Indian girl," "Cowboy Movie" could have been interpreted as an homage to his father's days as a cinematographer on westerns. In fact, it was Crosby's first, and most provocative, contribution to the group's habit of writing songs about each other—in this case, the story of the end of Crosby, Stills, Nash and Young, depicted as outlaws who turn on each other thanks to a Native American woman who drives them apart (and leaves them dead or in jail). The woman even introduces herself as "Raven," Stills' nickname for Rita Coolidge—who, when the song was released, was still with Nash. "It was about CSNY," Crosby says. "I took gigantic liberties with it and poetic license. I made Rita be the law but it's more the law of averages, not the law of the police. She was symbolic." (Says Nash of hearing it, "We all knew what it was about—it was obvious. That was just David's comment on what he thought Rita and I had done. He was almost comparing her to Yoko in a strange way, of having broken up the band. But, good song.") From Crosby's slightly hoarse voice to the pained, streaking guitars of Garcia and Young over a moody clopping beat, "Cowboy Movie" was brooding and pungent, with a whiff of dread.

The same couldn't always be said for the rest of *If I Could Only Remember My Name*, which, much like Crosby at the time, was encased in a hazy but rapturous stoner fog. "Song with No Words (Tree with No Leaves)" and "Tamalpais High (At About 3)," the latter rumored to be about the sight of teenage girls being dismissed at the end of the school day, were blissed-out dreamscapes; "I'd Swear There Was Somebody Here," Crosby's ghostly tribute to Hinton, amounted to layers of aching, overdubbed a cappella voices, all Crosby's and all recorded in one pained evening with engineer Stephen Barncard. "Music Is Love," a casual chant, had grown out of a jam with Nash and Young, who fleshed it out with extra instruments and returned it to him, a sort of musical gift. One of the strangest records by a major-label pop star of the time, *If I Could Only Remember My Name* puzzled many: *Rolling Stone* later called it out for "stupefying vagueness." But in the way the music balanced serenity with going into the deep end, the album captured Crosby's increasingly discombobulated life.

A few of the same players, including Garcia and Young, appeared on Nash's *Songs for Beginners.* Reflecting Nash's reputation as the stable, ever-reliable member of the band, the album was sincere and straightforward. ("If you accept Graham Nash on his own terms, which is simply as a nice guy who somehow wound up a musician, then you probably find him to be an agreeable sort," noted future Patti Smith Group guitarist Lenny Kaye in his review of the album in *Rolling Stone.*) A more produced version of "Chicago," complete with a choir chanting "We can change the world," was included, and "Military Madness," which touched on memories of his wartime childhood, pushed Nash into more aggressive territory, musically and lyrically. On that song, guest guitarist Dave Mason played a wah-wah pedal much as Stills would have. For the most part, though, Nash kept the arrangements sparse and uncluttered, extending his desire for a direct bond with anyone listening. His melodies were reliably accessible and uncomplicated. The sensitive-guy counterpart to Crosby's proudly subversive solo project, *Songs for Beginners* embodied the sound of a man who strove to be comforting and likable.

Beneath the sweet and sturdy melodies and female vocal harmonies (some courtesy of Coolidge), *Songs for Beginners* was laced with its share of turmoil over the events of the previous year. "I Used to Be a King" and the especially exquisite "Simple Man" sprang from his breakup with Mitchell (he had written and debuted the latter at the Fillmore East, Mitchell watching in the audience), and "There's Only One" offered a swipe at the heated pools of his superstar friends. "Wounded Bird" was his chin-up advice to Stills after the breakup with Collins, counseling him to swallow his pride and make amends with himself. (Revealingly, the album featured cameos by Crosby and Young—who asked to be billed as "Joe Yankee"—but not Stills.) "Man in the Mirror" proclaimed "two and two make four," triggered by the definition of freedom in George Orwell's *1984*—but could also be interpreted as alluding to the quartet. Even the cover photo was symbolic: Nash's self-portrait was taken through the window of Crosby and Hinton's home in Novato the day before Hinton was killed.

Like the man who made them, Stills' two albums, released within six months of each other, were musically catholic, relentless and sometimes guilty of overreaching. Featuring tracks cut during his early days in London, with Stills playing many of the instruments himself, *Stephen Stills*, which arrived late in 1970, opened with a souped-up, choir-laden version of "Love the One You're With," which became the first solo hit single for any of the four. The album didn't engage with Stills' roots in Latin music, but it managed to touch upon just about everything else in his repertoire. Those who wanted the sensitive singer-songwriter of "4 + 20" were rewarded with "Do for the Others" and "Black Queen," the ferocious white blues that showed his mastery of acoustic guitar and a hyena wail. Those blues roots also came to the fore in "Go Back Home," with that bee-sting Eric Clapton solo that almost threatened to take the song away from Stills. The unrequited feelings of "Suite: Judy Blue Eyes" returned in his song about Coolidge, "Cherokee." That song's incorporation of an electric sitar reinforced Stills as the leading musician of the four, the one most eager to shift to different rhythms and instrumentation. He was the one who was most up on the trends of the time: Stills tapped into the gospel-rock fever of the moment, which could also be heard in Joe Cocker's music, on "Church (Part of Someone)," which combined a choir and his razor-throated voice. The crowning moment of that style, and the album in general, came with the closing "We Are Not Helpless," where that choir, Ringo Starr's drumming and Stills' voice merged into one of the era's lost gospel-pop classics.

Stills set his musical ambitions far higher with *Stephen Stills 2*, out in the early summer of 1971. (The release was so rushed, to coincide with his upcoming solo tour, that some of the song lyrics were misprinted, forcing Atlantic to include a corrected sheet in later pressings.) Stills' initial hope to make the project a two-record set was nixed by Ertegun, but the songs assembled for *Stephen Stills 2* still captured the liberating creative rush he was experiencing when recording in London and Miami, even if some of its experimentation didn't pan out. "Change Partners," written three years earlier and once intended for Crosby, Stills and Nash, was reborn as a country waltz, with Jerry Garcia's honeyed pedal steel guitar making yet another appearance. Now, the song felt like Stills' commentary on the mothership group. Keenly aware of what his fans expected from him— lyrics about the environment and politics, and namely, the clash of left and right—Stills tapped into both with the horn-driven "Ecology Song" (which sported the album's clunkiest lyrics) and the strident "Relaxing Town," which name-dropped Jerry Rubin and Chicago's notoriously hardheaded mayor, Richard Daley, one of many symbolic enemies of the counterculture. "Word Game" worked itself up into a self-righteous barrage of anti-bigotry imagery. With everyone seemingly asking "What's your sign?" as part of the astrology boom (even the 1971 Ice Capades incorporated astrological signs into its presentation), Stills joined in with "Fishes and Scorpions," a dense jangle of guitars and astrological-sign lyrics that featured a spacy Clapton solo.

Never one to fully leave behind his folk roots, Stills paused periodically on *Stephen Stills 2* to bask in that unplugged style—the taut "Know You Got to Run" was centered around his banjo, and "Singin' Call," one of the songs he had written with his broken hand in Hawaii the year before, found him advising himself to slow down, at least for a bit. But it wasn't advice he always heeded, and more than he probably intended, *Stephen Stills 2* captured the sound of a man in a hurry, galloping from one style to the next, both enthralled and overwhelmed by his opportunities. In an odd and somewhat incomprehensible statement, the press release that accompanied the album alluded to Young, but not by name: "Stephen felt they needed someone in the group proficient enough not as a composer or singer but rather as a lead guitarist for him to hit from." Whatever those words meant, they didn't bode well for future collaborations.

To THE COLLECTIVE lament of the counterculture, 1971 was proving to be a debilitating capper to the last few traumatic years. The victories were growing smaller and the routs larger. The underground press, newspapers that operated outside the mainstream, would peak in the hundreds, if not thousands, around 1971, then start a sharp decline as the decade dragged on. (The phrase "underground press" was already being replaced by "alternative press.") Communes, which were striving to create a more open-minded model for society and land ownership, were also running into problems: "At present several thousand such groups are estimated to be in operation," reported *U.S. News & World Report* that summer, "though many break up after a few months in quarrels over sexual partners or household chores."

In an indication of how rapidly the music and times were shifting, "Suite: Judy Blue Eyes" was now considered an "oldie" on a radio station in Illinois. At the opposite end of the pop spectrum, the leading rock bands in the new decade, such as Grand Funk Railroad and Led Zeppelin, were louder, woollier and more visceral than those that came before—music almost born with arenas in mind. Succeeding Crosby, Stills, Nash and Young in the newly ascendant soft-rock terrain were the likes of James Taylor, Carole King and Cat Stevens, who amply reflected their generation's shifting priorities—less political, more inward thinking. In San Francisco that year, a former publishing salesman, Werner Erhard, launched EST (Erhard Seminars Training), a personal-best training program: as Erhard would write, "I am suggesting that the best way to learn about EST is to look into yourself, because whatever EST is about is in yourself." Soon enough, Tom Wolfe would label the era "The Me Decade."

Whether they wanted it or not, Crosby, Stills, Nash and Young were lashed to the bow of the times, and their disintegration, occurring just months after *Déjà vu*'s release, became, to their audience, another demoralizing sign of an idealized society gone wrong. At one of their summer 1970 shows, a fan had approached Nash and told him, "Please don't split up—we need you." When the breakup came, many took it as a personal betrayal. The attempted boycott of the band's Minneapolis show was one signal of the collective letdown, but other signs emerged by the summer of 1971. *Changes*, a New York–based rock magazine, blasted Crosby for owning "300 houses in Laurel Canyon," with "his fleet of

Mercedes and his yacht." Most of those accusations weren't true—the *Mayan* wasn't that high end, and Crosby wasn't a Southern California land baron—but the perception of Crosby, Stills, Nash and Young as pampered, bickering rock stars out of touch with their antiestablishment brethren was rapidly sinking in. *Rolling Stone* published a substantial interview with Stills, accompanied by photos of him horseback riding on his British estate. Although he never dressed in tie-dye and was less radical in his political views than Crosby, the article made Stills look, in his later estimation, like an elitist out of step with the non-mainstream world. "My definition is that blowing it up isn't going to work, I mean no way," he had told writer Ritchie Yorke, discussing his political views, in a prior interview in 1970. "I would like to take some of these people to Latin America and show them a real revolution. . . . The only way to do it is due process. We must patiently and carefully go about the process of voting these leaders out of office, man." The idea was reasoned and realistic—and completely out of step with calls for an overthrow of the American government.

As 1970 begat 1971, the Crosby, Stills, Nash and Young image was also beginning to take a hit. Rumors of onstage and offstage friction and contract riders—like a specially cleaned carpet they demanded at their concerts—began circulating. On their 1971 *Fillmore East—June 1971* album, one of the members of Frank Zappa's Mothers of Invention made a joke about "unreleased recordings of Crosby, Stills, Nash and Young fighting in the dressing-room of the Fillmore East!" While promoting the *Woodstock* movie, director Michael Wadleigh took aim at one of the band's signature strengths during an interview in the *Detroit Free Press*. "The first part of the song they did, 'Suite: Judy Blue Eyes,' was so bad," he said. "They were out of tune and mixed up." Wadleigh added that watching them "pull that song together" and emerge triumphant was noteworthy, but the damning quote still circulated. Cocaine was at times making them play faster and sing sharper. At the Fillmore East shows, drummer Johny Barbata saw the occasional front-row fan screwing up his or her face and shouting out, "You guys are too wired—you don't sound like the records!"

Perhaps taking their cue from *Rolling Stone*'s dismissive write-up of *Déjà vu*, newspaper critics covering dates on the 1970 tour had also begun voicing skepticism. A review of their show at Detroit's Masonic Temple made note of the way the group repeatedly slapped palms, and how Crosby raved about Barbata and Samuel the same way he had about the now-departed Reeves and Taylor. "So just how true are the onstage love scenes?" the reviewer questioned. "Maybe it's just good show biz." Writing up their Philadelphia show, *Philadelphia Daily News* writer Jonathan Takiff dubbed them a "super shuck" instead of "superstars," pointing to the way the group groused onstage about the enormity of the venue while still taking the money for the job. Takiff called the band "one case in many of the corruption of an art form. . . . [R]ock today seems less and less the idealistic form of expression and more a coldhearted, greedy business proposition." In his *Los Angeles Times* review of their first Forum show, onetime supporter Robert Hilburn wondered how dated their political songs would sound in a few years.

With the group in disarray, those grumbles only seemed to intensify with the rollout of *4 Way Street*. Almost six months after Atlantic had hoped to deliver it to record stores, the double LP arrived with appropriate fanfare in early April 1971; in its first week out, it was certified gold for $1 million in sales. (In the days of pre-electronic tabulation, such figures were generally suspect, but the appetite for the album was surely strong.) Like *Déjà vu*, it would eventually be perched at no. 1 on the *Billboard* album chart. But the press was far from welcoming. One of the band's local papers, the *Valley News* of Van Nuys, wrote off the album as a betrayal: "It demonstrates a great deal of thoughtlessness on the part of CSNY for their audience. They know the album will sell regardless of what it sounds like. . . . [It] contrasts sharply with the group's socially conscious stance." Hilburn, who had effusively praised *Déjà vu* as "easily the best new rock album of the year," switched gears in his write-up of *4 Way Street*, calling it "little short of a disaster" for the way its "worthwhile material has been handled better elsewhere." In the most stinging comment, he added, "CSNY—collectively and individually—seem to be making a lot of the wrong moves."

The capper was the belated release, a month after *4 Way Street*, of *Celebration at Big Sur*, the movie of the 1969 all-star California concert at which they'd appeared. With its scenes of Stills physically confronting the stoned heckler, the trio onstage in their fur coats, and Crosby reclining in a sauna with naked women, the movie, which collected far less at the box office than *Woodstock*, only reinforced the group's image as coddled rock stars.

Starting in the fall of 1970 with Young's *After the Gold Rush*, the solo albums rolled out one by one into the following year—Crosby's in February, Nash's in May and Stills' second in June. Each was certified gold, for half a million copies sold, the principal barometer of success in the industry at the time. But the comparatively muted reactions to the Crosby, Stills and Nash side projects lay bare that what they'd created as a group may not be repeated. It had become so mythological, so quickly, that they would have a difficult time topping it. In his *Rolling Stone* review of *Songs for Beginners*, Kaye acerbically referred to Crosby, Stills, Nash and Young as "the Alexandrian Quartet axis," as if they were pompous rock gods. *Billboard* dubbed "Music Is Love," Crosby's single from *If I Could Only Remember My Name*, an "infectious rock ballad loaded with Hot 100 potential," but the record didn't wander anywhere near Top 40 radio. Stills' instrumental dexterity—the way he would be credited playing multiple instruments on one song, as if he didn't need anyone else—was interpreted as egomania. "Stills has always come on as the ultimate rich hippie—arrogant, self-pitying, sexist, shallow," lashed out Robert Christgau in his *Village Voice* review of *Stephen Stills 2*. "Keep it up, SS—it'll be a pleasure to watch you fail." For all their declarations of sticking with their stated goal of being a freeform band that would record in whatever combinations they desired, fewer fans were listening. Rewriting the rules of the pop business was proving to be more arduous than they'd imagined.

Stills was the first to challenge—and bump up against—the assumptions of their fan base when, early in 1971, he announced a tour of his own accompanied by a "big band." When the shows got underway that summer, the audiences who took their seats in arenas around the country, expecting the lovelorn troubadour of "Suite: Judy Blue Eyes" and "Helplessly Hoping," were confronted with something very different. As Stills warned a crowd in Baltimore, he didn't want to repeat himself. What fans experienced that night and in other cities was an ambitious three-part show that marked the most adventurous undertaking of any of Stills' estranged bandmates. Anchored by the former group rhythm section of

Dallas Taylor and Fuzzy Samuel, the shows opened with a rock-and-roll set, followed by a folksier middle, and then a finale featuring a brassy six-piece horn section. The latter was more like the music encountered at concerts by big-band rockers like Chicago or Blood, Sweat & Tears than traditional Crosby, Stills, Nash or Young fare. Stills' planned opening act would be the Young-free Crazy Horse, who had just released *Crazy Horse*, an utterly charming and warmly melodic album spotlighting Danny Whitten's songs and voice and the lead guitar of Nils Lofgren. But Whitten had a worsening drug problem, and when Jack Nitzsche left the band, Crazy Horse bailed out of the Stills tour.

Given Stills' role in four straight best-selling albums and his status as one of rock's leading men of the moment—a sort of rugged, cigarette-puffing ranch-hand of pop—his tour should have been a victory lap. The fees he was receiving—$100,000 for a show at the Forum in Los Angeles—also attested to his stature. Yet as confident in his abilities as he was, he remained riddled with insecurities: as he told a Chicago audience, the show would be "a marathon where you watch the singer bleed while he tries to sing 18 songs in a row." The set lists ranged from his Buffalo Springfield contributions to songs from his two solo records. But for crowds expecting to hear his best-known Crosby, Stills, Nash and Young songs—and not a horn section playing, in one case, a Stax cover—the shows were often puzzling. Stills saw himself as a bluesman, musician and guitarist, not a wayward member of four troubadours; at some performances, he even adopted an unfamiliar Texas accent, referring to the audience as "y'all." (Adhering to his socially conscious voice, though, he donated half the proceeds of his Baltimore date to two drug treatment centers in Washington, the Blackman's Development Center and the Free Clinic.)

To calm his nerves, Stills took to drinking before the shows, resulting in erratic performances; one night, it took him a full five minutes to find his onstage stool during the acoustic set. "He was a nervous host," says Bruce Hensal, a former Bill Graham employee who became a member of Stills' crew for that tour. "It was a big show, a big band to lead, and he wasn't really the showman out there in front of it." (As Stills admitted to the *Los Angeles Times* in 1979, "In '71 and '72, I found that the various pressures on me from the business were too much to deal with, and I turned into a drunk for a while.") After a show in Oklahoma, he tore a knee ligament, forcing the cancellation of the rest of the tour.

But Stills, in search of lofty commercial and artistic goals, was already thinking ahead. By chance, members of the Flying Burrito Brothers, including frontman and former Byrd Chris Hillman, caught his show in Cleveland, and afterward, Stills summoned them to his hotel room and discussed an even more ambitious undertaking, and wanted to know if they wanted to be a part of it. At the moment, he showed scant interest in returning to the band whose success had allowed him to headline arena concerts on his own.

LATE IN THE DAY of June 10, 1971, Crosby and Nash pulled up to the Lido Boatyard in Newport Beach, where the *Mayan* was docked in preparation for an expedition. When the two noticed a few black sedans lingering nearby, Crosby joked about being busted by the feds, but he turned out to be right: before he knew it, a gun had been placed to his head and he was under arrest.

Hours before, a squad car driving by had noticed a parked van on the dock, its keys still in the ignition. The *Mayan* had just set sail, with some of Crosby's friends aboard. When the cop signaled to the boat's passengers, thinking the vehicle owner might be aboard, he smelled what seemed like a familiar, illegal odor. One of Crosby's friends on the boat would later say it was the smell of overcooked brown rice. Still, everyone on board panicked. Rattled by the sight of cops, they flushed a pound of pot and a smaller amount of hash down the toilet and turned on the bilge pump. Comically, the drugs bubbled up to the water's surface. "The only trouble with that move is that boats don't have sewer pipes," deadpanned a narcotics detective. Five of Crosby's friends onboard were arrested on charges of drug possession, and Crosby, upon his arrival, was also arrested, on the charge of selling marijuana. The charges were eventually dropped because the police didn't have a search warrant at the time of the arrests, but the incident, which culminated with Crosby clashing with a photographer at the court hearing, cemented his outlaw-rebel image.

Throughout 1971 and into the following year, Crosby and Nash would share more than busts and sailing expeditions. The first of the quartet to have bonded, during the Byrds and Hollies days, they again gravitated toward each other as friends and collaborators in the wake of their group's perhaps temporary implosion. Where others thought Crosby was abrasive and egomaniacal, Nash found him lovable and fascinating, as if Nash were living vicariously through his pushing-the-envelope friend. The two were still the closest in age (as of mid-1971, both were in the vicinity of thirty); they were also the ones most open to keeping the spirit of the band alive. Embarking on a series of concerts as an acoustic duo, they sat on adjoining stools, gazed fondly at each other and offered mini re-creations of Crosby, Stills, Nash and Young shows. Exhuming "Wooden Ships," "Teach Your Children" and "Déjà vu," and talking to and joking with the crowds between songs, the two casually rekindled the harmonies, hippie-campfire ambience and onstage indulgences of the 1969 and 1970 concerts. They made in-jokes (Crosby would refer to feeling under the weather as the "Lebanese flu," although everyone sensed what he *really* meant), and their self-deprecating cracks maintained the conceit that they were interchangeable from their fans. After they started a song in the wrong key at the Dorothy Chandler Pavilion in the fall of 1971, Nash said, "Superstars, right? No way."

For both men, the artistic hookup also offered a reprieve from the fraught quartet. "Graham and I found out we would work easily with each other," says Crosby. "Stephen wanted a career like Neil's. He's always been very competitive with Neil. But Nash and I were like Paul [Simon] and Artie [Garfunkel]—we sang scarily well together. And we liked each other. I always wanted to have a really good buddy-friend." (By then, Crosby's older brother, Ethan, who'd grown dissatisfied with urban sprawl and society at large, had begun his retreat into life in the wilderness. He would commit suicide about twenty-five years later.) Nash even designated a room in his San Francisco house the "Crosby Suite," complete with a collection of his friend's favorite snuff boxes. In every way, they sought sanctuary with each other.

As for Nash's relationship with Stills, it remained complicated by their falling-out over Rita Coolidge. Stills had even slipped a quick, coy reference to "Rita" into "Sugar Babe" on *Stephen Stills 2*, about a year after their breakup. But Crosby knew the freeze-out wouldn't last. "We have fights, but it's usually over a chick who goes from one member to the other," he'd told the *Detroit Free Press* the previous December. "When the chicks split, everything's cool." Their friend Bobby Hammer tended to agree. "They had girlfriends who went from guy to guy, and that caused tension," he says. "They would say, 'Stephen said Graham stole her' or 'David stole her from me,' but the truth was that the girls would go, 'I'm done with you, so I'm going to flirt with the other guy.'"

A year later, Crosby's prediction was proven right. Nash and Coolidge amicably parted, and Nash had a fleeting dalliance with Barbra Streisand, who was filming her comedy *What's Up, Doc?* in San Francisco. The two went on several dinner dates, leading to an item about them in the gossip column of one of the local newspapers, but according to Nash, they didn't sleep together. (Nash did, however, write a tune, "Another Sleep Song," in her Los Angeles home.) In fact, there was a general thaw in relations among all the band members, and they began making guest spots at each other's concerts. Nash joined Stills onstage at the latter's 1971 Madison Square Garden show, where the crowd erupted at the sight of even a partial regrouping. (Coolidge, who attended the show with Nash, stayed offstage.) Then, during Crosby and Nash concerts in the fall of 1971—one in Boston and two at Carnegie Hall in New York—Stills and Young appeared for unannounced cameos, with the crowds going suitably bananas at the sight. The afternoon of the second Carnegie Hall show, they reconvened offstage and in private: Crosby, Stills and Nash turned up at a New York studio to overdub harmony vocals to three songs—"Words," "Alabama" and "Are You Ready for the Country"—for Young's next album. "Alabama" was a scorching diatribe Young had written about the state and its backward image. Practically metallic in its feel, the song almost seemed written with their harmonies and sensibility in mind, and onstage at Carnegie, they had sung it together.

The quartet's grandest but most relaxed reunion of the year was around the corner. In the summer of 1971, as he was nearing completion of a new album called *Harvest*, Young was forced to finally have surgery for his back issues. At a hospital in Redwood City, near his ranch, he had several discs removed. When word of the operation leaked out, he was surely irritated to find his actress girlfriend Carrie Snodgress mentioned as well; the two had been a tabloid item since his trip to Nashville, where one gossip column noted, "Where Neil goes, Carrie goes," and now it was reported that she was "at his side constantly" during recuperation.

Young invited Nash to the ranch to hear *Harvest*, and the two went out into the middle of a lake on the property. Nash expected Young to haul along a cassette player, but Young had other ideas. On one side of the lake was his house, and on the other side, his barn-cum-recording studio, with massive speakers installed at both. The left channel of music boomed out of the house, and the right channel from the studio. When Young felt the balance wasn't right, he yelled out, "More barn!" ("It's just a little thing that happened one day and it keeps growing and getting crazier," Young later said of that moment. "Yeah, I think it was a little house heavy.")

In the purest manifestation that they were, at heart, a musical if dysfunctional family, Young then invited all three of his distanced comrades to his ranch for Thanksgiving dinner in 1971. Crosby, Nash, Joni Mitchell and their friend and photographer Joel Bernstein piled into a car and drove from San Francisco. On the way, Crosby announced he was in possession of something no one else had—not just the best pot, as usual, but an early tape of Jackson Browne's debut album (alternately known as *Jackson Browne* or *Saturate Before Using*), for which Crosby had contributed sterling vocal harmonies. As the music played, Mitchell asked who Browne was, and, in unison, Nash and Bernstein retorted, "Only your next boyfriend!" ("She was just a friend at that time and that's why we could say that," Nash explains of the ribbing.) In fact, their prediction turned out to be true: Browne and Mitchell would start an affair about two years later.

At the ranch, where Stills had also arrived, Snodgress cooked up a meal and everyone gathered around an oval wooden table. When dinner was over, each of them, Mitchell included, sang new songs for the others. Stills debuted a ballad, "Love Story," which shared a title with one of the biggest movies of the period, and Mitchell presented them with one of the songs she would soon include on *For the Roses*. No managers or music business types were in the house, and the air was one of mutual respect, not animosity. The experiment they had initiated three years before was working.

JUST BEFORE THAT communal meal, Stills had moved on to another, entirely different venture. In the middle of one of Criteria's studios in Miami, he had gathered together a small group of musicians and was recording,

of all genres, bluegrass and honky-tonk songs. With members of the Burritos—mandolinist Hillman, pedal steel guitarist Al Perkins, singer-guitarist Rick Roberts and fiddler Byron Berline—contributing, out came songs
that returned to Stills' early folk days as well as Hillman's pre-Byrds
years as a bluegrass player. The songs they practiced or recorded included Bill Monroe's "Uncle Pen," Leon McAuliffe's "Panhandle Rag" and
the '50s country hit "Dim Lights, Thick Smoke (and Loud, Loud Music)."

Although Ertegun had nixed Stills' plan to make *Stephen Stills 2*
a two-record set, Stills was determined to release a collection of that
length. Many of his peers—the Rolling Stones, Eric Clapton, George Harrison—had unveiled two- or three-LP sets: why shouldn't he? A double LP
would be the ultimate manifestation of his creative drive, and the Miami
bluegrass hoedown would be the first step in combining all his influences—rock, blues, Latin music, country and folk—into an epic undertaking, a grand statement that would finally set him on his own path. Starting
with his touring band, Stills began assembling musicians who could aid
in that quest: drummer Taylor, who had resumed working with Stills
after being fired from the quartet; bassist Samuel; twenty-three-year-old
Miami-based percussionist Joe Lala, a former member of the Blues Image
("Ride Captain Ride") who could bolster Stills' desire to delve further into
Latin rhythms; and keyboardist Paul Harris, who had briefly worked with
Crosby, Stills and Nash during their Sag Harbor woodshedding period
and had the chops to play nearly anything. Signaling that he was ready
to move on to a new and perhaps more permanent group, Stills soon
made an offer to Hillman, Perkins and Berline to join his new band as
well. Frustrated with the Burritos, who were straggling on without their
former and increasingly dissipated cofounder Gram Parsons, Hillman
contemplated the move. Determined to woo Hillman, whom he respected,
Stills sent Michael Garcia, his longtime friend and now employee, to Los
Angeles, where Garcia barged right into a Hillman recording session with
a rare, collectible mandolin as a gift from Stills. Hillman finally agreed.
Through his usual force of will, Stills had his lineup.

The country and bluegrass get-together was promising, but it was
only the beginning. Stills returned to the round-the-clock marathons he
preferred, recording with engineers Ron and Howard Albert. The Florida-
born brothers had already been through the rock-and-roll mill, working

on Eric Clapton's Derek and the Dominos project *Layla and Other Assorted Love Songs* and the Allman Brothers Band's *Idlewild South.* But Stills was an altogether different challenge. They kept up with the relentless pace by alternating shifts—one would work a full day, go home to sleep, and be replaced by the other sibling. Stills would simply never leave. "It was 24/7—or more like 72/7," says Howard Albert. "A short day would be fourteen hours. He had a lot of music in him and he wanted to get it out."

The rock-and-roll high life followed Stills and the band to Miami, where they rented a home in Coconut Grove and partook of crazed speedboat rides. Stills was writing songs at a furious pace. Both the new ones and the old ones left over from his previous two albums tried to grapple with the toll that success was taking on him. "Rock & Roll Crazies" was a warning to himself (and perhaps to Crosby, Nash and Young as well) about losing one's way amid sycophants and overindulgence. Dedicated to three guitarists who had recently died (Hendrix; Duane Allman, killed in a motorcycle crash that year; and Al Wilson of Canned Heat, who had died of a drug overdose in 1970), "Blues Man," a brooding solo march underscored by darkly brittle guitar, was a warning shot of its own. (As Stills told *Guitar Player*, he didn't use a pick but instead a combination of his index finger and thumb, and he achieved that needle-like guitar tone with his fingernail. His version of a flat pick, he said, was "a big callous.") In "Don't Look at My Shadow," he praised Colorado for saving him from the Los Angeles scene. The pensive "Johnny's Garden" paid homage to the groundskeeper at his English home and the peace the property brought Stills. (That gardener, whom Peter Sellers had hired when he lived there, would also be the inspiration behind the character of Chance, the simpleton-groundskeeper hero of Jerzy Kosiński's 1971 novel *Being There.* Later, it became a movie starring Sellers.)

In those songs, Stills also licked his wounds from the past year or three. He finally found a place for "So Begins the Task," his first farewell to Judy Collins, adding Perkins' steel guitar to a track cut in London. Each of the four sides of the two-LP set was given a title, with the rock-and-roll part dubbed "The Raven," his nickname for Coolidge. He also wallowed in the remnants of his broken heart in "Hide It So Deep," in a sublime duet with Hillman called "Both of Us (Bound to Lose)" that lurched from ballad to Latin rave-up, and in "Right Now," about a woman newly distanced from him thanks to a friend and his "games." (Although Stills has never admitted it, Nash is said to be the target of the song.) "Witching Hour," an outtake from this period, addressed how he felt he'd been taken advantage of by Crosby, Nash and Young—"like, 'I'm being used here, and I'm not sure why,'" he told writer Bill DeYoung. "And when it came time to get down to it, I'm the go-to guy." On tape boxes, he dubbed the singer-songwriter LP side "CSN," as if it were a genre, like "country" or "blues." That portion's standout track, "It Doesn't Matter," had started as a collaboration between Hillman and the Burritos' Rick Roberts, with Stills rewriting their original lyrics. In the seamless way it integrated Lala's timbales, Perkins' country steel guitar and the milky Hillman-Stills vocal synchronicity, it transformed into one of Stills' most affecting resigned love songs.

Luckily, Stills had musicians who could follow him in whatever direction he chose. The band was amazingly versatile, capable of playing any genre Stills dictated, and over the course of about two months, they rose to the occasion. With Stills as the benevolent but hard-driving dictator, they set those songs to blues shuffles, electrified Latin, hardwood-floor honky-tonks, ballads that landed Stills in balladeer territory, and bluegrass hoedowns. "What to Do" featured completely different instrumentation in each verse. Even for musicians accustomed to late hours, the work was challenging. Perkins encountered that new regimen for himself when they spent all night trying to get the right take on the crunchy "Rock & Roll Crazies," the frisky Latin rumble "Cuban Bluegrass" and the hardened blues "Jet Set (Sigh)." By four in the morning, they were still at it. "I was half asleep playing those takes," Perkins says. "But he wanted me to feel it, and it all seemed to work."

With Stills' new band, no one doubted who was in charge. "A band is a democracy up to a point; then somebody has to be in charge," Stills told the *Atlanta Constitution* as the album was about to be unveiled. "Everybody in this band understands that." (He added, "When Neil joined us on *Déjà vu*, it broke down. Everybody was doing his thing and we weren't together. . . . More than our sound changed. The music was good but the situation wasn't.") Yet for the first time since the Springfield, Stills was giving himself over to the band concept. He encouraged Perkins to play solos (slide guitar on a pedal steel, for a different, harsher sound) and Harris to take a piano or organ part. Stills' and Hillman's voices blended together naturally, with Hillman's earnest harmonies countering Stills' gruffer delivery. Stretching out to eight minutes, "The Treasure (Take One)," about an unnamed Rocky Mountain woman whom he followed eastward (a possible allusion to Collins), broke into a dramatic Stills wah-wah solo before shifting to a shuffle with alternating Stills and Perkins workouts. Stills also turned "Anyway" into a duet with Lala.

Yet for all his declarations in song that he was now a level-headed Coloradan, Stills' world only seemed to grow increasingly daft. Hanging with Stills during this period, Mickey Hart witnessed what he called his friend's love of "the edge—he liked to cut with a keen blade." Indeed, Stills had taken to unnervingly flashing a Bowie knife. In 1972, Hart, who had temporarily left the Grateful Dead after his father embezzled from the band, was making a record of his own, *Rolling Thunder*, in the Bay Area. He'd thought the album was done until Stills, a comrade-in-arms when it came to spending copious time in studios, came by and asked to hear the master tape. While appreciating the tracks, he immediately found things he didn't like about them. The two barricaded themselves in the studio for several straight days—"We had food and drugs brought in the back door by my girlfriend," Hart says—while Stills redid instrumental and vocal parts as Hart watched, helplessly. Finally, Hart had had enough and said, "Stephen, come on, man—let's just call it."

Without warning, Stills grabbed a Bowie knife from somewhere, held it to Hart's throat and pointed to the speaker: "Don't you *ever* tell me to stop! This music is *incredible*! This music is *great*!" Hart looked at him, shrugged and said, "Okay, man, all right—go ahead." Later, he would laugh it off. "Stephen was so extreme in everything," he says. "He was the only one who could really go to that place. He was relentless."*

---

*One outcome of Stills' habit of carrying a Bowie knife was a falling-out with the Rolling Stones camp. For a brief period, Stills and the Stones were bonded: Bill Wyman played bass on at least one track on *Manassas*, and Stills attended Mick Jagger's first wedding. But when Stills visited the hotel where the Rolling Stones were staying during their Denver tour stop in 1972, he and Keith Richards had a tense encounter, and, according to Wyman, each pulled a knife on the other. Manassas crew member Bruce Hensal also says Richards had tried to hire him away from Manassas, to Stills' displeasure. Relationships between

While Stills was recording his two-LP release, Young visited Miami and stopped by Stills' rented home with a tape of *Harvest.* The rapport between the two was cordial, if not overly touchy-feely. As the music played, Perkins, who was also present, felt a sense of their old competitiveness. Young's new band, the Stray Gators, featured pedal-steel player Ben Keith. (Counting Crazy Horse, his solo performances and Crosby, Stills, Nash and Young, the Stray Gators constituted Young's fourth musical platform in just over a year.) Afterward, Perkins wondered if he now had a job in Stills' band because he, too, played pedal steel. "I don't know if Stephen realized that Neil had started that group [the Stray Gators] or if he considered doing one himself because that's what Neil was doing," says Perkins. "In my opinion that's one of the reasons why Stephen wanted a group." If Young's new band had a steel player, Stills wanted one, too.

IT WASN'T THE QUARTET, but for Ahmet Ertegun in early January 1972, it would have to suffice. Visiting Wally Heider's studio in Los Angeles, where only three years earlier Crosby, Stills and Nash had conjured up their first album, Ertegun now found himself sitting between only Crosby and Nash. As the backing tape of a new Nash song, "Southbound Train," played, Crosby sang into one of Ertegun's ears and Nash into the other.

For the past year or more, Ertegun and his crew at Atlantic had been doing their best to jump-start a reunion of the full foursome. "Of course," says Crosby. "They made more money, back when people bought records. They wanted us back together." In July 1971, a label executive announced that the group would embark on a "farewell tour" in early 1972, decades before major rock acts routinely announced such undertakings. When the label heard that Halverson had taped the Crosby and Nash performances in New York and Boston, which included the surprise Stills and Young appearances, executives proposed releasing the tapes as *Crosby, Nash and Friends.* Neither the tour nor the album came to fruition. Stills, in particular, nixed the album idea, and justifiably so: since *4 Way Street* had arrived in stores just months before, the thought of

---

Stills and the Stones would never be the same. Stills and Richards did exchange a friendly handshake decades later at a Rock & Roll Hall of Fame ceremony.

releasing another concert record of similar material made little sense. Stills later told *Hit Parader* that Crosby and Nash took it as a "personal affront" when he clamped down on the idea; Nash has no recollection of Stills' objections.

Ertegun would have to settle for another offshoot project instead. In a natural extension of their snug duo performances and unforced relationship, Crosby and Nash had decided to make an album together. Starting in the summer of 1971, they recruited a core group of supple, supportive players—guitarist Danny Kortchmar, keyboardist Craig Doerge, bass player Leland Sklar and drummer Russ Kunkel, soon collectively known as the Section—who were fast becoming the leading session crew in Los Angeles. Some or all of them had played on Mitchell's *Blue*, James Taylor's *Sweet Baby James* and *Mud Slide Slim and the Blue Horizon*, and Carole King's era-defining *Tapestry* and subsequent *Music.* Those records were signature albums of the time, but Crosby and Nash (and Stills and Young) still dwarfed everyone else. Kortchmar—a street-savvy, cynical and very confident guitarist—couldn't believe his good fortune in landing the Crosby and Nash job. "I was thrilled beyond belief," he says. "I couldn't believe they called me for that."

Stretching out over several casual months, the making of the album called *Graham Nash/David Crosby* was a largely stress-free affair, especially compared to the patchwork aspect of *Déjà vu.* "David was in good spirits, and they were like, 'We can do this as a duo,'" says Halverson, whom they hired to engineer the album. The backup musicians watched as Nash would excitedly cheerlead a Crosby song they'd just recorded, then as Crosby did the same for a Nash song—leaving it to the band to diplomatically suggest trying one more take to improve it.

For the album, Nash had prepared a spiteful rocker, "Immigration Man," about the time he was detained at the Canadian border and was miffed by his treatment; "Girl to Be on My Mind," about a lonely night he'd spent on New Year's Eve 1971 at his house in San Francisco; and "Southbound Train," which, with its harmonica solo and generalized references to equality and freedom, had an earthy, folk-protest-song quality. An undercurrent of funereal French horns made "Strangers Room," a meditation on an affair, one of Nash's most evocative songs. Never the most prolific writer—and increasingly focused on sailing and women at that point in his life—Crosby excavated two tunes from his 1968 tape, "Games" and "The Wall Song." Thanks to the participation of Dead members Garcia, Phil Lesh and Bill Kreutzmann, "The Wall Song" churned like a restless sleep (Crosby would say that the lyrics, about someone stumbling "half blindly" through life could've described himself, but were "poetic license"). Crosby's other songs reflected a musician caught between grief and hedonism. As still as a wave-free body of water, "Where Will I Be?" embodied the way Hinton's death had left him numb, while "Page 43," which benefited from twinkling accompaniment from the Section, found him searching for reasons to carry on.

As much as their twosome concerts, *Graham Nash/David Crosby* felt like two men complementing each other. Nash's more melodic pop tendencies balanced out Crosby's less conventional, more angular approach to writing. Crosby's "Whole Cloth" had a sharp, accusatory edge in its lyrics and delivery, with the members of the Section pushing and jabbing the music into looser, limber new territory. Tracks like that offset the cloying moments, such as Nash's "Blacknotes," an improvised piano ditty recorded live onstage at Carnegie Hall the night Stills guested and Nash found himself alone at the keyboard, waiting for his bandmates to emerge. Overall, like the album Stills had completed in Miami, the album portended life after the mothership.

Although Nash had no idea that Stills was writing a song, "Right Now," about him, he was already preparing an answer. "Frozen Smiles," also recorded for the *Graham Nash/David Crosby* album, was his admonishment to an unnamed friend who he felt was traveling down the wrong road, using a reference to "dealers" to evoke both a card game and drugs. The title image came from the facial expression people would make while on cocaine. (It also conjured the Frozen Noses moniker that Stills and Crosby had once used.) At the time, Nash was coy about the target of the song, although the following year Geffen would say it was "a certain indication as to why they're not together any longer." As Nash recalls, "There was a lot of cocaine going on in those early days, and when people are doing it, everyone's smiling, those frozen smiles. I just wanted to help Stephen. I don't like talking. But in song, you can craft it and fire the arrow off." To perhaps soften the blow, the song was set to a jaunty melody.

Graham Nash/David Crosby, released in the spring of 1972, was dedicated to "Miss Mitchell," who visited them in the studio, when Ertegun was also there. At Nash's urging, Mitchell previewed "Free Man in Paris," a song she'd just written about David Geffen. In fact, Geffen was about to be free of Crosby, Stills, Nash and Young. Although Stills and Geffen had been partners in musical schemes during the band's formative days, even briefly rooming together in New York, they were now butting heads over the direction of Stills' career. Always the chemically straightest of the Geffen-Roberts gang, Geffen disapproved of Stills' lifestyle and his financially taxing solo tour of 1971. Moreover, Stills wasn't particularly open to Geffen's suggestions and wanted to control his own publishing. "When I see Stephen doing things that I think are wrong . . . I tell him so and he doesn't listen," Geffen told writer Roy Carr. "I certainly am not going to be a part of somebody ruining their career or doing those things that I think are tragically wrong things." After Geffen publicly criticized him in interviews, Stills printed up bumper stickers that read "Who is David Geffen and why is he saying those terrible things about me?," a play on the title of Dustin Hoffman's current film, *Who Is Harry Kellerman and Why Is He Saying Those Terrible Things About Me?* Depending on who tells the story, either Geffen fired Stills or vice versa.

In any case, it was Crosby who would be Geffen's last, most exasperating straw. When he and Nash were playing their two Carnegie Hall shows in the fall of 1971, Crosby called Geffen and demanded that his co-manager, who was about to fly from Los Angeles to New York to see the performance, bring along Crosby's preferred Mexican Oaxaca pot. Initially resistant, Geffen acquiesced, and a friend of Crosby's met Geffen at Los Angeles International Airport and handed him a manila envelope, which Geffen tucked into his suitcase. All went according to illicit plan until an airport security employee popped open the suitcase and saw seeds spilling out of the envelope. Geffen denied any knowledge of the package but was still arrested and spent the night in jail—right before the Jewish holiday of Yom Kippur, at that. Freed on bail by his brother, Geffen continued his journey to Manhattan and met up with Crosby at the Warwick Hotel, where Crosby (who confirms the story) demanded to know the whereabouts of his weed. He was incensed that Geffen had lost it. "Geffen was furious," says Nash. "Crosby's a hard man to face down, and so was Geffen. They got over it, but Geffen didn't want to be a personal manager after that. With good reason. We were a handful."

Geffen was nonetheless a presence during the making of the Crosby and Nash album. With Ertegun in town (and being trailed by a *New Yorker* writer), he dropped by the studio to haggle with the label head over how much Atlantic would reimburse the duo for their studio costs, ultimately agreeing on $5,000 for every $100,000 worth of units sold. Geffen also demanded a $50,000 fee for himself, to be paid in advance; he and Ertegun eventually compromised at $35,000. ("I need the money to run my company," Ertegun complained. Geffen shot back, "Ahmet, I'm your friend, and I love you, but don't squeeze the juice out of every situation.")

It would be one of Geffen's last business dealings with them. The previous year, 1971, he and Roberts had launched a new label, Asylum, home to Jackson Browne, the Eagles and other acts they felt they could nurture. Before long, however, and to Crosby, Nash and Young's surprise, Geffen sold Asylum to Atlantic and moved into a label job, giving up his stake in their management. Roberts would continue to manage Young—whom he clearly seemed to prefer—as well as Nash and Crosby, for the time being. But the consolidation of the music business was only beginning.

FEW GOT A closer view of the different band members' lives at this time than Guillermo Giachetti. After helping Young move into the Broken Arrow Ranch, he accompanied him on his early 1971 solo tour. It was such a low-key affair that Young tuned his own guitars, since Giachetti, who had been hired as a guitar tech, was inordinately green in the art of roadie work. At an auditorium in Edmonton, Canada, Giachetti witnessed how Young bonded even further with his fans when, after the show, many discovered that the plunging temperatures had literally frozen their cars. After they wandered back into the theater to await tow trucks, Young reemerged to play another set, even though his compact crew had begun tearing down the equipment. "It was magical," says Giachetti. "He was cool enough to just do that."

Once the tour ended, Giachetti was offered a similar crew job with Stills and jumped at the offer. The Northern California cold was getting to him, and, besides, he says, "I was twenty and just wanted sex, drugs and

rock and roll. With Stephen it would be bling, racecars and sailboats."
First, Giachetti flew from Young's ranch to New York, where Stills was
having an operation on his knee to ward off arthritis. From there, Stills
and his band and crew headed for Surrey, so Stills could recuperate and
rehearse the band for its upcoming first tour.

By now, the ensemble had a name, Manassas, inspired by a train
station sign in that town in Virginia. Since it was also the name of a Civil
War battle, in which the Confederate Army scored one of its major early
victories, it appealed to Stills' ongoing fascination with that period in
American history. (Once, during a break while horseback riding in Marin
County with Mickey Hart, he grabbed a bunch of pebbles and used them
to replicate the maneuvers of the armies at the Battle of Gettysburg.)
As Giachetti and others learned, that interest extended in other, more
mysterious ways. Later, back in Los Angeles, Giachetti picked up a journalist to interview Stills and later drove the writer back home. On the
way out, the writer asked Giachetti why Stills was talking about a certain
southern general and reincarnation. "I'm like, 'I don't know, man,'" says
Giachetti. "I wanted to keep my job. Creative people are off their rockers."

The military motif continued at Stills' Brookfield House estate. After
his break with Geffen, he'd recruited Dan Campbell, a Louisiana lawyer
and pal, to be a manager of sorts, but soon he settled on Michael John
Bowen, a short-haired, no-nonsense military veteran. When Bowen began working for Stills in Miami, he was stunned by his new client's work
habits: "God, what is wrong with this guy?" he said to a mutual friend
after visiting the studio and forcibly dragging Stills out with a rope after
he'd been working for several days straight.

With Stills and Bowen in charge, Manassas was soon modeled after
a battlefield operation. Each band member was given a Halliburton case
with his name and number stenciled on it, as well as a buck knife. (Stills
wasn't alone in his love of such weaponry. When a *New Yorker* reporter
visited the *Graham Nash/David Crosby* recording sessions, he noticed
that Crosby had a "small woodsman's knife" tucked into his belt.) At
Brookfield House, some of Manassas' musicians and crew slept in bunk
beds—"like army barracks," recalls Perkins—and Stills referred to Hillman
as his "first lieutenant." Bowen organized the band's touring schedule as
if it were a military campaign, with detailed itineraries that were ahead of

their time. ("Not that anyone read the printouts," says one crew member. "People would use them as cocaine bindles.")

At Stills' British estate, Manassas alternated between partying and rehearsing their new material, sometimes the former far more than the latter. Stills' double album was now named *Manassas*, and one of his goals in concert was to play the first side of the album, the rock-and-roll portion, in its entirety straight through. The musicians were accomplished enough to pull it off. Among the guests who stopped by to jam was Eric Clapton, who was then deep into his heroin addiction. "They picked him up and brought him to the house to get him out of his funk," says former crew member Bruce Hensal. (Unfortunately, none of those rehearsals were recorded.)

Once Manassas packed up and took its show on the road, the band was all business in the best way. The same versatility that was on display on the *Manassas* album—released in April 1972, a week before *Graham Nash/David Crosby*—was seen in their live sets. The shows were as ambitious as Stills' multipart 1971 shows, yet far more organic. At their debut, in Amsterdam, they opened with a sparkly cover of Buffalo Springfield's "Rock & Roll Woman" and ended, about three hours later, with a set of electric songs from *Manassas*—literally traversing Stills' career. In between were folk songs ("He Was a Friend of Mine"), country ("Fallen Eagle"), blues ("Go Back Home," from Stills' first album) and an unplugged version of "Love the One You're With," but only one song associated with his Crosby, Stills, Nash and Young days, "4 + 20." Hillman was a steady, low-key presence onstage, bolstering his boss but never threatening to overtake him. Although drug use in the band was prevalent—one reason why straight-laced fiddler Byron Berline opted out of joining them—everything felt marvelously on track, at least musically. As Perkins (who was Christian and didn't indulge in the same excesses as the rest of Manassas) recalls, "I had that feeling, 'Gosh, this could be a long-lasting group.'" Stills told someone he was only calling the ensemble "Stephen Stills and Manassas" for the time being; eventually, it would simply be "Manassas."

Manassas amounted to a prodigious display of peak-era Stills songwriting and singing, and favorable comparisons to Buffalo Springfield abounded. The reviews, even in the oft-critical *Rolling Stone*, were upbeat, and the album broke into the *Billboard* Top 10. The shadow of the old group still hung over them, however. "Crosby, Stills, Nash and Young ought to get back together for an album or two," wrote the *San Bernardino County Sun* in April 1972, in a review of *Manassas.* "Then maybe they would stop recording all this unspectacular material, like Crosby and Nash did recently and Stills has here." But at that moment, fans and the press craved that reunion more than the four principals did. In an interview with *Hit Parader*, Stills said that "chances are absolutely 100 percent" that he, Crosby, Nash and Young would reunite at some point. But the possibility remained vague.

THROUGHOUT 1972, THEIR old nemesis, Richard Nixon, was running for reelection, and signs of a growing rot in the country were emerging. That fall, two former Nixon aides, G. Gordon Liddy and E. Howard Hunt Jr., were among seven officials indicted on charges related to a break-in of the Democratic National Committee headquarters at the Watergate office complex in Washington, DC. Meanwhile, inflation was inching upward: the price of food was almost 4 percent higher than the year before.

Despite the Watergate scandal, Nixon retained a strong lead in the polls over his opponent, a thoughtful US senator from South Dakota named George McGovern. One survey showed that 62 percent of the voters preferred Nixon, and only 23 percent favored his Democratic opponent. Yet even the skeptical journalist Hunter S. Thompson referred to McGovern as "probably the most honest big-time politician in America." McGovern introduced a series of proposals that could have been lifted from a Crosby, Stills, Nash or Young song: they included bringing American troops home from Vietnam within three months of his inauguration and slashing $30 billion from the military budget. His appeal to liberal-minded creative types couldn't have been more apparent than in the planning of two benefit concerts on opposite sides of the country. In Los Angeles, Carole King, James Taylor and Barbra Streisand headlined the first. The East Coast show, at Madison Square Garden, symbolically reunited long-estranged show-business partners, including Simon and Garfunkel, Mike Nichols and Elaine May, and Peter, Paul and Mary.

A reformation of Crosby, Stills, Nash and Young would have been a natural addition to either McGovern benefit, but that was not about to happen. Instead, voter registration tables were set up in the lobby of a Manassas show in San Bernardino, California, and in May, Young released a pro-McGovern single, "War Song." With its lumpy tempo and clumsy lyrics, "War Song" was well intentioned but slight, noteworthy primarily for the musician co-billed on it—Nash, who sang harmony throughout. Unlike "Ohio," "War Song" didn't crack the Top 40 (it was banned by more stations than "Ohio" had been). In fact, it seemed to disappear as soon as it was released. The trifling nature of the song almost seemed like a metaphor for McGovern's increasingly damp campaign, which culminated in his election-night slaughter by Nixon in November.

Despite reuniting with Nash for "War Song," Young had clearly soared past all three of his erstwhile bandmates. After numerous production delays—Young wanted the cover to have the same sort of grainy feel as *Crosby, Stills & Nash*—*Harvest* had finally been released in February 1972. In terms of locales, it was far more scattered than any Crosby, Nash or Stills record; songs had been recorded in Nashville, London (with the London Symphony Orchestra, as Nash sat in the studio watching), and at Young's barn studio at his ranch. The jumble of tracks—from the desert-dry balladeering of "Out on the Weekend," to the portentous, orchestrated "There's a World" and "A Man Needs a Maid," to the scraggly, but crunching, rock-and-roll piece "Alabama"—should have made for an incoherent album. But again, it felt of a piece, held together by Young's singular audio personality.

Unlike his partners, Young also realized the power of mystique and used it to his advantage. Stills hurled himself into promoting *Manassas* with a grueling series of European and American shows, accompanied by numerous interviews. After playing a nearly sold-out concert at Honolulu's International Center Arena, he and the band held a press conference—at midnight. As teenage female fans scarfed down potato chips from bowls, and the Manassas members gulped Scotch directly from bottles, Stills answered the usual questions about his upbringing, musical influences and places of residence. Young, by contrast, didn't give a single interview to promote *Harvest*; other than a few guest appearances, including one at a festival and another at a Manassas show, he didn't play a full concert of his own all year. Even his photos inside of *Harvest* barely showed his face.

But in what would become a recurring refrain, the *Van Nuys News* announced that "it has become thoroughly evident by now that the one with all the talent in that conglomeration is Neil Young." *Harvest* struck a chord that none of his peers had managed. Sung by any other artist, the simplistic lyrics of "Heart of Gold" would have been laughable, but the firm, sulking chords and the arrangement, culminating in guest artist Linda Ronstadt's harmony rising up during the finale, made it undeniable. "The Needle and the Damage Done," about Danny Whitten's growing drug problems, was a warning shot about addiction, and in a year in which the South went for Nixon, "Alabama" would prove timely. A month after its release, both *Harvest* and "Heart of Gold" held down the no. 1 slots on their respective charts. As much as Crosby, Stills and Nash tried to tap into the zeitgeist with politically minded songs on their own albums, Young seemed to do it effortlessly; *Harvest* was steeped in loneliness, soul searching, anger and neediness, and Young's front-and-center voice, which exhibited a new frailness, perhaps stemming from his medical issues, was never more direct and penetrating.

Rather than take to the road, Young spent most of 1972 fine-tuning his directorial debut, *Journey Through the Past*. It wasn't unusual by then to see rock stars in films, but *Journey Through the Past* was the strangest and least coherent product of that budding genre. A grab bag of original scenes, found footage, and concert clips of Buffalo Springfield and Crosby, Stills, Nash and Young, the movie had nothing approaching a plot and came across like a student film project. Characters from throughout Young's recent life made appearances: he and Snodgress drove around aimlessly; Stills walked through a public park, spouting odd commentary at dawn after the quartet's 1970 show in Philadelphia; Young was seen rehearsing at his barn studio with the Stray Gators. Put in charge of props, James Mazzeo, now an entrenched member of Young's posse, had Young install a blacksmith shop at the ranch to construct lights and lamps for the film. Young told Mazzeo that the film, especially its scenes of an unnamed professor wandering around, had come to him in his sleep. "Neil would tell me his dream and I'd go create a set and get the actors to reenact what his dream was about," Mazzeo says. "Neil has a photographic memory when it comes to dreams. He remembers a lot of details. That whole movie was coming from one dream one night to the next two nights later." (Asked how Crosby, Stills and Nash, who each appeared in the film, fit into that framework, Mazzeo laughs: "I think those were the nightmares!")

The soundtrack to *Journey Through the Past*, released at the end of 1972, before the movie hit theaters, frustrated management: Gary Burden's gatefold-sleeve design virtually ensured that each of the two LPs would roll out onto the floor when the packaging was opened. It also confused many of the fans who had gobbled up *Harvest*, who were now confronted with two LPs of Young and Springfield songs along with the Beach Boys and Handel's *Messiah*. Due to legal entanglements with Snodgress—who had a contract with Universal Pictures, while Young's movie was released by Warner Brothers—the film was delayed for several months, until the spring of 1973. Even then, it was barely reviewed and virtually disappeared.

No matter: by then, Young was on to a new project, a belated tour in the early months of 1973 to promote *Harvest*. The plan was so ambitious that when the shows were first announced, John Hartmann of the Geffen-Roberts Company hinted that concerts in China and the Soviet Union were also possible. They weren't, ultimately, and all for the better: starting with Whitten's fatal overdose before the start of the tour—right after Young had been left with no choice but to fire him from the band for being too spaced out to play—Young was miserable. Audiences were screaming for "Heart of Gold" when he wanted to move forward and play a batch of songs no one, other than his band, had yet heard. As stragglers at the Baltimore show took their seats in the front rows, the stage lights shone right on them, and Young became distracted—to the point where he walked off the stage and stayed there for half an hour. In Tucson, during "Old Man," one fan strode right up to the front of the stage and began taking photos with a bright flash in Young's face. When drummer Barbata arrived to replace original percussionist Kenny Buttrey, who had provided a steady, but not heavy, beat on *Harvest*, he realized what he'd stepped into. "I didn't know Danny had died," Barbata says. "Neil goes into this big bummer and starts drinking shots of tequila and slurring his words. It just got weird."

There were occasional bright spots: During his January 1973 show at Madison Square Garden, after Young performed a somber new song called "Soldier," someone from his crew appeared onstage and handed Young a note. After reading it, he told the audience, to cheers, "The war is over." To the collective relief of the world, the United States, North and South Vietnam, and the Viet Cong had all formally signed an agreement to end the chaos.

The new songs he was playing were defiantly scrappy, the opposite of the typical Crosby, Stills, Nash and Young mode: "Don't Be Denied," a virtual autobiography set to a beautifully bedraggled melody, and "Time Fades Away," a manic shuffle, in which he and Ben Keith, who had emerged as his musical sidekick, traded guitar and slide parts and off-kilter singing.

But Young was drinking and stressing so much that, about halfway through the tour, he placed a save-our-ship call to Nash. "He said, 'I need friends and I'm lonely out here—what do you think?'" Nash recalls of the conversation, in which Young asked if he and Crosby would join him on the tour to sing backup on a few songs. Nash arrived only to find Young downing plentiful amounts of a drink that blended tequila, orange juice and lemon sweetener. "I don't know why success would freak him out," Nash says. "It wouldn't freak *me* out. But we helped him stabilize the situation. We were there for him and he knew it. He wasn't quite so alone." Years later, Crosby would still smile at the thought that Young, for once, needed *them*.

Crosby and Nash joined him onstage for "Southern Man" and "Alabama" and yakked with the crowd more than Young ever did. Not surprisingly, Young didn't spend much time with them offstage; he remained an enigmatic presence. But their coming-together moments would prove to be a forerunner of a far more ambitious plan—in even bigger venues, facing even larger crowds. Five fractious years after first becoming a band, they were about to remind the world, and themselves, how weighty a presence they had been in the culture.

CHAPTER 5

APRIL 1973-DECEMBER 1974

Starting with the day he was thrust into the group after Dallas Taylor's firing in 1970, Johny Barbata thought he'd seen it all when it came to Crosby, Stills, Nash and Young. That same year, Stills had recruited Barbata for his first solo album, and after a typically long night in the studio, Barbata arrived back home in the early-morning hours, exhausted, only to take a call from Stills asking him to turn around and come back—he had a few more musical ideas to get on tape. To what seemed like Stills' displeasure, Barbata passed on the request to return to work that same morning. "That's just the way he is," Nash consoled the drummer. "You did the right thing."

Now, in 1973, came another call from the Stills camp, again concerning Taylor, who by then had begun his deep, quickly debilitating dive into hard drugs, including experimentation with heroin. A roadie had introduced the drummer to the drug, and before long Taylor was shooting up alongside Keith Richards during work on an album by Bill Wyman of the Stones. Eager to help his bandmate—Taylor and Hillman were his wingmen in Manassas—Stills had paid for Taylor's rehab, but Taylor had relapsed. Without any explanation, Barbata found himself on a Lear jet heading for a Manassas show in Saratoga Springs, New York, in the summer of 1973. There, Stills told Barbata to set up his own drum kit by the side of the stage and be prepared to fill in for Taylor if he couldn't make it through the show. That scenario came to pass when, midway through, Stills ordered Taylor off the stage; Barbata then did his best to play on a song he'd never heard before.

Manassas' troubles were a microcosm of the problems Crosby, Stills, Nash and Young struggled with on their separate paths in the year that followed. If 1972 had demonstrated how each of them could survive and prosper outside the mothership band, 1973 would be a rude awakening about how much their fans were willing to endure while awaiting another group album or tour. Young's problem-plagued shows, culminating with his outreach to Crosby and Nash, made for an early barometer. Another was the sudden re-formation of the original Byrds.

In the years since Crosby had been fired from the band, the Byrds had gone through a string of personnel and musical changes, veering from barroom country to Americana rock; their prominent instrument became the twangy, lyrical lead guitar of Clarence White, who joined in 1968. The Byrds now sounded almost nothing like the ensemble that had once featured Crosby, although later songs, such as "Chestnut Mare," "Just a Season" and "Ballad of Easy Rider" (which *did* make that movie), demonstrated that Roger McGuinn, the sole surviving member by the end of the '60s, could successfully remake the band. By 1972, the Byrds had declined, with their albums limping along both creatively and commercially. Crosby and co-manager Elliot Roberts visited McGuinn at his home in Malibu and, according to McGuinn, Crosby said, "Some of this stuff you guys are doing with Clarence is pretty good, but some of it isn't." McGuinn agreed with him. With Geffen now in charge of Asylum, a plan was hatched to reconvene the original Byrds; in the post–Crosby, Stills, Nash and Young era, they could be marketed as something akin to a supergroup. Although Hillman was still a member of Manassas, the others were largely available and unrestricted by record contracts. Since the Byrds were still technically contracted to Columbia, Geffen only had to convince Clive Davis to let them go—which Davis did in exchange for a McGuinn solo album that Crosby would oversee.

In a sign of his industry clout, thanks to his success with Nash, Stills and Young, Crosby would serve as the producer of the Byrds reunion album. McGuinn, the nominal leader, would take a back seat to his former rival. "David was the boss, the big guy," says McGuinn. "I wasn't used to that. He did what he wanted. He was the bigger star and he was pretty much in charge. He had a lot of confidence." Thanks to Crosby's potent weed, the making of the album was, McGuinn says, "a great party." Unable or unwilling to return to their soaring "Eight Miles High" period, the Byrds instead opted for a folksier coffee-house approach. Gene Clark, in particular, shone on songs like "Full Circle" and "Changing Heart," which poignantly hinted at the personal and career problems he'd had since leaving the Byrds. McGuinn and lyricist Jacques Levy's "Sweet Mary" and a Crosby-fronted version of Joni Mitchell's "For Free" made the most of the group's harmonies, which felt almost gothic.

But because of the rushed nature of the project (Hillman still had commitments to Manassas), and the fact that some of the members withheld their strongest material for albums of their own, the final product was spotty. A remake of Crosby's "Laughing," from *If I Could Only Remember My Name*, was flabby and unnecessary. When the album, *Byrds*, was unveiled in March 1973, the group put on a stoic public face. "I had a wonderful time doing it, working with all of them," Crosby told *Rolling Stone*. "Stress that."

But expectations were inordinately high, and the reviews were middling to brutal. In *Rolling Stone*, Jon Landau called it "the most disappointing and one of the dullest albums of the year." (And it was only March.) Since he was credited as producer—even pictured front and center on the cover photo—Crosby absorbed the brunt of the criticism. Elaborate plans for a combined reunion tour of Crosby, Stills, Nash and Young along with the Byrds and the Hollies—a monumental organizational task to begin with—crumbled with the album's disappointing sales. In coincidental but biting timing, *National Lampoon Lemmings*—a play derived from the beyond-irreverent humor magazine *National Lampoon*—began performances off-Broadway. The show parodied a fictitious rock festival, openly mocking Crosby's political songs in "Lemmings Lament." *Lemmings* was up and running when the *Byrds* album arrived in stores.

For all its early promise and across-the-musical-universe shows, Manassas was simultaneously starting to spin out of control. Onstage and on record, the band effortlessly leapt from one genre to another; offstage, they adhered to their pure rock-and-roll lifestyle. Taylor was far from the only one dabbling. "People liked their snow and drink," says guitarist Al Perkins. On a 747 flight to Australia, the group smuggled aboard hash mixed in with cigarettes and openly smoked and drank.

When the band reconvened in Florida in late 1972 to make its second album, its members were more scattered and less inspired than the year before. Adhering to his vision of Manassas as a band as much as a vehicle for himself, Stills planned to make the record more of a group effort, with other members taking a greater role in writing and singing. The eclecticism of their debut resumed in the sparkly bluegrass of the hitchhiker's lament "Do You Remember the Americans," the low-rider funk paranoia of "Rollin' My Stone," and the tough-guy boogie rock of Hillman's "Lies." Without Stills, the rest of the band concocted "Mama Told You So," which sounded more like the then popular R&B band War than anything out of the Crosby, Stills, Nash and Young universe.

But overall, the material was weaker than on *Manassas*, and Stills seemed distracted. "We said, 'This isn't happening—it's not good,'" says Howard Albert, who engineered the album along with his brother Ron. "Stephen went, 'Okay, fuck those guys,' and finished it up with other people. He was at times drinking a lot. It wasn't good." Disciplined and not one to suffer fools or self-indulgence lightly, Hillman confronted Stills about the up-all-night recording schedule. Adds crew member Guillermo Giachetti, who was experiencing his first Manassas studio work, "Helping Stephen in the studio was the hardest thing I've ever done in my life. It was tough to keep up with him. He'd be in the studio for three days in a row and I'd go to sleep and go back the next day and he'd still be there." Part of Giachetti's job became convincing Stills to eat.

Having sold the Brookfield estate in England for a profit, Stills was now calling Colorado his home—he had bought a house in Rollinsville, outside of Boulder—and Manassas reassembled there for additional work. With his neighbor and new friend Joe Walsh playing greasy-spoon slide guitar, Stills wrote and sang "Down the Road," a startlingly candid white-blues catalog of his misadventures that rattled off cocaine and bourbon. Twice the album was submitted to Ahmet Ertegun; twice, Ertegun rejected it for containing too many tracks that didn't feature the star of the band. (In the shuffle, a few worthy songs—"Witching Hour" and "Thoroughfare Gap," the latter one of Stills' most thoughtful musings, set to banjo and mandolin accompaniment—fell by the wayside.) Relocating again, this time to California, Manassas kept recording, now with longtime Stills collaborator Bill Halverson on hand. "We were trying to get something the label would put out," Halverson recalls. "We recorded and recorded and got in other players to make Ahmet happy. But the stream was running dry. It wasn't CSN. They weren't bringing that kind of talent to the table."

Called *Down the Road*, the album meandered out in the spring of 1973, a month after *Byrds*, and suffered a similar critical and commercial fate. Like *Byrds*, *Down the Road* wasn't the complete debacle it would later be labeled. The mix was punchier than on *Manassas*; Stills' two Spanish love songs, "Pensamiento" and "Guaguancó De Veró" (the former a type of tango, the latter a version of a rumba), were fetching; and the anti–Vietnam War "Isn't It About Time" returned Stills to his politically aware roots. But the often sloppier *Down the Road* didn't do much to bolster Stills' reputation, which had already begun to take body blows. Two nights after his concert at Madison Square Garden in 1971, the venue was scheduled to host the all-star "Concert for Bangladesh," featuring co-organizers George Harrison and Ravi Shankar along with Ringo Starr, Eric Clapton, Leon Russell and other upper-crust rock luminaries. Given how quickly the concert had to be set up, Stills offered Harrison his sound system—and then heard he hadn't been invited to play. ("But then," Stills has said, "I'd gone to visit Ringo and was really hammered, so he probably warned them off.") Reviewing *Manassas*, and in particular songs like "Colorado," the *New York Times* called his music "the self-pitying cry of a wounded male chauvinist. . . . Obviously, it never occurs to Stills, whose field of vision too frequently encompasses only his own tortured adolescent soul, that women these days are becoming independent human beings." A *Rolling Stone* profile in 1973 started in the worst way imaginable, at least as far as publicity was concerned: "It's difficult to name a rock & roll star who's been put down, chopped up, dismissed and generally hated as much as Stephen Stills."

While Crosby, Stills, Nash and Young weren't paying attention, younger bands influenced by them—Eagles, America—were sprouting up and delivering more seamless versions of the kind of music the quartet had pioneered. America's first hit, "A Horse with No Name," was an unintentional but uncanny imitation of Young, who didn't know what to make of it when he heard it. America was also managed by Geffen-Roberts, who appreciated their attitude right away. "CSNY was pretty much a constant fight—'I think we should do this,' 'Well, I *don't!*'" recalls Leslie Morris. "America did pretty much what you wanted them to do. They were good clients."

Unbeknownst to any of them, a manager and trained violinist in New York, Hilly (short for Hillel) Kristal, was preparing to open a new club in downtown Manhattan in the fall of 1973. Like Crosby, Stills, Nash and Young, he loved folk music—he was even planning to call the club CBGB & OMFUG, an abbreviation for "country, bluegrass, blues and other music for uplifting gourmandizers." But that musical menu would soon change to a more bare-boned and influential form of rock and roll, and in their thickening fog, few in the Crosby, Stills, Nash and Young world would see it coming.

"CROSBY, STILLS AND NASH is a *myth*," Stills practically spat out at a reporter in 1973. If so, it was a myth that refused to die. In late 1972, music journalist Ritchie Yorke, who had solid access to the band, reported that Crosby, Stills and Nash had met with Elliot Roberts to discuss a new album and tour, possibly with Young's involvement. Another published report early in 1973 claimed the trio were already at work on a record to be released in April. But all of it was wishful thinking; Crosby and Nash were on the road with Young during that time.

Still, the start of an actual reconvening did occur in April in Hawaii. Crosby and Young had remained particularly close of the four, with Crosby counseling Young on his increasingly difficult relationship with Snodgress. During this period, Young referred to Crosby as "my guiding light." In return, during Young's tour, Young let Crosby use his tour plane to fly to Santa Barbara and visit his mother, who was dying of cancer (she would pass away that year, at the age of sixty-seven). It was a magnanimous gesture that Crosby would never forget.

After a lengthy sailing trip from the mainland to Hawaii once Young's tour ended, Crosby had arrived in the hippie-centric, former plantation town of Lahaina in western Maui, docking the *Mayan* off the Mala Wharf. Young arrived soon after and began spending time with Crosby. Even there, people in their business would put themselves out for the band. Tom Moffatt, a local DJ and promoter who was among the first to play rock and roll on Hawaiian radio, was asked to help bring contracts to Young and Crosby on the boat. Moffatt retrieved the packet at the airport, flew from Oahu to Maui, took a taxi to Lahaina and then was forced to hire a fishing vessel to take him the two miles out to sea to Crosby's boat—where Crosby and Young scrawled their signatures on the paperwork and sent Moffatt back on his way to land.

Later the following month, during a break in Manassas' unremitting tour schedule, a newly bearded Stills, along with Nash, also arrived in Maui. They took up residence in a house Young had rented, along with those who'd accompanied them on the trip. The musical-family aspect of their dynamic played out in multiple ways. Young was joined by Snodgress, and Crosby brought Debbie Donovan, his most regular female companion of the time. Stills arrived with his new wife, a vivacious French singer, songwriter and keyboardist named Véronique Sanson. The daughter of French Resistance fighters, Sanson, twenty-four, had first recorded as a teenager but was now in the first flush of her own career; her 1972 album *Amoureuse* had established her in her native country as a formidable proponent of flowing piano chords and emotive singing. She had met Stills soon after attending a Manassas show in Paris the previous fall, and the attraction was immediate. Stills asked her father for permission to marry, and on March 14, 1973, they wed at a ceremony, held not far from Brookfield House, that was attended by Nash and other rock luminaries, including T. Rex's Marc Bolan. A few days later, Ertegun threw the couple a wedding bash in New York. "Why did they get married? They were both singers," says Giachetti. "It was a beautiful thing." Many hoped it would be the stabilizing force that Stills appeared to need at that point in his life.

With their families in attendance and the West Maui mountains in the background, it was hard to imagine a less stressful scenario for setting up their first album since *Déjà vu.* Young brought "Human Highway," a folksy but disheartened ballad ripe for group harmonies. Among others, Nash had "Prison Song," which touched on both his father's imprisonment and modern drug busts. With an ambling melody that stretched out like yawning arms, Crosby's "Time After Time" captured the sense of contentment he was experiencing. The songs were worked up in a casual fashion, and the group—relaxed, hirsute, tanned—even posed on the beach for a photo (snapped by one of Nash's friends, Harry Harris) that would make an ideal album cover: the superstars in repose. But the idyll was shockingly brief. According to Young biographer Jimmy

McDonough, one of the roadies, Bruce Berry—formerly with Young, now working for Manassas—showed up with drugs intended for one particular band member who'd already had his fill, and the serenity exploded.

Nonetheless, the plan to start and complete an album proceeded, and the group reconvened at Young's studio on his ranch in the summer, joined by bass player Tim Drummond and drummers Barbata and Russ Kunkel. Aligning everyone's schedules proved to be the first major task. Stills, perennially an all-nighter, would sleep during the day, precisely when the others were awake and watching the most riveting television of the summer: the hearings of the Senate Watergate Committee, which was investigating that suspicious break-in from the year before at the Democratic National Committee headquarters. (Just as the recording sessions began, on June 28, US senator Howard Baker, a Republican, famously asked, "What did the president know, and when did he know it?") A few songs were put on tape, including Stills' "See the Changes," a modestly percussive ballad about the impact Sanson had had on his life. Meanwhile, Nash wrote down a list of possible tracks for the album and presented it to his friend Joel Bernstein.

But the time apart had taken its toll. Listening to each other's suggestions after being the bosses of their own bands was no longer palatable, and the work petered out. "It was Neil," says Crosby. "It was his choice. He didn't want to do it. He took another look to see if he would be happy doing it and it didn't look happy to him. He was happy with me and the sailboat. I don't think Nash helped. He wants Neil's power. Nash wants to be Neil and Neil wants to be Bob [Dylan]. Funny shit." To writer Bill DeYoung, Stills would credit the crash to "drug-induced confusion on everyone's part at the time." With its hopes for a long-overdue group album in the fall suddenly evaporating, Atlantic hastily announced it would instead push out a compilation, and record-store ads for *Crosby, Stills, Nash & Young's Greatest Hits*, complete with makeshift cover art featuring a photo of the group onstage at the Fillmore East in 1970, began appearing in newspapers. Demonstrating the ongoing chaos, that album was canceled at the last minute.

Two weeks after the group work crashed, Young embarked on another, very different journey. Reconvening what was left of Crazy Horse (Ralph

Molina and Billy Talbot), along with Ben Keith, Nils Lofgren and Young's gruff, opinionated producer, David Briggs, Young and his crew settled into Los Angeles's SIR studio in late August. In between shooting pool, drinking and coking it up, they recorded a series of hauntingly dissipated songs about, among other things, the overdoses of Danny Whitten and Bruce Berry. Berry had died on the mainland shortly after delivering drugs to the group.

From his mainstream AM radio breakthrough to the deaths of Whitten and Berry, everything around Young felt out of sorts, and the new material reflected that mood. Young and his musicians, dubbed the Santa Monica Flyers, made music the polar opposite of what Crosby, Stills and Nash had done, and even far removed from *Harvest*: vocals were occasionally out of tune, and the musicianship had a spontaneous, off-the-cuff feel. "Neil didn't want us learning the songs and working on parts too much," Lofgren recalls. "It was the antithesis of production. We'd play a song for half an hour and develop a part. Briggs kept saying, 'We're not gonna over-rehearse.' Me and Ralphie used to argue with Briggs—'Let me sing the harmony part.' We didn't even know the *words*. It was the roughest record ever made." The music, an album called *Tonight's the Night*, was so steeped in ennui and decay that the public wouldn't hear it for almost two years.

Simultaneously, Nash was entering a surprisingly cheerless era of his own. By the middle of 1973, he had a new live-in girlfriend, Calli Cerami, a transplanted college student who, coincidentally, had lived on the same Florida street where Stills had rented a house with Manassas. After meeting some of the members of that world in Florida and then moving to San Francisco to attend the California College of Arts and Crafts in Oakland, Cerami had been invited by Elliot Roberts to a party at Nash's home. She found Nash "very flirtatious from the word 'go,'" she recalls. She also sensed he was "kind and warm to everyone—very true to his lyrics." It wasn't long before Cerami moved in with him. Her father objected, telling her, "You're giving up the best years of your life—to this guy? He's not married and you should be married." But for Cerami, the new lifestyle into which she was suddenly thrust—lobster fishing on Crosby's boat, traveling to Crosby and Nash shows in Lear jets—was a magical, enticing place, the upscale counterculture of the early '70s on full display.

Yet in spite of his tastefully designed home and new relationship, Nash was in the early stages of a depression; according to one friend, his breakup with Mitchell was belatedly hitting him, three years later, and his cocaine use had increased. He was also eager to prove he could be on the same creative playing field as the likes of Young. *Wild Tales*, the record he began making within weeks of the collapse of the reunited CSNY project, would be that vehicle. Nash began recording songs that were several Laurel Canyons away from the cheeriness of "Our House." In addition to "Prison Song," he sang of his internal confusion (the haunted-dream melancholy of "Another Sleep Song," with an exquisitely woozy arrangement to match), his feelings about Mitchell (the snippy but upbeat country song "You'll Never Be the Same"), and his distaste for fame ("On the Line"). Stark, bereft and powerful, "I Miss You" brought out his lingering feelings for Amelia "Amy" Gossage, the daughter of advertising executive Howard Gossage (designer of a best-selling sweatshirt featuring the image of Beethoven), who had been Nash's companion for about a year and a half before their breakup in 1973. Using members of the most recent edition of the Stray Gators—Drummond, Keith and Barbata—Nash set those melodies to arrangements that were less adorned than those on *Songs for Beginners*; like Young, he even played more harmonica. Fueled by session man David Lindley's slide guitar, the title song was scrappy rock and roll, rougher than anything Nash had made before. (Opening with Drummond's Motown-tough bass, the title song would be one of the rawest tracks Nash would commit to vinyl.) Though not as visceral as Young's recent musical voyage, *Wild Tales* was its own journey into darkened territory.

The same month Nash and Young started work on their individual records, David Geffen sold Asylum to Warner Communications for $2 million in cash and $5 million in stock. His Asylum label and Elektra were merged under Warner's umbrella, with Geffen appointed chairman of the new Elektra/Asylum Records. Since the deal included rights to the artists' publishing, the shift rattled many Geffen-Roberts clients, including Crosby, Nash and Young. "We pretty much put Geffen in business," says Crosby. "It wasn't a good feeling." According to Cerami, "Graham and David were really pissed at Geffen. Nobody was happy."

The lure of the mothership still lingered in the waning months of 1973, when Stills and Manassas settled into San Francisco's Winterland theater for two nights in October. Ken Weiss, a Hillman associate now running Stills' Gold Hill publishing company, was backstage at the first show and glimpsed an unusual sight: Crosby, Stills, Nash and Young huddling together in a dressing room. Weiss couldn't hear what they were saying, but it became apparent soon enough. During the acoustic part of Manassas' show, a roadie emerged to place several stools onstage, and the crowd was stunned when Crosby and Nash suddenly appeared alongside Stills. (They were also likely baffled when Stills ordered Bill Graham to eject an inebriated Grace Slick, who was doing karate moves by the side of the stage during the first Manassas set.) "We're here for a while, just for a little while," Nash told them. They'd barely practiced, and at times it showed. Stills forgot the lyrics to one of his own songs, "As I Come of Age."

Yet the natural rapport between them was ageless as they slipped into versions of "Helplessly Hoping," "Wooden Ships" and John Lennon and Paul McCartney's "Blackbird." Nash's voice roamed to his traditional highs, particularly on "Wooden Ships." Returning to his usual organizational role, Nash also adjusted Stills' mic, announced songs, and bobbed and weaved while singing. (Other tendencies resurfaced as well: one of the members of Manassas nicknamed them "Crosby Smells of Hash" that night.) The crowd lustily cheered every moment and was further roused when Young materialized. "It's been a long time since this happened!" Nash noted, at which Young stood back up and gave an exaggerated "I quit!" What followed was startling: acoustic and fairly tight versions of new songs they had worked up over the past year together, including Young's "New Mama" (he and Snodgress had had a son, Zeke, the previous year), his doper anthem "Roll Another Number (for the Road)," and "Human Highway" (with Stills and Young trading lead vocals). Nash's "Prison Song" and "And So It Goes," a *Wild Tales* rocker that was melodically reminiscent of "Cowgirl in the Sand," both took on added gravitas. The performance, which lasted just under an hour, amounted to a public rehearsal—a frustrating hint of an album the public would essentially never hear.

Three nights later, back at Winterland, Stills seemed to acknowledge as much. In the midst of a solid performance with Manassas, complete with another Crosby cameo, he thanked the band for its work and told the crowd, "We ain't superstars, but we make good music," before adding, "To me, this band is home." Several nights later, in Long Beach, the group would give its final show. But others, from Hillman to Weiss, saw a hint of what was about to come. "You had Atlantic wanting it and the company willing to pay you whatever," Weiss says. "And here they were being friends. It felt like the natural order."

THE KID WITH the backpack, whoever he was, was drawn to the clatter emanating from deep in the woods. He surely recognized those familiar harmonies and songs, and he, like some others, may have simply thought a massive stereo was blasting old albums. But before he was able to see the source of the music for himself, one of Young's ranch hands found him and escorted him off the property. Other fans parked their cars on adjoining properties within a few miles and sat up in the hills. "Don't hurt 'em," the ranch hands told the property owners, who complied. They just wanted to hear the music.

Had any of them made their way through the forest during the late May and early June of 1974, they would have witnessed a remarkable sight: Stills, Nash, Crosby and Young, usually in that order, standing on a makeshift wooden stage about six feet above the ground. In the heat of the midday sun, sometimes shirtless and wearing shorts, they were practicing songs they hadn't played together in years as a run-up to their first full tour since 1970. Managers, road crew members and friends hovered around, taking in the rare sight. "The year before hadn't been so good, but this time they seemed to be getting along," says Cerami. "They all seemed to be pretty positive about it. I don't remember a lot of fighting. We were all pretty stoked."

In the months leading up to the rehearsals, numerous forces had finally welded them back together. Although plans for an album and a tour in 1973 had disintegrated, those preliminary proposals made everyone realize the likely financial windfall that could come of such a venture. "Elliot and Geffen were basically thinking, 'We're not going to *not* make this money,'" recalls a source close to the band. Thanks to friendly reunions like the get-together at Winterland, the timing now felt right, and another round of discussions began. Bill Graham had by then shut down his Fillmore theaters in New York and San Francisco; disillusioned by the increasing greediness of the music business, he had decided to take a break. But now he was back in the game, acting as the promoter for Bob Dylan's immensely successful comeback tour in early 1974. Knowing well the public appetite for a Crosby, Stills, Nash and Young reemergence, Graham pitched Geffen and Roberts—and the musicians themselves—an audacious plan: a tour that would mostly play outdoor stadiums. They had never before attempted something on that scale. Everyone agreed that, should it be undertaken, Graham would be the man for the job.

The tour, which promised millions in revenue, appealed to the band on multiple levels, starting with their finances. For Stills, the newly disbanded Manassas had been artistically rewarding but a money pit; a generous boss, he paid his band and crew well, but they lost thousands of dollars a night on the road. *Rolling Stone* reported that he had spent $36,000 on a Mercedes snowplow for his Colorado home. Barbata heard that Stills once had a private jet fly to Colorado to pick up two cases of his favorite Coors beer and transport them to a show. During his first meeting with Weiss, after a Manassas concert in Georgia in the spring of 1973, Stills confessed he was feeling the pressure of shouldering the band by himself. The poor sales of *Down the Road*—around 250,000, about half of what the first *Manassas* had sold—only reinforced his delicate financial state.

Young hadn't fared much better with his latest record, *Time Fades Away.* A clankety document of his trouble-plagued tour, it was a live album that, unlike almost every other concert collection of the time, contained not a single retread of an old hit. Instead, from the anxious title track to the monolithic finale, "Last Dance," pausing only for a few voice-and-piano songs, the album featured all new—and all wonderfully ragged—material. For some record buyers, that alone was challenging enough. But the songs were delivered in a voice that sounded sometimes hoarse and agitated, and the Stray Gators provided meaty but jumpy accompaniment. To the consternation of old and new fans, nothing on the album sounded remotely like "Heart of Gold," although "Don't Be Denied" was one of his most personal songs, and "L.A.," his love-hate ode to his former adopted home, had a draggy grandeur. One of Young's most remarkable records, *Time Fades Away* was like one long exposed nerve set to music.

And not counting the hodgepodge *Journey Through the Past* soundtrack, it also became his worst-selling album since 1969's *Neil Young*.

Young didn't seem to care—the art and the anti-commercial message were far more important to him than money—but Broken Arrow Ranch was not an easy property to maintain. About $30,000 was needed for asphalt roads and driveways, the studio in the barn needed to be upgraded, and he had to feed and maintain the animals living on the property. "One time in the '80s, Neil goes, 'Do you know what the cows need to live? $170,000 a month,'" says James Mazzeo. "Nineteen seventy-four was the beginning of all that." Nash still lived an upscale lifestyle at his home in San Francisco, but *Wild Tales*, to his dismay, peaked at no. 34 on the *Billboard* chart and sold only 150,000 copies, a fraction of what the band albums had moved. As for Crosby, he'd finally found property he wanted to call home—a nondescript, fairly isolated home on the outskirts of Mill Valley with a pool and a huge lot—but it was also ready for an upgrade. As his friend Kevin Ryan recounted, part of the budget for the makeover included checks made out to "a mythical Jose Gonzalez," which bought cocaine for construction workers.

When Crosby and Nash returned to playing duo shows in late 1973, they were met by largely supportive audiences—but at a show in Wisconsin there were hecklers. In Rochester, New York, Nash asked the crowd, "Do you want to hear an old song or a new song?" and someone tellingly yelled out, "Old!" Reviewing their show for the *Chicago Tribune*, critic Lynn Van Matre dubbed them "the most deadly-dull big-name duo of the year," adding that the performance was "like something out of the past, and not in the best way." The top-selling albums of 1973 belonged to the likes of Elton John, Alice Cooper and Led Zeppelin, who caught the arena showmanship zeitgeist of the moment far more than any of the Crosby, Stills, Nash and Young offshoots. With Bill Graham offering to run the day-to-day operation with his team, relieving a frazzled Roberts of that part of a huge undertaking, the tour would boost the quartet's bank accounts and return them to their upper-echelon status in the business. All they had to do was tolerate each other for a few months.

Although rumors began leaking in the press, Stills would ultimately break the news of the tour to the world. In the early months of 1974, he found himself back on the road, this time with a leaner post-Manassas band featuring a young, Texas-based guitarist named Donnie Dacus. Although Stills was still able to draw crowds, his standing was evident when, in Chicago, the marquee on his hotel spelled out, "Welcome American Dairymen" in huge letters, and "Welcome Stephen Stills Group" in noticeably smaller letters below. On the last day of the tour, he told writer Barbara Charone that he, Crosby, Nash and Young would be reuniting for shows starting July 4 in Tampa, Florida. He articulated an artistic reason as well: their musical collaborations. "I think that some of my records have suffered for lack of their influences, and some of theirs have suffered for lack of mine," he told Charone. "And we all kind of agree on that." He admitted that "the hardest part is going to be for everyone to remember how to sit and take orders—and me too," but added that he respected Crosby's vocal arrangements and Nash's ability to tell Stills not to overplay. ("And Neil and I," he paused, "well, that's another deal.") In May, Stills couldn't resist some of his usual impolitic bluntness when talking to a United Press International reporter about the tour (which, at the time, he said would only consist of ten shows). "Graham Nash doesn't like the style of my solo stuff—he thinks it's too loud and too lush," he said. "But then I think his album [*Wild Tales*] drags."

Crosby and Nash were less enamored of the idea of playing stadiums but went along with the plan. Nash later said he took a quaalude before an important meeting, and therefore wasn't able to voice his concerns about the size of the venues. "I heard Graham say, 'Well, Crosby and I, we do whatever Neil and Stephen want to do,'" Tim Drummond later told *Rolling Stone*'s Andy Greene. "And I thought, 'God-damn, how disappointing they have a life like that.'"

The expected musical negotiations followed. Stills wanted to hire Russ Kunkel as drummer, Kenny Passarrelli as bassist, and the former Manassas conga player Joe Lala, all members of his current band. But in a repeat of the way Stills and Young had divvied up the rhythm section in 1970, Young (and Nash) argued for Tim Drummond as their preferred bass player, and Drummond landed the job. As Stills later recounted to Greene, it was his suggestion to rehearse at Young's ranch, which meant Young abdicating some of his crucial privacy. "I kind of forced that down: 'Neil, we're coming to your ranch and we're going to build a stage across the road from your studio because we've got to learn how to play outdoors,'" Stills said. "He didn't want all those people in his house, but it actually worked."

In late May, musicians, managers and crew began assembling at Broken Arrow, with the crew crashing in a barn full of Young's vintage cars. "It was like going on a camping trip, but a high-end one," says Glenn Goodwin, a former serviceman in the Vietnam War who had started working for Nash and was now part of the crew. A full-size concert stage was erected across a dirt road from Young's studio, and the band would play for several hours a day, relearning old songs and figuring out how to rearrange their solo material for the group. While setting up every day, Goodwin saw their wildly opposing gear: Stills' super-potent Marshall amps contrasted with Young's Fenders and Nash's and Crosby's custom-built units. Clearly, this was no traditional band, but four men with distinctly separate sensibilities and crews. "It was a total mish-mash of stuff, all different brands," says Goodwin, who was assigned to Crosby, Nash and Drummond. "We purposefully stayed away from Neil's gear. We had our assignments."

While the band rehearsed, the business of preparing for one of the most ambitious tours in pop history was underway in the San Francisco offices of Bill Graham's FM Productions. Although not every one of the thirty-one planned shows (the number had quickly risen from the ten that Stills had mentioned) would be in outdoor stadiums, the amount of equipment and number of employees needed was still formidable. The tour would involve six trucks, a travel agency, carpenters, bus drivers and leap-frogging stages: while they were playing one city, another crew would arrive at the following city and spend the day erecting a stage there. Among the opening acts along the way would be Santana, the Band, the Beach Boys and Joni Mitchell—all headlining acts on their own who would now be subsumed by the collective Crosby, Stills, Nash and Young power grid.

Serving under Graham with the title "tour manager/artist services" was Chris O'Dell, a former employee of Apple Records who was now a seasoned industry pro; she had just worked with Graham on Dylan's tour. Flying into San Francisco, O'Dell arrived at the FM offices to find one of her coworkers sitting before boxes of cigarette cartons. Diligently, he unrolled each cigarette, replaced the tobacco with pot, then rolled them back up and replaced the plastic on each cigarette pack. Ginseng bottles were emptied and refilled with cocaine. Those and other sup- plies—including aspirin and toiletries—would be placed in a large trunk set up in the hospitality suite of each hotel on the road, available to anyone who asked. "That was my first realization of, 'Oh, my God, this is going to be an interesting tour,'" O'Dell says. "No one had ever catered to groups like that before. The idea was to make everything available."

In a radio interview before the tour commenced, Young sounded hopeful even when the disc jockey brought up the dreaded "supergroup" term. "We have a lot of past together," Young said. "We have a lot of mem- ories of each other. . . . We have a relating point from the past. Now the thing, uh, is that relating point still going to be sparkling now like it was then? . . . That's what we got together to find out and to get it going and see what's happening."

As Mazzeo watched the band play at Young's ranch, dutifully and with focus, he also caught sight of something equally unusual, even in this rock-and-roll circus: Stills and his manager Michael John Bowen conducting soldierly exercises on the stage. "It was all this military shit: 'Stand at attention!' 'Chest out!' All kinds of boot-camp stuff," Mazzeo recalls. Neither he nor anyone else involved doubted that the tour would be an unusual expedition.

As STILLS, YOUNG, and a teenage journalist, Cameron Crowe—on assign- ment for the *Rolling Stone* competitor *Crawdaddy* magazine—watched from the upper-floor restaurant of a nearby hotel, thousands of concert- goers began streaming into the Seattle Coliseum in the early afternoon of July 9. Although he'd been joking at first with Stills, Young turned quiet at the sight. In a few hours, the opening show of the tour would power up—coincidentally, four years to the day since the last show on the *Déjà vu* tour. Over 15,500 tickets had been sold for the Seattle show alone.

In context, the thought of a rock band in stadiums (something that had not been attempted since the Beatles' mid-'60s shows in venues of that size) made a twisted sense: by 1974, so much in popular culture felt oversized. The prog band Yes practically dared its fans to plow through the entirety of *Tales from Topographic Oceans*, a double LP with one extremely long and twisty song per side. Led Zeppelin launched its own record label, Swan Song, with elaborate parties in New York (complete with live geese) and Los Angeles. Two of the top-grossing movies of the year, *The Towering Inferno* and *Earthquake*, were overblown disaster epics—the latter was screened in some theaters in Sensurround, speakers that literally rattled viewers into believing they were in the midst of a quake. That fall, motorcycle daredevil Evel Knievel would attempt—and fail—to launch his rocket-fueled Skycycle X-2 up a 108-foot ramp and over Idaho's Snake River Canyon; one account of the festivities leading up to it called the event "a Woodstock on wheels." In light of the spectacles of the year, hardly anyone thought Knievel's stunt was remotely abnormal.

The Crosby, Stills, Nash and Young tour would reflect that grandeur in more ways than just its venues. Goodwin checked into one of the hotels one day and, preparing to crash, saw specially made pillowcases printed with Joni Mitchell's painting of the quartet. (The artwork would also grace the cover of *So Far*, a premature greatest-hits album that Atlantic released that summer to capitalize on the reunion.) "I go, 'You gotta be kidding me,'" Goodwin says. "Our luggage tags were leather embossed with Joni's art. I don't know if 'decadence' is the right word, but it was so over the top." Meals would be served on wooden plates that were also festooned with Mitchell's illustration. Limousines would be on round-the-clock call; a personal chef was prepared to whip up whatever meals the band members wanted. Decades later, such amenities would be commonplace, but in 1974, they represented nouveau riche rock culture.

The initial plan had called for the tour to start in Los Angeles, but when LA's county commissioners nixed the idea of booking an outdoor venue, Seattle received the kick-off honors. The four men who ambled onstage after an opening set by Jesse Colin Young, formerly of the Youngbloods, still comported themselves like ornery individuals. For that and most of the shows that followed, a now bulky-looking Stills, reflecting his love of football and a team spirit he wanted in the band, wore a succession of football jerseys. Young, with his sunglasses, summer-short haircut and occasional straw hat, resembled a carny barker. Both sported mutton-chop sideburns, as if they were competing for most imposing facial hair. Crosby's pronounced receding hairline was offset by a halo of curls atop his head. Nash was the most physically transformed: with his unkempt mane and beard, scarily thin at 120 pounds, and wearing patched jeans and army shirts, he no longer resembled the vest-clad British countryman of several years before.

As they took their places onstage, the show began as it always would: with Kunkel and Lala launching into a percussive rattle that led into Stills' blaring guitar and rivet-gun solos, and finally into his "Love the One You're With." As if they'd been holding in their elation since that last 1970 show in Minneapolis, the crowd unleashed a collective bellow.

During rehearsals at Young's ranch, it was decided to showcase not only the songs from *Crosby, Stills & Nash* and *Déjà vu* but also some of the work from their own albums and whatever new material they'd written. As a result, the first night in Seattle ran over three hours, encompassing more than forty songs. On that and subsequent nights, there was something for everyone. The oldies—a harmony-fueled "Suite: Judy Blue Eyes," a monstrous "Déjà vu" and the inevitable sing-along, "Our House"—were faithfully resurrected. Fans could now hear how some of the solo songs—such as "Change Partners," "Immigration Man" and "Cowgirl in the Sand"—would have sounded if they'd been group recordings, and how "4 + 20" and "Sugar Mountain" would come across with harmonies added. Lovers of *Harvest* heard Young play "A Man Needs a Maid." Behind them during the opening and closing electric segments, Kunkel, Lala and Drummond offered up a sturdy, unflinching backbeat; Kunkel's rubbery drumming, in particular, was a perfect match for that coliseum and the others to come.

In keeping with the excessive length of the show, they overdid it that first day: their voices were raw by show's end. The next day, in Vancouver, Crosby totally blew out his voice during "Almost Cut My Hair." For the rest of the set, he barely sang. The climactic "Carry On" jam session was stretched out to compensate for him, and Crosby, as Crowe witnessed, was nearly reduced to tears after the show. Later that night, they huddled with management to determine how to proceed. Someone brought up the story that John Lennon had supposedly wrecked his voice before the Beatles' taping of *The Ed Sullivan Show*, forcing Paul to vocally assist his bandmate. "What it meant was, Stephen, Graham and Neil had to basically cover for David," says Ron Stone of the Geffen-Roberts Company, who accompanied the band on the tour. "Four-part harmony would be three-part without anyone noticing."

As Bill Graham fended off regular calls from David Geffen, who wanted to make sure the band wasn't fighting yet, the tour posed any number of other challenges, starting with the outdoor stadium shows in Oakland, the third city on the tour. That summer, the Grateful Dead settled into a few stadiums with their enormous, towering Wall of Sound system, but they weren't playing an entire tour in those venues. The Crosby, Stills, Nash and Young team had to learn to do so on the fly. Sound systems remained primitive—in-ear monitors that allowed musicians to hear each other hadn't yet been invented—and the combination of open-air acoustics and competing ramped-up guitars were a recipe for sonic overkill. (Stills had turned the once acoustic "Black Queen" into a bludgeoning stomp that was perfect for stadiums, although it completely obliterated the subtlety of the original.) At times, Crosby and Nash could barely hear themselves, resulting in harmonies that could sound ragged and off-key. "We were dealing with the elements and other things that could impact the sound," says Goodwin. "So it could fall apart, and when it did, oh, my God—the harmonies [suffered]. How those guys could hear themselves sometimes was baffling to me. The volume was ridiculous. The sound system for the vocals had to be stronger than the band. It got to be a battle. It was scary and not fun."

The risks of playing quieter songs in such massive venues also became clear one evening—the acoustic set was cut short when overly excited, borderline belligerent fans started throwing bottles onto the stage, almost hitting Crosby. (When a live album from the tour was finally cobbled together in 2014, forty years later, the vocal shortcomings were a major issue. Nash and co-producer Joel Bernstein, along with engineer Stanley Tajima Johnston, spent considerable time cobbling together songs Frankenstein-style, using harmonies from one performance and the backing from another to construct perfect tracks.)

Nonetheless, they were off and running until the tour wound down in early September. After the second night, O'Dell was already exhausted. "I was in my room in Vancouver thinking, 'I'm going to *die*,'" she recalls. "All I could think about was how tired I was." Just under thirty more shows remained.

FOR ALL ITS overblown pop culture, the country remained in a depressed sulk. It was bad enough that 1974 had started with a gas shortage, which led to rationing and long, infuriating (and often fraught) lines at the pumps. One of the shows would take place in New Jersey, where residents could only buy gas every other day. The recession dragged down auto sales and drove up the price of household staples (by fall, the cost of sugar would surge 300 percent from the year before). By year's end, six million Americans would be out of work, the highest number in over a dozen years. The Watergate scandal, entering its second year of congressional hearings, made public the idea that the leader of the free world might be a criminal.

Not surprisingly, the culture began looking to the past for relief or escape. Sixties nostalgia had cast a melancholy over Don McLean's omnipresent 1971 hit "American Pie," a rousing but inherently forlorn look at the rise and fall of communal rock culture. More reflection followed, but without the angst. *Grease*, an originally rowdy but later cartoonish musical about teen life in the '50s, arrived off-Broadway in New York in 1971, followed in movie theaters in 1973 by *American Graffiti*, director George Lucas' alternately woolly and wistful glimpse of high school graduates in 1962. That movie's success prompted the far more sanitized TV sitcom *Happy Days*, set in an idyllic suburb in the '50s, starting in the first month of 1974.

In that context, a reunion of one of the most iconic acts of the previous decade took on a heightened import. For many in the arenas and stadiums, it would be their first chance to see one of pop's most storied bands in person. Audiences never failed to be juiced when Stills began playing the opening of "Suite: Judy Blue Eyes" or when Young picked the knotty, immediately recognizable notes of "Ohio" during the electric set. The songs that received the loudest cheers were the ones associated with nation-shattering events—Kent State, the Kennedy assassinations, the Chicago Eight. When the skies opened up during one outdoor show, a segment of the crowd burst into the "No rain! No rain!" chant that had been immortalized in the *Woodstock* movie. In Houston, an overzealous security guard at Jeppesen Stadium saw early arrivals pressing against the gates and sprayed them with mace. Charging onto the scene, Bill Graham reamed the guard and apologized to the fans. "What is this, Kent State?" one of them yelled back, angrily conjuring a memory straight out of the country's—and the band's—past.

Of the four, only Young had a new album to promote by the summer of 1974. Its enigmatic cover showed him standing on the sand in Santa Monica, facing the ocean; in the foreground, a newspaper sported the headline "Senator Buckley Calls for Nixon to Resign." And that was just the beginning. The record itself, called *On the Beach*, was a disconsolate, wintry collection of songs that were anti-nostalgic in just about every way. Another pivot from the strums and melodies of *After the Gold Rush* and *Harvest*, the album was like a bumpy drive on a bleak highway. "Walk On," a shout-out to haters, had a gawky guitar part and clackity feel that guaranteed it wouldn't find much of a home on AM radio.

The first half of the album painted a less-than-flattering portrait of the legacy of the country and the music business. The narrator of the spooked-out "Revolution Blues" was a leftover Weather Underground type itching to mow down celebrities; he wants to attack a factory that builds computer logs by unleashing doves instead. It was both scary and comical. "For the Turnstiles," featuring just Young on banjo and his musical sidekick Ben Keith on dobro, was an oblique take on the concert business that sounded as if it had been written on an Appalachian mountain that had inexplicably popped up in Hollywood. Indeed, it sounded like the album had been recorded in a druggy, alcoholic haze. The second, ravaged half of *On the Beach* addressed Young's discomfort with the media and the demands of his fans (the intentionally draggy slow burn of the title track) and his dissipating relationship with Snodgress ("Motion Pictures"). Set to a sulky melody lifted from British folk singer and guitarist Bert Jansch, "Ambulance Blues" was a comment on critics and the band he was about to tour with that very summer; a crack about peeing in the wind referred to what Elliot Roberts had supposedly barked at his ornery client after one of the aborted reunions with Crosby, Stills and Nash.

Hardly the type of sunny record one would promote on a stadium tour, *On the Beach* made it sound as if Young's own life and the country itself were drowning, rather than standing safely on the shore. Yet Young did coax his bandmates into playing a few of its songs on the road, sometimes with dazzling results. Young and Stills shredded back and forth in "On the Beach." Despite his objections to "Revolution Blues" ("too

Mansonesque," he says), Crosby had strummed along on "Revolution Blues" in the studio, and he played it onstage with Young as well.

If Young was coming to play mammoth venues where he could barely see most of the crowd, he would do it in his way, and not merely by playing *On the Beach* songs. When he sat down by himself with a guitar, anyone expecting to hear "Heart of Gold" was bound to be disappointed. Only three times during the thirty-one shows did he play his ubiquitous hit. Instead, the crowds were treated to Young tunes they'd never heard before: "Love Art Blues," a honky-tonk ramble about his dog; the melancholic "Star of Bethlehem"; or a song about his long-lost hearse, "Long May You Run."

Like the "Country Girl" assemblage from *Déjà vu*, another new song, "Pushed It Over the End," showed how Young could pull the other three into novel—almost novelistic—territory. Young had debuted the tune during a surprise set at New York's Bottom Line in May 1974, calling it "Citizen Kane Junior Blues," and it seemed be launched right out of the news. The month before, the publishing heiress Patty Hearst, who'd been taken hostage by a radical group calling itself the Symbionese Liberation Army, had been photographed taking part in a bank robbery—hence the Milly cradling a gun in the intro. The central character in Orson Welles' *Citizen Kane* had been based on Hearst's grandfather, William Randolph Hearst. Performed with the full band that summer, "Pushed It Over the End" was a majestic, epic piece, lurching over eight minutes through rise-and-crest tempo changes, with Young's lead guitar and Stills' electric-keyboard yawps also egging on the arrangement. "Neil would just pull one out of his ass—his hat or his ass, either or—and kick it out," recalled Drummond to Andy Greene. "The rest of them would grab on and hang on. That's how it worked. That's what made it so exciting." Along with *On the Beach*, Young's flurry of new and often topical songs was added proof that his creative rush, his ability to write fresh material, often at a furious pace, could overwhelm his partners. According to group historian Pete Long, one-third of the songs they performed on the tour were Young's.

Crosby, Stills and Nash couldn't hope to compete with that output. Crosby admitted as much at the first show, in Seattle, as he was about to play "Carry Me," partly about the death of his mother the year before.

Comparing their songwriting bursts, Young wrote "about three of 'em a day," as Crosby told the crowd. But they did their best, all of them hauling along newly written or very recent songs. Crosby had "Carry Me" and "Time After Time." Stills had the jazzy Latino shuffle "My Angel," which he co-wrote with Dallas Taylor; another Latino rocker, "First Things First," on which he would show off his timbales chops; and "My Favorite Changes," an attempt at autobiography (citing his struggles with fame in his twenties, which were almost over). Unfortunately, "My Favorite Changes" was played only at one show. But in a move almost as perverse as some of Young's, Stills also debuted his sullen piano ballad "Myth of Sisyphus"—in which he partly mocked himself—to stadiums packed with fans who surely wanted to boogie. For his part, Nash trotted out songs from *Wild Tales*. These included, with the others accompanying him, "Prison Song," which was tailor-made for a group sing-along, as well as the agitated "Fieldworker," about the Mexican laborers he had seen working, under wretched conditions, in Northern California, and "It's All Right," a piano serenade for Cerami that yearned to be the next "Our House." (In a worlds-colliding moment, he dedicated the song to Cerami at their Long Island show as Mitchell watched in the wings.) Combined with the dusted-off oldies, each show on the tour presented a body of work that signaled they were rock's most frustrating and yet most formidable band.

As the band tested the limits of its reinvention onstage, events in the outside world pressed in on them. On August 8, Richard Nixon, impeachment in the rear-view window, and Republicans bailing on him, resigned midway through their show in New Jersey. Nash announced the news to the crowd, and Bill Graham hastily arranged to have one firework set off to celebrate. A far more heartbreaking moment came on the morning after they'd played Houston, about a week earlier, when Graham somberly informed Nash and Kunkel, who was married to Cass Elliot's sister Leah, that their old friend, Mama Cass, who had first brought the trio together, had died. After playing the last of her shows at the London Palladium, Elliot had returned to the apartment where she was staying and was found dead in her bed the next morning. In an interview, a doctor on the scene implied that she had choked on a ham sandwich in her room, although it was later determined that the sandwich was untouched. The likely cause of death was heart failure, with Elliot's weight a factor. Only six years before, they had sung in her living room, but their lives had gone through many changes since then.

To the outside world—at least to writers invited along to report on the tour—the offstage atmosphere was composed and professional, the four men at its whirlwind core newly centered adults. "We're mature cats now—we've grown up a lot," Crosby told writer Michael Pousner before their show at Houston's Jeppesen Stadium, while lounging in the Safari Room (complete with a thatched bar) of the Whitehall Hotel. A report in *Time* described the backstage scene as "amazingly relaxed" and "all just a bit suburban," likening the band to "four affable, affluent businessmen bound for a Sunday afternoon of pro football."

When Bill Graham would invariably barge into whatever lounge they were in to round them up for the trip to the stage, they went along merrily (in Houston, though, Young opted for his own vehicle rather than accompanying the others). When Nash would run up to Stills before a show to hastily inform him of a change in the set, the two men, in front of one journalist or another, were amenable and cooperative. The same team spirit held as they stood onstage on their preferred Persian rug: Crosby and Nash would enhance Young's "Don't Be Denied" with high harmonies, and Young played jolly piano behind Nash's Watergate-chaos-inspired rocker from *Wild Tales*, "Grave Concern."

Yet that facade didn't always jibe with reality. To ship the musicians from city to city, Chris O'Dell generally booked them on commercial flights. But early on, she realized she wasn't being asked to purchase plane tickets for Young. As she soon learned, Young had bought a GMC motorhome so that he and his inner circle—Mazzeo, their friend "Ranger Dave" Cline, and Young's son Zeke—could drive from show to show. (Carrie Snodgress was an occasional and not always welcome addition.) Eventually, they switched to a $400 Cadillac he purchased in Chicago for half a dozen shows all located within a half-day's drive. As Mazzeo recalls, "Neil said, 'Look, we're not going to be part of this tour. We're going to show up for all the gigs, but that's it. We may have hotel rooms in the towns, but we're mostly going to be on our own.' He wanted to avoid all the shit he had on the tour with those guys four years before. He wanted to be with friends and family. Our thing was not to be on that tour as much as possible. And we did a great job of it."

For O'Dell, Young's private trips were a relief. "It was easier," she says. "We didn't have to worry about Neil." But for Crosby, Stills and Nash, they were the latest sign that Young was still operating in his own personal orbit. "Neil traveled separately and kept himself separate," Crosby says. "That was him being honest about how he felt. Neil is a very pragmatic guy when he's dealing with us. He knows what he's dealing with, with Stephen, with me and with Graham. And he uses us when it suits his purpose. I wish he wanted to be our buddy. But the music was good and that was what counted."

Young's aloofness extended to interviews to promote the tour: in essence, he didn't do any. The other three sat with numerous reporters during the trip, but always without their fourth wheel. "Neil Young doesn't talk to anybody—he has been burned," Nash told the Associated Press. "We fools, on the other hand, will try to communicate what it is we're really trying to do." Embedded with the band, Ben Fong-Torres of *Rolling Stone* was only able to get two sentences out of Young before their St. Paul concert. Young told him he was leaving right afterward for a lengthy drive to Colorado, adding, "You know, I'm not real good at giving interviews. But I'll tell you, I'm having a lot of fun and it's getting better every day." (Message: He didn't want to talk about it.) Even when he was onstage with the whole band, Young subtly communicated his separate space: at moments during the lengthy jam that followed "Carry On," he would turn to face Kunkel and play directly to him with his trademark piercing stare. Kunkel wondered how much the stance had to do with Young's intensity during performance and how much it was his search for a safe space onstage, away from the others.

As much as they wanted to change, each of the four remained personally driven, and when they were together, they easily set to bickering. "They were very explosive," says Giachetti, who was part of Stills' crew on the tour. "It should have been no big deal: you go on tour and play music. But there was a lot of competition. There are many ways to light a stage, and they would disagree about that. They would get angry and start fighting if a song ended in a black-out or a white-out or a spotlight. If one had sex with twins, the other guy had to have sex with twins."

Giachetti was most likely referring to Crosby's traveling arrangements. While Debbie Donovan remained at home, Crosby enjoyed the company of two women on the road: Nancy Brown, a Montana-born teenager who would celebrate her eighteenth birthday on the tour, and a mysterious Mill Valley groupie named Goldie Locks. "I wanted to be the center of attention and I was—because the girls loved me and wanted to make me happy," Crosby wrote in his memoir *Long Time Gone*, in which he also referred to himself as "a complete and utter pleasure-seeking sybarite." (Ron Stone, who was married and often took long drives with Crosby on the road, has said, "I lived vicariously through David on that tour.") One of the band's business associates realized he had become accustomed to the lunacy when he visited Crosby's hotel room during one stop. "Two women in dresses and no panties doing cartwheels around the room while I'm watching TV—and I'm annoyed because they're in the way," he says. "I said, 'Could you do that somewhere else?' After a while, the abnormal became normal and you stopped paying attention to the bizarre."

Naturally, other disagreements stemmed from the music. At times, frustrated over the lack of impeccable arrangements—the rough-hewn feel of some of the performances reflected Young's sensibility more than the others' deliberate choices—Stills would grow irritated and would feel the others were shooting him dirty looks if he overplayed. At one after-party, the letters "CSNY" were carved out in blocks of ice on a table with the usual ocean-sized portion of shrimp, and Stills, angry over how the others had reacted onstage to his playing, attacked the ice with "backfists and knuckle punches and karate," he told writer Bill DeYoung. "I took it apart in front of them. . . . I went through the 'N' with one punch and it just shattered."

By the time the tour made its way east, the sheer size of it all was starting to wear everyone down. O'Dell had already started drinking early on in the trek to ward off the anxiety. "It was the only tour I ever did where each member of the band had his own faction," she says. "It was them and *their* person who worked for them. It was very stressful." Upon arriving at the Plaza Hotel in New York, O'Dell was told to report to Crosby's quarters—he wasn't happy with the direction of the breezes wafting into the room and was threatening to go back home. Hurriedly they found a new room more to his liking. "Who knew he needed cross-ventilation?"

O'Dell recalls. "It wasn't in the rider." Meanwhile, Stills' voice, warbly and boozy, was showing wear and tear. Adding to the madness of the tour, he had also taken to regaling everyone with fanciful tales of serving in the armed forces. ("The crowded years," as Nash calls the in-joke that resulted from such talk.) In any other context, puzzling statements like those would have raised eyebrows, but during what Crosby would dub "The Doom Tour" that summer, they were par for CSNY's course.

Bob Dylan famously appeared at their Minneapolis show; afterward, he invited Stills and Drummond to hear the songs that would make up *Blood on the Tracks*. They sat on facing hotel beds as Dylan played the songs (Nash, irked, stood outside listening in). When Dylan was done, Stills made some vaguely critical comments. "And Dylan, being the arrogant man that he was, he said, 'Well, Stephen, play me one of your new songs,'" Drummond recalled to Greene. "And that was the end of it." (As Stills told Cameron Crowe that year, "I've been the most obnoxious superstar, arrogant. . . . I have a bad habit of stating things pretty bluntly. I'm not known for my tact.")

Yet it was the normally level-headed Nash who seemed most impacted by the craziness. O'Dell found Nash the easiest of the four to deal with: he had his own demands, but he wasn't belligerent about them. Yet, starting with his shaggy-dog look and his singing—which became unusually ragged and throaty, thanks to the onstage blare—Nash was going through major changes. "All my aware life, from age 16, 17, 18, I've been an object," he told *Rolling Stone*'s Fong-Torres during the tour. "A fucking object. That's why I try very hard to be as unrecognizable as possible." Even before the tour, cocaine was never far from him—a container with an ounce of it always sat in the medicine cabinet of his upstairs bathroom in San Francisco. The group only encouraged that habit—O'Dell saw a baseball-sized hunk of it in one band member's room—and by the time Nash checked into his own quarters at the Plaza, he was scrawny and gaunt, his ribs poking through his chest. With the help of Cerami, who snapped the photo, he took a self-portrait in his bathroom that showed him looking especially emaciated. During the same era, Allan Clarke, Nash's former Hollies friend and bandmate, recalls Nash showing up at his Manchester-area home in a red Mustang. "He came into the house with a big 'How ya doing?' and packing joints, and I said, 'Graham,

I've got kids in the house—if you're going to do that, you're going to have to leave.'" Nash heeded his wishes.

The American leg of the tour wrapped up on September 8 at Roosevelt Raceway on Long Island. The grounds were damp after several days of rain, but 77,000 fans still waited in the mud or wet grass to see the band along with Joni Mitchell (and the L.A. Express), the Beach Boys and Jesse Colin Young. Mitchell joined them for "Suite: Judy Blue Eyes," wrapping her elastic swoon around their harmonies. But the show was also hounded by sour notes. Before it began, Bill Graham informed the crowd, to boos and cheers, that the new president, Gerald Ford, had just pardoned Richard Nixon. Then, as the band was walking offstage after the last song, they were served with legal papers suing them for their only canceled show on the tour.

After their success planning and promoting the Summer Jam at Watkins Glen—a 1973 festival in upstate New York that outdrew Woodstock, featuring the Grateful Dead, the Allman Brothers Band and the Band—its East Coast promoters, Jim Koplik and Shelly Finkel, were eager to create a similar event on the West Coast. They wanted Crosby, Stills, Nash and Young as headliners, and the Beach Boys, the Band, Joe Walsh and Jesse Colin Young playing before them. The promoters picked Ontario Speedway, a 170,000-capacity raceway in Orange County, and put tickets on sale for an August 3 show. But the prospect of hauling out to the desert in the late-summer heat apparently didn't sit well with fans: out of 100,000 tickets, only 15,000 were purchased.

A new date, after the band's lone European show, was considered. Whether it was an accurate report or not, the promoters were told Young didn't want to return to California right after the overseas trip, and they were offered just Crosby, Stills and Nash for $150,000, instead of the entire group for $200,000. Koplik and Finkel declined and canceled the show. To recoup their expenses, they decided to sue the band, and Bill Graham asked them to serve the musicians the papers at the end of—not before—the Roosevelt Raceway show. "Bill let us go right to the stairs," says Koplik. "He made sure they would only walk back down one set of stairs so that we wouldn't miss them. Bill was being good to us. He had no stake in it."

Out of respect for Michael John Bowen, Stills' manager, who had been helpful in organizing the original show they had hoped to put on, Koplik and Finkel served the others but not Stills at that moment. In the end, the promoters settled out of court for $150,000. If the idea of mammoth outdoor stadiums hadn't appealed to the band before, it truly didn't now.

To EVERYONE'S RELIEF, the end loomed in sight when the band and crew flew to England a few days before September 14. For an aptly grandiose finale, the tour would wrap up at Wembley Stadium, a fifty-one-year-old venue in northwest London that could accommodate over 100,000. The opening acts would be Joni Mitchell and the L.A. Express and the Band. That year, Mitchell had intersected with the mainstream with *Court and Spark*, an album that managed to be both whisper-personal and radio-friendly, and she toured arenas to promote it. Despite their unpleasant breakup four years before, she and Nash had patched up their friendship and spent studio time together. She joined the band for two of their mega-shows; although she hadn't reached their stadium-show level of fame, she was by now one of the most rightly revered and influential singer-songwriters of the era. "As we got more successful Joni was like our mascot," Crosby says. "She would hang with us. But she was always a little resentful that she wasn't in the boys' club and that we had gotten so huge. She wanted to be a lot bigger. I think she felt she deserved to be a lot bigger, and she did, but her stuff is so good it went over the heads of most people."

At Young's insistence, the band would only do one overseas show. "They wanted us to go all over Europe," Drummond told Greene, "and Neil put his foot down and said, 'No, we'll do one show.' I wanted to go all over the damn place. But he was too exhausted or whatever." If there was only to be one show, it would be a big one. Mel Bush, the British promoter for Wembley, ensured that the band would be treated like the icons they were (and saw themselves as). Five mobile homes, one of which had previously been used by Elizabeth Taylor, were set up backstage, along with a catering van to supply them with whatever food they wanted. Each dressing room would be equipped with "one bucket of water and one woolen blanket" in the event of a fire. For reasons that were odd but in keeping with the recurring insanity of the tour, the venue's contract stipulated that no hypnotism would be allowed on the premises.

Rain had dogged the area for several days leading up to the show, right up to that morning. Gazing out at the throng stretched before him, Mazzeo saw what he recalls as "thousands of the whitest, skinniest English people you've ever seen in your life." The sound system combined the band's equipment with additions from a local company. At least the indulgences were the same, albeit even more potent: awaiting the band and their employees was a pile of Merck cocaine from European pharmaceutical labs, resulting in a truly pure stash.

The final show of the tour began the way it had in Seattle, with Kunkel initiating a beat that would lead into "Love the One You're With." But as he sat down at his kit, he was momentarily off his game. Kunkel had rolled with the craziness of the tour. Onstage, he had kept a watchful eye on Young, since Young seemed to lose himself in the songs, and it was never clear how long his solos would last. But at Wembley, as Kunkel took in the heaving ocean of people, the screaming and yelling was so overwhelming that he was thrown off at first; for a moment, he was worried he would blank on what he was supposed to play. "Oh, God, it was like being in a hurricane," he has said. "I'd never experienced anything like that before." A consummate pro, Kunkel didn't flub, and by then, the sun had broken through, as if the band had brought the California weather with it. By the end of the show, all those pale British bodies were sunburnt.

Yet the accumulated grind of the expedition announced itself on the Wembley stage. As in America, few in the crowd seemed to notice or care; the mere sight of the four men reunited—for their first group performance in the country since early 1970—was satisfying enough. But the band sang sharp and looked and sounded hopped up: by "Word Game," his acoustic blues from *Stephen Stills 2*, Stills looked like he was going to nod off. The patchwork sound system made it especially difficult for Crosby and Nash to hear their own singing, and the harmonies, especially on "Carry On," were often painfully out of tune.

The night and the tour ended in an appropriately rock-and-roll manner. Nash, Young, Stills and Cerami visited Paul and Linda McCartney at their home immediately after the show. McCartney danced to Jackson Five records, Linda showed off her prized art collection, and Stills, to the mortification of a few, gave the former Beatle pointers on how to play bass. At a party at Quaglilino's restaurant in London during their stay in town, Young and Stills, both clearly inebriated or chemically enhanced, jammed with Jimmy Page and John Bonham of Led Zeppelin.

With an eye toward an ABC-TV special to air in May 1975, the Wembley show was preserved on video. Watching the footage later, though, the band saw for themselves how mangy they looked and sounded and decided to shelve the special. "We were just too wrecked," Crosby says. "We knew it and watched the video after and said, 'Aw, fuck.'" The footage was relegated to the expanding vault of unreleased and aborted attempts at reconciliations.

"WE SEEM TO HAVE a two-month half life, and then it blows," Crosby told the *New York Times* backstage at Long Island's Roosevelt Raceway, as he watched Mitchell's set. "Actually, there are no hard feelings now. We just want to take a well-deserved rest, and then we'll go into the studio in November and record an album." Crosby's words were well considered, but as sensible as the plan sounded, they were pushing it. Most bands would make a new album, *then* tour behind it. Flouting the standard rules once more, Crosby, Stills, Nash and Young opted to spend four months in each other's faces on the road and then, despite the ensuing stress and anxiety, reconvene in a studio for months shaping and polishing new songs.

Given what they'd just put themselves through, the plan was, to say the least, risky. It didn't help the mood when the receipts for the tour were added up after the final show. At the time, much of rock was a cash business, so it wasn't unusual for Bill Graham and Geffen-Roberts employees to find themselves in a hotel room after a show, stuffing wads of bills into duffel bags and then waiting for an armored truck to haul the money to a bank. But once the production costs were added in, along with the lavish spending—including the ornate pillowcases and the teak plates—the estimated $10 million profit shrank. According to Nash, each man emerged with only about $300,000. (Stone disputes that figure, saying each made $1 million—but before expenses.) As Crosby says, "We were not sufficiently aware that we were being taken to the cleaners."

In that tainted-well atmosphere, the last thing they needed was to see more of each other, but starting in early December, they congregated at Rudy Records, the cozy studio in the basement of Nash's home in San Francisco. The week before, Young had been in Nashville. He was already at work on his own new album—a bleak series of songs ruminating on the end of his relationship with Snodgress, along with "The Old Homestead," a gently galloping piece that addressed, obliquely, how he was grappling with issues arising from the group's reunion. But he'd committed to the group album and dutifully showed up at Nash's house, along with the same rhythm section they'd used on the tour and Ron and Howard Albert, Stills' producers of choice.

According to studio paperwork, little happened during that session. Work began on one song—possibly Stills' "Thoroughfare Gap"—but the situation quickly deteriorated. As Young, Nash's neighbor and friend Joel Bernstein, and others watched, Stills and Nash got into an argument—"a coke-fueled, stupid-ass thing," recalls one of those present—over the placement of one note in a song. "Stephen wanted me to sing this vocal part and my body wouldn't physically let me do what he was asking," Nash says. "It didn't make musical sense, and every time I tried to do it, my body said, 'What the fuck are you trying to do?' I told him and he got infuriated with me."

In an adjoining part of the studio, Glenn Goodwin caught the tail end of the ruckus. "There was some yelling," he recalls, "and when the door opened, it looked like something had happened." Young was soon out the door, and Nash retreated to his bedroom on the third floor with Cerami. Stills raged on in the basement, threatening to cut up a tape of the recording with a razor blade. Unsure what to do, Nash called his assistant, Mac Holbert, who lived next door, and asked him to physically eject Stills from his house. "I was actually a little disappointed that Graham didn't go down and confront him, that he had someone else go first," says Cerami. "I thought, 'Hell, this is your house—what do you mean?' But I don't blame him." With Cerami's support, Nash put on an early copy of Bob Dylan's *Blood on the Tracks* (ironic, given Dylan had previewed those songs for Stills months before) and waited for his partner to be evicted from his home.

A few days later, about a week before Christmas, they decided to give it another go. Since Nash's home studio was fairly small, they reconvened at the Record Plant in nearby Sausalito, a more professional setting that should have made them focus. But on what may have been only the second day of work, someone forgot to turn off the talk-back microphone in the control room, allowing those in the recording room to hear what was being said about them. Exactly what was overheard remains vague: it may have been critical words about Young or about how much bass player Tim Drummond was being paid. As Nash recalls, "The Albert brothers were listening to us argue and someone came out of the control room and said something about what we'd been saying, and everyone got crazy."

Almost immediately, Drummond was gone. They replaced him with bass player Leland Sklar, a musician with a mountain-man beard and a caustic sense of humor who had been James Taylor's stalwart player as well as a contributor to *Graham Nash/David Crosby*. Sklar walked in and found, he says, "not the most comfortable atmosphere." Over the course of two days, they managed to record a full take of a new Crosby song, "Homeward Through the Haze." Built around Crosby's own murmuring piano, the song, which touched on Los Angeles and critical barbs they'd taken, had a glum stateliness, and two more Crosby songs, "Time After Time" and "Carry Me," both played on the recent tour, were also attempted. At some point, Bill Kreutzmann, the Grateful Dead drummer who lived nearby, was invited to play, but he was so dismayed by the vibe that he went back home. The band tried to bribe him to return with one of the fur coats they wore on the inside of *Crosby, Stills & Nash*, but Kreutzmann still begged off. Tellingly, the Crosby, Stills, Nash and Young world was too crazy even for a member of the Dead.

On the planned fourth day, December 20, crew employees showed up for work only to find John Talbot, a member of Young's organization (and the brother of Crazy Horse's Billy Talbot), packing up and carting away his boss' gear. Clearly, the work was over. "Neil could say, 'They drove me crazy and I couldn't stand to be around it,' or 'It was Stephen's fault for doing too much dope,' or 'It was Crosby's fault for being too much of a baby,'" Crosby says. "And I would agree with all of the above.

But for Neil, the music has to be exciting for him. You *should* follow the music and not the money. He's right." As Cerami adds, "I don't blame Neil. It wasn't pleasant."

As they later learned, Young had been driving to the studio when he realized he no longer wanted to put himself through the psychodrama. He turned the car around and drove back home. Returning to his ranch, he ran into his friend Mazzeo. "It was too much, too much," he told Mazzeo. He didn't have to say more. Young had been to that particular circus one too many times, and the merry-go-round was over.

CHAPTER 6

FEBRUARY 1975–AUGUST 1978

I f Crosby couldn't work with Nash, Stills or Young, there was always the Grateful Dead. By 1975, Crosby was living in the same Marin County town, Mill Valley, as Dead singer and guitarist Bob Weir, and in the early months of that year, he began dropping by the quirky, skylight-enhanced recording studio Weir had built above his garage.

The evening of February 20, 1975, illustrated the bonds—musical and otherwise—between Crosby and the Dead. In Weir's tight-quartered practice space, Crosby settled in with members of the band. At that point, the Dead were on sabbatical from live performances and in the early stages of working up material for their album *Blues for Allah.* Crosby broke the news that his girlfriend, Debbie Donovan, was nearly nine months pregnant (their daughter, Donovan, was born not long after), and Jerry Garcia asked Crosby if he was nervous. Before Crosby had a chance to answer, someone wondered if Garcia himself had been anxious when *his* children had been born, and he shot back, "*Oh* yeah."

Then came analyses of their favorite weed. Crosby's stash—stored under his house, as he and Nash's lawyer, Greg Fischbach, soon discovered—was still renowned as "pullover pot": if you were driving and took a hit, you'd be forced to pull over and stop to avoid an accident. Crosby's pot was also legendary for its absence of seeds; only rock stars seemed to be able to afford such a luxury.

"It's one of the best joints I've ever smoked in the last couple years," Crosby remarked about one of his preferred blends.

"I've still got some of that," Garcia said.

"Save it," Crosby urged. "That's for New Year's Eve and birthdays. You can't work on it. You can't drive on it."

Garcia agreed: "All you can do is go out into the zone."

Since they'd gathered in a working environment packed with amplifiers and instruments, it was inevitable they would start making music that was also out in the zone. Although he seemed to average only a few songs a year, Crosby nonetheless had two compositions he wanted the Dead to learn. He played one of them, "Low Down Payment," for Garcia, Weir, bassist Phil Lesh and pianist Keith Godchaux. Another song inspired by random emotions and events—Crosby awoke one morning to hear a lover in tears, an image that appeared in the lyric—"Low Down Payment" was typical of the way Crosby toyed with structure. It started in choppy, irregular 11/4 time, moved to 4/4, slowed down in tempo but remained in 4/4, then revved back to 11/4 for the finale. "We would play in odd time signatures," recalls the Dead's drummer, Mickey Hart, who was then on the verge of rejoining the band after several years on his own. "David was an easy jam. Unlike Stills, David didn't take command. He became part of what was going on, and he watched and listened. He had a different personality than Stephen."

When Crosby finished, Garcia nodded approvingly and said, "That's nice." Lesh and Godchaux joined in to work up an arrangement, and for over an hour, they tried making something of it. They also took numerous stabs at "Homeward Through the Haze," which Crosby had tried recording during the failed Crosby, Stills, Nash and Young sessions two months before.

During a break, Crosby mentioned working on what he called "live tapes."

"How's that coming?" he was asked.

"We did a lot of good shows," Crosby said. "I've heard enough for one side already."

Crosby was likely referring to a concert album culled from the previous summer's reunion tour. With a collection of new studio material scuttled after the Sausalito meltdown, a live record was the logical alternative, yet nothing about that idea would be simple, either. Roughly a third of the shows on the tour had been recorded, but Young balked at the idea of a tour memento. He'd written most of the new material they'd played on tour, and he feared that such a record would be top-heavy with his own tunes. "Listen, if they'd had new songs with the authority that their old songs had, we could've knocked off four or five of mine so that just the best two surfaced," Young later told *Mojo*. "That would have truly been CSNY. But it wasn't to be, so the record never came out." In the years that immediately followed, he would approve the release of only one song from the tour: "Pushed It Over the End," with overdubbed harmonies from Crosby and Nash, and even then, only on the B-side of a single released in Italy. If Young had wanted to downplay or even hide his participation in that reunion, he couldn't have picked a better way to do it.

The week Crosby gathered with the Dead to work out "Low Down Payment," the no. 2 song in the country was the Eagles' "Best of My Love," followed four spots below by America's "Lonely People." In the absence of new product from CSNY, devotees of SoCal soft rock had shifted their loyalty and record-buying dollars to their musical heirs. (David Geffen had even cobbled together an ersatz CSNY by recruiting former Buffalo Springfield and Poco leader Richie Furay, former Byrd and Manassas member Chris Hillman, and brooding singer-songwriter J. D. Souther for the Souther-Hillman-Furay Band; the group released two albums on Asylum before collapsing.) Rock itself seemed less urgent; it had been absorbed into mainstream culture. In *Billboard*, Bill Graham bemoaned the waning passion of rock fans. "I remember how kids waiting on line outside the Fillmores would tell me their whole week was empty until we opened up for another weekend," he mourned. "Now the kids outside my concerts tell me how much they enjoyed the last movie they saw or even how they got off on an evening of bowling or something."

As the magazine pointed out, rock and roll had gone from "an artistic lifeline for an entire generation to simply entertainment." A very different, more rhythmic, and less inhibited sound was also beginning to overtake the charts; that week, the Landmark Hotel in Las Vegas became the first major resort to open a disco. Not coincidentally, the *New York Times* reported that cocaine, while hardly new to the culture, had now become "the most fashionable drug in the United States," largely because it was cheaper than heroin. At the time, it was also seen as a nonaddictive sexual stimulant.

That spring, the Vietnam War, which had fueled some of the group's strongest political statements, was sputtering to a close. The city of Saigon fell, accompanied by the sight of Americans and South Vietnamese clambering aboard helicopters to escape the collapse of the country. On April 11, the US government announced it would be closing its embassy in Cambodia amid what it called "a seriously deteriorating military situation." Back home, Nixon was out of office, and a number of the former president's men had been indicted or convicted of various charges stemming from the Watergate scandal. A lawyer who had prepared Nixon's tax returns had also been indicted, on three counts of conspiracy to commit tax fraud. Gerald Ford, the new president, was an inoffensive placeholder who didn't inspire much of anything, including hatred and protests. He was a complacent commander in chief for a newly complacent time.

Crosby, Stills, Nash and Young, now men without a cultural context, again scattered in the wake of their failed Record Plant work. Early in 1975, *Billboard* reported that Young was ensconced at a studio in Toronto, working on overdubs for a new album—probably *Homegrown*, a collection of sober, reflective acoustic songs that would be the follow-up to *Harvest* that his fans had patiently been awaiting. Stills, eager to resume his own career, decided the time had come to sever his ties with Atlantic and Ahmet Ertegun. Like Crosby and Nash, he felt the label had sabotaged his records, by way of minimal promotion, in hopes that low sales would spur them all into reuniting. "I kinda felt like, 'Get the idiot back with those other three idiots. Why don't we let a couple of his records die and then he'll get the message?'" he told writer Barbara Charone that year. *Rolling Stone* reported that Stills was also irked that Ertegun hadn't attended his wedding (despite the fact that he had later thrown a party for the newlyweds), although Stills' manager, Michael John Bowen, denied that story.

Timing was on Stills' side. Columbia Records was eager to crack the lucrative Laurel Canyon market. Most of the community's biggest acts were signed to Geffen's Elektra/Asylum label or some other Warner-affiliated label. Michael Tannen, Stills' lawyer, brought a demo tape of Stills' new material to Bruce Lundvall, the head of Columbia. Impressed with what he heard, Lundvall offered a multi-album deal before he'd even met Stills. With the paperwork underway, Lundvall announced he wanted to finally shake hands with his new signing, who was recording at Criteria in Miami.

Tannen was alarmed. Tales of rock-star excess were making their way back to him, and Tannen was worried that if Lundvall and his team saw Stills in his current condition, the company could conceivably bail on the offer. With Lundvall and his crew already aboard a plane to Miami, Tannen and Bowen leapt into action, swiftly relocating Stills to the legendary Fame studio in Muscle Shoals, Alabama. When Lundvall arrived at Criteria, he and his team were told they'd *just* missed Stills, leading them to board yet another plane to Muscle Shoals. By the time they arrived there, Stills had again been transplanted, this time to San Francisco. At that point, the Columbia team gave up. "Eventually they just said, 'Fuck it,'" says Tannen, "and signed the contract." Tannen wasn't happy with the way the deal had gone down, but it was better than the alternative. (As a thank-you gesture, Bowen and Stills dropped a high-priced vase off at Tannen's office, which he would still have more than forty years later.)

On the other side of the country, Nash was coping with more of the encroaching darkness he had felt the previous year; the sinister side of the culture they had wrought was now staring him in the face. A delusional female fan who claimed she was related to Nash—she would sign her letters "sister of Willy Nash," after his nickname—materialized outside his home, sitting on a park bench across the street. It was later discovered that she had used cut-up parts of his album covers to construct an altar to him.

One day when Nash wasn't home, his friend Joel Bernstein, who lived next door, was looking after the place and heard a knock at the front door. There stood a policeman, the woman at his side, asking if her story about being a Nash family member was true. Before Bernstein had a chance to explain that she was likely deluded, the woman slipped past Bernstein, ran upstairs and locked herself in Nash's bedroom on the third floor. Bernstein had to climb up on the roof and enter the room through the window; he grabbed her and somehow dragged her out of the house. The woman probably didn't notice the hole in the wall opposite that same window in Nash's room. The damage had been inflicted a year or so earlier, when a man with a .350 Magnum had fired two blasts into the house. In another incident, Crosby, who had been staying in the house while his Mill Valley home was under renovation, had seen someone trying to steal the hubcaps off the Mercedes he'd parked outside;

he had let off a few shots in the air to chase away the thief. Everyone assumed that the person who fired into Nash's house was that same man who had tried to steal the hubcaps and that he was now seeking revenge, even if he had no idea that rock stars were living there.

By then, the Crosby, Stills, Nash and Young scene had already begun wearing on Calli Cerami, Nash's girlfriend since 1973. "When I first joined this group of guys, I thought they were all pretty cool," she says. "But then, slowly, everybody got crazier and crazier." Before long, Nash and Cerami's relationship petered out in what she calls "sort of a mutual agreement." As when he and Mitchell broke up, Nash wasn't alone for long. Lunching at a Hollywood pharmacy-cum-hangout called Schwab's, he was captivated by Susan Sennett, a twenty-three-year-old blonde actress who'd starred in Pepsi commercials and on TV (including a role as one of the daughters in the Nelson family TV reboot *Ozzie's Girls*). Sennett would soon be Nash's latest flame.

Before their breakup, Nash and Cerami experienced another, more ominous shock. Just before Valentine's Day in 1975, they were in Hawaii in an attempt to rescue their relationship when the disturbing news arrived: Amy Gossage, Nash's partner before Cerami, was dead. Described as a "sophisticated waif" with "the winsome look of a choir boy," Gossage embodied the free-spirit San Francisco lifestyle. But her brother had been traumatized by their father's death and, starting in high school, had become a serious drug user. That day in February, he had visited Amy in her North Beach apartment, and he later told police he'd found her body in a pool of blood; she had been stabbed and bludgeoned. A half-finished clay bust sat nearby (she was studying art). Amy was nineteen. In short order, police arrested her brother on murder charges. During his trial, it came out that the two siblings had had a heated argument over money—$5,000—connected to their late mother's estate. Her brother would claim his sister had lunged at him with a hammer and scissors, and that he had "overreacted" in order to disarm her. (Amy's friends doubted she would have taken such action.) Convicted of voluntary manslaughter, her brother was sentenced to fifteen years in prison, although he would eventually serve only three and later attend college and law school.

Gossage's brutal murder was devastating for Nash. "It really affected him in a terrible way," says Cerami. "He did care for her. Even thinking about it made you depressed." The enlightened, drug-enhanced world they had hoped to usher in with the '60s clearly now had a darker, more violent side.

IN THE AFTERMATH of the post-tour collapse, Crosby and Nash again gravitated toward each other. Their voices—Nash's clarinet-high reediness and Crosby's comparatively lower timbre—still made for a natural blend, and their approaches to work augmented each other as well. "Graham was the hardest working and David was lazier," says Leslie Morris, the former Geffen-Roberts assistant who, in late 1974, took on the challenge of managing Crosby and Nash after they parted ways with Geffen and Roberts. Crosby and Nash were ready to move on from the turbulent Stills, the noncommittal Young, and the issues that engulfed them: "We felt," Crosby says, "like we didn't want to be in their movie anymore." Jerry Rubenstein, a former Geffen-Roberts accountant who was now the newly appointed president of ABC Records, offered Crosby and Nash a sizable advance to leave Ertegun and Atlantic. When Crosby and Nash's lawyer, Greg Fischbach, called Ertegun to discuss a release, Ertegun hung up on him. But he called back several days later to finalize the arrangement, and Crosby and Nash became free men.

By the dawn of 1975, the two had a new label and nearly two albums' worth of substantial material. Crosby had "Carry Me" and "Homeward Through the Haze" from the aborted group album, along with "Low Down Payment." Continuing his tradition of veiled swipes in song at his bandmates, Nash had written the embittered "Take the Money and Run" about the previous summer's tour and the cash that had flowed in and out of its coffers. In his "Cowboy of Dreams," the friend with a home and a barn was Young. In his first draft of the song, Nash had written that he was "tired of the heartache and scenes" around Young, but when Larry "L.A." Johnson, a filmmaker who had worked with them—and who would go on to work with Young extensively in the years to come—heard the song, he told him, "You're not tired of Neil. You're *scared.*" Nash promptly changed "tired" to Johnson's word choice. Nash also finally completed "Wind on the Water," a paean to endangered whales he had started on his 1970 sailing trip with Crosby. The song was partly about Crosby. "David had spent a few years having the press not saying very nice things about him—throwing harpoons—so there's a lot of Crosby in that first verse," Nash says. "Nothing's just about the whales."

Nor was Crosby averse to portraying his bandmates in song occasionally. Composed the year before, "King of the Mountain," its theatrical melody enhanced by Craig Doerge's piano, painted a portrait of a lonely, solitary figure in a stadium—which, unstated, was Stills. "Nash and I were watching Stills go down the tubes and thinking 'Man, he's losing his marbles,'" says Crosby. "I was certainly going down the tubes myself, but it's easier to look at someone else than yourself." For reasons no one quite recalls, Crosby withheld the song from the new album, however; during this period, he only performed it in concert with Nash.

When the duo began recording in Los Angeles, and at Nash's home studio in San Francisco, the contrast with the last few Crosby, Stills, Nash and Young studio attempts was palpable. They recruited the same core group that had backed them on *Graham Nash/David Crosby*—Danny Kortchmar on guitar, Doerge on keyboards, Leland Sklar on bass, and Kunkel on drums, along with Nash's preferred bassist, Tim Drummond, and multi-instrumentalist string wizard (and Jackson Browne musical sidekick) David Lindley. With Crosby and Nash holed up at the Chateau Marmont during the LA sessions—possibly in one of the same bungalows where John Belushi would overdose a few years later—the finished takes rolled out effortlessly. Crosby's "Bittersweet," an elliptical meditation on being torn between shadows and light, was written and recorded in one session, a feat that would have been unimaginable with the full group. "It was night and day," says roadie Glenn Goodwin. "They were doing four or five tracks a day. It was *crazy*." With the aid of the studio pros, the two Crosby songs that hadn't been successfully put on tape by Crosby, Stills, Nash and Young sprang to life. "Carry Me" soared on intertwined guitar parts and harmonies, and "Homeward Through the Haze" was firmer than the group version, benefiting from a smidgen of harmony on the chorus from another friend, Carole King. As Crosby told Cameron Crowe in *Rolling Stone*, once the album was finished, "That's not like spending three bittersweet weeks in a studio and coming up with nothing on the tapes. The contrast is stark, to say the least. You talk about your black and white, man. It was glaring there."

Released in the fall of that year, *Wind on the Water* reflected its effortless creation: it was the most precision-tooled and forceful piece of music either man had made. The songs were enhanced by deft and understated touches: Lindley's doleful dobro on "Naked in the Rain," Doerge's country piano on "Cowboy of Dreams," and dueling solos between Kortchmar and Lindley during the finale of "Love Work Out," a ferocious (for them) stomper. The rockers, including "Take the Money and Run," had a clean, spare fluidity, while the dreamier songs, such as "Bittersweet," never drifted into a blur. Crosby's "Critical Mass," a dense, wordless vocal fugue he had recorded years earlier, now had newly added Nash harmonies. It served as a prelude to Nash's whale song, "Wind on the Water," which felt downright cinematic; the song even started with whale sounds.

Wind on the Water took everyone by surprise. *Rolling Stone* praised it as showing Crosby and Nash "at the height of their musical powers," calling it "their best studio work since *Déjà vu.*" Backstage at one of their shows, a Dallas DJ admitted to Crowe that he'd always considered Crosby and Nash the "George and Ringo" of the band, but added, "Guess I was wrong."

Onstage, too, Crosby and Nash were experiencing a rebirth. They hired most of the musicians who had played on the album to tour with them, renaming them the Mighty Jitters, both as a play on James Brown's Mighty Flames and as a none-too-subtle reference to cocaine. The players were costly, but they were worth the expense. Before each show, no matter the size of the venue or the crowd, Nash would say to Kortchmar, "Let's make history," an attitude that carried into the performances. When those musicians were backing James Taylor, Carole King or Jackson Browne, they provided tasteful, unobtrusive accompaniment, almost as if not to rattle the featured acts. Crosby and Nash weren't as concerned. "I can always remember Crosby saying 'Turn it up!'" says Kortchmar. "He was the first person to *ever* tell me that." Kortchmar, on guitar, and Lindley, on lap slide, would trade scalding solos (Lindley, in particular, would tear it up on "Fieldworker"), and the elongated, solo-heavy jams of "Déjà vu" would open with Kunkel dropping coins onto his snare drum for an added twilight-zone effect. "While they are not as spectacular on stage as Mr. Stills, nor as enigmatic, and therefore intriguing, as Mr. Young," wrote the *New York Times'* John Rockwell of one of those performances, "they have staying power."

Some things, of course, would never change. In the midst of a post-show interview, it was suggested by a reporter that Crosby ask Nash a question of his own.

Crosby didn't hesitate. "What do you think of the girl in the purple top all the way over to the left?"

Nash didn't pause: "I've got to admit that my main distraction was over to your stage right and through the trees. There was a lady lying down there who kept brushing her hair."

STILLS' TEAM WASN'T particularly devastated in the wake of CSNY's implosion; some of them saw the larger group as a distraction, and Stills himself was eager to move on and return to his familiar and comfortable role as boss. While Crosby and Nash were making *Wind on the Water*, Stills was cobbling together his first Columbia album. The working title was *As I Come of Age*; eventually, it was retitled *Stills*. Consisting of recordings made at various locales over the previous few years, the album addressed his struggles with fame and the seeming tranquility he now felt as a married man with a child ("My Favorite Changes"), his feeling of betrayal by unnamed friends ("Cold Cold World"), and a sense of feeling lost in general ("In the Way"). "To Mama from Christopher and the Old Man" was a bouncy ode to fatherhood; his son with Sanson had been born the previous year. The mood was that of a seemingly humbled man taking stock of his checkered past and promising future.

Like Crosby and Nash's *Wind on the Water*, *Stills*, released in June 1975, included more fully realized, more carefully produced versions of songs that could have been part of the never-completed Crosby, Stills, Nash and Young album. In "First Things First," he cautioned himself, to the accompaniment of a chugging Latin groove, about living too much in the past (the song also used Crosby and Nash harmonies recorded the year before). The sensual "My Angel" had a growling vocal that almost seemed like a nod to R&B love men like Barry White, and the stark, brooding piano ballad "Myth of Sisyphus" felt more apt for a solo than a group record. Thanks to engineer Bill Halverson, "As I Come of Age," Stills' litany of mistakes and regrets that he cut with Ringo Starr in 1970, finally escaped the vault: after Stills had spent years trying and failing to play the just-right guitar solo in its midsection, Halverson asked Donnie Dacus, who was also working with Halverson on another project, to add the part. Upon hearing it, Stills initially thought it was something he himself had played.

On the cover of *Stills*, in a photograph Joel Bernstein had taken during the group rehearsals at Young's ranch the year before, Stills appeared husky and hardened. On the back cover, in slippers and slacks, playing guitars on a patio with Dacus, he was the picture of contented fatherhood. Those contrasting images played out on the album as well. With their emphasis on suave keyboards and smothering harmonies, many of the songs had a maturity and sophistication not heard in Stills' earlier work, with few hints of the folk rock of the Springfield or his work with Nash, Crosby and Young. Sometimes, as in the gritty "Shuffle Just as Bad," the change-up worked. But some of the album's overly pillow-soft arrangements—as well as the double-tracking of Stills' vocals, which undercut the direct emotions in the songs—stifled the bite and tension. "Turn Back the Pages," a galloping rocker co-written with Dacus that became the album's first single, wasn't as brisk as it should have been.

Eager to please Columbia, Stills worked at being accommodating. He talked to reporters and even politely signed an autograph for fans who approached him while he was being interviewed during a meal. "I ain't the asshole everybody wants to make me out as," he told Barbara Charone in *Creem*, adding, "Basically CSNY were very sanctimonious. There was something about the vibe that bunch put out that was annoyingly sanctimonious, and I was a part of it, and yes, I'm equally guilty." Stills told another journalist that he felt a bit guilty about promulgating the image of drugs in the culture, saying, "I'm not going to be a hypocrite and defend anything, but I feel partly responsible and it kind of makes me feel a little ashamed."

Stills sold only modestly, and pop radio never embraced "Turn Back the Pages," but Stills toured with a large band that included Dacus along with singer, songwriter and former Flying Burrito Brother Rick Roberts. They were able to replicate, to some degree, the Crosby and Nash harmonies during electric band versions of "Suite: Judy Blue Eyes." The acoustic segments included full-throated versions of "Find the Cost of

Freedom" and a new piece, "Treetop Flyer," about a drug-smuggling pilot, that may have been based on a real acquaintance. Played with an acoustic slide guitar, the song had a sexy menace. But the shows didn't always sell out, and during one at the Hollywood Bowl, the audience screamed and talked so much during his acoustic segment that even the trade magazine *Cashbox* felt the need to weigh in: "While smoking grass at concerts has become a fact of life, poor manners are, in our opinion, a far worse offense." When Stills grabbed a swim at a hotel in the Berkshires before a show, a teenager in a Neil Young T-shirt sat by the side of the pool and cracked, "Stephen, why are you such an asshole?" Stills ignored him and continued on his way.

For all the maturity in his new material, Stills nonetheless seemed a little lost. His tour bus was dubbed "The Pleasure Dome," and he half-joked in one interview that he was a member of the "heathen defense league." Adhering to his military thinking, bandmates would refer to him as "Sarge." Young's buddy James Mazzeo was recruited as the tour manager; Stills even asked him to locate a motorhome just like the one Young had used the year before. But by the end of the tour, Mazzeo was so repelled by the atmosphere that he declined a free post-tour vacation to Hawaii with Stills and the crew. Mazzeo lied and said Young needed him back. "But," he says, "I just wanted to get the fuck out of there."

THE MOTORHOME WASN'T Stills' only link with Young. On *Stills*, he offered up a cover of Young's "New Mama" and declared he would now include a Young song on each of his records. Yet the real rapprochement between the two began when Young, while recovering from throat surgery, materialized onstage during several Stills shows in California that summer and fall of 1975. By the last one, at the University of California, Los Angeles' Pauley Pavilion, Stills shouted, "The spirit of the Buffalo Springfield is back!" Talking with the *Los Angeles Times* after Young's first appearance with him, at the Berkeley Greek Theatre in July, Stills admitted that a reunion of Crosby, Stills, Nash and Young probably wouldn't happen: "There is no real financial incentive for us to tour because we didn't make that much money on the last tour," he candidly explained. But he also let it out that he and Young had spent a weekend hanging out together and had talked about making an album and touring. All they needed, he said, was a rhythm section.

Of all the change-partner pairings they'd attempted over nearly a decade, a Stills and Young project was the one that had never seemed possible, given their competitive sides. But now it was, and according to a source in the Stills camp, the idea began with Young's management, which made a certain amount of financial sense. (The eventual album would also wind up on Young's label, Reprise, not Stills'.) After *Harvest*, Young had abandoned accessibility for albums like *Time Fades Away* and *On the Beach*. The records were roughhewn, scalding, often far from easy listening—and some of the most penetrating work of his life. Yet none had replicated the commercial success of *Harvest* and "Heart of Gold." On tour with the *Tonight's the Night* band (the Santa Monica Flyers) in Europe in 1973, band members recalled seeing Roberts huddled with Young in the back of a tour bus, berating Young for sticking with a project that was increasingly turning off ticket buyers.

By 1975, Young was emerging from a period of personal turmoil that included his final breakup with Snodgress. "I was pretty out there," he told biographer Jimmy McDonough. "Kinda lost." Moving out of his ranch and down to Malibu, which was now home to many wealthy superstar rockers, including Bob Dylan and members of the Band, Young finished *Homegrown*, the album he'd started right before the failed 1974 CSNY sessions. Here at last was the sequel to *Harvest*—until friends like the Band's Rick Danko heard the *Tonight's the Night* tapes at a party at Young's home and convinced him to release those recordings instead. As stark and intense as that record was, the public found it another head-scratcher.

By early 1975, Young had fully regrouped with Crazy Horse, thanks to the addition of guitarist Frank "Poncho" Sampedro to take over for the late Danny Whitten, and recorded a new album with them. As if blowing away the ennui of the past few years, *Zuma* was clear and lucid. (In publicity photos with Crazy Horse, Young was even grinning.) The songs emanated from different parts of his life: they included "Don't Cry No Tears," from his early Squires days, and "Pardon My Heart," from the previous year's quartet revival (but without Crosby, Stills or Nash on the track). "Cortez the Killer" evoked epic Crazy Horse jams like "Down by the River," but with even more mystical leanings. As with the previous Stills and Crosby-Nash records, *Zuma* also rescued a song from the 1974 tour rehearsals: "Through My Sails," the closing track, was a fragile lullaby of a song, with harmonies wafting in like a summer breeze. It was yet another tease for a group album that would never be.

Even though it was more straightforward rock than *Tonight's the Night, Zuma* peaked on *Billboard* at the same spot as that album, no. 25. Young didn't care, but others surely did, and the financial prospects for a first-ever Stills and Young album couldn't be denied. Artistically, each man knew what he could bring to the other: Stills' tendency to incessantly work over songs and arrangements could make Young's songs more radio-friendly, and Young's raw energy could temper Stills' perfectionism. Another, more emotional reason was also in play: Young rightly sensed that his old comrade was struggling creatively and could use a boost.

The two convened in Miami in January 1976, a mere two months after Young had joined Stills and his band onstage in Los Angeles. The record would be made on Stills' turf, at Criteria, and with his band: bassist George "Chocolate" Perry, drummer Joe Vitale, keyboardist Jerry Aiello and former Manassas percussionist Joe Lala. For over a month, the musicians took a crack at songs by both men. Stills and Young had first played "Long May You Run" onstage together during the 1974 tour; now they cut a warm band version of it. They worked up Young's "Traces," also from that tour, and Young brought in sunbaked ballads like "Midnight on the Bay." With producer Tom Dowd and engineer Don Gehman overseeing the sessions, they also tried, but didn't finish, Stills songs such as "One Way Ride" and "Treetop Flyer."

Perry, a twenty-three-year-old native Floridian, was familiar with the setting: starting in his teen years, he'd played on records by Betty Wright, Gwen McCrae and other artists on the scrappy R&B and disco label T.K. Records, which was also home to KC and the Sunshine Band. (Perry's nickname, "Chocolate," was derived not from his African American heritage but from his love of candy bars.) Yet the Miami sessions were his first taste of the Crosby, Stills, Nash and Young dynamic. In their drive for the ideal take, he sensed a similarity between Stills and Young. "Neil was exactly like Stephen," he says. "He wanted his songs to be *this* way, period, and they had to have a certain groove and feel. We'd be finished and he'd say, 'I don't like it—let's go back and do it again.' We did 'Midnight on the Bay' four or five times."

Yet, as much as they tried, the two leaders' oil-and-water worlds refused to mix. Young rented and lived on a funky boat docked in a nearby harbor. "How cool was that?" says Guillermo Giachetti, who was still a member of Stills' crew. "Instead of a hotel, he stayed on this boat. Stephen was different; he wanted the pool and the big house and convertibles. Two different lifestyles." Meanwhile, Stills' penchant for working until dawn—or past it—was anathema to Young. "You didn't see too much of them at the same time in the studio," says Perry. "When Neil was doing his stuff, we'd be in the studio with him. When Stephen was doing his stuff, we were in the studio with *him*. Most of the time, they weren't together."

In early April 1976, Young found himself back in the Bay Area, returning home after a series of Crazy Horse shows in Japan. One day he unexpectedly stopped into Nash's house in San Francisco. Nash and Crosby had barely spoken with Stills over the past year, but Nash and Young retained a connection. After the last show of the group reunion tour in 1974, Young and Nash, along with Cerami, Mazzeo, Joel Bernstein, Leslie Morris and Young's friend "Ranger Dave" Cline, had traveled to Amsterdam for a post-tour vacation (Young had driven there in a Rolls Royce he had bought in England). "I think we needed that, because of the craziness of that tour," says Cerami. During the getaway, Nash and Young bonded more than they ever had before.

Now, as they relaxed in Nash's basement studio, Young told Nash that he and Stills had been recording together and he had a tape of some of those songs. "You're standing in my studio," Nash replied. "Where's the cassette?" Young promptly played three or four songs he and Stills had cut in Miami. To Nash, the reason for Young's visit was clear. "Neil may have thought two things," Nash said. "That David and I would sound great on these songs. And maybe it would help him with his relationship with Stephen." Young wanted to know if he and Crosby were willing to come down to Miami, where he and Stills were recording, and take another shot at a group album.

Nash would have had good reason to hesitate about diving back into those choppy seas. With *Wind on the Water*, he and Crosby had finally found their outside-the-mothership voice. Promoting the album in *Rolling Stone*, Nash told Cameron Crowe, referring to the quartet's future, "We still might make another album one day, but now is not the time." *Wind on the Water* had peaked at no. 6 on the pop album chart—two spots lower than the high-water mark of *Graham Nash/David Crosby*, but nonetheless an impressive achievement, given the changes in pop during those three years. Its sales easily bested those of *Stills* and *Tonight's the Night.* The seeming cast-offs of the group were now the stars; maybe they didn't need Stills or Young after all.

As harmony singers, Crosby and Nash were also being validated in the world outside the group. Anyone listening to AM or FM radio during 1975 and 1976 would have heard their backup voices on records by Carole King, Art Garfunkel, Elton John and Jackson Browne. Their bond with James Taylor was particularly strong, and not simply because Taylor was not averse to his share of carousing at the time. One day in late 1974, journalist Robert Greenfield, a former associate editor in *Rolling Stone*'s London bureau and a casual friend of Crosby and Nash, was at Nash's home with his future wife when Crosby and Nash asked them to follow them down to Nash's basement studio. Excitedly, they cued up the tapes of two songs, "Mexico" and "Lighthouse," that they'd recorded with Taylor for his album *Gorilla*; their harmonies brightened the former and lent a sunset quality to the latter. "They were telling us they were going to go out with James, and it would be their next big ticket," says Greenfield. "They didn't say, 'He's going to replace Stephen.' But they think it's going to be Crosby, Nash and Taylor. The expectation was that they were going to be performing with him and they were jacked up about it." Nash confirms that story: "We absolutely thought about that. We'd sounded great together." But it was "just a fantasy," he says. Taylor was never informed of the idea.

Under the circumstances—a second wind few fully expected—Crosby and Nash were now taking control of their music and destiny in ways they hadn't before. Yet the lure of something magical, and lucrative, remained. Although they were deep into the recording of the follow-up to *Wind on the Water* when Young visited, Nash and Crosby soon packed their bags and stashes; they boarded flights to Florida the next morning. After several previous failed attempts, the next version of the great lost group album, the one they'd planned on calling *Human Highway*, was again in reach. Maybe the third attempt would be the charm.

JOE VITALE COULDN'T quite grasp what he was witnessing. Only a few months before, the scrappy twenty-seven-year-old drummer and multi-instrumentalist—who had been born in Ohio and was attending Kent State during the 1970 shootings—had been asked to join Stills' band after a stint with his college friend Joe Walsh (the former James Gang lead and future Eagles guitarist). With his *other* band seemingly history, Stills was determined to blast into a more raucous rock-and-roll life, and Vitale and Perry were along for the ride. "Stephen was like a battery on full," Perry recalls. "He didn't sleep very much. He was that kind of ambitious cat. He always felt like he had something to prove." When Stills, Vitale and Perry flew to Houston in January 1976 to join Bob Dylan and the Rolling Thunder Revue for a benefit for the imprisoned boxer Rubin "Hurricane" Carter, Stills' guitar was so loud during the sound check that Dylan commanded his bass player to ask him to turn down his amp for the show. The request was not honored.

But here Vitale was a few months later, on a mid-April morning in Miami, watching Crosby, Stills, Nash and Young all together. They had gathered in a studio with acoustic guitars and were playing a new Nash song, "Taken at All," that seemed to chronicle the band itself. The identity of people who'd "lost it on the highway" and were off in different directions couldn't have been more obvious. "I watched them do that song sitting around in a circle with a mic, singing and playing," Vitale recalls. "It was the foundation of what they do—the blend was perfect. It was a great thing to witness."

Over the next two weeks, Crosby and Nash added their voices to the already recorded Stills and Young songs. To make the record more of a group effort, they also tackled a few Crosby and Nash songs, including "Taken at All" and a wordless Crosby rouser called "Dancer" that dated back five or six years. Many mornings, Nash would meet Young for breakfast at the Mutiny at the Sailboat Bay Hotel, the infamous ground zero for the city's cocaine world. A semblance of normalcy, at least for them, settled over the project. Was it possible that this album, so long in the making, could be falling into place so fast and so efficiently? Was some version of *Human Highway* about to come to fruition?

Then one morning Young didn't show up for breakfast, and a hotel employee informed Nash that he'd left Miami. Young was on his way back to California.

Not for the first time, Nash was confused, but too many factors had been pulling the project apart before it was barely off the ground. Nash and Crosby had already informed Stills and Young that they needed to return to Los Angeles to complete their own album before finishing up the group project. Unbeknownst to them, Stills and Young had already mapped out a summer tour starting in July, which made it imperative to wrap up the album—whoever would appear on it—as soon as possible, so the release would coincide with the shows. "Neil came in with steam coming out of his ears," Stills told writer William Ruhlmann nearly fifteen years later, with Nash and Crosby in the room. Stills turned to Nash, "I got the impression that you two guys had a fight or something? You and Neil? Some kind of an argument or something." Nash agreed, noting that Young had probably been offended that he and Crosby were planning to depart in the middle of making a record. Nash rightly surmised that Young wouldn't have appreciated his and Crosby's lack of focus on a possible reunion record.

Crosby and Nash returned to California to resume work on their album. While they were there, Stills and Young made the friendship-crushing decision to revert to their original duo concept; as Nash learned during a call from Young, he and Crosby's voices were stripped off the songs. A few months later, Stills told writer Chris Charlesworth that he assumed Crosby and Nash would finish their record, and he and Young would finish their own. Either way, the Stills-Young backup players were called in to replace the Crosby and Nash harmonies. As Perry recalls, "I'd go home and come back and things would be different."

Young would voice some regret for the decision: "[Crosby and Nash] sang 'Midnight on the Bay' and it was great," he told writer Bill Flanagan a decade later. "It really was. I never should have erased that. But I thought I was doing the right thing at the time." Crosby and Nash were hardly in the mood for level-headed conversations. Both were taken aback by the decision, and Nash unleashed his anger in a hot-plate interview with *Crawdaddy*. "How many times can you keep going up and saying, 'Okay, I'll stand here while you hit me again, but just don't hit me as hard as you did last time!'" he vented. "It was dirty. I won't work with them again. I will not work with them again! Fuck 'em. They're not in it for the right reasons. They're in it for the bucks. I see Stephen's career going downhill and I see Neil's career going downhill, and I don't give a shit." (As Crosby notes, "Nash has a temper.") Even those in and around their universe who thought they'd seen it all were stunned. "I thought, 'This is not good,'" says Ken Weiss of Stills' Gold Hill publishing company. "Graham and David had every right to be upset. I thought, 'If CSNY didn't exist, it certainly won't exist now.'"

On May 8, Crosby, Nash and a few of the Mighty Jitters reconvened at a Hollywood studio to complete work on their own album, now called *Whistling Down the Wire* after a line in one of its songs. Nash's "Taken at All," rescued from the Miami reunion, took on a new mournfulness, as well as a more fleshed-out arrangement featuring Lindley's fiddle. Even more striking was "Mutiny." With its grunting guitar and bass parts, a screechy Kortchmar solo and an atypically yelping Nash vocal, the track, named after the Miami hotel where it all fell apart, was Nash's angriest song about his partners. It would be the testiest piece of music on their album.

STRUMMING THE OPENING CHORDS of the singer-songwriter legend Fred Neil's "Everybody's Talkin'," Young admonished the shrieking crowd at the Pine Knob Music Theatre in Clarkston, Michigan. "I just want to be able to hear myself, that's all," he said in a tone that tried not to sound irritated.

Even though their album remained unreleased, the newly named Stills-Young Band tour nonetheless had to begin as planned that night, June 23. The tour dates had been intended for Crazy Horse; now Stills and Young had commandeered the allotted concerts and rehearsed at Young's ranch. On paper, the set list amounted to any fan's wish list. There would be Buffalo Springfield songs like "Mr. Soul"; songs they'd played together during the 1970 Crosby, Stills, Nash and Young tour ("On the Way Home," "Southern Man"); highlights from their years apart ("Heart of Gold," "The Treasure [Take One]"); fresh material they were debuting (Young's intensely open-hearted song of devotion, "Like a Hurricane," making its stage debut); and songs from a duo album no one had yet heard. For the first time since 1968, the two of them would perform "For What It's Worth" together, Young reviving the haunted, harmonic single-note lick of the original recording.

The set also included a few songs from *Illegal Stills*, the record Stills had released that spring. Cut with most of his touring band, the album was more cohesive than *Stills*. Its inspired cover, designed by noted Columbia art director John Berg, displayed a bottle of moonshine emblazoned with Stills' face. Yet it was disconcerting to cue up a Stephen Stills album and, now and then, hear band member Donnie Dacus singing lead instead of his boss, which happened on pieces Dacus had composed. Dacus' songs ("Closer to You," "Midnight in Paris") were pleasant, middle-of-the-road pop, but hardly Stills' style. "Stephen had trouble writing," says Michael Tannen, Stills' lawyer. "There was a kid [Dacus] he was writing with and Stephen was leaning on him too much." (For a moment, Stills had considered renaming his band Stills-Dacus.) A bulldozer version of Young's "The Loner" stood out, and the Latin rocker "Buyin' Time" and the grinding "Circlin'" kicked up some dust. His affinity for military veterans emerged in "Soldier," the story of a wheelchair-bound vet set to a Latin shuffle. But *Illegal Stills* was another missed opportunity, a baffling vanilla wafer of a record.

As the first set of shows rolled along—coinciding with the national celebration of the country's two hundredth birthday, complete with "Bicentennial Minutes" on TV that reduced major historical events to dramatized sound bites—the makings of a memorable tour were alluringly within reach. Young led the band through the funky stomp of another new song, "Homegrown"; at various times, Stills' solo set would include gentle versions of "Helplessly Hoping," as well as the Springfield's "Four Days Gone," free of the gargling-whiskey voice that sometimes overtook him. Their guitar styles—Stills' coiled, Young's stinging—made for intermittently charged duels. They played before 17,300 concertgoers in Pittsburgh and 16,900 in Cincinnati, sizable crowds for musicians who hadn't had hit albums in recent years.

Yet, starting with ads that sometimes billed the ensemble as "The Neil Young–Stephen Stills Band," the Stills-Young Band trek was tainted from the start. For someone who valued control, Young must have felt frustrated. He was touring with Stills' band, not his own. In order to tighten up their performances, Stills insisted they stick with roughly the same set each night, but Young soon grew impatient with the format. (Stills would later admit the shows were a bit "static.") "[Young] got me in the dressing room before a gig and said, 'All right, man, you're holding back. I wanna see you get out there and hit it more,'" Stills told Charlesworth. One night, Stills berated Young's sound man, Tim Mulligan, in front of the crowd. And when Stills sometimes failed to remember a lyric or sang off-mic, the band was forced to compensate on a stanza's notice. "When he forgot a line, you knew to pick up when he started," Perry said. "Some nights, they would go sixteen bars, some twenty-four bars. I don't think Neil appreciated that." Between shows, Young flew back to Florida to continue work on the still-uncompleted Stills-Young Band album, which the tour had been intended to promote.

The July 17 issue of *Billboard* featured a full-page ad for *Illegal Stills*, touting Stills' "history-making tour with Neil Young that will take his powerful music all over the country for more than three months." Three days later, on the bus after a show in Columbia, South Carolina, Young decided he'd had enough and instructed his driver to head in another direction. (Stills was traveling with his band on one bus, Young with his team on another.) When the Stills band buses rolled into Atlanta and arrived at the appointed hotel the next morning, each musician was given a room key and a telegram from Young. Stills' read, "Dear Stephen, Funny how some things that start spontaneously end that way. Eat a peach, Neil" (a reference to their arrival in the Peach State). Even though about twenty shows remained on their itinerary, the Stills-Young Band experiment was shut down. Perry was stunned. "I had never been on a tour that just quit in the middle," he marvels. "When you're a side musician, you have your forecast of expected income. You're thinking about what you're going to do with the money when the tour is over. And the tour is over faster than you thought. I was making $250 a night. To lose that kind of money in one flash was shocking."

Young announced that he was coping with a recurrence of a throat issue that had led to surgery the previous year. But not everyone accepted that explanation. The road work and time with Stills had ceased to be enjoyable for him, and per his usual response, he was gone when the fun ended. Stills holed up in his hotel room, while his manager, Michael John

Bowen, spoke with each of the band members and arranged for their return trips home. When the musicians finally saw Stills, he wasn't in much of a mood to talk. "Stephen was heartbroken," Vitale says. "There were going to be lawsuits and all sorts of shit. He was almost in tears. It was very hurtful to him." Reached by phone at a hotel bar, Stills told Cameron Crowe—who was chronicling the tour for *Rolling Stone* but didn't yet know Young had bailed—"I have no answers for you. I have no future." Valiantly, Stills made up for a few of the nixed shows. On August 24, he played what had been planned as a duo performance at the Inglewood Forum in Los Angeles, but the *Los Angeles Times* called it a "disappointing substitute" for a Stills-Young show. That night, Stills sang "Long May You Run," a farewell to the tour, and to the album that had collapsed the month before.

A few weeks after that show, the Stills-Young Band album, *Long May You Run*, finally arrived. Disappointingly, it didn't recapture the feel of Buffalo Springfield as much as Stills had hoped it would. As in the recording sessions, the two men alternated songs and lead vocals on the album, but it still felt strangely lopsided. Most of Young's contributions—the trifling "Ocean Girl," the lulling "Midnight on the Bay," the quasi-country shuffle "Let It Shine"—were as casual as beachwear and about as weighty. (Stills' squawking lead guitar on "Ocean Girl" was lively, though.) Stills' songs, such as the underwater-dive tale "Black Coral" and the pained "12/8 Blues (All the Same)," with his grunting, sputtering solo, had a toughened intensity. "Fontainebleau," Young's swipe at that upscale Miami hotel, spewed vitriol and included some of his most furious guitar parts, and the title song, a tribute to Young's legendary hearse, featured Stills' sandpaper harmony and Aiello's calming organ. But mirroring the way it was made, the album sounded like the work of two different people. Only in the fading moments of the last song, the jazzy "Guardian Angel," did Stills and Young trade guitar parts—a thrilling moment that lasted all of twenty seconds.

Whether it was the bad karma around the tour or the uneven music, an album that should have been historic was greeted with indifference, only reaching no. 26 on *Billboard.* The reviews amounted to a collective pile of shrugs. Reflecting the media consensus that Young was now overtaking Stills in the quality of his work, in spite of the lightness of some of Young's contributions, *Crawdaddy* headlined its review "Stills Water Drowns Young."

Meanwhile, after a strong start of their own, Crosby and Nash were beginning to hit a rough patch. They parted ways with Leslie Morris, their manager of barely a year and a half. "You can't manage David," she says. "He didn't like me as his manager and I didn't like *being* his manager." *Whistling Down the Wire*, their follow-up to *Wind on the Water*, was rushed out in early summer. A blend of new material, including "Mutiny," and leftovers from *Wind on the Water*, it was a markedly more low-key and complacent affair. The record had much to recommend it: the duo's versions of "Time After Time" and "Taken at All" made the case that they could handle those songs just fine without Stills and Young, and Crosby and Nash's harmonies never felt more tender. But other songs felt slight, and the absence of the meaty arrangements of *Wind on the Water* didn't help. "Spotlight" captured the way their fans identified with them, but it also demonstrated how they backed away from their fans. (A press release for the album kept up the hope for a reunion of the four band members, declaring, "CSNY have recorded several songs together in recent years which are as yet unreleased, but a new CSNY album is projected in the near future.") Crosby and Nash had a potential hit in "Out of the Darkness," an atypically commercial ballad—it would have worked well on a romantic-movie soundtrack—but they declined to edit it for radio play, dooming its chances. (It never got higher than no. 89 on the charts.) Ironically, the album peaked at exactly the same position as *Long May You Run.*

They were still rock stars, and they still lived that life as much as possible, as David Rensin, a Los Angeles–based writer who covered rock and roll, observed. ABC Records had hired Rensin to coordinate on-the-road interviews for Crosby and Nash during the summer of 1976. He found them largely amenable. Their continuing prestige was apparent when the tour rolled into Tanglewood in Massachusetts and Rose Kennedy could be seen sitting in the bleachers with some of the Kennedy grandchildren. After a show in Akron, Ohio, on August 22, Crosby and his crew were late for a flight out of O'Hare. Crosby, his girlfriend Nancy Brown, a roadie, and Rensin made a crazed dash for the airport, their stash coming along for the ride. Since they arrived with only minutes to spare, there was no time to officially return the vehicle, so it was ditched at curbside. "We thought, '*Someone* will see it's a rental car,'" Rensin recalls. "So we just left it there."

Although almost no one in the world acknowledged it at the time, a very different sound was making its presence known in pop. That spring came the release of *Ramones*, the first album by four dressed-down guys from New York who preferred their songs short, terse and rivet-gun-like. They sang about Nazis, sniffing glue, and beating on brats with baseball bats. *Ramones* only sold seven thousand copies that year. But combined with Patti Smith's *Horses* from the previous fall, as well as singles drifting over to the States by the Sex Pistols, England's most confrontational punk band, the new album showed that rock was about to make an abrupt turn toward a leaner, angrier and spunkier style. Albums like *Whistling Down the Wire* and *Long May You Run* suddenly felt fusty, self-satisfied or both.

When Crosby, Nash and the Mighty Jitters pulled into Holmdel, New Jersey, to play two shows at the Garden State Arts Center in August, they found themselves face to face with another member of rock's new guard. By chance, Bruce Springsteen's lighting director was friends with Crosby and Nash's tour manager, Glenn Goodwin. When he learned Crosby and Nash would be playing on Springsteen's home turf, the Springsteen employee had an idea: a softball game. Springsteen and his band and his crew had formed a softball team, the E Street Kings, and they challenged Crosby and Nash, who quickly assembled a team of their own. In another coy pharmaceutical reference, they dubbed themselves the San Francisco Hoovers.

On the appointed day, the teams assembled at an empty mid-Jersey high school field for the private, no-press-allowed event. The mood was jovial, complete with an outdoor cookout and plenty of beer. But as crew members like Goodwin had feared, the E Street Kings proved to be far more experienced players once the teams took to the dusty field for the game. Nash kept catching the ball with his right hand while wearing his mitt on his left. "They kicked our ass," Goodwin says. "David wasn't super athletic and I don't know if Graham had ever played baseball before. We said, 'Let's make him the pitcher,' but he didn't know what to do with a glove or how to throw. It was the funniest damn thing." When Springsteen briefly left for a few innings, the Crosby and Nash team scored a few runs. But when Springsteen returned and saw the scoreboard, he whipped the Kings back into shape, and his team won. Afterward, the players assembled for a friendly group shot, but in a way, the day was a symbolic passing of the torch.

THAT AUGUST, THE FOURSOME never seemed more entrenched in separate corners. Crosby and Nash, working with their own band, remained embittered about the aborted Miami sessions. "I suspect it was Stephen more than Neil," Crosby says. "But the whole process was insulting enough to us that we went back and said, 'Okay, that's it, we're done.'" Young was holed up in Malibu recording a slew of strong new songs, including the troubled self-portrait "Hitchhiker," the surrealistic "Pocahontas," and "Powderfinger," which, with its lyrics about a family fighting off an unnamed enemy, felt like a mythological folk tale. He was also still coping with his breakup with Carrie Snodgress. Nash remained so angry with Young over the Miami episode that, according to one source, he didn't allow "Pushed It Over the End" to be included on *Decade*, a three-LP retrospective that Young was preparing.

Once more, Stills seemed to be isolated from the others; to make things worse, his world was unraveling. Neither *Stills* nor *Illegal Stills* had been hits, and the modest sales of *Long May You Run* made for a trifecta of middling success. (To rub a certain amount of salt in the wounds, his former label, Atlantic, also released two Stills albums, a concert record and a compilation, which Tannen, Stills' lawyer, interpreted as the label's way to spite Stills for leaving.) Taken aback by the excesses of the American rock-and-roll world, Sanson filed for divorce from Stills in August. Stills moved out of their Colorado home and holed up in the penthouse of the Beverly Rodeo Hotel on Rodeo Drive. With promoters calling for his and Young's heads in light of the canceled shows, Stills was forced to embark on a solo tour. (Young, meanwhile, his voice apparently recovered, would soon begin an American tour with Crazy Horse.) "It's a question of finances," Stills told *BAM*, a magazine covering Bay Area music. The article said he sounded "somewhat distant and melancholy" while discussing the upcoming tour.

Yet just when the group had arrived at what felt like a hard-to-conquer impasse, another chance at a revival materialized. On August 12,

Crosby and Nash were scheduled to play the first of two shows at the Greek Theatre in Los Angeles. At Stills' hotel room, Weiss argued that his friend should attend to show his support. Given how close the venue was to the hotel, it would be more than noticeable if he *didn't* show up. As Weiss knew, the risks were enormous. If Stills ventured backstage, Crosby and Nash could easily ignore him or unload on him. Yet Weiss also sensed that the power had shifted: Crosby and Nash were in a positive place in their careers, and Stills was humbled. Stills hesitated, but eventually he relented.

Before Stills left for the Greek, Weiss reached out to John Hartmann, the former Geffen-Roberts manager, who, along with his partner Harlan Goodman, was now handling Crosby and Nash's career. Weiss, who wouldn't be attending the show himself, wanted to ensure that Stills would be allowed backstage without any issues. He received assurances, yet throughout the night he still regularly called his contacts at the show for updates. Meanwhile, Nash warned his team that, should they spot someone wearing a football jersey, they should keep him away. Nonetheless, Stills made his way back—after Joel Bernstein saw him standing by the side of the stage—and he, Crosby and Nash wound up huddling in a dressing room. As Weiss predicted, the issues that had driven them apart a mere three or four months before weren't brought up. "What were we going to do, especially if people knew Stephen was there and that we didn't invite him onstage?" Nash says. "We said, 'Let's just do the encore and we'll be fine if they see us together.' Of *course* we were pissed at him, but . . . showbiz. 'You're here and we're here.'"

Stills ended up joining them onstage for "Teach Your Children" to a rapturous response. In another conciliatory gesture, Nash, at the suggestion of his girlfriend Susan Sennett, invited Stills to his second home in the Los Angeles area, where they got drop-down drunk together. "All I'd heard was what a monster Stephen Stills was," Sennett (later Susan Nash) told Crosby, Stills and Nash biographer Dave Zimmer. "And when I met Stephen, here was this shy man who didn't seem too terrible." When Stills eventually returned to his hotel on Rodeo Drive, Weiss thought he seemed like a different person, as if a burden had been lifted from his shoulders.

As inconceivable as it would have seemed weeks before, plans for a Crosby, Stills and Nash album were now again in the air. From the moment preliminary work on the album began in Los Angeles in December, a new sense of productivity was in the air. Nash and Crosby dropped by a Stills session, and Nash brought along "Just a Song Before I Go," a wispy ballad inspired by a dealer's dare for him to write a song in the few hours before boarding a flight. With Christmas less than a week away, the three men, accompanied by the CSNY tour rhythm section from 1974, nailed the song in a few takes; Stills' lead guitar conjured smoky barrooms. "There was a different vibe," recalls Vitale, who played vibraphone on the track. "CSNY was a project, but CSN was a band." The smoothness of the session made them decide to forge ahead with an album, but pointedly, Young was not invited.

The next month, the three flew to Miami, where everything had fallen apart only eight months before. Taking a cue from his Manassas days, Stills suggested they rent and live in the same house for camaraderie. Naturally, the arrangements had to be just so. Charged with setting up the living quarters, Guillermo Giachetti found a Miami mansion and installed Nash upstairs, Crosby on the first floor, and Stills on the same floor as Crosby, yet on the other side of the house. Giachetti needed to ensure that each room had something special to offer so that no one felt they were getting the short end of the luxury stick. "The main requirement was not to bruise anyone's ego by getting them a funky room," he says. Dinners were arranged in the house, followed by studio time until dawn. On more than a few occasions, the three would bump into each other sneaking a donut out of the refrigerator in the middle of the night.

On their first day of work, January 19, 1977, Miami was hit with a fluke snowstorm, its first of the century, which left snowflakes clinging to palm trees. But nothing, not even freak weather, could stop their reunion. "Everyone came in every day on time," says Howard Albert, who would co-produce with the trio and his brother Ron. "It was more down to earth and controlled, more 'Let's make the best record we can.'"

After so many derelict group efforts, making the best record they could was paramount; the public was starting to move on. Early in his career, Glenn Frey of the Eagles had studied the mistakes some of his predecessors had made. Those precursors had included Crosby, Stills, Nash and Young, and the lessons he and bandmate Don Henley had learned about maintaining and controlling a band had paid off; it was now the Eagles, not their mentors, who were America's leading band. The release of their massively popular *Hotel California* album dramatically underscored that shift. The same month, Crosby, Stills and Nash recorded "Just a Song Before I Go." Their reputation and legacy were at stake.

With the band working in Miami, and with the Alberts on hand, the situation catered to Stills' need to feel unthreatened, which helped him to be productive. "Graham and David let Stephen do his thing," says Howard Albert. "He was the driving force. There were fewer power trips going on." Born of both necessity and maturity, a sense of cooperation took over. The backup musicians included key players from both Stills' band and the Jitters. The days of Stills playing most of the instruments were over, and each man would have final say on the finished version of his songs. As a result, the blowups of old were largely missing in action. "I didn't see any arguments or negative vibes," says George Perry, who played bass. "We were actually having fun. David would come in and say, 'Are you ready for my part yet?' or 'Check this out, it sounds great.' I didn't see confrontation." At last they nailed a version of Stills' "See the Changes," which Crosby, Stills, Nash and Young had attempted at Young's ranch nearly four years before. (The song had outlived the marriage that inspired it.) Leaving behind the drums and the congas of the version with Young, the new rendition featured only one guitar and three voices. What emerged was an older, wiser sequel of sorts to "Helplessly Hoping," with a concluding high note from Nash as a dramatic capper.

Hedonism was always only a few doors away. For all the sensuous pleasures he was experiencing, Crosby was still coping with Christine Hinton's death and a growing emptiness. Although Crosby remained with Debbie Donovan when their daughter Donovan was born in 1975, he continued his relationship with Brown, even paying for her rent in a house near his. All three knew of the arrangement. Donovan would end up leaving with the baby, and Brown moved in to take her place. Crosby's downcast mood stemming from Hinton's death poked out in songs he'd been writing the previous few years: the fame-questioning "Homeward

Through the Haze," the dazed and confused "Bittersweet," the self-lacerating "Foolish Man" (the latter from *Whistling Down the Wire*). "We didn't
have any instruction booklet so we were dealing all the time with how
to deal with fame, money and loss," Crosby says. "How to deal with life.
We externalized everything. It was a cathartic deal with us. We would
come up against a problem and write about it and try to work through it.
That's how we processed it." For the reunion, Crosby also brought "In My
Dreams," a direct expression of his snowballing isolation from the world
as his drug issues deepened; the reference to various "nearby" versions
of himself suggested that different parts of his personality weren't communicating with each other.

Crosby's growing void also began expressing itself in harder drugs.
During the time the album got underway, he learned he had a perforated
septum from snorting too much cocaine, which opened the door to a new
experience, freebasing the drug. In Miami, Crosby's immersion in his
new habit quickly made itself known: he'd often be holed up in his room
rather than at the beach, only emerging later in the day for dinner and
nighttime studio work. As *Crawdaddy* reported, Stills actually challenged
Crosby to a race one morning. At the appointed time, Stills was ready
to go, outside the home where they were staying, and tore off down the
street. Crosby stayed in bed, blowing off the challenge. "There was a lot
of wretched excess," Crosby says. "There was a lot of cocaine. But there
was some good music that happened. The songs made it work."

While the band was crafting the record, their managers were assessing their bargaining power in the business. Technically, the collective
group was still contracted to Atlantic. Speaking with a reporter that year,
Ertegun admitted he had allowed them to record for other labels on their
own—"with the understanding," he added, in pointedly terse language,
"that when they recorded together again, they would be with us." John
Hartmann, working with Stills' manager, Michael John Bowen, had other
ideas and wanted to make sure the reconvened trio landed the most
lucrative deal possible. Despite Stills' connections with Ertegun, Hartmann let it be known to Walter Yetnikoff, the boisterous new president
of Columbia, that the band would consider leaving Atlantic. That suggestion also played into the ongoing battle between Columbia and Atlantic's
sister label, Warner Brothers: Yetnikoff had lured James Taylor away

from Warner Brothers, and now Paul Simon, with whom Yetnikoff didn't remotely get along, was on the verge of leaving Columbia for Warner.

After flying to Miami to hear the finished tracks, Ertegun decreed that the album was "very powerful." Then, at Hartmann's invitation, Yetnikoff and other Columbia staffers jetted to the studio to hear portions of the record for themselves. They liked what they heard. On the ride back, Yetnikoff asked Hartmann what it would take to sign them. Hartmann knew Atlantic's original deal with the band—which called for sixty-nine cents an album in royalties—was outdated and no longer adequate. Once Atlantic heard that another party was interested, Ertegun gave in, awarding Crosby, Stills and Nash one of the most lucrative contracts of the time: a $1 million advance on each group album, and complete artistic and creative control (even over the cover art). The royalties would double if they sold over a million records; those figures would also increase if the list price of the records rose. Even better, that rate would apply to their back catalog on Atlantic. Knowing well the band's history, Ertegun questioned how many more records they would actually make together, but he nonetheless flew out to Los Angeles for the signing of the contract.

During the making of the album, the band celebrated in its own way, leaving for a nearly weeklong sailing trip to the Bahamas along with several of their employees. They went scuba diving and snorkeled, and Bernstein, along for the trip, snapped photos of them onboard the boat for an album cover. Given Crosby's vampire-shift hours, it was the first chance Bernstein had had to shoot them in daylight. To their employees, the mood was noticeably relaxed, even hopeful. "Obviously they must have had a good time with that album," Giachetti says. "They went off on that trip instead of flipping each other off."

As THE FIRST Crosby, Stills and Nash album in eight years was nearing completion, Ron Albert took a break. He strolled out into Criteria's parking lot to clear his head and stay awake—a regular part of his and his brother's method of working with Stills. This time, he glimpsed a shadow by the shrubs, "some guy not exactly dressed for a prom, pissing in the bushes." When the man turned around, it turned out to be, of all people, Young. They invited him inside to listen to his erstwhile bandmates' new album.

David Crosby, early '60s. (Photo by Michael Ochs Archives/Getty Images)

Graham Nash during the early Hollies days, 1964. (Photo by
Derek Preston/Paul Popper/Popperfoto/Getty Images)

The Hollies, 1966: Bernie Calvert, Nash, Tony Hicks, Allan Clarke and Bobby Elliott. (Photo by Barry Peake/REX Shutterstock)

The Byrds arrive in London, 1967: Crosby, Chris Hillman, Michael Clarke and Roger McGuinn. (Photo © REX/Shutterstock)

Buffalo Springfield, 1967: (top row) Stephen Stills, Neil Young and Jim Fielder (filling in for Bruce Palmer); (bottom row) Dewey Martin and Richie Furay. (Photo by GAB Archive/Redferns Collection)

Neil Young at the Buffalo Springfield group house, Malibu, California, October 1967. (Photo by Michael Ochs Archives/Getty Images)

Outtake from the famous "couch album" photo shoot. (Photo by Henry Diltz/
Corbis via Getty Images)

Judy Collins and Stills,
San Francisco, 1968.

(Photo by Robert Altman/
Michael Ochs Archives/
Getty Images)

Mitchell and Nash arrive at
Heathrow Airport, 1969.

(Photo by WATFORD/
Mirrorpix/Mirrorpix via Getty
Images)

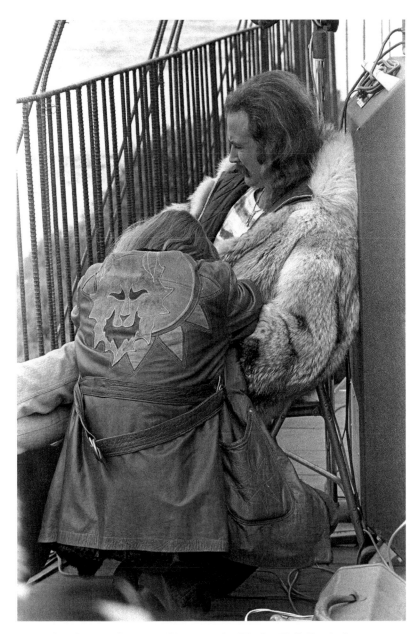

David Crosby and Christine Hinton at the Big Sur Folk Festival,
September 1969, a few weeks before her death. (Photo by Robert Altman/
Michael Ochs Archives/Getty Images)

John Sebastian, Stills, Nash, Joni Mitchell and Crosby at the Big Sur Folk Festival, September 1969. (Photo by Robert Altman/Michael Ochs Archives/Getty Images)

The group electric set at the Fillmore East, New York, June 1970. (Photo © Amalie R. Rothschild)

Young and Stills confer during the mammoth CSNY 1974 summer tour. (Photo by
New York Daily News Archive/Getty Images)

Crosby, Nash and Stills at the outdoor "No Nukes" rally in Battery Park, New York, during the week of the all-star Madison Square Garden MUSE concerts, September 1979. (Photo by Ebet Roberts/Getty Images)

Crosby, Nash and Stills during rehearsals for the troubled 1982 *Daylight Again* tour. (Photo by Henry Diltz/Corbis via Getty Images)

Crosby, Stills, Nash and Young at the audio-challenged Live Aid reunion 1985.
(Photo © Amy Sancetta/AP/REX/Shutterstock)

Stills' mother Talitha, group mentor Ahmet Ertegun and Stills, mid-1980s. (Photo
by Henry Diltz/Corbis via Getty Images)

Crosby and Jan Dance wed in May 1987, joined by Graham and Susan Nash (left) for their renewal vows. (Photo by Henry Diltz/Corbis via Getty Images)

Crosby, Stills and Nash, Woodstock 1994. (Photo by Henry Diltz/Corbis via Getty Images)

"CSNY2K" press conference for their first quartet tour in twenty-six years, October 1999. (Photo © Peter Kramer/STAR MAX Inc./Newscom/Mega)

The quartet gather at the 2008 Sundance Film Festival for the premiere of Young's *CSNY/Déjà vu* movie. (Photo by Jeff Vespa/Contour by Getty Images)

James Raymond (Crosby's son and band mate) joins his father and Nash at an Occupy Wall Street performance, 2011. (Photo © Adam Scull/Photolink.net/ Newscom/MEGA)

Stills, Nash and Crosby at the ill-fated Christmas tree lighting ceremony, December 2015. (Photo by Cheriss May/NurPhoto via Getty Images)

Young and James Mazzeo had recently arrived in Fort Lauderdale, where Young had settled onto his new boat, the *Evening Coconut*. He, Mazzeo and reclusive singer-songwriter Fred Neil would lounge aboard the boat as the sun went down while Young and Neil played each other's songs. Mazzeo eventually returned to California, but Young stayed in Florida. When Young found himself at Criteria that night, the four exchanged hugs and laughs, despite the disastrous attempt at a quartet album in that same studio less than a year before. Crosby, Stills and Nash proudly played Young the final mix of "Shadow Captain," the opening song on the album, and stood around him singing their parts live.

Written by Crosby and keyboardist Craig Doerge, whose unleashed-stallion piano would drive the track, the song was based on a semiautobiographical lyric that had come to Crosby fully formed in the middle of the night during a sailing trip down the coast of California. The melody and arrangement surged, crashed and receded like waves on a beach. In the way Stills' rough edges countered Nash's higher, purer parts, it was also a fitting showcase for their more mature harmonies. When the tape finished, Nash recalls Young loving the song. Vitale, also observing, saw another part of their dynamic at work. "It was, 'I hope you like this,'" Vitale recalls. "They were relieved and thrilled when he said, 'Man, I love this.' They wanted Neil's approval."

Stills and Young had patched up matters between them a few months before, when both showed up at the Band's farewell concert in San Francisco, "The Last Waltz," and participated in an end-of-show jam session together. Now, in Miami, Young was so intrigued by the reunion that they tried recording one of his songs, "Will to Love," a lo-fi, seven-minute epic about a fish swimming up a river. It was both loopy and exquisite. "We tried to learn it, but we could never get past it as a band song," Young later told writer Bill Flanagan. "I couldn't sing past the second verse without forgetting what I was doing, losing it totally and getting all pissed off because it didn't sound right. I couldn't get through it." The song was abandoned, and Crosby, although a fan of the tune, made the case that they should remain a trio, at least for the time being. Once again, Young parted ways with Crosby, Stills and Nash—but amicably this time.

In preparation for their relaunch, the band also got its first-ever logo, one that would endure for decades. Hartmann's younger brother Phil was the de facto art department at the Hartmann-Goodman office, where he had already designed album covers for clients like Poco and America. Although no one asked, Phil conceived a logo for Crosby, Stills and Nash that intertwined the first letters of their last names. "He chose the colors carefully, saying Crosby was red for his passion, Stills blue for his soul, and Nash green for his earthy honesty," recalls his brother John. Phil later dropped the second "n" from his last name and went on to become a brilliant comedian and mimic, especially during his time as a cast member of *Saturday Night Live.* He wasn't paid for his work on the logo, but Nash gave him a Martin D-45 acoustic guitar to express his appreciation. Hartmann treasured the guitar right up until his death in 1998.

In June 1977, the impossible came to pass: a new album by Crosby, Stills and Nash appeared. In its early stages, they'd considered calling it *Jigsaw Puzzle,* but they settled for the less inspired, more generic *CSN.* Depending on the pressing, their portrait on the cover (taken by Bernstein on the boat trip) showed them either dour or smiling. Either way, the record inside captured three very different men, now in their thirties, struggling to solve a puzzle: the search for common ground. A sense of compromise and conciliation had been there from the start. "Shadow Captain" kicked off the record with its rush of harmonies. In previous years, it would have been easy to imagine Stills playing an attention-craving solo on it. Instead, his slide guitar was undermixed, almost buried, taking a back seat to Doerge's piano.

So it went for most of the album, which was engulfed in a muted, morning-after sedateness appropriate for men who'd endured several lifetimes' worth of triumphs and train wrecks in the eight years since *Crosby, Stills & Nash* came out. From its emphasis on voices over intrusive instruments to Stills' terse, largely reined-in solos, the album captured men tip-toeing on eggshells for the sake of their careers and solidarity. Rattled by the soul-gutting experiences of his past year, Stills had set aside his wariness of psychiatrists and begun weekly sessions with a therapist in California, exploring his neuroses and self-destructive ways. ("I guess maybe I don't like myself," he told writer Peter Knobler for an article in *Crawdaddy.*) He came off as newly reflective in such *CSN* contributions as "See the Changes" and "Dark Star," said to be inspired by a long-past affair with Joan Baez. (Asked about it in 2017, Baez

confessed to being unfamiliar with it: "Do I know that song?") With its celestial bounce and a skipping-stones electric piano solo by Doerge, "Dark
Star" was brooding but effervescent, and Stills avoided the oversinging
trap he often set for himself.

His partners contributed sober or contemplative songs to match. Unlike his friskier earlier group contributions, Nash's "Cold Rain" and "Carried Away" were somber and elegiac, the former conjuring his parents'
working-class stasis. In the self-deprecating "Anything at All," Crosby
poked more than a few holes in his renowned ego, breaking into a quick
laugh that made the song all the more human. Nash's "Cathedral" was
initiated by a visit to England's Winchester Cathedral, where he was
tripping on acid and stumbled upon the grave of a soldier who'd died
on Nash's own birthday. Solemn in its verses and freaked out in its chorus, the song, complete with swirling orchestration, almost replicated the
highs and lows of a trip. The arrangement of "In My Dreams" marked
a group effort: Nash had suggested the extended finale, and Stills had
added a snappish acoustic guitar solo.

CSN lacked the sunshine-daydream joy of their first album together,
and it didn't try to airbrush the state of their music or their lives. In "Run
from Tears," Stills grappled with the breakup of his marriage, answering
his doleful words with bursts of lead guitar. "Fair Game," one of the album's few missteps, merged a forceful Latin groove by Stills with lyrics
about women on the prowl in singles bars. ("As Graham said to me once,
'David and I are above the waist, and Stills is below the waist,'" says
Bill Siddons, who would later become their manager. "Stephen was the
groove and rhythm and sex of the band, and Graham and David were the
ephemeral ones.") An even more desperate Stills breakup song, "I Give
You Give Blind," ended the album on a resigned but strong note. The song
was the grown-up version of the concluding "49 Bye-Byes" on *Crosby,
Stills & Nash*, but with its battle scars up front—much like the album itself.

The reviews of *CSN* were largely kind—"Crosby, Stills and Nash Recapture Magic," read the Copley News Service's wire story—although
John Rockwell of the *New York Times* noted, "Ultimately, one senses a
defeatism here. . . . This sounds like a tired last recourse—an attempt at
commercial success by three men whose egos make it hard for them to
collaborate, but whose relative lack of popular success by themselves

makes it difficult not to do so." The general public just seemed glad to have them back. "Just a Song Before I Go" went Top 10, and the album peaked at no. 2, held out of the top slot by Fleetwood Mac's ubiquitous *Rumours.*

Starting in early June, Crosby, Stills and Nash embarked on their full-scale first tour as a renewed trio. Keeping in mind their nitroglycerin nature, the crew had to determine exactly how far Stills' overpowering Marshall amp stacks had to be from Crosby and Nash. The length of the tour itself had to be carefully considered. "Anything more than four weeks was pushing it," says crew member John Vanderslice, who was on his first tour with the band. "It was almost like a chemical reaction. You can put these two chemicals together, and it would take this amount of time to corrode the case. So no more than six weeks. If you did eight weeks, something would happen." Fittingly, the first leg of the tour was restricted to a month.

The scale of the undertaking—and the rewards of a reunion—became apparent as two tractor trailers full of equipment pulled into the Pittsburgh Civic Arena on June 11 for the fourth show of the tour. The trucks carted amplifiers and 120,000 watts of lights that took sixteen roadies, two forklift operators and ten stage hands to unload and install. The rider in the trio's backstage contract called for a cutting board and knife (perhaps not only for food), a carton of Marlboros and plenty of liquor: two cases of Heineken beer, two bottles of Jose Cuervo Gold tequila, a bottle of Mouton Cadet wine and a bottle of Rémy Martin Cognac. The band would be paid $40,000 along with an unheard-of 85 percent of the ticket sales. At this show alone, they would play before 16,950 people. Backstage, Nash asked a visitor wearing a Mercedes Benz T-shirt if he could exchange it for his; naturally, the man complied.

At each show, backed by Vitale, Lala, Perry and Doerge, the band members worked at balancing nostalgia and modern times. The sets were peppered with songs from their own records but brought in the expected group favorites. In one high-tech touch, Stills was able to gallop around the rim of the stage by way of a wireless guitar pickup. (When Stills would periodically drop and break it, Giachetti would quickly have to scout out a replacement for a few thousand more dollars.) Nearly every review of the show mentioned Stills' self-discipline, Crosby's new girth ("bear-like," as one reviewer called it) and the spontaneous arena sing-alongs to "Our House," complete with flicked lighters. The hyper energy of the 1974 tour with Young was largely absent—again, for the greater good. "The dynamics were different," says production manager Glenn Goodwin of the shows compared to that tour. "It seemed like they were a tighter unit." Despite occasional shouts for Young, audiences seemed relieved to see at least three of them reunited on the same stage.

AT LEAST FOR the immediate future, there would be no arenas in Young's life—just the opposite, in fact. Returning to California, he reached out to Mazzeo, who had moved onto a communal farm in Santa Cruz with his guitarist friend Jeff Blackburn. A beach town roughly seventy miles south of San Francisco, Santa Cruz had a population of just over thirty thousand—a size that would have fit into one of the venues on Crosby, Stills and Nash's reunion tour.

Young told Mazzeo he didn't want to be alone on his ranch. "There were still a lot of Carrie vibes there," says Mazzeo. Mazzeo invited him over, and Young made himself at home on the farm. Blackburn had been playing local clubs with his eponymous band, and Young was fascinated. "I said, 'Buck has a band together,'" says Mazzeo, using Blackburn's nickname, "and as soon as he hit town, Neil goes, 'God, they need another guitar player.'"

"Will to Love," the salmon saga Young had tried recording with Crosby, Stills and Nash earlier in the year, finally appeared on record—without them—in June. The song was part of *American Stars 'n Bars*, which arrived the same month as *CSN*. The difference between the two albums spoke to the opposing creative approaches of the two camps. *CSN* was recorded in the same period with largely the same musicians, while Young's album, harking back to an approach he took with *After the Gold Rush* and *Harvest* (and parts of *Tonight's the Night*), was pieced together from sundry sessions with varied players over a longer stretch. The trio preferred a somewhat orderly process; Young thrived on the grab-bag approach.

In Young's case, the gamble usually paid off, and it happened again with the almost schizoid *American Stars 'n Bars*. Its first half was barnburner country rock featuring Crazy Horse, with Linda Ronstadt and

Nicolette Larson as backup singers; the two women added sisterly vocal firepower to "Bite the Bullet" and "Hold Back the Tears." The songs
brought out a looser, less monolithic side of Crazy Horse, much like the
one they'd shown on the Danny Whitten–led album in 1971. In addition to
"Will to Love" and the electric hoedown "Homegrown," the second half
was centered around "Like a Hurricane," which had morphed from the
solo acoustic rendition in the Stills-Young Band tour into a musical trip
into the Young cosmos. Goaded by his extended Morse-code-freakout
guitar and Poncho Sampedro's Stringman synthesizer—and stretching
out to over eight minutes—it was both vast and intimate, yearning and
erotic. The type of recording that felt like an immediate, eternal gem as
soon as it was heard, "Like a Hurricane" would become one of Young's
most popular and played songs.

Normally, an album with Crazy Horse would have meant a tour with
them, but much to the surprise of Jeff Blackburn and his band members (former Moby Grape bassist Bob Mosley and drummer Johnny
Craviotto), Young began rehearsing with them instead. In early July, the
newly renamed Ducks, after a duck's landing they saw in town, played its
first shows—in local bars in Santa Cruz. In what the *Santa Cruz Sentinel*
called "the worst-kept secret in town," the Ducks would drive to a club
and ask the opening act for their slot ("They were fine—they knew they
couldn't draw what we could," says Mosley). Charging only a few dollars
for admission, they would tear through sets of songs by Young and by
Blackburn. Young debuted new material like "Sail Away" and "Comes a
Time" in more electrified versions than were later heard on record. "It
was unfathomable," recalls Mosley. "Some of the guitar solos took me
into outer space. It was incredible shit." Starting in mid-July and ending
around Labor Day, the Ducks would play more than twenty gigs in bars
like the Back Room, the Crossroads and the Catalyst. Young's only stipulation was that they play within the Santa Cruz city limits (his contract
with Crazy Horse forbade him from touring without them). As Young
told local music writer Dan Coyro that summer, "I'm starting to get back
that certain feeling for playing my music. . . . It's like being born again."

Young eventually rented a home on East Cliff Drive, prompting the
Sentinel to call him "a full-fledged resident," and he was often spotted
riding his ten-speed up and down Seabright Avenue. "Neil loved that,"

Mazzeo says. "He was like a regular person. Neil knows he's not going to be anonymous, but he likes to *pretend* he's anonymous." Mosley doesn't recall Young ever mentioning Crosby, Stills and Nash, but to Mazzeo, the allure of a low-key Santa Cruz lifestyle (and band to accompany it) was more than obvious. "After the Stills-Young thing and the CSNY '74 thing, he just decided to come and hang out," Mazzeo says. "Neil would say to me, 'It's over, it's too fucking big.' This was all a reaction to that."

That summer, a series of robberies in the area rattled the community. On the night of August 17, a woman in her car outside of a bar called the Crow's Nest was robbed of her bag at gunpoint. Later, local police learned that one of the same men involved in the robbery had broken into Young's home and stolen guitars, tapes of gigs and what the police described as "new songs for Young's upcoming record albums." The burglar, it turned out, lived on the same street as Young. Newly disillusioned, Young was gone before anyone knew what had happened. "It was the end of the summer," says Mosley, "and he just disappeared."

REVIEWING CROSBY, STILLS AND NASH's show at the Inglewood Forum in late June, the *Los Angeles Times*' Robert Hilburn raised a critical red flag. "Whereas Crosby and Nash, who have toured and recorded as a duo, seemed relaxed and celebrative, Stills looked like a man uncertain about the reunion and its impact," he wrote. "The night's closing glow didn't erase the question mark over the band's future. . . . *CSN* revived its former glory well. The burden next time will be to come up with new reasons for the audience to believe in it."

Hilburn's words would prove to be eerily prescient. In October, the trio embarked on the second leg of the tour—again, for a mere five weeks, to ensure a degree of sanity and harmony. At the fifth show, at the Oakland–Alameda County Coliseum, Stills unleashed an abrasive solo during Crosby's "The Lee Shore." Crosby and Nash clearly did not approve. Sitting in the audience, writer Dave Zimmer noticed both men glaring at Stills. Some of their crew members weren't surprised. "Sometimes there would be amazing harmony, like a couple in a good mood who had a great dinner," says Giachetti. "And all of a sudden, it would be the opposite. Bad vibes. I would notice it would be clicking and the show would be fabulous, but there were shows when they'd be rushing through the songs." Crosby and Stills began arguing over who had the most songs in the set, leaving it to Nash to keep the peace. "Nash would always say, 'Fine, take out one of mine,'" says Vanderslice. "He was always the one to make a compromise."

But on multiple levels, the group was quickly coming apart. By the fall of 1977, Stills, who had briefly reunited with Sanson, had already begun work on a new album—his own, thanks to his obligations to Columbia. (As Stills would later tell *Goldmine* of *CSN*, "There was this feeling over in our end of the building that we were making the album of the year. And I didn't hear it.") Crosby's drug issues were also becoming more obvious, at least to their musicians. During their shows, Perry would watch as Crosby walked back to a speaker and pretended to drink a soda, when in fact he was snorting cocaine off the top of the can. "I didn't appreciate that at all," Perry says. "You know *somebody* saw it. It scared me." Perry was equally shocked when Crosby would return to the microphone and never miss a beat: "He played his parts! He sang his parts! How do you *do that*? Which was strange, cool and horrible all at the same time." Crosby was hardly the only one indulging in whatever at the time. On or around the same tour, as he later recounted to author Michael Walker, John Hartmann witnessed Stills having what seemed like a seizure—swallowing his tongue, eyes rolling back—thanks to a "mucus mass" in his chest. Only Hartmann's repeated pounding on Stills' chest appeared to save his life.

The tour over, they decided to quickly begin a new album. "Now let's hope it's not an accident—let's hope they're already putting together material for a more immediate follow-up album," wrote the *Democrat and Chronicle* of Rochester, New York, in a concert review. They certainly tried. In Los Angeles in late 1977, and then in Florida a few months later, Crosby, Stills and Nash reconvened with the Alberts for a follow-up. Material wasn't a problem: Nash had the whirring "Helicopter Song" and a pretty ballad, "Love Has Come." Crosby brought "Distances," one of his open-tuned meditations on broken connections, along with an escapist fantasy called "Drive My Car." Stills had, inconceivably, a disco pop song, "What's the Game."

In his concerns about whether the reconstituted group would make a *second* album under their new contract, Ertegun proved astute. Now that the three had a hit release under their belts, any sense of urgency or need to prove themselves as individuals evaporated. The sessions became so unfruitful that guitarist Danny Kortchmar, from the Mighty Jitters, was flown to Florida for added juice. "That was insane," Kortchmar has said. "They were having trouble getting along with each other and I guess they liked and trusted me." But too many cooks overtook the kitchen. "Everybody had their own set of guys, all good cats, but they came and went," says Vitale. "Everyone was 'I want to do this or that,' but there was no real focus. It just drifted along. Their priorities weren't lined up. It wasn't the focal point of everybody's lives." Crosby's former Byrd bandmates Roger McGuinn, Chris Hillman and Gene Clark were also at Criteria, working on what amounted to a Byrds reunion album without Crosby (or drummer Michael Clarke). McGuinn would see Crosby poke his head into their recording room. "He was kind of feeling it out: 'Do I want to do this?'" recalls McGuinn, who was under the impression that Stills had warned Crosby not to get involved and to stick with his obligations to CSN.

During this time, Stills had a brief, platonic reunion with Judy Collins. For all the hard feelings that had accompanied the end of their affair, they remained connected. She had written a song, "Houses," that was superficially about Stills' personality and wardrobe (along with the properties he owned). She also recorded her own version of "So Begins the Task." In 1978, Collins got sober after a two-decade drinking problem that had nearly destroyed her voice. She had just checked out of treatment when she ran into Stills in New York and invited herself down to Miami for a getaway. "He said, 'Don't come—you'll never stay sober down here,'" she recalls. "I'm sure he was absolutely right. But I was impressed that he said it and knew it." On his advice, she stayed north.

Everyone was so optimistic about a follow-up to *CSN* that a summer tour for 1978 was booked to promote it. The album was abandoned, but the tour—again, a mere five weeks—proceeded as planned. In repertoire and, for the most part, in musicians, it was a retread of the previous summer's shows. *Rolling Stone* noted as much in its review of their New York stop with the sarcastic headline, "Sentimental Journey."

The previous year, *Rolling Stone* had rhapsodized over *CSN*, calling it "honest and surprisingly humble." Of one of their concerts, it had said,

"Audience and band went home happy, having learned how easily dormant passions can be rekindled." But the about-face wasn't restricted to one publication, and it was emblematic of the media's revised attitude toward the genre the group embodied. The year 1977 would prove to be a banner moment for the California singer-songwriter rock that had dominated the decade: it was the year of *CSN, Rumours, Hotel California* (which, though released in late 1976, dominated 1977), Linda Ronstadt's *Simple Dreams*, James Taylor's *JT* and Jackson Browne's *Running on Empty*. Ronstadt made the cover of *Time*, while Crosby, Stills and Nash appeared on *People*. But overnight, with punk making the genre look and sound stodgy, their kind of music was deemed passé. In Crosby, Stills and Nash's case, their public images didn't help: between Stills' oversized aviator glasses and Nash's penchant for shag haircuts and mustaches, they couldn't have looked more like the picture of '70s fashion if they'd tried. The cover of *CSN*, depicting them on a boat, seemed to signify that they were now living wealthier, more upscale lives; certainly, they were no longer the down-home hippies of the *Crosby, Stills & Nash* cover.

In the midst of the latest round of Crosby, Stills and Nash disarray, Young released *Comes a Time* in the fall of 1978, complete with a cover image of what *Rolling Stone*'s Greil Marcus aptly described as "Huckleberry Neil." Recorded in Nashville with a large ensemble of pickers and string players, who overdubbed their parts onto his solo recordings, *Comes a Time* was mostly gentle; even the two tracks cut with Crazy Horse were largely unplugged. With its swell of multiple acoustic guitars, and Larson's harmonies providing a lush bed for Young's becalmed voice, the album returned him to *Harvest* territory in tracks like the wryly swinging title song, "Already One" (seemingly about his son, Zeke, and the bond they still had), and a version of Ian Tyson's "Four Strong Winds." (Thanks to the profits from Young's version, Tyson was able to buy a sizable ranch in Canada.) The placid tone of the album coincided with a major change in Young's life. In late 1974, he had met Pegi Morton, a born-and-bred California blonde who was working as a waitress. In the spring of 1978, the two were married in a low-key ceremony in Malibu. Afterward, they lived on his ranch, which had grown. Young had purchased property around the original ranch, and it now occupied a thousand acres.

Early in 1978, at an intimate San Francisco club called the Boarding House, Crosby temporarily became a Byrd again, joining McGuinn,
Clark and Hillman for an impromptu onstage reunion. Together they res-
urrected the songs—including "Mr. Tambourine Man" and "Eight Miles
High"—that had established them as rock's vanguard over a decade before.
But musically and electronically, Young was already several steps ahead
of all of them, even Stills. Three months later, he headlined the Boarding
House himself. For two shows a night over the course of five nights, he
debuted his now standard stash of previously unheard songs, including
"Thrasher," an exquisite but subtly brutal song about the now-distanced
trio. With its reference to those who were coddled and dead weight from
the past, "Thrasher" was a clear shot at life with Crosby, Stills and Nash.
"Well, at that point, I felt like it *was* kind of dead weight for me," he told
writer Bill Flanagan in 1985. "Not for them. They were doing fine without
me. It might have come off a little more harsh than I meant it, but once I
write it, I can't say, 'Oh I'm going to hurt somebody's feelings.' Poetically
and on feeling, it made good sense to me and it came right out."

Stills may have had a wireless unit that allowed him to bolt around
the stage while playing, but Young went one gearhead step further:
thanks to a miniature microphone tucked into his harmonica rack, he
was able to wander the Boarding House stage without constraints. Yet
he would soon be set apart from the others in the most dramatic of ways.
It would be the beginning of a long, complicated period of estrangement
that would threaten to destroy not only the band but also its most animated member.

PART THREE
WASTED ON THE WAY

CHAPTER 7
JANUARY 1979–NOVEMBER 1982

He wasn't the slightest bit thrilled that any of them were in his house, asking questions about the state of the band and the next reconciliation. But sometimes the job called for it, and in the early weeks of 1979, Stills had little choice but to tackle the task at hand.

With the trio once more at odds, Stills barreled along relentlessly with his music. The attempt at a *CSN* follow-up in Miami was barely old news when, in the fall of 1978, he released his third Columbia solo album, *Thoroughfare Gap*. Dating back to his use of horns and green-world lyrics on 1971's *Stephen Stills 2*, he had always kept one eye on the marketplace; this time around, that gaze was fixed on disco, the prevalent pop genre of the time. Radio and sales had been dominated by the Bee Gees and other acts with songs on the soundtrack to *Saturday Night Fever*, a 1977 movie about the youth disco subculture in Brooklyn, New York, starring John Travolta, that continued to draw people into movie theaters. Stills had first been drawn to the genre in 1976, while recording in Florida at the same studio where the Bee Gees worked. He and his preferred percussionist and close buddy, the gregarious Joe Lala, had shown up at a Bee Gees session for "You Should Be Dancing" and insisted on adding percussion to it. As Bee Gees drummer Dennis Bryon later recalled, the two, who seemed well lit, nailed the parts, which were used on the finished record. Stills steeped about half of *Thoroughfare Gap* in Studio 54 sonics, encasing his voice in fluttering flutes, sumptuous strings and burbling bass lines; he even recruited the youngest Gibb brother from the Bee Gees, Andy, to add harmonies. As Stills told the musicians who gathered in his home to record some of those tracks, he wanted "the most far-out disco sound you can imagine."

Thoroughfare Gap was one of the most privacy-be-damned albums Stills had ever made. In tracks like the desperately hopeful "We Will Go On," the grim and gnarled "Lowdown" and the Latino shuffle "Woman Lleva," he grappled with his failed marriage and subsequent depression, recasting the suffering-romantic aura that dated back to "Suite: Judy Blue Eyes." The remainder of the album was filled out with a sludgy remake of Buddy Holly and Norman Petty's "Not Fade Away" and "Can't Get No Booty." Stills and Danny Kortchmar had knocked off the latter, a flat-footed disco-parody novelty, in less than an hour, during an unproductive Crosby, Stills and Nash session earlier in the year. Only the vintage title track, which compared his life to an ongoing train and had a gently chugging arrangement to match, sounded like the Stills most of his fans were accustomed to hearing; not surprisingly, that song had been written and first attempted six years before, during the Manassas era.

The disco frivolity of the album's first single, "You Can't Dance Alone," clearly dismayed Crosby, Stills, Nash and Young's base, and the album became the first Stills solo album not to break into the Top 40, peaking at a sobering no. 83. With that flop, Stills had to subject himself to promotion, and reporters began showing up at his sizable home in Bel Air, with "SS" emblazoned on its wrought-iron gates. After walking down a hallway lined with gold and platinum album awards, then past a wood-paneled library, journalists would find themselves in a basement music den housing a bar, a pool table, multiple guitars and banjos, a piano and clumps of extinguished cigarette butts. For one interview, Stills fortified himself with what one writer called "a Tequila Sunrise in a glass chalice that looks more like a goldfish bowl." Every so often, a visiting writer could catch a glimpse of Stills' current girlfriend, actress Susan Saint James, known at the time for her role costarring with Rock Hudson in the TV detective series *McMillan & Wife*. Stills and Saint James had met months before and been instantly smitten with each other, and Saint James soon moved into Stills' house. By late winter, the gossip columns would be dotted with news of their summer wedding: "I know I'm good for him—why, I'm even going to get him off Coke!" she joked to a reporter. (The writer added, "The actress, a longtime vegetarian, is referring to the cola, not the powder.") By the spring, the romance had run its course. Saint James later attributed the breakup to incompatible schedules; Stills would generally be working in the studio while she was asleep. But during those early months of the year, they were still together, and he would momentarily brighten when she walked into a room during one of his interviews.

During the promotional interviews, Stills endured questions about his past but clearly preferred discussing songwriting, *Thoroughfare Gap* and the California Blues Band, a new electric rock and blues group he was taking on the road. With singer Bonnie Bramlett, formerly of Delaney and Bonnie, and former Dave Mason keyboardist Mike Finnigan on board, the band was grittier and more roadhouse than any he'd fronted before. Reporters asking for updates on his career with Crosby and Nash were met with curt, muted responses. "Ask Graham," was one. "Why all the boring CSN questions?" was another. "I haven't seen 'em," he told Dave Zimmer of *BAM* magazine. Stills did let it slip in one interview that Crosby, Stills and Nash had "half an album in the can," yet he failed to mention that hardly anyone had the will to finish it.

WITH ANOTHER ATTEMPT at a Crosby, Stills and Nash album in tatters—and the profits from the highly successful reunion album and tour still in their pockets—there seemed to be little reason to stay in touch. "There was no communication I can think of," says Guillermo Giachetti. In an unintentional return to the post–*Déjà vu* days of 1971, the four had again scattered, musically and geographically. Stills remained in Los Angeles. Nash and his girlfriend Susan Sennett had married in the spring of 1977, and they had their first child, a son named Jackson, in February 1978. By 1979, they were building a house in the Hanalei area of Kauai, in Hawaii, their new home base. Neil and Pegi Young were hunkered down at his Northern California ranch.

As for Crosby, he was a medium-length drive away from Young, in Mill Valley, becoming ensnared in an increasingly hermetic and unhealthy lifestyle. He and his new girlfriend, Jan Dance, had met when Crosby, Stills and Nash were making *CSN* in Miami in 1977; Dance's mother, Harper, was an indispensable part of Criteria Studios' operations, and her daughter had worked there as well, helping book studio time. A year later, when the trio was trying and failing to make their doomed sequel, Crosby and Dance—a sweet blonde with a sunshine smile—finally connected at the same studio. Soon afterward, he introduced her to free-basing and asked her to move into his home.

Once again, all four retreated to their familiar musical corners. Signing a new contract with Columbia, also home to Stills, Crosby and Nash decided to reboot the duo career. The two gathered together the songs they'd tried cutting with him, reconvened many of the musicians they'd used before and began cutting tracks. Given how productive they'd been together only a few years earlier, the work should have been productive. After sessions commenced in late winter, Columbia was so confident of a new Crosby and Nash album that the label penciled it in for a June 1979 release.

But Crosby's freebasing habit had begun to tighten its grip on him. Among his peers, he was hardly alone: by then, Jerry Garcia and many other '60s-rooted rockers were also becoming ensnared in drug addiction. Ever since his Byrds days, Crosby had prided himself on being able to get high while still making cogent music, and few suspected that blueprint would change. Yet it did. Working at Britannia Studio in Los Angeles, Crosby and Nash watched in a control room one day as the Mighty Jitters began working up an arrangement. Slipping into the room to join them, Crosby saw he had left his drug pipe atop a baffle between the musicians. The pipe fell down—either Crosby bumped into a baffle or the vibrations of the thunderous music shook it. Whatever the cause, the pipe hit the ground and smashed into fragments, and Crosby, who needed drugs to stay awake for the lengthy session, dropped to the floor and began gathering up the pieces. The music came to a dead halt. Nash wasn't above snorting cocaine himself, but seeing Crosby's habit literally wreck a possible track set him off; he told his friend he'd had enough and had to leave. Angry and in denial, Crosby stormed out of the studio, drove off with Dance and promptly crashed into a parked car. (His manager later tracked it down and paid for the repair.) Disgusted with Crosby, Nash decided to take his unfinished songs and make his own record. It was the first major breach in their friendship since they had become inseparable in 1968.

Despite the meager sales of *Thoroughfare Gap*, Stills plowed on. In 1979, he became one of the first musicians to record digitally, without audio tape, remaking "Cherokee," his nearly decade-old ode to Rita Coolidge, and he and his band flew to Cuba for a historic concert featuring American musicians (including Coolidge and her husband, Kris Kris-tofferson). If his irritable interviews were one indication that he had no interest in lingering in his musical past, his 1979 concerts were another. Show after show flummoxed his fans. Stills almost completely ignored the songs he'd cut with Crosby, Nash and Young and focused on material from his solo records (or blues covers highlighting Finnigan), singing in a voice that seemed to fray all too quickly by concert's end. Tickethold-ers would not hear "Carry On," "Suite: Judy Blue Eyes" or "Helplessly Hoping." They *would* hear "Love the One You're With"—but sung by his female backup singer, Brooks Hunnicutt. The move was nothing short of bold—and thrilling for those who yearned to hear him play Manassas tracks, such as the conjoining of "Rock & Roll Crazies" and "Cuban Blue-grass." But judging from the complaints of disgruntled fans as they left shows in New Jersey and New York, it was also career suicide. But like Nash, Stills had had enough of the past.

NOT FOR THE FIRST TIME, the founding trio would be thrown together by roiling times. The Vietnam conflict was over, but a new war raged on, this one against nuclear power. By early 1979, sixty-eight nuclear reactors around the country were generating just over one-tenth of the nation's electrical power, but the risks were becoming frighteningly clear. That year, the Nuclear Regulatory Commission would investigate 2,300 inci-dents at the plants, from inept inspections to poor management. Whether at a nuclear submarine base station in Bangor, Washington, or a site in Groton, Connecticut, antinuke protests were on the rise. The fears were increasingly reflected in popular culture. A January 1979 episode of *The New Adventures of Wonder Woman* found the series' superheroine going undercover to foil the sale of a black-market nuke warhead, and in the middle of March, a movie thriller about a reactor meltdown—*The China Syndrome*, starring Jane Fonda, Michael Douglas and Jack Lemmon—opened in theaters.

In a particularly unsettling example of life imitating art, a small blast of steam burst out of the Three Mile Island nuclear plant in Middletown, Pennsylvania, a mere twelve days after *The China Syndrome* opened. A malfunctioning cooling system had caused the reactor to overheat; in the worst-case scenario in such a situation, a reactor can become hot enough to destroy its concrete and steel casing, which can cause a leak of radioactive energy into the atmosphere. Over the next five days, mixed messages emanated from the plant and its operator, Metropolitan Edison. Even government authorities encountered difficulties getting straight answers, and the overly busy telephone lines didn't help. The news that eventually emerged was chilling: small amounts of radioactive material had periodically leaked out, and had wafted toward neighboring towns. Perhaps worse, a hydrogen bubble inside the reactor was threatening to burst. Residents within a ten-mile radius were ordered by the governor to evacuate by way of loudspeakers attached to trucks roaming through the streets. Five days later, the reactor was deemed stable. Presumably, the life-threatening emergency was over, this time. But the country—and the world—had been sufficiently rattled. Protests broke out not only in the United States but also in Europe and Asia. A week after the Three Mile Island incident, Columbia University dropped its plans to open a nuclear research reactor in upper Manhattan.

Nash had already been aware of the issue. Two months before the Three Mile Island catastrophe, he had joined Jackson Browne at the Forum in Los Angeles to protest the opening of the Diablo Canyon Power Plant two hundred miles north of the city. Three months after Three Mile Island, he again shared the stage with Browne, along with Joan Baez and others, to ram home the antinuclear point at "Survival Sunday II" at the Hollywood Bowl. (The first "Survival Sunday," held at the same venue the year before, had been a disarmament benefit featuring Peter, Paul and Mary, Arlo Guthrie and R&B singer Minnie Riperton.) But those events were a mere run-up to "No Nukes," five nights at Madison Square Garden in September 1979. The shows would benefit MUSE (Musicians United for Safe Energy) and spread the solar-power word with a lineup that included Nash, Browne, Bruce Springsteen and the E Street Band, the Doobie Brothers, Tom Petty and the Heartbreakers, Bonnie Raitt, Carly Simon and James Taylor. With disco peaking that summer, and the more radio-friendly new wave taking over from punk, "No Nukes" looked to be the last stand of what was becoming known as the classic-rock era.

Yet even with that lineup, the shows hit a snag: the planned fifth night didn't have a headlining act, and Browne told Nash it might have to be canceled. (Browne had tried to convince Joni Mitchell to come, but to no avail.) Finally, Browne asked Nash if he would consider calling Stills and Crosby for a one-shot reunion for the final evening; it could be the only way to salvage the show. Nash hesitated, realized he had little choice and put out the calls. Young was not considered: asked three years later by a French TV reporter what he thought of Browne and the No Nukes movement, he paused, then chuckled and said, "First of all, I think anyone who says that nuclear power is no good is just not looking forward. You have to look forward. You can't look back and say 'get a horse' every time someone has a new idea. That's why I'm not on an antinuke bandwagon. . . . I'm not out there saying, 'Build more plants.' I'm not like *that.* But I'm not saying, 'Don't do research.' We have to have power. Everything is dangerous."

Only a year had passed since Crosby, Stills and Nash had last performed together, yet tensions had run so high that, tellingly, the layoff seemed far longer. "We were like, 'Oh, my God—we thought this would never happen,'" recalls Danny Goldberg, a former journalist and ex-vice president of Led Zeppelin's Swan Song label who was co-producing and co-directing the movie being made of the event. "It seemed like an eternity since they'd been together."

Visiting the building where the group would be rehearsing, Goldberg decided to steer clear of Crosby and Stills, sensing a "wild look" in their eyes that terrified him. Rather than address them, or even get in their field of vision, he asked Nash to speak to them on his behalf. Yet as the three men converged at the space, they exchanged smiles and hugs and pulled together a set list of songs they knew well enough by then to play without much rehearsing, including "Love the One You're With," "Wooden Ships" and "Helplessly Hoping." The reunion would serve several purposes: it would prevent an embarrassing finale to the multi-night "No Nukes," it would lend another name act to the concert movie that was being planned, and it would help Stills with his increasingly thorny relations with Columbia Records. That year, he had recorded new material with his touring band, but Columbia had rejected the tracks and the situation remained at an impasse. Ken Weiss, Stills' new manager (Michael John Bowen had bowed out after seven years of working with him), felt that a strong performance would impress the Columbia executives in the arena that night. Stills delivered, even as he and Crosby acknowledged what they'd been through in an exchange during "You Don't Have to Cry": arriving at the line about fast going "crazy and old," Stills injected, "Check it out, Dave," and Crosby chuckled back.

But on the troubling side, people in the business had their first warning of Crosby's growing addiction that night. In the athletes' locker room, Crosby ordered his co-manager, John Hartmann, to seal up one of the shower stalls. Then Crosby dragged jars and bottles inside. "I walked in and said, 'David, you're stinking up the whole place—What are you doing?'" Hartmann recalls. Not completely to Hartmann's surprise, Crosby was cooking up freebase. When the shows were over, the three again went their separate ways.

MICHAEL STERGIS, A trumpet player through his college years at Southern Illinois University, had moved to Los Angeles and was playing guitar in pop singer Helen Reddy's band when his phone rang around midnight in late 1979. It was Stills, telling the lanky, shaggy-haired Stergis that he'd heard he was a talented guitarist and could he come to his house and help him write songs—immediately? Although Stergis hesitated for a minute, given the hour of the call, he went and wound up staying up with Stills until dawn, singing and playing. As with Donnie Dacus a few years before, Stills felt the need to turn to a younger musician—Stergis was twenty-seven—to help fire up his songwriting and inspiration. Later, when Stills offered Stergis the job as second guitarist in his band, Stergis watched as Stills phoned his current player, Gerry Tolman, and fired him on the spot.

Amid the manic energy of the Stills camp, it felt almost natural when, in March 1980, Stergis joined Stills at a John Denver–hosted celebrity ski race in Lake Tahoe, California, and Stills suggested on a whim that they drive the few hours to Nash's home in San Francisco. On the hurried drive, Stills and Stergis wrote a song for Nash and his wife, "You Are Alive," with Stills, behind the wheel, reeling off verse after verse as Stergis furiously wrote each one down. When they arrived at Nash's home, Stergis realized the visit was a complete surprise; Stills hadn't warned Nash they were coming. But Nash was welcoming, as always, and at one point Stills pulled Nash aside and told him Stergis was "the new David Crosby."

At first, Nash had greeted the new decade optimistically. Just before New Year's, he had unveiled a single, "In the '80s," whose chorus included an optimistic line about springing to life in the new decade. But whatever hope Nash had for rekindling his own career was quickly obliterated when *Earth & Sky*, the album that followed in February 1980, sank. A patchwork of new songs and leftovers from the Crosby-Nash and Crosby, Stills and Nash sessions, the album had had a troubled history from the start. It culminated with Nash switching labels, from Columbia to Capitol, when Columbia refused his demand to omit a bar code from the cover. Nash felt the small box would ruin the mood of Joel Bernstein's evocative photo of Nash in Hawaii, with a rainbow behind him.

Earth & Sky contained one of Nash's most forceful and gravest songs, "Barrel of Pain (Half-Life)," an antinuclear warning powered by an insistent female choir and Tim Drummond's deep-pocket bass thump. But the gentle ballads that made up a good portion of the album, such as "Magical Child," for Nash's first son, were out of step with the musical times, and the album never rose higher than no. 117 on the chart. During a low-key tour to promote it, Nash occasionally let his frustration spill out when greeted with lackluster audience reactions. "Can someone tune this goddamn thing?" he snapped at a roadie onstage in Florida while grappling with a malfunctioning guitar. Backstage that night, he was angry with his own performance. "Nobody sang 'Teach Your Children,'" he fumed. "That's incredible."

In what was now a decade-plus dance that the three (or four) men had been doing, few expected the next twist. In the summer of 1980, Nash and Stills reconnected in Hawaii: Nash was back home after his road work, and Stills was on vacation. Stills, too, had endured a rude music-industry awakening. After Columbia rejected his album, the label, rather than drop him outright, suggested he head back into the studio with an established producer who could right the ship. Stills had no choice but to cede control, and everyone mutually agreed on Barry Beckett, the Alabama-born keyboard player and producer who had played behind everyone from Aretha Franklin to Paul Simon; as co-producer, he had just helmed Bob Dylan's born-again records. Despite his control-freak tendencies, Stills went along with the suggestion. To the surprise of those who knew him, he almost seemed to enjoy handing over the reins to someone else.

Stills presented Beckett with a sturdy new song, "Southern Cross," which had a tangled creation of its own. Originally called "Seven League Boots," it had been written by two brothers, Richard and Michael Curtis, who had recorded it with Lindsey Buckingham of Fleetwood Mac. Weiss, who had signed the brothers to Stills' Gold Hill publishing company, heard the song and loved the music, but felt that something, namely the lyrics, wasn't gelling. Weiss played it for Stills, who agreed that the words weren't memorable: "Let me play around with it," Stills told him. A few days later, Stills had tightened up the arrangement and drafted new, nautically inspired lyrics. The Curtis brothers gave the rewrite their blessing, with all three men now sharing the credit. The reconfigured album, complete with "Southern Cross," was again submitted to Columbia. The company agreed it was better but added a stipulation: the label would only release it if, in the future, Stills agreed to work with outside producers. When Stills and his camp balked, Columbia shelved the album, leaving Stills, like Nash, at a creative and contractual impasse.

In Hawaii, Stills' aide-de-camp, Dave Rao, who attended to his boss' needs and errands, ran into Nash at a grocery store. Rao had good news: he told Nash that Stills had cut back on his drinking (to make sure, Rao marked a bottle with a grease pen and checked it regularly) and was in surprisingly good spirits. With nowhere else to turn and facing a suddenly indifferent and hostile music business, Nash and Stills found common ground. They finally reconciled, putting the friendship-destroying Rita Coolidge incident behind them. In July 1980, the two played a benefit for a mayoral candidate in Kauai. After Nash flew to Europe to join Stills and his band for a few European shows that summer, Nash's reservations about Stills melted away. "The man was totally overwhelmed with the strength of you and the professionalism of your show," wrote Rao to Stills that fall, referring to Nash. "His cautiousness is only related to the long run. He *knows* you are as stable and intelligent as they come and his rap was only for me to let you know how serious he is. He had given me the 'only one more shot left for this Limey' in Hawaii, but in the same breath, an exhilaration of the future of working with you again. . . . His trust factor is at an all time high." Rao added that Nash would be back in Los Angeles on October 5, and that Rudy Records, the studio Nash had opened when he moved from San Francisco, was booked for them starting October 13, 1980.

Knowing full well that their Atlantic contract called for a Crosby, Stills and Nash album, Stills and Nash began recording with the hope that Crosby, who was increasingly difficult to track down amid rumors of his escalating drug use, would eventually join them. Everyone assumed Ahmet Ertegun had heard the Crosby rumors, but they hoped he didn't know how dire the situation was becoming. But when Crosby stopped by Rudy to hear the preliminary work, he dismissed what he called the "bum band" (Stills' current lineup). He and Nash exchanged harsh words, and Stills and Nash decided to continue without him.

Given that Stills and Nash had never done an album together without Crosby, no one knew what to expect in terms of material or sound. Nash's new co-manager, Bill Siddons, who had famously overseen the Doors, was unsure: "What's a 'Stills-Nash' record? I didn't know." (Even *Rolling Stone* had a sarcastic "Random Notes" item about it.) One facet of the project, though, became immediately clear: the two had different lifestyles and working methods. With members of Stills' band as their backup, they began working at the new iteration of Nash's Rudy studio, a wood-paneled workplace in a courtyard in the heart of Hollywood (in the same compound as the Crosslight Agency, run by Siddons and his partner Peter Golden). Nash would regularly be the first to arrive and ready to work each morning; Stills would generally show up hours later. It wasn't uncommon to see Nash impatiently checking his watch while he waited for his partner to arrive. Nash preferred to head home to his new property in Encino at a reasonable hour; Stills stuck with his work-till-dawn fervor.

Susan Rogers, an enterprising twenty-something who had taken a night receptionist's job at the nearby University of Sound Arts and made her way into the audio recording world, had been hired as a maintenance technician at Rudy. (Among her earliest chores: replacing a knob in a Stratocaster guitar that Jimi Hendrix had given to Stills.) Rogers observed the contrast between Stills and Nash for herself. "Personality wise, they were incompatible," she says. "You couldn't imagine they would have chosen to be friends with each other outside of artistic collaboration.

Nash was a straight businessman and fairly sober. Stephen wasn't fastidious in the slightest. It didn't feel like they had much in common at all, but they needed each other."

Working with Nash in a studio environment for the first time, Stills' band members were also able to size up the differences between the two. "Graham will make anybody feel like a million bucks," says Stergis, who played on most of *Daylight Again.* "That's what he wanted to project the most and he wasn't projecting it falsely. That's what he wanted to be—that humble guy who made everybody say, 'That guy is just fantastic,' when they walked away. He would be invited over and do the dishes." Band members and Rudy employees saw other flip sides of the Stills and Nash dynamic, too—the way Nash was friendly but compartmentalized in his relationships, and the way the often withdrawn Stills could loosen up and invite employees like Rogers to his house for a cookout.

Yet for all their contrasts, Stills and Nash knew they had a job to do—in effect, they had to salvage their careers in a less forgiving new decade and industry environment. Nash noticed the difference without Crosby around. In that atmosphere, Stills, Nash and the other musicians, including Stergis, Finnigan and drummer Joe Vitale, remade "Southern Cross," from the canceled Stills Columbia album, into a richer, smoother-sailing version that made the best of Stills' huskier voice. "Stephen came alive without this underlying fear of whatever Crosby would have said to him if he sang something wrong," says Nash. "When you take that pressure off Stephen, he becomes much more involved in the work."

One of the songs under consideration was "Daylight Again," an expanded version of Stills' "Find the Cost of Freedom" with a longer introductory section about an unspecified war. Watching Stills record the crisp, trotting guitar part for it in the control room one night was John Partipilo, then known as "Jay Parti," a photographer whom they had unexpectedly hired to work as an assistant engineer on the project. "The name 'Daylight Again' was a joke between us," says Partipilo. "It seemed like every time we went into the studio, it was daylight again when we came out." Yet even so, as Stills cut the track, Partipilo saw a hint of what could be. "Even though we were looking through bleary, bloodshot eyes," he says, "something like that would happen and we'd go, 'Wow,' and get goosebumps."

Since Crosby wasn't available—and was feeling hurt that he had been left out of the proceedings—famous-friend singers were recruited to help replicate his contributions. They included Finnigan (whose soul-shouter moves bolstered Stills' singing in concert), Eagles bassist Timothy B. Schmit and Nash's longtime friend Art Garfunkel. Garfunkel's arrival at the studio prompted Nash to warn workers not to joke around or waste time. Garfunkel took recording seriously, so an air of professionalism, despite the omnipresent drugs and alcohol, had to be maintained. In Hawaii, Nash had written the best of his new songs, "Wasted on the Way," a rumination on how much music and energy the group had thrown aside over the years. Stills immediately liked the song, and they cut a demo with Schmit singing the Crosby part; Schmit then replicated it on the final version. "It's about all four of us," Nash told writer David Fricke, referring to CSNY. "Not just the three of us. The four of us have to take equal blame for the lack of CSNY-ness, or CSN-ness. As much music as we've made, a tremendous amount got totally wasted."

When work shifted to Hawaii to finish up the album, Stills and Nash got high together one day and had a brainstorm: instead of putting their own names on the cover of the album, they'd use a band name, Volkano, playing off the recent eruption of Mount St. Helens in Washington that May. The idea was in keeping with one-name rock bands of the time, like Foreigner and Toto, but it was also perhaps a sign that they saw a Crosby-free future for themselves. Few seemed to know where he was anyway.

BAM's DAVE ZIMMER was at home in Pacifica one spring evening in 1980 when his phone rang. To his surprise, the caller was Crosby. Zimmer had seen his first group-connected show (Manassas) in 1973, and he had begun writing about the four of them in 1977. In the preceding months, he had visited Crosby at his home in Mill Valley several times for interviews for a possible feature story. Crosby had been warm and friendly. People were on his case for doing drugs, he said, but he maintained that he'd made some of his best music while high. In between anecdotes about his life, Crosby's attention would periodically drift off.

The Crosby on the phone that evening was more focused: he hated to ask, but he needed money and could Zimmer lend him some? Zimmer, who only knew Crosby professionally and wasn't really a friend, found the request unusual, but Crosby seemed desperate. The journalist dutifully drove to an ATM, withdrew $50 and took the hour-plus drive to Crosby's home. On his front porch, Crosby thanked Zimmer: "I'll pay you back. You're a lifesaver. I gotta go." Then he went back inside. (He did pay Zimmer back, in full, a month later.)

The jarring and somewhat alarming request signaled that Crosby's life was unraveling at an alarming rate. Unless he had the occasional show or food run, he stayed inside his house in Mill Valley, using heroin and freebasing cocaine. Looking pale and sore-splotched, he would sometimes be seen walking the streets of Mill Valley clasping a mysterious bag and looking furtive. Few of his Crosby, Stills, Nash and Young associates knew any details, but what they heard, especially after the aborted Crosby and Nash sessions in 1979, was troubling. "We were always expecting that call—'Crosby's dead,'" says Rao. "You woke up every day and thought about it." During an interview in London with writer Johnny Rogan, Crosby freebased constantly. When Rogan asked Crosby how much time he thought he had left, Crosby replied, "About five years or so." Crosby's friends grew concerned enough to orchestrate a surprise intervention, and Nash, Grace Slick, Paul Kantner and others, including Crosby's friend Carl Gottlieb, a screenwriter known for his work on *Jaws*, showed up at his home. Crosby seemed to take it all in—until Nash found him in the bathroom trying to get high during a break in the intervention.

The situation eerily paralleled a screenplay that Crosby and Gottlieb had worked on in 1979: called *Push Play*, it centered around a supergroup band member who dies and leaves behind a tape of an unfinished album, with the plan that his former bandmates would reunite and complete it without him. Crosby was hoping to not only score the movie but play the deceased musician, although the script wasn't ultimately picked up for production. (During this same period, Crosby co-wrote another script, *FZ Tango*, with journalist Robert Greenfield. A drug-riddled action movie, it depicted a Vietnam War veteran and chopper pilot who grew entangled in a rescue mission with a sleazy defense contractor. Crosby's "What Are Their Names?" was penciled in for its soundtrack.)

Whether recording or in live performance, music never completely abandoned Crosby, who had still managed to sign a solo deal with

Capitol Records. Although the free-form days of *If I Could Only Remember My Name* were behind him for the moment, Crosby managed to string together stray songs he'd been writing and recording, including "Melody," a sparkly ode to the way music could salvage a man who had become a "patchwork." Bobby Colomby, the Capitol A&R man assigned to the project, saw potential in some of the music, particularly "Delta," a languid, piano-based ramble about someone drawn to the dark side that Jackson Browne had forced Crosby to finish, without drugs, at their friend Warren Zevon's house. Colomby helped secure additional funding for the album using Crosby's house as collateral.

But if drugs had fueled *If I Could Only Remember My Name*, they were now proving a hindrance to Crosby's long-delayed second solo record. Friends and collaborators, including engineer Stanley Johnston, keyboardist Craig Doerge and bassist Leland Sklar, pitched in, trying to pull the strongest and most focused performances out of him, but Crosby wasn't in any shape, physically or vocally, to deliver. He was easily distracted by his addiction (Johnston would half-jokingly refer to Crosby's paraphernalia as "Dave's chemistry set") and could often be found barricaded in recording booths, where he would be doing anything but singing. "He was locked in the vocal booth basing his brains out," recalls guitarist Waddy Wachtel of the one session he was hired to attend. "It was a fucked-up day. I don't recall anything getting done." To Sklar, those booths "smelled like a cat box that hadn't been emptied for eight months." With the help of punching in—recording vocals line by line, sometimes word by word—Crosby's voice could still rise to its former glory, as when he cut "Might as Well Have a Good Time," co-written by Doerge and his wife, singer-songwriter Judy Henske. Even though he hadn't written it and didn't connect with one of its lines—about staying ashore as opposed to sailing—Crosby threw himself into the song; its depiction of a wandering, lost soul almost felt as if it had been written for and about him.

Capitol, which didn't seem particularly taken with having Crosby on its roster to begin with, ultimately passed on the album, as Columbia had done with Stills. "It wasn't a normal record," Crosby admits. "There was a lot of really good stuff on it, like 'Kids and Dogs' [a vintage take with Jerry Garcia]. The label guy said, 'I don't give a *fuck* about Jerry Garcia.' But I was wrecked and it was easy to be critical of me, and he had

people whispering in his ear." When Capitol threatened to take control
of Crosby's house, Colomby argued that the label couldn't afford the bad
press, and the threat was dropped. Crosby told a club crowd in Virginia
Beach in May 1981, "The record company won't accept my new album.
They feel there's no audience for my kind of music now." Of his other
band, he added, "The chances of us getting back together as a group are,
well, not probable."

YET, IN A perverse way, the timing would prove to be ideal for a group
reunion. By the middle of 1981, reports of a Stills-Nash album, with contributions from Garfunkel and Schmit, were leaking to the press, leading
Nash to comment, "David was being a little difficult about certain things.
We didn't feel like hassling." When Stills and Nash decided to release the
album under their names without Crosby, it was left to their managers
to inform Atlantic. In a phone call with label executives, including Ahmet
Ertegun, Weiss told them that Crosby was driving Stills and Nash crazy.
Nash, in particular, was fed up, and they would be proceeding with a
Stills and Nash album.

The answer from one executive was unequivocal: "That's not going
to work." Stills and Nash had already spent nearly half a million of their
own dollars to finance the record. Ertegun now made it clear that he
would fork over their contractual $1 million advance—which would help
pay the men back—but only if the album was going to be a Crosby, Stills
and Nash project. When word of the meeting trickled out, the musicians
who'd played on the record so far were stunned. "I thought, 'Is this the
end?'" says Vitale. "'They don't have a record deal for this thing?' It was
disheartening. I thought about looking for another job."

On the beach in Hawaii, Stills, Nash and their musicians watched
the sunsets and grappled with how to proceed. It had become glaringly
obvious that Crosby, Stills, Nash and Young fans were far less interested
in their individual work than in group reunions, and now their own label
was similarly unresponsive. Eventually, they knew what they had to do,
half-heartedly or not: in order to recoup their investment and release
the music they'd slaved over for the better part of a year and a half, they
would have to ask Crosby to be part of the album. Nash telegrammed
Crosby with the invitation, and Crosby agreed to contribute. "Ahmet said,

'You can't do it without him. It's not a record. You do that and I'll put it out,'" Crosby recalls. "So they called me." To ensure that Crosby still had a singing voice, given his freebasing, Stills was in the audience when Crosby and his band played the Golden Bear in Huntington Beach in the fall of 1981.

Starting with Nash, everyone involved in the record felt apprehensive about Crosby's arrival at Rudy Records that fall. Since none of the local hotels were likely to give Crosby a room, because of his growing reputation, Nash recruited Susan Rogers to use his credit card and check into a room. After securing one, Rogers drove across town, picked up Crosby and Dance and sneaked them into the hotel by way of a back entrance and service elevator. To Rogers' dismay, Crosby carried a cardboard box that read "David's Clothes." In the room, Crosby lit up and started free-basing, burning a hole in the mattress.

On the designated day in late 1981, Crosby arrived wearing a parka. Stills wasn't there, but Crosby and Nash locked eyes and embraced. Crosby had a chillier introduction to Stergis: although Crosby shook the guitarist's hand, he also imitated pouring a can of soda on Stergis' lap. "All I knew was that I was there in case he died on the road, to take his place," Stergis says. "I was the insurance policy, and David didn't like it at all."

Starting with Nash's "Song for Susan," Crosby began attempting to add his voice to the already finished tracks. To Zimmer, who was observing the proceedings, the lyrics of that devotional song—about someone deceiving himself about "how to exist"—seemed to impact Crosby emotionally. But finding a place for his voice wasn't as easy as it had once been, and he spent the next few days searching for the right harmony parts. "He was real humble and like a scared kitten," recalls Vitale. "He knew he was in the shit. But he wasn't arrogant or any of that. He was, 'Yeah, I'll try that.' You could tell the poor guy just wanted back in and wanted to prove himself. But it wasn't like on *CSN*. Here he had a problem staying focused and remembering words. It wasn't the same." When Crosby would take bathroom breaks, Nash would grow agitated.

During those rest periods, Crosby would sometimes retreat to free-base in the tech shop where Rogers worked. "It was a place where I could get high and not get in their face," he says. "But I was wrecked.

I had come down just far enough to do good work and then I'd go out and get high again. 'Wasted on the Way' is absolutely true. We could've made so much more music if we hadn't wasted time arguing with each other or being 'fuck those guys!' or being too smashed to work. Which I frequently was."

A few short years later, Rogers would find herself working for Prince, but in 1981, she was already a fan and had hung a poster of him in bikini underwear and trench coat (from his *Dirty Mind* album) on the wall of her office. During a later visit to her shop, Crosby looked up at the poster and asked Rogers why she liked Prince. "I said, 'Why *wouldn't* I like him?'" she recalls. "'He's a clever musician with a guitar. That was you. What's not to like?' My intention wasn't to be mean. My intention was to say, 'He's like you.' But I did use the past tense." Crosby didn't respond.

Since drama was still part of the group's DNA, no matter the configuration, the album naturally did not wrap up when planned. "Feel Your Love," one of Stills' songs, had a midtempo dance-floor sway and one of his most tender vocals. After the song was finished and added to the record, Rogers walked into the studio as it was playing and told Nash how much she loved the song. Confused, he asked what she meant; it was the first time he had played it for all of the crew to hear. Rogers began singing the melody of the disco band Rose Royce's 1978 hit "Love Don't Live Here Anymore," and Nash's face turned white. After Rogers was asked to run out to buy a copy of the record, they realized Stills had inadvertently copied the song. (Garfunkel also pointed out the similarity to Nash in a separate encounter later.) A musicologist hired by attorney Greg Fischbach to compare the two numbers determined that a lawsuit was likely, so "Feel Your Love" was yanked from the album at the last minute. In its place, Nash inserted a dark, throbbing rocker, "Into the Darkness," about Crosby's addiction and physical condition. (In Crosby's 1988 memoir *Long Time Gone*, Nash insisted the song had been inspired by a screenplay he'd been given. But he now admits he told a white lie: "It sounds like I was evading answering the question. But no, it was completely about David.") Crosby glared at Nash when he heard the song—although he later came to understand and somewhat appreciate why Nash had written it—but the band had to fill the void left by Stills' accidental infringement somehow. When Siddons realized the mastering engineer for the album had just left for a two-week vacation in the woods, he scrambled to track him down and paid him $1,000 in cash to redo the album at the last minute. "That," Siddons says, "was a high-melodrama day."

In light of the way it had been cobbled together over several years, with and without Crosby's participation, *Daylight Again* was a seamless marvel. Each song easily glided into the next. Only those with a predilection for reading liner notes would have noticed that Crosby's two contributions didn't feature any instrumental work by Stills or Nash, or, for that matter, by any of the musicians who played on the rest of the album—a sure-fire indication they had been recorded separately. It was also their first album without photographs of each man on the cover; in place of a group portrait was "Celestial Visitation," a painting by artist Gilbert Williams depicting three hovering spaceships. Again, only an insider would have known that corralling all three for a group photo in 1982 would have been next to impossible.

By force of will—and creativity—Stills had traditionally placed the most songs on their albums, but this time he clearly dominated. He had written or co-written five of the eleven songs, not counting two outtakes. His tracks ranged from the middle-of-the-road balladry of "You Are Alive" to the semi-boisterous rocker "Too Much Love to Hide." Nash's input, especially the way he counterbalanced Stills' musical overkill, was apparent in the way those songs were sung and played: there was nothing close to an off-key note or overly indulgent guitar solo. Thanks to Nash, *Daylight Again* was far less grizzled than *Thoroughfare Gap*, although Stills' presence—including his lead guitar on "Into the Darkness"—added a hint of grit that had been absent from Nash's *Earth & Sky*.

With its buffed polish, *Daylight Again* was more impeccably produced and easier on the ears than 1977's *CSN*. Yet it also had little use for the snug harmonizing that had drawn so many listeners to their sound. The elongated "Daylight Again" ended the new album, and in doing so brought them full circle to their earliest days together (even if Art Garfunkel largely replaced Crosby on the recording). But it was also the only purely unplugged moment on the album. Now sporting fulsome harmonies and a chunkier, more airtight arrangement that made it an instant group standard, "Southern Cross" was aimed squarely at radio airplay and hit that target, breaking into the Top 20, following up the success of the album's first single, Nash's "Wasted on the Way." Yet the *type* of radio that took those songs to its bosom was also revealing. By the early '80s, a new format, "adult contemporary," or AC, had come into the world. It mirrored the aging of the baby boomers, who were now approaching or into their forties. On so-called "Lite FM," out went ballads crooned by the likes of Andy Williams and Robert Goulet. In came ballads crooned by the likes of Lionel Richie, ex-Eagle Glenn Frey and Chicago, signifying the settled-down phase of many baby boomers. Each of those acts had Top 10 AC hits in the fall of 1982, where they were soon joined by "Southern Cross."

Much of *Daylight Again*, including the modest trot of "Wasted on the Way," wandered into similarly plush, unthreatening musical territory. Other than "Daylight Again," the two songs that most conjured the trio's formative days were, ironically, Crosby's. "Delta" had the zoned-out beauty of his best earlier songs, while his poignant rendition of Doerge and Henske's "Might as Well Have a Good Time," accompanied by Doerge's piano, was the album's most human and most relevant track. In light of the legal issues that would soon ensnare him, the song took on the air of a burnout's graceful farewell.

Before the album was unveiled, it became imperiled by one final legal complication. As everyone knew, Stills had cut the first version of "Southern Cross" for an album Columbia had shelved two years before. A provision in Columbia's contract, standard for most such deals, asserted that artists could not remake any song made for the label within five years of recording. Since Columbia had failed to release "Southern Cross," the issue seemed a moot point—to everyone save Columbia's legal department. Rather than risk another lawsuit or a delay in the album's release, Atlantic negotiated a monetary settlement with Columbia. In exchange for allowing Atlantic to release the Crosby, Stills and Nash version of the song, Columbia would also collect a substantial royalty from future album sales. It seemed like a small price to pay for a reunion—to some degree, anyway—of one of the label's most significant acts.

STARTING WITH THE *Los Angeles Times*, the what-about-Neil questions started to arise as soon as *Daylight Again* appeared in June 1982. "It's hard to approach him," Nash told the paper. "We're so afraid of rejection.

We're scared of him. I swear we are. We've had so much heartbreak with him. Who wants to be rejected by a mad musician? It's grief I don't need." Later, Nash added, "Maybe Neil doesn't think CSN music is very good. I don't know how he feels. I haven't asked him."

By that summer, communication between Young and the Crosby, Stills and Nash camp had reached its lowest point. Employees and friends of the trio never saw Young in their vicinity; some, like Stergis, would never meet Young at all. "Those were the years when David had an issue with drugs and Neil didn't want any part of it," says crew member John Vanderslice, who had worked on Crosby, Stills and Nash's 1977 tour before switching over to Young's team the following year. "Neil wasn't interested in that side of things. He was more music oriented. And also, Neil had lost some friends [as a result of drugs] along the way." Never one to withhold his opinions, Crosby articulated some of those conflicts during his solo performance in Virginia Beach in 1981. Describing each of his occasional bandmates to the crowd, he said Nash "lived a tough life, grew up very poor," described Stills as "tough, macho, the drinker," and summed up Young with "a totally isolated guy who hangs out only with the people who work for him. And only those people."

But Young had already begun outpacing them on several levels. On their own tours in the late '70s, Crosby, Stills and Nash would broadcast footage of whales to the accompaniment of the prerecorded "Critical Mass." Their technology was decidedly low rent: Vanderslice would find a seat behind the stage, pray that it aligned with the center of the screen, and press "play" on a projector. On tour in 1978, Young was several tech-savvy steps ahead of them. One set featured an oversized microphone and amp—and scurrying roadies dressed in brown-hooded garb, in homage to the Jawas scavengers in *Star Wars*. Young could even control his amps with a volume switch on his guitar.

Young was taken with the energy and vitality of punk rock, a genre that appalled most of his peers. With the help of the Ducks' Jeff Blackburn, who provided the key line about it being better to burn out than to rust, Young had written "Hey Hey, My My (Out of the Black)," which referenced Johnny Rotten of the Sex Pistols. On that same tour with Crazy Horse in 1978, Young largely ignored *Comes a Time*, the album he was ostensibly promoting. Instead he blasted out songs like his Blackburn collaboration, along with happily primitive pounders such as "Welfare Mothers" and "Sedan Delivery." None of them were punk, to be sure, but they shared a musical primitivism and volume with that genre. Dispensing with another trademark of his hippie days, Young even chopped his hair short. The combination of proud musical crudity and his stage's technical savvy spoke to the many contradictions in Young's persona—and again set him apart from his erstwhile partners.

Although few outside his immediate circle knew it, Young had other, more urgent reasons to stay in Northern California and avoid the choppy Crosby, Stills and Nash waters. In November 1978, he and Pegi had their first child, Ben, but Ben was soon diagnosed with cerebral palsy; he was also quadriplegic and unable to speak. Already dealing with his son Zeke's diagnosis of mild cerebral palsy, Young was sent reeling. Then, in early 1980, Pegi had surgery for a congenital arteriovenous malformation in her brain, which had affected her ability to speak. She gradually recovered, slowly learning to speak like her old self. Months later, the Youngs began welcoming volunteers into their home to help with Ben. At the time, little or none of this utterly tragic situation made it into the press. Young's manager, Elliot Roberts, capably kept the label executives in the dark.

While Crosby, Stills and Nash coped with music industry rejection, addiction issues and internal psychodramas, Young, grappling with his own harrowing family struggles, almost heroically continued to churn out new music. Between 1979 and 1982, he completed five albums while his partners struggled to patch together one. In June 1979, when Crosby and Nash split asunder and Stills was trying to relaunch his separate career, Young took his usual approach of combining separate recordings from different periods, this time to major effect. The first half of *Rust Never Sleeps* focused mostly on songs from his tech-enhanced Boarding House run, while the flip side featured onstage live cuts with Crazy Horse from months later. With one half of it hushed and the other thunderous, *Rust Never Sleeps* took each side of Young's musical personality to its extreme, but the experiment paid off. On the unplugged songs, which included his biting Crosby, Stills and Nash evaluation "Thrasher," his acoustic guitar was so ethereal it sounded like wind chimes. Combined with surreal tall tales like "Pocahontas" and "Ride My Llama," the music was almost mystical. The Crazy Horse side managed to be both more crunchy and thinner-sounding than they were on stage, but "Powderfinger," his river gun-battle ballad from 1976, was so cinematic it didn't need a screenplay. Young's guitar sliced through that song as well as the intentionally thumpier stomps, such as "Sedan Delivery," where the guitars clomped like prehistoric monsters emerging from the woods in a sci-fi movie. "My My, Hey Hey (Out of the Blue)" worked beautifully as a woodsy folk song; its electric version, "Hey Hey, My My (Into the Black)" sounded like natural heavy metal, or at least Young's version of it. The *Village Voice*'s annual Pazz & Jop poll of nationwide critics voted it the no. 2 album of the year, behind Graham Parker's *Squeezing Out Sparks.*

Around the time Stills and Nash were starting what became *Daylight Again,* in late 1980, Young unveiled *Hawks & Doves,* an album that was half folkie gentility, half frisky honky tonk about unions and the bonds of love. On it, he finally unleashed "The Old Homestead," his 1974 song about the Crosby, Stills, Nash and Young reunion that year. During the period when Crosby returned to Nash's studio to finally contribute vocals to that project, in the fall of 1981, Young released *Re-ac-tor,* a lumpy but intermittently forceful record with Crazy Horse (including the splattering "Shots" and the locomotive-tug "Get Back on It"). In retrospect, his work on that album revealed how pressing his family matters had become—they were beginning to distract him from his music. Leaving his longtime home and supporters, Reprise Records, for a new deal with Geffen Records, which his former co-manager had now founded, Young relocated to Hawaii in 1982. There, he recorded a more traditional but lightweight folk-rock set, *Island in the Sun,* with a ragtag band that included veterans of all his previous ensembles: Nils Lofgren, former Buffalo Springfield bassist Bruce Palmer, Crazy Horse drummer Ralph Molina and Stills-Young Band percussionist Joe Lala.

But by the dawn of the '80s, facile folk-pop was no longer the commercial force it had been, and Geffen knew it, leading him to reject *Island in the Sun.* Although stung by the news, Young returned to a project he'd begun before that record, songs using regular synthesizers as well as a vocoder—essentially a voice synthesizer that would make him sound like a talking or singing robot. On several levels, computer-driven music spoke to Young—as a way to communicate with his son Ben and as outlet for his rebellious streak. "A lot of that . . . singing through the vocoder and everything . . . people not being able to understand what I was saying, was a representation of what I thought it must be like for [Ben]," Young later told Patrick Doyle of *Rolling Stone*. "It may be a little bit, um, complex for people to understand where I was coming from with that."

Intentionally or not, it was a savvy decision. In the early years of the Reagan era, electronic-driven pop was nearly everywhere, from New York dance clubs to the radio, where hits in the new style—including the Human League's "Don't You Want Me" and Soft Cell's "Tainted Love/ Where Did Our Love Go"—were dominating the charts by the summer of 1982. Outside and down the street from Nash's Rudy Records studio, employees could see massive billboards advertising new albums by the Cars and Talking Heads. "The excitement in LA about the new style of music was evident, and it was so visible in Hollywood," says Susan Rogers. "A new day had arrived." For now, there was little the rock establishment could do about it except occasionally rail: at a solo show at the Greek Theatre in the summer of 1980, Stills made a crack about "the guys with skinny ties" who were trying to overtake him and his peers.*

In interviews, Young began praising bands like the Human League as modern folk music, and those comments extended to his early promotion for *Trans*, his computer-pop record. In August 1982, with the record nearing completion, Young invited writers like David Gans of *Record*, *Rolling Stone*'s offshoot music magazine, to his ranch to talk up his change in sonic direction. At times, Young, at thirty-six, sounded startlingly like a Cali-rock-dismissing punk rocker. Discussing new wave bands like Devo and the way they were rewriting the rules of pop music, Young told

---

*In 1979, Stills' band was involved in a highly publicized fracas with Elvis Costello. When both acts were on tour, they wound up in the same hotel—and same hotel bar—in Ohio, where a very drunk Costello goaded the Stills band by insulting Ray Charles and James Brown. "They just seemed in some way to typify a lot of things that I thought were wrong with American music," Costello told *Rolling Stone* several years later. "And that's probably quite unfair. But at the exact moment, they did." Bonnie Bramlett slugged Costello; Stills was in his room at the time.

Gans, "The more of the past you have, the less validity you have. And I really understand that concept." When talk turned to acoustic music, Young slammed his own past. "It's like having Frank Sinatra and Perry Como come back and try to do a concert for us," he said. "It's bullshit. It's what their parents like. . . . They don't care what Perry Como thinks."

When Gans pressed Young about his musical heritage, Young publicly unleashed on his former partners: "But Neil Young's Perry Como! It's the same thing, you know. Neil Young from the '60s and early '70s is like Perry Como," Young said. "That's the way I look at it. If I was still taking that seriously, I'd be where Crosby, Stills and Nash are today." ("I remember reading that," says Rao. "I'm sure he felt that way at the time. *I* felt that way at the time. But I thought, 'Jeez, would you guys mature? It's not third grade.'") He also took a swipe at CSNY's irregular work habits: "It wasn't like a band that got together and played." In every way, it felt like an era was over—an energizing thought for Young, a crippling one for Crosby, Stills and Nash.

As a valued art director and photographer and a member of the Los Angeles music community, Jimmy Wachtel, the brother of session guitarist Waddy Wachtel, thought he knew what to expect when dealing with Crosby, Stills and Nash. He'd designed the cover for *Replay*, an unnecessary 1980 compilation that Atlantic had released in lieu of a new album; he had done the same for *Daylight Again*, down to hiring a company to build a six-foot-high neon sign with the trio's name. (The contraption implied a group cohesion that the album itself lacked.)

But when Wachtel arrived at Studio 2 of the Zoetrope film lot in Hollywood, he realized he didn't know at least *one* thing about the band in 1982. The musicians were rehearsing on the long part of an L-shaped structure; on the shorter end lay a seemingly out-of-place, one-room structure, like a rent-a-shed found at hardware stores. "I said, 'What's that?'" Wachtel says, "and they said, 'That's where Crosby goes.'" The unit would be a place for Crosby to retreat to freebase without having to leave the studio compound. "That was extreme, even for the times," Wachtel says. "I know a lot of people who were out of control, but *that* was out of control."

Even before the album was released, the litany of horror stories around Crosby seemed to grow by the day. On March 28, he was driving a rented Granada to the nuclear plant in San Onofre, where he was scheduled to join Stills and Nash at a protest concert. On the 405 freeway, Crosby had a seizure, and his car drifted from the right lane to the center, and finally into the concrete divider. When the police arrived, Crosby was miraculously unharmed, but officers found a .45, a film canister with white powder inside, quaaludes and drug paraphernalia. Crosby was charged with carrying a concealed weapon and driving under the influence of drugs or alcohol.

About two weeks later, on April 12, Crosby, on one of several solo tours he did for desperately needed cash, was in a makeshift dressing room at a Dallas club called Cardi's, waiting to play the second set of the night, when two police officers, who were in the area to assist with another call, decided to conduct a "routine inspection" of the club. Approaching a black curtain to the side of the stage, they pushed past an assistant—who warned them not to enter—and came upon Crosby holding a propane torch and a glass pipe. They also found a gym bag with a .45 in it. A roadie who worked for Crosby tried to knock the pipe out of Crosby's hand to convince the police it wasn't his boss', but it was too late. Once again, Crosby was cuffed on drug and weapons charges; once again, he was out on bail. When the group attempted another reunion, at a "Peace Sunday" rally and benefit concert in June, Crosby attended, and his voice was reasonably strong during a performance of "Long Time Gone." But few were happy to see him there. "David was like a bad penny at Peace Sunday," says Rao. "He was persona non grata. When he did show up, they didn't flock to him. It was very stressful."

Once *Daylight Again* had finally been cobbled together, the band—or at least Nash—put the best possible public face on the project. The reasons for Crosby's initial lack of involvement were glossed over or ignored. "When we put all the songs together, we realized that a lot of them were CSN songs in disguise," Nash told the *Los Angeles Times*. "We needed Crosby's voice. We could force the album through as a Stills-Nash album and forever hear in our heads what these songs should really sound like or, we could get Crosby." When "Wasted on the Way" was unveiled as the first single, few listeners knew that they were probably not hearing Crosby at all. "Stephen and Graham had a mask on as far as the public," says Vitale. "But it was their band and their family. One of the members of their family was screwing up. They wore it well on the outside, but inside I could tell it was tearing them up."

A tour was the inevitable next step to promote the album, but the logistics and even the morality of working with Crosby's addiction offered no easy solution. One night at Rudy, Nash agonized over whether to take Crosby on tour with them—and risk having him die on the road—or not supporting his family. (He and Susan had two boys—Jackson, then four, and Will, two—and were expecting a daughter, Nile, in July.) "I remember thinking what a terrible moral dilemma it would be," says Rogers. "For the need of money, you need to risk your friend's life." That income was considerable: individually, Crosby, Stills or Nash could command, at best, $15,000 to $20,000 a night, but together, they could now earn as much as $100,000 a show.

Nash remained torn. Although dates had been booked starting on the last day of July, Siddons was prepared to send telegrams to promoters saying that the tour was being canceled due to an unspecified illness. "I didn't know David that well," Siddons says. "So I said to Graham, 'What do you get when you get David clean?' He said, 'You get a *clean* asshole!'" They laughed—though Crosby could be taxing, he was still endearing—but a decision had to be made. The tour, if undertaken, would employ forty crew members. To haul people and equipment, they would need five tour buses and three tractor-trailer trucks.

Finally, Nash gave the go-ahead. He wanted to see if they could make it work, and part of him also hoped the demands of having to perform would set Crosby straight. (Others in their camp also felt Atlantic was exerting pressure.) The band hired Richard "Smokey" Wendell, who had worked as a drug-abuse enforcer for John Belushi, to keep Crosby from overdosing; Wendell had also been a Secret Service agent for Richard Nixon. At a picnic table at Rudy, Wendell came by to meet Crosby, who stiffened and flashed a wary look. Charged with making the intros, Rao explained that Wendell would be living with Crosby, adding that Wendell had worked for Belushi—who had overdosed a few months before. Crosby looked at Rao and said, "Great reference." Stills and Nash would refer to Wendell by his code name, "Mr. Washington," and to Crosby as "George's guy"—sometimes in front of Crosby, who didn't grasp the reference.

When a young woman visiting Zoetrope heard the band rehearsing and asked who it was, she replied, when told, "Really? I didn't know they were still *alive.*" Not surprisingly, the scene inside the studio was productive but often tense. Stills would often call out Crosby for being late or missing notes. "There were some big arguments, yelling and screaming, at Zoetrope," says Vitale. "Typical stuff in any band, but more intense because of Crosby's condition. After a while it gets to the point where you go, 'Why can't we be a *normal* band and have just a few arguments and not full-blown warfare?' It was intense."

Once the tour began, the change in Crosby was more than noticeable. In his long-sleeved flannel shirts, he looked heavier than he'd ever been. Even more shockingly, he talked to the audience far less than he once had. Music critic Geoffrey Himes, reviewing their Baltimore show, noted Crosby's "immobile, untalkative presence," and Crosby sang fewer lead vocals than ever. The most movement anyone saw from him would be his lips. As Vitale recalls, "David was up there like a prop so people who paid money to see CSN could see CSN. It was very disheartening."

The crowds flocking to the arenas to see the band's first tour in four years were unaware of the on-the-road arrangements that had been made to accommodate its ailing third wheel. A special room dubbed "Jump Street" was added to the side of the stage near Crosby to ensure he could take a break twice during every show to get high. Crew members were told to be respectful of Crosby and not to expect lengthy, in-depth conversations. On his first tour with the band, Crosby's guitar tech, Mason Wilkinson, would see Crosby get a certain look in his eye and realize it was time for him to take a break. "Nobody knew if he was coming back for the next song or the fourth song or the rest of the show," says Wilkinson. To ward off any bad notes or strums emanating from Crosby, the engineer working the sound board, Stanley Johnston, became expert at turning the volume of Crosby's voice down and replacing it with the voice of the keyboardist, Michael Finnigan. (He did the same with Stills if he was singing flat.) Johnston could also turn down Crosby's guitar and replace it with Stergis'. Stills and Nash had hired their biggest band to date—three guitarists, two keyboardists, a rhythm section and an added percussionist—to ensure that they would be able to compensate for Crosby's occasional missing-in-action guitar or voice.

In spite of everyone's concerns, Crosby made it to every show; the band was never forced to cancel, even though at times he would appear backstage at the last minute. But one musician who had been recruited for the tour, bassist George "Chocolate" Perry, saw the difference in him. "David and I used to lock on stage and look at each other eye to eye and groove to each other as Stephen was soloing," Perry says. "I'd stand in front of David, and he'd dig that. All of that went away when David was spaced on stage. We didn't have any of that face-to-face playing anymore. I used to look at him and say, 'Hey, turn around and jam!' and he was staring into the crowd or past the crowd." Before many of the shows, Stergis, feeling a bit guilty about his backup role, would drop by Crosby's dressing room and offer his support.

When the band played New Jersey's Brendan Byrne Arena in August, coinciding with Crosby's forty-first birthday, Crosby was nowhere to be found when they wanted to celebrate it with cake. Ertegun asked Stills to get him, and Stills begged off. Ertegun himself went up to Crosby's hotel room and dragged him down for the cutting of the cake. Crosby posed for a few over-the-top photos sticking the knife into the cake, but within minutes he was gone, back to his room.

Despite the difficulties and the worry, and the fallow years that had preceded it, the tour demonstrated that the ties between the band and its audience, if anything, had strengthened. The crowds would roar during every note they hit—or almost hit—during "Suite: Judy Blue Eyes." They forgave Crosby's muted presence, Nash's tight, zebra-striped T-shirts and new-wave buzzcut, and the rough patches in the vocal harmonies. The payoff would be simple: that moment, every so often, when an inert Crosby would break into a small, blissful smile after a moment of harmony or an audience response. It was a small gesture, but one that communicated something all too real: hope.

THE *Daylight Again* tour began to wind down in the middle of November 1982. *Rolling Stone* reported that Stills was so unhappy on the road with Crosby and Nash that he was eager to reform Buffalo Springfield (which he later denied, attributing the rumor to a Springfield reunion meeting that didn't lead anywhere). After the band's November 14 show in Iowa, Stills checked into his room at a nearby Radisson. He indulged in military rifle drills with his guitar for a while, then settled down to examine a series of photo proofs under consideration for a Crosby, Stills and Nash biography that Dave Zimmer was writing, with accompanying photographs by Henry Diltz.

Using a small magnifying glass, Stills focused on a series of photos taken behind the Shady Oak property in Los Angeles in 1969. One shot especially grabbed his attention. "You can tell by the way Neil is looking in this shot that he's saying, 'Man, I'm here, but I'm not really part of this group and I'm gonna break your heart again, Stephen,'" Stills said to Zimmer, his voice radiating disappointment. Asking Diltz not to use the photo, Stills marked it with an X with such force that the pen ripped through the proof.

By that point, Young was no longer even in the same country. What came to be known as the Trans Band had worked on its repertoire in California clubs before heading to Europe for a theatrical presentation unlike anything Young had yet attempted, complete with a stage that jutted out into the audience. To play the new material from the album *Trans*, he would make use of a vocoder. The tour had been a chore from the start. Returning guitarist and keyboardist Nils Lofgren had to sit down and patiently play Young standards with an addled Bruce Palmer over and over again to make sure he remembered them. "One day Neil says, 'I need you to do me a favor. After rehearsal, go to [Palmer's] house and sit there and play the songs for a few hours with him,'" Lofgren says. "So we played 'Cowgirl in the Sand' over and over. It was an exercise in helping Bruce with muscle memory." It was just a prelude to a chaotic tour that baffled audiences who were hearing synthesizer-dominated material from an album that wasn't even out yet.

Crosby, Stills and Nash coped with at least one last stage challenge before the *Daylight Again* tour stumbled to a close. Their three nights in November at the Universal Amphitheatre in Los Angeles should have been relatively easy to get through; they would be playing in their hometown, before friends, family and industry supporters. But they would still have to work around Crosby's issues, and the pressure had been turned up a notch: the band had been offered a six-figure sum by Universal to film the shows for cable or video distribution, a cash infusion no one was eager to turn down. (In one of the earliest signs of the growing affluence of the baby boomers, higher-priced tickets for the first twenty-five rows included dinner at a restaurant in Huntington Beach and a bus ride to the theater.) Nash joked to Siddons that they might have to use a cardboard cutout of Crosby for the filming, but deep down, everyone knew the situation was fraught. Nash secretly hoped the idea of being filmed for posterity would help Crosby focus. Before the show, Crosby himself was nervous, and a makeup artist lathered him with a putty-like substance to cover the sores on his face.

Once again, they made it through the performances. But the editing process that soon began turned out to be even more arduous. Working with a production team, Nash did his best to keep the camera from lingering on Crosby while ensuring he was present in enough shots to show them singing together. Stopping by the editing room, Susan Rogers heard cries of "Pull it back, pull it back!" when the shot zoomed in on Crosby. Even in the fleeting close-ups of the final video, it was hard to miss Crosby's glazed-over expressions. Watching the film, Vitale—who, sitting at the drum kit all night, had only seen the backs of his bosses' heads—was shocked at how Crosby looked. "I thought 'What the hell is wrong with Crosby?'" he recalls. "Until I saw that video, I had no idea that was the look on his face the whole night."

As with *Daylight Again*, Nash, with input from Stills and their team, was able to cobble together a viable product that again attempted to demonstrate that Crosby, Stills and Nash were a unified front. But by then, even Nash's faith in them was fraying. "It was a mess to deal with," he says. "We were trying our best to put this face up to the world that we were together and everything was okay. But it wasn't. It was rotting from the inside." Somehow, all four of them had made it through a troubling patch. What they didn't realize, together or separately, was that the rot would only grow deeper in the years to come.

CHAPTER 8

MARCH 1983-DECEMBER 1985

I f I happen to walk offstage, I'll be right back," Young warned the 5,500 concertgoers staring at him inside the Commonwealth Convention Center in Louisville, Kentucky. It was the night of March 4, 1983, and to the disbelief of the crowd, his prediction came to pass very soon after he had made it.

About an hour into his performance, Young felt ill, left the stage and passed out in his dressing room. The Jefferson County coroner, who happened to be in the audience, was asked to hurry backstage to check on him; after determining that Young couldn't resume, the coroner took the stage and told the thousands in the hall that Young had to cancel the rest of the show. (Later, it was determined that he had been suffering from a bout with the flu.) What followed was an unusual sight for a Young concert: already peeved by the long lines they'd endured just to get into the venue—fewer doors than usual had been opened before the show—some of the incensed Kentuckians threw beer cups and chairs at the stage, hitting some of the members of Young's crew in the process. Three people were ultimately arrested for inciting a riot.

As unexpected as that debacle may have seemed, though, it was not completely surprising: Young was walking a narrow tightrope at that point in his career. A few months before the show, he'd released *Trans*, his computer-music hoedown. The cover art—side-by-side illustrations of Young trying to hitch a ride in a classic '50s Cadillac on the right, and a holographic Young trying to do the same in a futuristic vehicle on the left—made the point that he was venturing into innovative territory. The music proved the claim: "Mr. Soul" was reconceived as vocoder-driven synth pop, and throughout, Young's voice was transformed into an electronically chirping bird ("Transformer Man"), a cattle-rustling android

("Computer Cowboy") and a lovestruck robot ("Sample and Hold"). Those tracks were disquieting but also weirdly beautiful—computer-music art. But unwilling to commit entirely to the concept, Young had offset those tunes with more conventional—and more insubstantial—pop. "Little Thing Called Love" was as tossed off as his later contributions to Crosby, Stills, Nash and Young albums. The public was generally confused; critics used words like "interesting" and "challenging" as they grappled with *Trans.* Wisely, Young's early 1983 tour offered something for everyone: acoustic sets of classics, segments where he strapped on his headset and played the electro version of "Mr. Soul" and, for the true believers in the crowd, footage of Buffalo Springfield and Crosby, Stills, Nash and Young to accompany "Don't Be Denied." During "After the Gold Rush," he changed the reference to "in the 1970s" to "the '80s."

But the ground was shifting around Young and his former bandmates in so many ways that it was hard to know how to move forward. For a few years, at least, they'd had a friend—or, at least, a like-minded politician—in the White House. In the early afternoon of June 9, 1977, Crosby, Stills and Nash had been invited to meet Jimmy Carter. Carter was their kind of president—an unabashed rock devotee who had quoted Dylan at the previous year's Democratic National Convention. His friends in the Allman Brothers Band had played benefit concerts for his campaign. Thanks to Stills' connections with the Democratic Party, the trio—along with their managers John Hartmann and Michael John Bowen—were awarded five minutes in the Oval Office at exactly 1:00 P.M., in between Carter hosting a luncheon on Middle Eastern policy with Hubert Humphrey and a meeting to hammer out appropriations for NASA. Stills donned a three-piece suit; true to his threat not to dress up for the occasion, the ever contrary Crosby arrived wearing a suit jacket but no tie. Nash would recall Hartmann taking a hit of a joint "by the open window" before Carter arrived, just for the sake of doing it, although Hartmann would decline to comment.

The election of Ronald Reagan, who'd been the reactionary, hippie-bashing governor of California in the days when Crosby, Stills, Nash and Young had come together, had come as a surprise to them. Starting with his haircut, which made him look like a high school principal from 1955—a vivid contrast to Carter's more up-to-date over-the-ears coif—Reagan was a throwback to a time they thought they'd never see again. Early in 1983, the era of fallout shelters and "duck-and-cover" fire drills in schools threatened to resume as Reagan goaded America into a new arms race with the Soviet Union. The same month that Young was in Kentucky, Reagan addressed the public on TV to propose the Strategic Defense Initiative (SDI), popularly known as "Star Wars." Under the proposal, he wanted the military to develop a defense system that could intercept a nuclear missile heading toward the United States. Meanwhile, First Lady Nancy Reagan's antidrug "Just Say No" campaign was a rebuke to the lifestyles that Crosby, Stills, Nash and Young and their generation had long practiced.

Just as dismayingly, the changes they'd fought and sung for hadn't arrived. The "No Nukes" concerts were barely half a decade old, and some of that mission had been accomplished. Nuclear power plants were historically unpopular; in 1982, plans for eighteen such facilities were canceled. The following year, the US Supreme Court upheld California's ban on building new plants, and the ruling extended to seven other states. But it was also dawning on Nash that concerts and rallies were not going to shred the military-industrial complex, and he found himself in the early stages of despair. "I went through a period where I would get depressed and feel that the environmental movement wasn't making the strides forward that I thought it would, that my vote didn't count," Nash said years later. (Although he held dual citizenship, Nash had become an American citizen in 1978.) "I wondered whether benefit concerts made any difference. It was causing paralysis."

In their own business, the old standards no longer seemed to apply. In January 1983, *Daylight Again* was certified platinum, for a million sales. But in the new era of blockbuster releases, that figure was no longer as significant as it once was. Michael Jackson's *Thriller*, the album that loomed over all of pop in the early months of 1983, was selling 300,000 copies every five days. The Jackson Five's first Motown single, "I Want You Back," had been released the same year as *Crosby, Stills & Nash*, but Jackson had reinvented himself in ways that the trio couldn't seem to pull off. MTV had become pop's leading influencer, and music videos were now such a part of the business that video production was eating up 30 to 45 percent of the time at Hollywood soundstages. Crosby, Stills and Nash had ventured into that territory with a clip of "Southern Cross," their faces mostly in shadowy silhouettes to ensure that their ages—early forties and late thirties—wouldn't turn off MTV viewers.

In further technological shifts, 1983 also marked the debut of the first cell phone, Motorola's DynaTAC 8000X, and the introduction of *Mario Brothers*, which would revive the flagging video game industry. The vinyl LP, the medium so associated with CSNY music—and their generation—was giving way to the compact disc; throughout 1983, CD players and discs would be unveiled in about seventy-five stores across the country. "The sooner the compact disc replaces the conventional black vinyl LP, the better as far as I'm concerned," a PolyGram executive said that spring. When WEA (Warner/Elektra/Atlantic) announced the first batch of albums to be transferred onto CD and available to record buyers that August, the list included vintage albums by Joni Mitchell; Emerson, Lake and Palmer; and Rod Stewart, but none by Crosby, Stills, Nash and/or Young. They'd have to settle for the sight of *So Far* topping *Cashbox*'s budget-oldies chart over Carole King's *Tapestry*, the Who's *Live at Leeds* and the first Doors album.

In general, the '80s would rarely be kind to musicians of their generation; in the new world of music videos and synthesizers, they were considered overnight dinosaurs. But Crosby, Stills, Nash and Young weren't always kind to each other, either. The same month Young fell ill on the job, the new issue of *International Musician and Recording World*, containing a feature story on Crosby, Stills and Nash, arrived on newsstands. Writer Steven Dupler had interviewed the trio not long after David Gans' interview with Young had been published in *Record*, and the strain between the two camps erupted publicly. "We could get blasé and say like Neil does in a lot of ways, 'My past is off in a box somewhere,'" Nash groused. "But then, his new tour is 90 percent old stuff, you know?" Stills told Dupler, "I'm more of a team player, man. I always was, and I always will be. That was always the frustrating thing about Neil. . . . He ain't into being in a band. He never was and he never will be. . . . The problem was when he would sit there and lie about it. And then he'd go gripe to our friends." Only Crosby kept his emotions in check, referring to Young as "a very nice man—I love him a lot," and "a very brave guy" with "a great deal of courage."

Crosby had reasons not to insult Young. During this time, Young had offered up a house on his ranch to Crosby to give him a place to detox. "Neil tried one time," Crosby says. "God bless him. He did make an attempt, and I loved him for it." Along with friends like Jackson Browne and, at times, Nash, Young had given up in disgust when Crosby proved unwilling to help himself. (Stills seemed exasperated with Crosby but hopeful that he would work things out for himself and survive.) Young had enough on his plate; Crosby's issues now had to take a seat way in the back.

Yet it was Crosby's legal and personal situation that would be the most jarring sign of the times, the embodiment of the crash and burn of the '60s. On June 3, 1983, a little over a year after he was busted in his dressing room in Dallas, Crosby found himself in a plaid jacket and baggy corduroys in a Dallas courtroom, about to hear a state district court judge in Texas, Pat McDowell, announce his verdict in the jury-free trial. Setting the tone for most of the coverage, the *New York Daily News* described Crosby as "a husky, extroverted Californian whose hippie language, shoulder-length hair and Fu Manchu beard seemed to lock him into a '60s time capsule." (Crosby didn't have a beard, but the remainder of that description was accurate at the time.) In the most shocking development of their fifteen-year saga together—which was saying something, given all they'd been through—Crosby was found guilty of cocaine possession and "unlawfully carrying a handgun in a tavern" (the loaded .45 that had been found in his bag backstage at Cardi's). The verdict was a decisive victory for the assistant district attorney in the case, Knox Fitzpatrick, who turned out to be Crosby's worst nightmare: a hardened southern lawyer who was not especially fond of law-flouting renegades.

Crosby, who at times had dozed during the trial—to the point where one member of his legal team had had to jostle him to stop him from snoring—faced thirty years in jail. The repercussions—to the band, for its income, and even in terms of its image—could be sizable. "I was sitting in front of my TV in Hawaii watching my friend fall asleep in front of the fucking judge," recalls Nash, who was even more startled when he saw

Crosby's mug shot. "He was wearing a CSN jacket. I thought, 'Oh, fuck!'"
It was not the sort of advertising or public image Nash wanted to present
to the world. For now, however, the scope of the fallout was still uncertain: the sentencing would come a few weeks later.

TOWARD THE END of June, days after the verdict, a private plane carrying
Crosby, Stills, Nash and their musicians and employees began its descent
into Rome. With or without Young, the trio hadn't performed in Europe
as a group following their last show at the Wembley Arena almost a decade before. Since they'd neglected the continent for so long—and were
about to release a new album that would benefit from overseas promotion—the Crosslight Agency had set up a month-long tour that would
encompass shows in France, Germany, Italy, Switzerland and England.

The flight to Rome, which occurred later in the trip, was rock touring
business as usual—with one flagrant exception. A short while before
the tour had begun, one of the Crosby, Stills and Nash crew had found
himself in a difficult situation when an accountant had asked for proof
of purchase after the roadie had bought drugs for one of the band members. "This sleazy guy would show up and give you the drugs, so how
do you account for that?" the crew member says. "The accountant said I
had embezzled seven grand. I just couldn't prove it. You can't put it in a
statement." The crew member was soon dismissed.

Rightly sensing they shouldn't attempt to smuggle contraband through
customs, everyone aboard the plane realized it would be best to use up
all the drugs on the plane before landing. The result was a last-minute
frenzy of excess. "We had to put the wheels down but we hadn't quite
snorted it all and there was a lot left over," Nash recalls. "The toilet on
that plane was one of the most drug-infested toilets ever."

Given how long it would take the three or four of them to fashion new
music together, it was hardly surprising that an immediate follow-up to
Daylight Again was nowhere in the cards. But the band, largely Stills
and Nash, pieced one together anyway: *Allies*, the most haphazard record the trio would ever make. "It was bolted together for cash-flow
reasons," Bill Siddons says, and it showed. The album was a patchwork
of concert recordings (from the same fall 1982 Los Angeles show that
had been filmed for their cable special), two new studio recordings, and

two live recordings featuring Crosby that dated back to 1977, before his voice began to fray from drug abuse. The album had moments of glory, like a 1977 version of "Shadow Captain," the first live recording released from that reunion tour, and the trio's version of Nash's antinuke "Barrel of Pain (Half-Life)," a revival of a song on the verge of being forgotten. But it was hard to envision a less inspiring record than *Allies*, which personified the dysfunction of the band at that collective low point. The two new songs on the album didn't even feature Crosby. Stills' "War Games," propelled by a huffing and puffing synthesizer but with enough of a hook that it could have been a hit, had been slated for the film of the same name, a nuke-age thriller starring Matthew Broderick, but ultimately it was barely heard in the movie. The music video they released for the song, which included zero footage of the band, received negligible airtime on MTV, since it was deemed to be too much like a trailer for the film. Nash's "Raise a Voice" was intended as a rousing call to arms—it even resurrected the opening lines of Stills' "We Are Not Helpless" from his first solo album, conjuring memories of a now long-ago time when they had tapped into the political zeitgeist. But with its placid, even-tempered melody, the song was the musical equivalent of Nash's despair over the state of the antinuke movement: it could barely rouse itself.

The promotional materials for *Allies* seemed to depict a band in denial. All the photographs showed Crosby, Stills and Nash between 1969 and 1977, as if the previous six years—and Crosby's problems—hadn't existed. A press release claimed they would record a new album "in the fall," an optimistic statement, at best, given Crosby's legal obstacles. Even the album cover was compromised. The original artwork, conceived by art director Jimmy Wachtel, was hilarious: a photo of Franklin Roosevelt, Winston Churchill and Joseph Stalin at the 1945 Yalta Conference at the end of World War II, but with Crosby, Stills and Nash's heads on their bodies. Fearful that the doctored photo would offend fans in Europe, their managers decided to replace the artwork with a patchwork of distorted concert photos. After all, they wanted Europeans to buy tickets to their concerts.

As the band awaited the next stage of Crosby's bust—sentencing and perhaps an appeal—they headed to Europe. Their management now included Jeff Wald, the fast-lane former husband and manager of pop singer Helen Reddy. Wald was now overseeing Stills' career, while Siddons and Peter Golden handled Nash (and, although not officially, Crosby). Extraordinary precautions were put in place. According to Wald, the budget included about $2,500 a night in case Crosby's freebase torch set fire to hotel rooms. In light of the numerous border crossings that would be involved, avoiding busts was also vital. In each city, they arranged for a local dealer to buy whatever was required and stash it in a safe deposit box until the drugs were needed at concerts or hotels. It wasn't the first time something along those lines had been attempted; when Crosby and Nash toured Japan in 1976, they had been warned not to bring anything illicit into the country, but, according to one crew member, "we found somebody in the country, for pot more than anything else." (The precautions paid off: even Nash's harmonica case was checked for contraband.) But the 1983 European tour took that plan to its queasy extreme.

Logistically, the individual-dealer scheme made a certain demented sense: no one wanted to find Crosby wandering around alone in search of drugs. But the scenario was still too much of a risk for some. After seven years of working with Stills and then the trio, drummer Joe Vitale quit, fearing a bust was imminent. "I wasn't about to go to Europe with someone carrying that many drugs," he says. "They had dogs and checkpoints. It was serious. I could see this thing going to hell in a hand-basket." George Perry, their regular bass player, stayed, but he, too, had reservations about the tour; he'd heard rumors that law enforcement officers were always hovering around venues. "We were nervous—Are we next?" he said. "I'm sure everyone felt the same way. We thought [the police surveillance] was centered around the whole band, not just David. When we got back to LA, I didn't leave the house for a *long* time. And I was nice to everybody: 'Yes, sir!' 'Yes, ma'am!' For a good while."

Crosby was by no means the only one in the organization given to partying. Once, a formidable pile of cocaine was delivered to a crew bus, courtesy of Crosby. "That *never* happened," says one crew member, who was puzzled by the gift. He and his road mates soon learned why it had been sent their way: the cut was poor, and therefore useless for a solid freebase high. (Nevertheless, the crew didn't turn down the offer.) Stills would later admit to *The New Yorker* that he was having his own issues at the time. "I never drank until later, because my father was such an object lesson in how not to act," he said. "And, lo and behold, in the '80s, I turned into him!"

Yet, as hard as it was to imagine, the tour was even more stressful than the previous year's reunion. Accompanying the trio for part of it, Crosby's friend Carl Gottlieb thought Crosby was the one who was the most in command of the three at a show in Toulouse. But thanks to poor sales and a less-than-reliable promoter, concerts in France and Spain—Barcelona and Madrid among them—were canceled. When an audacious plan to commandeer Wembley Arena for three nights fizzled on account of low sales, the shows were collapsed into one. Since the Wembley show could have been their last, in light of Crosby's upcoming sentencing, Nash later told writer Dave Zimmer that Wembley was one of their strongest. But the trek was still unsettling for all involved. "We did what we had to in order to make it work," Siddons says. "It's amazing we got through it and didn't all go to jail. It was completely dysfunctional. And very scary." When they arrived back in the States, with the less welcoming '80s very much in full swing, their future was more uncertain than ever.

IN A BRIEF RESPITE from the chaos, Nash picked up the pieces with his previous band. In 1981, a condensed medley of old Hollies hits had been a left-field sensation in the UK. The band—at that time, Allan Clarke, Tony Hicks and Bobby Elliott—decided to patch up its differences with Nash and record their first album with him in about fifteen years, although, in light of Nash's earlier departure from the band, unease between Nash and Clarke lingered. The reunion album, *What Goes Around . . .*, released in mid-1983, was not a return to their '60s glory days; it swamped the group's harmonies in generic synth-pop arrangements designed to make them sound modern. But at least Nash had one breather from everything that was encircling his main band.

On August 5, 1983, Crosby and Nash were reunited, in a way, in a courtroom. Crosby's sentencing day had arrived, and he again turned up in the best shape he could manage, in a jacket and pressed blue jeans. Before the sentencing was handed down, one of Crosby's defense lawyers attempted to explain that his client had been left "paranoid" by

John Lennon's murder in 1980. Another read aloud a letter from Nash to the court that stated, in part, "I truly believe that what David needs at this junction of his life is help, guidance and professional supervision. I believe that confinement in a prison would probably kill him." In a biting response, prosecutor Fitzpatrick observed that Crosby had made "very fine music," but pointed out that Nash had "a financial interest in having Mr. Crosby [out of prison] and on the concert circuit with him."

When the time to announce his decision arrived, Judge McDowell had the ultimate rebuttal. Crosby's legal team was hoping, at worst, for three years behind bars. Instead, he was handed a five-year sentence for cocaine and three years for gun possession; the sentences would run concurrently, so Crosby would only face five years in prison. Thanks to an immediate request for an appeal, he was released on an $8,000 bond. But the scenario was bleak. It was only compounded when, in the same month, *People* magazine published a devastating cover story on Crosby with the headline "Cocaine Casualty." In the interview, conducted at his Mill Valley home before sentencing, Crosby came across as a last-legs contender, financially and physically: "His torso is bloated and heavy, his fingernails are black and bitten, and his arms are scarred with wounds and bruises." The story reported that Crosby's phone service had been cut off for lack of funds; as a result, he had to drive a motorcycle into town to use a pay phone. For years, the group had fought publicly and trashed each other in the press and in song, but they had still managed to keep their personal lives out of the media, for the most part. Crosby's very public fall, embodied by the *People* story, revealed the darkness behind the harmonies and appearance of brotherhood.

A month and a half later, in one of the few times he publicly acknowledged Crosby's plight, Young dedicated "Only Love Can Break Your Heart" to his former bandmate at a show in Nashville. Although his own life had been far removed from Crosby's situation, Young had also struggled in the new decade. *Trans* had alienated the longtime faithful, but it hadn't lured in any new, younger followers. In response to the creative and personal turmoil engulfing him, Young made another wheels-spinning U-turn and decided to record a country album. (That fall, he was also hit with an unexpected expense: by decree of the Los Angeles Superior Court, he would have to pay his former partner, Carrie

Snodgress, $10,000 a month; in addition, he would have to spend as much as $300,000 to upgrade her home in Los Angeles, where she lived with their son, Zeke.) When Geffen executives expressed ambivalence toward the country music idea, Young changed courses yet again; in a pithy comment on their desire to see him play more rock and roll, he recorded a collection of reverb-drenched, loopy '50s rock covers and originals, as if he and his white bucks were fronting a rockabilly band. To ram the sarcastic point home, he called the album *Everybody's Rockin'.*

Starting with a cover depicting a slicked-back Young in a white suit, *Everybody's Rockin'* affectionately harked back to Young's teen rock-band days in his native Canada. Renditions of period oldies, such as Junior Parker and Sam Phillips' "Mystery Train" and Jimmy Reed's "Bright Lights, Big City," were bloodless, but his own "Kinda Fonda Wanda" was lascivious fun. The sentiments in "Payola Blues," another Young original that sported a '50s ducktail, spoke to Young's frustrations with radio. The album was droll, but it was also something a Young record hadn't been before—a novelty. Even the sonics were jarring; with echoey reverb encasing every track, the music felt as if it could be blaring out of a malt shop several blocks away.

Everybody's Rockin' could have tapped into the retro rockabilly revival propelled by new, freshly pompadoured bands like the Stray Cats. The punk and subsequent new wave scenes owed a debt to the woolliness of early rock and roll, and so did Young. But the album, which didn't even make it into the Top 40, was ultimately a misfire: it made the most authentic and least trendy of rockers seem suddenly inauthentic. The best part of the album was director Tim Pope's oddball, out-of-sync video for "Wonderin'," which demonstrated that Young's dry sense of humor remained (though, to Nils Lofgren's puzzlement, the new version sounded nothing like the one he'd cut with Young over a decade before).

In May 1984, Young and his wife, Pegi, welcomed their first daughter, Amber Jean, but Young's work would only grow more baffling. David Geffen, now on the other side of the record company fence, had been angered by Young's seeming unwillingness to make a traditional Neil Young–style album instead of a series of what felt like gimmicks. Geffen Records had scored a few hits since its 1980 launch, but was struggling following failed albums by Donna Summer and Elton John. The last thing its founder needed to hear was the sound of another former superstar crashing. In late 1983, he sued Young for $3.3 million for making supposedly uncommercial music. "One day, I show up and I hear all this hubbub with Elliot Roberts," says Lofgren. "I hear that David Geffen is suing Neil because he's too 'un-Neil Young-like.' I'm thinking, 'How can this happen?'" Young countersued. Both suits would be dropped about a year and a half later, but the tumult was another sign of how off course Young seemed to be.

Young remained undeterred in following his muse, and in late 1984, he completed his country album, *Old Ways*. Revved up by his new friendship with Willie Nelson and another new lineup—the International Harvesters, which included his longtime allies Ben Keith and Tim Drummond along with fresh recruits, such as the Cajun fiddler Rufus Thibodeaux—Young decided to go all in on the genre. Gone were the sunglassed tech guru of *Trans* and the slickly dressed greaser of *Everybody's Rockin'*. With his sleeveless T-shirts, floppy hats and amiable grin, Young now reinvented himself as a guy at a feed store who also happened to play guitar.

Old Ways wouldn't be released for another year, but Young road-tested his new lineup and material by playing on a double bill in the summer of 1984 with veteran hell-raiser Waylon Jennings and his singer-songwriter wife, Jessi Colter. The move was somewhat risky: Jennings had little patience for phonies, especially those seeking to switch over to his genre for commercial gain. But Young won him over—Jennings saw him as an unruly fellow maverick—and Colter was impressed at the sight of Young whipping up fresh beverages on his tour bus for his son Ben, who was accompanying him. "To live with that and deal with it and get down on his knees with him and administer to that child, Neil was very compassionate," Colter recalls. To endear himself to a potentially wary Nashville, Young also agreed to do things he rarely did in the rock world; he appeared on talk shows (in Nashville, no less) and invited reporters onto his tour bus for interviews.

In some ways, Young's move toward country music was natural. He had had an affinity to the music dating back at least to his cover of Don Gibson's "Oh Lonesome Me" and the Cali honky-tonk portions of *American Stars 'n Bars*. But this time he brought almost too much energy to the idea: as played onstage with the International Harvesters, "Powderfinger" and "Are You Ready for the Country" felt abnormally jaunty, stripped of their underlying unease. Young's stock had fallen so low—or he left people so confused—that when he played Shreveport's Municipal Auditorium in September 1984, the local newspaper described him, first and foremost, as "a performer at Woodstock."

Even more disconcerting were interviews Young gave that year, in which he insisted he was done not only with rock but also with the values long associated with him. "Reagan—so what if he's a trigger-happy cowboy?" he told a reporter in New Orleans. "He hasn't pulled the trigger. Don't you think it's better that Russia and all these other countries think that he's a trigger-happy cowboy than think it's Jimmy Carter who wants to give them back the Panama Canal? I mean, we built the canal." He also took jabs at welfare ("You can't always support the weak") and the naïveté of his generation ("It makes me mad when people have that attitude—very idealistic, don't hurt anybody"). Crosby was possibly headed for prison, and Young appeared to be preparing for a Republican rally, and it was hard to say which was more unsettling.

Now a convicted felon, Crosby tried to scare himself straight in the months after his sentencing. Jan Dance, his girlfriend, was also ensnared by drugs, and mysterious, seedy characters circled around them. One day, two crew members were told to drop off one of Crosby's cars with a drug dealer, who was handed the keys. "It was hard to watch that and see how scumbags like that took advantage of David," one of the crew recalls. "But David owed him money for various things and he didn't have it. [The other employee] said, 'Just move on, man. Forget about it.'"

To his credit, Crosby attempted to quit drugs some half-dozen times. That November, while his case was still being appealed, he and Dance agreed to enter a drug rehab program at Ross General Hospital, not far from Crosby's Mill Valley home. At the time, according to an admission report he later publicly shared, Crosby—described as "a disheveled man who appears to be his stated age and is slightly obese"—was admitted for "chemical dependency, opiate and cocaine." His conditions included "chills and sweats five to six times a day" and being "constipated chronically." Four of his teeth were "broken and badly carious," and there were "multiple burns on his fingertips" (related to the use of freebasing equipment). Unfortunately, Crosby felt like the center's staff "didn't like" him, and he bailed on the program within days.

A month later, he tried again, checking himself into Gladman Memorial Hospital, a psychiatric facility in Oakland. Their report on Crosby astutely determined that deep psychological issues, not just a wanton lifestyle, had dragged him into addiction. "This patient has used drugs over the years to contain his agitations and his depressions—although he, himself, may not be fully aware of this. . . . There are strong suggestions that even as a youngster he has not coped well with external strictures imposed upon him or with rules and regulations in general." The report called Crosby "an intrinsically intelligent—though not disciplined—and sensitive man who has, however, never found peace with himself nor gratification in his relationships with others." (In other words, Christine Hinton's death in 1969 wasn't the only reason he had resorted to getting high so often.) When Crosby told his hospital handlers that he "felt tremendously depressed, even suicidal," he was placed on suicide watch. Crosby changed his mind and convinced administrators he wouldn't take his own life. But after cocaine and heroin were sneaked into his room, Crosby left that facility as well. Promises he had made to Nash and to his managers in the music business that he would kick drugs went unfulfilled. "I always thought that because of the massiveness of it, David was not there," says Siddons. "This was his physical manifestation, but I was talking to the demon. I never thought I was talking to David Crosby."

To earn extra cash, Crosby and a band of his own returned to the road, playing clubs and dives (and occasional prestige outlets, such as the Beacon Theatre in New York). His innate professionalism often overcame his bad habits, and the fans were always ready to shout their approval; at the Red Creek Inn in Rochester, New York, they cheered when he told them, "They tried to keep me from coming and singing for you, but I'm out here anyway." Yet the money would never completely suffice; he barely made enough to support his small band and crew, never mind his habit. Always in need of funds, Crosby resorted to confronting promoter Bill Graham: "You've made a lot of money off me, and I need some money," he demanded. Graham turned him down, telling Crosby he wasn't about to give him cash that would be handed straight to a dealer. "I was not happy," Crosby says. "But looking back, I respected him all the more for it." Siddons gave his credit card number to a Marin grocery store so Crosby could have food; that way, Crosby would have something to eat but no access to cash for drugs.

With Crosby's possible imprisonment still looming, the group took a series of steps to plan for the future. Quietly, Nash bought Crosby's publishing company for $25,000, so that his friend wouldn't lose a valuable source of future income to dealers or to anyone else to whom he owed money. (In the end, he would sell it back to him.) To fulfill their contract to Atlantic, Nash had begun rounding up whatever individual songs were lying around: recordings of his own (songs like "Lonely Man" and his plea for a cleaner world, "Clear Blue Skies"), tracks from Crosby's unreleased 1980 solo album, and a few Stills leftovers, including a group version of "As I Come of Age" from 1981. The album was such an arm-twisted requirement that employees at the Crosslight Agency referred to it as *Contractual Obligation Album*. But after plowing about halfway through the project, Nash abandoned it. "Atlantic wanted an album," he says. "They weren't getting legal with us, but it was well known they would love another record soon. I tried but it didn't work. It felt like a patchwork thing, which is what it was."

Solo albums had always been part of their game plan, but they took on an added significance during a dire and uncertain time. "There was nothing anybody could do for David," says Debbie Meister, who worked for Siddons at the Crosslight Agency. "They tried so many different kinds of interventions. But everybody has their own rock bottom they have to reach before they can make that change. That's why they started doing solo projects, just in preparation. Nobody knew what was going to happen."

Stills' *Right by You* tumbled out in time for a Crosby, Stills and Nash summer 1984 tour. As always, the album spoke to his versatility. Several of the songs had guitar solos by Led Zeppelin's Jimmy Page overdubbed separately in England; in particular, "50/50" proved Stills could still concoct a crisp Latin shuffle. A remake of the Lonnie Donegan–associated Cold War warning, "No Hiding Place," was both relevant and a welcome nod to Stills' Manassas bluegrass side. (Chris Hillman, who had returned to bluegrass after a reunion with Roger McGuinn and Gene Clark had fizzled, played on the track as well.) A lush cover of Young's "Only Love Can Break Your Heart" was nicely underproduced (and included a newly written verse by Stills, as if he were trying to prove he could write as well as Young). But the album had no center. Continuing a trend that had started on *Daylight Again*, some of it drifted into uninspired adult-contemporary banality. As commendable as it was for Stills to update his sound, the electronic handclaps and techno-pop synths that peppered other tracks came off as clumsy. The music felt coated in a fog of cigarette smoke and libations, leaving songs with potential–the boogie rocker "Flaming Heart" and the bubbly "Stranger," co-written with Stills' ten-year-old son Christopher, for example–sounding muddy, and precious little of his guitar poked through the arrangements.

The album rose no higher than no. 75 on the *Billboard* chart, but in addition to touring, publishing remained a lucrative form of income. Stills continued to pull in additional funds through his Gold Hill company, which administered the rights for hits like Firefall's "You Are the Woman" and "Just Remember I Love You." But each of the three had growing children–including Stills' son Christopher, Nash's three children and Crosby's daughter Donovan–and Crosby, Stills and Nash remained the steadiest, most lucrative source of income for them. So, despite the nightmare of the recent European trek, they toured again that summer. Again, accommodations were made to ensure that Crosby could make it through an entire two-hour concert, including, again, Crosby's own offstage room. "It was almost like a dog biscuit," says one road-crew member. "'If you come onstage and don't leave in the middle of the show or the middle of the song, you'll get a little extra dog biscuit at the end of the night.' They had a show and they weren't concerned what shape he was in as long as we could get him there."

As always, Nash put on his best positive face for the media, although it was getting harder to pretend all was well. "What can I say?" Nash told the *Democrat and Chronicle* in Rochester that October when asked about Crosby. "The man likes to get high. I've done what I can. But he's a 43-year-old man and he can do what he wants. Believe me, this is not something David wants to have happen, and it weighs heavily on him." That December, after finding himself at another drug-plagued party, Nash swore off cocaine.

"ENVISION THIS," WROTE Zach Dunkin of the *Indianapolis News* in September 1984. "Neil Young on stage with David Crosby, Stephen Stills and Graham Nash for the first time in 10 years at the Sports Center Monday night." After all, Dunkin noted, Young was playing in Muncie on a Sunday night, then had a day off—the same day the trio were playing at the arena. "Hey, give him a call," Nash told Dunkin when it was brought up in an interview; the writer then tried, without success, to reach Young's manager, Elliot Roberts, for comment. What Dunkin called "the most-desired reunion in pop music history next to the Beatles" would not happen that weekend.

In the fall of 1983, Nash had joined Young onstage in California for a rendition of "Ohio." But for most of the early to middle part of that decade, Crosby, Stills and Nash continued to operate in a separate universe from Young. Appearing on a Nashville TV show in the fall of 1984, Young had been dismissive of the trio, saying he wasn't working with them anymore, in part due to different "lifestyles." Soon after, Stills participated in a political benefit at Rockefeller's, a two-hundred-seat club in Houston. As he tuned up and prepared to play "Daylight Again," he paused. "I understand that my Canadian friend, Mr. Neil Young"—he started, although he had to pause when the crowd broke into cheers at the mere sound of Young's name—"made some rather, shall we call them, um, ill-considered remarks to the press. Well, the, uh, funny part about it is that the press don't know when it's been *had!*" More applause. "You see, they're so busy taking themselves seriously that they actually believe this . . . small boy. He *does* that, too, man. I've known him for a long time. Look you right in the *eye* and lie to your motherfuckin' ass! *Lie!*" He then imitated Young: "'I don't believe that any more, man. Nuke 'em! Nuke the gay whales! I mean can you dig it?'" Stills then relaxed a bit. "He's just poking fun at me and Nash for doing all this shit, y'know." Chuckles emerged from the crowd. "I appreciate it myself. How else could we get any press?" In between playing songs he rarely unearthed with the group—"Do for the Others," "Thoroughfare Gap," all in fine voice—he lambasted Reagan's lack of military experience and sang the antinuke "No Hiding Place." Much of the verbiage and the set list could be interpreted as a subtle dig at Young's newly professed politics.

In December 1984, a reprieve arrived when, in a startling and hopeful development, Crosby's conviction was overturned on the grounds of an illegal search of Cardi's. Citing the Fourth Amendment—which protects "the right of the people to be secure in their persons, houses, papers, and effects, against unreasonable searches and seizures"—the appeals court determined that Crosby had been entitled to privacy in his dressing room, no matter what he was doing in it. Crosby was far from a free man. Just two months earlier, in October 1984, he had been pulled over after illegally passing cars on his motorcycle in the San Francisco suburb of Ross; police found drugs, a dagger and a revoked driver's license. In light of lingering charges, Judge McDowell offered to let Crosby undergo treatment in lieu of going to jail, and Crosby agreed to take him up on the offer. His psychiatrist selected the plush Fair Oaks Hospital in suburban Summit, New Jersey, where John Phillips of the Mamas and the Papas (and his daughter Mackenzie), Robert Kennedy, Jr., and others from the ranks of the rich and famous had gone to clean up. After putting off his admission as much as possible—and getting deliriously high in his motel room the night before checking in—Crosby finally went to Fair Oaks to be admitted on January 10, 1985. He was far from happy about it, especially after he found he would not be permitted to have a musical instrument in his room. Crosby also tried to smuggle drugs into the hospital in his cheeks, squirrel-like.

Nevertheless, he started to make progress—until, seven weeks into the program, someone he would later describe as "a really bad guy" offered to help him escape. During one of his allowed walks on the grounds, Crosby jumped into a waiting car and went to New York City with his accomplice. It was yet another blown chance. "Being addicted takes over, like fire takes over a burning building," says Crosby. "And at a certain point you can't get off the elevator. You go, 'This is not right and I'm going to take my life and go this way.' But you have no control. It's not about you anymore. It's about the drug."

A day later, US Drug Enforcement Agency investigators and New York City cops hunted Crosby down in an apartment in Greenwich Village, after he'd bought cocaine. "I was just about to turn the corner," he told the *Dallas Times Herald*. "I blew it—it was my mistake." On March 6, 1985, Judge McDowell ordered Crosby to jail, denying him bond. With no way left to escape, Crosby had to enter the Lew Sterrett Justice Center in Dallas, where he mopped floors and delivered meals to fellow inmates.

After stealing a bit of bacon, he was placed in solitary confinement. But again, he was soon saved, at least momentarily: when an appeals court ruled he couldn't be held without bond, Crosby was released on May 1, 1985. Nash and Siddons helped raise the bond money. But the release would prove to be another false start. Returning to Los Angeles, Crosby immediately hurled himself back into his addiction. And on June 11, the Texas Fifth Court of Appeals, in a nine-to-four decision, upheld his conviction and sentence—essentially, overturning the reversal of ten months before—by asserting that police *did* have the right to search his private space at Cardi's. Crosby's legal team requested a review by the Texas Court of Criminal Appeals just as Crosby, Stills and Nash prepared to start a summer tour two weeks later.

Despite his fondness for Crosby and his concern, Young still had a full plate of his own to deal with, including career and personal matters. That summer, he finally rolled out his country album, *Old Ways*, over two years after he'd first started it. The record offered up some lovely tunes—his song for Ben, "My Boy," was inordinately touching—and only Young would make an album for country fans that included a spaced-out epic, "Misfits," that was five minutes of story songs about falling space stations and hookers. But schmaltzy arrangements swamped some of the material, the gone-to-the-fishing-hole mood of other songs felt forced, and his Willie Nelson duet "Are There Any More Real Cowboys?" plodded along like a tired horse. Ironically, the album was more of a successor to the laid-back Young of *Harvest* and *Comes a Time* than anything he'd done since those records, but it became one of his two lowest-charting records of the decade.

That same summer of 1985, Young's past finally caught up with him when he was forced to confront the possibility of a quartet reunion, and a very public one at that. To continue the African famine-relief efforts they'd started with the 1984 benefit single "Do They Know It's Christmas?," the British rockers Bob Geldof and Midge Ure, working with the likes of Bill Graham, had hastily organized Live Aid, two benefit concerts to be held nearly simultaneously in London and Philadelphia on July 13, 1985. The lineup for the two stages—including David Bowie, Queen, Tina Turner, Bob Dylan, Elton John, U2, Madonna, Mick Jagger, all playing for free—was formidable, and Young signed on with his country ensemble, the International Harvesters. Knowing Crosby, Stills and Nash wanted in, their management pushed for the group to be included; in the end, the trio spent $16,000 of their own money to fly from Oklahoma, where they were gigging the night before.

Realizing they and Young would be on the same stage at Philadelphia's JFK Stadium, albeit at different times of the day, Nash thought the time was right to push for an onstage reunion. The trio performed first, doing a three-song set in the late morning in which each man looked as if he were in his own separate world. Crosby appeared immobile and frowny, Stills wore an army outfit and headband for no discernible reason, and Nash appeared slim and coiffed. Because of faulty monitors, they could barely hear themselves, but somehow they made it through "Southern Cross," "Suite: Judy Blue Eyes" and "Teach Your Children." Just before "Teach Your Children," Stills ordered Crosby to hand over his guitar so he could play it himself. Crosby was rarely seen on the live telecast; tellingly, the cameras focused more on Stills and Nash. "It was a little less than perfect," Nash told a reporter in the days that followed.

Then Nash made his way to Young's trailer, situated near those of Jagger and Turner. "Graham was beside himself about what to do," says Tim Foster, Young's road manager. Nash broached the idea of an impromptu quartet performance, and Young was open to it. Well aware of Crosby's condition, Young still needed proof that they could coalesce enough to pull it off. The fact that the show was being broadcast around the world, to 1.5 billion people in 100 countries, ramped up everyone's desire to avoid embarrassment. "They said, 'We have to be as good as we can be,'" says Siddons, who left the negotiations to Nash and Young for what could be the quartet's first stage performance in eleven often difficult years.

After Young had played his own set, the four gathered in Crosby's trailer. "Neil cautiously came back to see if any of this was going to work," says Nash. As Siddons and Joel Bernstein watched, the four sang together for the first time in nine years, warming up with Young's "Only Love Can Break Your Heart." For all the apprehension in the air, which included bodyguard "Smokey" Wendell standing guard outside of Crosby's vehicle, their vocal memory kicked in. "It was one of the few times I was actually star-struck," says Siddons. "One of the highlights of my career was watching them sing live in that trailer. I thought, 'This is amazing.'" With that, Young was on board for the onstage reunion. "Once Neil heard it, he was okay," Nash says. "It wasn't a tour or a record. It was just two or three songs."

Thanks to some rejiggering of the schedule, they would hit the stage in about an hour, but everything about the performance felt last minute. At 8:30 P.M., the four materialized in front of a striped curtain. "Together again, Crosby, Stills, Nash and Young," someone announced after they were already onstage. "How y'all doing?" said Nash (in a black MTV T-shirt and leather pants), adding, "Surprise," with only some of his usual zest. In a sleeveless white T-shirt, Young looked like the healthiest of the bunch, but he had trouble hearing his guitar as they began. Nevertheless, they proceeded with "Only Love Can Break Your Heart," followed by "Daylight Again" (with a revised lyric about world hunger) and "Find the Cost of Freedom."

All of six minutes, the performance was over before many knew it had begun, but perhaps that was for the best. Due to microphones that fed back into the massive speakers behind them, they had hearing issues and were not entirely in tune. Coming immediately after a Led Zeppelin reunion (with Phil Collins sitting in on drums), the performance felt anticlimactic. Decades later, Pegi Young, who left Live Aid before the performance, would have no memory of it even happening. As Neil Young told writer Nick Kent ten years later, "Damn, you'd have thought our performance on Live Aid would have been enough to finish off any wave of nostalgia, wouldn't you?" The trio flew to their next show, and Young once again went his own way.

THE SUMMER OF 1985 would bring another slew of Crosby, Stills and Nash shows and another round of hope-for-the-best interviews. As Nash bluntly told the *Pittsburgh Press* that July, "We're trying to get as much touring and recording done as we can in case David goes to jail." To upgrade its sound for the '80s and also cover more for Crosby, the band now employed three keyboard players. Fans continued to buy tickets; with Crosby's imprisonment still a possibility, many went thinking it would be the last time they'd ever see the trio onstage. "The drama might have only been a few years, but it seemed like lifetimes," says Dave Rao, who continued to work for Stills and the band until that summer. "Every day was such agony."

As much as everyone tried to manage the situation, times could still get tense. Fed up with Crosby, Stills considered filing papers to legally dissolve the trio, but he never followed through. On a few occasions, Crosby left the stage unexpectedly; in Pittsburgh, he vanished during one of Stills' songs, "Stranger," and didn't return until eight tunes had passed. In Philadelphia, Crosby disappeared for forty-five minutes. Usually on those occasions, Stills and Nash would gamely rearrange the set to play more of their own material. But in Philadelphia, as Nash began playing a song or two of his own, Stills decided he had had enough. Stomping into the backstage dressing room, he found Crosby lying on a couch. Walking over to the food table, Stills took the beer and soda cans out of a tray of ice water and promptly dumped the water and the tray on Crosby: "Never walk off the stage during a performance!" he yelled, along with other warnings, as crew members looked on. Stunned by the cold water, Crosby moaned, "What's the problem?"—or something to that effect—before crew member John Partipilo and other employees helped him, soaking wet, back onto the stage. "It was pretty shocking," says Partipilo. "Stephen was pissed, really upset. It was hard on us to watch it go down. I wondered, 'How much worse can this get?'"

Crosby looks back on those tours in the middle of the decade with regret. "I was a massive disappointment to everybody, and I was fucking with their money," he says. "They wanted to keep me alive and working so that we could continue to make that money. I think they did care about me. But I don't know how much of it was job security and how much of it was they cared about *me*. But I was certainly the one who went the furthest and lowest with drugs. And I'm sorry for putting that in the way of us making more music."

The madness of 1984 and 1985 made the 1974 reunion tour (the one dubbed "The Doom Tour" by Crosby) seem like a walk in the rock-and-roll park. And yet something astonishing was happening: the shows were hardly train wrecks. The summer before, discerning *New York Times* critic Stephen Holden, reviewing one of the trio's concerts, noted, approvingly, "Their harmonizing was remarkably precise and consistent over the course of a demanding two-and-a-half-hour set." Notices like that, some with headlines like "Crosby, Stills & Nash Keep Suite Sound Coming" and "The Magic's Back for Crosby, Stills & Nash," followed them throughout the summer of 1985. Employees at the Crosslight Agency gathered around one day to watch the group on a morning talk show; to their astonishment, Crosby snapped to attention. "Our minds were blown," says Meister. "He was always like that. It didn't matter how fucked up he was. If he had his mind set on being articulate, he was articulate."

Even odder, the crowds were as supportive as ever, if not more so. CSN fans had already lived through nearly two decades of the group's hills and valleys, and by now they glimpsed bits of themselves in all three (and Young as well). Like the band, they were now older and a little heavier. Many of them, like Crosby, Stills and Nash, were coping with the excesses of their youth or trying to keep up with the musical and cultural changes of the '80s. In Crosby, they saw a counterculture outlaw who was clearly in the grip of hard times, and they concluded that he needed their encouragement. Walking into a stadium with the band, Siddons saw fans leaning over a balcony and cheering Crosby on. "I remember feeling so weird about that—that he was in that condition and they didn't care," Siddons says. "It was unnerving," Siddons adds, that somebody could make "mistake after mistake," and it only "made him more worshipped. . . . But they loved him. It made him more of the anti-hero they wanted." It wasn't uncommon for Crosby to receive a standing ovation merely for walking onstage; at a show in Iowa, the fans jumped to their feet in support of him *several* times throughout the evening.

For those in the band and crew, every small victory helped them make it through another day. They adjusted their expectations accordingly. "With the Eagles, every note was played exactly the same way every night," says crew member John Vanderslice. "They wanted it to sound exactly like their records. CSN were more concerned about trying something better than worrying about being perfect. They'd try to grab a note. When they hit it, it sounded great. When they missed it, they'd miss it, live on the spot without a net. As Crosby would say, 'The imperfection in the weave guarantees you the uniqueness of the cloth.' A lot of other artists wouldn't show their vulnerability or limitations. That was a real human aspect of these guys. They weren't afraid to belly-flop."

When Crosby would rouse himself for a version of "Long Time Gone" or sit down at the piano and find his way into and out of "Delta," Stills or Nash would give him a high five or smile in his direction. Part of it was show business as usual, but another part of it wasn't. They knew those triumphs could vanish at a moment's notice.

IN 1976, WHILE promoting *Whistling Down the Wire*, Crosby had been asked what he would have done had he not become a musician. "I'd be in jail," he shot back, adding that it was not because of illicit substances, but because he was "too much of a punk" with "too little respect for the law."

Nearly a decade later, in the fall of 1985, that premonition was bearing down on him with crushing intensity. Working with a legal team that included Alan Dershowitz—fresh from victories in the trials of porn star Harry Reems and accused socialite murderer Claus von Bulow—Crosby was awaiting a decision in an appeal of his sentencing. But once again, he pressed his luck. In October, he drove his 1985 Ford Thunderbird into a fence at a nearby house in Mill Valley; police found the usual combination of drugs and a gun in his car, and Crosby was arrested for leaving the scene of an accident and released on another bond, for $5,000. The incident prompted another hearing in Texas.

To support himself and his habit, Crosby continued to play club shows, and his performance at the Stone in San Francisco in November played like his own last waltz. Looking overweight and wheezing ("like the worst nightmare of a lifelong smoker," one reviewer noticed), Crosby sang in a voice that was clearly shot from freebasing. The crowd shouted loyal, encouraging words throughout, and Crosby, overcome with emotion, broke down in tears. He walked offstage before composing himself and returning. Any attempts to look and sound upbeat with Stills and Nash were gone; the public was now witnessing his complete and utter breakdown. The scenario was likely to repeat itself on November 30, when Crosby was booked to play the Golden Bear club in Huntington Beach.

Crosby would never make that date. Thanks to the hit-and-run incident, Judge McDowell demanded that he appear at a hearing in Texas on November 25 to make a case against the court revoking his appeal bond. Crosby was already on three years' probation for a traffic violation in

Ross, California, a year earlier. Convinced he would most likely end up in jail, Crosby stayed in California rather than make the trip to Texas, and the judge issued a warrant for his arrest. "I hope it doesn't end tragically," one of his lawyers, David Vogelstein, told reporters outside the Dallas court. By the time authorities arrived at his Mill Valley home, Crosby had sold his piano for $5,000 and fled with Jan Dance. He would later write that he identified with "underdogs and outlaws"; for now, he was one himself.

In the early days of his new life as a fugitive, Crosby took refuge in the homes of, among others, the Grateful Dead's Mickey Hart. "Everybody was hiding him out," Hart says. "He was going from place to place. He'd lost everything. The base will take anybody's mind and soul. It took David's." Crosby also hid out at the home of a member of the Crosby, Stills and Nash crew. Using their contacts, Siddons and Golden began tracking Crosby and Dance's whereabouts on a map, and it became clear that he was making his way to Florida. Unbeknownst to them, Crosby was planning to return to the *Mayan* and sail off, possibly to Costa Rica, despite the warnings of the likes of Siddons that such an escape could never be permanent. (Later, the authorities wondered if Crosby had fled to Florida to join in on a sad, partial reunion of the Byrds, now a tattered cover band featuring only Gene Clark and Michael Clarke from the original lineup; they were playing a club in Fort Lauderdale. But Crosby's escape to Florida had nothing to do with that show.)

At first, Crosby didn't listen to anyone's advice. "Jan and I were so happy—we were together, we were high, we were running away together," he wrote. But ultimately, broke and strung out, he realized he couldn't run anymore. He and Dance were out of money, their friends in Florida refused to take them in, and the *Mayan* was in serious need of repair, making any plan to escape the country by sea impossible. In a moment of clarity, broke and shoeless (although not, he claims, sporting wigs, as was reported), Crosby realized he had reached "the end of my line." He adds, "You get to a point where you look at your life and it's a shambles and you've screwed everything up, and you make a choice. You say, 'I have to take whatever's coming and make it right.'" At 3:45 P.M. on December 12, as the *Mayan* sat miles offshore, he found a ride to the FBI office in West Palm Beach, Florida; without telling Dance what he was doing, he turned himself in. The FBI alerted Texas officials, who admitted they had no idea he was in Florida.

As Crosby was led off in handcuffs, he told reporters, "Wish me luck," adding, "This seemed like the best thing I should do." He sported a red T-shirt in the crowd with "David's Tour" printed on the front, but there would be no more concerts, at least for a while.

CHAPTER 9

JANUARY 1986–DECEMBER 1988

The path back to the quartet began when the front doors of the Texas Department of Corrections in Huntsville opened on August 8, 1986. After serving nine months behind two different sets of bars, Crosby was officially released. Bill Siddons, who was still involved in overseeing the remnants of Crosby's career, had flown to Dallas and driven to Huntsville to pick up his client. As he waited outside the daunting red brick building, Siddons caught sight of a portly, clean-shaven guy with short hair, his stomach pushing up against his white-collared shirt. "Who the fuck is that?" Siddons thought to himself before realizing it was his client. So much of Crosby's image had been tied up in his bushy hair and mustache; now, despite the change, at least he was a free man. Siddons hoped he would be free of his former addictions as well.

The previous nine months had been difficult for everyone in the group's world. Young had watched *Old Ways*, his venture into country, fade as quickly as his earlier Geffen releases, and relations between him and David Geffen remained tense. To satisfy his label boss' demands for a rock album not drenched in irony, Young hired producer and guitarist Danny Kortchmar. Although largely recognized as James Taylor's former backup guitarist, Kortchmar was now also known as the co-producer and co-captain of Don Henley's solo hits after the Eagles. Starting in late 1985, Young and Kortchmar hunkered down in Los Angeles with Steve Jordan, a brash and extroverted drummer who had been a member of the original house band on *Late Night with David Letterman*, and Niko Bolas, a scrappy, twenty-nine-year-old California native who had cut his teeth working with James Taylor and Warren Zevon. Despite his knowledge of the LA rock world, Bolas was barely familiar with Young, as he discovered on his first day on the job. "This hippie came walking in the studio and I said, 'Who the fuck is this guy and where's Neil Young?'" he recalls. "He had the fringe jacket. I called him 'grandpa granola.'"

As soon as Young plugged in, Bolas heard the loudest, most aggressive guitar he'd ever experienced, and the engineer soon understood why. Geffen had cut the budget for the album; Bolas even recalls the label calling to say it would decrease the preorder shipments, even though the album was still in the works. Young had to take out his frustration somehow, and he seemed undaunted by the legal and industry hassles around him. "It hurt people but it also inspired everybody," Bolas says. "He said, '*Fuck* that' and showed up with even more fire in the belly. He said, 'Somebody told me I can't do this, so I'm gonna do it twice as loud.'" The album also featured more synthesizer than Young had used on any record since *Trans.*

Landing on Water, released in the summer of 1986, floated, but barely. "Touch the Night" was Young's best synth-rock hybrid, drummer Jordan's visceral beats were like cannon shots, and "Hippie Dream," set to a gloomy synthesizer throb that wouldn't have been out of place in a period prison movie, was Young's comment on a certain former bandmate. Castigating Crosby for being in such dire shape, Young called the idea of wooden ships just a "hippie dream"; toward the end of the song, he seemed to pledge that he wouldn't fall victim to the same fate. The song was even more cutting than his earlier "Thrasher," about Crosby, Stills and Nash. But *Landing on Water* was largely anemic and only sold marginally better than *Old Ways.* Released about two weeks before Crosby was let out of jail, the album was a dismaying sign that Young's career was nearly as precarious as Crosby's.

While Crosby was in prison, Nash remained hopeful. "I never thought David would die or overdose," he says. "I thought he was smarter than that. I knew that it would take a year or so to get over this and him going to prison and starting again. I didn't lose faith in the fact that he would come out and still be great." But with his musical partner of about fifteen years out of the picture, Nash was forced to confront a creative future on his own, and he revived his dormant solo career in an appropriately—or, in fact, inappropriately—'80s way. "It doesn't have David or Stephen on it, and it doesn't sound like anything they might have done," Nash said when the album, *Innocent Eyes*, arrived, a few months before *Landing on Water*. Featuring songs by outside songwriters and a synthesizer-heavy production more suitable for pop stars twenty years younger, *Innocent Eyes* was even more contrived than Young's record. Tellingly, its most affecting moment was "Glass and Steel," a song of support for Crosby that offered him the power to "carry on." For once, Nash wrote sympathetically, not accusingly, of one of his bandmates.

Among the musicians he hired to back him at those sessions was guitarist Waddy Wachtel, who got a glimpse of the ongoing wackiness that continued to encircle the group. During a break, Wachtel was lying on a couch when Stills, who wasn't playing on the record at all, suddenly burst in. "Oh, man, I'm glad you're here!" Stills exclaimed. Startled, Wachtel jumped up and asked why, and Stills demanded to know who had sold Wachtel the Les Paul guitar he was playing, suspecting it had been stolen from him. Wachtel had to remind Stills that he himself had bought the guitar from Stills, for $350, back in 1969 when they all shared a rehearsal space. "*You* sold it to me!" Wachtel shot back.

Of course, none of them had had it rougher than Crosby. In a Dallas courtroom on January 6, 1986, he had again faced Judge McDowell after turning himself in, handcuffed for the hearing. Crosby's team had offered to send him back to Fair Oaks in New Jersey, but McDowell had rejected the request and ordered Crosby to jail on the weapons and drug charges from 1982. At first he was sent to the Lew Sterrett Justice Center in Dallas; since that prison did not allow musical instruments, and the state prison in Huntsville did, Crosby ultimately requested—and was granted—a transfer. In state prison, he would also be able to get credit toward release (three days' credit for each day served) if he stayed on good behavior.

In Huntsville, he was forced to kick drugs the hard, cold-turkey way. Initially, he was given his own cell (prison officials were worried that a fellow inmate could try to harm a celebrity), and he was allowed only three hours of exercise a week. "I'm in a room about the size of your closet and they won't let me out to eat," he told a *San Jose Mercury News* reporter visiting him in March. "They just shove the food through a hole in the door." Wearing white overalls with "Dallas County Jail" stenciled on the back—and now sporting a graying beard—Crosby told the newspaper he'd been clean for one hundred days, and he spoke encouragingly about his treatment and his desire to get out. "I would very much like to be out of here," he said, "but it feels great just to not be strung out all the time." He was so optimistic that he said he and Nash were planning to make a duo album that summer in Los Angeles.

In jail, Crosby talked daily with Jan Dance, whose previous few years had been as grim as Crosby's. Her bad fortune had culminated on the day a biker held her hostage and beat her up (resulting in two broken ribs) while Crosby, Stills and Nash were away on the road. After Crosby turned himself in, Dance, then barely ninety pounds, had entered a rehab clinic in Salinas, south of San Francisco. Thanks to her detox efforts, she was able to avoid jail time stemming from charges of drug and gun possession when she'd boarded a plane from Kansas City to Denver in August 1984. But now, both she and Crosby were simultaneously attempting to straighten out their lives. As Crosby told the Crosslight Agency's Debbie Meister, "She has to clean up, too, because we can't come back together if one of us isn't clean." Through his management, Crosby arranged to have flowers delivered weekly to Dance at her rehab center.

Crosby's transfer to state prison was approved in March. During Crosby, Stills and Nash's 1983 European tour, Crosby and his friend, screenwriter Carl Gottlieb, had gathered in a hotel room to watch the 1972 Steve McQueen movie *The Getaway*, parts of which were filmed at the prison in Huntsville, which was nicknamed the "Walls Unit." Now, three years after watching that film and wondering if he'd end up there, Crosby found himself on a bus with seventy other inmates, all on their way to the one-hundred-year-old red brick building, where he would complete his prison term.

Behind the locked doors of the prison, Crosby worked at the inmate mattress factory. But he also managed to stay in touch not only with Dance but with Nash, Stills, Jackson Browne and Joni Mitchell. The Dead's Mickey Hart mailed him a cassette player and a tape he had produced of dense vocal choir recordings by Tibetan Gyuto monks; Hart felt the music would help focus and calm him. Other faces from the past reemerged. In 1978, Crosby's former Byrds frenemy Roger McGuinn, who'd become enmeshed in cocaine use of his own, had been rattled when he saw what drugs had done to Elvis Presley. Kicking alcohol, weed and cocaine, McGuinn had become a born-again Christian, and he mailed a few Bible verses to Crosby in jail for encouragement. "It rolled off his back," McGuinn says. "He's an atheist." But in one of his replies to McGuinn, Crosby mentioned he was forming a prison band. The make-shift group was one sign that Crosby might still be able to create music. Although he was not allowed to have pen and paper, Crosby still man-aged to write a song, "Alexander Graham Bell," about his lifeline to the outside world, the telephone. Eventually, he wrote another song, "Com-pass," which had a typically diffuse melody and lyrics that looked back over the wreckage of his previous decade. It was better than "Alexander Graham Bell," which would never be recorded, and served as a beacon of hope. "That's the first thing I wrote when I was still in prison," Crosby says, "that made me think I was going to be able to write again."

In July, thanks in part to credit he received for his earlier time at the treatment center in New Jersey, Crosby was finally approved for parole, with his release date set for the following month. As two dozen fans waited outside, Siddons ushered Crosby out of Huntsville, and Crosby was shuttled to a halfway house in Houston. About two weeks later, Nash was playing a Houston club with his new, synth-centered backup band—a musically radical move that amounted to his version of Young's Trans Band outing, but in smaller venues. Before launching into his whales song, "Wind on the Water," the tape of Crosby's vocal piece "Critical Mass" was cued up, and to the audience's surprise, the curtain opened to reveal the newly free Crosby. Nash shouted, "Mr. David Crosby, ladies and gentlemen!" Recalls Nash, "We set it up showbiz-wise. You can recognize the silhouette of Crosby anywhere. It's like Alfred Hitchcock." Crosby debuted "Compass" and told the audience, "Thinking about this night kept me going."

After receiving approval to serve out his parole in California, Crosby boarded a flight heading west with Siddons and Nash, who realized that reentering society wouldn't be easy for their friend. Due to delays, the flight sat on the runway for several excruciating hours. Crosby, still de-compressing after his months in jail, became increasingly agitated—to the point where Siddons asked the pilot if he would let them out. Pointing to a small, round access panel on the floor of the cockpit, the pilot informed Siddons that was the only exit now that the doors had been sealed. A worried Siddons offered to pay a $3,000 fine to unseal the doors, but eventually Crosby calmed down and the flight proceeded.

Realizing that his client had two equally important needs—cash and the sound of an adoring crowd—Siddons quickly booked club shows for both Crosby and Nash, and Crosby on his own. (Siddons warned Crosby he had to stay clean until December, when the first shows would take place.) The shows also made up for performances Crosby had canceled during his time before jail. Again, despite all his travails, his horrifying descent into addiction, and his physical decline, Crosby was received warmly. At the Catalyst in Santa Cruz, fans screamed "We love you!" and "Welcome back!" In a loose shirt that helped hide his prison weight gain, Crosby tried to make light of his fall from grace. "As far as I'm concerned, I've got the solution for the state of Texas: we give it back to Mexico," he joked. At the Miramar Beach Inn in Half Moon Bay, California, he called himself "fat and sassy," borrowing a phrase from Wavy Gravy. But his voice and guitar playing, on both recently and rarely played songs— including "Distances" and "Drive My Car"—were better preserved than anyone had a right to expect. Crosby also cashed in on his life experience by signing a contract with Doubleday for a memoir, reportedly for a $500,000 advance.

Soon after the Half Moon Bay show, he headed to New York with Stills and Nash to play "Crack Down," an anti-crack benefit at Madison Square Garden organized by Bill Graham. There, the crowd gave Crosby, Stills and Nash a standing ovation—but booed rappers and hometown heroes Run-DMC. In 1986, there was no question which of the two acts was more culturally relevant, yet Crosby's astonishing comeback—the way he was now a visceral symbol of his generation's rise, fall and re-surgence—trumped everything in its path.

BY OCTOBER 1986, the world of Crosby, Stills and Nash was still largely foreign to Pegi Young. Since her husband had fundamentally kept his distance from the trio from the late '70s through the mid-'80s, she had rarely seen them. After the Youngs had married and settled onto his ranch, raising their son, Ben, and their daughter, Amber Jean, family and Neil's work took precedence. Pegi would have no memory of meeting Crosby, Stills or Nash until the middle of the '80s, when she recalled the time Crosby and Dance, in the midst of their addiction, had visited during a possible intervention. Her lasting memory of meeting Nash during this period would be his brown leather pants.

Then came her calamitous first meeting with Stills, probably in early 1986. Young had reconvened the original members of Buffalo Springfield to see if their cherished old chemistry could be ignited again, and he, Stills, Richie Furay, Dewey Martin and Bruce Palmer assembled at Stills' new, more compact home in Encino to play together. But each was in a different zone, physically and chemically; the jam sessions were loose, friendly and largely unproductive. Dropping by the reunion one day, Pegi walked into Stills' house and accidentally tripped over an extension cord for a computer that was on a table in the next room. ("I'm a bit of a klutz," she says.) Stills came rushing down the stairs in a panic, thinking all his files had been lost, and Pegi apologized profusely. Given Stills' oncoming hearing loss, she wasn't sure if he heard her, but ultimately the computer files were salvaged and they eventually became friends. Otherwise, Pegi had had little interaction with the three of them, which made it all the more surprising when, on the night of October 13, 1986, she looked around and there they were all together again.

That year, working with a recreational therapist, Jim Forderer, and a speech and language pathologist, Dr. Marilyn Buzolich, Pegi had opened the Bridge School, a learning institute in Hillsborough, California, for developmentally challenged kids unable to communicate verbally. To raise money for the school, the Youngs organized a benefit at the Shoreline Amphitheatre in Mountain View, not far from the Broken Arrow Ranch. The staging was minimal, and the only rule was that the acts had to perform acoustically, with no electric instruments. In addition to Young, who would fly in from a show in Wisconsin the night before, the lineup included Bruce Springsteen, Don Henley, Tom Petty, Nils Lofgren and Robin Williams. To Pegi's shock, Crosby, Stills and Nash were suddenly backstage as well. "They surprised me," she recalls. "I don't know why Elliot [Roberts] didn't tell me. I don't know if Neil knew or not, but it was a surprise to me." Equally surprised, if more lighthearted, was Robin Williams, who saw Crosby backstage and exclaimed, in a southern preacher voice, "Good God almighty, free at last!"

During his set, Young announced the arrival of "old friends," and his unbilled older bandmates were suddenly back onstage with him. Looking corpulent but cheery, his mustache and hair already growing out, Crosby appeared nervous at first, sticking his hands in and out of his pockets while singing tentatively on "Only Love Can Break Your Heart." (Of his weight gain, one critic cracked in print, "Prison food must be better than we are led to believe.") The quartet also sang Stills' "Change Partners" and Young's "Ohio," during which Crosby became more animated, making it the highlight of their set. They harmonized behind Springsteen as well, on "Hungry Heart." ("Those guys sing pretty good!" Springsteen enthused when it was over.) Given everything they'd been through the past few years, especially with Crosby, the mood was celebratory. "They seemed really happy to be together," Pegi says. "I know there was concern on Neil's part about David's health and what he was doing, so everyone was pleased to see him doing so well. They did seem to have a good time."

With Crosby freed from prison only two months before, the performance amounted to a trial run for a group reunion that Young, always the most tentative, had roped himself into. While promoting *Everybody's Rockin'* on disc jockey Jim Ladd's syndicated radio show *Rockline* in the fall of 1983, Young had taken calls from listeners, and one of them had asked about his wayward and clearly troubled bandmate. "Everybody's concerned about David, you know," Young responded. "He's having a bad time and he's a very unique person and he has a lot of problems that are unique to him. And he's having a rough time. It's too bad. He really took a bad turn. And I hope he gets himself together. I told him now if he does get himself together and straightens up that I'll join the group again and we'll do something together. And uh, that's all I can do. That's all I can do, you know. . . . He knows everybody loves him. And everybody's concerned. Everybody's been telling him that, but there's something else happening there." In his most encouraging comment, Young ended his response with, "The building's still standing. It didn't burn down or anything."

Whether Young remembered his promise or not, Crosby—and Nash—certainly took it to heart. During his jail interview with the *San Jose*

Mercury News in early 1986, Crosby brought up the idea of a possible reunion. "If I manage to stay off drugs—which I'm going to do—Neil's going
to come back with us also," he said. "I spoke to him about it and told him
I'm serious about it. There's going to be a CSNY record, which should
be really exciting." Crosby wasn't exaggerating: during the recording of
Landing on Water, Niko Bolas had taken several calls from Crosby, who
was still behind bars in Texas and eager to speak with Young. While promoting *Innocent Eyes* that summer, Nash had brought up the possibility
of reconvening, too, saying he had "big plans" for the four of them.

Once Crosby was released, those designs, historic by their standards,
moved forward one careful step at a time. It had been a dozen years
since the four had worked together for any substantial period of time,
and few were sure the old camaraderie could be recaptured after one
abbreviated set at a Bridge School benefit. On February 6, 1987, they reunited again onstage, playing two sets at a Greenpeace show. Thankfully,
they sounded more rehearsed and cohesive than they had at the Bridge
School event. Young and Crosby, along with Jan Dance and Pegi Young,
solidified their bond by sailing to Panama on Young's schooner, the *W. N.
Ragland.* At a Crosby, Stills and Nash show at the Shoreline Amphitheatre in August, Young emerged for the encore, joining them for "For What
It's Worth," "Teach Your Children" and "Find the Cost of Freedom"—repertoire standards that didn't need much rehearsal time. That month, Stills
predicted that they would begin recording a new album in the fall and
tour the following spring.

Young's potential participation was all the more crucial in light of
the trio's failed attempt to make their own record to fulfill their revised
1977 contract with Atlantic. To everyone's pleasant surprise, freebasing
had not completely ravaged Crosby's singing. After one early performance with Nash, Nash had jokingly snapped, "Fuck you, Crosby! How
do you still have your voice?" For their first truly all-aboard effort since
1977's *CSN*, Crosby, Stills and Nash had hired Bill Szymczyk as producer.
Szymczyk had survived years of working with the hard-to-please Eagles,
and the trio reunited members of their touring band, including Joe Vitale,
for the sessions.

From the first day of recording in March 1987, Szymczyk realized he
faced as many challenges as with the Eagles. Crosby, Stills and Nash

didn't have many songs prepared—one was Stills' "Treetop Flyer," which was by then over a decade old. Nash worked to keep things on track and in focus, but Stills seemed, in Szymczyk's words, "all over the map." Crosby struck him as cranky, perhaps because he was still adjusting to his sober lifestyle. "They were quite fragile," the producer recalls. "The early flush of success had been over for quite a while, and I got the feeling they were treading water. They were not in top shape at the time." (Joe Vitale insists the band was careful about having any recreational substances around Crosby during this period: "None of us were walking around in front of him smoking joints. We had a lot of consideration for what he'd gone through. We didn't want to fuck up that recovery. We were so proud of him.")

Even though he'd been part of the group on and off for a dozen years, bassist George Perry was astonished when he glanced into the control room and saw Stills and Crosby in an overheated argument. "I'd seen so many fights between Stephen and Neil and David and Graham, but this was the most confrontational I'd ever seen," Perry says. "They were raising their arms and screaming at each other. I'd never seen them argue face to face." In the past, such blowups would evaporate by the following day's work, but in this case, there would *be* no next session. In a surprise equal to Young bailing on the Stills-Young Band tour, Perry was told, along with the other players, to pack up and go home after about two weeks of sporadic work. The trio informed Szymczyk they needed to leave for a few days to record "Chuck's Lament," a gauzy but agreeable pop ballad for the soundtrack of the movie *Amazing Chuck and Grace*, but they never returned. "It turned into seven days and then ten and then it was, 'Nah, we're not coming back,'" Szymczyk says. "And that was the end of that."

In the midst of the turmoil, Szymczyk sensed that the three did share at least one common goal. During the downtime, he would hear Stills and Nash talk about working with Young again. "I'd hear snippets, like, 'Well, he doesn't want to do it now, but maybe . . . ,'" Szymczyk recalls. "They were really hoping to get back together with Neil."

ON THE SUNNY but hazy morning of May 16, 1987—ironically, toward the end of President Reagan's "Just Say No to Drugs Week"—more than two hundred people, including Stills, Bonnie Raitt and Grace Slick, filed into the Church of Religious Science in Hollywood to witness a sight they probably never thought they'd see: the wedding of David Crosby and Jan Dance.

Since they had emerged from prison and rehab, respectively, the couple had worked hard at transforming their lives, as the Crosslight Agency's Debbie Meister had noted upon her first sight of Dance after her recovery. "I did a double take," she says. "The last time I had seen them, they were wearing knit caps when it was ninety degrees in LA, covering up every part of their body, because of the sores. But when Jan came back from rehab, her hair was glowing. Her *face* glowed. You looked at them and you just knew there's no way they were going to go back to that other life." Stills gave away the bride; wearing a morning coat to match Crosby's, Nash joined the couple to renew his vows with his wife, Susan. The gesture was both a show of support and a sign that, after a decade of marriage, the Nashes had hit a rough patch. The vows had the feel of a renewal for both couples: at a post-ceremony party at Nash's house in Encino, the Nashes and the Crosbys jumped into the pool. Another guest, Roger McGuinn, was amused to notice waiters serving nonalcoholic wine.

Crosby was also in the early stages of clearing up the wreckage of his finances. In January 1987, he had filed bankruptcy papers that included a list (without specific amounts) of everyone he owed money to, including their management, Atlantic Records, a Harley-Davidson shop in Glendale, a pool-cleaning service and even the Crosby, Stills and Nash corporation. During that same period, Nash, feeling he needed to be more in touch with the business, had returned with his family to Los Angeles after a decade in Hawaii. He and Crosby were now neighbors in Encino, and a Crosby, Stills and Nash tour, their first with a sober Crosby, was being planned for the summer. "They were happy because I was back functioning and because they do could CSN and make a bunch of money again," says Crosby. "It's the only way any of us ever make any money."

Also in attendance at the wedding festivities was Vicki Samuels, a producer for the CBS TV newsmagazine *West 57th.* Just before the wedding, Samuels had been approached by the trio's publicist to see if the show would be interested in a segment on Crosby's comeback pegged to their upcoming tour. The series *60 Minutes* was also interested in a

Crosby profile, she was told, but the group was worried that *60 Min-utes* might be too tough on the band. Though it was left unsaid, they assumed a *West 57th* segment would be frothier. Samuels and *West 57th* correspondent John Ferrugia were both admirers of the band, but they pushed for a story on the whole group, not just Crosby. The band agreed, and filming began at the wedding.

Their first taped interview would be with Nash, at his home; on sub-sequent days they were scheduled to go to Crosby's home and then Stills'. When Ferrugia brought up stories about Stills' "drug and alcohol problem" (Ferrugia's words) with Nash, Nash smiled nervously, paused and said, "What are you going to say next?" Then, on camera and with no further prompting, he admitted that Stills' issues were hurting the band, but said he felt Stills could overcome them the way Crosby had. Sam-uels and Ferrugia, who both had been expecting an upbeat story, were stunned. "That was the turning point of the interview," recalls Ferrugia, who, with Samuels at his side, listened as Nash lit into Stills, citing his "egotistical quest to be better than anybody" and how he and Crosby had felt they had been treated as "backup singers." At his home the next day, Crosby was more diplomatic, admitting to his own troubled past. But a new, different angle for the piece—what had started as a "coming-of-age story for boomers," as Ferrugia puts it—was now emerging. "I loved their music," Ferrugia says. "But the tragedy was that you have these people with incredible talent and yet they couldn't get it together."

Of the three, Stills remained the most discreet and the least willing to talk about his personal life, which became glaringly clear when the *West 57th* crew arrived at his home. Years later, Stills would explain to Dan Rather that John Lennon's assassination in 1980 had triggered issues for him. "The end of my enjoyment of my success happened [on] December 8th, 1980," he told Rather. "And I believe I poured myself into a bottle of whiskey for about 10 years. And pretty much missed the '80s." (Recalling that era in a 2010 interview, Stills said he was working on a memoir; he joked that each page in his chapter on the '80s would only feature the words, "I think I had a good time.") As a wary Stills rocked precariously back and forth on a chair, looking as if it were the last place in the galaxy he wanted to be, Ferrugia brought up what Nash had said. Begrudgingly, Stills admitted that he liked "fine wine and good scotch." When pressed, he bluntly stated, "I like to party, all *right*? . . . That's my own thing to deal with, and I'm not going to do it publicly." Ferrugia tried to follow up, but Stills interrupted him ("'But' my *ass*"). Ferrugia moved on to talk about music, yet the reporter felt he had captured a revealing moment. "You could see where the relationships in the band had broken down," Ferrugia says. "He said it was nobody's business and that's exactly what was going on in the band: 'It's none of your business and it's none of *their* business.' That's what Graham and David were talking about and we saw that in that comment. The contrast between this harmonious music, this public persona, and a dysfunctional relationship was stunning to me."

To complete the filming, the crew also appeared at a rehearsal for the band's tour, which would launch two days later. Stills had a tendency to be late. ("He wasn't good with time—it wasn't like he was careless about rehearsal," says Vitale.) As Young would tell *Rolling Stone* the following year, Stills also had a regular habit before each extended road trip: "Every tour that CSN has ever done, Stephen has gone out the window—he blows out before he goes on the road. He blows out heavily." Both habits seemed to merge that day. The band and the TV camera crew waited and waited at a rehearsal studio. Finally, Stills showed up, hours late and looking a bit glazed over. The musicians started to rehearse, but Stills didn't initially join in. Nash, who could erupt when pushed, finally ripped into him, saying he would "trash the fuck" out of him if he didn't put on his guitar and practice. "When there's a TV crew from CBS and you're three hours late and don't tell anybody, that's just not right," Nash recalls. "So we were fucking furious with him before he walked in." (Adds Siddons: "Graham wasn't a milquetoast. He was volatile and powerful himself. He could push them around when he needed. He would yell and scream and speak the truth, and in their hearts, they knew he was right.")

As the tongue-lashing began, a cameraman filming the practice lowered his gear, but Samuels ordered him to resume. "I said, 'Shoot this!'" she recalls. "He says, 'But they're CSN.' I said, 'This is a news story—turn it on now!' Never had I expected that the idols of youth had all this anger and animosity." Crosby stuck his hand in front of the camera, but it was too late: enough of the spat had been captured on tape. "It was bad timing," says crew member John Vanderslice, who was observing helplessly from the sidelines. "The people from the show were sitting around waiting and they get the footage of the century when Stephen walks in. More dirty laundry in front of people. We thought, 'Well, there goes *this* tour.'" Despite the flare-up, the group reluctantly agreed to one more segment for the TV show, and Samuels was able to watch them sing and play acoustically as if nothing had happened.

As the trio hit the road that summer, the mere sight of a beaming, if chunky, Crosby was enough to elicit "a thunderous, emotional outpouring," as one critic put it, at the show at Irvine Meadows in California. That scene would repeat itself throughout the season. At numerous stops, Crosby would refer to his prison time, saying he wouldn't preach often but that "if you've watched my life for the last ten years, it should take you about two seconds to figure it out." (In an interview during the tour, Stills encouraged fans to see them "now that Crosby is awake.") Stopping in backstage at a New York–area show, Meister saw the three palling around as if they'd never had any issues with each other, even in recent months. "You would never think there had ever been a harsh word that passed through anybody's lips at that point," she says. "It was like brothers who don't always get along, but in the end, you know they're your brother and it's going to work itself out."

The *West 57th* story wouldn't air until October, so fans were spared the sight of the bickering until the tour was over. But running into Nash some twenty years later, Ferrugia realized that the segment, and Nash's candid comments, hadn't been accidental. Nash told him he had never uttered such critical words to Stills' face; the interview was his way of communicating directly with his bandmate and trying to force Stills to work through his problems. "He said, 'I said things that may have been hurtful to Stephen, but thank God I said them,'" Ferrugia recalls. (Several months later, Stills got married for the second time, to model Pamela Anne Jordan, in a Washington, DC, ceremony. Crosby, Nash, Ahmet Ertegun and members of the Kennedy and Carter families attended.)

Talking with *Rolling Stone* months after the *West 57th* segment was broadcast, Young was hardly taken with it: "The thing that surprised me was the fact that CSN actually did the show. I mean, what are they gonna do next, *Geraldo*? . . . What kind of stupid move is that?" But plans were already proceeding for a recorded reunion with all four.

NATURALLY, YOUNG WOULD set the guidelines for what everyone hoped would be the first fully realized Crosby, Stills, Nash and Young album since 1970. He told Bolas it would be done on his turf—the studio on his ranch—and with his crew, including Bolas and Young's longtime co-producer and engineer Tim Mulligan. Young was juggling several other projects, so the sessions would happen when they happened—over months, if that's what it would take.

What Young couldn't control were the business entanglements that complicated the project. In a timely reprise of their head-butting of 1968, David Geffen and Ahmet Ertegun were now facing off again. As of late 1987, Young was still signed to Geffen Records, while Crosby, Stills and Nash remained with Ertegun and Atlantic. Both labels were part of the same corporate family, but Ertegun insisted the album be released on his label. During an interview with author Fredric Dannen for his music-industry book *Hit Men*, Geffen took a call from Ertegun, which eventually involved negotiations for the reunion album. To Ertegun's dismay, Geffen was demanding a 50 percent cut for Young. "Crosby, Stills and Nash are old, fat farts!" Geffen screamed at Ertegun as Dannen listened. "The only one with any talent is Neil Young!" According to Siddons, that demand didn't make it far, and Geffen never actually wanted the album. (Geffen did not respond to interview requests for this book.) In the end, the project ended up on Atlantic, deemed part of their obligation to the label.

Just before he fully reengaged with his bandmates, Young was feeling musically rejuvenated—but with an entirely different group. After tours and a few attempts at an album, he and Crazy Horse finally managed to finish a record, 1987's *Life*. But it was a largely listless, dispiriting affair. The album was sprinkled with standouts, such as "When Your Lonely Heart Breaks," but many of the songs were swamped in gauzy production. ("Prisoners of Rock 'N' Roll," though, was a bludgeoning anti-record-company statement of purpose.) A fraught European tour with the band, dogged by low ticket sales and a riot, ensued. Although Young was dissatisfied with the Horse's playing, he filmed the tour for a movie, *Muddy Track*. Under the circumstances, it was hardly surprising that Young was soon in search of another creative outlet. Not long after that, Bolas suggested that Young go in a different direction and use trumpets or saxophones on a new project. "The next thing I know," he says, "there were six guys with horns and they were called the Bluenotes." Two of the horn players—Young's longtime musical sidekick Ben Keith and a guitar tech, Larry Cragg—weren't even accomplished on those instruments. But Young was reinventing himself again, this time as a black-hatted, somewhat sharply dressed type named Shakey Deal, who backed a blowsy big band playing brassy variations on Chicago blues.

It was too much for Crazy Horse's Ralph Molina and Billy Talbot, who stuck with it for two weeks before deciding it wasn't up their musical alley. Taking Molina's place was a Memphis-raised drummer, Chad Cromwell, who had been playing with former Eagle Joe Walsh. Arriving in Los Angeles, Cromwell saw how inspired Young was by his latest makeover: within an hour of arriving at the studio, the entire band was putting songs on tape, and within two weeks, an album was in the can. "It was really unpredictable—you didn't even know what song you were going to do," Cromwell says. "I conceptualized Neil as a folk guy, a singer-songwriter, but he was a lot more rock and roll."

This Note's for You wasn't entirely rock and roll; it alternated between swaggering tracks that had a romping *Tonight Show* feel ("Ten Men Workin'," "Life in the City") and songs that evoked middle-of-the-night restlessness ("Coupe De Ville," "Twilight"). The title song, a dig at the way corporate sponsorship was eating into rock, had a snarky bite and a parody video to match. The concept may have bordered on gimmicky, but the kinetic energy of the music was undeniable; for the first time on record in years, Young felt alive, even allowing himself a jubilant bit of Blood, Sweat & Neil pop called "Sunny Inside." His take on a cheating song, "Married Man," brought out the never-before-heard white blues in Young's guitar. (Alas, the album didn't include "Ordinary People," an epic that painted a portrait of a society falling apart; it was almost too intense for the album and wouldn't be released for another twenty years.) The album was the sound of Young reemerging from the creative fog that had overtaken him for much of the decade, as it had his comrades.

With the joyful experience of the Bluenotes ringing in Young's ears, one last, crucial test had to be passed before the Crosby, Stills, Nash and Young album could proceed. Given their contrasting lifestyles (Young had hardly sworn off weed but was now employing a personal trainer) and their past head-butting, everyone needed confirmation that Stills and

Young could work alongside each other in a studio. After all, it would be the first time they had really attempted to do so in about a dozen years—a lifetime when it came to the quartet. "The relationship between them had been solidly fragile, if that's possible," says Nash. "With mercurial personalities, you need to know they're on the same page or else it's madness. When they're on the same page, it's still madness, but slightly more enjoyable madness."

At Nash's suggestion, Young invited Stills to the ranch for what Bolas calls "test runs" without Crosby and Nash. Their management agreed. "Crosby would do whatever it took to make that happen, and Graham is a compromiser by nature," says Siddons. "But Stephen didn't like that Neil was holding the cards. Graham saw that the thing to do was to get the two of them to work together and see if they could find a one-on-one relationship. We didn't know whether it would work." Stills called Vitale to tell him he was going to Young's ranch to see "if this thing can fly."

The Crosby, Stills and Nash camp held its collective breath. Tim Foster, Young's longtime production manager, printed up jokey T-shirts that rearranged the group's initials—"SYNC—It's Time for a Change"—implying Stills was now in charge. After Stills and Young had spent a week palling around and jamming at the ranch, the word came down that the coast was more or less clear. The work would begin in February 1988, almost eighteen very long years to the month since *Déjà vu* had been wrapped up.

"CAN IT HAPPEN AGAIN?" Abbie Hoffman wrote during this era, referring to the decade of the '60s. "No way. It is never going to happen again. The music is never going to be that good, the sex is never going to be that free, the dope is never going to be that cheap."

Crosby, Stills, Nash and Young wanted it to work; they wanted to conjure the best, not the worst, of their golden era as a unit. Yet the sense that everything about the quartet could be large scale was rammed home as soon as work on the album began and Crosby, Stills and Nash descended upon the Broken Arrow Ranch with their crew and equipment. There were guitars, amps and separate recording equipment for Stills, all in a twenty-four-foot truck that had to navigate along a goat trail on the property. In time, dozens of employees—engineers, guitar techs and so on—would settle in. A $1 million advance from Atlantic was hanging in the balance, and preparations had to be just right.

On paper, the setting was properly idyllic. The barn studio, now called Redwood Digital, had a view of nearby canyons. Goats and peacocks wandered about, some of the latter descending on the group's BMWs parked outside. Arriving for work one day, Bolas had to wait for sixteen cows to pass by. Another day, he found himself squeezed between Young and Nash in the front seat of Young's pickup truck, with Stills and Crosby sitting behind them. One by one, they passed cassettes to Bolas to pop into the tape deck. Each cassette contained one of their songs for consideration. As the truck rattled around Young's woodsy acres, fresh music filled the car. "It was, 'This is what I've got, here are my ideas,'" Bolas recalls. "We were playing songs as Neil was driving over the hills."

During an early day of recording, Crosby sat alone in the barn playing "Compass," the song he had composed in prison. It would be one of the emotional highlights of the album, but to everyone's amusement, they had to wait until a peacock outside the studio stopped squawking before they could resume work. Still, in the first month, "Compass" would be one of six completed songs for the record. "It was like putting on a well-worn shoe," Crosby says. "I knew I could do it again." Accompanied by Vitale on drums, Bob Glaub on bass, and the other musicians they had brought to the ranch, they also tackled another new Crosby song, "Nighttime for the Generals," co-written with keyboardist Craig Doerge. The song would be the first to allow for alternating guitar solos by Stills and Young. The two also concocted "Drivin' Thunder," a huffing-and-puffing rocker with lyrics that captured Stills' my-way-or-the-highway attitude of the time. (It was the musical equivalent of his *West 57th* interview.) With Young, they were able to finally nail a version of Nash's "Clear Blue Skies"; with its blending of Young's harmonica, a Stills guitar solo and some of the most distinctive harmonies on the album, the song was an example of what they could still accomplish when more or less acting as a team. They also worked on two Young songs: "Name of Love," a vague antiwar song he had tried to teach Crazy Horse onstage the previous year, and "American Dream," inspired by the demoralizing tale of Senator Gary Hart of Colorado, who had been a leading Democratic presidential contender in the 1988 race until a widely publicized affair with a younger model derailed his career.

Not long after the sessions commenced, Young's album with the Blue-notes, *This Note's for You*, was released. Adding to its second-wind feel, the record found Young back on his former label, Reprise; Roberts had negotiated a way for his client to leave Geffen (complete with accompanying pay cut for Young). Happy to promote the album for Reprise, Young made himself available for interviews, one with writer Dave Zimmer, who was still working with *BAM*. Sitting in Young's car, Zimmer brought up the rumored Crosby, Stills, Nash and Young album in the works, and, to Zimmer's surprise, Young said they already had five songs in the can. "It's very productive and it's been very good," Young said after a pause, calling the music "magnificent." He expressed relief that Crosby was "not strung out" and "very alive," adding, "I really believe it's a great record. I don't know how long it's going to take to finish, but we're dedicated to finishing it."

Revealingly, Young remarked that he didn't see himself as an "add-on" in the band anymore. "Now," he told Zimmer, "I'm the driving force in the band. And basically, that says it." The comment hardly came as a surprise to Pegi Young, who caught glimpses of the men at work but was mostly preoccupied with family matters. "Neil has some difficulty giving over the reins to anybody else," she says. "He has clear ideas about how things should be done and the sound he's looking for. I would say that Neil [at that time] would probably have been the leader of the group." If Young wanted to record during a full moon, which meant the others would have to wake up at two in the morning, so it would be.

As the relative youngster in the crew, Bolas received his first up-close look at the band, observing Young's daily juggling act. "When they walked in the door, you never knew what would happen," he says. "David wears life casually, like a loose piece of clothing. Graham was very analytical. Stephen, there were four of them in there, and which one showed up, you never knew. Neil sees this all and decides, 'What am I going to deal with and what am I going to walk away from?' Nobody was best friends with anybody, but they wanted it to work." Having worked with expressive singer-songwriters like Zevon, Bolas was accustomed to hearing confessional songs, but he was still struck by the group's ability to get, in his words, "totally naked behind a lyric–they were willing to risk."

Hints of what had once been would periodically emerge. When Chad Cromwell, the Bluenotes drummer, was invited to join them at the ranch, he found himself playing shuffles with Stills and Young on the first day of recording, as Crosby and Nash stood on the sidelines watching. By the end of the day, the jam had morphed into a new Stills song, a peppy strut called "That Girl." "When it was happening, holy shit, it was so great," Cromwell says. "There they were, those four guys. It was really beautiful to see how good they could be together, on a good day."

Yet as work on the record dragged on into summer, challenges–different ones from the past–began to arise. Bolas had to learn when to push them and when to hold back, which was never easy to determine. "You're not going to produce them," he says. "They are who they are. I'm not going to tell them how to sing a bridge. I will say, 'It's a bit out of tune, so can I make the headphones different?'" If Crosby was upset with his headphones and began screaming at Bolas, the engineer had to learn not to take it personally and let Crosby get it out of his system. Stills appeared jumbled–Crosby would later describe him as "toasted" in his second memoir. As a result, Young would be forced to finish some of the incomplete songs Stills had brought with him. They would share writing credits on the creamy pop number "Got It Made" and "Night Song," a brooding, croaked-voice dirge that captured the dark night of Stills' soul better than any interview could. (It was originally written for a reboot of the *Twilight Zone* TV series.) "I don't remember a *bit* of it, and I'd rather not discuss it," Stills told a VH1 interviewer a decade later about the making of the album.

Plugging *This Note's for You* in the British magazine *Q* that spring, Young joked that the album in progress would be called *Geriatrics' Revenge*. But the line wasn't always so funny. Crosby, carrying extra weight, would tire easily and needed to take extended stretches on a couch in the studio. Even during ear-splitting playbacks, he could be seen and heard snoring away. "You spend too much time in a jail and all you do is lie down on your cot," says crew member John Vanderslice. "He'd always revert to that, go back and lay down. It was that decompression out of the prison life." Yet Nash sensed Young's frustration when he ordered all the couches in the studio removed. "When he did that, I knew he was pissed at Crosby and therefore not happy about the whole thing," Nash says. "To have all of us there all the time gets a little weird for Neil, and those small things to Neil are gigantic."

Soon after the couch incident, Joel Bernstein stopped by the ranch to hear some of the album. At the time, Bernstein was working for Prince, and he couldn't help noticing the difference between the two camps: Prince would be tightly controlled and regimented, whereas Crosby, Stills, Nash and Young were disorganized and their days ill defined. When they played one of Young's songs, "This Old House," for Bernstein, Bernstein was struck by how shiny the harmonies sounded, thanks to new technology that ran their voices through electronics. It made them sound bright yet strangely unnatural.

It didn't help matters when, in the midst of the sessions, Nash approved the licensing of "Our House" for a Sears ad that would pay him over $100,000. (It would also later be featured in a sausage commercial.) Siddons suggested that Nash notify Young of his decision; after all, Young's name was on the recording, and in light of "This Note's for You" and its accompanying video, which mocked the likes of Michael Jackson for plugging products, the idea that Young would be even remotely linked to such an advertisement could be awkward. Nash agreed and called Young, resulting in a heated argument: Nash pointed out that Young hadn't sung or played on the original record and that it was his right to decide what to do with it. In the end, Nash prevailed, and his bank account benefited from it; his royalties from the song doubled.

The work didn't wrap up at Young's ranch; for finishing touches, they regrouped in Los Angeles. When he stopped by the studio, Siddons found them gathered around a pile of popsicle sticks, each representing songs and writers. Nash explained it was their way of figuring out the sequencing; they had to make sure the songs were apportioned equally. Crosby was irked that at least one of his contributions was dropped for what he felt were inferior songs by the others. "Neil and Stephen abused the privilege," Crosby says. "They stuck songs on there that absolutely should not have been on the record. 'Drivin' Thunder,' no fucking way. It was a game of politics. Neil and Stephen decided they were running things, and they jammed those on there to get the publishing, which is dumb." But Young was in charge, and no one opposed him.

At a listening session, Stills, who felt they never found the "right rhythm section," told them, "It ain't there. If you want to put this out, do so over my objections." The tapes were then shipped to Young's ranch for final mixing and tweaking. While Crosby, Stills and Nash's management played what they thought was the finished record for Ertegun and the president of Atlantic, Doug Morris, word came down—while everyone was listening—that Young wanted to tweak it further. "We were on pins and needles the whole time," Siddons says. "We didn't know if they would finish it or if Neil would approve it." Finally, Young signed off, and a release date of November 1988 was penciled in.

During the making of the album, in the spring, Stills had given an interview to a New Orleans newspaper in which he noted, with all seriousness, that the record would be billed to "SYNC," after Tim Foster's joke. In not quite the same spirit, Nash playfully wore one of the gag T-shirts when Crosby, Stills and Nash played at a fortieth anniversary concert for Atlantic Records that spring. (Young was invited to participate, but he declined for unspecified reasons.)

In the end, the billing would be as usual, Crosby, Stills, Nash and Young, but they would be a group in name only. Photographer Aaron Rapoport, an experienced professional who'd shot Steven Spielberg and others for *Rolling Stone*, was hired to shoot the band for the album jacket, with a caveat: he was told upfront he wouldn't be able to get them in the same room and would have to make the best of it. Rapoport photographed Crosby, Stills and Nash at Stills' house one afternoon. On another day, he took shots of Young at a Los Angeles hotel, but he wound up taking a trip to Young's ranch for a follow-up session because Young wasn't pleased with the initial images. On the cover, photos from the two separate shoots were fused to give the impression they had all been in the same place at the same time. A more revealing photo would be tucked inside the CD packaging: Crosby, Stills and Nash gathered around a microphone, as Young, his head resting on his hand, sat glumly on a nearby chair.

WHEN IT CAME to a Crosby, Stills, Nash and Young revival, it would have been hard to find a sweeter spot than the fall of 1988. For most of the decade, the survivors of what was now called "classic rock" had been cluelessly at sea, making hapless attempts to sound synth-enhanced and "acting" in music videos—assuming they even had record contracts by then. Crosby's former Byrds bandmate Chris Hillman escaped that fate by going full-on country with his Desert Rose Band, and Roger McGuinn returned to folk clubs as a solo act, but they were among the few who avoided mortification.

By the time the new CSNY album, *American Dream*, had been adjusted to Young's specifications, classic rock no longer felt like an embarrassing guest who wouldn't leave a party overrun by teenagers. The techno-pop that had dominated at the dawn of the decade had peaked, and '60s rock veterans now exuded a weathered, badge-of-honor aura. The year before, George Harrison and the Grateful Dead had returned with albums that made sonic concessions to the times but retained their innate sound and charm. Harrison's Traveling Wilburys project, teaming him with Bob Dylan, Tom Petty, Roy Orbison and ELO's Jeff Lynne, revived the idea of a supergroup and was publicly embraced. Steve Winwood's new coif, lacquered sound and beer commercial made him palatable to those who may not have even been born when he was in Traffic. With Stevie Ray Vaughan and Robert Cray ramming blues rock onto the pop charts, even the dormant Allman Brothers Band began discussions about a reunion that would come to fruition the following year, as would a comeback by another once-left-for-dead survivor, Bonnie Raitt. Meanwhile, punk and new wave bands like the Clash and the Cars had either dissolved or were on the verge of doing so.

Even the political climate, if nowhere near as charged as during the late '60s, offered a way in for *American Dream*. By the fall of 1988, the country had been through its share of shocks to the system. Distrust of government and the military was making something of a comeback. A year before, the stock market had crashed, and the Reagan administration had reluctantly admitted it had sold weapons to Iran (which was technically illegal) in order to use the money to support the contra rebels in Nicaragua, a pet passion of Reagan's. The president's glossy "Morning in America" campaign was undercut by a growing sense that the country was rotting from within. Michael Dukakis, a liberal Democratic governor from Massachusetts, was about to run against Reagan's designated heir, George H.W. Bush, offering hope for the first Democratic president since Jimmy Carter. To tie in *American Dream* with current events, Atlantic prepared a groan-worthy press release for the album's unveiling: "The Election May Be Over, but Atlantic's 'Four' Fathers Crosby, Stills, Nash & Young Have the New American Dream," it blared. Below was an "absentee ballot" checked "Yes!" next to the group's name.

But the optimism, starting with Democrats, was short-lived. On Election Day, Bush trounced Dukakis. *American Dream* would be a similar letdown. In the least likely way imaginable to kick off a Crosby, Stills, Nash and Young record, the title song opened the album with a blast of imitation flute (actually a synthesizer played by Stills) and a Motown-evoking bass part from Glaub. The mood was the polar opposite of the phrase "public porch"—the exquisite term concocted by poet and group pal Charles John Quarto to describe the unplugged intimacy of the original band. And the album only continued down that confounding path.

None of their previous albums, recorded either as a trio or a quartet, had shied away from each man's singular personality, mood and state of mind. Yet each record had still managed, miraculously, to sound cohesive: they weren't a traditional band, but they played one on record. Reflecting the vast amounts of time they'd spent apart, combined with their divergent musical tastes by the time of the Reagan years, *American Dream* was a conflicting grab bag of sounds and styles—nothing if not a discordant listening experience. Stills and Nash were interested in modernizing their sound by way of electronic instrumentation, but those efforts contrasted sharply with Young's largely organic leanings after his experiments with *Trans* and *Landing on Water*. His folksy "This Old House," a leftover from his country band days that tapped into the economic anxiety of Middle America, was somehow on the same album as Nash's "Shadowland," a piece pushed along by synthesizers that aimed to evoke the rice paddies of the Vietnam War. Nash's "Don't Say Good-Bye" was sentimental and affecting, but Stills' electric lead guitar solo elbowed its way into it, one of many examples of how the music lurched from one tone to another.

American Dream wasn't without merit. From his lone acoustic guitar to the group harmonies behind him, Young's "Feel Your Love" came off as an adult sequel to "Through My Sails." Stills' "Got It Made," which became a minor adult contemporary hit, had an undeniable hook in its chorus. Crosby's "Nighttime for the Generals" showed they could work up plenty of righteous antimilitaristic anger two decades after "Ohio," and the song felt even more timely with former CIA head George H.W. Bush having just won the presidency. (On that song, Young had won a particular battle: he insisted the group replace the synthesized bass they would use when playing the song in concert with an actual bass guitar for a more natural feel.) And in its way, *American Dream* was unflinchingly honest. They sounded like what they were: grown men in their forties without much in common. As heard in Stills' creaky voice on "Night Song" and "That Girl," that honesty wasn't always easy to handle. If *The Traveling Wilburys, Vol. 1*, was easy listening, *American Dream*, its troubled counterpart, was uneasy more often than not.

And as with the Stills-Young Band's *Long May You Run*, Young didn't give the impression he'd donated his best songs to the project; "American Dream" and "Name of Love" both felt slight. Bolas had the feeling that some of the four were saving their best material for solo albums. Indeed, the day after a group session in July, Young reconvened with his own musicians and recorded two of his other songs, "Someday" and "Ordinary People." Bass player Rick Rosas would later tell Vitale that Young and Crazy Horse's Frank Sampedro had co-written a gripping new rocker, "Rockin' in the Free World," during this same period but that it had been reserved for Young's own record.

The music trade magazine *Cashbox* was enthusiastic about the single "American Dream," saying it was "filled with the bitterness and beauty about a youth gone to pot." (Never had the phrase "back-handed compliment" meant more.) *American Dream* was certified platinum, for a million sales. But in the years before record sales were electronically tabulated, that number was questionable, especially since the album didn't crack the Top 10. And starting with the *New York Times*, the reviews were generally dismissive. "What's missing beyond the failings of any individual contribution is a sense of shared purpose or even identity," wrote John Rockwell. "This record does not sound as if it were impelled by a burning artistic vision." A review in the *Baltimore Evening Sun*—"If the quartet had made music this limp and turgid 20 years ago, they wouldn't have become stars"—was typical. "Everybody was hoping for an explosion of the fond memory rather than the reality of the humans," says Bolas in defense of the record. The lone music video made for the album, for "American Dream," didn't help. Directed by British filmmaker Julien Temple, it played off the song's themes of politics and the media, depicting Young as a paparazzo, Nash as a sleazy politician sleeping around, Stills as a gun-toting officer in the mode of Iran-contra heavy Oliver North, and Crosby as a wheelchair-bound corporate titan. The fact that they were outside the MTV demographic was only heightened when makeup used to age each man actually made them—Stills and Crosby especially—look older.

A few weeks before the arrival of *American Dream*, Crosby was in New York doing publicity for his book, *Long Time Gone*, an unflinching and candid autobiography that laid out his addiction in graphic detail and described the toll it had taken on him and Dance. A reporter from the *Daily News* asked him about the forthcoming group reunion and how fans would take heart, seeing all of them as having survived the ravages of an era. "Well, *some* of us have," Crosby muttered without explaining further. (He then talked up some of the songs he admired on the album, citing his, Nash's and Young's but none of Stills'.) Again stirring the pot, Nash plugged *American Dream* in a joint interview with Crosby for writer Gary Graff. Asked about the state of the band, Nash said, "Stephen could use some help," before Crosby (and Siddons, who was listening in) pulled him aside to stop him from talking about it further.

Even before the album was finished, Young was backing away from the idea of partaking in a full-fledged tour to promote it. During his spring interview with Dave Zimmer of *BAM*, he waved off the idea: "It wouldn't be a consistently great thing every night," he said, presumably alluding, at least, to Crosby's recovery issues. "When they see CSNY, even if it's a nostalgia trip, I want them to believe that their life is worth living and that the rest of their life is going to be better than the first part. But if we were going to go out now and it wasn't happening. . . . I don't want to be any part of that kind of show and I will not be a part of it." Expressing similar reservations to *Rolling Stone*, Young brought up a comparison to an aborted Rat Pack reunion: in March 1988, Frank Sinatra, Dean Martin and Sammy Davis Jr. had launched a "Together Again" tour, only to see

Martin drop out almost immediately due to kidney issues. "If we go out there and fall on our ass, what are we?" he told *Rolling Stone.* "Dean Martin? All the alcoholics who went to see him, they didn't say, 'Wow, look at Dean. He used to drink so much, but he got himself together and now he's strong, up there with Frank and Sammy.' I feel sorry for the guy. He's in the fucking hospital. . . . That's a weird comparison, but in some ways it's very true. They're just another generation's heroes. So I think we have a responsibility, and I don't think we've lived up to it yet."

Young had kept his word to make the group album; he was now doing the same about not touring behind it. When *American Dream* was released, he consented to just one radio interview, joining the others by phone—the audio equivalent of the conjoined album cover photo. "Neil recognized the album wasn't very good, and he behaved as if it wasn't," says a source in the trio's camp. "If he'd made noise about the record, everyone would have gotten on board. But Neil was committed that nothing was going to happen and that's how he behaved. It was tamped down." Asked about the album a year later, Young told the *Village Voice,* "It could've been great. I did it to keep a promise," and said nothing more. Young had already lined up another tour with the Bluenotes. As Pegi Young says, "I think his actions were indicative of what he was feeling about that experience. He may have moved on to something else in his head."

For Crosby, Stills and Nash and their team, a reunion trek with Young would have meant a financial windfall, and the news that there would not be a tour with Young was disappointing. "It would have helped sell the record," says Vitale. "He promised he would make a record, and he was a man of his word. And that was the end of it." Nash conceded later that the album wasn't "earth shattering": "It wasn't like, 'We can't wait to play these songs live.'" The group's management scrambled to book the trio for its own shows that fall. To avoid any awkward overlaps, Siddons and Gerry Tolman—who had once been Stills' backup guitarist but was now managing him—met with Lookout Management, Young's overseers, to ensure that Young's Bluenotes concerts wouldn't be in the same area or cities as the Crosby, Stills and Nash shows on the same nights.

In the weeks after the release of *American Dream,* Young agreed to join them for precisely two public performances: "Graham Nash's Children of the Americas Radiothon," a benefit concert to alleviate childhood hunger in North and South America, and the next Bridge School benefit. Backstage at the former—a Jerry Lewis "Jerry's Kids" type of benefit, but featuring classic rockers like Jackson Browne and Randy Newman— Nash was asked about a tour now that *American Dream* was out. "I don't know, I truly don't know," he replied, adding that Young had told them he wanted to finish another record with them before he would consider going on the road together. In terms of how long it had been between Crosby, Stills, Nash and Young albums by that point, that answer amounted to: Don't expect to stand in line to buy tickets anytime soon.

Their performance at the Bridge School benefit, at the Oakland Coliseum on December 4, 1988, betrayed little, if any, friction. With his hair and mustache now fully grown out, Crosby exuded a leonine benevolence; Stills and Young shared a microphone during parts of "Love the One You're With." Although they played without a backup band, they threw themselves into an unplugged "Southern Man" that included acoustic guitar solos from both Stills and Young (along with Nils Lofgren, who reprised his piano part from the original recording). In another glimmer of the old days, Crosby's feisty rendition of "Long Time Gone" was accompanied by the sight of Stills playing with a cigarette in his mouth. Audience members were left wanting more, but the performances didn't change Young's mind about a tour.

Nash would be left with one haunting visual memory of that period. After one recording session for *American Dream*, Young drove back to his ranch alone while Crosby, Stills and Nash followed him in their own car. Watching Young pull away from them, Nash grabbed a camera and snapped a few shots. "I saw him driving along this lonely road," he later told Andy Greene of *Rolling Stone*, "and I thought, 'This is a perfect image of Neil Young.'" It was also the perfect reminder of one of their most painful missed opportunities—a reunion that nearly closed the door on Young working with them ever again.

CHAPTER 10

DECEMBER 1988-NOVEMBER 1994

s a member of the Bluenotes and a contributor to *American Dream*, drummer Chad Cromwell had already experienced the musical whiplash inherent in Young's constant pursuit of new musical adventures. But he wasn't ready for another pivot so soon after the CSNY reunion. A week before Christmas in 1988, with *American Dream* stalling on *Billboard*'s album chart, Cromwell found himself on the other side of the country from Young's ranch, playing yet another iteration of his boss' music. For several late nights at a studio in New York's Times Square, he, Young, and bass player Rick Rosas made a feisty, amped-up racket. "We were in Manhattan recording power-trio punk music and keeping Keith Richards hours, for some reason," Cromwell recalls. Each night when they left the studio, they were greeted by a jarring sight: "It was so cold, and you were stepping over guys bundled in boxes and sleeping bags."

Matching the ambience, the songs Young brought along, including "Heavy Love" and "Cocaine Eyes," were also agitated. "I'm thinking, 'These aren't blues tunes anymore,'" Cromwell says. "They were a commentary of some kind." In some cases, the connection was clear. They cut a blaring, crunchy version of the old Drifters hit "On Broadway," with lyrics, contrasting the glitter of that street and being broke, that fit the atmosphere surrounding them, and "Cocaine Eyes" was interpreted by some in Young's circles as a devastating commentary on one of his erstwhile bandmates. The songs wouldn't be available to the general public for another year, but Young wasn't stopping. The next month he was pushing Old Black, his preferred and oft-punished electric guitar, to even louder extremes on the road with an expanded band he called, appropriately, the Restless.

The contrast with the music he had been making on and off for months with his former colleagues could not have been more apparent, and Young was not one to hide his feelings. "It only lasted a while," he said to a French TV reporter about *American Dream.* "Then it was over. We made a record . . . but I've gone so far, I've gone all over the place and they're still doing what they've always done. Coming back together wasn't as easy as I thought it might be."

Easier, at least on some levels, was compiling another album of his own, *Freedom*, which arrived in the fall of 1989. (*Eldorado*, an EP—for extended play, shorter than an album but more than a single—also arose from that New York session, preceding *Freedom* by a few months, and some of the EP made it onto the final album.) The tracks for *Freedom* were pulled from sundry times and places: the openly dissipated "Too Far Gone" had been written in the mid-'70s, whereas "Someday" was cut at his ranch during downtime from work on *American Dream.* Yet from the sturdiness of the songs to the directness of his delivery—no persona, no synthesizers—*Freedom* was the model Neil Young album that David Geffen had dreamed about but never received. It had everything one could have wanted, especially after a decade of strangeness. "Rockin' in the Free World," heard in both acoustic and electric versions, harked back to the dual takes on "My My, Hey Hey (Out of the Blue)" and "Hey Hey, My My (Out of the Black)" on *Rust Never Sleeps*, but with an added infusion of righteous, Bush-era anger. Even though it was more produced than past takes, "Too Far Gone" evoked Young's hangdog country-bar moments, and the naked balladry beloved by fans of his singer-songwriter side returned in the wistful "Hangin' on a Limb" and the mawkish "The Ways of Love."

For all its touchstones, though, *Freedom* also conveyed a man pondering his wayward previous decade and, true to the album's title, trying to break free of it. Bleak and shadowy, "Wrecking Ball" seemed to implore people to stay with him. In concert, "Crime in the City (Sixty to Zero Part 1)" could extend to as much as twenty minutes, but even in the truncated version on *Freedom*, its tableau—beleaguered cops, robbers and musicians pondering what had become of society, culminating with autobiographical comments on Young's broken home and upbringing—was still gripping. Although not specific, "No More" amounted to a list of his recent personal and artistic struggles; the moment the song slammed to a pause, with Young spitting out the title phrase, was one of the most chilling moments on any of his albums from the decade.

While Young was putting the finishing touches on *Freedom*, his newly abandoned partners were attempting to pick up the pieces and find a way forward. Despite the physical weaknesses he was still dealing with after addiction and imprisonment, Crosby began the process of making up for lost and wasted time. He quickly followed his book *Long Time Gone* with an album with the optimistic title *Oh Yes I Can*; the cover portrait revealed a newly upbeat, smiling, less mentally and physically ravaged Crosby to the world. The album, released not on Atlantic but by way of a new deal with A&M, found him picking up where he'd left off: with members of the Section and the Crosby, Stills and Nash band helping out, he remade songs like "Melody" and "Flying Man" that had been intended for his canned, freebase-debilitated solo album of a decade before. The inconsistent production undercut some of those songs, but the freshly written "Tracks in the Dust" was a startling return to form. Framed as a conversation between opposing parts of his personality—the hopeful and the cynical—it was essentially a dinner party with himself. The melody, augmented by the shimmery tones of his friend Michael Hedges on guitar, brought out the conversational quality of Crosby's voice.

The trio still existed, and when forced, they could rise to the occasion; in the fall of 1989, they played an acoustic benefit at the United Nations. There, they generally stayed on track, doing, among others, Crosby's "Tracks in the Dust" and Stills' pared-down version of "Got It Made." But in light of the commercial and artistic disappointment that was *American Dream*, the division in the group that had been exposed in the all-too-revealing *West 57th* show—pitting Crosby and Nash on one side, Stills on the other—intensified. Despite being the founding two members of the band, Crosby and Stills had never been especially close; now, in light of Crosby's sobriety, their lifestyle differences had never been further apart, making for a new degree of conflict. "I knew they weren't getting along," says Roger McGuinn, who opened for a few Crosby, Stills and Nash shows during this period. "They had arguments. Both very strong personalities." As Crosby put it a year later, "Stills and I butt heads a lot. We kind of disagree on a lot of things."

During an interview with *Billboard* to promote *Oh Yes I Can*, Crosby revealed that he and Nash had started recording for what would be their first album as a duo in more than a dozen years. Reveling in modern studio technology and recruiting a bevy of collaborators, the two created heavily produced tracks with layers of keyboards and often electronic drums. They gladly recorded other writers' material, including "If Anybody Had a Heart," by JD Souther and Danny Kortchmar, and called in lead guitar players like Peter Frampton and session man Michael Landauto to play parts Stills normally would have tackled. Nash heard one of Joe Vitale's songs—a synth-poppy rocker called "Live It Up," written for potential use on a soundtrack—and immediately asked to include it, despite the fact that it was markedly unlike anything one would expect from them. "Graham really liked it and said, 'I'd like to sing that song,'" says Vitale. "To this day, I don't know why. We got a lot of grief for that." (Vitale's original recording of the song would turn up a few years later in a *Saved by the Bell* TV movie, where the synth-pop arrangement felt more at home.)

But in a replay of the *Daylight Again* experience, the project would morph into a trio album. Although Ahmet Ertegun remained patient when it came to coaxing a new record out of them, Atlantic had a new label head, Doug Morris, and the time had come for another Crosby, Stills and Nash album. Early in 1990, almost a year after the start of the Crosby and Nash sessions, the duo became a threesome again when Stills began arriving for work. With help from Vitale, Stills labored at home to finish his songs while Crosby and Nash continued without him. When they would go home for the night, Stills would arrive with his team and lay down his own material, like "Tomboy," or overdub his parts onto the Crosby and Nash songs.

For the first time, the situation was noticeably impacting Nash. He had begun to feel guilty about being away from his children while on tour and being unfaithful to his wife, Susan, along the way. In a misguided attempt to look more youthful, he had grown a mullet, which he spent painstaking hours combing backstage before shows to ensure its

luster. The agonizing creation of yet another group album only added to
his stress. "We were trying to do the best album we could, but it was
a fight all the way," Nash recalls. "It was a piecemeal album, and it was
the beginning of me realizing it was different between me and David and
Stephen. It used to be the three of us without question. Now it was three
individuals. We had begun to lose it."

The absence of a group mindset continued to the end of the project,
when an album cover had to be submitted. According to Nash, neither
Stills nor Crosby wanted their photos on the front of the package. "You
should have seen what David and Stephen looked like during that time,"
Nash says. (In a group interview the following year, Crosby cracked,
"We're not handsome—we're not sex gods," and Stills added, "We made
a vow this year not to use our pictures anymore.") With no one willing
to make a firm decision, Nash went with his first choice: what he admits was a "fucking weird image" by artist David Peters of hot dogs (on
sticks) on the moon, the earth in the distance. For Nash, the image had a
veiled association: when he received US citizenship, Stills, as a joke, had
taken him to Pink's, the iconic hot dog stand in Los Angeles. To subtly
update the original artwork, Nash asked Peters to insert a fourth hot dog,
floating away from a broken stick, to signify Young. "Those sticks are
very fragile," he says. "They can be used as a weapon or they can fail
when you really need them."

According to Nash, no one was thrilled with the idea, but options
were not forthcoming. "I said, 'Fine, let's find something else,' but they
never said shit at the time," he says. "There was no time to make better
choices." Bill Siddons, their co-manager, was livid. "That was the only
time I ever yelled at them," he says. "I said, 'Are you guys idiots? You're
one of the most revered institutions and you're going to put out an album
with hot dogs on the moon? It's going to destroy you!' They just laughed
at me. They wanted to do something different and take the piss out of
themselves, I guess."

When the album, *Live It Up*, emerged in June 1990, the cover was met
with bemusement at best, and sometimes mockery. ("Blame Nash, not me,"
deflects Crosby.) The music inside was no less incongruous. Starting with
the pumped-up electronic pulse of the title song, *Live It Up* smothered

many of their best qualities—harmonies and intimacy—in forty-eight-track wide-screen production. A few of its songs reinjected political awareness into their music: Nash's "After the Dolphin," cowritten with Craig Doerge, documented a British bar bombed during World War II, and "Yours and Mine," co-written by Crosby, Nash and Doerge, probed gun violence, marrying its lyrics to a sky-high chorus. But capable pop tracks like "Straight Line" didn't sound much like Crosby, Stills and Nash, and although most of Stills' songs had rhythmic hooks, they felt weightless. The only time the three gathered around the same microphone was on "Haven't We Lost Enough?," a collaboration between Stills and an unlikely partner, REO Speedwagon frontman Kevin Cronin, that pared the trio's sound back down to voices and one guitar. A return to Stills' distraught-romantic side, it was both the best song he'd devised in years and the standout on the album. "That song was from the heart," says Siddons. "But the other stuff was formulaic and soulless." The reviews were mixed or dismissive, and at least one, in the *Tampa Tribune*, zeroed in on what was absent, calling Stills "uncharacteristically subdued."

The album was mean to signify a rebooted, 2.0 version of Crosby, Stills and Nash, a modernization of the band, and the arena tour planned to accompany it reflected that goal. "We thought this year we should bring CSN into the '90s," Nash told a reporter. The plan involved a costly stage set utilizing carefully choreographed video imagery to accompany many of the songs, and they hired Jules Fisher, a lighting designer who had won multiple Tony awards, including one for *Pippin*, to help with the project. "I wanted to up the game—we were burning out markets by doing the same show every night with no new presentation," says Siddons. "You needed to do something completely different to transform the Persian-rugs-and-three-flashlights mentality to the modern era." During "Wooden Ships," a sailboat would flash overhead; a stained-glass window would appear during "Cathedral."

The band went along with the concept, but, as with the production of *Live It Up*, the revamped staging became bogged down in unnecessary gimmicks. The tour would involve bigger crews, five trucks, and over $1 million in cost overruns—what Siddons calls "a million-dollar mistake." The trio's band couldn't help but roll its eyes. "It's CSN, not Pink Floyd," says Vitale. "They didn't need a giant production. Their fans didn't want to see all that crap. They were treating it like a Broadway show. The band guys, we hated it." Onstage, the members of the band would snicker among themselves at various times, as when a slide show of children was brought up during "Teach Your Children."

As the four-month-long tour began to wind down at summer's end, another attempt to introduce Crosby, Stills and Nash to the video generation arrived in the form of an invitation to perform for MTV's new series, *MTV Unplugged.* Although they were barely given any airtime on MTV, the network thought hiring them for the show would show its commitment to heritage artists. On a humid August day, they pulled into the Ed Sullivan Theater to tape their segment, which would be followed by sessions featuring Aerosmith and the LA hard rockers Ratt that same day. The first hiccup arose when Stills showed up with a sinus infection, chest cold and the flu. Rather than cancel, they decided, against Stills' wishes, to stick with the schedule and tape the episode; to help Stills feel better, MTV got him chicken soup and found a nearby gym with a hot shower. Stills sounded froggy, and a stylist had to constantly apply powdered makeup to all three of them to ward off a shine from the humidity. Nevertheless, they performed eight songs, five of which would air in the finished show. The episode would be only one of three—the other two featured Nirvana and the grunge band Live—that were filmed straight through, with no retakes or reshoots.

Before the taping, Stills warned them to expect bad reviews, yet the write-ups barely materialized. In the era before *Unplugged* became must-see television, thanks to later shows by Eric Clapton and Paul McCartney, the Crosby, Stills and Nash episode wasn't panned so much as ignored. The acoustic format may have been surprising for Steven Tyler and his bandmates in Aerosmith, but the format came across as strummed business as usual for Crosby, Stills and Nash. "There was nothing different about it from any other appearance they would make with those songs," says *Unplugged* producer Alex Coletti. "It was just a great performance that was their stock-in-trade. Plugging them in would have been interesting." As a result, Coletti says, it would become "the most forgotten *Unplugged*" in the series' history.

AMERICAN DREAM MAY have been comatose on arrival, but another dream never died. A headline in the March 1, 1990, *Los Angeles Times* pronounced: "CSN&Y to Reunite." For all the lingering disappointment over the making and unmaking of their reformation album, they were still capable of brushing aside the strain and resentments and climbing onstage together for a worthy cause. In the early months of 1990, that cause was their long-troubled original drummer, Dallas Taylor.

Then approaching forty-two, Taylor had become one of the earliest and most frighteningly visible signs of the toll their lifestyles could take. In 1979, he had briefly returned to the Stills band, but he was still battling drug addiction and was soon replaced. Taylor sued Stills for allegedly not paying him royalties that were due on the Manassas albums he co-produced and drummed on; when he was offered $10,000 to settle, in an arrangement stipulating that he sign away all future royalties on Crosby, Stills, Nash and Young records, Taylor readily agreed. To the disgust of his lawyer, he then cashed the check at a nearby bank and spent all the money on drugs within five days. At one point he was living with two prostitutes at the musician-friendly Tropicana Motel in West Hollywood. After bottoming out in the '80s, he entered rehab and emerged clean, with a new career as a drug counselor. But the experience left him weakened—John Sebastian recalls Taylor as "physically incapacitated, with a lot of pain involved," when the two tried playing together at a drug rehab benefit—and in November 1989, he was diagnosed with a failing liver; his doctor placed him on a waiting list for a new organ.

The March 31, 1990, benefit at the Santa Monica Civic Auditorium, intended to raise funds to offset Taylor's $200,000 medical bill, was billed as a Crosby, Stills, Nash and Young reunion. Don Henley and Stills' fellow former Manassas cohort Chris Hillman also played with their own bands. Taylor later wrote that during Henley's opening set, he observed Stills and Crosby "watching from behind the curtain at the edge of the stage, hidden from the audience." He thought he "could read envy and a certain amount of awe on their faces." Henley was enjoying a post-Eagles solo success of the type that Crosby, Stills and Nash had each craved but never achieved. No matter what they did on their own or how high the quality, the clamor for the group overshadowed it.

After a combination of solo and group songs, the moment no one imagined would ever happen again arrived: Taylor, who had been fired unceremoniously from the band twenty years before, anxiously sat down at a drum kit and played "Wooden Ships" with them. (Three weeks after the show, he received his liver.)* The following night at the same venue, the four came together again for another benefit (promoting the California Environmental Protection Act), and Young even invited them to Farm Aid, the annual family-farm benefit he had been involved in since 1985. There, Stills and Young exchanged hugs before they played "This Old House." In a moment that demonstrated what a well-oiled machine Crosby, Stills and Nash could be, Nash stuck his hand in his pocket and handed Stills a guitar pick midway through "Suite: Judy Blue Eyes."

Given how intertwined they were financially, business would yank them back together. Starting in the mid-'80s, the former Buffalo Springfield rhythm section of Dewey Martin and Bruce Palmer had anchored a tribute band using its original name. In May 1990, Stills, Young and Richie Furay jointly filed for the trademark for "Buffalo Springfield," which was granted to them two years later; the cover band, with Young's and Stills' begrudging permission, was able to continue under the name Buffalo Springfield Again. (A similar scenario had taken place in 1989 and 1990, when Crosby and his former Byrds compadres McGuinn and Hillman played a few concerts to establish their legal right to the band name after their fellow former Byrds Gene Clark and Michael Clarke started touring as the Byrds; after a drawn-out legal contest, Clarke, who died in 1993, was awarded the name.) Once more defying Young's wishes, Nash gave Fruit of the Loom permission to use a newly recorded version of "Teach Your Children" for $500,000. But nothing in those transactions resulted in as many hard feelings as the creation of a planned boxed set tracing their interconnected music and careers.

---

*The concert wasn't the end of their story. In 1996, Taylor again sued the band for whatever unpaid royalties he was still due, despite his earlier agreement with Stills; he claimed that subsequent payments (for, among other things, their 1991 boxed set) had been cut off after the publication of his 1994 memoir *Prisoner of Woodstock*, which contained mildly salacious group stories. The suit left such a bad taste in the trio's mouths that when *Crosby, Stills & Nash* was reissued in a deluxe CD edition a decade later, Taylor's image on the back cover was mysteriously absent.

Starting with landmarks like Bob Dylan's *Biograph* in 1985, multidisc boxed sets had become the heftiest way to capitalize on CD reissues and boomer nostalgia. By 1991, with Nash and band comanager Gerry Tolman at the helm, it was Crosby, Stills, Nash and Young's turn. After the critical and commercial drubbing of *Live It Up*, such a collection also felt necessary, a way to remind people of the band's music, legacy and impact when they all appeared to be fading.

Knowing that Crosby and Stills would have little patience for wading through boxes of tapes and outtakes, Nash grabbed the reins. He and Tolman went to work as co-producers, compiling four discs of well-known and unreleased material of the solo, duo, trio and quartet recordings. Alongside the expected hits and favorites were a slew of rarities that defined the appeal of the boxed-set vogue: the original, extended jam version of "Almost Cut My Hair," a live take of "Man in the Mirror" from one of their 1970 Fillmore East shows, the version of "Suite: Judy Blue Eyes" with Taylor's never-used drum part on the first section, and Crosby's original "Guinnevere," with Jefferson Airplane's Jack Casady on bass. Young gave Nash permission to use a certain number of songs, and they were sequenced into the collection—which, at least for a time, was being billed as a Crosby, Stills, Nash and Young anthology.

But the experience of reliving their troubled two-plus decades together was not always a pleasant experience. Writer Steve Silberman, a devoted Crosby fan who had seen the band in concert numerous times—even during Crosby's dark period in the early '80s—witnessed just how difficult it was for them to grapple with the contents of the set. Silberman was working a restaurant day job when he received a call from a pal who was also a friend of the band. What was Silberman doing right now? It turned out that Crosby, Stills and Nash were in a hotel in nearby Los Gatos meeting about their boxed set, and they could use help figuring out what their best unheard material was; Silberman had been suggested as a knowledgeable outsider. To his astonishment, he suddenly found himself face to face with his musical heroes. Crosby struck him as initially guarded, as if still tentative about reentering the world after his jail time.

Silberman strongly felt that one song in particular needed to be unearthed and included: the one he thought was called "Wordless Song," from Crosby's shelved solo album. Nash told him the track's title was

"Kids and Dogs," and he had a copy of it in his car. Retreating to the vehicle, Nash popped a cassette into its sound system, and the beautifully remixed recording of Crosby's guitar and stacked voices and Jerry Garcia's crystalline acoustic guitar, making for an ageless, psychedelic folk melody, filled the air. After years of hearing only a bootleg version, Silberman reveled in the glistening, improved sound quality until, less than a minute in, Nash switched it off. "I just can't listen to it," he said. "That time [circa 1980, when Crosby included it on his rejected solo album] was so horrible." As gorgeous as the track was, and despite the fact that it had been recorded in the early '70s, during the experimental PERRO days, it reminded Nash of Crosby's struggle with addiction and his own mixed feelings about it.

"Kids and Dogs" didn't end up on the compilation and, as Nash soon learned, neither would most of Young's contributions. Just as the set was sequenced and ready to go, Nash received word from Lookout Management that Young had changed his mind. Nash was gobsmacked. "Neil said, 'You can use whatever you want,'" Nash says. "I had it all planned out, but Elliot calls me and says, 'You can only use six with Neil.' Well, that fucks up my entire trip. I had to take out the Neil songs and rearrange the discs. I didn't think that was nice at all. I mean, come on—we're trying to do a fucking job here. Help me out. I'm not trying to rob you. I'm trying to show what the addition of you meant musically." Part of the reason for the change of heart was financial: Bill Siddons, Crosby and Nash's manager, had devised a deal in which the group would receive a relatively small advance upfront but a larger cut of the royalties. The arrangement didn't remotely please Young's manager, Elliot Roberts, who would tell writer Jimmy McDonough, in his biography of Young, that it was "a shit deal . . . and they wanted us to be part of the shit deal." He also felt that Crosby, Stills and Nash were "totally using Neil" by including his name on the cover. Young ultimately granted permission to include "Helpless" and "Ohio," but only those two songs.

Now called *CSN*, thus sharing an uninspired title with their 1977 studio album, the boxed set made the most of the format. Over four discs, it bobbed between familiar studio versions, alternate takes, unreleased material and highlights of group and offshoot albums. Since the set was arranged chronologically, at Ertegun's urging, the fourth disc suffered. But the set nonetheless made its point: it reminded the world that, despite two decades of often disappointing band and solo albums, the group had helped reinvent the sound and sensibility of pop. In typical form, nothing would be perfect: in the offices of the Crosslight Agency, Debbie Meister received aggrieved phone calls from family members—none of their wives had been thanked in the credits. "I had a lot of very angry women calling me," says Meister. "I didn't get thanked either. Nobody got thanked." The booklet was reprinted in future pressings to include the omitted names.

When the collection was rolled out in October 1991, Crosby, Stills and Nash dutifully promoted it in joint interviews, where they could be almost comically combative. Why weren't there more Crosby songs on the set? "It's just that his songs are so insufferably long," Stills retorted. Talking with the Associated Press, the three of them debated the precise location of their first harmonizing. Stills stuck with his memory of Cass Elliot's house: "I can see it, in her dining room, which looked out over the pool, and John Sebastian was swimming in the pool while we were singing."

Crosby brusquely retorted: "Just because you remember doesn't mean it happened. You were as high as the rest of us." At that point Nash intervened, cutting Crosby off before the conversation grew too heated. Only when Young's name came up did their fragile unity return. "When we say, 'What about the greater good?' he gets this glazed look," Stills said. "It's absolutely foreign to him." Crosby then high-fived Stills.

FOR CROSBY, THE night of January 16, 1991, should have been celebratory. At New York's Waldorf-Astoria hotel, the five original Byrds were to be inducted into the Rock & Roll Hall of Fame. Given their fractious history and relationships, a degree of awkwardness was guaranteed. A few months before, Crosby had broken a shoulder, an ankle and a leg when his motorcycle crashed while he was going around a curve on the road near his house in Encino. (He eventually sued the manufacturer for $1.2 million, using the money to pay off some of his debts.) But Crosby had recovered enough to travel, and at the Waldorf, he was in a wheelchair. Crosby was being so demanding that Chris Hillman, who was wheeling him around, made a crack about the '40s noir thriller *Kiss of Death*, in which a woman in a wheelchair gets pushed down a flight of stairs. "Don't do it," Crosby said to Hillman.

At the dinner table, drummer Michael Clarke, who was extremely drunk, rebuffed Crosby's invitations to help him get clean. Crosby, still newly sober, was visibly incensed when Quincy Jones—during a rambling speech as part of the induction of Ahmet Ertegun's brother Nesuhi Ertegun—appeared pretty liquored up himself. "Get off the stage!" Crosby said. "How *dare* you!" When the band went onstage to reunite, Clarke was so inebriated that the house drummer was used instead. "It was very awkward seeing the other guys in the Byrds," Crosby told *Rolling Stone* in 2009. "There were not a lot of warm, fuzzy feelings. But everyone handled it well and we were certainly proud to be there."

Another distraction overshadowed the night: while attendees were filing into the Waldorf ballroom, word began making its way down the line that the United States had started bombing Iraq. At 9:00 P.M., in the midst of the ceremony, George W. Bush's national address was broadcast live on screens inside the ballroom. In another era, such a cataclysmic event would have brought Crosby, Stills, Nash and Young together. But now, each wound up handling the situation separately.

A month after the Byrds' induction, Young had publicly reconciled with Crazy Horse. Crosby, Stills and Nash were baffled by the decision: "I thought it was dumb," Crosby says. "Nice guys, but [imitating their sound] 'boom boom cap, boom boom cap.' 'Now I'll use the *other* string on the bass.' You know he had something in mind and he wanted it that simple or he wouldn't have done it." But Young kept being drawn back to Crazy Horse in spite of his own frustrations with them, especially on the enervating European tour in 1987. *Ragged Glory*, the album he'd made with them early in 1990 and released that fall, extended Young's revitalized streak. No longer as sludgy as they had been on 1987's *Life*, Crazy Horse sounded refreshed: the combination of their own straightforward but clean musical lines and Young's Old Black guitar resulted in what sounded like a long-lost sequel to albums like *Zuma*. Whether it was monolithic (the ten-minute "Love and Only Love"), merry (a version of "Farmer John") or down-home ("Country Home"), *Ragged Glory* testified to the way Crazy Horse made Young feel sonically at home and at ease. With them, he finally nailed a version of "White Line," a loping, cocaine-alluding rocker

Young had written and first performed in the mid-'70s, and none of his other bands would have played a more appropriately lumbering version of a song like "Fuckin' Up." At a time when mainstream rock and roll had become defined by pre-grunge hair metal (and the remnants of the indie rock scene of the '80s), Young and Crazy Horse sounded spikier than most of their younger competition. As Kurt Loder opined in his *Rolling Stone* assessment, "I guess Neil Young is the king of rock & roll."

Ragged Glory handily outsold *Live It Up*, and the tour designed to promote it returned Young and Crazy Horse to arenas. With the first Iraq War now underway, Young used the platform for his most political statements up to that point. When he played a version of Bob Dylan's "Blowin' in the Wind," the stage set incorporated both a yellow ribbon and a peace sign. For added new-decade relevance, Young and his management cannily arranged for another change-up that would have a lasting, decisive impact on his music and image: they invited Sonic Youth and Social Distortion, both younger, punk- and indie-minded bands, as opening acts. Young's fans often didn't know what to make of them, especially Sonic Youth, who reveled in harsh, often grating tunings and a disdain for rock-showmanship clichés. But Young was never less than supportive, telling the band he would listen to one of their twistiest songs, "Expressway to Yr. Skull," before he started his own set.

Starting with the realization that their volume had been lowered by Young's crew, Sonic Youth found the experience eye-opening as well. When the band's manager complained about it, the sound was adjusted, but Young's crew gave them dirty looks afterward, and the members of Sonic Youth were often chased away from the side of the stage when they wanted to watch Young's set. As they no doubt noticed, his team was hardly as mellow as his most delicate music. Guitarist Lee Ranaldo, a fan of Young and Stills who had learned to play songs like "4 + 20" during his teen years, brought Stills' name up a few times, but in the ongoing aftermath of *American Dream*, Young gave the impression he wasn't interested in discussing any of that.

To PROMOTE THEIR largely Young-free boxed set, Crosby, Stills and Nash once again took to the road. By now, touring was an obligation and a necessity, rarely a passion. "CSN had fallen into bad habits," says Siddons.

"They never had a common objective. They toured to make money because Crosby and Stephen were always broke and Graham was happy to go along. It was driven by considerations other than 'We work together and love each other.'"

But to change things up in the way Young would do from time to time, the trio threw themselves a curveball. On and off for over a year, they embarked on their first-ever purely trio tour—no backup musicians, no production or staging, just the three of them. It was the type of show that Nash, in particular, had envisioned them giving in 1969, back in the days when he thought their first album might be purely folkish. More than two decades later, their voices were grainier and not as reliable; Stills could no longer hit the son-of-a-preacher high notes, and the devious-choirboy purity of Crosby's '60s voice was lost to history (and drug use). Deprived of instrumentation and rhythm sections that could cover up their shortcomings, their harmonies would have to be pinpoint accurate, and Stills would have to ensure that his guitar tone and parts were extra focused to fill up the space.

To everyone's surprise, even at times their own, they mostly pulled it off. Forced to up their game and not embarrass themselves, they rallied and gave some of their more inspired performances of the decade. They relied too heavily at first on songs they had played on thousands of nights, but by the time the tour entered its second year they were also freshening up the set with unheard material. While staying at New York's Plaza Hotel on a previous visit, Crosby had been watching *The Fisher King*, a movie about a homeless man named Parry (played by Robin Williams) who becomes deluded after his wife is senselessly killed, then imagines himself as a knight in search of the Holy Grail. Attacked by muggers, he lies in a catatonic state until a friend (played by Jeff Bridges) sneaks into the hospital and gives him a trophy representing the legendary chalice. Parry awakens from his coma and asks, "I had this dream, Jack. I was married. I was married to this *beautiful* woman . . . I really missed her. Is that okay? Can I miss her now?" At that point in the story, Crosby broke down, wailing and overcome to the point where his wife, Jan, thought she would have to take him to an emergency room. "What's going on?" she told him. "Is it Christine?" Crosby said it was—his feelings of guilt and loss over Hinton's death over two decades before had suddenly come to the surface—and she talked him through it. The next day he wrote a song—initially called "Fisher King Song," but later "Somehow She Knew"—that became a meditation on Hinton's loss. "It was freeing and cathartic," he says, "and I felt much better."

It wouldn't be the only new song they played on the tour. In "Thousand Roads," Crosby turned his troubled years into a parable with no easy answers. Nash's delicate "Try to Find Me" was inspired by the sight of a boy and girl, both with cerebral palsy, comforting each other at one of Young's Bridge School benefits. Stills brought the energized "It Won't Go Away," a screed against political divisiveness that Crosby touted as a possible new "For What It's Worth" when they began playing it live. They also included rarely performed deep tracks like "Bittersweet" and "Taken at All," the latter for the first time as a trio onstage. "It was very successful," Nash recalls of the tour. "We were trying to find out whether that magic we had in the beginning still existed on any level, since I was seeing the band I loved and helped create crumble before my eyes." In late June 1992, they played New Haven, Connecticut; about a hundred miles to the north, in Lenox, Massachusetts, Young was doing one of his own acoustic shows. But the closest the two camps came to merging was when the trio's opening act, Michael Hedges, performed a medley of Young's "Cinnamon Girl" and "When You Dance, I Can Really Love."

Nothing would ever be 100 percent harmonious, of course. In reviewing the performance filmed at San Francisco's Warfield Theatre, Stephen Holden in the *New York Times* called Stills "a remote, sullen figure." As borne out by his next project, a degree of distance remained between him and the other two. With his occasional producers Ron and Howard Albert, Stills traveled to Florida and cut a record at the brothers' studio; per its title, *Stills Alone*, it stripped his music down to voice and guitars. "We thought, 'Let's make a record as if Stephen was over for dinner and pulled out his guitar and played a few songs,'" says Ron Albert. Although Stills' voice was weathered, and the album only included two new songs, alongside remakes of his and others' vintage material, *Stills Alone* marked a long-overdue return to his folk roots. Yet the fact that he was playing unaccompanied, on an album that came out on an indie label owned by the Alberts, only seemed to reinforce how isolated Stills had become from the others by the second year of the '90s.

EVEN WHEN THEY went out of their way to avoid each other, they still brushed close, like airplanes almost touching wings in a near collision. Starting in late 1993 and extending into the following year, Young made a rare decision to record in Los Angeles, rather than at his ranch. At nearly the same time, Crosby, Stills and Nash began making their first record as a true working ensemble in years at Ocean Way, a studio in Burbank all of twenty miles away.

While Crosby, Stills and Nash were trying to regroup in every sense of the word after the botch of *Live It Up,* Young had been enjoying a second wind of epic proportions. *Ragged Glory* became one of his most acclaimed albums, and in typical form, he lurched in the opposite direction for its follow-up, 1992's *Harvest Moon.* Released in the twentieth anniversary year of *Harvest,* the new record shared more than a word in the title with its predecessor: for the occasion, Young recruited the remnants of his *Harvest* band, even inviting that album's backup singers, James Taylor and Linda Ronstadt, into the fold again. *Harvest Moon* captured everything about the softer side of his musical persona—its sweetness, sentimentality and occasional corniness. Particularly at moments like "Unknown Legend" and the over-the-top, treacly "Such a Woman," the album felt like one long, awestruck love song to Pegi Young, with stops along the way to engage in ambiguous antiwar commentary ("War of Man") or stray into dead-pet territory ("Old King"). A decade earlier, he'd compared Crosby, Stills and Nash to sweater-vested crooner Perry Como; in interviews to plug *Harvest Moon,* he was bringing up Como's name to describe himself and the mellow sound of the album.

Harvest Moon was clearly an album his fans had been clamoring for; in no time, it had sold a million copies, rare at that point in his career. His renewed profile extended to the underground as well. Although his often openly sentimental and earnest songs were the polar opposite of the ironic or emotionally garbled message of indie and alternative rock, Young's credibility with a new generation of noise-prone musicians was unstoppable. In 1989, a slew of indie rockers—Sonic Youth, the Pixies and Nick Cave among them—had contributed to a Young tribute album. In the new decade, he taped his own episode of *MTV Unplugged.* Unlike Crosby, Stills and Nash's segment, his was perfectly timed; the series was now highly rated and could make best-selling albums. The crowning moment came when Young and Pearl Jam, a Seattle band that worked furiously hard at the pent-up-guys-with-guitars tradition, joined together at an MTV ceremony in late 1993. That meeting would later result in a collaborative album, *Mirror Ball*. Young and Eddie Vedder, Pearl Jam's lead singer, had been born nearly two decades apart, but from their vocal timbres to their flannel shirts, they were a relaxed fit.

Young and Pearl Jam's "Rockin' in the Free World" was merely the latest in a string of TV bookings that reinforced Young's stature as he approached fifty. His 1989 *Saturday Night Live* appearance, pegged to *Freedom*, found him playing a hopped-up rendition of that same song that would be one of the most exhilarating musical moments in the show's history. At 1992's Bob Dylan tribute concert at Madison Square Garden, he carjacked the stage during a raucous version of "All Along the Watchtower." By comparison Crosby, Stills and Nash were, to their mystification, never even invited on *Saturday Night Live*. Reviewing a Young show in the fall of 1992, the *Los Angeles Daily News* couldn't help but note, "By comparison, Young's sometime collaborators Crosby, Stills and Nash have a tinge of the golden oldie about them these days."

Of the original trio, Crosby had the most juice during this time. After befriending Phil Collins and singing on his hit "Another Day in Paradise," he'd made a polished, if largely unremarkable, album of originals and covers, *Thousand Roads*, complete with a Collins cameo. (Nash guested on it, but Stills was nowhere to be heard.) But in the CSN world, Young's continued relevance, culminating with his work with Pearl Jam, was confounding. Young teamed up with cred-heavy director Jim Jarmusch to record a spooky, gnarled instrumental soundtrack for *Dead Man*, an oddball western starring Johnny Depp. For their venture into soundtracks during the same period, Crosby, Stills and Nash chose to contribute a wordless vocal piece to the opening credits for a movie version of the '60s dolphin-adventure series *Flipper*. "What was frustrating was how Neil could stay current without even really trying," says Debbie Meister. "He was really smart, picking the right bands to perform with, like Pearl Jam. I still wonder how he was able to do that. CSN would want to do things like, 'Let's try to get an opening act that would be [current].' That would've done it, but I don't think they could agree on one."

The trio did, however, absorb the debacle of the fractured, contrived creation of *Live It Up*. In a concession to Atlantic, they consented to work with an outside producer for the first time since the early Paul Rothchild sessions in 1968. One of the most distinguised in the field, British producer Glyn Johns worked on enough classic-rock albums to fill up the airwaves of any FM radio station, including records by the Who (*Who's Next*), the Eagles (their first two albums) and Eric Clapton (*Slowhand*). He'd also had a hand in dozens of others by the Rolling Stones and the Steve Miller Band, among others, along with solo albums by Nash and Young. To test the waters, Johns was offered $30,000 to produce four songs for Crosby, Stills and Nash. "We knew we'd get something that was right," says Siddons, "and I'd have a shot at breaking the record with the label because the last two were such disasters."

Declaring he wanted an album "true to the sound" of the band, Johns insisted that all three men be in the studio at the same time rather than adding their parts separately. Once they agreed to those terms and began working in Los Angeles, a sense of collaboration returned; Stills could even be found in the kitchen of one of the studios, cooking up a bouillabaisse for the band. "Glyn Johns is fearless—he will say what he thinks," says Crosby. "If you don't like it, tough shit. He wanted the best shot at making a good CSN record." In terms of its material, the potential was there. Stills had "It Won't Go Away." Nash's "Unequal Love" and the becalmed "After the Storm," about a hurricane in Hawaii, felt cozier than his songs had in a while, and his "Find a Dream" made up for its premise—life advice to youngsters—with a somber, elegiac melody and delivery. When Crosby couldn't devise a chorus for "Camera," about his father and his photographic interests, Stills came to his aid, and their blended voices and Stills' lead acoustic guitar on the track brought back the mood of their 1977 *CSN* reformation. "We all knew what we could be doing if we all concentrated," says Nash. "Glyn was a strong personality and he needed to be strong to keep the three of us from killing each other."

But when management submitted the album to Atlantic in the late spring of 1994, the label's lack of enthusiasm was immediately clear: no one called with any feedback. After a week of disheartening silence, Siddons finally spoke with an upper-tier label executive who told him, "Wow—when these classic acts lose it big, it's stunning, isn't it?" Driving to the band's rehearsal space, Siddons delivered the disheartening news. The label wasn't excited and, at the very minimum, they needed to add at least one new track to the record. As he had with "Carry On" on *Déjà vu*, Stills rose to the occasion, pulling a new song seemingly from out of nowhere. Announcing he had a leftover, unfinished tune, he played them "Only Waiting for You," a springy, piano-driven ode to renewed love. (Stills and his second wife divorced during this period, and Stills was in a new relationship.) With a hoped-for release date less than a month away, everyone reconvened to record it in a last-minute attempt to salvage the album.

On the day they pounded out "Only Waiting for You," a *Los Angeles Times* writer was on hand to witness Crosby, Nash, and Mike Finnigan, on keyboards, record harmonies for the song. "We sound like church geeks," Crosby groused about the "oohs" they were attempting; he and Nash suggested "aahs" instead. After hearing the change, Stills, in the control room, looked distinctly unhappy: "Good God—not so much Bruce Lee," he moaned. As always, Nash finessed the situation and worked out a vocal line that would please both Crosby and Stills. And with that, the album was finally ready, and Atlantic accepted it, albeit half-heartedly.

Even then, they couldn't escape Young's shadow. By the most unlikely of coincidences, Crosby, Stills and Nash's album, *After the Storm*, was released on the same day in August 1994 as Young and Crazy Horse's *Sleeps with Angels*—an album that, naturally, didn't even remotely try to capitalize on the peaceful-uneasy feeling and success of *Harvest Moon*. One of Young's most experimental records, *Sleeps with Angels* yanked Crazy Horse in many different directions, almost as if to demonstrate that they weren't anything close to a one-note band. There were ballads that sounded as if they could have been played in Old West saloons; terse and sputtery rockers, including "Piece of Crap"; and protracted, serpentine explorations, such as "Change Your Mind," which stretched out to fourteen numbing minutes.

The title track, the last one recorded for the album, was Young's reaction to the suicide of Kurt Cobain from Nirvana, who had shot himself in the head in April and left behind a note that quoted, in part, from "My My, Hey Hey (Out of the Blue)." (For that reason alone, Young, anticipating questions about that day and the note, declined any interviews to promote the album; he also passed on touring.) With a moody pulse that gave way to a spasmodic chorus, "Sleeps with Angels" was murky and unsettling, a vibe that extended to the album's most compelling tracks. The homeless imagery in "Safeway Cart" and the mysterious deaths in "Driveby" and "Trans Am" were made even creepier by Crazy Horse's muted, subdued accompaniment; they sounded as if they'd been recorded playing under burlap sacks. Crazy Horse sounded spooked themselves, and Young pulled equally muffled tones out of his solos. It was hardly pop or even classic-rock radio material—and yet *Sleeps with Angels* became his first Top 10 album since *Rust Never Sleeps* fifteen years prior.

Billboard deemed *Sleeps with Angels* "another jewel in the crown of a brilliant and enduring artist"; it also noted, in an overly optimistic separate review, that Crosby, Stills and Nash were "indeed sounding young again" on *After the Storm*. While Young did nothing to promote his album, Crosby, Stills and Nash offered themselves up to any interview or TV gig that would have them, including *The Tonight Show with Jay Leno* (where they played a forceful "Find a Dream" with bandleader Branford Marsalis sitting in on sax). The host of *Later*, Greg Kinnear, took a question from the audience: If they were to hear one of their songs done up as Muzak, which would it be?

"Let's make it one of Neil's songs!" Nash quipped, as Crosby visibly groaned.

When Kinnear broached the idea of a quartet reunion, Nash added, "We're not holding our breath."

ON FRIDAY, AUGUST 12, 1994, the Crosby, Stills and Nash tour buses lurched out of Stowe, Vermont, lugging along guitars, amps and the lava lamps and incense they required for their dressing rooms. They had the day off, but little time to relax. They had to drive 245 miles to the Catskills in New York and prepare for an event they were equally anticipating and dreading: the twenty-fifth anniversary of Woodstock.

For original Woodstock co-organizer Michael Lang, life after those three days in the rain and mud had only briefly involved more festivals. "Woodstock was an idea and a concept and I didn't think it could be repeated," he says. "I wasn't looking to be in the festival business." His role at Altamont, standing onstage and watching Hells Angels beat people with pool cues, only solidified that feeling. After that event, he had started a record label and moved into managing—trying to handle Joe Cocker, who was still battling his drinking-problem demons years after his career-making spot at Woodstock. But with Woodstock hitting its quarter-century anniversary, Lang had a change of heart. He reconvened with Joel Rosenman and John Roberts, two of his partners from 1969, to begin planning a sequel, this time on an 840-acre dairy farm in Saugerties on a site that had been considered for the original Woodstock. In a revealing indication of the cultural and financial changes since the first concert, the festival now had a corporate sponsor (Pepsi). The production costs soared to $30 million, and tickets were $135 each (and had to be bought in blocks of four).

Smartly, Woodstock '94, a three-day festival, was dominated by musicians—Green Day, Nine Inch Nails and so forth—who would draw younger festival goers. But Lang wanted to invite as many of the surviving original acts as he could, so the event would be sprinkled with the likes of Cocker, Santana, Country Joe McDonald and members of the Band. At the top of Lang's list from the start were Crosby, Stills, Nash and Young. "I was definitely into it," Lang says. "But they were not."

In this context, "they" was not much of a mystery. Lang approached Young's management and was told in no uncertain terms that he would only do the festival by himself or not at all, and certainly not with Crosby, Stills and Nash. "It had to be either Neil or them, but it couldn't be both," Lang says. ("We were not aware of that," Nash says. "There's a lot of things with Neil we're not aware of.") Young's aversion to blatant nostalgia and commercialism surely played as much of a role in that decision as any personal issues he had with CSN. In the end, Lang and his partners in Woodstock Ventures chose Crosby, Stills and Nash. "They were so heavily associated with the film and festival that it made much more sense to do that," he says. "I love Neil, but it was more a historical choice than a musical one." The others weren't surprised. "Neil knew as I did that it wasn't going to work—it wasn't going to be like the first one," says Crosby. "But the money was good." The band was offered second-tier level, $250,000, on the second night, August 13. (The biggest acts received $350,000, although Young was reportedly offered $1 million for his own spot.)

Once their buses pulled onto the grounds, everyone was immediately aware that Young wasn't anywhere near Woodstock '94, and the question of his attendance came up at a press conference. "Who gives a shit what Neil thinks?" Nash snapped. "The last time we checked, he still goes out and plays for money." Nash tempered his startling comments with an attempt at humor: "Neil's doing a benefit for brokenhearted penguins. He can't make it." But Young's distance from them on what could have been a notable day clearly stung.

Before their set, despite a power line falling on Crosby's parked bus, the communal atmosphere seemed welcoming. Stills stood by the side of the stage taking in a performance by the LA hip-hop act Cypress Hill, who integrated Latin rhythms into their hardened beats and weed rhymes. Backstage, they ran into their old friend and fellow Woodstock veteran John Sebastian. He was still in the area, living in a house he had bought with earnings from his theme song to the *Welcome Back, Kotter* TV series. They asked him to introduce them and, at the last minute, to join them onstage to re-create his harmonica solo in "Déjà vu." Since Crosby's fifty-third birthday was the following day, Jan arranged to bring a cake out onstage and have the crowd acknowledge the occasion. Crewmember John Vanderslice suggested the three men be rolled out on stage in wheelchairs by "three sexy girls in nurse outfits" to play off their veterans-of-Woodstock image. Nash loved the idea, Stills didn't, and it went nowhere.

By the time Sebastian introduced them (referring to them as "the old guys"), security seemed nonexistent, and a mosh pit had developed in front of the stage. In spite of the organizers' efforts to re-create the feel of the original festival, everything—the sound of rock, politics (Bill Clinton, a Democrat, was in the White House rather than Nixon), current events (there was no war)—was different in 1994. Crosby, Stills and Nash didn't stand a chance.* Their set was in the middle of the afternoon, soon after

---

*That summer, the trio found themselves on a flight to Washington, DC, with David Geffen, their former co-manager and occasional nemesis. At Hillary Clinton's request, they'd been hired to be the surprise entertainment at Bill Clinton's forty-eighth birthday. The animosity between the two camps seemed to vanish. They bantered with Geffen on the ride down and sang on the South Lawn of the White House.

the teeth-grinding Rollins Band and before the industrial-strength Nine Inch Nails, although there was a brief lull in the musical storm provided by Melissa Etheridge, who played immediately before Crosby, Stills and Nash.

Compared to those more pent-up modern musicians, Crosby, Stills and Nash couldn't help but look like reminders of another era and generation. Their set that day, with its marked emphasis on the oldies, embodied much of what alternative rock was rebelling against. (A reference to a cracked vinyl album and a turntable needle in "It Won't Go Away" may well have baffled the CD-geared crowd.) The audience was respectful, seemingly recognizing "Long Time Gone" and other FM-radio favorites, but barely rousing when the band rolled out songs from *After the Storm.* "It was awful," Crosby says. "You can't re-create anything no matter what you try to re-create. We were playing to a mosh pit trying to do 'Helplessly Hoping.' Bunch of people slathered out of their minds—drunk, stoned, fucked up, muddy. Almost being animals. It was an abortion."

But Crosby was facing bigger problems than that. His year had been fraught from the start: the IRS had come calling, demanding $1 million for back taxes and placing a lien on his income. He was forced to sell his home in the San Fernando Valley and rent another near Santa Barbara, where he had spent time as a child. During the making of *After the Storm,* he would arrive at the studio and end up lying on the couch, plagued by stomachaches and feelings of bloat that went beyond his weight concerns. "I felt like someone hit me with a ton of bricks," he says. Nash would have to wake him up to sing his parts. On the road in the summer, Nash and Stills asked him why he had missed a particular musical cue, and Crosby was so ill he didn't make their show in Utah in July. A doctor at Johns Hopkins in Baltimore diagnosed him with liver disease from hepatitis C. On the bus at Woodstock, his legs cramped up, as a side effect of the liver medication he was taking to reduce the fluids in his stomach, and crew members had to help him offstage.

Once the tour was over and Crosby returned to Los Angeles, the diagnosis grew even more dire: basically, he was dying. In November, he was admitted to UCLA Medical Center with a quickly deteriorating liver and placed on a transplant list. On one predawn morning, Nash received a phone call: a new liver had been found, and the surgery would take place that day. Nash drove to the hospital with Crosby's doctor, who lived in his neighborhood. Once there, to cheer Crosby up, Nash looked at him on the gurney and said, "You leave me with fucking Stills, I'll kill you." Crosby was laughing and singing "Amazing Grace" as they wheeled him in and closed the door.

All their plans for a comeback—the album, the Woodstock anniversary, *The Tonight Show*—fell by the wayside. Despite its relative quality compared to other recent efforts—it was the most cohesive and natural-sounding record they'd made since *CSN*—*After the Storm* didn't break into the Top 40. Anyone visiting the New York offices of Atlantic that fall would have noticed a box in an empty office that contained a stack of unsent CDs of the album's planned next single, "It Won't Go Away." Young was storming on, but Crosby, Stills and Nash CDs were literally gathering dust, and one band member was now close to losing his life.

PART FOUR
ON THE WAY HOME

CHAPTER 11
APRIL 1995-APRIL 2000

O n an April afternoon in 1995, the backyard of Nash's home in Encino was transformed into the soft-rock capital of the world. Jackson Browne and former Doobie Brother Michael McDonald milled
about; Crosby and Stills were also in attendance. But more than a few
heads turned when in walked Young. Although Nash had invited him and
Pegi, no one knew whether he would attend. "It was a little bit of a surprise," says Debbie Meister. "People were pretty excited he was there."
Crosby called it "a wonderful, happy afternoon" to writer Dave Zimmer.
"Everybody was in good spirits and very comfortable."

The reunion was the lesser of several miracles being celebrated in
that backyard that day. The mere fact that Crosby was actually alive,
defying death once more, was the first. When he'd been admitted to the
UCLA Medical Center the previous November, his future had been ten-
uous at best. At that moment, Los Angeles County was running short of
his blood type, O positive, and his name was on national and local waiting lists for a new liver for thirty-nine days; during this time, a potential
replacement liver was found, but it turned out to be cancerous. Finally,
with Crosby perhaps a week away from death and feeling as if he were
dying a little bit each day, a compatible liver was discovered in a thirty-
four-year-old African American man who had died in a car accident. After seven hours of surgery, Crosby had yet another chance—his second,
possibly third—at life. (He was criticized by some, who thought he had
received preferential treatment, but UCLA spokespeople pointed out that
thirty-nine days was the average wait time for a new liver.) Three weeks
later, Crosby was released from the hospital and returned home.

When Crosby had first been given the grim news of his liver disease,
he and Jan also learned that, after months of trying to start a family, she

was pregnant. The April 1995 get-together at Nash's house was a baby shower, and for the occasion, Young brought his family. (Django Dance Crosby would be born a month later, May 9, 1995.) The party marked the first time the four had been in the same space since playing a free out-door concert in San Francisco's Golden Gate Park for Bill Graham in late 1991, after the legendary promoter was killed in a helicopter accident. At Graham's tribute, the strains in their relationship showed; they looked tired and sweaty, and the performance felt perfunctory. But time was healing their wounds, as Young admitted to *Spin* soon after the shower: "If I was going to play with CSN it wouldn't be that big of a jump. I really like those guys. We're in touch." For Meister and others, it felt like a new beginning. "Maybe it was a harbinger of hope," she says. "I'll bet you ten to one that Neil was thinking, 'Well, David's cleaned up and now having a baby in his life will make things more stable for him to possibly get all of us together again.'"

Any such thoughts would have to wait, however; in the aftermath of his surgery, Crosby needed at least a year to recuperate, and the Crosby, Stills and Nash machine ground to a halt for reasons other than ego clashes. The medications Crosby was taking made his mood swings sharper; even stranger, he told Nash, he was suddenly interested in foot-ball, making them both wonder if the donor had been a sports fan.

Crosby's surgery and reputation aside, an air of stasis hung around the group family tree. Young remained his inscrutable self. He and his family continued to live on the Broken Arrow Ranch amid an array of cattle, peacocks and llamas, and with at least one "private property" sign done up in psychedelic lettering. Journalists seeking interviews were instructed to follow the usual procedure: arrive at the Mountain House restaurant in La Honda, not far from his ranch, at which point Young would take the reporter for a drive in one of his vintage cars, such as his prized 1956 Lincoln Continental Mark IV. Young resuscitated Crazy Horse for *Broken Arrow*, an album that, thanks to lengthy, slithering-snake tracks that meandered for up to nine minutes, felt like one very long, often exasperating, song.

In the wake of the commercial crash of *After the Storm*, Crosby, Stills and Nash seemed at an equal impasse; their relationship with Atlantic was adrift, and in 1995, they fired Bill Siddons, Crosby and Nash's manager of over fifteen years. By then, Siddons felt he'd done all he could have done for them anyway. "I realized that everything I knew in my career about how to do things didn't matter," Siddons says. "It affected me for the next three or four years. I lost my ability to make things happen." Classic rock remained a formidable presence despite the rise of hip hop, alternative rock and dance music in the '90s. The highest-grossing tour of 1996 was the reunion of the original members of Kiss, followed, after comparative newcomer Garth Brooks, by Neil Diamond, Rod Stewart and Bob Seger. With 1997's *Time Out of Mind*, Bob Dylan reaffirmed that boomer rock stars in their fifties, still a new concept, could be resurrected artistically and in the business; he even walked away with a Grammy for Album of the Year. But it was still unclear where Crosby, Stills and Nash would fit in that larger picture.

In theory, the full quartet was scheduled to cross paths again on the night of May 6, 1997. As part of its twelfth annual induction ceremony, the Rock & Roll Hall of Fame would be honoring Buffalo Springfield and Crosby, Stills and Nash alongside Joni Mitchell, the Jackson 5, the Bee Gees, Parliament-Funkadelic and the Rascals. To make sure they arrived on time, the trio drove to Cleveland in the midst of their spring tour. But in keeping with his mercurial tradition, Young had his own plans. Two years earlier, he'd been inducted on his own into the Hall of Fame by Pearl Jam's Eddie Vedder. Young's acceptance speech included shout-outs to his wife Pegi as well as to Crazy Horse; his producer, David Briggs; Kurt Cobain; Elliot Roberts; Mo Ostin of Warner Brothers; and Ahmet Ertegun of Atlantic Records (whom he thanked for allowing him to leave the label so that he and Stills wouldn't have solo careers with the same company). Pointedly, Crosby, Stills and Nash were not mentioned.

Given Young's participation in the ceremony, which was broadcast on the VH1 network, Joel Gallen, who produced and directed the taping, was hoping for what he calls "a CSNY moment" at the 1997 event, especially since Young would be inducted alongside Stills in the Springfield. But Gallen's hopes were demolished when Young issued a statement: "The VH1 Hall of Fame presentation [*sic*] has nothing to do with the spirit of rock and roll. It has everything to do with making money. Inductees . . . are forced to be on a TV show for which they are not paid, and whatever comments they would like to make . . . are all subject to the VH1 editor.

Someone who has absolutely no right to interfere." Gallen was puzzled. "He was there two years before, onstage jamming with Eddie Vedder and Led Zeppelin, and that aired on VH1," he says. "And he had no problem with that." Young was supposedly also irked by the high cost of tickets, which topped out at $1,500 a plate.

Once more, Stills was left holding the bag, this time during the Springfield induction. At a press conference afterward, Stills turned to Richie Furay and cracked, "Well, Neil didn't show again." In an unexpected reprise of thirty years before, when Crosby sat in with the Springfield at Monterey Pop, helping to launch Crosby, Stills and Nash, Crosby again joined Stills on "For What It's Worth" as Dewey Martin and Bruce Palmer stood onstage and clapped along. But Young was nowhere near the stage—or even the state.

BACKSTAGE AT THE Rock & Roll Hall of Fame induction, a Crosby, Stills and Nash representative made the media rounds, talking up the trio's renewal to any reporter who would listen. "It's the rebirth of the band," he would say, and press releases from the firm's office claimed they "aren't surviving . . . they're thriving."

During group concerts that spring and into the following year, the trio did seem newly invigorated—Crosby more robust, Stills more animated. Their set lists continued to rely heavily on the overplayed hits and passed over many of the gems written and recorded for their solo and duo projects, which required too much additional rehearsal. (A rare and welcome exception was Crosby's "Thousand Roads," which allowed Stills to inject a blues-steeped solo in keeping with the song's uncharacteristically low-down groove.) Yet a fair share of new material continued to creep in: Nash's haunted, solemn "Half Your Angels," written in the aftermath of the Oklahoma City bombing that took the lives of 168 people in 1995; Crosby's "Morrison," a lyrical contemplation of the Doors' late singer; and Stills' defiant and rowdy "No Tears Left." "I think we're more compassionate with each other now," Nash told one writer, Gary Graff. "We're friendlier, more understanding of each other's failures and weaknesses and we try to amplify all the good." After Crosby played one of his songs, Stills told Nash backstage, "Man, he nailed the *fuck* out of that."

In public, some of the sniping of old lingered. Promoting their tour in the summer of 1996, Nash admitted, "Sometimes you don't like your brother or sister. Sometimes I don't like David or Stephen. In those moments, we can't make music." In an interview with Steve Silberman for *Goldmine*, Crosby, reflecting on his mixed feelings for Stills, said, "I like him—no, I love him. I'm not sure I like him, but I definitely love him." But Crosby's near-death moment had shaken the band anew; for once, it made them all appreciate the group and its fragility. Although Crosby and Stills continued to grate on each other, they also began to value each other a little more. Stills had brought freshly made chicken soup to Crosby's hospital room after his transplant, and he had issued a rare supportive statement about his bandmate to the press. Posting online during this era, the summer of 1998, Crosby addressed someone who had disparaged Stills: "The guy who feels he has to put down Stills viciously in order to show how cool Neil is . . . Neil (who is my friend) *never* says that shit about Stephen. I am much more critical and even I don't say mean stuff like that. Stephen has problems . . . I had problems . . . and if you were living out here in front of everybody you might turn out to have a few too."

But beginning with their status in the business, the resurgence their team was hoping for remained a goalpost far in the distance. Atlantic, their home of nearly thirty years, was entering a new phase of profitability. Riding a wave of pop, from singer-songwriter Jewel to the loosey-goosey pop band Sugar Ray to the R&B and hip-hop-oriented soundtrack of *Space Jam*, the label was on its way to earning $750 million in global sales in 1997. (One of those multimillion sellers, Jewel's *Pieces of You*, was produced by Ben Keith, Young's longtime sideman.) Yet in the aftermath of the mediocre sales of *American Dream*, *Live It Up* and *After the Storm*, Crosby, Stills and Nash's relationship with Atlantic had deteriorated. Although Ertegun remained co-chairman of the company, he was even less involved in its daily operation than before. In 1996, discussions began between the company and the band to end their affiliation. After a tense meeting with executives over a meal, with a typically feisty Crosby confronting them about their lack of knowledge of the band's history with the label, the group asked to be released. In March 1997, after nearly three decades, Crosby, Stills and Nash were no longer affiliated with Atlantic. "It was our choice," says Crosby. "Ahmet wasn't there anymore. He was our cat, our mentor. Without him, they were just another record company. Usually a bunch of guys who couldn't make it selling shoes, so they went into the record business."

Without the advances they would have received from Atlantic, cash was now a pressing concern, and the trio, along with Gerry Tolman—who had once managed only Stills but was now guiding the trio after Siddons—went in search of any and all opportunities to generate income. Nash launched Manuscript Originals, which sold framed, handwritten lyrics of his songs, and some by Crosby ("Guinnevere") and Grace Slick ("White Rabbit"), for $9,500 each. In the fall of 1997, San Francisco's Triton Hotel overhauled room 620, renaming it the Graham Nash Suite. For as much as $299 a night, guests could kick back in a room that, the hotel declared, was "remarkable for its selection of comfortable, stylish furnishings made and upholstered with industrial hemp." Nash himself supplied some of the furniture from his own home, along with platinum album plaques and vintage concert passes; the bathroom featured Hollies album covers and mounted, handwritten "Our House" lyrics. For a proper British ambiance, the room also came equipped with a tea set and instructions on the best steeping methods.

Stills continued to exploit his back catalog, licensing "For What It's Worth" to a Miller Beer ad ("it paid a year's taxes," he told writer David Fricke) and allowing it to be sampled by the rap group Public Enemy as the basis for their single "He Got Game." Meanwhile, once-crass ideas, such as casino gigs and corporate functions, were no longer ruled out. In 1997, the trio played two nights at the Circus Maximum room at Caesars in Lake Tahoe. The following year, they would play the iconic Fillmore in San Francisco—but this time for employees of the telecommunications companies WorldCom and MCI, which had announced a $50 billion merger and wanted to celebrate. As Tolman told the *Hollywood Reporter*, "There's a wealth of opportunities out there right now—not only in the traditional sense but certainly within the investment community."

Coincidentally, classic rock had begun to leverage its future. In early 1997, David Bowie had made headlines in the financial press with what were called "Bowie Bonds"—a deal wherein Bowie partnered with

Prudential to raise $55 million by issuing bonds secured by future royalties from much of his back catalog. The thought of instant cash immediately appealed to Crosby, Stills and Nash, and soon enough, their camp had reached out to David Pullman, the New York–based banker who had engineered the Bowie transaction. "After the Bowie deal was announced, they were the first in line to talk about it," says Pullman, whose Pullman Group would potentially handle the deal in a joint venture with an investment bank, Fahnestock and Company. The company would assess Crosby, Stills and Nash's various revenue streams, from record royalties to publishing revenues and foreign album sales, to determine their worth.

Before long, Pullman was flying to Los Angeles to lunch with Crosby, Stills and Nash at the Sunset Marquis. After being escorted into a private dining room, Pullman glimpsed the group dynamic at play. Nash suggested Pullman order a healthy fruit salad; Crosby went for the meat dish. All three were affable and fascinated with the bonds idea, but Nash exhibited the sharpest grasp of the intricacies of the proposal. To Pullman's amusement, Crosby stood up and gave what amounted to a vigorous, animated monologue about the band's need for independence, bringing up the resolutely indie singer-songwriter Ani DiFranco as an example they should follow. Pullman also sensed their disappointment with Atlantic. "It was uncomfortable for them that things were changing," he said. "They created what we consider modern music. So this was very painful for them to go through."

Among the profit-making ideas discussed at the table that day was one that was misguided but potentially commercially viable: an album of remakes of songs from their pasts, which would deprive Atlantic of some of the profits from the old songs and increase their own royalties. They had already made one such attempt, recording, but not releasing, a new version of the Byrds' "Turn! Turn! Turn!" (For similar reasons, Nash had cut an entirely new version of "Our House" for use in a commercial.) In the decades that followed, many other pop acts would do the same, rerecording their own songs with similar windfalls in mind. But Crosby was opposed to the remake-album idea, telling Fricke it "will be perceived badly."

Given that three writers were involved, a Crosby, Stills and Nash bond would have been more complex than the Bowie arrangement, and it also carried risks. In the end, the band passed. "We didn't think it was a great idea," says Nash, "and after the Bowie bonds took a dive [two years later], the idea of maximizing publishing and writing and turning it into stock that would be bought and sold didn't make sense to us." At one point, Pullman, unaware of the group's split camps, asked whether Young would be part of any such deal. "It was like, 'Well, we're never really sure if he's in or not,'" Pullman recalls. Pullman later approached Young and Roberts about a similar arrangement, but nothing was worked out.

That carrot—was Young part of them or not?—was dangled again a few months after their lunch with Pullman. In September 1997, Crosby, Stills and Nash played a week of non-corporate shows at San Francisco's Fillmore. On the day of the third night, September 16, Stills ran into Neil and Pegi at a nearby restaurant; in the oddest of karmic coincidences, they wound up being seated at adjoining tables. To Stills' surprise, Young said he was interested in joining the band onstage later in the week, for the simple reason of wanting to hear them all play together once more.

That same night, during the first encore, the band launched into "Ohio," as it had started doing that year without Young (beginning with a performance on the Kent State campus for the twenty-seventh anniversary of the shootings). Nash was facing the crowd when he heard what he calls "this big roar" from the audience. Initially, Nash thought a fan had made his way onto the stage, but the guy in the rumpled jacket and trucker's hat who materialized next to them was Young, who joined them not only for his own song but also "Carry On" immediately after. It was the first time he had played either song with the three of them in nearly twenty-five years. When it ended, Stills grabbed Young in a bear hug and pecked him on the cheek. Band members like Joe Vitale who had never shared the stage with all four at once were thrilled.

Crosby, Stills and Nash hoped—practically assumed—Young would join them the following night, and their crew arranged for a special backstage area for Young's gear and dinner. But Young didn't materialize; as show time approached, he was driving back to his ranch. Backstage, the others sighed, rolled their eyes and again returned to the stage without him.

BY THE LATE '90s, Crosby was beginning to chafe at the trio's lack of experimentation, the way it was settling into an oldies revival. "All bands start out really excited with each other and with the material and having a blast," he says. "And at a certain point it's 'turn the machine on and play the hits,' because that's where the money is. It had started to happen [with Crosby, Stills and Nash] in the late '70s. And it kept getting more that way."

At the same time, another lead guitarist became part of the Crosby, Stills and Nash universe. Jeff Pevar, a strapping, square-jawed musician from Connecticut, had witnessed his parents' breakup when he was ten and channeled his energy into guitar. Working his way into the New York music scene, he met James Taylor, who later advised the budding singer-songwriter Marc Cohn to hire a band and include Pevar in the lineup. Cohn had a hit with "Walking in Memphis" in 1991, and he landed an opening-act slot with Crosby, Stills and Nash in the summer of 1992. Crosby, especially, became a vocal supporter of Cohn's work. During the sound check at their first show, in Cleveland, Pevar, then thirty-five, saw Crosby, and to get his attention, began playing the chords to "Triad"; Crosby, no stranger to flattery, was intrigued. Early in the tour, Crosby and Nash took to joining Cohn during his opening set, where they were able to play with Pevar as well.

Pevar was far from the first to sense that the Crosby, Stills and Nash rapport was pitted with landmines. One night, he spied Stills backstage and decided the time had come to introduce himself and express his admiration. Reaching out his hand, Pevar was taken aback when Stills, who tended to be withdrawn backstage, seemed to barely look at him and walked away without returning the handshake. "This is not going to be easy," Pevar thought to himself. During one West Coast Crosby, Stills and Nash show, Crosby invited Pevar to join him and Nash during their duo portion of the set. Returning to the stage for the group portion, Stills said, into the microphone, "So am I fired now?" (It was one of many examples of how he could be easily hurt by perceived criticism.) Pevar felt terrible, since he didn't want to imply he could take Stills' place.

In the summer of 1997, after a heated argument with Stills and Nash, Crosby walked out on the band. For two weeks, they were in limbo, but after Stills and Nash issued an apology, Crosby returned. (Crosby has no recollection of this event.) But by then, a possible exit—or, at least, reprieve—had arrived. During Crosby's hospitalization and liver transplant surgery, small mountains of fan mail arrived at UCLA. Among them was a letter from John Raymond, a broker from San Bernardino who wanted to let Crosby know, in case he didn't recover, that Raymond and his wife had adopted a boy who was actually Crosby's natural-born son. Named James, he was the baby Crosby and then girlfriend Celia Ferguson had conceived in 1961, causing Crosby to flee to the other side of the country. Soon after the baby arrived in May 1962, Ferguson had put him up for adoption. Thirty years later, John Raymond asked his son—a musician himself—if he was interested in knowing the identity of his birth parents. A social worker informed James that his father was, in fact, "David Van Cortlandt Crosby." At first, James hesitated to reach out; he wasn't very familiar with Crosby, Stills and Nash's music and didn't want to be someone who showed up unexpectedly, claiming to be a child of a celebrity. He also wasn't sure what he would be getting into. One evening he and his wife, Stacia, who were expecting their own child, were watching Crosby on a talk show, joking about an acid flashback. "James looked at me like, 'Yeah, I don't know—I don't know about this,'" she recalls.

Through a mutual friend, James Raymond reached out to Mike Finnigan, the keyboardist for Crosby, Stills and Nash, who in turn passed the message to Crosby, and one day the phone rang in the Raymonds' home in Altadena, northeast of Burbank. Father and son were soon reunited in the UCLA Medical Center cafeteria—Crosby was there for a postsurgery checkup—and Crosby, who was nervous and not sure what to expect, learned that his son had "absolutely no baggage at all" about his wayward father. Raymond didn't especially resemble Crosby—the short-haired musician looked more like jam-band rocker Dave Matthews than a Crosby offspring—but the two shared a love of jazz. Raymond, an accomplished keyboard player, had already put in time in studios and studied with a session guitarist, Larry Carlton (who, in another example of their overlapping circles, had played on Joni Mitchell's *Court and Spark* along with Crosby). Crosby soon gave Raymond a set of lyrics he'd written—"Morrison"—and Raymond set them to music and invited Crosby to his home. Feeling his car stereo system was better than the one in his house, Raymond sat with his father in the front seat of his 4Runner in the driveway, the windows rolled down, as he played his tape. From inside their home, Stacia Raymond watched as Crosby's face lit up and he exclaimed, "Play it again, play it again!" "What could have been an ugly narrative turned out to be one of the most positive things in David's life," says longtime Crosby friend Leland Sklar, the bass player. "It gave David a whole new impetus for writing and recording. CSN were resting on their laurels."

With that—and a call to Pevar to see if he would join them—Crosby had a new band, dubbed CPR, after their initials and, in a sly reference, Crosby's near-death experience. With CPR, Crosby had a new and far more open-minded avenue for his songs. In April 1998, the three signed a contract with Samson Music, an Omaha-based independent label. Crosby's delight at taking a break from the fraught Crosby, Stills and Nash scene, and being in a band with his long-lost son, was palpable from the start. "I think David sought refuge from the CSN craziness in CPR," says Pevar. "He was enjoying not having to deal with other people's egos and he was enjoying the opportunity of being of service to his son. It was easy." Crosby took Pevar for a sail on the *Mayan* and, in a mailing to his fan base, wrote that Pevar "has long been my absolute favorite guitar player." (One wondered what Stills thought if and when he ever read that line.) "It's the night before we start recording," Pevar posted in the early morning hours of August 4, 1997. "We're all very excited. New songs are *still* coming. . . . There's been such a natural groove surrounding the fledgling ensemble."

Unlike the often disjointed Crosby, Stills and Nash sessions of the past decade or more, CPR material arrived in a joyful rush; songs were often recorded in one or two takes. One day, Crosby handed Pevar lyrics for a song called "Little Blind Fish." Crosby, Stills, Nash and Young had attempted to record it—it was the only song co-written by all four—on Young's ranch two decades earlier, to no avail. In its first incarnation, it was a lumpy semi-blues piece, with each man taking a verse. Pevar, who was completely unaware of the earlier version, took the lyrics home and merged them with a bluesy fingerpicking melody and, almost overnight, CPR had finished a song that the quartet never could.

Released in 1998, *CPR*, the trio's debut, was a strikingly precision-tooled work, far more so than any of the recent Crosby, Stills and Nash records. With Raymond's sparkly keyboards and Pevar's snaky guitar leading the way, it veered more toward jazzy pop than rock; Crosby's admiration for

Steely Dan came through more than ever before. The emotional center-piece of the album, "At the Edge," found him surveying the previous few years of his life and giving thanks for surviving, and its choral harmonies were vintage Crosby. Later he would call it his favorite piece of music out of everything he had ever made.

In interviews, Crosby would frequently refer to Crosby, Stills and Nash as "my day job." Yet as creatively invigorating as CPR was for Crosby, it would not prove to be an escape hatch from his more famous but often frustrating band. *CPR* sold modestly, not helped by the fact that Samson, in spite of proclaiming itself "The Strongest Name in Music," couldn't compete with the major labels for distribution and radio play. That October, Crosby wound up back in the hospital; while singing, he had pushed so hard with his diaphragm that his sutures broke. He and CPR would continue for a bit longer, but for Crosby, it would be back to the world of Crosby, Stills and Nash—although with a twist that few, Crosby included, would have expected.

Sitting in the control room at Conway Recording Studios in the Korea-town section of Los Angeles in January 1999, Bill Halverson was wit-nessing a sight he thought he'd never see again. Crosby, Stills and Nash were gathered around a microphone; on the other side of the glass were Halverson and Neil Young. "You guys are sounding pretty good," Halver-son recalls Young telling them as he watched his onetime partners sing. "Maybe you can put some vocals on a few of my tunes."

A few months before, Halverson had returned to his home in Nashville to find a voice message from Crosby asking if Halverson would be willing to help him, Nash and Stills out. The call arrived nearly thirty years after the producer and engineer, now fifty-seven, had huddled with the trio at Wally Heider's in Los Angeles to piece together their first album. Halver-son had worked with them sporadically afterward, on *Déjà vu* and on a handful of their '70s solo and duo projects. But by the '80s, he'd burnt out on the scene and had left California. Crosby, Stills and Nash, however, had never forgotten the way Halverson had brilliantly captured their harmo-nies on tape, and now, decades on, they offered to fly him to LA to work similar magic. Halverson soon found himself at Conway, a studio that, with its thicket of surrounding trees, guaranteed a degree of privacy. (In the years to come, Britney Spears would record there, fending off paparazzi as she walked in.) Crosby, Stills and Nash were industry outcasts without a record deal, but they had proceeded with a new album anyway, financing it themselves, and the engineer was confronted with bits and pieces of songs that had been cut at various locations beginning in early 1998.

Initially, Halverson had only been hired for a week, but everything changed when, early in 1999, he saw a vintage car pull into the parking lot. Young, carrying a guitar, emerged from it.

Young's arrival was not completely unexpected. For nearly a decade, a Buffalo Springfield boxed set had been discussed and planned, but Young and Stills had only recently settled into the project, congregating at Young's ranch to sift through vintage tapes and reminisce. In the early days of Crosby, Stills, Nash and Young, the two had butted heads the most, but as the years wore on, they grew closer and took on the air of brothers who tolerated each other's idiosyncrasies. "There was always a competitiveness," says Pegi Young. "Their *mothers* were competitive. Rassy [Young] used to say, 'I'm the mother of the star!' And Tai [Stills] would say, '*I'm* the mother of the star!' The apples didn't fall far from those trees. But over time they learned how to give each other room and space and play to each other, not *at* each other." In May 1996, Stills had married for the third time, to Kristen Hathaway, his children's one-time governess. (Crosby and Nash attended the wedding, which was held in Florida while all three were on tour.) They eventually had two sons, Henry (named after Henry Diltz) and Oliver Ragland, whose middle name was also Young's mother's maiden name.

During the Springfield archive-digging meeting, Stills played Young "Acadienne," a Cajun-inspired romp he'd worked on with Crosby and Nash, and asked if Young would consider adding a part to it. Stills also confided to Young that he felt his new songs weren't going over well with Crosby and Nash, and Young promptly gave Stills a pep talk about self-worth and offered to pitch in on the Crosby, Stills and Nash record that was in progress. Nothing was pinned down, however, so Stills was surprised when, one day at Conway, he was told Young was on the phone. "I'm on my way," Young declared. Stills offered to send a car to pick Young up at an airport, but Young said, "No, you don't understand—I'm in the car." He had driven from his ranch to Los Angeles.

Young was drawn back to his old partners for a variety of reasons. "*American Dream* was an attempt that failed to reach anything like its true potential," he told *Mojo* in 1995, "but that's no reason for me not to try it again sometime." Not having to be the center of attention may have played a factor, along with the idea of fresh inspiration. The year before, 1998, had been a creatively low-key one for Young. For the first time in ages, he hadn't gone on tour or released a new album; when he played his annual spots at the benefits for the Bridge School and Farm Aid, he sported a gray beard that implied he'd been off the grid. He'd spent the decade cycling through most of his past backup bands, as well as Crazy Horse and a new version of the Stray Gators. He'd played unaccompanied. Other than resurrecting the International Harvesters, his country band, or one-shot moments like the Ducks or the Restless, Crosby, Stills, Nash and Young were the only configuration he hadn't revisited in recent times. The idea that his former bandmates were making a new album on their own dime, with no record deal or corporate backing, also appealed to him. "He admires it when people continue to make music," says Pegi. "And they weren't sitting around waiting on his call. They were doing their own thing." Young would tell *Los Angeles Times* writer Robert Hilburn that he just went with his gut. "I don't know why I felt this was the time," Young said. "But I knew it was going to work. I just went with my instincts."

At Conway, Young heard a tape of a new Nash song, "Heartland," a grandiose epic about workaday people, and wound up overdubbing guitar parts onto it. He did the same with Stills' aggro-blues "No Tears Left." But the work didn't end there. Although he had just completed a new album, a largely low-key, acoustic affair called *Silver & Gold*, Young offered the group the chance to cherry-pick a few of its songs for their own album. "I have no idea why," Crosby said. "It *was* out of left field, but that's how it is with Neil. He shows up and says, 'I want to do this,' and we say yes. Yes, I want the money, but I love it that he's always pushing the envelope. And he very often has great songs. Not always, but often."

Naturally, Young would never make it easy for any of them. One of the Young songs they selected was "Slowpoke," a beautifully wrenching ballad—appropriately, about middle or late age—with references to slowing down but also wising up. The song had a languorous beauty, and its chorus cried out for harmonies. As Young and Halverson sat side by side in the control room, Crosby and Nash gathered at the micro-phone; Stills was relaxing in a nearby lounge. "Why aren't they singing together?" Young asked Halverson, who replied that this system seemed to work for them, especially in light of Crosby's relatively recent liver transplant. "David doesn't always have the energy and can run out of gas before Stephen can learn his part," Halverson told Young. It was best if Crosby and Nash nailed their parts and added Stills in later. Stills' hear-ing issues also made it logical to separate him from the others.

Young nodded and accepted the reasoning but soon grew fidgety as Crosby and Nash tried to devise a harmony for the song. "David, can you go into the lounge and get Stephen and have him sing with Graham?" Young said through the talk-back button. "Let's see how that works."

But that approach didn't do it for Young either, so he ordered Nash to bring Crosby back; Stills was given a break, and Crosby and Nash vocalized together again. Still not hearing what he was hoping for, Young then joined the duo at the microphone himself. After they had suffi-ciently practiced, Stills was again roused and asked to sing, this time with Crosby and Nash for the full trio effect. "See how that sounds," Young was heard saying to them. After all the permutations had been exhausted, the harmony blend that wowed the world reappeared. Halv-erson was stunned: they suddenly sounded as if twenty-five years hadn't flown by.

Young wasn't about to let the work dissipate. For the next several hours he had them repeatedly work on harmonies for his song.

"You make the whole album sound like that," Young finally said, "and I'll stay."

Halverson, who hadn't spent much time with all four of them in the studio, even during Déjà vu, belatedly caught a glimpse of Young's skill at coercing them into doing what he wanted. "Neil has this way of acting like a bumbling kid, awkward and talking in half sentences," he says. "He fumbled his way into tricking them. It was masterful. He knew exactly what he was doing." When their former manager, Bill Siddons, visited Conway, Nash played him some of the songs. "How come this sounds so much better than anything during *my* era?'" he asked Halverson, who said it was all a matter of having them sing to each other—a physical reminder of their bond after so many highs and lows.

With almost no planning, a new Crosby, Stills, Nash and Young album suddenly seemed like a possibility. Perhaps Young felt bad for his former comrades, now seemingly exiled from the music business. But he informed Howie Klein, then president of Reprise, about his new plans. "He came to me and said, 'I'm doing a record with CSNY that's going to be a classic, incredible album and tour,'" says Klein. "What was there for me to say? If Neil wanted to do it, we did it." Once Young came on board and brought along his record company, the financial concerns eased up. Crosby was able to fly back and forth to his new home in the ranchlands of Santa Ynez, outside Santa Barbara, instead of making the grueling three-hour drive from Los Angeles.

The album in progress, under the working title *Heartland*, recalled the days of *Déjà vu*, when Crosby, Stills and Nash recorded material without Young while Young worked on tracks on his own. This time, with Halverson back on board, Young added parts to songs Crosby, Stills and Nash recorded, and the trio overdubbed harmonies onto Young's barn-recorded numbers. The process, Nash says, was "a little weird. It wasn't a real album." Yet the long-dormant chemistry between them began to reappear. Using Crosby's son James Raymond as well as drummer Joe Vitale, they settled in to work on one of Crosby's new songs, "Dream for Him," a wafting lullaby to his son Django, who was then preschool aged. Recorded in the morning, when Crosby's voice was still at full strength, the song was gentle and fluid, the rhythms cresting and receding like waves. (It felt like a belated companion piece to the group version of "The Lee Shore.") Stills and Young added dots-and-dashes electric guitars. "They couldn't generate the magic all the time," says Halverson. "It came and went. But when they got the blend going, it would blow their minds that they could sound like they had thirty years ago."

The past revisited in other ways. As he used to do, Crosby rolled joints for anyone who wanted to partake. At one point, another guest from the early years arrived. Nash and Halverson were working at the studio when a limousine pulled up, and, with the help of his driver, out stepped Ahmet Ertegun. At seventy-six, the Atlantic chairman was frail but dapper as always, and Nash eagerly played him songs from the work in progress. Knowing that Reprise had the rights to the album, Ertegun listened attentively without commenting, then headed out after half an hour.

Yet the sessions also laid bare a number of changes—some obvious, some subtle—since the days when they had first come together. Crosby, now fifty-seven, often looked and sounded fatigued from his operation. "If you hadn't made me sound so good back in the day," he snapped at Halverson after one grueling session, "you'd be gone by now." After decades of ear-drum-decimating amplifiers, Stills was now saddled with two hearing aids. Even Young, although only fifty-three, had a senior moment as he was leaving Conway after a day's work. In the next studio, the modern punk band Green Day was working on an album. As Young walked by in the courtyard, one of the bandmates shouted out that the remake Young and the others had just cut sounded fantastic. Young had no idea what he was talking about—but soon realized the Green Day dude was referring to the Crosby, Stills, Nash and Young version of "White Line," from 1990's *Ragged Glory*. Young had completely forgotten he'd cut the song nearly a decade before. The quartet version, which Halverson felt wasn't as strong as Crazy Horse's, was relegated to the archives.

As committed as he was to the album and to the prospect of resurrecting the decades-old partnership, Young remained his unpredictable self. He would periodically bolt for home. When he would step out for a break, no one was absolutely sure if and when he would return. His stubborn nature reared its head during the recording of Crosby's "Stand and Be Counted," a call to political action co-written with Raymond. A grownup reboot of "Almost Cut My Hair," it was similarly primitive—a thunderous crunch closer to Crazy Horse's sound than the quartet's—and would also provide an opportunity for Stills and Young to let loose with alternating solos. As the tape rolled, no one noticed that the sliding glass door of Crosby's recording booth had accidentally been left ajar, resulting in noisy leakage in the background of the finished take. The band wanted to take another stab at it, but Young was insistent that it stay the way it was; much as with "Almost Cut My Hair," he relished the raw energy of the performance. "You replace it and I'm outta here," he told them, and the matter was settled.

By summer, the album was finished, or so they thought. Just as the mastering was set to begin, Nash received a call from Young; he and Stills were back at the ranch and felt the record needed more work. Crosby and Nash hauled up north, Halverson driving the tapes from Los Angeles. "Neil wasn't hearing an 'Our House,'" says Nash. "He told me, 'Hey, man, write a song like "Our House." We need it for this one.'" The musicians stayed in houses on the property and Young's chef whipped up meals; Halverson was given a personal tour of Young's massive toy-trains set. (Thanks in part to his sons, he'd become an obsessive Lionel Trains collector and, several years before, had been part of an investment group that had bought the company.) With Stills banging along on a cowbell, they bashed out Young's "Queen of Them All," the silliest song the four of them had ever concocted, and an acoustic Nash lullaby, "Someday Soon," inspired by a teenage fan of the group who'd died of cancer (it also hinted at some of Ben Young's recent health struggles). Nash played a tape of "Sanibel," an island-breezy outtake from *Live It Up* that Neil and Pegi Young both liked so much that it was included on the album, with Young singing one of the verses himself.

The songs were whittled down to a workable sequence, leaving at least two gems on the studio cutting-room floor. With its gentle, loping interplay between acoustic and electric guitars, Crosby's "Climber" was even looser and more mystically inclined than "Dream for Him," but it was cut loose, along with Nash's "Half Your Angels." Another Crosby song, "Kings Get Broken," was attempted and left out, but later revived by CPR. Perplexingly, they stuck with Stills' "Seen Enough," a cranky-old-man talking blues about the Internet, the military-industrial complex and internet addiction. In a freakish replay of his *Daylight Again* accidental copyright infringement, someone realized the verses of "Seen Enough" bore a melodic resemblance to Bob Dylan's "Subterranean Homesick Blues." In this case, the song stayed on the album—but with a credit saying it was "inspired by Bob Dylan," who also took a cut of the royalties.

When the music was finally completed, family and friends convened at Conway for a listening party. Sitting on the floor and wearing his train engineer's hat, Young seemed content; Pegi Young snapped a photo of young, blond Henry Stills. In another sign of Young's clout, the album title was changed at the last minute, from *Heartland* to *Looking Forward*, and Nash's planned cover design—a logo-type image of a rooster, inspired by coffee-bean bags in Young's studio—was replaced with the photo of Henry that Pegi had snapped. ("It was out of our hands," says Nash.) The encouraging vibrations continued when the band invited various Warner Brothers and Reprise executives to Conway to hear the album. On a bright, blue-sky Los Angeles afternoon, all four men ate, drank and hobnobbed with label representatives. They'd rarely looked or acted more like an actual band.

THE MORNING OF October 12, 1999, in New York City brought two equally jolting sights. Crosby, Stills, Nash and Young were once again on the same stage—this time, at Madison Square Garden. And one of them was rolled onstage in a wheelchair.

After *American Dream* had stumbled out of the gate eleven years before, Young had told the band he didn't intend to tour behind it until they'd made another album. Eleven years later, he was living up to that vow. Even before *Looking Forward* was completed—before Young had even fully committed himself to it—speculation about the first quartet tour since 1974 had started bubbling up. On January 31, 1999, just a few weeks into Young's participation on the project, the *Los Angeles Times* reported that promoter Michael Cohl, who had worked with the Rolling Stones and other heavyweights, was offering the quartet a guarantee of $500,000 per show, twice the amount many of their peers were commanding at the time. The following month, Nash confirmed a fall group tour in an interview.

When the details were rolled out months later—for a tour to start in 2000, and thus coyly dubbed "CSNY2K"—Young's impact on the band's income couldn't have been more apparent. For the first time in over a decade, Crosby, Stills and Nash would be playing arenas, with tickets priced as high as $200. "When it's CSNY, it bumps up twenty notches as opposed to just CSN," says Bill Bentley, then Young's publicist at Reprise. "I used to make a joke: just add a zero on the end for the guarantees for the live shows." When Crosby ran into an old business associate and was asked what it was like working with Young again, he acknowledged the difference between $60,000 a night and $600,000. Later, Crosby again readily admitted to the Neil Young effect. "It changes the money," he says. "It changes how you travel. It changes the size of the venues. It makes sure you can have your own catering and stay in good hotels. A lot of ancillary benefits you love if you're out there on the road."

Several stumbling blocks had emerged. Health issues involving Ben Young delayed the planned tour launch until early 2000, and a freak boating accident also threatened to sink them. In the years leading up to CSNY2K, each man had had a mishap. During a Crosby, Stills and Nash tour of South Africa in January 1996, Stills had slipped in a hotel bathroom and broken his nose. A year and a half later, Young had been forced to postpone five weeks of European shows with Crazy Horse after accidentally slicing his left index finger while making a sandwich; the injury had left him temporarily unable to play. But nothing compared to September 12, 1999, when, on a sailing trip with his wife, Susan, their son Will, and some friends, Nash's powerboat had smashed into an unexpected wave in Hanalei Bay on Kauai. The boat had dipped, and when a second wave hit, Nash had been thrown up in the air. He landed hard on deck, breaking both legs and smashing his right ankle, and had to endure a two-hour ride to the nearest hospital and four hours of surgery.

As serious as Nash's injuries were, plans for the CSNY2K tour proceeded. By the time of the press conference announcing the shows, he still needed a wheelchair to get around. It was far from the only sign that they were all advancing in years—both Crosby's and Nash's hair had gone Alps-white. Yet, gathered at a long table onstage at the Garden, they still exuded their anti-group individuality: Stills, who by now had a goatee in the style of his mentor Ertegun, donned a sports jacket, while Young wore a black Route 66 T-shirt and one of his Lionel Trains caps. As they answered questions from a battery of reporters, they did their best to keep the mood jocular. "I'm taking a slightly different approach in that I'll be awake," Crosby joked. "We really want to play," he added. "We're not good at anything else."

"You can see *that* from this press conference," Young joked.

Young's renewed investment in the band continued in the weeks that followed. In the past, he had rarely made an effort to promote the group when he was part of it, but now, that stonewalling fell by the wayside, perhaps because nothing could be taken for granted. The pop music landscape had been shaken yet again; it was now dominated by expertly choreographed acts like Britney Spears and boy bands capable of selling a million copies of an album in one week. Rock itself had shed any pretense of sunshine and light in favor of rage; a new wave of rap-influenced hard rock bands had engineered a hostile takeover of the music. When the third Woodstock festival took place in the summer of 1999, the overheated crowd, egged on by acts like Limp Bizkit and Kid Rock, trashed vending booths, lit bonfires and bashed cars in the vicinity.

The concept of four men gathered around stools and microphones, holding acoustic guitars and harmonizing, never seemed more old school, and making the public aware of the reunion was never more urgent. With Reprise footing the bill, reporters were invited to hotel rooms in New York, San Francisco and London to meet all four and chat up *Looking Forward* just before its release on October 26. Deferring to Young's wishes, vintage hotels were chosen, and the coffee tables in each room were covered with candles and flowers as *Looking Forward* played on stereos. ("We had to test the sound system," recalls Bentley. "Oh, my God—heaven forbid it didn't sound good in the room.") Whether intentionally or not, the meet-and-greet at San Francisco's St. Francis Hotel was held in the General MacArthur Suite, which had been named after the decorated military man renowned for his World War II speech and its phrase "I shall return."

The group interviews had their expected moments of amusement and only hints of the old friction. "I love how you dress, but I can't stand the food you eat," Crosby told Stills as *USA Today* reporter Edna Gundersen looked on. Startled, Stills replied, "What?" (Given Stills' auditory issues, Nash would often stare Stills in the face and repeat questions so that his partner could answer.) Crosby groused about meat, Nash deadpanned about how they'd tour with individual hairdressers, and Young, eager to shut down the silliness, added, "We'll have really good organic food of every type for everybody. A healthy variety." During an interview with *Guitar World*, Nash and Stills took to joking while Young rolled his eyes. In another interview, Young mentioned the "White Line" mix-up and Crosby chided, "See how much we like you? We didn't even rag on you."

Demonstrating how fully he could commit to group projects when he chose to, Young remained effusive. "This is gonna be a great tour," he said at the Dorchester Hotel in London, the same place they'd stayed in early 1970. "We've never reached our potential and I think we can now." His mood hit a small speed bump during another interview, when Stills unexpectedly brought up the day Young bolted from Buffalo Springfield just before they were scheduled to perform on *The Tonight Show.* "I bailed on the Carson show because at that point we were very young and I think we'll leave it at that," Young replied curtly. "Let's move on." Yet Young still participated in group chats and posed with all three for photos, something he had rarely done in thirty years. In a few of the shots, he was even grinning. (For the back cover of *Looking Forward,* photographer and longtime workmate Henry Diltz coerced them into loosening up by telling them a bawdy joke.)

Asked by a European reporter at a press conference why he was working with Crosby, Stills and Nash again, Young responded, "I mean, God only knows why. I really don't. But I'm glad it happened." He added, "It's one day at a time, one song at a time." As he had at the New York press conference announcing the tour, he said the group was already at work on a follow-up to *Looking Forward.* The idea seemed fantastical, but stranger things—like the first Crosby, Stills, Nash and Young tour in twenty-six years—had happened.

ON A SOUNDSTAGE outside San Francisco in December, the four were in the midst of practicing for their upcoming shows when the moment Crosby half-expected finally arrived. Huddling with the other three, out of earshot of their backing musicians, Young said, "There are three guys on stage here who aren't us." Crosby thought to himself, "Uh, oh—here it comes."

In preparation for the CSNY2K tour, the wants and needs of both camps needed to be fulfilled. John Vanderslice, who had worked in the road crews of both camps, was rehired, this time to be Nash's assistant and help with his post-accident recovery. By the time of the rehearsals, Nash was miraculously walking again, but on tour he would need to exercise consistently and take regular walks. Young required a small upright piano in each of his hotel rooms in case a new song needed to burst out. The staging had to be fashioned to each man—or team's—liking. Stills and Young would continue to stand on opposite sides of the stage.

Crosby, Stills and Nash preferred in-ear monitors that allowed them to hear themselves and adjust their voices while singing harmonies; Young craved a wall of sound around him, to literally lose himself in the music. "It was like Ford and GM putting a merger together," says their production manager, Mason Wilkinson. "Two successful businesses that went on for years and you had to figure out a way for them to work together. Neil had to be comfortable, and so did CSN."

Those adjustments proved to be minor compared to the one that became necessary as soon as rehearsals began. At the outset, everyone had agreed that the band would include Vitale on drums and Finnigan on keyboards—both were long-standing members of Crosby, Stills and Nash's touring and recording band—as well as Donald "Duck" Dunn, the veteran bass player who had recently recorded with Young. As in the past, Stills would get his drummer, Young his bass player. Over the course of a month, the collective diligently rehearsed songs from *Looking Forward* as well as chestnuts like "Southern Man" and "Southern Cross." At one point, Vitale noticed a microphone hanging over his kit but didn't give it much thought. But the feel wasn't right for Young. "It's not that Neil didn't think they were accomplished musicians," says Vanderslice, "but he said, 'I don't want this to be a jukebox tour, playing the same hits the same way they've been played forever.'"

At a group meeting, Young announced that he wanted to switch up the backup players. Stills, who had utilized Finnigan and Vitale the longest, wasn't happy and made his feelings known. But he was outvoted, just as he had been in 1970 with the firing of Dallas Taylor at Young's request. "We knew Neil didn't want Joe or Finnigan," says Nash. "They didn't play simply enough. When Neil says, 'He can't play my shit,' you have to take notice of that. What are we going to do—force Neil to play with a drummer he doesn't like? It was very hard." In the production office, where he was making calls to organize hotel rooms and transportation, Wilkinson heard the news. "We were like, 'Uh, *what?*'" he recalls. "You're not exactly starting from scratch, but it was a scramble."

When the musicians returned to their hotel, Nash visited Vitale and Finnigan to inform them that, at Young's request, their services were no longer required. Both were stunned. Vitale soon heard a theory about the microphones dangling overhead: he'd been secretly recorded so that the tapes could be sent to a replacement drummer to learn his parts. "That was a pretty low blow," Vitale says. "It destroyed friendships for a while. It went away, but that night I hated all of them. It was, 'Fuck all of you.' That really hurt." As Crosby recalls, "It was a mess."

Young already had a beat-keeper in mind: Jim Keltner, a well-regarded drummer best known for his work with the various Beatles after their breakup. The Tulsa-born Keltner had an impressive and eclectic resume—those were his drums on Steely Dan's "Josie," Gary Wright's "Dream Weaver," Bob Dylan's "Knockin' on Heaven's Door," the two Traveling Wilburys albums, even the Ramones' *End of the Century*, to cite only a few of hundreds of examples—but he was also Young's kind of player, direct and unfussy, and with an endearing straightforwardness to boot. Young had worked with him off and on in the '90s. Young's suggestion—to replace two Crosby, Stills and Nash players with his own rhythm section of Dunn and Keltner—was the most indisputable evidence that Young was master of the group domain. "From the CSN side, the underlying sense was: Neil has to be happy," says Vanderslice. "If he ain't happy, it ain't gonna happen. If Neil wants it to be a certain way, they're the ones who blink." Asked about the incident a few months later, Young was somewhat apologetic but unyielding. "It may seem to be a little harsh and disruptive to make a change like that," he told David Fricke, "but it's like anything else—you have to go with your gut feeling and the music is number one."

Young now had his players in position, and the tour was scheduled to begin early in 2000. An even more rigorous round of rehearsals began a few days before Christmas 1999, and Stills invited Keltner to his home for two days so the two could get acquainted. (Keltner felt Stills wanted to ensure the drummer could play his songs the way Stills wanted.) Rearranging some of the harmonies to include Young's voice took time. "Neil will always sing in tune," recalls Keltner, "but they were working hard on the vocals and sometimes they were really bad." In the new year, the hard labor continued: the entire band regrouped in San Mateo for more practice, followed by four days at the empty LA Forum.

The clash-of-titans Stills-Young dynamic reemerged while they were working up Stills' "Dark Star." Keltner's drum part varied from the recording of twenty-two years before, which pleased everyone except Stills, who preferred that it replicate what Vitale had played on the original recording. Young made it clear he sided with Nash and Crosby. "It wasn't a bad fight, just a verbal exchange," recalls Keltner. "Neil liked it and I got my way. Neil doesn't like the beat to be real tidy. He wants a vibe. A sound and a beat but for it to be swimming."

Stills backed down, and the impact of that exchange carried over into the band's new version of "Love the One You're With," which had a bumpier, grittier rhythm than normal. Keltner was worried that Stills would again be displeased, but this time he said nothing, and the altered beat stayed in the set. "If Stephen saw Neil was upset in any way, he'd back off," Keltner says. "I remember hearing somebody say, 'They're all concerned about keeping Neil happy. If he goes, there goes the tour.'" Young's elevated stature was also felt in the set list, which included songs from his solo career—"Cinnamon Girl," a newly relevant "Old Man," and "Rockin' in the Free World." Yet aside from Stills' "Love the One You're With" and one attempt at Nash's "Chicago," the list didn't include songs from any of the others' non-group records.

Still, Young could be unusually protective of his former bandmates. One day, Keltner expressed his concerns about playing one of Nash's songs, which he found uninspiring. Young immediately defended Nash. In Keltner's mind, that made the situation acceptable: if Young could handle that material, then Keltner and Dunn could as well.

STARTING IN LATE JANUARY 2000, the band and their crew hunkered down in another empty arena—the Convocation Center at Cleveland State University—to continue warming up. The concerts would revive the format they'd used in 1974—an electric band opening, a mid-show unplugged segment and then a return to the full band. In another throwback to their first tours, they covered the stage floor with a Persian rug. (This outing, however, they decided to open, rather than close, each show with "Carry On," fearing their voices would be worn out if they reserved it until the very end.) By the time they arrived in Cleveland for final rehearsals, most, but not all, of the kinks had been worked out to Young's satisfaction. In a red flannel shirt and baseball cap, he had everyone bear down on "Old Man," pressing Crosby, Stills and Nash to keep refining their harmonies and shooting alternately appreciative and disapproving looks at them.

"Old Man" was far from the only song they tweaked in the days leading up to the first show, five days later, in Auburn Hills, Michigan. Young
instructed Nash to play "Someday Soon" on his guitar with his fingers,
not a pick. "The pick makes it seem too busy," Young said, before using
Nash's nickname. "We just have to remember to be soft and gentle with
it, Willy. This is a great song." He ordered them to get "in the groove" with
"Marrakesh Express": "It's not swinging," he opined. While working up
"Wooden Ships," Stills went into one of the standard Crosby, Stills and
Nash concert shticks—holding the last syllable in the word "language" in
the introduction as long as possible while looking at his watch. "Wait a
second—what the fuck is this?" Young snapped, and that gimmick was
now out of the show. With little time to waste, Young taught Stills to play
the riff to "Cinnamon Girl."

The first night, at the Palace in Auburn Hills, had its share of stum-
bles: they lost their way momentarily during "Cinnamon Girl." But the
audience—a blend of fans who'd seen them in the '60s and '70s and those
who weren't born until then—stayed with them for the entire show,
which lasted three hours and forty-five minutes. On subsequent nights,
the harmonies that Keltner felt needed more work didn't always rise to
the occasion. When they played "49 Bye-Byes" onstage with Young for
the first time ever, it lacked the sinuous groove of the original. So did the
revamped and newly joyless "Love the One You're With." At the Staples
Center in LA, Stills looked irked when Young walked over and made a
set change, leading to additional tech issues. "One Buffalo Springfield
song and we're already tuning for an hour," Young cracked.

When Crosby and Nash took over the stage as a duo for the inevitable, clear-as-a-mountain-stream version of "Guinnevere," Young would
exit but tell the crowd, "I'm gonna leave you with Crosby and Nash. Don't
worry, they'll take care of you. You're in good hands." But Young could
still be irked when the others almost literally patted themselves on the
back—or gave each other high fives—after a song, or by the way Nash
exclaimed "David Crosby!" after they'd played a song Crosby had written
(and vice versa). One night, Nash offered an unsolicited plug for the
upcoming Springfield box, and Young shot back, into the microphone,
"That was a commercial, an advertisement!" Stills remained given to at-
tention-getting gestures—gesticulating during his acoustic guitar solo on

"Someday Soon," for one—but the show actually did need the occasional jolt of visceral energy, given how much less movable Nash and Crosby could be.

Backstage, everyone had separate quarters, as if socializing could exhume lingering antagonisms. The less time spent in each other's company, the less chance someone would blurt out the wrong opinion or request at the wrong time. During breaks in the set, Young would retreat to his offstage area with Keltner and Dunn; Dunn and Young would share a joint, and Keltner observed that Young would have precisely one shot of tequila. (On his tour bus Young would regale Keltner with tales of the Stills-Young Band fiasco: "Stephen used to bug the shit out of me—he always wanted me to change this or that," Young would say.)

Yet as the tour progressed, moments of the wired-up energy of the 1970 and 1974 excursions surfaced. "Mr. Soul," nearly thirty-five years old, was revived, with Keltner slamming down on his kit while Young and Stills blasted away; Stills even re-created his counterpoint harmony. Stills and Young also wailed back and forth at each other during "Almost Cut My Hair." Recalls Nash, "Neil really loves Stephen, and there was one particular time on stage when Stephen played a great solo and Neil came up to me and said, 'That's why he's here, man—I can't do that.' And he was right." Keltner opened "Ohio" with a martial drum beat. When Young sat down at his pipe organ for "After the Gold Rush," with Crosby and Nash joining in, the crowds still whooped it up when he arrived at the line about getting high.

Onstage, they looked and sounded like men who'd survived more than three decades of punishing road work and self-indulgence, but during moments like "After the Gold Rush," the decades of roiling disharmony seemed to dissipate. "No matter what else was going on around them, politics or whatever, when they got on that stage it all disappeared," says promoter Arthur Fogel of The Next Adventure, the touring division of Live Nation that promoted the tour. "They were kind of intuitive or instinctive about meshing their voices. After a few shows, it started to come back." The encore was always given over to an acoustic version of "Long May You Run," taking them full circle back to voices and guitars—and on a song that had ripped them apart nearly a quarter century before. It was now a love song not just to a car but to the idea of the quasi-band itself.

At times, they could still make each other laugh, often at Crosby's
expense. Just before the start of the tour, a February 2000 cover story
in *Rolling Stone* answered one of pop culture's pressing mysteries: Who
was the biological father of the children of singer Melissa Etheridge and
her partner at the time, filmmaker Julie Cypher? To the shock of the
planet, the sperm donor turned out to be Crosby, at his wife Jan's suggestion. Backstage at CSNY2K, Crosby was teased mercilessly about the
news, with the others dubbing him "The Sperminator." "Watch out, you
might get pregnant!" Stills roared at a backstage visitor talking to Crosby.
Just before their encore at the Tacoma Dome, Nash, Stills and Young
held back before returning to the stage, leaving Crosby to walk out alone.
During one introduction, Young said, "This is a Crosby song, but we're
gonna do it anyway."

The set also included a good chunk of the new material on *Looking
Forward*, which had been released in late fall, a few months before the
start of the tour. *Looking Forward* would never make anyone forget *Déjà
vu*. Their harmonies were gruffer, less giddy and, in cases like Stills'
"Faith in Me," compressed to the point of sounding flattened. Nor did
the album resolve the central creative conflict between the two camps:
Young's love of the primitive versus the others' love of polish. That contrast was especially jarring when the album lurched from the gangly
rhythms and harmonies of Young's "Queen of Them All" to the studio
perfection of the *Live It Up* leftover "Sanibel."

Yet given the Frankenstein's-monster way in which it was bolted together, *Looking Forward* was far more cohesive than the all-together-now
mood they had attempted on *American Dream*. Young's title song, "Slowpoke," and "Out of Control" (the latter an exquisite modern parlor song
that grappled with keeping a relationship going after years of trials) had
an autumnal feel befitting the musicians' ages and tribulations. On each,
Crosby, Stills and Nash's harmonies fit so snugly and seamlessly that
they sounded as if they'd all been together when the songs were taped.
The album was better than anyone had a right to expect: looser, more
natural (no synthesizers), more self-aware. Whether it happened organ-
ically or was the result of overdubs, it offered moments of their vintage
blend, like the sound of Stills and Nash harmonizing on "Heartland" as
Young peeled off lead lines behind them.

To launch the album, Reprise couldn't decide whether radio would take to Nash's "Heartland" or Crosby's "Stand and Be Counted," so the label released both. *Billboard* was withering about the former: "Of such colossal musical and lyrical banality that it defies belief," read its review, which added that Young's solo "is so timid that it sounds as if he just wanted to leave the room." "Heartland" didn't make much of an impact, along with the album itself, which peaked at no. 26. At their shows, songs from *Looking Forward* were greeted politely, in line with its tepid sales. Perhaps public fatigue played a role: after *American Dream* and *Live It Up*, fans' hopes for a triumphant return on record may have been extinguished.

By the time of the final performance, in St. Louis on April 19, the initial estimates of the tour's potential profitability proved accurate. The tour wound up grossing $42 million, averaging $1 million per show in arenas holding between ten thousand and fifteen thousand concertgoers. As in 1974, rumors of extending the shows to Europe progressed no further than talk. A mere two weeks after the last CSNY2K show, Young was already looking forward to resuming his own career; he headed for New York to do *Saturday Night Live*. *Looking Forward* would have benefited from such a plug; instead, that showcase went to Young alone, who played two songs from his new solo album, *Silver & Gold*. "Neil had his own career to look out for," said a source close to him at the time. "Maybe he and Elliot thought, 'Let's protect the brand.'"

Just as discussions of more concerts faded, so did any attempt to quickly make another album together, as they'd hinted at their press conferences. "It's not goodbye—we're not done yet," Young told Halverson at the last session, at Broken Arrow Ranch. But Halverson would never hear from him again, at least as of 2018. Rather than push it, they would let it rest after accomplishing something they'd never done before: they'd spent months on the road together without melting down.

CHAPTER 12

MAY 2001-SEPTEMBER 2006

T he seeds of what would perhaps be their last union were planted nearly five years before, during an unexpectedly dark and troubled time for the country. Once the CSNY2K tour had wound down, Young again followed his muse, this time pointing him in the direction of members of Booker T. and the M.G.'s, the durable instrumental band heard on so many classic Stax R&B records. After playing with them at the Dylan tribute in 1992, Young had toured with the combo; now, in another complete about-face after two years in the Crosby, Stills and Nash vortex, he wanted to deep-fry his new material in their Memphis grooves again.

Over the course of several months in the fall of 2001, Young flew the band's surviving original members—"Duck" Dunn and keyboardist Booker T. Jones as well as the M.G.'s' current drummer, Steve "Smokey" Potts—to the Bay Area. The songs—like the bouncy ode to his daughter, "You're My Girl"—managed to avoid the novelty side of his past forays into rockabilly and Chicago blues. One song in particular stood out for Potts. "It didn't hit me the whole time we were recording," Potts recalls. "Then Neil was saying it was for that guy on the plane. And I was like, 'Oh my God, that's what he's singing? Wow.' It didn't hit me until later."

The man in question was Todd Beamer, the field rep for the Oracle tech company who, on September 11, 2001, had led the charge into the cockpit on United Flight 93, which ultimately smashed into a Pennsylvania field. Called "Let's Roll," after Beamer's words to his fellow passengers, the song sounded like David Bowie's "Fame" put through a hard-rock grinder. Young and the M.G.'s recorded it in the middle of November, and by the end of the month, Young knew the best context for it; he called Crosby, Stills and Nash individually to suggest a post-9/11 series of reunion shows.

Given the typically lengthy gaps of time between tours, the suggestion caught them off guard, but it also made sense: in a country suddenly
shaken by an attack that left three thousand people dead in New York
City alone, familiar faces singing comforting songs about peace and unity
(even if peace and unity sometimes escaped the band itself) had the
potential to be a comforting balm. Again in a holding pattern—no new
album in the works, no new record deal after Atlantic—Crosby, Stills and
Nash readily signed on. They'd been on the road themselves on September 11 and had canceled the remainder of their shows and returned
home. About two weeks after "Let's Roll" was recorded, a Crosby, Stills,
Nash and Young 2002 tour was confirmed. "Neil has always called the
shots, economically," Crosby confirms. "He has that power. When he
says, 'Let's get together,' we come. Neil puts as many people in a building
as we can by himself, so if we get together, he has that power behind
him. It's part of the dynamic."

In light of how quickly this next go-round was set in motion, there
would hardly be time to rehearse—a mere two weeks—and Young would
again be in charge. Not only would Dunn, Jones and Potts be the backup
band, but Jones would be assigned the title of "musical director." The set
would include at least four songs from *Are You Passionate?*, the still-un-
released album Young had recorded with the M.G.'s. Still, in the context
of another bout of Crosby, Stills and Nash inertia, an arena tour with
Young, with tickets priced at as much as $200 a seat, was a welcome
prospect. (When *Chicago Tribune* music critic Jim DeRogatis confronted
Crosby about those prices, Crosby retorted, "I guess you don't understand how much it costs to put a tour on the road. Well, my advice to you
is don't go. . . . If you don't want to pay the money, you should definitely
not come. As a matter of fact, we won't miss you, because all the seats
will be sold.") Stills and Nash talked optimistically about working with
the changed-up rhythm section: Stills and Jones had run in the same circles two decades before, when Stills was dating Rita Coolidge and Jones
had partnered up with Coolidge's sister Priscilla, and Jones had played
and sung on Stills' first solo album.

Of all the tours the quartet would embark upon, the 2002 Tour of
America would prove to be the least memorable. It lacked the freshness

of the 2000 shows, and new Young songs like "Goin' Home" and "Let's Roll" weren't always a natural fit for the other three. The set list contrasted Young's nonstop creativity with the relatively meager output of his partners. The other three offered up few new songs—Stills' ersatz reggae "Feed the People," which had been kicking around for nearly two decades, was an exception, along with Nash's "Half Your Angels," the Oklahoma City tribute that took on a new context after 9/11.

On the road, Young continued to make jokes at the others' expense. "Ladies and gentlemen, the lion from *The Wizard of Oz!*" he said by way of introducing Crosby one night. Crosby zinged him back later, in Hartford; after they'd played "Woodstock," Young cracked, "Anybody here go to Woodstock?" When some in the arena responded with a lusty cheer, Young deadpanned, "I didn't." Crosby shot back, "Yes, you were there." Yet it remained clear that Young pushed them hard, whether by resurrecting the entire "Carry On" and "Questions" merger onstage for the first time in decades or making them play sets that lasted three and a half hours. Two years earlier, Nash told Robert Hilburn of the *Los Angeles Times*, "When you play together for 30-odd years the way David, Stephen and I have, it's easy to get into bad habits and let the audience reaction be your standard. As long as the audience is applauding, it's very easy to think everything is okay. But Neil doesn't have any interest in that." Young was clearly still holding their feet to the musical fire.

When the tour ended, they again had heftier bank accounts: its forty shows grossed $35 million, almost as much as the $42 million they'd made from CSNY2K. But to the surprise of absolutely nobody who knew them, the message of unity they conveyed during the tour ended with the last performance. Two weeks after the show, in an echo of the way he'd promoted *Silver & Gold* as soon as the CSNY2K dates wrapped up, Young was on *The Tonight Show* playing songs from his newly unveiled *Are You Passionate?*

IN WHAT COULD be seen as a revolt against playing the oldies with Crosby, Stills and Nash, Young grabbed the wheel and drove it into even more adventurous terrain as soon as the Tour of America finished. His Booker T. and the M.G.'s period would be another fleeting phase. After only a few concerts with them in Europe in the summer of 2002, Young was gone;

drummer Potts would never hear from him again (as of 2018). Instead, Young turned his attention to a relic from the '60s and '70s—the concept album. Set in a fictional town of the same name, *Greendale* told the story of a multigenerational family trying to come to grips with a changing twenty-first-century world. Instead of using different singers or actors, Young himself sang each song in the voice of a character: the cranky, outspoken Grandpa Green; his artistic son, Earl; Earl's eco-activist daughter, Sun; and drug dealer and black sheep of the family Jed. A devil lingered around the fringes, waiting to suck in anyone and everyone.

The *Greendale* album had a casual, jam-session scruffiness. The songs weren't monumental, but they were the grainiest, earthiest he'd put on record in years. Played by Young with the reunited Crazy Horse rhythm section of Ralph Molina and Billy Talbot, they shuffled and scraped along in an unhurried, loping way. If all that wasn't enough new information to digest, Young took the show on the road, with a stage set replicating a front porch, and performed the album from start to finish to an audience that was most likely expecting reprises of "Cinnamon Girl" and "After the Gold Rush." As he told *Relix*, he didn't want the crowd to like him just "because I've been around for a long time and as part of something they related to years and years ago." The Young classics would arrive, but, to the bafflement of some audiences, only during an encore.

In the immediate years after the two reunion tours with Young, Crosby, Stills and Nash rehired Joe Vitale and Mike Finnigan, who'd been dismissed by Young, and resumed their own grueling roadwork. By 2004, they were still without a record contract, and the modest sales of *Looking Forward* (which didn't even hit 500,000 copies) hadn't improved their market viability. As with many of their fellow classic rockers—such as James Taylor, who half-joked during this period that touring constituted the first nine of ten sources of his income—the road was their primary paycheck.

Dating back to the days when crew members would drop a miniature replica of Stonehenge onto the stage as Nash sang "Cathedral"—making them crack up at the homage to the disastrous prop in *This Is Spinal Tap*—moments of levity arrived periodically. On their way to a stage in the Bay Area, they marched past a backstage lavatory and joked with each other, "We spent a million dollars in that bathroom!" Crosby laughed along, but for him, life in Crosby, Stills and Nash was still creatively maddening. He remained inspired by working in CPR with his son James Raymond and guitarist Jeff Pevar: in 2001, they had released a second album, *Just Like Gravity*. Written by Crosby and Pevar, "Katie Did," one of the album's highlights, was a conscious attempt to return Crosby to a rock patch and managed a degree of radio play. But it didn't help the album sell any more copies than its predecessor, and Crosby wound up funding the group's tours himself with little financial reward. "It meant everything," Crosby says of the group and meeting Raymond. "But nobody heard of us, and calling ourselves Cardio Pulmonary Resuscitation didn't help. It seemed like a good idea at the time, but we should have just called it 'David Crosby.' The music probably went over most people's heads." With CPR far from a moneymaking proposition, Crosby had no choice but to return to the mothership. For a while, he, Stills and Nash valiantly included *Looking Forward* material, including "Faith in Me" and "Dream for Him," in their set, but inevitably the songs were dropped, and they returned to concentrating on the oldies the audience wanted to hear.

By that time, Crosby and Nash had accumulated a small pile of new material, along with songs written or co-written with Raymond and the other musicians, including drummer Russ Kunkel. In 2002, Nash had included some of his fresh tunes on *Songs for Survivors*, which, like Crosby's earlier *Thousand Roads*, flattened its songs (like "Lost Another One," partly motivated by the heart-attack death of Jerry Garcia in 1995) under a layer of overproduction. In the next telltale sign of the trio's dysfunction, Nash and Crosby opted to record their latest material as a duo, leaving Stills out in the cold. Recruiting a group of their own, which included Pevar, Raymond and session guitarist Dean Parks, they set up in a cozy, living-room-style Los Angeles studio and began working them up. "Whenever Stephen hears a Crosby song, he throws his hands up," says Nash. "He can't figure it out. We had a lot of music that I knew would make Stephen throw his hands up, and we had Pevar and Dean Parks. We didn't need Stephen."

Although they'd tried nailing it with Stills and Young, Crosby and Nash finally produced the definitive version of "Half Your Angels," now slower and almost ghostly. Raymond supplied the album with two of its best songs: "Lay Me Down," which sported a vintage-Crosbyesque acoustic flow, and "Puppeteer," with a tense, accusatory tone that was neither vintage Crosby nor Nash but welcome nonetheless. Crosby resurrected an out-there a cappella piece "Samurai" from the late '70s and riled himself up in modern protest songs, including the anti-one-percent "They Want It All" (and the anti-fracking "Don't Dig Here," written by Nash, Raymond and Kunkel). The arrangements were as impeccable as a freshly cleaned suit, every note neatly in place. At twenty songs, the resulting double CD, *Crosby-Nash*, overstayed its welcome, a fact the duo almost seemed to acknowledge when they followed it with a single-disc distillation. And with its tasteful adult-rock varnish, the record could have used a few injections of Stills' sandpaper voice. But the album, which arrived in 2004, contained some of the best recordings either Crosby or Nash had made in a decade, and it would remain Nash's favorite of the albums he made with Crosby.

When the time inevitably came for Crosby, Stills and Nash to crank up a summer tour, Crosby convinced all involved to make room in the band for Raymond and Pevar, with an eye toward slipping some of the *Crosby-Nash* songs into the set. To ensure that Stills felt comfortable with another, flashier, lead guitarist in the band, Pevar spent time playing blues with Stills at his home. "I likened it to going into the lion's cage and pulling out the thorn," says Pevar. "That's what it was like for me. Certain musicians are threatened or insecure or just not that gregarious. I wanted to let him know I was a bro."

But given the personalities and the delicate egos involved, taking the show on the road did not always go as smoothly as the Stills-Pevar jamming. As many as eight new Crosby and Nash songs were included in the set, during which Stills would regularly leave the stage and hand over the guitar chores to Pevar. The band, one of their largest to date, now had two keyboard players and four guitarists, making for a frequently cluttered sound, and tensions began to build. "I think Stephen saw Jeff as a threat," said Nash. "Jeff is a big guy, a big presence on stage, and quite possibly Stephen didn't like that." (As Stills told author Dave Zimmer soon after that tour, "There are just so many notes. With guys like Pevar . . . you put him and Finnigan in the same band, and you're going to quickly use up all of 'em. Two years ago, I vowed never to allow another guitar player in the band—except Neil.") Vitale, still nursing wounds from his firing by Young, also sensed that Stills was less than happy with another guitarist onboard. He also found it puzzling that the band was being asked to learn and play songs from a Crosby and Nash album.

Yet Crosby, Stills and Nash shared the bond of remaining outcasts in the same business that had made them stars. In 2005, Young reupped his arrangement with Reprise Records, signing a multiple-record contract worth millions. *Crosby-Nash*, meanwhile, was released on the British-based indie label Sanctuary, which would fold within a few years; a year later, *Man Alive!*, Stills' first full-on album in two decades, was released by the Florida-based indie Pyramid, home to veteran rock and rap acts. Returning to the genres he'd explored on his early solo records and with Manassas, *Man Alive!* dipped into folk, blues and Latin music, adding a touch of reggae ("Feed the People") and old-timey country (the traditional "Different Man"). Slowly and painstakingly compiled over a period of years, *Man Alive!* included recordings dating back nearly thirty years. As motley as *Crosby-Nash* was cohesive, *Man Alive!* swerved from the Rolling Stones riffs of 1976's "Ain't It Always" to the taut, menacing acoustic blues of "Piece of Me." Recorded mostly in 1979 and shelved thereafter, "Spanish Suite" was an ambitious, multipart work reminiscent of "Suite: Judy Blue Eyes," and featured a glistening piano part by Herbie Hancock. The later recordings on *Man Alive!* revealed how Stills had gravitated over the decades toward garrulous rock and blues—as well as how thick-tongued his singing had become over time (even as his electric guitar retained aspects of its old bite).

While promoting the album, the office of Stills' manager, Gerry Tolman, emphasized to reporters that they shouldn't ask Stills about his past—but in at least one moment on *Man Alive!* he commented on his past anyway. "Round the Bend" found him recounting the time when he'd met Young and formed Buffalo Springfield, and then when he'd joined another band of well-known men and had seen it all go to pieces thanks to hangers-on. (Nash contributed a harmony and melodic part to "Wounded World," but Crosby was nowhere to be heard on the album.) For a bonus dab of nostalgia and electricity, Young overdubbed a guitar part onto the song as well. "Round the Bend" marked the first time Stills had squarely addressed the quartet in any of his songs—and with roughhouse hard-rock boogie diametrically opposed to just about anything Crosby and Nash would ever write or sing.

BY THE MIDDLE of the 2000s, they had each either entered or were approaching their sixties, and age and old habits continued to dog them. On March 6, 2004, CPR, on its last legs, had just played a college in New Jersey, and Crosby was preparing to board the band's bus out of Manhattan when Pevar stopped by his room for a talk. Pevar was feeling increasingly isolated in the group. "It's a very unique situation—David and his son making up for lost time," Pevar says. "And I was feeling like I was kind of getting pushed aside. It's David's scene and who the hell am I? But I saw it as a democracy and it was changing." The two had an emotional conversation lasting so long that, at the last minute, they realized they had to check out immediately to make the tour bus. Thanks to that rush, Crosby left behind one of his bags. As the bus drove off, he told his bandmates he needed to go back and retrieve it—it contained a .45, a knife and a small amount of weed. "I go, 'What? This is crazy!'" Pevar recalls. "I said, 'Why don't you forget about it?'" But at 1:00 A.M., Crosby did return—and was promptly arrested as soon as he walked into the hotel. A housekeeper had found the bag and a hotel employee had opened it.

Appearing in court the next day, wearing a T-shirt that read, "A Man in His Truck Is a Beautiful Thing," Crosby was quiet as he was charged with criminal possession of a weapon in the third degree (a felony) and three lesser charges: possessing a knife with a blade longer than four inches, possession of ammunition, and unlawful possession of marijuana (which he had never fully given up and now found medicinal). Nash was in London when he got the call. "David was being stupid," he says. "You don't go back for the bag. Don't you think it's possible the hotel would look inside the bag? Of *course* they would." After posting a $3,500 bond, Crosby was freed to resume the CPR tour. When it was learned that the gun had been purchased legally, an assistant district attorney suggested a $5,000 fine (the pot charge was dismissed). Yet in light of his comeback, the incident was painfully embarrassing and again made Crosby the butt of jokes; he himself felt awful and later called the move "completely stupid." When they heard Crosby had decided to return to his hotel, Young and his manager, Elliot Roberts, had a good, long laugh at the absurdity of it.

More seriously, Crosby received another ominous diagnosis—diabetes—and in 2005 had surgery for a blocked artery that almost killed him. Stills also received bad news: he was diagnosed with prostate cancer and underwent surgery. (In another example of the way Nash could rattle the cages despite wanting to keep things copacetic, he announced Stills' condition during a TV interview, which mortified his bandmate.) Stills gave up tequila and other hard alcohol in 1999, but the arthritis in his knees was starting to cripple him. His hearing problem was starting to impact the others: during shows, Crosby and Nash would regularly walk over to Stills and ask him to lower the volume on his electric guitar. "We said, 'Sorry, but if you want to work with us, turn the fuck down,'" Crosby says. "He would get all pissed. It's not that he was trying to do the wrong thing. He just didn't *know* how loud he was playing." Crosby also lost a degree of hearing, but just in his right ear.

Other signs of mortality were starting to hit them or those around them as well. On New Year's Eve, 2006, Gerry Tolman, still managing Stills and Nash, was killed in a car accident in Los Angeles. He was fifty-two. Given their shared history, Tolman had a deep understanding of their dynamic and had worked hard to protect them; given his tenure as a member of Stills' band, he could also speak to them on musicians' terms. In the late '90s, he'd approached writer Dave Zimmer, who had written an authorized biography of Crosby, Stills and Nash, first published in 1984 and subsequently reissued two times. Although the band had final say over its contents, they were still commendably frank in their interviews with Zimmer, and the book didn't shy away from their excesses and disagreements. Tolman, worried about the band's image, decided the time had come to clean that story up; he offered Zimmer a nominal fee for the rights to the book, with the goal of republishing it after the band members edited out parts they didn't like. In the contract offered to him, Zimmer would also have been required, bizarrely, to sign off on any rights to ancillary revenue from group merchandising—including, in the words of the contract, "electronic games, toys, comic books [and] apparel"—as well as "theme park rights." Taken aback by the curious offer, Zimmer declined and retained the rights to his book.

In light of such relentless oversight of their career and image, Tolman's death rattled the band. "He took care of Stephen, meaning it took a lot of that pressure off me and David, so it was a terrible loss," Nash says. "Gerry kept us together." The impact was equally clear to those who worked for them. "Gerry kept the energy going and had all these ideas and excitement and thoughts about moving forward," says Vitale. "He was a real positive thinker. Always left the band with a great feeling that we were a good band. He was the coach of the team." Stills signed up with Young's manager, Elliot Roberts, but the group together would now be managed by the wife-and-husband team of Cree and Buddha Miller, who also worked with their friend Jackson Browne.

Not long before Tolman's death, in March 2005, Young had a life-rattling experience of his own while he was shaving in his hotel room in New York. The night before, he had inducted the Pretenders into the Rock & Roll Hall of Fame, sitting in with them on "My City Was Gone." But now, looking in the bathroom mirror, he noticed what he thought looked like "a piece of broken glass" in his eye and was quickly diagnosed with an aneurysm. In typical Young style, he stuck with his plan to fly to Nashville and record a new album, *Prairie Wind*, even penning several new songs on the flight down. He completed most of the work before returning to New York for surgery. (Whether or not it was a result of his health issues, *Prairie Wind* would also be one of his most uncentered records, an odd lot of singer-songwriter ballads, horn-driven vamps and some of his least noteworthy songs of the decade.) Although he later busted an artery during a postsurgery stroll, he miraculously recovered. Adding to his life complications, his father, Scott Young, died in June.

"All I know is, I don't want to die," Young told *Time* after his operation. "I have a lot left to do. I don't feel like people are giving up on me, and I won't give up on them." At that moment, he wasn't going to abandon his old friends, either.

IT WOULD TAKE another war, another photograph and another connection to Ohio to weld them together again. In late March 2006, Young and his wife Pegi visited their daughter, Amber Jean, then in her early twenties, at Kenyon College in Gambier, Ohio. Copies of *USA Today* were distributed at the Youngs' hotel, and one article and its accompanying photos—"Lifesaving Knowledge, Innovation Emerge in War Clinic"—immediately seized his attention.

Almost three years before, America had gone to war yet again. For reasons that would be contested for years to come, George W. Bush had signed off on an invasion of Iraq following the September 11 attacks in New York and Washington. Bush, along with his defense secretary, Donald Rumsfeld, and just about everyone else in his administration claimed that the Iraqi dictator, Saddam Hussein, had weapons of mass destruction, and American missiles were fired into Baghdad in 2003. Since Iraq had little or no connection to the September 11 strikes, the focus on that country made almost no sense, beyond a way for America to flex its military muscles *somewhere*, but the country still rushed into battle. By the time the Youngs arrived in Ohio, more than 1,700 American soldiers had lost their lives in Iraq. In November 2005, US Marines had killed as many as 24 unarmed Iraqi civilians, including, horribly, girls between the ages of one and fourteen. A presidential commission concluded that "the intelligence community was dead wrong in almost all of its prewar judgments" when it came to whatever weapons had existed inside Iraq before the invasion.

The *USA Today* story reported on two American hospitals and numerous field hospitals in Iraq—modern versions of the ones depicted in the TV series and movie *M*A*S*H*, set in the Korean War. Reading the article, Young learned about how the doctors had been ordered to carry weapons while operating, and the breakthroughs in medical technology to help soldiers recover from the gruesome advances in warfare: a "portable heart-lung machine," bandages that could stem bleeding, and new clotting drugs designed to prevent extensive hemorrhaging in soldiers who had been shredded by roadside bombs.

Everything—the incursion, the casualties, the disquieting reasons behind the invasion itself—felt eerily familiar. Returning to his hotel room, Young was so disgusted that, as with "Ohio," he felt compelled to set his thoughts to music. Out tumbled "Families," about an American soldier yearning to come home and finally doing so—with the unspoken implication that he was returning in a coffin. Then came another song, then another: his first full onslaught of what could be called protest songs, from a songwriter rarely known for them. Given their back catalog of odes to war, ecology and social justice, it would always irk Crosby, Stills and Nash that "Ohio" made Young seem more like a topical songwriter than they were, but in one creative outburst, he made the case that he could speak out about current events as fiercely as they could.

Back at the ranch after the Youngs' trip, Niko Bolas, who was still working for Young as an engineer, took a call at the studio from Young, asking him to come over for dinner. Bolas had grown accustomed to his boss' whims and spontaneity, so the request was not surprising. During a post-meal drive, Young asked, "Man, how come no one's doing protest records?"

"I don't know," Bolas replied. "Kids aren't like how we grew up."

"We gotta do something," Young replied.

A few days later, Young arrived at the studio with bassist Rick Rosas and drummer Chad Cromwell, his old Bluenotes players, and the three straightaway worked up and recorded two of Young's new antiwar songs; by the fourth day, they had eight. Between March 29–a week after he'd seen the USA Today article–and April 16, they had made almost an entire album. In one day alone, March 31, Young pounded out the intentionally incendiary "Let's Impeach the President" before he'd had breakfast, followed by "Lookin' for a Leader" (options included Colin Powell and Barack Obama, who was then a US senator) and "Roger and Out," written in the voice of a soldier addressing the buddy with whom he'd signed up for service–and who was now seemingly dead. The process reminded Cromwell of the fast-and-furious creation of the 1989 EP *Eldorado*, when the same three musicians had cranked out equally ferocious songs. "He'd go back home or someplace else on the property, write the song and then come back to the studio and we'd jump in and track it," Cromwell says. "And it went that way until the record was complete." Bill Bentley, Young's publicist, was in touch with Young during this time and recalled his outrage. "He was sick of the war and sick of Bush," says Bentley. "He was pissed. He wanted to register how he was feeling."

In light of his adopted country attacking another country for reasons that turned out to be scurrilous at best and illegal at worst, Young's rage was understandable, and he channeled his indignation into his fiercest album in years. From its thunderous power-trio arrangements to Young's equally roiling guitar, *Living with War* bristled and jabbed.

On its best songs—the semi-apocalyptic "After the Garden"; the protest-anthemic, Dylan-referencing "Flags of Freedom"; and "Shock and Awe," which looked back on Bush's premature "Mission: Accomplished" photo op with seething sarcasm—he and his musicians sounded as if they'd been rewired for added voltage. (A choir overdubbed later onto some of the songs added an eerie undercurrent.) Young later admitted the songs were rudimentary for a reason; as he would say, he didn't want to waste stronger, more worked-over melodies on George Bush. But what the recording lacked in sophistication it more than made up for in an urgency lacking in his music over the previous decade.

Unlike with "Ohio," Crosby wasn't around to witness the writing of *Living with War*, but he and Nash learned about the material soon enough. In April, they received a call from Young asking them to join him at the five-star Hotel Bel-Air near Beverly Hills; he had something he wanted them to hear. Although Crosby, Stills and Nash had appeared with Young at the Bridge School benefit concerts in 2003 and 2005, it had been four years since their last tour, and communication between them was once again sporadic. Crosby and Nash, who both happened to be in Los Angeles, arrived at the hotel expecting to spend time in Young's room, but instead they piled into one of his vintage cars and began tooling around the hills and canyons of Topanga.

The locale was home to hundreds of memories—Young's old house, for one, was still tucked away there—but little about the drive was nostalgic. With Crosby and Nash side by side in the back seat, Young blasted *Living with War*. As the songs played, the two nodded at each other, making mental notes of where they could insert harmonies. Young's goals were unclear, but when the music stopped, he told them he wanted to play the songs on tour with them. "I don't know if Stephen had heard any of it," Nash recalls. "But Neil is good at playing the game. He knows that if he gets me and David in, what choice does Stephen have?" They told Young they would help him out in whatever way he wanted, and then called Stills to tell him he had to hear the songs too.

BY THE SPRING OF 2006, news correspondent Mike Cerre had experienced more than most men and women his age, starting with serving in Vietnam and then as a war reporter in Iraq and Afghanistan. But he was still taken aback when he received a call from Lookout, Young's management, asking if they could purchase footage from his time embedded with American troops in Iraq in 2003. The buyer would be Neil Young, and the footage would be used for a tour—but, as Cerre was told, not "a regular tour but something more meaningful."

If anyone could help channel Young's feelings about the war, it would be Cerre. As a forward air observer in the Marines during the Vietnam War, Cerre, who had a tough but regular-guy demeanor, helped coordinate medevacs, air strikes and reconnaissance missions with American troops who confronted enemy soldiers. In that role, he flew 110 missions until he was sidelined when shrapnel penetrated his cockpit, resulting in chest and arm wounds and a ripped tendon. The camera skills Cerre exhibited while aboard his plane led to him working on TV documentaries, and decades later, the ABC series *Nightline* recruited him to tag along with Marines and special forces in Afghanistan immediately after September 11. With a Marine division, he then ventured into Iraq in 2003, winning an Emmy for his role as lead correspondent on an ABC special, *Brothers in Arms: The Untold Story of One Marine Company in Iraq.*

As Cerre soon learned, Young was building a Crosby, Stills, Nash and Young tour around his freshly spewed antiwar songs, but Young was being particularly sensitive to the situation on all levels. "They were very concerned about this tour being antiwar," Cerre says. "They wanted it to be antiwar but not anti-troop. Neil was very concerned about how he was going to walk that fine line. Once he told me, 'Who am I to tell people about this? I'm Canadian and didn't serve in the war.'" Cerre was reluctant to sell the footage but offered to film new pieces about veterans to show the ways in which war forever changed those who'd served in it.

By that point, Young had been technically savvy for decades, using wireless microphones and guitar-controlled volume switches for his amplifiers during the *Rust Never Sleeps* tour in 1978, and learning about computers, both for his music and to help his son Ben. Now, seeing himself as a modern town crier, he wanted to spread the word about *Living with War* and his visceral dislike of Bush as quickly as possible. Although he had an active hatred of MP3s and digital audio, he bit that particular bullet. By the last week in April, less than a month after he'd recorded it, the *Living with War* songs were streaming for free on his website—and as a continuous stream, forcing people to listen to the entire record. He also launched a website, the Living With War Network, complete with video footage, protest songs by a wide range of other musicians and a logo meant to resemble that of CNN.

Still, Young knew from the start that that plan wasn't enough; he needed a larger forum in which to deliver his message—hence his decision to take Crosby and Nash on the Los Angeles ride. "He realized he has a certain audience of a certain number, but if you want to spread an idea like *Living with War*, it would be more powerful and the message would get around to more people with the four of us," says Nash. "It's a much bigger deal when the four of us do it." Stills came onboard, and the same week *Living with War* went up on Young's website, a Crosby, Stills, Nash and Young Freedom of Speech Tour was announced, starting July 6, 2006, and continuing through just after Labor Day. "When there's a vast amount of money to be made and a message to be delivered," Nash says, "it can move pretty fast."

Everyone in Young's world and in the Crosby, Stills and Nash camp, musicians and managers alike, knew the financial ramifications of any such reunion. One northeastern show—in the same venue where Crosby, Stills and Nash had only taken home $125,000—would gross $800,000. But for once, a financial windfall wasn't the only motivation. "He wanted us for legitimacy and to spread out the responsibility," Crosby says. "He wanted his brothers in arms when he took on the US president."

Even more than in any previous group tour, Young laid down his particular laws about nearly every aspect of the shows, starting with a call to Cromwell about his participation. "I said, 'Tell me about the band,' and he said, 'Hang tight, I'll get back to you and tell you who's doing what,'" Cromwell recalls. "He called back and said 'Here's the band.'" The backup musicians consisted of Young's current, non–Crazy Horse unit: Cromwell, Rosas, Ben Keith and keyboardist Spooner Oldham. "It was fair to assume he was calling the shots," Cromwell says. "Presumably there wasn't a lot of discussion going on [with Crosby, Stills and Nash] about that. It was, 'This is who it's going to be, okay, fellas?' What were they going to say?"

Within weeks, the musicians were assembled at a rehearsal space in the San Fernando Valley, and the production manager, Tim Foster—who had first worked with Young in 1973–faced a challenge. For the stage floor, Young wanted the words to the US Constitution written out on a canvas sixty feet wide and forty feet deep. Foster had to scramble to find a set designer who could assemble it in a matter of weeks. Stills wanted his usual small patch of wooden flooring that would allow him to move around, and the designer had to ensure he wouldn't slip and fall on the Constitution canvas. When sound modifications were needed during rehearsals, Stills suggested parachutes to diffuse the sound and offered to reach out to his connections in the military; in the end, Foster and the crew were able to work around the problem.

Young also had a laser-focused plan about the songs they'd play and the way the band would communicate with the audience. He decreed that the set list would consist almost entirely of their political or social-awareness material. While the quartet had a number of songs that easily fit that bill–from "For What It's Worth," "Ohio" and Nash's "Southbound Train" up through recent material, including Stills' "Wounded World," Crosby's "They Want It All" and Nash's "Milky Way Tonight"–it still took time for them to wrap their heads around that idea. "They kept trying to break the mold and go, 'We'd like to do a song about the whales,'" Young told *Mojo* later. "No way. I said, 'We're doing songs about war and politics and the human condition, that's it. Don't let people off the hook, don't give them any relief, just keep slamming them with the same information.'" ("'Wind on the Water'–why not?" Nash would muse later. "Neil doesn't like people singing with him. We love it.") To make sure everyone remembered the lyrics, a few teleprompters were rented.

Although Stills had deeply held political beliefs–and even campaigned for local Democrats along the route of the tour–Young had to work especially hard to convince him that such a concept would work. (Some in the Crosby, Stills and Nash camp rolled their eyes at other parts of the show, like Neil slapping his strings with flip-flops to call attention to a line in "Let's Impeach the President.") More than any of the four, Stills needed regular affirmation and encouragement to do his best work, and the idea that some audience members might be rattled by the absence of nonpolitical material left him with feelings of "misgivings and ambivalence," as he later told *Mojo*. He also worried such a show would only serve to galvanize Republicans. Even when it came to the name of the undertaking—the Freedom of Speech Tour—Stills retorted to a reporter, "I wasn't at the meeting" when that decision was made.

In the end, Young prevailed, as always. "When he has a head of steam like that, you have to go with it," Nash says. "We said, 'Okay, you're the boss of this—we're with you.'" During rehearsals, they drew up lists of pertinent songs and, in a sign of cooperation, offered to remove some of their own material to make room for that of others. "What I clearly saw from Neil was, 'Hey, man, if we're going to do this shit, we've gotta kill it,'" Cromwell says. "He had to make them do that." Crosby's wife Jan and their son Django (then eleven) were recruited, along with the crew member and musician Larry Cragg, to hoist aloft one of the gigantic old *Rust Never Sleeps* microphones as if they were all raising the flag at Iwo Jima; some in the crowd didn't realize it would also serve as a call for the audience to sing along.

During the first electric set they would play four straight numbers from *Living with War* ("After the Garden," "Living with War," "The Restless Consumer" and "Shock and Awe"). In the second set, they would veer back to unplugged chestnuts that, while not antiwar, were songs the audience would want to hear ("Helplessly Hoping," "Our House," "Only Love Can Break Your Heart" and others), lulling the crowd into a nostalgic haze before hitting them with "Let's Impeach the President" toward the end of the show. Young put an end to the standard between-song patter of Crosby, Stills and Nash, which could range from political commentary to self-congratulatory information about who wrote what tune; he wanted the songs to speak for themselves and avoid any pontificating. The move would also be a protective measure: if the group went from one song right into another, it gave the more conservative members of the audience less time to react against what they'd just heard.

After filming a few interview segments with veterans to show Young, Cerre showed up at rehearsals, but, to his annoyance, was kept waiting outside a dressing room for two hours. He had the distinct impression, right or wrong, that Lookout Management was not as jazzed about the tour as Young was. Finally, Cerre barged in, holding a videotape, and said, "Here's a great fucking story!" and walked out. Young dragged him into a bathroom and told him he'd back him completely and take care of management's concerns. "I really respected Neil for that," Cerre says.

"He said, 'I think there's something there not fully baked but let's keep doing it.'" With that, Cerre would be officially embedded in many of the Freedom of Speech shows.

In the four years since they'd last performed together on tour, additional rust had set in, and the first weeks of rehearsal had more rough patches than usual. "It took those guys time to get their chops up, to really get back to form," says Cromwell. "The first week was like the wheels were rusted up and we're not sure how we can get them to turn so let's keep banging on it and greasing it until something happens. I was wondering there for a minute when it would start sounding great." But after a few weeks of relentless pounding, it began to come together during a run-through of "Wooden Ships," which always fired up Stills' and Young's guitars.

ON THE SIXTH NIGHT of the tour, at the Xcel Energy Center in St. Paul, Minnesota, Crosby was in the midst of a dressing-room interview with *Rolling Stone*'s Andy Greene. "When we do it right, they fucking get it," he was saying. "To me that's us being valid, like we were in the beginning. That's us doing what we were put here to do."

Then came a knock on the dressing room door and in burst Young, dressed in his stage garb—fatigues and floppy hat—that made him resemble a South American rebel fighter. Young said "Excuse me" to Greene and then went into the third verse of "Families," singing the "Oooh ooh" part. In his mind, the others weren't singing it correctly.

"Do you wanna go through it?" Crosby said.

"Yeah," Young said, singing the part, "I'm going back to the U.S.A."

"Oh, that'll be brand new," Crosby replied. "I'll try to remember the 'U.S.A.' one."

"Don't remember it—do it," Young said curtly.

"Do you want it from Willy to the end?" Crosby asked, using Nash's longtime nickname.

"You keep on doin' it," Young said. "Just do it like you're doin' it, short but very effective: 'Oooh, oooh . . . '"

"How about we do it in the next verse too?"

With a trace of irritation in his voice, Young said, "That's the one I told ya. Once you come in, you never get out. Two sets in and 'U.S.A.'"

"Look at me funny when we get close," Crosby said before Young was gone. No sooner had Young departed than a visibly rattled Nash dashed into the room; he'd received his own visiting lecture from Young. With very little time to spare until the show started, the two rehearsed the harmonies Young had just laid out for them.

Young had always been a tough taskmaster, but his emotional investment in the Freedom of Speech Tour was especially marked, permeating every aspect of the expedition. A few hours before he had crashed into Crosby's dressing room, the musicians and their family members had congregated in a cinder-blocked backstage room for dinner, talking, laughing and eating. Crosby and Pegi Young, who was along for some of the shows, conversed warmly. When Young walked in, the room immediately quieted—and largely remained that way while he ate. The usual backstage jokes were never hurled in his direction. "I saw the rest of them teasing each other," says Cromwell. "But nobody beat up on Neil. I never saw that." The minute the St. Paul show ended, Young was in an SUV being driven to the airport. Stills wanted more time so he could shower at the venue and continued to insist on it—until he was told, point-blank, that there was no time: everyone had to meet Young at the airport, now. Stills consented.

When Cerre caught up with the tour, in Philadelphia, he saw firsthand how Young reminded everyone, in schoolteacher tones, about the no-chatter rule between songs. "He told Crosby in no uncertain terms, 'No political patter, no ad-libbing. Let the music speak for itself,'" Cerre says. "Crosby didn't say anything. I could see him holding himself back. It was tough." ("Maybe I don't agree with the way he says things, not always," Young later said to *Mojo* about Crosby, "but we are all coming from the same place." As Crosby says, "There were a lot of rules.")

The rusty moments that dogged rehearsals carried over into the early leg of the tour; as Young would later admit, "We had some shows that were a little rough." With their rumpled clothes and scraggly hair, the band members usually looked as if they had just rolled out of bed. (After his *Rolling Stone* interview in St. Paul, Crosby walked right onstage in the clothes he was wearing.) At the Toronto concert, less than a week before St. Paul, Stills—who had put on additional weight before his prostate surgery—tripped over wiring and fell onstage. Joking about his weight gain later, Stills cracked, "I even made Crosby look good," but the moment when he had tumbled wasn't funny for anyone. The backup musicians held their breaths, wondering if they would be playing the rest of the tour without Stills, but Stills stood up and went on with the show.

Yet the intensity that drove Young invested the shows with a crackling vitality missing on the previous reunion jaunt. The impetus behind them made "Ohio" and "Wooden Ships" transcend nostalgia. The back-and-forth solos between Stills and Young in "Wooden Ships" and "Déjà vu" felt more robust and extra-metallic, the two now resembling elderly lions hurling their chests at each other with guitars. By including songs they hadn't played much together in decades, such as Nash's "Southbound Train" and Crosby's "Carry Me," they sounded less rote than if they had merely worked their way through the hits. "They've been singing about things they've believed in," Young told *Billboard* later, "and also just singing a lot of love songs, and a lot of songs that people enjoy, so it could become kind of like date night going to see them." They even exhumed Crosby's "What Are Their Names?" from *If I Could Only Remember My Name*, which Crosby had rarely performed live before. Now it was an a cappella piece, with the audience keeping time with its applause, and the lyrics about the mysterious men who controlled the country hadn't sounded that relevant in decades. Pegi Young hadn't heard the song before and cried every night they performed it.

The emotional highlight of every show was "Find the Cost of Freedom," which they sang against a backdrop of photos of soldiers who'd been killed in the Middle East. With Stills fingerpicking the lead parts and the four locking into harmonies, the performance came as close as humanly possible to re-creating a night from 1970. "It was very emotional," says Cerre. "It gave them a great sense of purpose." While interviewing audience members for the movie Young was making, Cerre encountered older, graying fans who had brought their children to the show. They wanted them to see and hear what a '60s concert was like.

THE ALARMING NEWS hit while the band and crew were slogging from West Palm Beach to Atlanta. On August 10, British authorities announced they had foiled a potentially horrifying new attack: a plan to detonate liquid explosives on as many as ten flights from London to various cities in the

United States, including New York and Chicago. Since the plot had called for smuggling the explosives in carry-on bags, security at US airports was ramped up. The Department of Homeland Security had raised the threat alert, and liquids and lotions of any kind over a certain amount would now have to be checked with luggage. Some American Airlines flights along the eastern seaboard were canceled. Talk radio exploded; here, those hosts argued, was proof that America was still at war, even nearly five years after September 11. The day felt almost like a repeat of September 12, 2001.

In light of how quickly the tour had been conceived and scheduled, it was inevitable that the routing—the city-to-city order of the shows—would be complicated. "It was almost like a Star of David tour, all over the place," says Nash. "It was pretty brutal." The trip from Florida to Georgia was expected to be one of the more manageable legs of the journey, but, with his eye on the news, and given his own broadcasting background, Cerre sensed that Atlanta could be volatile for them, and not only because they were now deep in the red states. Cumulus, a conservative-leaning radio conglomerate, was based in that city and owned several stations there. Three years before, the company had taken it upon itself to ban the Dixie Chicks from its stations after they had dissed Bush during a concert in London. Cerre told Young he wanted to leave Florida for Atlanta earlier than the band so he could visit conservative talk show hosts in town and ferret out the mood of the city. Young and others told him he was just being a "negative news guy," and that they weren't concerned. But Cerre and his crew stuck with their plan. When they dropped by stations to interview talk-show hosts, such as Neal Boortz, they found, as they had predicted, that few were thrilled to have Crosby, Stills, Nash—and especially Young—in town. In their minds, who were these old liberals to tell them what to do now that the country was newly under siege?

Thanks to an hour-long delay and the extended crowd drinking that resulted from it, the thousands who gathered at the Philips Arena in Atlanta were already in a volatile mood by show time. The first signs of trouble came early, during "Families," which was accompanied by footage of dead soldiers in coffins. At least a few in the hall were offended and screamed back at the band or left. "We knew there were bound to be people who weren't going to like what we were saying," says Nash, who, like the others, couldn't always see or hear what was happening in the crowd that night. "If you buy a ticket to a CSNY show, what the fuck do you expect? Lovey-dovey shit all the way through?" The parade of hits that followed appeared to settle them down, even if the jostled audience members didn't grasp that "Déjà vu" (which immediately followed "Families") was now a commentary on the times rather than merely a favorite song from their second album.

But when the band started in on its first encore, "Let's Impeach the President"—with its lyrics displayed on a large screen behind the band to encourage a sing-along—a small but loud contingent unleashed its anger. Some tossed water bottles at the stage, others flashed middle fingers, and at least one-tenth of the house began angrily streaming out. Those who opted to stay began yelling at the ones leaving. "We knew in Atlanta we'd piss off a shitload of people," says Crosby. "We knew that would happen: 'I wanna kill that sumbitch Neil Young! You can't say that about a great American!' Some funny shit."

At that moment, though, it wasn't very amusing. "Probably because of the previous two CSNY tours, it caught people off guard," admits promoter Arthur Fogel. "It was a shock to the system." To capture the disruptions, Cerre sent a crew to film people near the exits, the most well-lit areas of the arena. The cameramen bore the brunt of the rage as people pushed them against the wall; fortunately, one of Cerre's soundmen was able to catch one of the cameras before it smashed to the ground.

When the main set ended soon thereafter, the group hurried backstage only to find Young's manager, Elliot Roberts, screaming at him, "No fucking encore!" Young responded in kind, announcing they *would* be doing one; after all, he retorted, this was called the Freedom of Speech Tour for a reason. Young led the musicians back out for one more song—"Woodstock"—but the tension didn't subside when the music ended and the lights went up. Instead of jumping onto tour buses, the musicians and Cerre were driven out of the venue and straight to a nearby airport in SUVs flanked by a motorcade of Georgia state troopers. Since the major airlines had shut down their flights as a result of the terrorist threat, a DC-10 was quickly chartered, and nearly two dozen musicians and crew members piled on for the flight out. "They were really shaken but also invigorated," says Cerre, who joined them on the plane. "It was like, 'Yeah, that is what music is about, and I guess we got people's attention.' And at the end of the day, it could have gotten much worse. Nobody got hurt and it didn't turn into a riot."

FOR THE FIRST TIME on the tour, Young was rattled. He and the group were confronted with a startling new reality: that some portion of their fan base, solid counterculture types from the Vietnam era, no longer shared the group's political leanings. In 1972, according to an American National Election Study, 51 percent of eligible-voter boomers identified themselves as Democrats, and 29 percent as Republicans. But in a similar poll that would be published in 2008, two years after the Freedom of Speech Tour, the number of Republican-leaning boomers would jump to 48 percent. The unnerving aftermath of the '60s hadn't just revealed itself in drug casualties or Gordon Gekko–style career changes, but in voting habits as well.

Especially after the Atlanta fiasco, the implications of this generational drift were immediately felt. In Young's hotel room in Washington, DC, before the next show in Bristow, Virginia, security guards poked behind the curtains in search of unwanted intruders. Before they went onstage, the four men had a long-standing tradition of a band handshake, which replaced the shared joint of years before. That evening, at the Nissan Pavilion concert in Bristow, Young huddled with Crosby, Stills and Nash and instead told them how nervous he was. They slapped him on the back and did their best to comfort him. "We got your back," Stills responded. For a moment, at last, Young no longer needed them just for musical or financial reasons; he needed them for emotional support.

That night, as bomb-sniffing dogs were ordered up for that and future shows, some booing again erupted during "Let's Impeach the President." But showing a fortitude that had escaped him during the Stills-Young Band tour of three decades before, Young gave no thought to canceling. "We thought, 'Let's just keep going,'" recalls Pegi Young. "If we stopped, would the terrorists win?" The shows weren't Pegi's first encounters with hostile fans; she still recalled the extremely vocal reactions to her husband's *Trans* tour decades before. But another month of shows awaited them, and those in the touring party who weren't accustomed to those responses made peace with the new normal. Fans in Missouri also walked out during "Let's Impeach the President," and the bomb detectors continued to try to protect them. "The first time I saw the bomb squads, I thought, 'This is not good,'" says Cromwell. "I thought, 'Is this going to be the gig where the bomb goes off? Is this how it will end?' I was nervous, but after a few more gigs, it wasn't that bad. Everyone settled into it." The set list never changed, and "Let's Impeach the President" remained the first encore.

At the Theater at Madison Square Garden in New York, about two weeks after the Atlanta showdown, they were greeted with an unusual sight: Patti Smith, Donald Trump and Salman Rushdie all seated near each other in the first few rows.* Finally, on September 10, they played their final show of the tour, in Burgettstown, Pennsylvania. Young made sure there would be no concert booked on September 11; even for him, that would be tempting fate—and audience reactions—too much.

For the first time in years, if not decades, the quartet had a cultural and political reason to exist. After the last concert, Nash hoped Young would extend the tour in one form—or country—or another. The Iraq War was hardly over, and, as it turned out, American troops would remain there for another five years. Young begged off—although this time, his decision wasn't entirely due to the exhaustion involved with dealing with the Crosby, Stills and Nash world. The entire experience had left him shaken: they had met the enemy, and some of them were their own kind. "No amount of protection or bomb-sniffing dogs make you feel like you're covered," he later told *Rolling Stone*'s Greene. "It was a very emotional journey and very tiring. It wiped me out for a long time." Other than his regular appearance at the Bridge School benefits in the fall and a few cameo spots with other artists, Young barely performed for the rest of the year. Nor would he take to the road again until the fall of 2007, a year after the last Freedom of Speech shows. He'd made his point, and the trio had served its purpose.

---

*Trump, who had been an admirer of Young's music for years, had appeared backstage at several of his concerts: "He always came with an entourage and usually a lovely lady on his arm," Pegi Young recalls. "When we were playing in Atlantic City, Neil was in his dressing room and I said, 'Neil will be out in a few minutes.' Trump didn't seem to like that very much." Crosby later retweeted a photo of Young and Trump together from 2014, before Young and Trump had a public falling-out over Trump's use of "Rockin' in the Free World" at campaign rallies. "Everybody makes mistakes sometimes," Crosby tweeted, of Young.

CHAPTER 13

JANUARY 2008–SEPTEMBER 2018

Time refused to stand still for them, but for a moment in 2008, it nearly did. Grabbing scarves and wool caps, the four united again, this time at the Sundance Film Festival on January 25. As they assembled for group photos, chuckling at inside jokes, they looked like Mount Rushmore versions of themselves. Their faces were weathered, their clothes rumpled, and Stills' glasses lent him the look of a craggy college professor who taught counterculture history. But if one squinted, it was still easy to conjure up the same young men who would gather for photo shoots at the Shady Oak house in Los Angeles, flashing peace signs and goofy, stoned grins some forty years before.

The Freedom of Speech Tour, Young's most provocative project since the computer-voiced songs on *Trans*, had wound down over a year earlier. Although it wasn't the biggest tour moneymaker of 2006—it came in sixteenth place—it had still grossed $32 million. But the work wasn't done. The documentary about the entire, sometimes fraught undertaking needed to be assembled, and Young huddled with his co-director, Benjamin Johnson—son of Larry "L.A." Johnson, Young's close friend and documentarian, and Leslie Morris, Crosby and Nash's former manager—to whittle down the hours of concert footage, audience interviews and profiles of Iraq War veterans that Mike Cerre had collected. Once the film was finished, and before the Sundance festival, Crosby, Stills and Nash were invited to an early screening in Santa Monica of *CSNY/Déjà vu*.

Of the three, only Nash was able to make the trip, but he wasn't happy with what he saw. To his displeasure, Young included footage of the moment Stills had tripped and fallen onstage, and Nash found the ending unsatisfying. During one of the nightly performances of "Find the Cost of Freedom," with its backdrop of deceased soldiers, the cameras zoomed in on Karen Meredith, whose son Ken Ballard, an army first lieutenant, had been killed by friendly fire in Iraq in 2004. When her son's photo materialized in the montage, Meredith broke into tears. Nash thought the film should have ended there; instead, it concluded with footage of a veteran navigating curvy highway turns on a motorcycle. Others in the CSN camp would later agree with Nash on these issues. But even though some of the profits from the Freedom of Speech Tour had been used to finance and complete the movie, they were told that no changes would be made; as the director, under his Bernard Shakey pseudonym, Young had final say. "It was wrong," Nash says. "We should have had input into that movie. If it's about the four of us but three of us have no say? Gee, thanks. Like we don't have a fucking opinion about our involvement in this? That's not right."

By the time of Sundance, where *CSNY/Déjà vu* would premiere, Crosby, Stills and Nash had suppressed whatever mixed feelings they had about the movie and Young's filmmaking skills for the greater good. They posed for their group shots and joined Young for a press conference at the first screening and for interviews. Even there, Young asserted his dominance. Talking with the Associated Press, Crosby joked: "Don't you think it'd be a good idea if we had a law saying you can't have control of nuclear weapons unless you can pronounce the word 'nuclear'? I'm just asking." (He was mocking Bush's tendency to pronounce the word as "nu-cu-lar.") Having none of it, Young reprimanded Crosby in front of the reporter: "That comment is a polarizing comment. It doesn't have to do with the grass roots of the country in the Midwest. It takes people and separates them." When Young maintained in the same conversation that younger musicians weren't writing protest songs anymore, Nash interjected about Eminem's "Mosh," but Young ignored him and kept talking—as he also did when Crosby brought up another Bush-era musical commentary, "Dear Mr. President" by pop singer Pink. At the festival, Young invited Josh Hisle, a two-tour combat veteran and part-time singer-songwriter, to perform; when Hisle launched into a fervent version of "Rockin' in the Free World," Nash, biting some part of his tongue, emerged from the wings to shout along on the chorus with Hisle and Young.

The movie tumbled out into theaters, along with a companion live album that qualified as the first Crosby, Stills, Nash and Young record in nearly a decade. *CSNY/Déjà vu Live* delivered Young's dive-bomber guitar in "Military Madness" and group versions of *Living with War* tracks like "After the Garden" and "Families." But the quasi-soundtrack didn't fully capture the wallop of the shows; dumped unceremoniously on the market, it felt like an orphaned child. (It spent exactly one week on the *Billboard* chart, at no. 153, before dropping off entirely—an ignominious end to the tour.) By then, Young had already moved on. "After an album like that," he told *USA Today*, "you kind of have to cleanse your soul. You can't go around saying, 'This is how I feel' for the rest of your life, especially when there's so much else to talk about." Those concerns included the environment, audio quality (eventually resulting in his short-lived Pono high-res audio player), and writing his first memoir.

But for the first time since their 1977 reunion, Crosby, Stills and Nash were given a chance to shine without Young. At a meeting of Columbia Records executives in early 2008, Steve Barnett, the label's co-chairman, mentioned that the company needed a viable fourth-quarter release by an established act—a record that would essentially sell itself without the promotional dollars that labels usually spent breaking in new artists. By chance, Jay Landers, a veteran A&R man who had long worked with Barbra Streisand, one of Columbia's legacy acts, had been obsessing over Henry Diltz's *California Dreaming* coffee-table book of LA rock photos, many of which included Crosby, Stills and/or Nash. Landers, who didn't know the group personally and had no idea if they were even on speaking terms, thought they could be the veterans Barnett had in mind. Inspired by Diltz's book, he also had what he considered the perfect idea for them: an album of versions of songs by their California rock peers, with the working title *Laurel Canyon*.

Barnett, who turned out to have fond memories of Crosby, Stills, Nash and Young, was thrilled with the idea, and in almost no time, Landers found himself meeting Nash at the home of their managers, Cree and Buddha Miller, to fill them in on his concept. The next day, Nash called Landers and said, "Jay, you've come up with the first idea my partners instantly agreed to in forty years." With hardly any effort on their part, the trio had their first major-label record deal in over a decade—two albums, one of covers, the other a Christmas collection, with a combined, respectable six-figure advance.

By the time the deal was announced in the summer of 2008, a new and even more exciting twist was attached to it. Early in the discussions, Landers and Barnett brought up a natural choice for a collaborator on the covers album: Rick Rubin, who'd recently been appointed co-chairman of the label. Rubin, who was all of six years old when *Crosby, Stills & Nash* was released, had made his name in the '80s with hip hop; as co-owner of Def Jam Records and a fledgling producer, he had worked with LL Cool J, the Beastie Boys and Public Enemy and, in the '90s, had sonically reshaped bands like the Red Hot Chili Peppers. Germane to Crosby, Stills and Nash, he had also rebirthed Johnny Cash with a series of to-the-bone albums that salvaged Cash's recording career and connected him to a new generation by way of smartly chosen covers of alternative rock songs. If Rubin could take the same tack with Crosby, Stills and Nash—and if the label could use the album to remind everyone of their place in rock history without Young, as they insisted—the trio could be similarly reborn, similarly retro "cool."

Rubin and Landers began a series of phone conversations to discuss which songs from that era the trio could tackle; two of Landers' early suggestions were Jackson Browne's "Jamaica Say You Will" and "Rock Me on the Water." Landers was therefore surprised when Nash called him one day to ask why he hadn't attended a meeting with Rubin and the group. Landers had no idea the get-together had even been scheduled and soon deduced that Rubin wanted to produce the record himself. In light of Rubin's track record and reputation, Landers understood and stepped aside. The changeover made sense on certain levels, but it would also prove the undoing of the trio's last chance at remaking itself in the new century.

"Lots of opportunities for us to fall on our asses!" Stills wheezed half-merrily as he made his way into a crowded rehearsal space in Manhattan.

With the Rubin project still in its early stages, Crosby, Stills and Nash had taken a break. On a midafternoon in October 2009, they gathered in a windowless space in the Chelsea neighborhood with members of their band as well as Bonnie Raitt, Jackson Browne and James Taylor. In a few short days, they would all be taking part in a concert celebrating the twenty-fifth anniversary of the Rock & Roll Hall of Fame, into which all four members of CSNY had been inducted (CSN as a trio, Young as a solo act, and individually as members of the Byrds or Buffalo Springfield). The concerts, presenting two nights of start-to-finish rock legends, including Mick Jagger, Bruce Springsteen, Lou Reed, Simon and Garfunkel, U2, Jerry Lee Lewis and many more, offered up the latest possibility of a Crosby, Stills, Nash and Young reunion.

That summer, they had had a close call when the trio and Young were slotted to play on consecutive days at the Glastonbury Festival in England. Posters for the event hinted that the four might end up on the stage together. "Of course, the festival had to promote the 'reunion,'" Stills grumbled to Greene of *Rolling Stone*. "They had a whole spread, a picture of the four of us. I kid you not. It's totally misleading." The Hall of Fame concerts a few months later afforded another, far more concrete opportunity. As planned from the beginning, each segment of the shows would focus on one artist or genre and include guest appearances by fellow musicians or predecessors in that field. (Simon and Garfunkel's spot, for instance, would include an appearance by some of their doo-wop heroes, such as Dion.) Early on, it was decided that one segment would be devoted to singer-songwriter rock—and, in a perfect world, would be centered around Crosby, Stills, Nash and Young, along with appearances by some of their peers.

The concert organizers included Jann Wenner, the editor and founder of *Rolling Stone*, and Joel Gallen, a television director and producer. They had a feeling Young might not be inclined to join in, especially after his criticisms of the TV tapings of the annual Hall of Fame induction ceremony for VH1. But they asked his manager, Elliot Roberts, anyway; Roberts didn't say no and said he would pass along the invitation to Young. Assuming Young would ultimately decline, Wenner reached out to the likes of Browne and Raitt. As the weeks and months went by, no further updates arrived. In the days leading up to the concerts, Gallen held out hope that Young would show. "I didn't think there were tremendous odds it would happen, but we always felt there was some possibility," he says. "Neil can be a last-minute guy." Finally, the word came down that Young would not attend. No reason was ever given, so no one knew if he didn't want to be on the same stage with certain people or simply didn't feel comfortable with the concert and presentation. (Young tended to revel in nostalgia only on his own terms, as in his reunion tours with Crazy Horse.) Young was then offered a guest spot during a "Crosby, Stills, Nash and Friends" segment, so he wouldn't have to play with them the entire time, but that offer didn't elicit a response, either.

Still, the mood at SIR Studios on West Twenty-Fifth Street was bustling and upbeat, with musicians, managers, technicians and stone-faced security guards clogging up the various practice rooms and doorways. As Crosby, Stills, Nash and James Taylor milled around in one room, waiting for their equipment to be set up, they heard a roar in the outside hallway: Bruce Springsteen had entered the building. Nash went out and stepped onto a chair to snap a few photos of the parting of the seas. When Elvis Costello arrived, Crosby immediately made his way over to him to chat. Nearly thirty years after the infamous bar fight between Costello and members of Stills' band, these musicians were pretty much in the same boat in a twenty-first-century sea of hip hop, electronic dance music and indie rock. Everyone was a "rock veteran" now, and the old generational barriers no longer applied.

They finally assembled in one of the rooms and rehearsals for "Crosby, Stills, Nash and Friends" got underway. The musical director of the concert, Robbie Robertson, looked on. Stills had arrived a day late; his youngest son, Oliver, was turning five, so he had flown to New York the day after the birthday party, with Nash's okay. Crosby approached one of the cameramen to talk about his father's career in cinematography and how he'd visited the *High Noon* set as a child, adding that his dream job would have actually been to play a role in the much later western *Silverado*. Springing into take-charge mode, Nash announced, "Okay, we're going to run through 'Teach Your Children,'" and Taylor, Raitt and Browne took their places in front of microphones, concentrating with unblinking focus on each word as they sang. "Sounds good," Nash said when it was done. "That *could* be a hit song!" Meanwhile, Stills shouted over to Taylor, who stood at the opposite end of the lineup with his guitar, and gave him instructions on a particular chord change. Stills then went over to Taylor and slapped him playfully on the upper right arm, as if he were a bar-room buddy. Taylor seemed genuinely startled. After everyone left the room for a food break, he stayed in place with his guitar, playing the chords over and over like a student worried about letting his professor down.

After "Teach Your Children" had been rehearsed to everyone's satisfaction, Nash approached Crosby and Stills. "Guess what?" he told them. "Jackson wants to do 'The Pretender' again." They thought they'd rehearsed Browne's contribution enough already, but apparently not. Crosby dropped his chin to his chest and sighed, and Stills put a hand on Crosby's shoulder, grinned and said, in his salty-dog way, "I feel the same way, buddy!" Taking two bites of a roast beef sandwich and a swig of soda, Crosby returned to the practice room, where Browne began putting them through their paces. Stills walked in sporting a grin and a "sleeping baby" sign he'd borrowed from Cree Miller, who had brought her infant to the studio. Browne looked at the sign, smiled patiently and shook his head. He didn't know Stills as well as he knew Crosby and Nash and was ascertaining how to work with him.

The rehearsal spotlighted what Crosby, Stills and Nash could accomplish when goaded. Along with Browne and the members of both of their bands, they began working up "The Pretender," which Crosby and Nash had sung with Browne on record in 1976. After one take, Browne stopped the band and said, "It shouldn't be so loud at the end," referring to the delicate balance of dynamics and changing instrumental volume in the song. Nash walked over to make sure Stills, who was grappling with hearing issues, had heard Browne's instructions. They started up once more, and Browne again shut it down so Crosby and Nash could further polish their harmonies. After a few more warmups, their voices sounded almost ageless. Meanwhile, Stills, cradling his electric guitar, sat glumly near an amp at the other end of the stage, unhappy at the lowered volume of his guitar. "I'll split the difference 'cuz right now I'm *inaudible,*" he grumbled. After they played the song through one more time, complete with a Stills solo that tastefully fit in with the arrangement, another break was called. Stills went over to Browne's microphone and sang in a throaty, theatrical way, "Nobody *knows* the trouble I've *seen . . .*"

Onstage at the Garden a few nights later, "Crosby, Stills, Nash and Friends" came off with no major gaffes. "The Pretender" was flawless, as was Taylor's reunion with Crosby and Nash on his "Mexico." Raitt accompanied them on slide guitar during "Midnight Rider." ("I don't own the clothes I'm wearing," Browne said, quoting a line from that song as he watched the rehearsals with Raitt. "They are that guy. Each one of them has *been* that guy.") When the segment ended, everyone congregated in the Crosby, Stills and Nash dressing room, watching the rest of the show on a monitor and chatting away. Off to the side of the room, looking disconnected from it all, sat Stills. As was often the case after one of their performances, the shyest member of the band would be the first to leave and return to the tour bus while Crosby and Nash reveled in the attention.

THE RUN-THROUGHS OF "The Pretender" would be nothing compared to the groundwork for their Columbia debut. After his first gathering with the trio, Rubin called Landers to bring him up to speed. "He went, 'It was a struggle—they really need to practice,'" Landers says. "He was saying something about Crosby not being as cooperative as he had hoped."

In Rubin's mind, the project shouldn't be limited to California singer-songwriter pop. What if it also included contemporary rock and roll they could have sung back in the late '60s while practicing at one house or another? Thus began the ritual of the lists. Rubin and the group (with help from photographer and musician Joel Bernstein, a longtime friend of the band) would compile names of possible cover versions, and Bernstein helped work up acoustic arrangements. The trio would go off, learn the tunes, then sing them for Rubin, who would choose the ones he liked before handing them another list. Eventually the inventory included material by the Beatles ("Blackbird," which they'd been performing on and off for forty years), the Rolling Stones ("Ruby Tuesday"), Bob Dylan ("Girl from the North Country"), Fred Neil ("Everybody's Talkin'," which they'd also worked up in the past), the Beach Boys ("In My Room"), the Grateful Dead ("Uncle John's Band") and the Who ("Behind Blue Eyes"). It was arduous work for a band unaccustomed to being put through such paces—and with a producer who was, to say the least, unconventional. Rubin, a soft-spoken, bearded music guru, listened more for vibe than technical aspects, and was rarely seen at the newly renovated Sony Music building in Los Angeles.

During its summer 2009 American tour, the trio began road-testing some of the cover versions onstage, and the response was largely positive. It was unusual, to say the least, to hear them play Who and Stones classics alongside their own songs, but the crowds certainly recognized the oldies and seemed open to the interpretations. Asked about the project during a break in the tour, Crosby tried to stay on the positive tip. "It's fun singing this stuff," he said. "Rick's as smart as everyone says he is. He's brilliant. He can really definitely hear well." Asked if Rubin was familiar with their work, Crosby replied, "You know, I'm not sure. I know he knows who we are. But I'm not sure which parts of who we are he is familiar with. He has said he's interested in our contemporaries. Beatles, Joni, Dylan, James [Taylor]. How that's going to pan out, I don't know."

As upbeat as he tried to be, Crosby didn't sound wholly convinced the album would come together, and Rubin's out-of-the-gate concerns about his connection with Crosby (and the work they'd have to put into evoking the olden days) would soon play out. Given the numerous projects he routinely juggled, Rubin wasn't always able to work with them steadily, and the group began to feel disrespected, as if they weren't worth his undivided attention. (Rubin declined comment for this book.) Among other suggestions, Rubin, who undoubtedly sought to make the best possible album with them at this stage of their careers, wanted the trio to sing together on the same microphone rather than record separately and combine the parts digitally. If they were standing next to each other—as Young had learned during the *Looking Forward* sessions— Rubin may have felt he could recapture their essence, but they were no longer accustomed to working that way. "I tried to reason with them and say, 'Let it go and just do it—trust someone,'" says drummer Joe Vitale. "And it was like, '*No.*' They weren't going to sit back and do what Rubin said."

According to Nash, the breaking point arrived when Rubin suggested they learn three other songs: "Morning Has Broken" by Cat Stevens, "Summer Breeze" by Seals and Crofts, and "Ventura Highway" by America. Nash says they simply could not sing the Stevens song given Stevens' 1989 comment that "[Rushdie] must be killed," after the publication of Salman Rushdie's *The Satanic Verses*, when the Ayatollah Ruhollah Khomeini of Iran had issued a *fatwa* calling for Rushdie's death (although Stevens, now using the name Yusuf Islam, later walked back his comments). The choice of "Ventura Highway" baffled everyone: They were being asked to work up a song by a band that had followed and somewhat copied them? "Some of the songs Rick wanted us to do were insane," Nash says. "How the fuck can you stand there and ask CSN to do 'Ventura-fucking-Highway'?" The group wanted to cover two Beatles songs, "Blackbird" and "Across the Universe," but Rubin preferred they limit it to one; Crosby insisted that he and his bandmates, not Rubin, should make that call. "Without being unkind to Rick, it was the wrong chemistry," Crosby says. "It was never going to work. I didn't have a good feeling about it right from the get-go." Asked about the progress of the album in early 2010, Stills almost uttered something, then mimed closing an imaginary zipper across his mouth.

Before any official recording sessions had taken place, the project collapsed. "I was relieved when it ended," Crosby says. "There wasn't a record there. I didn't think the choice of songs was correct at all. And that highlighted the fact that they were coming from Rick. Wrong guy." Crosby, Stills and Nash weren't the only ones who were thankful: Sony, Columbia's parent company, was so eager to be done with the project that the executives allowed the group to keep their $300,000 advance, a highly unusual move.

The end of the deal was announced in January 2011. (Rubin himself, who never quite gelled with the label, would exit Columbia the following year.) Without Rubin, they tried to keep the covers concept afloat, renting out Browne's studio and recording a few of the remakes themselves, but it soon petered out. "We cut five things in four days," says Crosby. "It was relatively easy. Still, there wasn't a record there. We'd already spoiled the pie." The Christmas album never even got that far. The rebirth of the band was over before it had barely begun.

TALKING WITH A FRIEND, Young was asked about the possibility of working with Crosby, Stills and Nash again. "Yeah, you can *do* that," he replied wryly, "but then you're dealing with David Crosby. And Stephen Stills. And Graham Nash." The thought of it—the internal politics, the psycho-dramas, the ego-juggling—could be overwhelming. But another possibility remained tantalizingly out of reach. Vitale first heard about it while on tour with Crosby, Stills and Nash in the summer of 2010, when Stills asked him during a bus ride if he was interested in becoming the drummer in Buffalo Springfield.

Despite its exceedingly brief run, the Springfield had remained close to the heart for both Young and Stills; for all the drama in *that* group, both looked back with doting fondness on the band, those years and their youth. The original Springfield had regrouped every so often, mostly for casual jam sessions, but with the annual Bridge School benefit approaching in the fall of 2010, Young gave the revival more serious thought. By then, two of the founding members had died: Bruce Palmer had succumbed to a heart attack in 2004, and Dewey Martin to unspecified natural causes five years later. That still left Stills, Young and Richie Furay, who had become a conservative-leaning pastor in Colorado. Young reached out to the other two, who were up for a Bridge School reunion. Per tradition, Stills and Young divvied up the rhythm section: Stills was able to use Vitale, while Young recruited one of his bass players, Rick Rosas. Working up songs they hadn't played in decades—including the multipart "Broken Arrow"—the group rehearsed at an empty theater in San Francisco. In a bar after one practice, Young approached Rosas and Vitale and said, "So what's it like to be in the Springfield, guys?" It was all happening so quickly; it felt too good to be true.

As Crosby, Stills and Nash were grappling with the Rubin project, Young immersed himself in his usual bevy of projects, rolling out a new album nearly every year. He also became obsessed with fuel conservation, converting his 1959 Lincoln Continental into LincVolt, a vehicle that would run on electricity or natural gas. With songs titled "Get Behind the Wheel" and "Fuel Line," his 2009 album *Fork in the Road* was nearly a concept album about that project; "Just Singing a Song" argued that saving the planet was more important than making music. For the follow-up, he, like Crosby, Stills and Nash, opted to work with a younger, authenticity-inclined producer: in his case, Daniel Lanois, who frequently collaborated with U2 and Dylan. *Le Noise*, a play on the producer's name, was both familiar and singular. At heart, it was the sound of Young singing and playing, backed only by his guitar. One of the tunes was also recognizable: written in 1976 and long bootlegged, "Hitchhiker" was a detailed and far from flattering chronicle of his mid-decade ennui, although the *Le Noise* version included an updated verse in which he expressed thanks for his kids and loyal spouse. Other, brand-new songs returned to recognizable topics: "Love and War" recalled the tales of soldiers in *Living with War*, and "Peaceful Valley Boulevard," a history of America from the takeover of Native American lands to the impacts of climate change, continued the bullet-scarred landscapes in everything from "Down by the River" to "Powderfinger" to "Driveby." (Crosby may have been the gun-toter of the band, but Young, interestingly, wrote about weapons and their lethal implications far more regularly.) But Lanois swathed Young's voice and songs in waves of electric guitars, which rumbled and whooshed around Young as if he were turning himself into a one-man Crazy Horse. The sonic boost transformed *Le Noise* into a haunted, gothic-forest album, a welcome return to form after undistinguished 2000s records like *Prairie Wind* and *Fork in the Road*.

Though rarely one to dwell in the past, Young had spent the preceding decade dipping into it more than usual. The Springfield boxed set of 2001 was one such move. In 2009, he rolled out the first volume of his long-in-the-works *Archives* retrospective, eight CDs with 128 songs, some released, some surfacing for the first time. Young had been shaping his own retrospectives as far back as 1977's *Decade*, but *Archives*, accompanied by an inches-thick scrapbook of lyrics and photos, took his self-cataloging to a new, hippie-librarian level of fastidiousness. To the surprise of Crosby, Stills and Nash, it also included several live recordings and concert footage from their 1970 Fillmore East shows. "Without asking our permission," Nash shrugged later. "It's Neil's world."

Stills remained aware of the vastly different public perceptions of his work compared to Young's. "Who knew that Neil would step in there and keep coming back?" he told *Uncut* in 2009. "He makes this whole succession of really bad albums, and then pops up a good one and suddenly he's preeminent again." A portrait of Young taken by Nash (the same one later appeared on the cover of Jimmy McDonough's Young-authorized biography, *Shakey*) was mounted in Stills' living room, but he could also still be competitive with him. Starting in 2006, separate boxed sets devoted to the solo works of Crosby, Stills and Nash began rolling out. Nash's and Crosby's each contained three discs, but when Stills learned of the massive size of Young's *Archives*, he made sure that his collection contained at least four CDs. Called *Carry On*, it made the case that he had been unjustly underrated; as a special treat, it contained the version of "Black Coral" from the aborted 1976 Crosby, Stills, Nash and Young recordings with Nash and Crosby's harmonies still intact—apparently, their voices hadn't been wiped out completely.

Over the course of two rainy nights at the Shoreline Amphitheatre in Mountain View, California, in October 2010, Buffalo Springfield rumbled back to life—even though only with acoustic guitars and a rhythm section—and the songs, from "Nowadays Clancy Can't Even Sing" to "On the Way Home," survived the more rugged voices singing them. The shows went so well that the band regrouped six months later for a handful of West Coast shows (Tom Petty sat happily in the first row at one of them), as well as a performance at the Bonnaroo Music and Arts Festival in Tennessee in mid-2011. A full thirty-show East Coast tour was planned for the fall of that year. Stills opted out of a summer Crosby, Stills and Nash tour as a result, and Vitale canceled other work assignments to clear the way for the Springfield.

But the group's twisted history repeated itself when Young changed his mind and canceled the fall trek, and Buffalo Springfield again became extinct. Later, a source told *Rolling Stone* that Young was "disappointed with their playing," but whatever the reason, the other band members, Stills in particular, were stunned or livid, particularly over the loss of income. "Neil's doing what will take the music to a place he wants it to go," Crosby says. "He's been pretty consistent about that. He runs over people and fucks people over when he's doing it, but that's not his primary concern. His concern is making sure the music goes where he wants it to go. Looking at it from the outside, it's easy to say, 'Neil, what the fuck?' But in his mind, he's following his muse. It's led him astray sometimes, but it's also led him into some great areas."

Young further baffled his Springfield comrades by returning to Crazy Horse, with whom he recorded not one but two albums: an idiosyncratic collection of folk and rock oldies called *Americana* and a two-disc set of new material, *Psychedelic Pill*. The latter resurrected the fluid, long-and-winding Horse jams of the past, albeit to lyrics that were bizarrely stream of consciousness even when painting a portrait of a booze-soaked relationship ("Ramada Inn") or saluting Dylan and the Dead ("Twisted

Road"). Its most compelling number, "Walk Like a Giant," described the dashed hopes of his generation; it was one of the most resigned songs Young had ever written.

Perhaps in keeping with that song, Young's interest in the quartet seemed to dim considerably. In 2013, they regrouped one more time at a Bridge School benefit, but the performance was under-rehearsed, and Young spent much of it wandering around behind the trio as they sang. Pegi Young thinks he may have been "playing to the kids," the physically challenged students who sat behind the stage, but for Nash, "it was a little nerve-wracking. I wasn't crazy about Neil walking all over the place." The following year, *CSNY 1974*, a boxed set of live recordings from that year's tour painstakingly pieced together by Nash, Bernstein and loyal engineer Stanley Tajima Johnston, was finally completed. With its inclusion of new material by all four, the album dispelled the notion that Young was the only one who was actively creative at that time. And with its group versions of "Carry On," "My Angel" and "Pushed It Over the End," among others, it was the closest anyone would ever come to hearing the aborted *Human Highway* reunion album. Not surprisingly, Young, who had long expressed his disillusionment with that tour and the way he had written the bulk of its new material, signed off on *CSNY 1974* but didn't consent to even a single interview to promote it.

In the 2010s, the Crosby, Stills and Nash road machine carried on with added technological help. Stills had been talked into using in-ear monitors so he could hear himself better, and his singing and guitar playing, while not quite at 1970 levels, recovered enough. The additional musicians now included a new guitarist, seasoned British musician Shane Fontayne, who was less obtrusive on stage than his predecessor, Jeff Pevar, and knew how to take a low-key role when playing in the band. The other musicians continued to join in on the harmonies to bolster the group's sometimes shaggy vocal sound.

They could still get into testy public debates. Visiting the *Rolling Stone* offices in 2008 to talk about their fortieth anniversary, their first singing session came up. Stills still insisted it occurred at Cass Elliot's house. Crosby immediately shot him down: "You are welcome to it, man, [but] you're wrong. But it's okay, we love you anyway." Shooting Crosby a look that wasn't quite loaded with affection, Stills retorted, "Yeah, well, then quit with a smug look, 'cause you're wrong."

"No, I'm not," said Crosby.

In light of the collapse of the Rubin album and their own subsequent effort to salvage it without him, the odds of another record emerging from them seemed slim to none. With record sales sinking, thanks to streaming and downloading, many of their peers were beginning to feel the same way about recording and releasing new material: Why bother if the sales would be minimal and there wouldn't be much of an industry to support it? Instead, Crosby, Stills and Nash opted to follow the example of Jackson Browne and launch their own label. Next to the possibility of a Rick Rubin–helmed record, the first release on CSN Records, a live album called *CSN 2012*, was a considerable letdown, a largely redundant retread of the old hits.

Thanks to a startling turn of events few would have expected—even given the decades of dysfunction—CSN Records would exist for a total of one release. The disorder began in the summer of 2013, when Nash published his memoir, *Wild Tales*, with help from writer Bob Spitz. Surveying his life from childhood through the later days of the band, the book placed particular emphasis on Crosby's decline and fall (although not in as much candid and often squeamish detail as Crosby himself had done in *Long Time Gone*, his first memoir). Nash says he had the trio's managers send advance copies to Crosby and Stills for their approval; if they had any objections, material could be removed. Stills had a few concerns, but Crosby claims he never received the advance copy; by the time he read it (and asked his friend Bobby Hammer to fact-check it), he was told it was too late to make changes.

Up to that point, the bond between Nash and Crosby had appeared to be unbreakable. Starting with Crosby's addiction and his friends' failed interventions (and then his imprisonment), their alliance had survived more than anyone could have expected. After Crosby was released from prison, Nash had helped him and Jan find a house by cosigning a lease and lending them rent money. The two still gravitated together musically, embarking on duo tours in the 2000s that made little money but allowed them to play songs outside the group standards. That bond could fray at times. One evening in the late '90s, James and Stacia Raymond had an unexpected midnight visit from the Crosbys. Crosby, still wearing the suit and tie he had donned for an industry event with Nash, told them he had had an argument with his old friend. According to Stacia, Crosby was "completely freaked out and shaking," although she didn't ask specifically what had caused the fight. As in other breakdowns, though, Crosby and Nash managed to patch it up. As recently as 2007, Crosby had told *Classic Rock* magazine that Nash was "a wonderful man, a true Renaissance man . . . an honorable man, which is rare, very rare. He's been as good a friend to me as a human being could be."

Wild Tales extended Nash's tradition of both upholding the band and upsetting their apple cart. But starting with Crosby's reaction, it would have several band-shattering ramifications. In an interview with *Rolling Stone* six months after the book's release, the normally talkative Crosby went silent when asked about *Wild Tales*. But friends sensed Crosby felt betrayed by the emphasis on Crosby's foibles over Nash's own exploits, although Nash was unapologetic. "I copped to all the drugs I took and copped to being unfaithful," he responded. "I don't know what dirt there was about me that I needed to say. One thing David doesn't understand is that every fucked-up decision he made affected *me* and that's what I wrote about. It affected me on a very deep level. He was my best friend."

As always, they shelved their discontent and went on tour in the summer of 2014. But another, weightier shoe dropped months later. To the astonishment of many in the music community, not to mention Young's fans, Young filed for divorce from Pegi that season, after thirty-six years of marriage. "We were having a rough patch," Pegi admitted to *Rolling Stone* two years later. "But I never would've thought in a million years we would be getting divorced. So, yeah, there was a bit of a shock value there." Young had a new partner, actress and activist Daryl Hannah. The year before, Hannah had accompanied Young for part of a cross-country drive in his LincVolt. One newspaper report described her as a "friend," but the two had clearly connected.

In interviews—and now on social media platforms—Crosby was rarely known to hold back; his Twitter swipes at everyone from the Doors ("the band never swung once") to Kanye West ("useless as tits on a bull") to Taylor Swift ("shallow") would give his account must-read status. At times, his public comments stirred up more than he'd hoped, no more so than in September 2014. During an interview with the *Idaho Statesman*, he was asked about Young's divorce and relationship with Hannah. "I happen to know that he's hanging out with somebody that's a purely poisonous predator now," Crosby said. "And that's karma. He's gonna get hurt. But I understand why it happened. I'm just sad about it. I'm always sad when I see love get tossed in the gutter." Crosby later claimed he had been talking off the record (the reporter, Michael Deeds, says Crosby gave no indication he was doing so), but the damage was done; the quote went viral almost immediately.

Dating back to the earliest days of the quartet, Young and Crosby had had a mutually supportive friendship. Young admired Crosby's cheerleading ability with the band (if not, most likely, his dismissive comments toward Crazy Horse), and Crosby's rebel-king attitude appealed to Young's anticonformist ways. Crosby had been there for Young when support was needed, and Young had repaid the favor, as much as he could, during Crosby's addiction days. Even if *American Dream* had been a dissatisfying experience, Young's pledge to rejoin the band if Crosby cleaned up was a sincere offer to help. In 2010, *Rolling Stone's* Andy Greene asked Crosby if there was any truth to rumors of a Crosby, Stills, Nash and Young tour. "God, I wish it were [true], you know," Crosby replied. "It's really exciting music and it's one of the ones that I like to do really a lot. I love working with Neil because he pushes the envelope. I feel really good making music with him. I love it." Young similarly had fond words for Crosby in his 2012 memoir, *Waging Heavy Peace*, where he also made room for flattering comments about Stills' musicianship and Nash's harmonies. Having seemingly mellowed about the group compared to earlier, harsher comments, Young now wrote glowingly about his time with the trio.

Crosby's remarks about Hannah, though, shattered his alliance with Young, at least in the immediate months and years that followed. Niko Bolas, the engineer and producer who'd worked with Young on and off since the '80s, was driving to Capitol Studios in Hollywood to work on Young's next record when the musician called to tell him about Crosby's comments. Young, Bolas says, was "less than enthused," to put it mildly. "Big-time pissed" is the way Young's longtime friend James Mazzeo puts it. According to Bolas, the comments didn't break Young's concentration. "Nothing affects Neil when it comes to the work," he says. "Everything fuels it." Young told Bolas he hadn't written a new song in years but, in part because of his relationship with Hannah, he had a fresh batch ready to go. After singing his tunes to Bolas, Young returned to perform them, live, in front of an orchestra, even unearthing Barbra Streisand's microphone for added vintage feel. "Neil was fearless," Bolas says. "He's standing in the middle of the room with ninety people around him all looking at his music. You talk about the willingness to be naked. I know very few human beings who can do that." Young's concentration only seemed to be broken occasionally when he would call Hannah on his tablet. "Put the iPad down—we have to sing," Bolas would order him. On the 2014 album that came to be known as *Storytone*, string arrangements lent Young's songs a dreamy, romantic feel unlike anything he'd done in years.

Shortly before the album came out, and about a month after Crosby's reported comments, Young was asked about the state of the band at a public interview during the annual New Yorker Festival. "Nash, Stills and Young?" he replied, straight-faced. He denied any "feud" and spoke glowingly of Stills as his "brother"—"There will never be another Stephen Stills"—but couldn't even bring himself to utter Crosby's name.

Eight months later, Crosby would apologize to Hannah while appearing on Howard Stern's satellite radio show. In the spring of 2017, he amplified those comments: "I'm not in a position to criticize anybody. I've made more mistakes than anybody I know of who's still alive. So I apologized for it. I didn't have any right to criticize his choice. I called Neil up and said, 'Listen, Neil, that was wrong. I said it off the record but I don't think I had the right to say that.' It was a mistake but not the worst I've ever made." Nash, meanwhile, wondered why it took Crosby so long to offer an apology, further imperiling any future CSNY reunion tours.

In November 2015, Hannah threw Young a seventieth birthday party in Los Angeles. Stills and Nash were invited and attended; Crosby was noticeably absent. Whether it was coincidental or not, Young's 2016 concert album *Earth* included a new version of "Hippie Dream," his devastating flame-throwing of Crosby during his low point as an imprisoned addict. It had not appeared on a record of his since 1986.

NASH's *Wild Tales* would rattle another relationship close to the band. In the book, he wrote glowingly of his wife, Susan, and their enduring marriage, which had survived his frequent infidelities. In chronicling it all, though, Nash experienced a life-changing realization. "It was only after it came out that I began to really absorb what I had done with my life," he says. "I began to realize that what I thought were the happiest parts of my life in fact weren't. I said, 'Look, how much longer is my life going on? I can just settle and coast through it or I'll follow what my heart said I should be doing.' Which is what I did."

Backstage at a Crosby, Stills and Nash concert at the Beacon Theatre in New York in 2014, Nash, then seventy-two, met Amy Grantham, a photographer, artist and cancer survivor who was almost exactly half Nash's age. Within months, Nash had separated from Susan and was spending time with Grantham on the East Coast, where she was based. It wasn't long before divorce proceedings between the Nashes began. "I was getting older and I wasn't in love with Susan anymore," Nash says. The separation shook Nash's family. "I understand the pain I've put them through, but I had to save *my* life," Nash explained. "There's only *me* in here. And I've got to be whatever 'happy' is, because I'm coming to the end of my life."

Simultaneously, Nash, long credited with trying to hold the group together as a working band and business, even during its bleakest years, lost patience with them. The collapse of the Rick Rubin album was one of the first points of exhaustion. "It was actually getting to be typical," he says. "It almost felt like the myth of Sisyphus, in a way, pushing a big rock up a hill. And it's slipping back occasionally and pushing it further and it's slipping back." The way he, Stills and Crosby were excluded from the making of the *CSNY/Déjà vu* movie provoked Nash to send a long, enraged email to Young in 2010, in which he resurrected all the ways he'd felt disrespected over the decades: the time Young pulled songs from the 1991 *CSN* boxed set, the argument over Nash licensing songs to commercials, and now the movie. "I asked him who made him king of the world," Nash recalls. "There's *four* of us here. And I've always felt that Neil in a way treated us as background singers. It wasn't nice." According to Nash, Young wrote back, "What a load of shit," but later sent a follow-up note saying he had been coping with the sudden death of his friend and musical soulmate Ben Keith.

In addition, onstage and off, Nash and Crosby were suddenly being sharp with one another, like an old married couple who could no longer tolerate each other's idiosyncrasies. In September 2015, the trio took part in a cruise on the *Queen Mary 2*, where fans paid a minimum of $1,499 per cabin to sail with them (and see them perform on the boat) from New York to Southampton, England. Aboard the boat, Crosby seemed uncommonly subdued, and to a friend who was there, Nash compared the trip to the *Titanic*. (Stills, on the other hand, grew unusually animated during one shipboard dinner, sharing stories and laughs with Crosby's daughter-in-law Stacia, who had never seen him lighten up that much.) To the bafflement of the fans aboard, the trio didn't eat or mingle with them during the entire trip.

Then, on December 3, 2015, the trio were invited to perform at the annual tree-lighting ceremony at the White House, joined by an odd-lot lineup that included the emo-punk band Fall Out Boy, the US Coast Guard Band, and Miss Piggy from *Sesame Street*. Putting off their song choice until the last moment, Crosby, Stills and Nash settled on "Silent Night," the simplest and quickest Christmas carol to learn. But silent would not be the word for what followed. At the beginning of the performance, each man was supposed to say his name and state his favorite national park, with the help of a teleprompter. By mistake—although others weren't so sure—Crosby began his part and kept going, reading everyone's lines. Confused and realizing Crosby was talking over him, Stills shot his partner a sharp look and flicked a guitar pick at him in disgust—all as the event was being live-streamed. "I can't *believe* you," Stills said to Crosby, for all to hear, as they were about to start singing. If that wasn't uncomfortable enough, the microphone feeds were not properly synced, leading to cringingly out-of-tune harmonies. "It was horrifying," Crosby says. "They had mixed up the monitor feeds so Stills was getting Nash's feed and I was getting Stills'. Stills couldn't hear himself and didn't know what he was doing. They had some words we were supposed to say in sequence and I didn't get the sequence right. Stills was really mad at me."

To Stacia Raymond, it was a telling sign of the bandmates' long-simmering resentments. "When you let hurtful things go by without addressing them and just let them fester and pile up, then of course a couple years later someone's going to lose their shit," she says, recalling how one of the trio's tours in the mid-2000s almost shut down early after a blowup. "And that's what happens. And it's so violent and it's so bad when it happens that it makes it harder and harder each time it does happen to ever come back from that. They're human and they're allowed to make mistakes. They're allowed to hurt each other. But then what do you do afterward?"

That night, tensions truly boiled over. In the backstage green room afterward, Stills and Crosby had words: Stills snapped at Crosby for speaking his lines, and Crosby shot back about Stills not singing in key. Nearby but with his back to them, Nash heard someone gasp—and turned around to see Crosby and Stills lunging at each other. A member of their management team jumped to attention and pulled the two apart. All the strains that had been simmering between them for decades—dating back, at the very least, to the Stills and Crosby shouting match that had been captured on film at the Shady Oak house in the summer of 1969—erupted like a geyser.

Asked by *Rolling Stone* in 2008 whether they would still be a working band in another ten years, Crosby had replied, "I just don't know, man. The answer is when it isn't fun, we won't do it." Nash added, "And when that is, we have no idea." The day after the Christmas tree ceremony, they knew.

BY THEN, THE rhythm of their lives and interactions—the coming together, the collision, the breakup, the reconsolidation—were like twisted clockwork. Even after a successful reunion, it would only be a matter of time before one of the wheels would come off their bus. Now, fifty years on, they had come full circle to where they were before they banded together.

Back in the late '60s, Crosby and Nash, while having already met, were still in their own worlds—Nash in the Hollies and Crosby looking for a life and career after the Byrds. They were living thousands of miles apart. Now, all these decades later, the two men were once more living separate lives. Nash had fully relocated to New York City and lived in an apartment in the East Village, just blocks away from the former location of the Fillmore East. Shortly after his break with Crosby and Stills in 2016, he returned to his own career—much as, during his waning days with the Hollies, he'd felt it was time to express himself. In another repeat, divorcing his longtime wife, Susan, and moving far away to be with a new partner echoed how he'd left his first wife, Rose, in England and moved to America, where he eventually moved in with Joni Mitchell. With Fontayne as his new collaborator and co-songwriter, he pounded out a slew of songs that addressed his new love and the uncertain road he was now navigating personally and professionally. The album, *This Path Tonight*, arrived only months after Crosby, Stills and Nash had essentially disbanded.

About fifty years before, Crosby had been booted out of the Byrds and was forced to forge a new sound with new partners. Now that he and Nash were no longer on speaking terms, that cycle, too, repeated itself. Knowing full well that his ravaged body could betray him at any moment, Crosby—who had undergone bypass surgery in 2014—began urgently making up for lost time, fashioning the albums of his own music that he'd neglected to make over the dissolute decades. On 2014's *Croz*, collaborators like Fontayne and James Raymond supplied him with crisp guitars ("Set That Baggage Down") and smooth hooks ("Radio"), and new Crosby songs, including "Time I Have," which grappled with balancing contentment and anger, addressed his mortality. He began working with the New York–based multi-instrumentalist and producer Michael League—who, despite being forty-two years younger than Crosby, shared the same inclination toward the experimental, jazzy and abstract. League, who also fronted the band Snarky Puppy, produced and played on Crosby's next album, *Lighthouse*, which focused on Crosby's voice and acoustic guitars—no drums or electric guitars. *Lighthouse* evoked the loose-fitting, hazy-days mood of *If I Could Only Remember My Name*, and though it lacked that album's moments of gorgeous intensity, the bossa-nova feel of "Look in Their Eyes," and songs like his springy ode to New York, "The City," were the kind of delicate beauties Crosby had concocted decades before. When Crosby recruited League and singer-songwriter-musicians Michelle Willis and Becca Stevens for

his touring band, he had a new part-time group, and the addition of female voices added a never-before-heard element to his music. Reteam-
ing with Raymond, with Jeff Pevar on guitar, Crosby then completed
Sky Trails, his third album in three years, which reveled in smart Steely
Dan–style pop. Crosby was now dubbed one of the founding fathers of
"yacht rock," as pop-culture ironists called the soft rock of the '70s and
'80s. It was hard to imagine a more unexpected second–third? fourth?–
wind in pop music.

Just as Crosby and Nash had returned to their separate corners, replicating the days before they met, Stills and Young also circled back to life
circa 1967 and 1968. With his ex-wife, Pegi, taking over the ranch after their
divorce, Young moved south to Los Angeles–for the first time since the
mid-'70s–to be with Hannah; in doing so, he began reconnecting more
with Stills. The odds of another Buffalo Springfield resurrection were
slim (in fact, a 2018 Springfield tribute concert in Los Angles included
only Richie Furay), but the two began spending more time together than
they had in years, and Young participated in Stills' annual Light Up the
Blues benefits for autism. (Stills and his wife Kristen's oldest son, Henry,
had been diagnosed with the condition.) Given all the upheavals in his
own life, Young appeared to find new comfort in playing guitar onstage
alongside Stills, who was one of a dwindling group of his musical compadres and collaborators. By then, the long, sobering list of deceased
musical collaborators and backup musicians (for Young and any of the
trio) included their old art director Gary Burden, producer David Briggs,
former Manassas percussionist Joe Lala, Young's longtime sideman and
touring partner Ben Keith, bassists Tim Drummond and Rick Rosas,
Young's filmmaking collaborator Larry "L.A." Johnson, and former group
drummer Dallas Taylor.

Even before the group fallout of 2015, Stills had been tooling around
new avenues. He'd been approached about re-creating *Super Session*,
the 1968 surprise-hit jam album he done with Al Kooper and the late
Mike Bloomfield. When Kooper wasn't available, ideas for other guitarists
were bandied about, and they settled on the youngish sparkplug Kenny
Wayne Shepard, along with a keyboardist, Barry Goldberg, who had also
been part of the original *Super Session* project. Thus was born the Rides,
which finally gave Stills a full-on outlet for the blues-warrior side he

had long had to suppress in Crosby, Stills and Nash. The group made two blues and boogie albums; the second one, *Pierced Arrow*, featured "Virtual World," a Stills-sung lament on the impact of social media that, unlike "Seen Enough," was fluid and touching. Stills seemed both cognizant of and embarrassed by his past exploits, but given that people in the music business had been predicting his demise since the '70s, at least he could say he'd outlasted and outlived his dark periods.

In an even more striking example of the circle-game aspect of this point in all their lives, Stills was suddenly reunited with his great lost love of 1968, Judy Collins. The two had remained friends in the decades since; in 2009, they had cut a remake of Tom Paxton's "The Last Thing on My Mind" for one of Collins' albums. (At Collins' studio in New York, Stills noticed the corns on her feet and was immediately reminded of how her feet had looked back then.) In 2017, they finally made their first complete album together, *Everybody Knows*. Then they embarked on a series of tours in which they played songs about each other, from a bit of "Suite: Judy Blue Eyes" to Collins' "Houses" and Stills' "So Begins the Task." During the duo's summer 2017 tour, Stills looked and sounded more relaxed onstage than he had during his later years with Crosby and Nash, and his guitar playing, while not fully recapturing the lucidity of his '60s and '70s work, regained some of its delicate nuances. Like Crosby, he also dropped some of the extra weight he'd been carrying for years. "He's very relieved," Collins says brightly when asked how Stills was holding up in light of his group's collapse. "He's taking care of himself now. When you're faced with autism, you grow up a lot." Collins also seemed to know instinctively that confronting Stills would not pull the best out of him. (Young had once told Crosby not to criticize Stills if he played badly, but only to encourage him.) When Collins and Nash ran into each other at a concert in New York just before the start of the Stills-Collins tour, Nash said, "Stephen is so wonderful and he's the last person to know it." Collins detected a degree of envy on Nash's part that she, not he, would be hitting the road with Stills.

In 2018, fifty years after he'd met them, Young circled back as well, reconvening with a revised version of Crazy Horse: Ralph Molina on drums, Billy Talbot on bass and, substituting for Frank "Poncho" Sampedro on guitar, Nils Lofgren, who himself had first worked with Young and the

Horse all those decades ago. Young began opening up even more of his archives, thanks to a relaunched website, and he continued pumping out albums at a pace that shamed every one of his boomer-rock peers. The albums were spotty and made one wonder how David Briggs—Young's producer, friend and quality-control gatekeeper, who succumbed to lung cancer in 1995—would have felt about them. But Young refused to sit still. When making *Peace Trail* in Los Angeles in 2016, he invited Jim Keltner to the studio to try out a few new songs. One day turned into four, and Keltner was shocked when Young used an early run-through of one of the songs—not even a fully practiced tape—for the album. "With Neil, you usually get the first take, maybe the second," Keltner says, "but in this case, not even a take. I was still learning the song. And, of course, that's what goes on the record." It would have been unimaginable for Crosby, Stills or Nash to release anything so unpolished; half a century later, the keen differences in record making between the two camps were still in effect.

They had now shifted archetypes: Nash was the rebel, Crosby and Stills the domesticated husbands, but Young was still the ornery loner, traversing his own proudly idiosyncratic route (and eventually marrying Hannah in the summer of 2018, although he would lose his home in the devastating California fires that fall). During the making of *Peace Trail*, Young played a guitar part that struck Keltner as unlike any sound he'd made before. "You're playing different," Keltner said.

"*Everything's* different now," Young said, not unhappily.

IN THE FALL OF 2017, Nash sat in a coffee shop a block away from his new Manhattan home. Confirming his worst fears, he scrawled through the lyrics to Young's new album, *The Visitor*.

In the months that followed the Christmas concert debacle, Nash continued upending his life, telling any reporter who would ask that Crosby had wrecked the band and that he, Nash, was never going to sing with him again. Nash had said similar things about Stills and Young exactly forty years before, but now his words had a rattling finality to them. Although he mostly held his tongue publicly, Crosby did take a few digs at Nash's book on his Twitter account, as well as in a 2016 newspaper interview. The back and forth was just another extension of the barbs they had all shot at each other over the decades—ones that would eventually be forgotten—but with a new Crosby-versus-Nash twist. This go-round, Crosby never went as far as Nash had and claimed he would eagerly work with the quartet again (but not the Crosby, Stills and Nash configuration), but longtime friends and associates remained stunned at the latest, least expected turn in the saga.

As ever, Young had continued to chug along without them. With Hannah in the director's chair, he returned to movie making, acting and performing in an oddball western called *Paradox*. On tours, he was joined most often by Promise of the Real, a scruffy roots band fronted by Willie Nelson's son, a scruffy singer, songwriter and guitarist named Lukas, with Lukas' brother, Micah, sometimes participating. They were younger, more energized and less prone to internal drama and baggage than Crazy Horse. And with their prodding, Young was giving newly revved-up shows that dug deeper into his back catalog. His anger toward the corporatization of the country spilled out into the first record he made with them, 2015's *The Monsanto Years*. Starting with *Living with War*, Young had become a late-bloomer protest songwriter, and *The Monsanto Years* aimed its arrows at Walmart, Starbucks and Chevron, while also announcing he was in love again.

Young recorded another album, *The Visitor*, with Promise of the Real during the first year of Donald Trump's presidency. In it, he issued a series of calls to resist those in power, oppose the "Boy King" running America, and fight for the planet, the environment and women's rights. The songs weren't as specific in their targets as those on *The Monsanto Years*, and neither record had Young's most memorable melodies, but *The Visitor* was nevertheless another topical-song grenade.

In light of the Freedom of Speech Tour, it would have been easy to imagine Young singing those songs with three people in particular. But it wasn't to be. Looking at the lyrics to *The Visitor* in an email on a cellphone, Nash, who still sported a sizable wave of hair, read slowly, carefully and quietly, absorbing every word. His demeanor was somber. Finally, he put down the phone. "Normally, with this, he would've been calling us to go out and do this," he finally said of Young. "Interesting that he's made no such approach to us. Very sad."

He continued: "I don't know what's going to happen next. Maybe it's all finished. Maybe it's crumbled to a nonexistent entity now. When you're forty, you make rash decisions. But when you're seventy-five, it may be completely over. And now that I've seen Neil's words, which we should've been singing with him, it's another sign it's over."

By that point, he and Crosby had not spoken in two years, a once unimaginable thought. (By the end of 2018, that breach would extend to three years.) Months earlier, in January 2017, friends, family and associates of Nash's long-standing engineer, Stanley Tajima Johnston, had gathered in Los Angeles for a memorial; Johnston had died suddenly on Thanksgiving. Stills, Nash and sundry members of their old band and crew attended, but Crosby, who was in town finishing up *Sky Trails*, told friends he was too busy working to make the memorial. Instead, the mourners heard the Beatles' "In My Life" sung by Nash, Stills—and Joel Bernstein.

In the spring of 2018, Crosby spent several weeks in New York making yet another new album—his fourth in four years—with League, Stevens and Willis. Released that fall, the glistening, harmony-laden *Here If You Listen* was his first collaborative group effort since the headiest days of Crosby, Stills, Nash and Young. Crosby traded songwriting and lead vocals with the others, and the album even sported a song, "Vagrants of Venice," that was a lyrical counterpart to "Wooden Ships." (This time it was climate change, not nuclear weapons, that would wreck the planet.) The East Village studio where Crosby was working was probably a ten-minute walk from Nash's apartment, yet they never connected in any way during Crosby's visit. Nash didn't even know Crosby was in town until someone told him.

BY THE FALL OF 2018, fifty years had elapsed since that evening at the Whisky a Go Go and the first night Crosby, Stills and Nash had sung together, wherever it was. Since then, they had embodied so much about their generation, from rock and roll to substance abuse to a wanton lifestyle to multiple partners. Now in their seventies, they had survived it all: later-life health scares, near-fatal accidents and overdoses, financially crippling divorces, the invading armies of punk rock, the ravages of drug and alcohol abuse. Three of them were now grandparents. Like many their age, they were coping with receding hairlines, hearing loss, and aches and pains all over their bodies; they also remained proud political

JANUARY 2008–SEPTEMBER 2018

progressives, as seen by a new, Hannah-directed video for "Ohio," released in the fall of 2018, that protested the NRA.

After years in which the group's legacy seemed to dim, it received a vote of confidence from a new generation. A fresh wave of harmony-inclined bands like Fleet Foxes and Dawes openly admitted to CSNY love. "For What It's Worth" became a folk protest standard, covered in the new century by everyone from Ozzy Osbourne and Rush to Lucinda Williams and Heart's Ann Wilson. Nash's *Songs for Beginners* was the subject of an indie tribute album featuring the likes of Bonnie "Prince" Billy covering all of its songs, while Crosby's *If I Could Only Remember My Name* was acknowledged as a misunderstood cult stoner classic.

Whether they would ever work together again, or ever even assemble together in the same room, remained almost as unknowable as the locale of Crosby, Stills and Nash's first harmonies. Newly apart, they seemed more comfortable in their own skins. They could look back on their past foibles with a sense of head-shaking humor. They had made their contributions to rock history, and they had the awards, the album sale plaques and the Rock & Roll Hall of Fame inductions to prove it. At this point, they simply wanted to do what they wanted to do and make the most of what was left. Their generation understood that, too—about themselves and about these men.

By way of social media, their followers asked them on a daily basis to reunite, but not even the musicians themselves were sure if and when that would happen. "Very hard decision this time," Crosby admits of parting ways with the others. "We had a good band. It was easy. I made a good paycheck. But we had gotten to the point where we didn't really like each other. I don't have bad feelings, but Nash and Stills dislike me intensely. And it was unpleasant. It had gotten to the point where it was just awful." As Nash would put it, "If CSN and CSNY never play another note of music, look what we did. As complicated as it was, we made some pretty good music and we talked to a lot of people about shit we felt was important. If it never happens again, so be it. Things come to life and they come to an end."

Those who were close to them could only imagine a reconciliation happening for financial reasons. Except for Young, the days of playing large venues were gone; on their own, they were headlining clubs and small theaters. Revenue from CDs and streaming services was minimal. As a result of that changing business model, Crosby toured three separate times in 2018 in order to pay his bills. By then, he had also sold the *Mayan* for financial reasons.

But even after the most tumultuous era in a career filled with them, it was impossible to break the bond between them. They'd been through too much together, so a surprise reconciliation, for a tour or a one-shot show, could never be ruled out. Given their history, in fact, it could almost be expected. Even though he seemed utterly content with Hannah and working with Promise of the Real, Young refused to publicly rule out another go-round. In 2017, he told *Mojo* "a lot of things have to be settled" before a reunion but "that's what brothers and families are all about. . . . I'm open." A year later, he admitted to *Huffington Post*, "I don't plan things like that. . . . I want to make music with people who want to make music—that have the same sensibilities that I have. I don't care who they are." For all their disagreements, Nash and Young remained in touch and even met for a New York meal during this period.

In early 2018, Crosby participated in a night of protest songs at New York's Carnegie Hall, joining League, mandolinist, singer and radio host Chris Thile and others. At the end, all the participants came together and performed "Ohio." Young was nowhere near New York and probably wouldn't have joined in if he were. But the song and the performance—which could be interpreted as Crosby's olive branch to Young—were still chilling and newly relevant, especially in light of the spate of police shootings over the previous few years. The future of the Crosby, Stills, Nash and Young experiment was in doubt. Yet the performance proved that the legacy would endure.

ACKNOWLEDGMENTS

Every journalist knows that each story he or she tackles has the potential to be Rashomon-like, but the saga of Crosby, Stills, Nash and Young takes that prospect to a new level. Not only is the tale inordinately tangled, but after five-plus decades, everyone who participated in it has his or her own slightly different take on what happened and when. Ferreting out the truth—or something close to it—was challenging, but also, I have to admit, a lot of fun.

For their time, let me first thank Graham Nash and David Crosby, who graciously agreed to be dragged through this story and tolerated my questions and follow-ups. My gratitude also to Amy Grantham and Jan Crosby for allowing me into their homes in order to grill their respective partners.

Despite several inquiries, I was, unfortunately, not able to speak with either Stephen Stills or Neil Young for this project. According to his camp, Stephen is at work on his memoir and prefers to save his memories for that book. I wish him all the best and look forward to his telling of this tale, which should be fascinating. I've done my best to communicate their points of view by integrating interviews with fellow writers and associates, and I hope I've adequately captured their states of mind at particular moments in this story. I certainly never lost my admiration for their talent along the way.

In terms of secondary interviews, Bill Halverson, Bill Siddons, Joe Vitale and Ken Weiss were especially giving of their time and helped fill in many blanks. For their insights and recollections, I'd like to thank, in alphabetical order, Ron and Howard Albert, Stephen Barncard, Bill Bentley, Niko Bolas, Calli Cerami, Mike Cerre, Allan Clarke, Alex Coletti, Judy Collins, Jessi Colter, Chad Cromwell, Lillian Davis, John Ferrugia, Greg Fischbach, Arthur Fogel, Tim Foster, Joel Gallen, Felix Giachetti, Danny Goldberg, Glenn Goodwin, Bobby Hammer, Mickey Hart, John Hartmann, Bruce Hensal, Jim Keltner, Howie Klein, Jim Koplik, Jay Landers, Michael Lang, James Mazzeo, Roger McGuinn, Debbie Meister, Bob Merlis, Leslie Morris, Bob Mosley, Mark Naftalin, Chris O'Dell, John Partipilo, Al Perkins, George Perry, Jeff Pevar, Franco and Maureen Pietoso, Jerry Pompili, Steve "Smokey" Potts,

David Pullman, Dave Rao, Aaron Rapoport, Stacia Raymond, David Rensin, Susan Rogers, Sally Mann Romano, Salli Sachse, Vicki Samuels, Rowland Scherman, John Sebastian, Ron Shapiro, Bill Siddons, Leland Sklar, Michael Stergis, Ron Stone, Bill Szymczyk, Michael Tannen, John Vanderslice, Jimmy Wachtel, Waddy Wachtel, Mason Wilkinson and the late, amazing Pegi Young. All helped clarify and elaborate on this saga, and I'm grateful for their time.

Several sources spoke with me only on background, and I thank them for their assistance as well.

Four books in, Ben Schafer at Da Capo Press remains as enthusiastic and emboldening as always. Thank you to Michael Pietsch, who not only fully supported this project but doubly impressed me with his reference to "The Lee Shore" in one of our first emails about this book. My agent Erin Hosier of Dunow, Carlson & Lerner—and Young, as I sometimes like to add—fought the good fight as always and offered guidance and encouragement along the way. Thanks also to Justin Lovell at Da Capo for helping out with various vital duties.

A number of fellow writers and historians offered advice, tips and transcripts. I'll start with Dave Zimmer, whose groundbreaking *Crosby, Stills & Nash: The Biography* I absorbed during train commutes to my first job back in 1984. Despite the thought of another writer diving into this terrain, Dave was gracious and accommodating, even allowing me to cart off his vast archives of clippings and memorabilia on loan. Dave, who knows as much about this story as anyone on the planet, was also kind enough to read through my manuscript and catch more than a few factual glitches.

Joel Bernstein's dedication to the CSNY cause is indisputable, and I thank him for allowing me to pick his brain and logbooks to ensure chronological accuracy. A shout-out as well to Henry Diltz for his research help in the past, and to Stefano Frollano for sharing his own archival research into the group's recording dates.

My *Rolling Stone* colleagues Andy Greene, David Fricke, Patrick Doyle and Brian Hiatt were kind enough to share story notes, transcripts and insights, and I can't thank them enough for their generosity (especially Andy, my comrade in CSNY dissection and scrutiny). Thanks to Robert Greenfield for his insights (and script!). For feedback, contact information and sundry tips, shout-outs to Steve Silberman, David Fear, Joel Peresman, Sheila Weller, Fred Goodman, Greil Marcus, Steve Knopper, Justin Kreutzmann, Martin Porter, David Yaffe, Michaelangelos Matos, Jesse Jarnow, Michael Deeds, Bill Flanagan and Daniela Tijerina. My sister Colette Browne and her husband,

Howard McPherson, filled me in on aspects of Hawaiian history from their many years there. Meredith Rutledge-Borger and Jennie Thomas at the Rock & Roll Hall of Fame helped with document excavation.

Thank you to everyone at *Rolling Stone*, especially Jann S. Wenner, Jason Fine and Christian Hoard, for their support and for allowing me the extra time to work on this project.

Thanks to Michael Jensen, who warned me about the challenges in tackling a book on this topic but never deterred me. For their help in connecting me with important sources, thank you to Carrie Davis at Live Nation, Katherine DePaul, Michelle Gutenstein, Rob Krauser, Camilla McGuinn, Connie Bonner Mosley, Maureen Raffety, Rose Solomon, Mark Spector and Brittnee Walker at BMI.

Kathy Heintzelman and Katherine Streckfus sharpened, tightened and improved my manuscript with exceptional skill. Many thanks to Christine Marra for making all the trains run on time. Corinne Cummings came to my fact-checking rescue and saved me from several embarrassments, and Breanne Springfield ably and swiftly transcribed interview tapes. Deb Dragon excavated all the photos you're seeing inside. Doug Silver helped me navigate through tempo changes, time signatures and other musical notations. For additional tips and pointers, thank you to Barry Ollman, David Gernert, David Silver, Francesco Lucarelli and Ron Simon. Shout-outs to Jeff Ogden at the Admiral Farragut Academy and Michelle Zarin, Bob Edwards and Tom Scott, all formerly of the Record Plant.

As always, many, many hugs and my love to Maggie and Maeve for tolerating the nonstop Crosby, Stills, Nash and Young music around the house for over two years (even *Trans*, Mags!). Their love, humor and strength inspired me daily, especially during a particularly difficult stretch of time in the early stages of this book. They truly helped me carry on.

BIBLIOGRAPHY

For this book, I interviewed approximately 120 people in the Crosby, Stills, Nash and Young universe between the summer of 2016 and the fall of 2018. A handful of those interviews, as indicated below, preceded that research and were for articles in *Rolling Stone* and my book *Fire and Rain: The Beatles, Simon & Garfunkel, James Taylor, CSNY, and the Lost Story of 1970* (Da Capo, 2011).

In addition to the newspaper and magazine articles and websites cited below, I regularly returned to certain key volumes and am indebted to all those writers and scholars for their work.

Dave Zimmer's *Crosby, Stills & Nash: The Biography*, 3rd ed. (Da Capo, 2008), is an essential guide to their tangled tale, and his reporting on their childhoods and teenage years remains definitive. David Crosby and Carl Gottlieb's *Long Time Gone: The Autobiography of David Crosby* (Doubleday, 1988) and *Since Then: How I Survived Everything and Lived to Tell About It* (G. P. Putnam's, 2006); Graham Nash's *Wild Tales: A Rock & Roll Life* (Crown, 2013); and Neil Young's *Waging Heavy Peace: A Hippie Dream* (Blue Rider, 2012) and *Special Deluxe: A Memoir of Life and Cars* (Blue Rider, 2014) were indispensable reads for their insights into each man's life and music. My understanding of Young's early years and career was greatly enhanced by Jimmy Mc-Donough's *Shakey: Neil Young's Biography* (Random House, 2002) as well as John Einarson's *Neil Young: Don't Be Denied; The Canadian Years* (Quarry, 1992) and *Mr. Tambourine Man: The Life and Legacy of the Byrds' Gene Clark* (Backbeat, 2005). Johnny Rogan's *Crosby, Stills, Nash & Young: The Visual Documentary* (Omnibus, 1996) is unsurpassed for its week-by-week, sometimes day-by-day, chronicling of their world.

Other worthwhile volumes included the Zimmer-edited *4 Way Street: The Crosby, Stills, Nash & Young Reader* (Da Capo, 2004); Sheila Weller's *Girls Like Us: Carole King, Joni Mitchell, Carly Simon—And the Journey of a Generation* (Atria, 2008); Fred Goodman's *Mansion on the Hill: Dylan, Young, Springsteen and the Head-on Collision of Rock and Commerce* (Vintage, 1997); Joe Vitale's *Backstage Pass* (Hit Records, 2008); Barney Hoskyns' *Hotel California* (Wiley, 2006); editor Holly George-Warren's *Neil Young: The Rolling Stone File* (Hyperion, 1994); John Capouya's *Florida Soul* (University of Florida Press, 2017); Johnny Rogan's *Byrds: Requiem for the Timeless*, vol. 1 (Rogan House, 2011) and his *Complete Guide to the Music of Crosby, Stills, Nash & Young* (Omnibus, 1998); and Bill Graham and Robert Greenfield's *Bill Graham Presents: My Life Inside Rock and Out* (Doubleday, 1992). The Sugar Mountain and HyperRust websites were valuable tools for set lists and other show details.

SOURCE NOTES

CHAPTER 1: EARLY YEARS—DECEMBER 1968

3   Crammed next to each other: Richard Drew, "Hollies Turn on 'Names' of Pop Music," *Independent Star News* (Pasadena, CA), February 17, 1968. Young's appearance is noted in Sandy Gardiner, "Off the Record," *Ottawa Journal*, March 8, 1968.

4   Asked if nuclear bombs: "A-Arms Not Needed Now: Wheeler," *New York Daily News*, February 15, 1968.

4   An eighteen-year-old living: "Say Killing in Defense of Mother," *Independent* (Long Beach, CA), February 14, 1968.

5   "I don't know, though": Mike Ferguson, "Buffalo Bustup," *Courier-Post* (Camden, NJ), June 29, 1968.

5   "Maybe we can steal him": David Fricke interview with Stephen Stills (SS), 1997.

6   "We came offstage": Author interview with Allan Clarke.

6   Adolf Hitler had spared Blackpool: Mark Tran, "Hitler's Plans to Turn Blackpool into Nazi Resort Come to Light," *Guardian*, February 23, 2009.

7   "I definitely wasn't cool": Author interview with Graham Nash (GN).

7   Once their schooldays had ended: These and other details on Stills' childhood from Dave Zimmer, *Crosby, Stills & Nash: The Biography* (Da Capo, 2008).

7   "We're the Hollies": Author interview with Clarke.

8   "We went along with the flower-power": Ibid.

9   "I had better pot": Author interview with David Crosby (DC).

9   "The producer told us": Author interview with Clarke.

10   "A lot of it was my own natural": Author interview with DC.

10   "I had never heard an orchestra": Ibid.

10   His father, Floyd, came from: These and other family details from David Crosby and Carl Gottlieb, *Long Time Gone: The Autobiography of David Crosby* (Doubleday, 1988).

10   "a really good parent": Author interview with DC.

11   "I knew my father": Ibid.

11   "dubious moral character": Ben Fong-Torres, "David Crosby: The *Rolling Stone* Interview," *Rolling Stone*, July 23, 1970.

12   "I'm really horrible": Crosby and Gottlieb, *Long Time Gone*.

13   "He was a little bit unruly": Author interview with Roger McGuinn.

13   Unable to handle the news: This and other early chronology from Zimmer, *Crosby, Stills & Nash*.

13   "He wanted to be in the band": Author interview with McGuinn.

15   "Change is where it's at": Author interview with Mark Naftalin.

15   "Rev it up *loud*": Sylvie Reice, "Byrds Fly High in World of Teens," *Los Angeles Times*, May 24, 1966.

15 "literally made the chapel doors": David F. Wagner, "Byrd Singing Debate at Lawrence University Show," *Post-Crescent* (Appleton, WI), March 8, 1966.

16 "I was into Eastern religion": Author interview with McGuinn.

16 "Can you do that?": Ibid.

16 Williams Stills, his father: Zimmer, *Crosby, Stills & Nash.*

16 "an entrepreneurial kind of guy": Fricke interview with SS, 1998.

17 "had to change countries": David Cavanagh, "Fame Is a Subtle, Dangerous, Seductive Thing . . . ," *Uncut,* July 2009.

17 After Illinois: Zimmer, *Crosby, Stills & Nash.*

17 "I loved the drill": Fricke interview with SS, 1998.

17 falsely accused: Zimmer, *Crosby, Stills & Nash.*

17 construction of storage tanks: Fricke interview with SS, 1997.

18 "Stephen was head and shoulders": Author interview with John Sebastian.

19 westward migration: Tom Gray and Robert Scardamalia, "The Great California Exodus: A Closer Look," Civic Report, Center for State and Local Leadership at the Manhattan Institute, September 2012, https://www.manhattan-institute.org/pdf/cr_71.pdf.

21 "Stephen and Neil both respected": Author interview with Nurit Wilde, 2010.

22 "We just couldn't hack him": Mike Gormley, "Neil Young: On His Own in His Own Special Way," *Detroit Free Press,* February 28, 1969.

22 "It was all about the fact that": Author interview with Lou Adler, 2013.

23 "They were at a point": Ibid.

23 "so grumpy at us": Author interview with McGuinn.

23 "He was going beyond the scope": Ibid.

23 "Ah, they suck—I don't like them": John Einarson and Richie Furay, *For What It's Worth: The Story of Buffalo Springfield* (Cooper Square, 2004).

23 "I liked the Springfield right away": Author interview with DC.

23 "My lick": Ibid.

24 "Stephen asked me": Ibid.

24 "One just didn't do that then": Zimmer, *Crosby, Stills & Nash.*

24 "stunk to high heaven": Einarson and Furay, *For What It's Worth.*

24 "He sat in with us": Ferguson, "Buffalo Bustup."

25 "We may be breaking some rules": Tom Paegel, "Pop Jam Session Held at Hullabaloo Club," *Los Angeles Times,* July 6, 1967.

25 "I want to retire in five years": Reice, "Byrds Fly High."

25 "We thought, 'Oh, really?'": Author interview with McGuinn.

25 "It wasn't *my* plan": Author interview with DC.

25 "complying with a request": Diane Morgan, "The Disc Seen," *Press Democrat* (Santa Rosa, CA), November 20, 1967.

25 "They asked me to resign": Peter Tork interview with Brian Hiatt, 2007.

26 "It was a bad marriage": Author interview with McGuinn.

26 "There was regret": Author interview with DC.

27 "just another blonde": Estrella Berosini to Sheila Weller, *Girls Like Us: Carole King, Joni Mitchell, Carly Simon—And the Journey of a Generation* (Atria, 2008).

27 "You walk into a club": Author interview with DC.

27 "I discovered sensimilla": Ibid.

28 "This is *nuts*": Author interview with Bill Halverson.

29 "like a brotherhood or a marriage": Author interview with DC.

29 "The Byrds could swing": Ibid.

29 "It wasn't just about Bobby": Ibid.

30   "We could've done without that": Ibid.

30   "[Cocaine] started happening": Andy Greene, "The Oral History of CSNY's Infamous 'Doom Tour,'" *Rolling Stone*, June 19, 2014.

30   an estimated $5 million on cocaine: Martin Waldron, "Drug Use in America," *New York Times*, January 12, 1968.

30   "I probably wasn't the only one": Author interview with Sebastian.

31   "I was pretty down": Author interview with GN.

31   "Which one of us is gonna steal him?": Zimmer, *Crosby, Stills & Nash*.

31   "I thought everyone": Author interview with Clarke.

32   "David sent me": Ibid.

32   "He is aware and alert": "The Hollies a 'Group's Group,'" *Ottawa Journal*, March 1, 1968.

32   Christine Gail Hinton: Crosby and Gottlieb, *Long Time Gone*.

32   "Joni found out about that" and "it was a very 'goodbye David' song": Author interview with DC.

33   two recognizable figures: Author interview with Waddy Wachtel.

33   "I didn't think much of the Hollies": Author interview with DC.

33   "Do it—that's all I'm going to tell you": Fricke interview with SS, 1997.

33   "Who will steal him?": Jim Ladd interview with SS, *Rockline*, 1982.

33   "They called out": Author interview with Sebastian.

34   "We took it 'on the road'": Author interview with GN.

34   "I'm going to ask you something": Author interview with Waddy Wachtel.

34   Clarke was therefore stunned: Author interview with Clarke.

35   "on the grounds of her misconduct": "Graham Nash Wins Divorce," Associated Press, January 28, 1971.

35   "He said, 'I want to leave'": Author interview with Clarke.

35   "I was thinking, 'Oh my God'": Author interview with Chris O'Dell. Also cited in her *Miss O'Dell: Hard Days and Long Nights with The Beatles, The Stones, Bob Dylan and Eric Clapton* (Touchstone, 2009).

35   "He wasn't in *my* dressing room": Author interview with Clarke.

35   "Crosby, Stills and Nash were already established": Author interview with O'Dell.

35   "They didn't get it": Author interview with DC.

36   Acerbic and enamored: Details of Roberts and Geffen, including the Laura Nyro story, draw from Thomas L. King, *The Operator: David Geffen Builds, Buys and Sells the New Hollywood* (Random House, 2000).

36   "Elliot we knew": Author interview with DC.

37   "animals": King, *Operator*.

37   "Capitol wouldn't touch it": Author interview with Leslie Morris.

37   called Furay: Michael Wale interview with SS, 1972.

37   "Sort of like a baseball deal": Ibid.

37   "Ah, man, the trouble": Ibid.

38   "Geffen manipulated the outcome": Author interview with Ron Stone.

38   In the last month of 1968: Author interview with Jerry Pompili.

38   "David Crosby of the Byrds": Ralph J. Gleason, syndicated column, December 29, 1968.

CHAPTER 2: JANUARY 1969–DECEMBER 1969

39   "That's the sound": Author interview with Halverson.

40   "We worked with Rothchild": Author interview with DC.

40   "He was very bitter about that": Author interview with Dave Rao.
41   "Stephen was pushing them": The quotation and the other information in this paragraph from author interview with Dallas Taylor, 2009.
41   "At the time we were very rebellious": Author interview with DC.
41   Nash would pen: Author interview with GN.
42   "Once you realize": Author interview with Sebastian.
42   "I got a little brushes thing": Ibid.
42   "That was normally what happened": Author interview with GN.
43   "It was a lot better": Author interview with DC.
43   "It was amazing to watch": Author interview with Sebastian.
44   "Cut his [Taylor's] hands off": Author interview with Taylor.
44   "Graham and David would come": Author interview with Halverson.
44   "Stills . . . had his eyes down": Ellen Sander, *Trips: Rock Life in the Sixties* (Scribner's, 1973).
44   "Yes, that's absolutely true": Author interview with GN.
45   "bugged Anderle": Author interview with Judy Collins.
45   Collins recalls bringing along a copy: Ibid.
46   "A huge influence on me": Author interview with DC.
46   "Stephen didn't like therapy": Author interview with Collins.
46   "It was just thrilling": Ibid.
47   "It was a struggle": Ibid.
47   "He must have been reading": Ibid.
47   "If you have a band name": Author interview with DC.
47   "the latest trend in groups": Dennis Douvanis, "Country Joins Rock for 'Now Sound,'" *Morning Call* (Allentown, PA), March 8, 1969.
48   referred to the trio as "Stills-Crosby-Nash": "Atlantic Plans Disk Action for New Coast Acts," *Billboard*, February 22, 1969.
48   "Try saying it any other way": Author interview with DC.
48   "Stephen was pissed": Author interview with GN.
48   "At the time": Author interview with DC.
49   "We were panicked": Author interview with Stone.
49   "It was the first album": Author interview with Henry Diltz, 2010.
49   "Needless to say": Author interview with Binky Philips.
50   At the all-black Dudley: James T. Wooten, "Troops Disperse Carolina Snipers," *New York Times*, May 24, 1969.
50   "Ahmet signs our paycheck": Author interview with Halverson.
51   "structural triumph": Robert Christgau, "The Byrds Have Flown—But Not Far," *New York Times*, June 8, 1969.
52   "It was that intimacy": Author interview with GN.
52   "as perfect": Christgau, "Byrds Have Flown."
52   "nothing short of a treasure": Ellen Sander, "Crosby, Stills and Nash: Renaissance Fare," *Saturday Review*, May 31, 1969.
53   "Do you want to pack it in, luv?": This and other quotes in this passage from Susan Gordon Lydon, "In Her House, Love," *New York Times*, April 20, 1969.
53   As Crosby recalls it, Young asked: Author interview with DC.
53   "a newly formed combination": "Tom Jones to Open Greek Theater Year," *Los Angeles Times*, May 8, 1969.
54   Stills and Taylor ran into George Harrison: Author interview with Taylor.

54 "Winwood was scared to death": Ibid.

54 Naftalin later had no memory: Author interview with Naftalin.

54 During a dinner with Stills and Geffen: Zimmer, *Crosby, Stills & Nash.*

54 as Crosby would recall in his first memoir: Crosby and Gottlieb, *Long Time Gone.*

54 "There's something about Neil Young": Zimmer, *Crosby, Stills & Nash.*

55 Born in Toronto on November 12, 1945: Details of Young's childhood from John Einarson, *Neil Young: The Canadian Years; Don't Be Denied* (Quarry, 1992); Neil Young, *Waging Heavy Peace: A Hippie Dream* (Blue Rider, 2012); and Jimmy McDonough, *Shakey: Neil Young's Biography* (Random House, 2002).

57 During a group interview in Connecticut: Margaret Rhodes, "Buffalo Springfield: Eastward Stomp," *Hartford Courant,* November 25, 1967.

58 "I went, 'Why would we *do* that?'": Author interview with SS, 2010.

58 "kind of silly": Dave Zimmer, "Stephen Stills Carries On," *BAM,* April 6, 1979.

58 "I knew this was going to be a monster": Fricke interview with SS, 1997.

58 "sounded like a new car": Young, *Waging Heavy Peace.*

58 "overplay": Thomas L. King, *The Operator: David Geffen Builds, Buys and Sells the New Hollywood* (Random House, 2000).

58 "I thought, '*That's* an odd pairing'": Author interview with Sebastian.

59 "Neil wasn't a superstar then": Author interview with GN.

59 "I said, 'Oh, shit!'": Author interview with DC.

59 "We said, 'Wow, that was great'": Author interview with Taylor.

59 "Nothing Neil does is an accident": Author interview with DC.

60 "They had the tiger by the tail": Author interview with Stone.

60 "If the heavens ever descend": *Detroit Free Press,* June 20, 1969.

61 "There was nude swimming": Author interview with Salli Sachse.

61 James himself would recall: Rick James with David Ritz, *Glow: The Autobiography of Rick James* (Atria, 2014).

61 "We always wondered": Author interview with Taylor.

61 James knew his protégé: James with Ritz, *Glow.*

62 "It was some silly thing": Author interview with Bobby Hammer.

62 "You walked out": Footage from *Crosby, Stills & Nash: Long Time Comin'* (Rhino, 2005).

62 "It wasn't shocking": Author interview with Sachse.

63 "Geffen knew what he had": Lang quotations and details on the planning of Woodstock from author interview with Michael Lang; Michael Lang with Holly George-Warren, *The Road to Woodstock* (Ecco, 2009).

63 Stills would later tell: Alan di Perna, "Turn Back the Pages," *Guitar World,* May 2013.

64 "Golly, we needed that": "Relaxing with Crosby, Stills . . . ," Lew Harris, *Chicago Tribune,* August 18, 1969.

66 "They're looking around": Author interview with Sebastian.

66 "I thought, 'Okay'": Author interview with DC.

66 "smug, English face": Dallas Taylor, *Prisoner of Woodstock* (Thunder's Mouth, 1994).

66 "He was quiet": Author interview with Greil Marcus.

67 "That was remarkable": Author interview with Lang.

67 "Neil would threaten": Author interview with GN.

67 "a huge mistake": Author interview with DC.

67 "a bullshit gig": McDonough, *Shakey.*

67 Young had recorded a few tracks: Neil Young Archives website, https://www.neilyoung archives.com.

67　"The sales pitch": Author interview with Stone.

67　"a triumph": Robert Hilburn, "Crosby, Stills, Nash and Young at Greek," *Los Angeles Times*, August 27, 1969.

68　"features Crosby, Stills and Nash": "Bayou West: A Different Store," *Chula Vista Star News*, November 9, 1969.

68　"Wasn't that great?": Author interview with DC.

68　"I did give him a knee": Ernest Leogrande, "Stephen Stills Still Temperamental," *Asbury Park Press* (Asbury Park, NJ), March, 8, 1974.

69　"Stills was ministered to": Robert W. Neubert, "A Year of Woodstocks," Chicago Tribune-New York News Syndicate, November 8, 1969.

70　"She rolled the best joints": Author interview with Hammer.

70　On the way, Crosby saw: Crosby and Gottlieb, *Long Time Gone*.

70　"like the Mummy" and "It brought everybody down": Author interview with Mickey Hart.

71　"Things like that": Author interview with Sachse.

71　"His entire world had been yanked": Author interview with GN.

72　"It was frightening": Author interview with Stephen Barncard.

72　"Usually one or two reels": Ibid.

72　"Mind-boggling": Author interview with Lang.

73　"There was steam": Author interview with Barncard.

73　"It's as if I had done it before": Author interview with DC.

73　"Until you forgive your mother": David Yaffe, *Reckless Daughter: A Portrait of Joni Mitchell* (Sarah Crichton Books, 2017).

73　"He was madly in love with her": Author interview with Hammer.

74　"crazy, love-filled": Author interview with Collins.

74　"David thought it was perfect": Author interview with Barncard.

74　"I didn't want anyone": Author interview with DC.

75　"It's like, 'What was wrong'": Author interview with SS, 2010.

75　"Mistakes—lots of mistakes": Author interview with DC.

75　"Neil was all business": Author interview with Barncard.

75　"It was bedlam, man": Author interview with SS, 2010.

76　"Graham was easygoing": Author interview with Sachse.

76　"Stephen and Neil were back at each other": Author interview with Taylor.

76　"By the time we got to *Déjà vu*": Author interview with GN, 2010.

76　"From day one": Author interview with Stone.

77　"The door flies open": Author interview with Nils Lofgren, 2009.

78　"When the managers would come in": Author interview with Halverson.

78　"Crosby's face was so sad": Author interview with Robert Greenfield.

78　"almost to a man bell-bottomed": Lynn Van Matre, "Crosby, Stills (etc.) 'Right On,'" *Chicago Tribune*, December 15, 1969.

78　Young showed up late: Wayne Harada, "A Mystic Movement at CSNY Concert," *Honolulu Advertiser*, November 24, 1969.

78　"Politics is bullshit": Ben Fong-Torres, "Crosby, Stills, Nash, Young, Taylor and Reeves," *Rolling Stone*, December 27, 1969.

79　"Leo worked his ass off": Author interview with Hammer.

79　"Streams of blood streaked": Joel Selvin, *Altamont: The Rolling Stones, the Hells Angels, and the Inside Story of Rock's Darkest Day* (Dey Street, 2016).

79　"just wide-eyed": Author interview with Hart.

79　"It went really fast": Author interview with Sachse.

80　"I could feel the music dying": Young, *Waging Heavy Peace*.

CHAPTER 3: JANUARY 1970–JANUARY 1971

81   "Henry Diltz Fan Club" and ham-radio calls: Author interview with Henry Diltz, 2010.
82   "Ahmet would whine": Author interview with SS, 2010.
82   "joined the Junior NRA": Crosby and Gottlieb, *Long Time Gone.*
82   sales of fretted: George Knemeyer, "Country Sound in Rock Boosts Sale of Guitars," *Billboard,* July 3, 1971.
82   "I hear a group like CSN": "Rock Groups Translate Emotion into Music, Words," *Poughkeepsie Journal* (Poughkeepsie, NY), February 22, 1970.
83   "It was perfect": Author interview with Lang.
83   Two Guys: Advertisement, *San Bernardino County Sun,* March 15, 1970.
83   "That was tragic": Author interview with SS, 2010.
83   "I'd committed the sin": Author interview with GN.
84   someone to lease Brookfield: Details of the estate from author interview with Ritchie Yorke, 2009; Ritchie Yorke, "Stephen Stills Cuts His 'Super' Album in England Without Crosby, Nash, Young," *Philadelphia Inquirer,* June 7, 1970.
85   "Stephen came to me full of praise": Peter Tork interview with Brian Hiatt, 2007.
86   "a clear, direct sound": Author interview with Lofgren.
86   "CSNY was this storm": Ibid.
87   "It was just unpleasant": Author interview with GN.
87   "Elliot was freaked": Author interview with DC.
88   "Crosby and I were watching": Author interview with GN.
88   Richard Nixon's approval rating: "Nixon Popularity Increases in Poll," *New York Times,* June 7, 1970.
89   "too perfect to be true": Langdon Winner, *Déjà vu* review, *Rolling Stone,* April 30, 1970.
90   "He was a bit eccentric": Author interview with Hammer.
90   "He did something that": Author interview with SS, 2010.
90   "Being a medicine man": Dolf van Stijgeren, "4 Way Site Catches Up with Greg Reeves," 4WaySite.com, 2014.
91   sneaked aboard a flight: Author interviews with Calvin "Fuzzy" Samuel, 2010, and Stone.
92   "Remember all those stories": Barbara Charone, "Stephen Stills: A Sympathetic Self-Portrait," *Crawdaddy,* October 1975.
93   "If the music's not there": Author interview with GN.
93   Taylor pledged his allegiance: Author interview with Taylor.
93   "the sore throats": *Billboard,* May 30, 1970.
93   As dance students: "SSC Group Plans Peace Benefit," *Press Democrat* (Santa Rosa, CA), May 20, 1970.
93   a survey of Indiana: "'Teach Children' Takes Top 10 Spot," *Indianapolis News,* July 17, 1970.
93   Atlantic rushed out a statement: "Crosby, Stills Not Breaking Up," *Billboard,* June 6, 1970.
93   "We told Elliot": Author interview with GN.
94   "The deal had already happened": Author interview with Taylor.
94   "Dallas was canned": Author interview with DC.
94   Taylor also claimed: Dallas Taylor, *Prisoner of Woodstock* (Thunder's Mouth, 1994).
95   "They were a bit in disarray": Author interview with Johny Barbata, 2009.
95   "Like a dummy, I did it": Author interview with Taylor.
96   "I went to the end of it": Author interview with DC.
96   "It was like the four of them": Author interview with Halverson.
97   "It was entertaining": Author interview with SS, 2010.
97   "It was destructive": Ibid.

98 "needlessly bitter barbs": Jack Lloyd, "CSN&Y Appears at Last: Near the End as Team?," *Philadelphia Inquirer*, June 11, 1970.

99 "No one can afford": Mike Steele, "What Price a Crosby, Stills, Nash, Young Concert," *Minneapolis Star Tribune*, May 10, 1970.

99 "Crosby writes about": Ibid.

99 "Well, that takes care of the sound check": Author interview with Charles John Quarto, 2010.

100 "Well, my heart": David Yaffe, *Reckless Daughter: A Portrait of Joni Mitchell* (Sarah Crichton Books, 2017).

100 "I said okay": Author interview with Rita Coolidge, 2010.

101 "brooding": Lew Harris, "Like Old Times Again," *Chicago Tribune*, July 6, 1970.

101 A writer for *Hundred Flowers*: *Hundred Flowers*, no. 11, June 10, 1970.

101 "We got through it okay": Author interview with SS, 2010.

101 "They didn't do a lot of rehearsing": Author interview with Halverson.

101 "various energies": Author interview with Diltz, 2010.

102 Standing in the back: Author interview with James Mazzeo.

102 "He told me he really didn't like": Ibid.

103 made as much as $7 million: Caroline Boucher, "The Pop Aristocrats," *Disc and Music Echo*, March 20, 1971.

103 "In the spring of 1967": Liner notes, Buffalo Springfield (box set) (Rhino, 2001).

103 $340,103 in cash: Jimmy McDonough, *Shakey: Neil Young's Biography* (Random House, 2002).

103 "When I saw that, I went": Author interview with GN.

103 "He looked like a wreck": Author interview with Felix Giachetti.

103 "Crazy thing to do": Ibid.

103 the *Mayan*, now docked: Crosby and Gottlieb, *Long Time Gone*.

104 "I was stoned and happy": Author interview with DC.

104 "The floor was all water": Author interview with Ron Albert.

104 "sixties radicals found it easier": Bruce J. Schulman, *The Seventies: The Great Shift in American Culture, Society and Politics* (Da Capo, 2002).

104 "in the same general area": Author interview with Stone.

105 "Stephen was adorable": Author interview with Coolidge, 2010.

105 "Mr. Sex of the Hollies": David F. Wagner, "They Couldn't Just Go Home Again," *Green Bay Press Gazette*, September 7, 1969.

105 "It's a terrible thing": Author interview with Diltz.

105 "It didn't help": Author interview with DC.

105 "she didn't break us up": Author interview with SS, 2010.

105 "crawling along the floor": "Rock Singer, Woman Booked in Drug Case," *Los Angeles Times*, August 20, 1970. Report of fine: "Rock Guitarist Stills Fined for Drugs," UPI, April 28, 1971.

106 "When Stephen was in the studio": Author interview with Halverson.

106 "He was more and more obsessed": Ibid.

106 "Neil was very focused": Author interview with Lofgren, 2009.

106 drove his Mercedes: Details of Stills driving trips from Diltz journals.

107 "It was so much fun": Author interview with SS, 2010.

107 To his shock: Graham Nash, *Wild Tales: A Rock & Roll Life* (Crown, 2013).

107 "It was wild times": Author interview with SS, 2010.

107 admitted to a Los Angeles hospital: Ritchie Yorke, "Neil Plans Solo Tour Then Year Off," *Ottawa Journal*, January 15, 1971.

107 "We were like a couple of groupies": Author interview with Giachetti.

108 "As good as Neil was": Author interview with DC.

109 Young was busy planning: Yorke, "Neil Plans Solo Tour."

109 "Neil likes to play in groups": Ibid.

109 Young was searched: Alex Cramer, "Neil Young in Concert: A Triumphant Return," *Ottawa Journal*, April 17, 1971.

110 "They'd had their big moment": Author interview with Morris.

110 Nash recalls "Southern Man": Author interview with GN.

110 "We made the mistake": Author interview with SS, 2010.

CHAPTER 4: FEBRUARY 1971–MARCH 1973

115 "I'd heard of CSNY": Author interview with Ben Keith, 2010.

116 "Whoever showed up": Author interview with DC.

117 "snorting up a long line": Steve Parish, *Home Before Daylight: My Life on the Road with the Grateful Dead* (St. Martin's Press, 2003).

117 During one jam: Author interview with Hart.

117 "It was about CSNY": Author interview with DC.

117 "We all knew what it was": Author interview with GN.

118 "stupefying vagueness": Bud Scoppa, dual review of *Graham Nash/David Crosby* and *Manassas*, *Rolling Stone*, May 25, 1972.

118 "If you accept Graham Nash": Lenny Kaye, *Songs for Beginners* review, *Rolling Stone*, July 22, 1971.

120 even the 1971 Ice Capades: Joe Baltake, "Ice Capades Dilemma," *Philadelphia Daily News*, February 12, 1971.

120 "Stephen felt they needed someone": John Robertson, *Neil Young: The Visual Documentary* (Omnibus, 1995).

121 "At present several thousand": "End of the 'Youth Revolt'?" *U.S. News & World Report*, August 9, 1971.

121 "I am suggesting that the best way": Werner Erhard, www.wernererhard.net.

121 "Please don't split up": Vicki Wickham, "Graham Nash: 'We May Fight, But the Music Wins,'" *Melody Maker*, June 1970. Reprinted in *4 Way Street: The Crosby, Stills, Nash & Young Reader*, edited by Dave Zimmer (Da Capo, 2004).

121 "300 houses in Laurel Canyon": Tom Newton, "Rapping," *The Signal* (Santa Clarita, CA), July 17, 1970.

122 "My definition is that blowing it up": Ritchie Yorke, "Stephen Stills Cuts His 'Super' Album in England Without Crosby, Nash, Young," *Philadelphia Inquirer, June 7, 1970.*

122 "The first part of the song": Mike Gormley, "Meet the Man Behind the Movie 'Woodstock,'" *Detroit Free Press*, April 26, 1970.

122 "You guys are too wired": Author interview with Barbata, 2009.

123 "So just how true": Mike Gormley, "2 Happenings Make Exciting Weekend," *Detroit Free Press*, June 16, 1970.

123 "one case in many": Jonathan Takiff, "So They Took 25Gs, Played a Little—and Then They Split," *Philadelphia Daily News*, June 25, 1970.

123 wondered how dated: Robert Hilburn, "Crosby, Stills, Nash & Young at the Forum," *Los Angeles Times*, June 29, 1970.

123 "It demonstrates a great deal": Mike Davenport, "The Jazz Scene," *Valley News* (Los Angeles), May 14, 1971.

123 "little short of a disaster": Robert Hilburn, "One Delight and a Near Disaster," *Los Angeles Times*, May 2, 1971.

124 "Stills has always come on": Robert Christgau, *Stephen Stills 2* review, *Village Voice*, October 14, 1971.

125 "a marathon": Linda Winer, "A Marathon with Stills," *Chicago Tribune*, July 19, 1971.

125 Adhering to his socially conscious: James D. Dilts, "Stills, Memphis Horns Provide New Sound," *Baltimore Sun*, August 2, 1971.

125 one night, it took him a full five minutes: Ernest Leogrande, "Stephen Stills Still Temperamental," *Asbury Park Press* (Asbury Park, NJ), March 8, 1974.

125 "He was a nervous host": Author interview with Bruce Hensal.

125 "in '71 and '72, I found": Dennis Hunt, "Stills: Back on the Strip Again," *Los Angeles Times*, January 21, 1979.

126 "The only trouble": "Rock Singer Nabbed on Drug Count," UPI, June 11, 1971.

126 which culminated with Crosby clashing: Crosby and Gottlieb, *Long Time Gone*.

127 "Graham and I found out": Author interview with DC.

127 "We have fights": Bob Talbert, "Record Notes," *Detroit Free Press*, December 19, 1970.

128 "They had girlfriends": Author interview with Hammer.

128 "Where Neil goes, Carrie goes": Red O'Donnell, "Nashville Sound . . . and Others," *Indianapolis Star*, November 7, 1971.

129 "It's just a little thing": Todd Van Luling, "Neil Young Finally Confirms the Most Popular Legend About Him," *Huffington Post*, June 21, 2016.

129 "She was just a friend": Author interview with GN.

131 "It was 24/7": Author interview with Howard Albert.

131 "a big callous": Lowell Cauffiel, "Stephen Stills," *Guitar Player*, January 1976.

132 "Like, 'I'm being used'": Bill DeYoung, liner notes for *Manassas Pieces*, 2009.

132 "I was half asleep": Author interview with Al Perkins.

132 "A band is a democracy": Peter Potterfield, "Manassas Is Like a Ball Team, and Stills Calls All the Plays," *Atlanta Constitution*, May 20, 1972.

133 "the edge": This and subsequent quotes from author interview with Hart.

134 "But when the Stones visited": Bill Wyman, *Rolling with the Stones* (DK, 2002) and Robert Greenfield, *Exile on Main Street: A Season in Hell with the Rolling Stones* (Da Capo, 2006).

134 "I don't know if Stephen realized": Author interview with Perkins.

134 "Of course . . . They made more money": Author interview with DC.

135 "personal affront": Tony Tyler, "Stephen Stills," *Hit Parader*, October 1972.

135 "I was thrilled beyond belief": Author interview with Danny Kortchmar for *Rolling Stone*, 2013.

135 "David was in good spirits": Author interview with Halverson.

136 "poetic license": Author interview with DC.

136 "a certain indication": Roy Carr, "Will CSNY Ever Re-Unite and Find True Happiness?," *New Musical Express*, July 29, 1972.

136 "There was a lot of cocaine": Author interview with GN.

137 At Nash's urging: Author interview with Halverson.

137 "When I see Stephen doing things": Carr, "Will CSNY Ever Re-Unite."

137 Crosby called Geffen and demanded: "Inventing David Geffen," *American Masters*, Season 26, episode 6, December 20, 2012.

138 "Geffen was furious": Author interview with GN.

138 Geffen was nonetheless a presence: Details of Ertegun's visit to Crosby and Nash session from George W.S. Trow Jr., "Eclectic, Reminiscent, Amused, Fickle, Perverse (I and II)," *New Yorker*, May 29 and June 7, 1978.

138 "It was magical": Author interview with Giachetti.
138 "I was twenty": Ibid.
139 "I'm like, 'I don't know'": Ibid.
139 "small woodsman's knife": Trow, "Eclectic, Reminiscent."
139 "like army barracks": Author interview with Perkins.
140 "They picked him up": Author interview with Hensal.
140 "I had that feeling": Author interview with Perkins.
141 "Crosby, Stills, Nash and Young ought to get back together": Henry Mendoza, "Sound-ings," *San Bernardino County Sun*, April 27, 1972.
141 "chances are absolutely 100 percent": Tyler, "Stephen Stills."
141 One showed that 62 percent: Jack Rosenthal, "New Survey Finds Nixon Is Leading McGovern 62–23%," *New York Times*, September 25, 1972.
142 As teenage female fans: Beverly Creamer, "Stills Fights Loneliness with Music," *Hono-lulu Star Bulletin*, April 17, 1972.
143 "it has become thoroughly evident": Mike Davenport, "The Jazz Scene," *Van Nuys News*, May 5, 1972.
143 "Neil would tell me his dream": Author interview with Mazzeo.
144 John Hartmann of the Geffen-Roberts Company: Robert Hilburn, "Neil Young Sched-ules Concert Tour," *Los Angeles Times*, December 30, 1972.
144 As stragglers at the Baltimore show: Steven R. Henderson, "Neil Young Offers Good, Solid Music," *Baltimore Sun*, January 22, 1973.
144 "I didn't know Danny had died": Author interview with Barbata, 2009.
145 "He said, 'I need friends'": Author interview with GN.
145 "I don't know why success": Ibid.

CHAPTER 5: APRIL 1973–DECEMBER 1974

146 "That's just the way he is": Author interview with Barbata, 2010.
146 Taylor was shooting up: Dallas Taylor, *Prisoner of Woodstock* (Thunder's Mouth, 1994).
146 Without any explanation: Author interview with Barbata; Johny Barbata, *The Legend-ary Life of a Rock Star Drummer* (DJ Blues Publishing, 2005).
147 "Some of this stuff": Author interview with McGuinn.
147 "David was the boss": Ibid.
148 "I had a wonderful time": Judith Sims, "Reunion of Old Byrds: A Time for Peace," *Roll-ing Stone*, January 4, 1973.
148 "the most disappointing": Jon Landau, *Byrds* review, *Rolling Stone*, April 12, 1973.
148 "People liked their snow and drink": Author interview with Perkins.
149 "We said, 'This isn't happening'": Author interview with Howard Albert.
149 "Helping Stephen in the studio": Author interview with Giachetti.
149 "We were trying to get something": Author interview with Halverson.
150 "But then . . . I'd gone to visit Ringo": Author interview with SS, 2010.
150 "the self-pitying cry": Loraine Alterman, "Steve Stills–a Male Chauvinist?," *New York Times*, September 10, 1972.
150 "It's difficult to name": Judith Sims, "Stephen Stills: The Reformation of a 'Jive' Artist," *Rolling Stone*, September 27, 1973.
150 "CSNY was pretty much a constant fight": Author interview with Morris.
151 "Crosby, Stills and Nash is a *myth*": Jim Girard, "The Myth of Crosby, Stills & Nash," *Hit Parader*, January 1978.

151 In late 1972, music journalist: Ritchie Yorke, "Crosby, Stills & Nash Are Back Together," *Boston Globe*, December 16, 1972.

151 "my guiding light": Neil Young, *Waging Heavy Peace: A Hippie Dream* (Blue Rider, 2012).

151 Tom Moffatt, a local DJ: Eddie Sherman, "Typewriter Ribbons," *Honolulu Advertiser*, April 24, 1973.

152 "Why did they get married?": Author interview with Giachetti.

152 According to Young biographer: Jimmy McDonough, *Shakey: Neil Young's Biography* (Random House, 2002).

153 "It was Neil": Author interview with DC.

153 "drug-induced confusion": Bill DeYoung, "Stephen Stills," *Goldmine*, October 5, 2001.

154 "Neil didn't want us learning": David Browne, "Nils Lofgren Recalls Touring with Bruce, Writing with Lou Reed," *Rolling Stone*, April 3, 2014.

154 "very flirtatious": Author interview with Calli Cerami.

155 "We pretty much put Geffen in business": Author interview with DC.

155 "Graham and David were really pissed": Author interview with Cerami.

156 Weiss couldn't hear: Author interview with Ken Weiss.

157 "The year before hadn't been so good": Author interview with Cerami.

158 Barbata heard that: Barbata, *Legendary Life*.

159 "One time in the '80s": Author interview with Mazzeo.

159 As his friend Kevin Ryan recounted: Crosby and Gottlieb, *Long Time Gone*.

159 In Rochester, New York, Nash asked the crowd: Tom Teuber, "Supergroup Relives the 'Old Days,'" *Democrat and Chronicle* (Rochester, NY), October 30, 1973.

159 "the most deadly-dull big-name": Lynn Van Matre, "Crosby & Nash: A Dullsville Duo," *Chicago Tribune*, November 13, 1973.

160 "I think that some of my records have suffered": Barbara Charone, "CSNY Reunion: July 4th," *Zoo World*, April 25, 1974.

160 "Graham Nash doesn't like the style": Bruce Meyer, "Stereo Scene: A Tour and Album," *Daily Independent Journal*, May 31, 1974.

160 "I heard Graham say": Andy Greene interview with Tim Drummond, 2014.

160 "I kind of forced that down": Andy Greene interview with SS, 2014.

161 "It was like going on a camping trip": Author interview with Glenn Goodwin.

161 "It was a total mish-mash": Ibid.

162 "That was my first realization of": Author interview with O'Dell.

162 "We have a lot of past together": Radio interview, unknown outlet, bootleg.

162 "It was all this military shit": Author interview with Mazzeo.

162 As Stills, Young, and a teenage journalist: Cameron Crowe, "Crosby, Stills, Nash and Young Carry On," *Crawdaddy*, October 1974.

163 "I go, 'You gotta be kidding me'": Author interview with Goodwin.

164 The next day, in Vancouver: Crowe, "Crosby, Stills, Nash and Young Carry On."

164 "What it meant was": Author interview with Stone.

164 "We were dealing with the elements": Author interview with Goodwin.

165 "I was in my room in Vancouver": Author interview with O'Dell.

166 cost of sugar: "Soaring Sugar Prices Spur Record Profits," *New York Times*, November 3, 1974.

166 overzealous security guard: Michael Pousner, "The Man Who Makes It Go—Bill Graham," *New York Daily News*, August 15, 1974.

167 "too Mansonesque": Author interview with DC.

168 "Neil would just pull one out of his ass": Greene interview with Drummond.

170 "We're mature cats now": Michael Pousner, "From Sparks and Fumes, the Music Zooms," *New York Daily News,* August 13, 1974.
170 "amazingly relaxed": "Return of a Supergroup," *Time,* August 5, 1974.
171 "Neil said, 'Look, we're not going'": Author interview with Mazzeo.
171 "It was easier": Author interview with O'Dell.
171 "Neil traveled separately": Author interview with DC.
171 "Neil Young doesn't talk to anybody": Mary Campbell, UPI, August 23, 1974.
171 "You know, I'm not real good": Ben Fong-Torres, "The Reunion of Crosby, Stills, Nash & Young: The Ego Meets the Dove," *Rolling Stone,* August 29, 1974.
171 "They were very explosive": Author interview with Giachetti.
172 "I wanted to be the center of attention": Crosby and Gottlieb, *Long Time Gone.*
172 "I lived vicariously": Author interview with Stone.
172 "backfists and knuckle punches": DeYoung, "Stephen Stills."
172 "It was the only tour": Author interview with O'Dell.
173 "Who knew he needed cross-ventilation?": Ibid.
173 "And Dylan, being the arrogant man": Greene interview with Drummond.
173 "All my aware life": Fong-Torres, "Reunion of Crosby, Stills, Nash & Young."
173 "He came into the house": Author interview with Clarke.
174 "Bill let us go right to the stairs": The quotations and other details from the canceled concert and lawsuit from author interview with Jim Koplik.
175 "As we got more successful": Author interview with DC.
175 "They wanted us to go all over Europe": Greene interview with Drummond.
175 "one bucket of water": Roy Carr, "The Coming of Archie, Betty, Jughead and Veronica," *New Musical Express,* September 17, 1974.
176 "thousands of the whitest": Author interview with Mazzeo.
176 "Oh, God, it was like being in a hurricane": Author interview with Russ Kunkel, 2012.
177 "We were just too wrecked": Author interview with DC.
177 "We seem to have a two-month half-life": John Rockwell, "80,177 Jam Roosevelt Track for Summer Rock Finale," *New York Times,* September 9, 1974.
177 estimated $10 million profit shrank: Nash and Stone comments about finances from author interviews.
177 "We were not sufficiently aware": Author interview with DC.
178 "Stephen wanted me to sing": Author interview with GN.
178 "There was some yelling": Author interview with Goodwin.
178 "I was actually a little disappointed": Author interview with Cerami.
179 "The Albert brothers were listening": Author interview with GN. (Ron and Howard Albert have no memory of this moment.)
179 "not the most comfortable atmosphere": Author interview with Leland Sklar.
179 Over the course of two days: Studio logs courtesy Joel Bernstein.
179 "Neil could say, 'They drove me crazy'": Author interview with DC.
180 "I don't blame Neil": Author interview with Cerami.
180 "It was too much, too much": Author interview with Mazzeo.

CHAPTER 6: FEBRUARY 1975–AUGUST 1978

181 stored under his house: Author interview with Greg Fischbach.
182 "We would play in odd time signatures": Author interview with Hart.

182 "Listen, if they'd had new songs": Nick Kent, "Neil Young at 50," *Mojo*, December 1995.

183 "I remember how kids waiting": Nat Freeland, "Rock Fans Picky, Says Graham," *Billboard*, February 22, 1975.

183 "the most fashionable drug": Nicholas Gage, "Latins Now Leaders of Hard Drug Trade," *New York Times*, April 21, 1975.

184 "a seriously deteriorating": Bernard Gwertzman, "Last Americans Leave Cambodia; Embassy Closed," *New York Times*, April 12, 1975.

184 a lawyer who had prepared Nixon's tax returns: Eileen Shanahan, "Two Men Indicted over Nixon Taxes," *New York Times*, February 20, 1975.

184 "I kinda felt like": Barbara Charone, "Stephen Stills: A Sympathetic Self-Portrait," *Crawdaddy*, October 1975.

185 Tannen was alarmed: Author interview with Michael Tannen.

185 "Eventually they just said": Ibid.

185 delusional female fan: Author interview with Joel Bernstein.

186 "When I first joined this group": Author interview with Cerami.

186 Amy Gossage, Nash's partner: "SF Heiress Slain–Brother Booked," UPI, February 14, 1975.

186 "sophisticated waif": Victoria Graham, "Amy Gossage Lived, Died Dramatically," Associated Press, March 23, 1975.

186 "overreacted" in order to disarm: "California Youth Guilty in Killing," Associated Press, May 2, 1975.

186 "It really affected him": Author interview with Cerami.

187 "Graham was the hardest working": Author interview with Morris.

187 "We felt": Author interview with DC.

187 When Crosby and Nash's lawyer, Greg Fischbach: Author interview with Fischbach.

187 "You're not tired of Neil": Author interview with GN.

187 "David had spent a few years": Ibid.

188 "Nash and I were watching Stills": Author interview with DC.

188 "It was night and day": Author interview with Goodwin.

188 "That's not like spending": Cameron Crowe, "Crosby & Nash: 'More Kick-Ass Than Anyone Expects,'" *Rolling Stone*, October 23 1975.

189 "at the height": Stephen Holden, *Wind on the Water* review, *Rolling Stone*, December 4, 1975.

189 "George and Ringo": Cameron Crowe, "One Half of a Supergroup No More," *Rolling Stone*, January 1, 1976.

189 "Let's make history": Author interview with Kortchmar for *Rolling Stone*, 2013.

189 "I can always remember Crosby": Ibid.

189 "While they are not as spectacular": Robert Palmer, "Crosby and Nash Catch On," *New York Times*, September 11, 1976.

190 "What do you think of the girl": Miles Hurwitz and Mark Schroeder, "Nice Guys Finish First," *BAM*, September 1976.

191 "I ain't the asshole": Charone, "Stephen Stills: A Sympathetic Self-Portrait."

191 "I'm not going to be a hypocrite": Lowell Cauffiel, "Stephen Stills Grows Up," *Creem*, November 1975.

192 "While smoking grass": "The Artist and the Audience: No Excuse for Poor Manners," *Cashbox*, August 9, 1975.

192 "Stephen, why are you such an asshole?": Charone, "Stephen Stills: A Sympathetic Self-Portrait."

192 "heathen defense league": Cauffiel, "Stephen Stills Grows Up."

192　"I just wanted to get the fuck out of there": Author interview with Mazzeo.

192　"There is no real financial incentive": Dennis Hunt, "CSNY: To Tour or Not to Tour," *Los Angeles Times*, August 3, 1975.

193　"I was pretty out there": Jimmy McDonough, *Shakey: Neil Young's Biography* (Random House, 2002).

194　"Neil was exactly like Stephen": Author interview with George Perry.

195　"How cool was that?": Author interview with Giachetti.

195　"You didn't see too much of them": Author interview with Perry.

195　"I think we needed that": Author interview with Cerami.

195　"You're standing in my studio": Author interview with GN.

195　"Neil may have thought two things": Ibid.

196　"We still might make another album": Crowe, "Crosby & Nash: 'More Kick-Ass.'"

196　"They were telling us": Author interview with Greenfield.

196　"We absolutely thought about that": Author interview with GN.

197　Joe Vitale couldn't quite grasp: Author interview with Joe Vitale.

197　"Stephen was like a battery": Author interview with Perry.

197　Stills' guitar was so loud: Bob Spitz, *Dylan: A Biography* (McGraw-Hill, 1989).

197　"I watched them do that song": Author interview with Vitale.

198　"Neil came in with steam": William Ruhlmann, "Crosby, Stills and Nash: The Story So Far," *Goldmine*, January 24, 1992.

198　Crosby and Nash would finish their record: Chris Charlesworth interview with SS, Just Backdated blog, http://justbackdated.blogspot.com.

198　"I'd go home and come back": Author interview with Perry.

198　"[Crosby and Nash] sang 'Midnight on the Bay'": Bill Flanagan, "The Real Neil Young Stands Up," *Musician*, November 1985.

198　"How many times can you keep going": Ted Joseph, "Nasty Nash: Pre-Road Downers, Post-Album Dumping," *Crawdaddy*, September 1976.

199　"Nash has a temper": Author interview with DC.

199　"I thought, 'This is not good'": Author interview with Weiss.

200　"Stephen had trouble writing": Author interview with Tannen.

201　"[Young] got me in the dressing room": Charlesworth interview with SS.

201　Stills berated Young's sound man: McDonough, *Shakey*.

201　"When he forgot a line": Author interview with Perry.

201　"history-making tour": *Billboard*, July 17, 1976, advertisement.

201　"I had never been on a tour": Author interview with Perry.

202　"Stephen was heartbroken": Author interview with Vitale.

202　"I have no answers for you": Cameron Crowe, "The Actual, Honest-to-God Reunion of Crosby, Stills and Nash," *Rolling Stone*, June 2, 1977.

202　"disappointing substitute": Steve Pond, "Stills Static Without Young," *Los Angeles Times*, August 26, 1976.

203　"You can't manage David": Author interview with Morris.

204　"We thought, '*Someone* will see'": Author interview with David Rensin.

204　"They kicked our ass": This and other information about the softball game from author interviews with GN and Goodwin.

205　"I suspect it was Stephen": Author interview with DC.

205　"It's a question of finances": "Steve Stills Solo, for What It's Worth," *BAM*, November 9, 1976.

206　"What were we going to do": Author interview with GN.

206　"All I'd heard was what a monster": Zimmer, *Crosby, Stills & Nash*.

207 "There was a different vibe": Author interview with Vitale.

207 "The main requirement": Author interview with Giachetti.

207 "Everyone came in every day": Author interview with Howard Albert.

208 "Graham and David let Stephen do his thing": Ibid.

208 "I didn't see any arguments": Author interview with Perry.

208 Although Crosby remained with Debbie Donovan: Crosby and Gottlieb, *Long Time Gone.*

209 "We didn't have any instruction": Author interview with DC.

209 Stills actually challenged Crosby: Peter Knobler, "Dark Star: Working the Vampire Shift with Stephen Stills," *Crawdaddy,* December 1977.

209 "There was a lot of wretched excess": Author interview with DC.

209 "with the understanding": Trowe, "Eclectic, Reminiscent, Amused, Fickle, Perverse (I and II)," *New Yorker,* May 29 and June 7, 1978.

210 Then, at Hartmann's invitation: Author interview with John Hartmann.

210 "Obviously they must have had a good time": Author interview with Giachetti.

210 "some guy not exactly dressed for a prom": Author interview with Ron Albert.

211 "It was 'I hope you like this'": Author interview with Vitale.

211 "We tried to learn it": Flanagan, "The Real Neil Young."

212 "He chose the colors carefully": Author interview with Hartmann.

212 "I guess maybe I don't like myself": Knobler, "Dark Star."

213 "Do I know that song?": Author interview with Joan Baez.

213 "As Graham said to me once": Author interview with Bill Siddons.

213 "Crosby, Stills and Nash Recapture Magic": Jack Williams, Copley News Service, November 7, 1977.

213 "Ultimately, one senses a defeatism": John Rockwell, "Neil Young—As Good as Dylan?," *New York Times,* June 19, 1977.

214 "Anything more than four weeks": Author interview with John Vanderslice.

214 The rider in the trio's backstage contract: This and other Pittsburgh show information from Deborah Deasy, "Back Stage: Many Pitch in to Let Show Go On," *Pittsburgh Press,* June 26, 1977.

215 "The dynamics were different": Author interview with Goodwin.

215 "There were still a lot of Carrie vibes": Author interview with Mazzeo.

215 "I said, 'Buck has a band together'": Ibid.

216 "the worst-kept secret in town": Greg Beebe, "Ducks Band Plays Two Solid Sets," *Santa Cruz Sentinel,* August 1, 1977.

216 "They were fine": Author interview with Bob Mosley.

216 "I'm starting to get back": Geoffrey Dunn, "The Story of Neil Young's Short-Lived Santa Cruz Band the Ducks," *Good Times,* August 15, 2017.

216 "Neil loved that": Author interview with Mazzeo.

217 "After the Stills-Young thing": Ibid.

217 "new songs for Young's upcoming record albums": "Police Nearly Nab Robbery Suspect," *Santa Cruz Sentinel,* August 22, 1977.

217 "It was the end of the summer": Author interview with Mosley.

217 "Whereas Crosby and Nash, who have toured": Robert Hilburn, "Crosby, Stills & Nash Reunion," *Los Angeles Times,* June 30, 1977.

217 both men glaring: Zimmer, *Crosby, Stills & Nash.*

217 "Sometimes there would be amazing harmony": Author interview with Giachetti.

218 "Nash would always say": Author interview with Vanderslice.

218 "There was this feeling": DeYoung, "Stephen Stills."

218 "I didn't appreciate that at all": Author interview with Perry.

218   "He played his parts!": Ibid.

218   Hartmann witnessed Stills having: Michael Walker, *Laurel Canyon: The Inside Story of Rock-and-Roll's Legendary Neighborhood* (Faber and Faber, 2006).

218   "Now let's hope it's not an accident": Jack Garner, "Finally, Back on Record," *Democrat and Chronicle* (Rochester, NY), July 24, 1977.

219   "That was insane": Author interview with Kortchmar.

219   "Everybody had their own set of guys": Author interview with Vitale.

219   "He was kind of feeling it out": Author interview with McGuinn.

219   "He said, 'Don't come'": Author interview with Collins.

219   "honest and surprisingly humble": Peter Herbst, *CSN* review, *Rolling Stone*, June 17, 1977.

220   "Audience and band went home happy": Michael Aaron, "Easy the Way It's Supposed to Be: CS&N Piece It Together Again," *Rolling Stone*, August 11, 1977.

221   "Well, at that point, I felt like": Flanagan, "The Real Neil Young."

CHAPTER 7: JANUARY 1979–NOVEMBER 1982

225   "the most far-out disco sound": Anthony Fawcett and Henry Diltz, *California Rock California Sound* (Reed, 1978).

226   "a Tequila Sunrise": Rob Sanford, "Straight Talk from Stephen Stills," *Songwriter*, August 1979.

226   "I know I'm good for him": Bill Royce, "Peopletalk," *Philadelphia Inquirer*, February 2, 1979.

227   "Ask Graham": Sanford, "Straight Talk."

227   "Why all the boring CSN questions?": Ibid.

227   "I haven't seen 'em": Dave Zimmer, "Stephen Stills Carries On," *BAM*, April 6, 1979.

227   "There was no communication": Author interview with Giachetti.

227   He and his new girlfriend: Details about DC and Jan Dance based on Crosby and Gottlieb, *Long Time Gone*.

228   Working at Britannia Studio: Information about Crosby and Nash sessions from author interview with GN; Crosby and Gottlieb, *Long Time Gone*.

229   the Nuclear Regulatory Commission: "2300 Reported at Nuclear Plants in 1979," *New York Times*, July 14, 1980.

231   "First of all, I think anyone": Young interview, YouTube, "Neil Young–Interview," YouTube, posted March 29, 2015, https://www.youtube.com/watch?v=frSgDeNjfgo.

231   "We were like, 'Oh, my God'": Author interview with Danny Goldberg.

231   "wild look": Ibid.

232   "I walked in and said": Author interview with Hartmann.

232   Michael Stergis, a trumpet player: Author interview with Michael Stergis.

232   "the new David Crosby": Ibid.

233   "Can someone tune?" and "Nobody sang": Robert Ely, "Show Termed Excellent, But Nash 'Misunderstood,'" *Tampa Bay Times* (St. Petersburg, FL), May 9, 1980.

234   "The man was totally overwhelmed": Author interview with Rao.

235   "bum band": Crosby and Gottlieb, *Long Time Gone*.

235   "What's a 'Stills-Nash' record?": Author interview with Siddons.

235   "Personality wise": Author interview with Susan Rogers.

236   "Graham will make anybody": Author interview with Stergis.

236   "Stephen came alive": Author interview with GN.

236   "The name 'Daylight Again' was a joke": Author interview with John Partipilo.

237 "It's about all four of us": Fricke interview with GN, 2005.
237 *BAM*'s Dave Zimmer was at home: Author interview with Dave Zimmer.
238 "We were always expecting that call": Author interview with Rao.
238 "About five years or so": Johnny Rogan, *Crosby, Stills, Nash & Young: The Visual Documentary* (Omnibus, 1996).
238 Crosby seemed to take it all in: Crosby and Gottlieb, *Long Time Gone*.
238 called *Push Play*. Ibid.
238 *FZ Tango*: Script courtesy Robert Greenfield.
239 "He was locked in the vocal booth": Author interview with Waddy Wachtel.
239 "smelled like a cat box": Author interview with Leland Sklar.
239 "It wasn't a normal record": Author interview with DC.
240 "The record company won't accept": Joni Norris, "David Crosby Moving on with His Music," *Daily Press* (Newport News, VA), May 10, 1981.
240 "David was being a little difficult": Christopher Connelly, "Random Notes," *Rolling Stone*, reprinted in *Fort Lauderdale News and Sun-Sentinel*, August 21, 1981.
240 In a phone call with label executives: Author interview with Weiss.
240 "I thought, 'Is this the end?'": Author interview with Vitale.
241 "Ahmet said, 'You can't do it'": Author interview with DC.
241 Nash recruited Susan Rogers: Author interview with Rogers.
241 On the designated day: Author interview with Zimmer.
241 "All I knew was that I was there": Author interview with Stergis.
241 "He was real humble": Author interview with Vitale.
241 "It was a place where I could get high": Author interview with DC.
242 "I said, 'Why *wouldn't* I like him?'": Author interview with Rogers.
242 After the song was finished: Author interviews with GN and Rogers.
242 A musicologist hired: Author interview with Fischbach.
242 "It sounds like I was evading": Author interview with GN.
243 "high-melodrama day": Author interview with Siddons.
244 "It's hard to approach him": Dennis Hunt, "Crosby, Stills and Nash Bury the Hatchet Again," *Los Angeles Times*, November 27, 1982.
245 "Those were the years": Author interview with Vanderslice.
245 "lived a tough life": Norris, "David Crosby Moving on with His Music."
248 "A lot of that": Patrick Doyle interview with Young, 2016.
248 "The excitement in LA": Author interview with Rogers.
248 "They just seem in some way": Greil Marcus, "Elvis Costello Repents," *Rolling Stone*, September 2 1982.
249 "The more of the past you have": This and subsequent quotes from David Gans, "Neil Young: A New Phase," *Record*, October 1982.
249 "I remember reading that": Author interview with Rao.
249 "I said, 'What's that?'": Author interview with Jimmy Wachtel.
250 On March 28, he was driving: "Singer Crosby Arrested on Drug, Weapon Charges," UPI, March 30, 1982.
250 About two weeks later, on April 12: Details of the arrest at Cardi's from Texas Court of Appeals, "David Van Cortlandt Crosby, Appellant, v. The State of Texas, Appellee," 750 S.W.2d 768 (1987); Crosby and Gottlieb, *Long Time Gone*.
250 "David was like a bad penny": Author interview with Rao.
250 "When we put all the songs together": Hunt, "Crosby, Stills and Nash Bury the Hatchet Again."
251 "Stephen and Graham had a mask on": Author interview with Vitale.

251 "I remember thinking": Author interview with Rogers.
251 "I didn't know David that well": Author interview with Siddons.
251 "Great reference": Author interview with Dave Rao.
252 "Really? I didn't know": Dave Zimmer, "Crosby Stills & Nash Together Again," *BAM*, July 30, 1982.
252 "There were some big arguments": Author interview with Vitale.
252 "immobile, untalkative presence": Geoffrey Himes, "CS&N Is No Fine Wine," *Baltimore Evening Sun*, August 6, 1982.
252 "David was up there like a prop": Author interview with Vitale.
252 "Nobody knew if he was coming back": Author interview with Mason Wilkinson.
253 "David and I used to lock on stage": Author interview with Perry.
254 "You can tell by the way Neil is looking": Author interview with Zimmer.
254 "One day Neil says": Browne, "Nils Lofgren Recalls Touring with Bruce, Writing with Lou Reed."
255 "I thought 'What the hell'": Author interview with Vitale.
255 "It was a mess to deal with": Author interview with GN.

CHAPTER 8: MARCH 1983–DECEMBER 1985

256 "If I happen to walk offstage": Details of Young Louisville concert from Cheryl Devall, "Crowd Goes into Frenzy When Illness Forces Singer to Leave Stage," *Louisville Courier-Journal*, March 5, 1983.
257 five minutes in the Oval Office: Files of "Jimmy Carter Presidential Daily Diary," Jimmy Carter Presidential Library and Museum collection, Atlanta, Georgia.
258 Nuclear power plants were historically unpopular: Doug McInnis, "Nuclear Utilities Plagued by Costly Equipment Breakdowns," *New York Times*, October 10, 1982.
258 "I went through a period": Malcolm MacKinnon, "Graham Nash Rockin' for the Planet," *Hemp Times*, February/March 1998.
259 "The sooner the compact disc replaces": Mike Hennessey, "Compact Disc Launches in U.K.," *Billboard*, March 5, 1983.
259 "We could get blasé": This and other quotes in this passage from Steven Dupler, "Crosby, Stills & Nash: A Look at the Legend," *International Musician and Recording World*, March 1983.
260 "Neil tried one time": Author interview with DC.
260 "a husky, extroverted Californian": "Rock Star Crosby Is Guilty on Cocaine and Pistol Raps," UPI, June 5, 1983.
260 "I was sitting in front of my TV": Author interview with GN.
261 "We had to put the wheels down": Ibid.
261 "It was bolted together": Author interview with Siddons.
262 "in the fall": Atlantic Records, *Allies* press kit, 1983.
263 Extraordinary precautions: Details on drug arrangements for 1983 tour from Crosby and Gottlieb, *Long Time Gone*, and author interview with anonymous source.
263 According to Wald: Jeff Wald as told to Kim Masters, "A Gritty Account of Life as a Famous Hollywood Drug Addict," *Hollywood Reporter*, May 30, 2011.
263 "I wasn't about to go to Europe": Author interview with Vitale.
263 "We were nervous": Author interview with Perry.
264 "I never drank until later": John Seabrook, "Judy Collins and Stephen Stills' Old Romance," *New Yorker*, September 25, 2017.

264 "We did what we had to": Author interview with Siddons.

265 "I truly believe that what David needs": "David Crosby Free on Bail, Will Appeal Convictions," *Dallas Morning News*, August 7, 1983.

265 In a biting response: "Singer David Crosby Sentenced," Associated Press, August 7, 1983.

265 "His torso is bloated and heavy": Peter Carlson, "Cocaine Casualty," *People*, August 29, 1983.

265 By decree of the Los Angeles Superior Court: William Plummer, "'Mad Housewife' Carrie Snodgress Sues Rocker Neil Young for Support of Their Handicapped Son," *People*, September 26, 1983.

267 "One day, I show up": Browne, "Nils Lofgren Recalls Touring with Bruce, Writing with Lou Reed."

267 "To live with that and deal with it": Author interview with Jessi Colter.

268 "Reagan—so what": "Neil Young Is Backing Reagan," Newhouse News Service, October 12, 1984.

268 That November, while his case: This account and excerpts from this and subsequent medical reports are based on Crosby and Gottlieb, *Long Time Gone*.

269 "I always thought that because": Author interview with Siddons.

269 "They tried to keep me from coming": Andy Smith, "Crosby, Solo Now, Hasn't Forsaken His Musical Roots," *Democrat and Chronicle* (Rochester, NY), March 9, 1984.

269 "You've made a lot of money off me": Author interview with DC.

270 "Atlantic wanted an album": Author interview with GN.

270 "There was nothing anybody could do": Author interview with Debbie Meister.

271 "What can I say?": Andy Smith, "Crosby, Stills & Nash: Breaking Up Is Hard to Do for This Band," *Democrat and Chronicle* (Rochester, NY), October 22, 1984.

271 Nash swore off cocaine: Author interview with GN.

272 "Envision this": Zach Dunkin, "CSN&Y: Could It Happen?," *Indianapolis News*, September 14, 1984.

273 After putting off his admission: Crosby and Gottlieb, *Long Time Gone*.

273 "Being addicted takes over": Author interview with DC.

273 "I was just about to turn": Cope Moyers, "David Crosby Feels Music, Daylight During Stay in Jail," Los Angeles Times Service, March 13, 1985.

275 "Graham was beside himself": Author interview with Tim Foster.

275 "They said, 'We have to be as good'": Author interview with Siddons.

275 "Neil cautiously came back": Author interview with GN.

275 "It was one of the few times": Author interview with Siddons.

276 "Once Neil heard it": Author interview with GN.

276 "Damn, you'd have thought": Kent, "Neil Young at 50."

276 "We're trying to get as much touring": Justin Mitchell, "Crosby, Stills & Nash Still Rockin' Despite Personal Problems," *Pittsburgh Press*, July 28, 1985.

276 "The drama might have": Author interview with Rao.

277 In Philadelphia, Crosby disappeared: Ann Kolson, "A Life of Song and Trouble," *Philadelphia Inquirer*, August 9, 1985.

277 "It was pretty shocking": Author interview with Partipilo.

277 "I was a massive disappointment": Author interview with DC.

277 "Their harmonizing was remarkably": Stephen Holden, "Folk-Rock: Crosby, Stills and Nash Sing," *New York Times*, August 16, 1984.

278 "Our minds were blown": Author interview with Meister.

278 "I remember feeling so weird": Author interview with Siddons.

278 "With the Eagles, every note": Author interview with Vanderslice.

279 "I'd be in jail": Miles Hurwitz and Mark Schroeder, "Nice Guys Finish First," *BAM*, September 1976.
279 "like the worst nightmare": Barr Nobles, "A 'Fat and Sassy' Comeback," *San Francisco Chronicle*, November 1, 1986.
280 "I hope it doesn't end tragically": "Lawyer Is Fearful for David Crosby," Associated Press, November 29, 1985.
280 "underdogs and outlaws": Crosby and Gottlieb, *Long Time Gone*.
280 "Everybody was hiding him out": Author interview with Hart.
280 "Jan and I were so happy": Crosby and Gottlieb, *Long Time Gone*.
280 "the end of my line": Author interview with DC.
281 "Wish me luck": "Rock Singer David Crosby Surrenders to FBI," Associated Press, December 13, 1985.

CHAPTER 9: JANUARY 1986–DECEMBER 1988

282 "Who the fuck is that?": Author interview with Siddons.
282 "This hippie came walking in": Author interview with Niko Bolas.
283 "It hurt people": Ibid.
283 "I never thought David would die": Author interview with GN.
283 "It doesn't have David or Stephen on it": Lynn Van Matre, "Graham Nash Tries a True Solo Album Without Hint of Crosby, Stills or Young," *Chicago Tribune*, July 27, 1986.
284 During a break, Wachtel: Author interview with Waddy Wachtel.
284 "I'm in a room about the size": David O'Brian, "Straight Time," *San Jose Mercury News*, March 6, 1986.
285 "I would very much like to be": Ibid.
285 whose previous few years had been as grim: Crosby and Gottlieb, *Long Time Gone*.; Tom Leyde, "End of Cocaine Habit Is Addict's Beginning," Gannett News Service, May 14, 1986.
285 "She has to clean up, too": Author interview with Meister.
285 The Dead's Mickey Hart: Author interview with Hart.
286 "It rolled off his back": Author interview with McGuinn.
286 "That's the first thing I wrote": Author interview with DC.
286 "We set it up showbiz-wise": Author interview with GN.
286 A worried Siddons offered to pay: Author interview with Siddons.
287 "fat and sassy": Barr Nobles, "A 'Fat and Sassy' Comeback," *San Francisco Chronicle*, November 1, 1986.
288 "I'm a bit of a klutz": Author interview with Pegi Young.
288 "They surprised me": Ibid.
289 "They seemed really happy": Ibid.
289 "Everybody's concerned": Tape of *Rockline* interview, 1983.
290 "If I manage to stay off drugs": O'Brian, "Straight Time."
290 "big plans": Thom Duffy, "No Nukes This Time Around in Nash's Solo Traveling Show," *Orlando Sentinel*, August 24, 1986.
291 "all over the map": Author interview with Bill Szymczyk.
291 "None of us were walking around": Author interview with Vitale.
291 "I'd seen so many fights": Author interview with Perry.
291 "It turned into seven days": Author interview with Szymczyk.
292 "I did a double take": Author interview with Meister.

292 "They were happy": Author interview with DC.

293 "That was the turning point": This and other quotes in the paragraph from author interview with John Ferrugia.

293 "I loved their music": Ibid.

293 "The end of my enjoyment": Dan Rather interview with SS, *The Big Interview*, March 10, 2014.

293 "I think I had a good time": Author interview with SS, 2010.

294 "You could see where": Author interview with Ferrugia.

294 "He wasn't good with time": Author interview with Vitale.

294 "Every tour that CSN": James Henke, "Neil Young," *Rolling Stone*, June 2, 1988.

294 "When there's a TV crew from CBS": Author interview with GN.

294 "Graham wasn't a milquetoast": Author interview with Siddons.

294 "I said, 'Shoot this!'": Author interview with Vicki Samuels.

294 "It was bad timing": Author interview with Vanderslice.

295 "now that Crosby is awake": Cathy Beckham, "Switching Strings for Suits," *Statesman Journal* (Salem, OR), July 31, 1987.

295 "You would never think": Author interview with Meister.

295 "He said, 'I said things'": Author interview with Ferrugia.

295 "The thing that surprised me": Henke, "Neil Young."

296 "Crosby, Stills and Nash are old, fat farts!": Fredric Dannen, *Hit Men: Power Brokers and Fast Money Inside the Music Business* (Crown, 1990).

296 "The next thing I know": Author interview with Bolas.

297 "It was really unpredictable": Author interview with Chad Cromwell.

298 "The relationship between them": Author interview with GN.

298 "Crosby would do whatever": Author interview with Siddons.

298 "if this thing can fly": Author interview with Vitale.

298 "Can it happen again?": Abbie Hoffman, *The Best of Abbie Hoffman* (Four Walls Eight Windows, 1989).

299 "It was, 'This is what I've got'": Author interview with Bolas.

299 "It was like putting on": Author interview with DC.

300 "It's very productive": This and other quotes from Dave Zimmer, "Neil Young: Blue Notes from a Restless Loner," *BAM*, April 22, 1988.

300 "Neil has some difficulty": Author interview with Pegi Young.

300 "When they walked in the door": Author interview with Bolas.

301 "When it was happening": Author interview with Cromwell.

301 "You're not going to produce them": Author interview with Bolas.

301 "toasted": David Crosby and Carl Gottlieb, *Since Then: How I Survived Everything and Lived to Tell About It* (G. P. Putnam's, 2006).

301 "I don't remember": *VH1 Legends*, VH1, 2000.

301 *Geriatrics' Revenge*: Tom Hibbert, "Shakey's Last Stand," *Q*, June 1988.

301 "You spend too much time in a jail": Author interview with Vanderslice.

301 "When he did that": Author interview with GN.

302 "Neil was doing everything possible": Author interview with Bernstein.

302 "Neil and Stephen abused the privilege": Author interview with DC.

303 "It ain't there": David Fricke interview with SS, 1998.

303 "We were on pins and needles": Author interview with Siddons.

303 he was told upfront: Author interview with Aaron Rapoport.

306 "What's missing beyond the failings": John Rockwell, "Old Timers Out for a Spin Cut a Couple of Disks," *New York Times*, November 13, 1988.

306 "If the quartet had made": Michael Anft, "From Here to Bulgaria, It's Been a Good Year for the Voice," *Baltimore Evening Sun*, December 8, 1988.

307 "Everybody was hoping": Author interview with Bolas.

307 "Well, *some* of us have": Author interview with DC, 1988.

307 "Stephen could use some help": Gary Graff, "It's Deja Vu as Strife Makes More Fine Music for Crosby and Crew," *Detroit Free Press*, December 25, 1988.

307 "It wouldn't be a consistently great thing": Zimmer, "Neil Young: Blue Notes."

308 "If we go out there": Henke, "Neil Young."

308 "Neil recognized the album": Author interview with anonymous source.

308 "It could've been great": Jimmy McDonough, "Fuckin' Up with Neil Young: Too Faroz Gone," *Village Voice Rock & Roll Quarterly*, Winter 1989.

308 "I think his actions were indicative": Author interview with Pegi Young.

308 "It would have helped sell": Author interview with Vitale.

308 "earth shattering": Author interview with GN.

309 "I don't know": Steve Pond, "Nash & Friends Raise Money for Hungry Kids," *Los Angeles Times*, November 14, 1988.

309 "I saw him driving": Andy Greene, "Graham Nash's Photographs," *Rolling Stone*, April 11, 2013.

CHAPTER 10: DECEMBER 1988–NOVEMBER 1994

310 "We were in Manhattan recording": Author interview with Cromwell.

310 "I'm thinking": Ibid.

311 "It only lasted a while": Interview cited in Nick Kent, "This Young Will Run and Run," *Vox*, November 1990.

312 "I knew they weren't getting along": Author interview with McGuinn.

313 "Stills and I butt heads": Wayne Bledsoe, "Music in the Pink with David Crosby," *News Journal* (Wilmington, DE), June 20, 1990.

313 "Graham really liked it": Author interview with Vitale.

314 "We were trying to do the best": Author interview with GN.

314 "You should have seen what": Ibid.

314 "We're not handsome": Ruhlmann, "Crosby, Stills and Nash: The Story So Far."

314 "fucking weird image": Author interview with GN.

314 "Those sticks are very fragile": Ibid.

314 "I said, 'Fine'": Ibid.

314 "That was the only time": Author interview with Siddons.

314 "Blame Nash": Author interview with DC.

315 "That song was from the heart": Author interview with Siddons.

315 "uncharacteristically subdued": Michael Dunn, "Records," *Tampa Tribune*, July 20, 1990.

315 "We thought this year": Kathy Haight, "Crosby, Stills, Nash Still Having Fun," *Pittsburgh Press*, July 5, 1990.

315 "I wanted to up the game": Author interview with Siddons.

315 "million-dollar mistake": Ibid.

315 "It's CSN, not Pink Floyd": Author interview with Vitale.

316 "There was nothing different": Author interview with Alex Coletti.

317 Taylor sued Stills: Dallas Taylor, *Prisoner of Woodstock* (Thunder's Mouth, 1994).

317 living with two prostitutes: Cynthia Sanz, "Finally Drug-Free, Drummer Dallas Taylor Hopes for One More Miracle: A New Liver," *People*, April 2, 1990.

317   "physically incapacitated": Author interview with Sebastian.

317   "watching from behind the curtain": Taylor, *Prisoner of Woodstock*.

320   "I just can't listen to it": Author interview with Steve Silberman.

320   "Neil said, 'You can use'": Author interview with GN.

320   "a shit deal": Jimmy McDonough, *Shakey: Neil Young's Biography* (Random House, 2002).

321   "I had a lot of very angry women": Author interview with Meister.

321   "It's just that his songs": Ruhlmann, "Crosby, Stills and Nash: The Story So Far."

321   "I can see it, in her dining room": Larry McShane, "Crosby, Stills & Nash Remain Friends After 22 Years of Volatile Partnership," Associated Press, November 1, 1991.

321   "When we say, 'What about'": Ibid.

322   "Don't do it": Author interview with Chris Hillman for *Rolling Stone*, 2009.

322   "It was very awkward": David Browne, "Back to the Garden," *Rolling Stone*, September 17, 2009.

322   "I thought it was dumb": Author interview with DC.

323   "I guess Neil Young is the king": Kurt Loder, *Ragged Glory* review, *Rolling Stone*, September 20, 1990.

323   "CSN had fallen into": Author interview with Siddons.

324   "What's going on?": Author interview with DC.

325   "It was freeing and cathartic": Ibid.

325   "It was very successful": Author interview with GN.

325   "a remote, sullen figure": Stephen Holden, "Three Music Specials with Images of Middle Age," *New York Times*, March 7, 1992.

325   "We thought, 'Let's make a record'": Author interview with Ron Albert.

327   "What was frustrating was how": Author interview with Meister.

328   "We knew we'd get something": Author interview with Siddons.

328   Stills could even be found: Author interview with Zimmer.

328   "Glyn Johns is fearless": Author interview with DC.

328   "We all knew what we could be doing": Author interview with GN.

328   "Wow—when these classic acts": Author interview with Siddons.

329   "We sound like church geeks": This and other details in this passage from Chuck Crisafulli, "*Déjà vu* All Over Again," *Los Angeles Times*, July 24, 1994.

330   "Woodstock was an idea": Author interview with Lang.

331   "I was definitely into it": Ibid.

331   "It had to be": Ibid.

331   "We were not aware of that": Author interview with GN.

331   "They were so heavily": Author interview with Lang.

331   "Neil knew as I did": Author interview with DC.

332   "Who gives a shit?": "Woodstock '94: The Best and Worst," Associated Press, August 22, 1994.

332   "three sexy girls": Author interview with Vanderslice.

333   "It was awful": Author interview with DC.

333   $1 million for back taxes: David Crosby, "Second Chance," *People*, February 20, 1995.

333   "I felt like someone hit me": Author interview with DC.

334   "You leave me": Author interview with GN.

CHAPTER 11: APRIL 1995–APRIL 2000

337   "It was a little bit of a surprise": Author interview with Meister.

337 "a wonderful, happy afternoon": Zimmer, *Crosby, Stills & Nash*.

337 He was criticized by some: Bill Laitner, "Crosby Transplant Stirs Debate," Knight-Ridder Newspapers, December 3, 1994.

338 "If I was going to play with CSN": Eric Weisbard, "Not Fade Away," *Spin*, September 1995.

338 "Maybe it was a harbinger": Author interview with Meister.

339 "I realized that everything": Author interview with Siddons.

339 "a CSNY moment": Author interview with Joel Gallen.

340 "I think we're more compassionate": Gary Graff, "Crosby, Stills & Nash Carry On," Reuters, May 22, 1997.

341 "Sometimes you don't like": Rex Rutkoski, "Crosby, Stills and Nash Endure with the Times," Gannett News Service, June 25, 1996.

341 "I like him—no, I love him": Steve Silberman, "An Egg Thief in Cyberspace: A Conversation with David Crosby," *Goldmine*, July 7, 1995.

342 "It was our choice": Author interview with DC.

342 "It paid a year's taxes": Fricke interview with SS, 1998.

342 "There's a wealth of opportunities": "CSN to Carry on Without Atlantic," *Hollywood Reporter*, March 12, 1997.

343 "After the Bowie deal": Author interview with David Pullman.

343 "It was uncomfortable for them": Ibid.

344 "We didn't think it was a great idea": Author interview with GN.

344 "It was like, 'Well, we're never'": Author interview with Pullman.

344 played a week of non-corporate shows: Details of Fillmore show from notes courtesy David Fricke.

344 "this big roar": Fricke interview with Nash, 1998.

344 "All bands start out really excited": Author interview with DC.

345 "This is not going to be easy": Author interview with Jeff Pevar.

345 In the summer of 1997: Notes courtesy David Fricke.

346 Among them was a letter: This and details in the next two paragraphs from author interviews with DC and Stacia Raymond; Crosby and Gottlieb, *Since Then*.

347 "What could have been": Author interview with Leland Sklar.

347 "I think David sought refuge": Author interview with Pevar.

348 "You guys are sounding pretty good": Author interview with Halverson.

349 "There was always a competitiveness": Author interview with Pegi Young.

349 During the Springfield archive-digging: Notes courtesy David Fricke.

350 "*American Dream* was an attempt": Kent, "Neil Young at 50."

350 "He admires it when people": Author interview with Pegi Young.

350 "I don't know why I felt": Robert Hilburn, "CSNY: More Than Deja Vu," *Los Angeles Times*, February 12, 2000.

350 "I have no idea why": Author interview with DC.

351 "Why aren't they singing together?": This and following paragraphs from author interview with Halverson.

352 "He came to me and said": Author interview with Howie Klein.

352 "a little weird": Author interview with GN.

352 "They couldn't generate the magic": Author interview with Halverson.

353 "If you hadn't made me sound so good": Ibid.

353 "You replace it": Ibid.

354 "Neil wasn't hearing": Author interview with GN.

355 "It was out of our hands": Ibid.

355 a guarantee of $500,355: Steve Hochman, "Promoter Floats CSNY Tour," *Los Angeles Times*, January 31, 1999.
355 "When it's CSNY": Author interview with Bill Bentley.
356 "It changes the money": Author interview with DC.
356 But nothing compared to: Author interview with GN; Tim Ryan, "Nash Suppressed Pain by Envisioning a Sunset," *Honolulu Star Bulletin*, September 20, 1999.
357 "We had to test the sound system": Author interview with Bentley.
357 "I love how you dress": Edna Gundersen, "CSNY Rediscovering a Four-Part Harmony," *USA Today*, October 25, 1999.
357 "See how much we like you?": Joel Selvin, "*Déjà vu* All Over Again," *San Francisco Chronicle*, October 9, 1999.
358 "I mean, God only knows why": European press conference, October 1999.
359 "It was like Ford and GM": Author interview with Wilkinson.
359 "It's not that Neil didn't think": Author interview with Vanderslice.
359 "We knew Neil didn't want": Author interview with GN.
359 "We were like, 'Uh, *what?*'": Author interview with Wilkinson.
360 "That was a pretty low blow": Author interview with Vitale.
360 "It was a mess": Author interview with DC.
360 "From the CSN side": Author interview with Vanderslice.
360 "It may seem to be a little harsh": David Fricke interview with Neil Young, 2000.
360 "Neil will always sing in tune": Author interview with Jim Keltner.
361 "It wasn't a bad fight": Ibid.
361 "If Stephen saw Neil was upset": Ibid.
361 Starting in late January 2000: This paragraph and the two paragraphs that follow from notes courtesy David Fricke.
363 "Stephen used to bug": Author interview with Keltner.
363 "Neil really loves Stephen": Author interview with GN.
363 "No matter what else": Author interview with Arthur Fogel.
365 "It's not goodbye": Author interview with Halverson.

CHAPTER 12: MAY 2001–SEPTEMBER 2006

366 "It didn't hit me the whole time": Author interview with Steve "Smokey" Potts.
367 "Neil has always called the shots": Author interview with DC.
367 "I guess you don't understand how": Jim DeRogatis, "Carry On for Love and Money," *Chicago Sun-Times*, April 25, 2002.
368 "When you play together for 30-odd years": Robert Hilburn, "CSNY: More Than Deja Vu," *Los Angeles Times*, February 12, 2000.
369 "because I've been around for a long time": Jeff Waful, "Neil Young into the Source," *Relix*, August–September 2003.
370 "It meant everything": Author interview with DC.
370 "Whenever Stephen hears a Crosby song": Author interview with GN.
371 "I likened it": Author interview with Pevar.
371 "I think Stephen saw Jeff": Author interview with GN.
371 "There are just so many notes": Zimmer, *Crosby, Stills & Nash.*
373 "It's a very unique situation": Author interview with Pevar.
373 "I go, 'What?'": Ibid.
373 "David was being stupid": Author interview with GN.

373 "completely stupid": Crosby and Gottlieb, *Since Then*.

374 "We said, 'Sorry'": Author interview with DC.

374 "electronic games, toys": Author interview with Dave Zimmer.

375 "He took care of Stephen": Author interview with GN.

375 "Gerry kept the energy going": Author interview with Vitale.

375 "a piece of broken glass": Josh Tyrangiel, "The Resurrection of Neil Young," *Time*, September 26, 2005.

375 "All I know is": Ibid.

375 Copies of *USA Today* were distributed: Gregg Zoroya, "Lifesaving Knowledge, Innovation Emerge in War Clinic," *USA Today*, March 27, 2006.

376 "the intelligence community was dead wrong": Report of the Commission on the Intelligence Capabilities of the United States Regarding Weapons of Mass Destruction, March 31, 2005, archived at White House: President George W. Bush, https://georgewbush-whitehouse.archives.gov/wmd.

377 "Man, how come no one's": Author interview with Bolas.

377 "He'd go back home": Author interview with Cromwell.

377 "He was sick of the war": Author interview with Bentley.

378 "I don't know if Stephen": Author interview with GN.

379 "a regular tour": Author interview with Mike Cerre.

379 As a forward air observer: John Hickey, "An Interview with '69 Domer Mike Cerre," University of Notre Dame blog, http://notredameclassof1969blog.blogspot.com/2017/07/an-interview-with-69-domer-mike-cerre.html.

379 "They were very concerned": Author interview with Cerre.

380 "He realized he has a certain audience": Author interview with GN.

380 "When there's a vast": Ibid.

380 "He wanted us for legitimacy": Author interview with DC.

380 "I said, 'Tell me about the band'": Author interview with Cromwell.

380 "It was fair to assume": Ibid.

381 "They kept trying to break the mold": Martyn Palmer, "I Want Out," *Mojo*, May 2008.

381 "'Wind on the Water'—why not?": Author interview with GN.

381 "misgivings and ambivalence": Palmer, "I Want Out."

382 "I wasn't at the meeting": Jon Bream, "Four Strong Winds," *Minneapolis Star Tribune*, September 1, 2006.

382 "When he has a head of steam": Author interview with GN.

382 "What I clearly saw": Author interview with Cromwell.

382 "I really respected Neil for that": Author interview with Cerre.

383 "It took those guys time": Author interview with Cromwell.

383 "When we do it right": This and details of Young-Crosby exchange from notes courtesy of Andy Greene.

384 "I saw the rest of them teasing": Author interview with Cromwell.

384 "He told Crosby": Author interview with Cerre.

384 "Maybe I don't agree": Palmer, "I Want Out."

384 "There were a lot of rules": Author interview with DC.

384 "We had some shows": *CSNY/Déjà vu* (Lions Gate, 2008).

385 "I even made Crosby look good": Alistair McKay, "The Never-Ending War," *Uncut*, July 2008.

385 "They've been singing about things": Wes Orshoski, "Neil Young: The *Billboard* Q&A," *Billboard*, June 24, 2008.

385 "It was very emotional": Author interview with Cerre.

386 "It was almost like a Star of David tour": Author interview with GN.

386 "We knew there were bound": Ibid.

387 "We knew in Atlanta": Author interview with DC.

387 "Probably because of the previous two": Author interview with Fogel.

387 "No fucking encore!": Author interview with Mike Cerre.

387 "They were really shaken": Ibid.

388 In 1972, according to an American National Election Study: Karlyn Bowman and Andrew Rugg, "As the Boomers Turn," *Los Angeles Times*, September 12, 2011.

388 "We thought, 'Let's just keep going'": Author interview with Pegi Young.

389 "The first time I saw the bomb squads": Author interview with Cromwell.

389 "No amount of protection": Andy Greene, "Neil Young's Rough Ride: A Look Back at the Freedom of Speech Tour," *Rolling Stone*, January 29, 2008.

CHAPTER 13: JANUARY 2008–SEPTEMBER 2018

391 "It was wrong": Author interview with GN.

391 "Don't you think it'd be a good idea": This and subsequent quotes from "Young Keeps Rockin' in New Documentary," Associated Press, February 26, 2008.

392 "After an album like that": Edna Gundersen, "Young Doesn't Scrap His Old Songs," *USA Today*, November 14, 2007.

392 "Jay, you've come up with": Author interview with Jay Landers.

393 "Lots of opportunities for us": Author reporting from Rock & Roll Hall of Fame rehearsals, 2009.

394 "Of course, the festival had to promote": Andy Greene interview with SS, 2009.

394 "I didn't think there were tremendous odds": Author interview with Gallen.

395 They finally assembled: Quotations in this section from author reporting, 2009.

397 "He went, 'It was a struggle'": Author interview with Landers.

398 "It's fun singing this stuff": Author interview with DC, 2009.

398 "I tried to reason with them": Author interview with Vitale.

399 "Some of the songs Rick": Author interview with GN.

399 "Without being unkind": Author interview with DC.

399 "I was relieved": Ibid.

399 "We cut five things": Ibid.

401 "Without asking our permission": Author interview with GN.

401 "Who knew that Neil": David Cavanagh, "Fame Is a Subtle, Dangerous, Seductive Thing . . . ," *Uncut*, July 2009.

402 "disappointed with their playing": Patrick Doyle, "Inside Neil Young's Nature-Themed Opus," *Rolling Stone*, July 5, 2016.

402 "Neil's doing what will take": Author interview with DC.

403 "playing to the kids": Author interview with Pegi Young.

403 "it was a little nerve-wracking": Author interview with GN.

403 "You are welcome to it": Andy Greene, "Track by Track: Crosby, Stills & Nash on Their Self-Titled Debut," *Rolling Stone*, August 18, 2008.

405 "completely freaked out": Author interview with Stacia Raymond.

405 "a wonderful man": Kevin Murphy, "Life, Death and the Universe," *Classic Rock*, May 2007.

405 "I copped to all the drugs": Author interview with GN.

405 "We were having a rough patch": David Browne, "Pegi Young on Life After Neil, Heart-break-Inspired New LP," *Rolling Stone*, November 17, 2016.

406 "I happen to know that he's hanging out": Michael Deeds, "Crosby Says He's Still Got It, and It Makes No Sense to Me at All," *Idaho Statesman*, September 7, 2014.

406 "God, I wish it were [true]": Greene interview with DC, 2010.

406 "less than enthused": Author interview with Bolas.

406 "Big-time pissed": Author interview with Mazzeo.

407 "Nothing affects Neil": Author interview with Bolas.

407 "Neil was fearless": Ibid.

407 "I'm not in a position to criticize": Author interview with DC.

408 "It was only after it came out": Author interview with GN.

408 "I was getting older": Ibid.

408 "It was actually getting to be typical": Ibid.

408 "I asked him": Ibid.

409 "It was horrifying": Author interview with DC.

410 "When you let hurtful things": Author interview with Stacia Raymond.

410 Nearby but with his back to them: Author interview with GN.

410 "I just don't know, man": Greene interview with Crosby, Stills and Nash, 2009.

413 "He's very relieved": Author interview with Collins.

414 "With Neil, you usually get": Author interview with Keltner.

414 "You're playing different" and "*Everything's* different now": Ibid.

415 "Normally, with this": Author interview with GN.

417 "Very hard decision this time": Author interview with DC.

417 "If CSN and CSNY": Author interview with GN.

418 "a lot of things have to be settled": David Fricke, "The Situation Begins to Be Described," *Mojo*, January 2017.

418 "I don't plan things like that": Lauren Moraski, "Neil Young Chimes in on a Crosby, Stills, Nash & Young Reunion," *Huffington Post*, April 3, 2018.

INDEX